MW01493765

FOOD LAW IN THE UNITED STATES

As the modern food system continues to transform food – its composition, taste, availability, value, and appearance – consumers are increasingly confronted by legal and regulatory issues that affect us all on a daily basis. In *Food Law in the United States*, Michael T. Roberts addresses these issues in a comprehensive, systematic manner that lays out the national legal framework for the regulation of food and the developing legal tools that fill gaps in this framework, including litigation, state law, and private standards. Covering a broad expanse of topics including commerce, food safety, marketing, nutrition, and emerging food-systems issues, such as local food, sustainability, security, urban agriculture, and equity, this book is an essential reference for lawyers, students, nonlaw professionals, and consumer advocates who must understand food law to advance their respective interests.

Michael T. Roberts is the founding Executive Director of the Resnick Program for Food Law and Policy at UCLA School of Law. He has previously worked in private food law practice and served as consultant to the United Nation's Food and Agriculture Organization and World Food Law Institute. He is also the founder of the *Journal of Food Law and Policy*.

Food Law in the United States

Michael T. Roberts
UCLA School of Law

CAMBRIDGE
UNIVERSITY PRESS

CAMBRIDGE
UNIVERSITY PRESS

University Printing House, Cambridge CB2 8BS, United Kingdom

One Liberty Plaza, 20th Floor, New York, NY 10006, USA

477 Williamstown Road, Port Melbourne, VIC 3207, Australia

4843/24, 2nd Floor, Ansari Road, Daryaganj, Delhi - 110002, India

79 Anson Road, #06-04/06, Singapore 079906

Cambridge University Press is part of the University of Cambridge.

It furthers the University's mission by disseminating knowledge in the pursuit of education, learning and research at the highest international levels of excellence.

www.cambridge.org
Information on this title: www.cambridge.org/9781107545762

First published 2016

A catalogue record for this publication is available from the British Library

Library of Congress Cataloging in Publication data
Roberts, Michael T., author.
Food law in the United States / Michael T. Roberts, UCLA School of Law
    pages   cm
Includes bibliographical references and index.
ISBN 978-1-107-11760-0 (hardback) – ISBN 978-1-107-54576-2 (paperback)
1. Food law and legislation – United States.   I. Title.
KF3875.R63   2015
344.7304'232–dc23   2015019149

ISBN 978-1-107-11760-0 Hardback
ISBN 978-1-107-54576-2 Paperback

Contents

Acknowledgments

Regulation of US Food

When approached by Professor of Law Steve Sheppard some years ago to write a food law treatise, I responded with a high degree of reservation and skepticism. I was still trying to define in my own mind precisely what constituted "food law." I also fully recognized the amount of work and effort that would go into breaking new ground and defining and framing this emerging field. However, Steve's gentle persistence prodded me to think more and more about the prospects of such a treatise. I also realized that my almost schizophrenic approach to food law, back and forth from private practice to academia, along with my work in the food policy community, put me in unique position to see food law from multiple angles. And, so, I capitulated and the work commenced.

It is very appropriate that Cambridge University Press publish this treatise. It was in 2006, when I taught an international food law class as part of a summer law program at Downy College at Cambridge, I formulated the goal of developing a food law and policy program for a reputable law school. I have since then kept a picture of the students in that 2006 class visible in whatever offices I have occupied as a reminder of this lofty goal. I appreciate very much the generosity of the Resnick Family Foundation in funding the Resnick Program for Food Law and Policy at UCLA School of Law and for Dean Rachel Moran and the law faculty at UCLA in giving me the opportunity to serve as the founding executive director of this unique program.

My story of how I came to "food law" is too long to tell here;[1] however, this path has been populated by wonderful scholars, peers, students, and friends on whose shoulders I sit, having provided meaningful and much needed encouragement and support. It is here that I would like to acknowledge those who had a hand in the publication of this treatise.

I owe a great debt to the students who have worked tirelessly in researching supporting law and checking sources. This group includes highly capable UCLA law students Scarlettah Schaefer, Ben Leonard, Sara Ahmed, Max Leeds, and Han-Hsien Hsieh. I especially appreciate the remarkable contributions of Lauren Dunning, attorney for the Los Angeles Country of Public Health, whose insights on local and municipal regulations affecting food have been particularly helpful. This treatise would not have gotten off the ground without the organizational and logistical assistance of Julia Dalzell in the

---

[1] Such an account can be found in Michael T. Roberts, *Beginnings of the Journal of Food Law & Policy*, 11 JOURNAL OF FOOD L. & POL., 1 (2015).

early stages of drafting while we worked together in our food law and policy think tank prior to the inception of the UCLA program. I am grateful that the ever-competent Randi Kusumi from UCLA picked up where Julia left off and managed the logistics superbly.

I thank the editors of Cambridge University Press, including Matt Gallaway and his colleagues, for their careful and tireless editing.

I owe an enormous debt to food law colleagues and scholars, who have collaborated with me and encouraged me through this process – Jacob E. Gersen, Susan A. Schneider, Neil D. Hamilton, Marsha Echols, Craig Cooper, Edison Tang, Kim Kessler, and Margot Pollans, to name a few. I will always appreciate Keith G. Meyer, who taught a summer law class on agricultural law 26 years ago as a visiting law professor that inspired me to pursue a niche in food law a decade later. I also add my name to the long list of folks who are indebted to Peter Barton Hutt, a renown food and drug law expert; his early support of my foray into this field as a new academic provided much needed confidence. I also thank my foreign law professor friends – Ferdinando Albisinni, Yu Yangyou, Liu Yuan, Dean Han Dayuan, and Zhu Xiao – who have forged their own paths in food law and who have helped me grasp the global dynamic involved in food law

Finally, I acknowledge a noble family heritage grounded on a small farm where values of healthy food, sustainability, and hard work were instilled in my consciousness early in life. I also thank my family for their encouragement, support, and endless patience, as the manuscript for this treatise was ever present on weekends, holidays, and vacations.

Due to the flux in food law in the United States, the reader is advised that the coverage of food law in this treatise is current to August 1, 2015.

Table of Abbreviations

AA	Agreement on Agriculture
AB	WTO Appellate Body
ABA	American Bakers Association
ABC	American Broadcasting Companies, Inc.
ACA	Affordable Care Act
ACEP	Agricultural Conservation Easement Program
ADAA	Animal Drug Availability Act of 1996
ADI	Acceptable Daily Intake
ALDF	Animal Legal Defense Fund
ADUFA	Animal Drug User Fee Amendments of 2008
AFDO	Association of Food and Drug Officials
AFO	Animal feeding operation
AFSIC	Alternative Farming Systems Information Center
AHC	American Humane Certified
AIB	American Institute of Baking
ALJ	Administrative Law Judge
AMS	Agricultural Marketing Service
APA	Administrative Procedure Act
APHIS	Animal and Plant Health Inspection Service
ATTRA	Appropriate Technology Transfer for Rural Areas project
AWA	Animal Welfare Act
AZPDES	Arizona Pollutant Discharge Elimination System
BBC	British Broadcasting Corporation
BFRDP	Beginning Farmer and Rancher Development Program
BPI	Beef Products, Inc.
BRC	British Retail Consortium
BSE	Bovine Spongiform Encephalopathy (mad cow disease)
CACFP	Child and Adult Care Food Program
CAFO	Concentrated animal feeding operation
CARU	Children's Advertising Review Unit
CBP	Customs and Border Protection
CCA	Commonsense Consumption Act
CCRVDF	Codex Committee on Residues of Veterinary Drugs in Food
CDC	Center for Disease Control and Prevention
CDFA	California Department of Food and Agriculture

CDSL	Commission on Dietary Supplemental Labels
CERCLA	Comprehensive Environmental Response, Compensation, and Liability Act
CES	Cooperative Extension System
CFBAI	Children's Food and Beverage Advertising Initiative
CFR	Code of Federal Regulations
CFS	Committee on World Food Security
CFSAN	Center for Food Safety and Applied Nutrition
CFSC	Community Food Security Coalition
CFSP	Commodity Supplement Food Program
CIG	Conservation Innovation Grants
CISG	United Nations Convention on Contracts for the International Sale of Goods
CNPP	Center for Nutrition Policy and Promotion
COOL	Country of origin labeling
CPSC	Consumer Product Safety Commission
CRA	Corn Refiners Association
CRC	Chicago Rabbinical Council
CRFC	California Retail Food Code
CRP	Conservation Reserve Program
CSP	Conservation Stewardship Program
CSPI	Center for Science and Public Interest
CSR	Corporate Social Responsibility
CSREES	Cooperate State Research, Education, and Extension Service
CTA	Children's Television Act
CTAP	Conservation Technical Assistance Program
CUCL	California's Unlawful Competition Law
CVM	Center for Veterinary Medicine
CWA	Clean Water Act
DDT	Dichloro-diphenyl-trichloroethane
DHEW	Department of Health, Education and Welfare
DHHS	Department of Health and Human Services
DOJ	Department of Justice
DOL	Department of Labor
DPCIA	Dolphin Protection Consumer Information Act
DRV	Daily reference value
DSB	Dispute Settlement Body
DSHEA	Dietary Supplement Health and Education Act
DSU	WTO Dispute Settlement Understanding
DV	Daily value
EA	Environmental assessment
EBT	Electronic benefit transfer
EC	European Commission
EFSA	European Food Safety Authority
EIR	Establishment Inspection Report
EIS	Environmental Impact Statement
EMA	Economically motivated adulteration

EPA	Environmental Protection Agency
EPIA	Eggs Product Inspection Act
EQIP	Environmental Quality Incentives Program
ERS	Economic Research Service
EU	European Union
FAAMA	Food Allergy And Anaphylaxis Management Act
FALCPA	Food Allergen Labeling And Consumer Protection Act
FAO	Food and Agricultural Organization
FBDO	Foodborne-disease outbreak
FCN	Food Contact Notification
FCS	Food contact substance
FDA	Food and Drug Administration
FDAMA	Food and Drug Administration Modernization Act
FDCA	Food Drug & Cosmetic Act
FDLI	Food and Drug Law Institute
FDPIR	Food Distribution Program on Indian Reservations
FIFRA	Federal Insecticide, Fungicide, and Rodenticide Act
FMI	Food Marketing Institute
FMIA	Federal Meat Inspection Act
FMNP	Farmers' Market Nutrition Program
FMNV	Foods of Minimal Nutritional Value
FNS	Food and Nutrition Service
FOIA	Freedom of Information Act
FOP	Front of package labeling
FQPA	Food Quality and Protection Act
FSA	Farm Services Agency
FSIS	Food Safety and Inspection Service
FSMA	Food Safety Modernization Act
FTC	Federal Trade Commission
GAO	General Accounting Office
GAP	Good Agricultural Practice
GATT	General Agreement on Tariffs and Trade
GE	Genetically engineered
GFPP	Good Food Purchasing Pledge
GGP	Good Guidance Practice
GI	Geographical Indications
GMA	Grocery Manufacturers' Association
GMO	Genetically modified food
GMP	Good manufacturing practice
GRAS	Generally recognized as safe
GFSI	The Global Food Safety Initiative
HACCP	Hazard Analysis Critical Control Point
HARBPC	Hazard analysis and risk-preventive controls
HFCS	High fructose corn syrup
ICCPR	International Covenant on Civil and Political Rights
ICESCR	International Covenant on Economic, Social, and Cultural Rights
IDF	International Dairy Federation

IFT	Institute of Food Technologists
IOC	International Olive Council
IOM	Institute of Medicine
ISO	International Organization for Standardization
ISSC	Interstate Shellfish Sanitation Conference
IWG	Interagency Working Group on Food Marketed to Children
JEFCA	Joint FAO/WHO Expert Committee on Food Additives
KORUS FTA	United States-Korea Free Trade Agreement
LAFPC	Los Angeles Food Policy Council
LDL	Low-density lipoprotein
LFTB	Lean finely textured beef
LGMA	California Leafy Green Products Handler Marketing Agreement
MDEQ	Michigan Department of Environmental Quality
MRL	Maximum Residue Limits
MTA	Metropolitan Transit Authority
NAA	National Aquaculture Act
NADA	New animal drug application
NAFTA	The North American Free Trade Agreement
NAIS	National Animal Identification Program
NAOOA	The North American Olive Oil Association
NARC	National Advertising Review Council
NASA	National Aeronautics and Space Administration
NCA	National Canners Association
NEPA	National Environmental Policy Act
NFP	Nutrition Facts Panel
NGO	Non-governmental Organization
NHTSA	National Highway Traffic System Administration
NIAA	National Institute for Animal Agriculture
NJCFA	New Jersey Fraud Act
NLEA	Nutrition, Labeling, and Education Act
NLRB	National Labor Relations Board
NMFS	National Marine Fisheries Service
NMP	Nutrient Management Plan
NOAA	National Oceanic and Atmospheric Administration
NOAEL	No-observed-adverse-effect-level
NOP	National Organic Program
NOSB	National Organic Standards Board
NPDES	National Pollutant Discharge Elimination System
NPR	Notice of Proposed Rulemaking
NRCS	Natural Resources Conservation Service
NRDC	National Resources Defense Council
NSIL	National Seafood Inspection Laboratory
NSLP	National School Lunch Program
NSSP	National Shellfish Sanitation Program
NYSRA	New York State Restaurant Association
OCC	Office of Chief Counsel
OECD	Organization for Economic Cooperation and Development

OEM	Office of Environmental Markets
OFPA	Organic Food Production Act
OIE	World Organization for Animal Health
OIG	Office of Inspector General
OMG	Office of Management and Budget
ORA	Office of Regulatory Affairs
OSHA	Occupational Safety and Health Administration
OSTP	Office of Science and Technology Policy
OTC	Over the counter
PCA	Peanut Corporation of America
PCA	Pesticides Control Amendment
PDFA	Partnership for a Drug-Free America
PDO	Protected Designation of Origin
PDP	Principal display panel
PFDA	Pure Food and Drug Act
PGI	Protected Geographical Indication
PHC	Public Health Council
PHSA	Public Health Service Act
PMO	Pasteurized Milk Ordinance
POP	Point of purchase
PPIA	Poultry Products Inspection Act
PPNP	Preliminary Proposed Nutrition Principles
QPRAM	Quantitative Predictive Risk Assessment Model
QRA	Quantitative Risk Assessment
QSVP	Quality Systems Verification Programs
RACC	Reference amount customarily consumed
RASFF	Rapid Alert System for Food and Feed
RAW	Raw agricultural commodity
RCED	Resources, Community, and Economic Development
RCPP	Regional Conservation Partnership Program
RCRA	Resource Conservation and Recovery Act
RCT	Randomized controlled trial
RDI	Recommended daily intake
RFR	Reportable food registry
RFRA	Religious Freedom Restoration Act
RNR	Recall Notification Report
SARE	Sustainable Agriculture Research and Education
SCNT	Somatic cell nuclear transfer
SHU	Solitary Housing Units
SKU	Stock keeping unit
SNAP	Supplemental Nutrition Assistance Program
SPB	School Breakfast Program
SPS	Sanitary and Phytosanitary
TBT	Technical Barriers to Trade
TEFAP	The Emergency Food Assistance Program
TMRC	Theoretical maximum residue contribution
TRIPS	Agreement on Trade-Related Aspects of Intellectual Property Rights

TSCA	Toxic Substances Control Act
TTIP	Transatlantic Trade and Investment Partnership
UCC	Uniform Commercial Code
UDAP	Uniform and Deceptive Acts and Practices
UDHR	Universal Declaration of Human Rights
UK	United Kingdom
UL	Upper intake levels
UNCLOS	United Nations Conference on the Law of the Sea
UPC	Universal product code
USAIP	United States Animal Identification Plan
USCG	United States Coast Guard
USDA	United States Department of Agriculture
USP	United States Pharmacopeia
USPHS	United States Public Health Service
USPQ	United States Patents Quarterly
USPTO	United States Patent and Trademark Office
USTR	United States Trade Representative
VFD	Veterinary feed directive
VQIP	Voluntary Qualified Importer Program
WEMA	Working Group on Economically Motivated Adulteration
WHO	World Health Organization
WIC	Special Supplemental Nutrition Program for Women, Infants and Children
WTO	World Trade Organization

1 Introduction

§ 1.01 Definition of Food Law

[1] *Adaptation of Food Law*

Food law is both old and new. From the beginning of recorded history, societies have sought to regulate the production, trade, and consumption of food. This historical fact makes sense given the important roles of food: food sustains life; food affects quality of life; food shapes societies; food manifests cultural values. The modern food society has transformed food – its composition, taste, availability, value, and appearance – raising novel societal issues that affect the lives of consumers. In response, food law is adapting and developing into a distinctive area of law. Indeed, if the measure of the importance of law is how it affects the lives of people on a daily basis, then food law as it has developed is of paramount significance.

The adaptability of food law reflects the notion articulated by legal historian Lawrence M. Friedman, in *The History of American Law*, that modern law mirrors society and moves with its times so that it is always new.[1] Friedman explains that "[i]n traditional cultures, law was basically static: a divine or time-honored body of rules. It defined people's place in the order of society. In modern times, law is a tool, an instrument; the people in power use it to push or pull toward some definite goal."[2] While it is true that law also influences society and promotes change, the adaptation of food law to the modern food system and to the interest of consumers is why food law is new, as well as provocative: the adaptation requires new rules and fresh ideas and the two subjects – the modern food system and the interest of consumers – are not always in sync. In other words, the goal is not always definite. As a result, palatable tensions in food law provoke divisive issues (proposed mandatory labeling for genetically modified food, zoning rules for the production of backyard chickens, and proposed restrictions on sugar-added beverages, to name just a few) that make food law interesting and relevant to modern civil society.

[2] *Phases of Food Law*

[a] Phases: Sequential and Cumulative

The field of modern, emerging food law could be organized in diverse ways. This treatise divides food law into five topical phases: commerce, safety, marketing, nutrition,

---

[1] *See* LAWRENCE M. FRIEDMAN, THE HISTORY OF AMERICAN LAW XI–XX (Simon & Schuster., 3d ed. 2005).
[2] *Id.* at XX.

and systems.[3] These phases constitute the chapters presented in this treatise. This phase by chapter approach provides a historic framework that accepts Friedman's notion that modern law adapts to social change. Each phase started and has evolved in response to problems and challenges in the food system. In addition to addressing problems in the food system, each phase also reflects societal values and perceptions of food and underscores that food law is a dynamic, emerging field. Although the phases are for the most part sequential, they are also cumulative: the phases build on each other, creating overlap and spillover effects. The phases are distinctive enough, however, to justify separate attention. A brief summary of each phase is presented in the following sections.

[b] Commerce

Food has been at the heart of commercial activity since the days of antiquity. The oldest recorded food laws were designed to preserve the integrity of food commerce and fair play among purveyors of food by preventing food fraud and also to promote the trade of food in order to feed rising urban populations. The colonies followed suit and enacted food adulteration laws to prohibit economically motivated adulteration, a principal form of food fraud. The trade of food evolved in response to social and economic conditions to where today the US food system is part of a global food production and commercial trading network that relies upon trade to ensure for consumers the availability of an abundance of whole foods and food ingredients from around the world. Modern food commerce raises the same issues of fraud and market access that confronted ancient societies. The response of the law in the United States has been to enact domestic laws against economically motivated adulteration and to help develop a global trade legal architecture based on international legal instruments in the forms of treaties and international institutions that promote among participating countries free trade and harmonization of food quality and safety standards. Resolving trade conflicts within this architecture is one of the biggest challenges facing the international food trade system.

[c] Food Safety

Although food law in previous societies and early in the United States recognized the connection between adulteration of food and public health, scientists did not begin to understand bacteria, and their relationship to disease, until the late nineteenth century. It was recognized that food spoils, but the reasons for that and the potential for becoming ill from food were unknown. The history of food safety regulation is really the history of discoveries and inventions enabling regulatory responses to emerging safety problems, including sophisticated forms of contamination, various food additives, new pesticides, and scientific changes in the composition of food. Today, the technical intricacies in the making and handling of food raise safety risks at each segment of the supply chain, including the production, manufacturing, processing, packaging, marketing, distribution, and consumption of food. Lives depend on the efficacy of a wide range of federal, state, and local legal tools employed from the farm to the fork to safeguard food at each

---

[3] See Peter Barton Hutt, *Government Regulation of the Integrity of the Food Supply*, 4 ANN. REV. NUTR. 1 (1984) (Peter Barton Hutt, an eminent food and drug law scholar, has previously noted that food regulation has evolved over the centuries into the three phases of food fraud, food safety, and nutrition).

of the critical points along the supply chain. These laws continue to expand the government's role in the inspection of food product and in the enforcement against violations of law. These laws also continue to expand the responsibilities of food enterprises to keep records, follow safety rules and protocols, and develop preventive control standards. Increasing attention is being paid to imported food. The development of other forms of law besides regulatory law – such as litigation and third-party verification – are also increasingly used as legal tools to help ensure safe food.

[d] Food Marketing

Radical changes in the nineteenth century to the food system that were driven by technology and consumer demand – the creation of new types of food that were convenient and appealing to consumers on the move, improvements in preservation and transportation, and the economics of mass production and mass marketing – triggered a phenomenon that has since then challenged the application of food law: the rise of the brand name.[4] From the beginning, brand-name foods were marketed to consumers on the basis of "purity, convenience, quality and reliability, and the consumer bought the promises as well as the product."[5] The ever-changing composition and nature of food and the competitive environment in which food is marketed has necessitated laws that regulate the conveyance of information to consumers about food through marketing (labeling and advertising). These laws require food enterprises to tell the truth, to warn, and to educate. In an attempt to restrict commercial speech, marketing laws often generate novel conflicts over the First Amendment and over fundamental questions of what consumers need to know. Recent legal activity in the form of class action litigation against marketing claims has developed as a gap filler in some respects where regulations fail to provide clear direction or where enforcement falls short.

[e] Nutrition

While the link of food to nutrition has long been established, the public health consequences of the modern food system has generated an increase in nutrition regulation, starting in the 1960s in the United States. Although there are numerous facets to the response of law to nutrition issues, three general categories take shape: (1) the regulation of dietary supplements; (2) nutrition labeling; and (3) legal responses to malnutrition and obesity. While the regulation of dietary supplements and nutrition labeling is covered by detailed regulations, the outcome of the consumption of food or lack thereof in the modern food system has generated a plethora of nutrition policies, initiatives, and programs from multiple levels of government that address and legislate both obesity and hunger, plights that afflict millions of consumers in the United States and the world. Public health advocates adapt strategies from tobacco litigation for use in litigation against the food industry. Legal theories range from inadequate disclosure of health risks, misleading advertisements, targeting of children, and deceptive practices used. The approach of food law to the obesity epidemic is complicated by the debate over

---

[4] *See* REAY TANNAHILL, FOOD IN HISTORY 328–31 (1988).
[5] *Id.* at 331.

personal responsibility. Legislative and regulatory actions, such as restricting junk food in schools, controlling the portion size of soda drinks, mandating menu labeling, altering industry marketing practices, and taxing junk food are contested by critics, who invoke personal responsibility and express concerns over a "nanny state."

[f] Food Systems

Notwithstanding the industrialization of food, the act of eating has never been nor likely ever will be a simple exercise of satisfying a basic physiological need. Culture has always mattered. The governance of food is shaped by cultural, political, and sociological norms articulated by consumers and communities, the force of which has intensified with growing concerns about the modern food system. Concerns over sustainability, access to healthy food, localness, the right to certain information about food, the treatment of animals intended for food, monoculture, food justice and equity, and food security are generating new laws and recasting the debate over the role of law in the basic acts of making and eating food.

The food systems approach bespeaks of a growing recognition by consumers of the importance and relevance in their daily lives of food systems – local, regional, national, and global food systems. The focus on issues within these systems includes safety, marketing, and nutrition; however, the focus is couched with the context of food systems. For example, recent class action litigation over the claim "natural" on food products that have been genetically modified has less to do with the safety of these products and more to do with the methods, processes, and outcomes of the modern food system.[6] A food systems orientation raises challenges for a food regulatory system that is built on science; hence, nonregulatory law, such as private standards, voluntary standards, and litigation are emerging as legal tools to meet the expectations and demands of consumers. However, there are signs that cultural, religious, and proscriptive meanings can affect government policy and regulation. For example, policies such as food security can play a role in the use of law to support regional food systems and the US trade policy.

[3] *Expansion of Food Law*

[a] Building on Traditional Food Law

The expansion of food law by its adaptation to societal concerns builds on traditional food law, which is a discipline that has historically been coupled with drug law via the federal government agency charged with a central role in the regulation of food consumed in the United States – the Food and Drug Administration (FDA). The focus of FDA regulation of food is on public health.[7] Hence, the governing statutes and implementing regulations, rules, and standards that are generally oriented toward the prevention of unsafe

---

[6] *See generally* Michael Pollan, Vote for the Dinner Party, N.Y. Times Mag., October 10, 2012 at MM62.
[7] *See* Margaret A. Hamburg, M.D., Comm'r of Food and Drugs, Address on Effective Enforcement and Benefits to Public Health (August 6, 2009) (emphasizing FDA's responsibility to take swift and aggressive action to protect the public health).

and misbranded food are all intended to protect public health.[8] Although food safety has materialized as the top priority of the FDA, emerging concerns of malnutrition and obesity have expanded the FDA's regulatory scope to include nutrition, which generally involves regulating the dissemination of information to consumers about the properties and composition of food products. The regulations promulgated by the Federal Trade Commission (FTC) (advertising of food); the Food Safety and Inspection Service (FSIS) (safety of meat, poultry, and egg products), an agency in the US Department of Agriculture (USDA); and the Environmental Protection Agency (EPA) (pesticide residue on food) are also part of a tapestry of agency-regulated food law that focuses primarily on the safety and marketing of food.

Food law under the rubric of FDA food and drug law is the practice of a corps of law firms and lawyers who represent food enterprises engaged in the manufacturing, packaging, labeling, advertising, and distribution of food products. Many of these lawyers are organized in food and drug law practice groups in law firms located in Washington D.C., Chicago, and other large metropolitan areas. These lawyers typically participate in the Food and Drug Law Institute (FDLI)[9] and represent food and drug companies of all sizes. The practice of food law by these lawyers is mostly administrative law and is rich in its complexities. The literature relied upon by these lawyers are FDA-centric. The *Food and Drug Law Journal*, published quarterly by the Food and Drug Law Institute, for more than sixty years has offered scholarly articles providing insight into the actions of the FDA, as well as the FTC and USDA. The highly regarded casebook, *Food and Drug Law*, published by Foundation Press,[10] has been a mainstay in Law School food and drug law courses taught in US law schools, often by adjunct law professors who practice in the area.[11]

[b] Distinguishing Agricultural Law

Traditional food law is to be distinguished from agricultural law, which is rooted in the concept of agrarianism or "agricultural exceptionalism."[12] The Thomas Jefferson creed that "[t]hose who labour in the earth are the chosen people of God, if ever he had a chosen people" has translated into the societal goal to preserve and protect farms.[13] Agricultural law has been the legal tool to accomplish this objective: the use of legal exceptions, protections, and programs has been advanced to preserve the agricultural industry. Examples of agricultural exceptionalism via the law include protections afforded

---

[8] *See, e.g.*, 21 U.S.C. § 393(b)(2)(A) (FDA is to protect public health by ensuring that "foods are safe, wholesome, sanitary, and properly labeled").

[9] Founded in 1949, FDLI is a nonprofit organization that provides a forum for discussion of food and drug issues through conferences, publications, and member interactions.

[10] *See* Peter Barton Hutt, Richard A. Merrill & Lewis A. Grossman, FOOD AND DRUG LAW CASES AND MATERIALS (Foundation Press, 3d ed. 2007).

[11] Another text, *The Regulation of Food*, offers a pedagogical approach to the study of food regulation, geared to food regulatory scientists as well as food lawyers. *See* Neal D. Fortin, FOOD REGULATION: LAW, SCIENCE, POLICY, AND PRACTICE (2009).

[12] *See* Susan A. Schneider, *A Reconsideration of Agricultural Law: A Call for the Law of Food, Farming, and Sustainability*, 34 WM. & MARY ENVTL. L. & POL'Y REV. 935, 946 (2010).

[13] *Id.* at 939 (quoting THOMAS JEFFERSON, NOTES ON THE STATE OF VIRGINIA 170 (Frank Shuffelton ed., 1999) (1785)).

to farmers in labor, bankruptcy, and international trade; exceptions to environmental and antitrust regulations; and, programs based on subsidies, loans, and education.

Agricultural law has spawned law practices, largely in rural areas, that represent farms as well as agricultural enterprises, such as seed and chemical input companies. The academic approach to agricultural law started in the 1940s, where law schools at Harvard, Yale, Texas, and Iowa initiated short-lived agricultural law studies.[14] Agricultural law really took hold in the 1970s, a period of economic hardship for farms and rural communities. In 1979, the *Agricultural Law Journal* was first published. In 1980, the American Agricultural Law Association was formed to provide a forum for presentation and networking among lawyers of agricultural law. A year later, the LL.M. Program in Agricultural Law was founded at the University of Arkansas School of Law. In 1981, the fifteen-volume Agricultural Law treatise was published.[15] In 1985, the casebook, *Agricultural Law: Cases and Materials*, was published by West Publishing Co.[16] The authors of *Agricultural Law: Cases and Materials* define agricultural law as a multidoctrinal approach: "It is our view that agricultural law is not just a bit of contracts, a bit of torts, a bit of land use, a bit of commercial law, a bit of regulated industries, a bit of this and a bit of that. Rather, it is a complex and highly integrated field of law held together by certain broad themes."[17] These themes, according to the authors, include land use, economic regulation, and the promotion of family size farms. The authors conclude that agricultural law is the study of laws and institutions that have developed to reflect unique characteristics of agriculture and the need to preserve the farms. The contents of the textbook serve this purpose and include the financing the ownership of agricultural land, farm leases, warehouses, operational financing, animals, commodity futures contracts, agricultural cooperatives, agricultural employment, soil and water management, and farmlands preservation.[18]

Traditional food law is distinguishable from agricultural law in three ways. First, agricultural law focuses on the regulation of the production of agriculture, whereas food law traditionally focuses on the postproduction regulation of food – the processing, manufacturing, labeling, advertising, distribution, and consumption of food. Second, agricultural law focuses on the producer of food and the inputs that go into the production of food, whereas food law has a decided slant toward the interests of the consumer. Third, the practitioners of food law – typically urban lawyers in large metropolitan areas, who practice food and drug law – are a vastly different group in location of practice and cliental than agricultural law practitioners – typically lawyers in rural areas, who represent the interests of agriculture enterprises.

[c] Reframing Food Law

In the twenty-first century, there arose in the United States a nascent, social movement geared toward transforming the global food system.[19] Although the food movement has been at the forefront of conversation, it has often evaded definition. The movement has

---

[14] *Id.* at 941.
[15] *Id.*
[16] *See* Keith G. Meyer ET AL., AGRICULTURAL LAW: CASES AND MATERIALS (West Publishing Co. 1985).
[17] *Id.* at XIX.
[18] *See generally* MEYER ET AL., *supra* note 16.
[19] *See* Michael Pollan, *The Food Movement, Rising*, N.Y. TIMES REVIEW OF BOOKS (June 10, 2010).

concerned itself with changing social norms and includes numerous directions in addition to basic food safety and marketing concerns, such as GMO labeling, nutrition, food waste, sustainability, new farmers, farmland preservation, food sovereignty, school lunch reform, local food, food access, urban agriculture, farm bill reform, initiatives to create gardens and cooking classes in school, farm worker rights, nutrition labeling, obesity, hunger, animal welfare, and environmental issues.[20]

This growing interest in food has reframed food law in American society by creating aspirations that extend beyond the reach of traditional food law. As Michael Pollan points out, "[i]t would be a mistake to conclude that the food movement's agenda can be reduced to a set of laws, policies, and regulations, important as these may be."[21] According to Pollan, the food movement is "about community, identity, pleasure, and, most notably, about carving out a new social and economic space removed from the influence of big corporations on the one side and government on the other."[22] In essence, the food movement has set out to foster new norms for civil society. It should be noted that the food movement carries with it equity concerns in that minorities are underrepresented, especially among farmers' markets and community-supported customers.[23]

Notwithstanding the transcendent nature of the food movement, modern law has responded to emergent concerns of health, environmental, and economic impacts of the modern food system in two ways: first, the addition of new laws that emanate from the traditional food law regime of the FDA-USDA-FTC-EPA cluster of laws, rules, and standards; second, an addendum of new laws and tools that source from outside the traditional regulatory regime.

Addition – The traditional food law regime has generated significant legal activity in recent years. For example, the 2011 Food Safety Modernization Act (FSMA) has been heralded as the most important food law since the 1938 Food Drug & Cosmetic Act (FDCA), as it attempts to deal with growing imports of food and systemic food safety problems in the global food supply chain. Through FSMA, the traditional food law regime is also reaching for the first time the farm where value-adding activities on farms generate food safety concerns and attention from regulators.

Addendum – New, distinctive food laws that fall outside of government regulation law include laws that are developed by litigation, voluntary standards, contracts evoking private standards, and municipal laws that govern urban agriculture and local food. New government programs that shape the way food is produced, marketed, and distributed also generate and shape new legal relationships among stakeholders. All of these new laws operate as filler law where traditional regulatory law falls short in addressing problems and issues. These new laws also encompass innovative ideas on the promotion of issues important to the food movement, including the extension of SNAP benefits to farmers' markets and favorable zoning laws to promote aquaculture in blighted communities. These new laws are transformative to the extent that they shape the modern food systems approach. The food systems approach bespeaks of a growing recognition and concern by

---

[20] *See id.*
[21] *Id.*
[22] *Id.*
[23] *See* Julie Guthman, *"If They Only Knew": Color Blindness and Universalism in California Alternative Food Institutions,* 60 Prof. Geographer 387, 392 (2007).

consumers of the importance and relevance in their daily lives of food systems – local food systems, regional food systems, national food systems, and the global food system. A food systems approach encompasses the cultural values of food, from food production to consumption. In addition to commerce, safety, marketing, and nutrition, these values include community building, connection to food sources, and sustainable practices in the food system. These values incentivize consumers to desire information about food from the farm to the fork. Hence, new marketing laws on animal welfare claims or environmental practices on the farm connect the interests of consumers and farmers. Even laws that are intended to attract new and beginning farmers are part of food policy and affect consumer interest.[24] To a degree, a food systems approach is a convergence between agricultural law and food law.[25]

[d] Expanded Audience

The expansion of food law also broadens the invested audience. The first group is the legal bar, which includes the traditional FDA bar of attorneys whose practices are affected by the pressures and challenges imposed on their food enterprise clients by demands from consumers, litigation, and additional regulation. The food law bar also includes trial lawyers who engage in class action or other litigation involving food on issues not adequately addressed by regulation. Government counsel are increasingly being involved in city planning and public health issues on zoning of food desserts, community gardening, and farmers' markets, food access issues of food trucks, public health issues concerning nutrition programs, obesity, and even food and beverage taxes designed to change public consumption habits. Lawyers who represent advocacy groups, state and local food policy councils, pro-bono activities, and foundations have an interest in setting food policy.

A second group is the legal academy. Law schools are increasingly paying attention to food law and policy, an approach that examines the food system holistically and evaluates legal tools to address the problems from the modern food system.[26] Law schools are beginning to address issues about the food system through launching new courses, clinics, and centers.[27] Traditional law courses, including health law, environmental law, international law, public policy law, and intellectual law courses have components of food law and policy in their curriculum. Even traditional FDA law courses are well served by a larger contextual approach to food law and policy.

---

[24] *See* Neil D. Hamilton, *Greening Our Garden: Public Policies to Support the New Agriculture*, 2 Drake J. Agric. L. 357, 361 (1997).

[25] Susan Schneider, the director of the LL.M. program at the University of Arkansas, has called for a convergence of sorts between agriculture law and food law: a food-based agricultural law that reconciles the interest of farmers with the public good of society, advancing sustainability, food safety, health, and nutrition. *See* Schneider, *supra* note 12, at 946. In a similar vein, Neil Hamilton makes the case that farmers have an important role in food law and policy. *See* Neil D. Hamilton, *Keeping the Farm and Farmer in Food Policy and Law*, 11 J. Food L. & Pol'y 9 (2015).

[26] *See* Baylen J. Linnekin & Emily M. Broad Leib, *Food Law & Policy: The Fertile Field's Origins and First Decade*, 2014 Wis. L. Rev. 557 (2014) (documents the history of the development of food law in American law schools).

[27] Representative programs include the UCLA Resnick Food Law & Policy Program, the Harvard Food Law Lab, the University of Arkansas School of Law Agricultural and Food Law LL.M. Program, the Drake Law School Agricultural Law Center, the Howard University School of Law World Food Law Institute, and the Vermont Law School Center for Agriculture and Food Systems.

Additional groups comprise the audience of expanded food law. As jurists are increasingly hearing food law cases, a food law approach that is broad and contextualized helps in the decision making. Policymakers are increasingly cognizant of the importance of food law in not only adapting to changes in social food values, but also in the potential of law to shape food consumption priorities and habits. Finally, an assortment of nonlaw professionals – health advocates, urban planners, community organizers, and consumer advocates – are interested in the intersection of food law and their respective interests.

[e] Distinctive Discipline

The vastness of "food law" subject matter raises a legitimate question as to whether food law is not a discipline in and of itself, but merely a subsection of other forms of law – administrative, environmental, consumer protection, international, tort, zoning, animal welfare, constitutional, and intellectual property. However, the case to consider food law as a discipline (albeit multidoctrinal) in and of itself is strong. Its value lies in focusing attention on how law governs food from the field to the table. The challenges posed by a modern food system unlike anything that the world has experienced have generated attention on the governance of food to warrant a legal field and discipline such as food law. Moreover, by recognizing how law governs food, improvements can be made and dynamics can be better understood.

Finally, food law also has a framework, a fact occasionally overlooked by well-meaning practitioners and scholars when latching onto a food policy topic for the first time. It is this pre-existing framework that distinguishes emerging modern food law from other start-up law disciplines that are dismissed "as just another example of 'the law and …' problem."[28] This treatise explains how this framework has expanded as traditional and emerging legal doctrines operate and interact in response to changes in society that affect food and consumers. Whether this expanded field of "food law" is coherent and distinctive enough to evolve into a permanent discipline of law is a question that only time can answer. This treatise makes no pretense as to what the answer to this question ultimately will be. Instead, this treatise simply lays out the law governing food in order to equip the practitioner and scholar with an expanded legal framework to address the complexities and challenges of the modern food system.

The first stop in the framework is the analysis of the subject matter of food law – food – which raises the issue of how does the law define food.

§ 1.02 Legal Definition of Food

[1] *Statutory Definition*

Section 321(f) of the 1938 Food, Drug, and Cosmetic Act (FDCA) defines "food" based on the use of the article in question: "(1) articles used for food or drink for man or other animals, (2) chewing gum, and (3) articles used for components of any such article."[29] The impact of the changing attitudes about food has influenced this statutory

---

[28] A. Dan Tarlock, *Is There a There in Environmental Law?*, 19 J. Land Use & Envtl. L. 213, 228 (2004).
[29] Federal Food, Drug, and Cosmetic Act (FDCA), ch. 675, § 201(f), 52 Stat. 1040, 1040 (1938) (current version at 21 U.S.C. § 321(f)).

definition, wherein as taste became an important characteristic of food, the cultural concept of food began to embrace condiments and confectionary more clearly; hence, Congress expressly listed chewing gum so as to "eliminate[] any doubt as to whether or not [it is] food."[30]

As FDCA provides the FDA with jurisdiction over all foods that are not exclusively regulated by the USDA (meat, poultry, and eggs), the Section 321(f) definition covers most "articles" consumed by people or animals. The acts that grant food regulation responsibility to the USDA do not define "food" as a general term due to the limitation of regulatory jurisdiction for the USDA to specific food products. The Federal Meat Inspection Act (FMIA) defines "meat food product" as "any product capable of use as human food which is made wholly or in part from any meat."[31] The Poultry Products Inspection Act (PPIA) defines "poultry" as "any domesticated bird, whether alive or dead."[32] The Egg Product Inspection Act defines "egg" as "the shell egg of the domesticated chicken, turkey, duck, goose or guinea."[33]

[2] *Dual Classification: Food and Drug*

In addition to providing the FDA with responsibility over food, the FDCA provides the FDA with different degrees of power over nonfood categories of products, including drugs, cosmetics, devices, and biological products.[34] The determination of a product as a "food" distinguishable from these other products, especially drugs, as defined by Section 321(f), controls the regulatory approach the FDA will impose upon that product. While the distinction between food and drugs is not always clear, the fact that the FDA has greater authority over drugs renders the categorization a critical consideration.

Rather than focus on the actual use of an article as does Section 321(f), Section 321(g) defines "drugs" by focusing on the intended use of the product. Section 321(g)(1)(B) defines "drugs" as "articles intended for use in the diagnosis, cure, mitigation, treatment, or prevention of disease in man or other animals."[35] Under the rather imprecise definitions of "food" in Section 321(f) and "drug" in Section 321(g)(1)(B), a single substance may appear to qualify as a food or a drug. Honey, for example, is an article normally used for food, and thus constitutes a food under Section 321(f)(1). If, however, the intent by the producer or manufacturer is for honey to be used as a panacea for various ailments, the product may also fall within Section 321(g)(1)(B) of the drug definition. Thus, under the FDCA the terms "food" and "drug" are not mutually exclusive. Courts have universally accepted that there is some overlap between the terms and have delineated intent

---

[30] Lewis A. Grossman, *Food, Drugs, and Droods: A Historical Consideration of Definitions and Categories in American Food and Drug Law*, 93 CORNELL L. REV. 1091, 1112-1113 (quoting statement of Walter G. Campbell, chief of the FDA).

[31] 21 U.S.C. § 601(j).

[32] 21 U.S.C. § 453(e). Because "poultry" is defined as "domesticated" birds, game birds (like game animals) are regulated by the FDA.

[33] 21 U.S.C. § 1033(g).

[34] *See* 21 U.S.C. §§ 301-399. This coupling of food and drug has historical resonance in that for over 2,000 years. From the time of Hippocrates, little distinction was made between the two categories. The practice of medicine consisted largely of the wise choice of natural food products. *See* Barton Hutt, *supra* note 5, at 1.

[35] 21 U.S.C. § 321(g)(1)(B).

as the touchstone of Section 321(g)(1)'s drug definition.[36] Even though a substance may qualify as a food, the FDCA will regulate the substance as a drug if the manufacturer intends it for consumers to use for therapeutic purposes.[37]

Although FDCA appears to contemplate dual classification and looks to intended use to determine whether a substance is a drug, Section 321(g)(1)(C) expressly excludes food articles from the coverage of the drug definition. Section 321(g)(1)(C) augments Section 321(g)(1)(B) by defining "drugs" as "articles (other than food) intended to affect the structure or any function of the body of man or other animals."[38] Thus, the FDCA seems to mandate that if a product is "intended to affect the structure or any function of the body," yet at the same time qualifies as a food, the FDA cannot regulate that product as a drug even if a manufacturer promotes a product exclusively for its physiological effect. If a manufacturer of a food product, such as tea, for example, promoted the product exclusively for use as a stimulant, the act's drug provisions still might not apply.

The Section 321(g)(1)(C) food exclusion was addressed by the Seventh Circuit in *Nutrilab, Inc. v. Schweiker*, where the issue was whether "starch blockers," which were tablets and capsules containing a protein extracted from raw kidney beans, should be classified as an unapproved new drug or a food.[39] Incorporating a cultural understanding of food directly into law, the court interpreted the food exclusion to apply to "common sense" foods: "articles used by people in the ordinary way most people use food – primarily for taste, aroma, or nutritive value."[40] The court determined that the starch blockers were subject to regulation as a drug because the product was intended to affect a bodily structure or function by way of improved digestion, but was not consumed primarily for taste, aroma, or nutritive value.[41]

[3] *Emerging Subclassifications*

The expanding concept of "food" has limited the applicability of *Nutrilab*.[42] For example, as noted in Chapter 4, in 1990, the Nutrition, Labeling, and Education Act of 1990 (NLEA) permitted foods, under certain conditions, to make explicit disease prevention claims without being subject to the drug regulations.[43] The NLEA coincided with changing conceptions of food articulated by Michael Pollan as follows:

---

[36] *See* Nutrilab, Inc. v. Schweiker, 547 F.Supp. 880, 883 (N.D. Ill. 1982), aff'd, 713 F.2d 335, 336 (7th Cir. 1983); Millet, Pit & Seed Co. v. United States, 436 F.Supp. 84, 89 (E.D. Tenn. 1977).

[37] *See* United States v. Article of Drug Consisting of 47 Shipping Cartons, More or Less, "Helene Curtis Magic Secret," 331 F.Supp. 912, 917 (D. Md. 1971) (delineating a two-pronged test to ascertain whether there is therapeutic intent).

[38] 21 U.S.C. § 321(g)(1)(C).

[39] *See Nutrilab*, 713 F.2d at 335.

[40] *See* Grossman, *supra* note 30, at 1132 (quoting *Nutrilab* at 338) (The FDA has referred to the "taste, aroma, or nutritive value" formulation numerous times in the Federal Register).

[41] *See id.*

[42] Following *Nutrilab*, the FDA developed the position that plant stanol and sterol esters have nutritive value because they affect the digestive process, which is one of the metabolic processes necessary for the normal maintenance of human existence. The substances function by blocking the body's absorption of cholesterol, an effect that is seemingly similar to the effect of the starch blockers addressed in *Nutrilab*. *See* 65 Fed. Reg. 54,685, 54,688 (September 8, 2000).

[43] *See* Nutritional Labeling and Education Act of 1990, Pub. L. No. 101–535, 104 Stat. 2353 (codified in part at 21 U.S.C. §§ 343(i), (q), and (r)).

It was in the 1980s that food began disappearing from the American supermarket, gradually to be replaced by "nutrients," which are not the same thing. Where once the
familiar names of recognizable comestibles – things like eggs or breakfast cereal or
cookies – claimed pride of place on the brightly colored packages crowding the aisles,
now new terms like "fiber" and cholesterol and "saturated fat" rose to large-type promi-
nence. More important than mere foods, the presence or absence of these invisible substances was now generally believed to confer health benefits on their eaters. Foods by
comparison were coarse, old-fashioned and decidedly unscientific things – who could
say what was in them, really?[44]

The expansion of what constitutes food coupled with evolving consumer expectations
has also precipitated the development of subclassifications of foods under the jurisdiction of both the FDA and USDA. Some of these subclasses are expressly carved out by
statute; others are not defined by statute or regulation, but exist due to technological creation and consumer demand. All of these foods have particular meaning to consumers
and reflect the increasing frequency that consumers have looked to foods with particular
health constituencies and to foods that have been produced in a particular way that meet
cultural expectations. The more prominent of these emerging subclasses of food are
listed in the following pages.

- Dietary Supplements

Under the Dietary Supplement Health and Education Act of 1994 (DSHEA),[45] a group
of products that include vitamins, minerals, herbs, botanical products, and amino acids,
which are usually sold in tablet, capsule, liquid, or powder form, constitute what are
known as dietary supplements and are deemed a food (even if it is not a common sense
food under *Nutrilab*). As shown in Chapter 5, the DSHEA does impose certain unique
requirements on supplements that are different from conventional foods.

- Medical Foods

Medical foods became part of the statutory lexicon of the FDA when the 1983 Orphan
Drug Act defined "medical food" as food that is formulated to be consumed or administered enterally under the supervision of a physician and which is intended for the specific
dietary management of a disease or condition for which distinctive nutritional requirements, based on recognized scientific principles, are established by medical evaluation.[46]

- Foods for Special Dietary Use

Special dietary needs due to specific health conditions, such as celiac disease, lactose
intolerance, or obesity give rise to a demand for foods described as "special dietary use

---

[44] Grossman, *supra* note 30, at 1137 (quoting Michael Pollan, *Unhappy Meals*, N.Y. Times Mag., January
28, 2007 at 41.)

[45] *See* Dietary Supplement Health and Education Act (DSHEA), Pub. L. No. 103–417, 108 Stat. 4325
(1994) (codified in scattered sections of 21 U.S.C.).

[46] *See* 21 U.S.C. § 360ee(b)(3).

foods." Although the FDCA does not define this term, the act recognizes the concept that there are certain foods that are formulated to meet special dietary uses and it establishes labeling requirements for such products.[47]

- Functional Foods

In response to consumer demand for healthy food, the food industry has created a class of products commonly known as "functional food." There is no statutory or regulatory definition of what constitutes a functional food. In essence, functional foods provide health benefit beyond basic nutrition. As noted in Chapter 4, increasing attention to functional foods by the FDA may result at some point in the creation of a distinct legal category and definition for functional food.

- Food Additives

The FDCA defines "food additives" broadly as any substance "the intended use of which results or may reasonably be expected to result, directly or indirectly, in its becoming a component or otherwise affecting the characteristics of any food."[48] Substances as food additives include "any substance intended for use in producing, manufacturing, packing, processing, preparing, treating, packaging, transporting, or holding food."[49] Excluded expressly from the definition of food additive are pesticide chemicals, color additives, and dietary supplements.[50]

- Organic Food

The Organic Food Production Act (OFPA)[51] claims that foods are designated organic if they are produced, handled, and certified under a well-defined process established by the National Organic Program (NOP).[52] The "organic" label attaches to the organic food product in various categories, as explained in Chapter 4.

- Natural

Although the descriptor "natural" (or "All Natural" or "100% Natural") is commonly found on food product, neither the FDA nor USDA regulations define the term (despite repeated requests by the food industry, consumer groups, and even courts) and unlike with organic food, there is not a national uniform program that establishes processes by which a food can be considered natural. The agencies have instead issued informal and

---

[47] See COMM'N ON DIETARY SUPPLEMENT LABELS, THE REPORT OF THE COMMISSION ON DIETARY LABELS 11 (2014).
[48] 21 U.S.C. § 321(s).
[49] Id.
[50] See id.
[51] See Organic Foods Production Act of 1990 (OFPA), Pub. L. No. 101–624, 104 Stat. 3935 (codified as amended at 7 U.S.C. §§ 6501–6523 (2006)).
[52] See National Organic Program (NOP), Final Rule, 65 Fed. Reg. 80,548, 80,663–664 (December 21, 2000) (codified at 7 C.F.R. pt. 205 (2008)).

unbinding definitions of natural that are vague and indecisive, leading to consumer confusion, uncertainty, and an explosion of litigation.[53]

- Genetically Modified Food

No food classification has created as much controversy in the modern food system as food that has been genetically modified or genetically engineered, notwithstanding the fact that an estimated 70 percent of all processed US foods likely contain some genetically engineered material. There is no statutory definition of what constitutes genetically modified food (GMO). The term GMO on its face is an inaccurate descriptor due to the fact that most foods do not contain organisms. As a matter of policy, the FDA considers GMOs as equivalent to conventional food and defines "genetic modification" as the alterations of the genotype that occurred using any technique, whether conventional plant breeding or new biotechnology techniques.[54] Under this definition by the FDA, virtually all cultivated food crops could be considered genetically modified. However, the World Health Organization and common usage considers a GMO food as a food whose genetic make-up has been altered through the insertion of a gene from a different organism.[55] As noted in Chapter 6, the NOP standards for organic food forbid GMOs or food that is genetically engineered to be designated as organic.

The complexities of legally defining these last three food categories – genetically modified food, natural, and organic – are evident by the following syllogism: organic food will always be natural; natural food will not be organic unless the process by which the natural food is developed and handled comport with the NOP; genetically modified food by definition cannot be organic, but may be natural, although class action litigation as shown in Chapter 4 has challenged this notion.

§ 1.03 Forms of Food Law

The forms of food law in the United States are manifold. These forms encompass the legal tools used to regulate food commerce, food safety and quality, food marketing, nutrition, and food systems.

[1] *Government Regulation of Food Product*

[a] Fragmentation

Government regulation of food via public health and safety laws and consumer protection regulations is a patchwork of federal and state laws.[56] This patchwork is primarily a product

---

[53] *See, e.g.*, Holk v. Snapple Beverage Corp., 575 F.3d 329, 333, 341–2 (3d Cir. 2009); Lauren Ries v. Hornell *Brewing Co., Inc. et al.*, No. 10-cv-1139, 2010 U.S. Dist LEXIS 86384, at *6 (N.D. Cal. July 23, 2010).

[54] *See* Statement of Policy: Foods Derived from New Plant Varieties, 57 Fed. Reg. 22,984, 22,984 n.3 (May 29, 1992).

[55] WORLD HEALTH ORG., 20 *Questions on Genetically Modified Foods*. Similarly, the United Nations defines GMOs as "organism[s] that [have] been transformed by the insertion of one or more genes." FOOD & AGRIC. ORG. OF THE UNITED NATIONS, Glossary Definition of Genetically Modified Organisms, *FAO Glossary of Biotechnology for Food & Agriculture,*

[56] The US Supreme Court in POM Wonderful LLC v. Coca-Cola Co., 134 S. Ct. 2228 (2014) referred to the public health and consumer protection role of the Food, Drug, and Cosmetic Act (FDCA) by stating

of two historic points: first is US federalism, which allocates sovereign powers both to the federal and state governments; second is the federal and state governments' piecemeal approach to food legislation. The consequence of these two developments is a jumble of discrete, although often interrelated and overlapping, federal and state laws. Federal and state food law historically has had an uneasy coexistence. Because the Supremacy clause of the Constitution requires that federal law supersede or "preempt" conflicting state law,[57] the constitutional viability of state food laws are often called into question.[58]

Federal food law derives from Congress's constitutional power to regulate domestic commerce.[59] As with federal consumer laws in general, federal food laws are of relatively recent vintage. Prior to the twentieth century, the federal government rarely legislated food; instead, food regulation was the province of state and even municipal governments. Around the turn of the twentieth century, several factors led to congressional intervention. Rapid industrialization created an ever-expanding national market for manufactured or processed consumer food and nonfood goods. Because states had no jurisdiction to regulate conduct outside their borders, state law became increasingly ineffective at regulating food products that were distributed nationwide by out-of-state companies. In addition, there were several highly publicized incidents involving tainted food, including the accounting of awful conditions in meat packing plants detailed in the wildly popular novel, *The Jungle* by Upton Sinclair in 1905.[60]

As a result of these events, Congress enacted the first two federal food laws: in 1906 the Pure Food and Drug Act (PFDA)[61] and in 1907 the Federal Meat Inspection Act (FMIA).[62] The significance of these two acts has been far-reaching. The acts changed forever the traditional constitutional understanding that public health and safety was the province of several states. On a practical level, the acts ordered that federal regulators for the first time oversee the inner workings of the US food industry: the FMIA, for example, required every enterprise that processed meat products for interstate sale to submit to continuous federal inspection.[63]

Under the PFDA and FMIA and subsequent federal food acts, the bulk of federal responsibility for the direct regulation of food in the United States has primarily been delegated to the FDA and the USDA. However, a number of other federal agencies have become involved in the regulation of food, including the Environmental Protection Agency (EPA), which set pesticide tolerance levels; the Centers for Disease Control and

---

that the FDCA's "statutory regime is designed primarily to protect the health and safety of the public at large. The Supreme Court has previously acknowledged, however, that the agency is responsible under the FDCA to issue certain regulations to "promote honest and fair dealing in the interest of the consumer." *See* 62 Cases of Jam v. United States, 340 U.S. 593, 596 (1951).

[57] U.S. CONST. art. VI, § 2.

[58] *See, e.g.*, Quesada v. Herb Thyme Farms, Inc., Case No. B239602 (2d App. Dist., December 23, 2013) (court found that the federal Organic Foods Production Act (OFPA) preempted state law claims related to organic certification where Herb Thyme labeled its products as USDA Organic, but sold products with organically grown herbs mixed with conventionally grown herbs. The putative class action, alleging that the UCL was violated under California's separate, but federally certified, organic program was dismissed because the label met USDA's certification requirements).

[59] U.S. CONST. art. I, § 8.

[60] UPTON SINCLAIR, THE JUNGLE (Penguin Classics Deluxe ed. 2006).

[61] Pure Food and Drug Act, ch. 3915, § 6, 34 Stat. 768 (1906) (repealed 1938).

[62] Federal Meat Inspection Act, Pub. L. No. 59–242, 34 Stat. 1260 (1907).

[63] This requirement of continuous federal inspection was not included in the PFDA or in any of the subsequent acts that cover food regulated by the FDA.

Prevention (housed in the Department of Health and Human Services), which investigates foodborne illnesses; the Department of Commerce's National Marine Fisheries Service, which regulates seafood; the Alcohol and Tobacco Tax and Trade Bureau, which regulates alcoholic beverages, except wines containing less than 7 percent alcohol; the Department of Homeland Security, which coordinates agency action to prevent deliberate contamination; and the Federal Trade Commission, which regulates false advertising of food products. According to the General Accounting Office (GAO), fifteen agencies have emerged with regulatory responsibilities over food per thirty main statutes.[64] In addition to these federal agencies, over 3,000 state and local agencies oversee the food supply, with jurisdiction over retail food establishments such as supermarkets and restaurants.[65]

The division of responsibility between the two primary agencies – the FDA and USDA – is by food category. The FDA has been housed in a number of different agency configurations and has undergone numerous name changes.[66] The FDA today is an agency of the US Department of Health and Human Services (DHHS), one of the US federal executive departments. The USDA was created in 1862 during the presidential tenure of Abraham Lincoln. The USDA is an executive department within the president's cabinet that encompasses seventeen numerous agencies and organizations.[67]

USDA is responsible for various activities related to meat and poultry while FDA is responsible for all other food, as well as animal drugs and animal feed. However, the jurisdictional lines outlined by governing statutes and agreed upon by agencies are often arbitrary, producing peculiar results. An oft-cited example is pizza, which is regulated by the FDA unless topped with 2 percent or more of cooked meat or poultry, in which case it is USDA-regulated.[68] Even the regulation of meat can be disjointed: while the USDA regulates under FMIA[69] and the PPIA,[70] the FDA regulates the rest; beef and chicken are thus under USDA regulation while the FDA oversees venison, quail, and pheasant.[71]

As part of the executive branch of the government, the federal administrative agencies – e.g., FDA, USDA, FTC, and EPA – are subject to the requirements of the Constitution, the enabling statutes, and a number of procedural statutes, including the Federal Advisory Committee Act,[72] the Freedom of Information Act,[73] and most importantly the

---

[64] Renée Johnson, CONG. RESEARCH SERV. RS22600, THE FEDERAL FOOD SAFETY SYSTEM: A PRIMER, summary page (January 17, 2014) (see appendix A for listing of major food agencies, their responsibilities, and primary authorities).

[65] Id.

[66] See About FDA History, U.S. FOOD & DRUG ADMIN. (May 29, 2013).

[67] In fiscal year 2013, USDA had about 100,000 employees and delivered public services through its more than 300 programs worldwide. See Financial Report Fiscal Year 2013, U.S. DEP'T OF AGRIC. (2013).

[68] See INSTITUTE OF MEDICINE AND NATIONAL RESEARCH COUNCIL, ENSURING SAFE FOOD: FROM PRODUCTION TO CONSUMPTION 27 (1998).

[69] 21 U.S.C. §§ 601–695.

[70] Id. §§ 451–471.

[71] 21 U.S.C. § 601(j). The major divisions of regulator responsibility between the USDA and FDA are described in this statutory definition: the FDA's authority extends to products containing small amounts of meats and to those kinds of meat (e.g., game such as venison) not listed as within the USDA's jurisdiction. See also U.S. GEN. ACCOUNTING OFFICE, GAO/RCED-00-195, FOOD SAFETY: ACTIONS NEEDED BY USDA AND FDA TO ENSURE THAT COMPANIES PROMPTLY CARRY OUT RECALLS 6, n.1 (August 2000).

[72] Federal Advisory Committee Act, Pub. L. No. 92–463, 86 Stat. 770 (1972) (codified as amended at 5 U.S.C. app. (2012)) (Enacted as law in 1972 to define how federal advisory committees operate. The law has special emphasis on open meetings, chartering, public involvement, and reporting).

[73] Freedom of Information Act, Pub. L. No. 89–487, 80 Stat. 250 (1966), originally signed into law by President Lyndon B. Johnson on July 4, 1966, replaced by Pub. L. No. 90–23, 81 Stat. 54 (1967), amended

Administrative Procedure Act.[74] The Administrative Procedure Act (APA) provides for basic procedural safeguards in the federal regulatory system and establishes and defines judicial review authority over the federal regulatory agencies.

[b] FDA: Administrative Procedures Act

Notwithstanding the fragmentation of food regulation, the FDA has the most important consumer protection role in the regulation of food. The FDA has long performed its public health mandate based on science. It is believed that a principled adherence to science insulates the agency from overly political decision making, including agency capture.[75] The FDA's identity as a science-based agency permeates almost every aspect of its structure. The scientific method's primacy is enshrined not only in the statutes the agency implements and the regulations it has promulgated, but also in its programs, offices, and laboratories.[76] In dispensing its science-based responsibilities to protect public health, the FDA relies on a number of legal tools to regulate food, including orders and rules, rulemaking, public and private meetings, guidance documents, petitions, and enforcement actions.

The regulatory activity of the FDA reflects the development of the modern US administrative state as well as the uniqueness of the FDA's regulatory regime. During the first half of the twentieth century and the New Deal, regulatory philosophy shifted from a laissez faire approach to the regulating commerce.[77] Over time, the modern US administrative state has evolved where Congress delegates a great deal of interpretative and regulatory authority to administrative agencies by enacting broad statutes with the expectation that the agencies will fill in the gaps. Like other agencies, the FDA uses a variety of policymaking tools to fill these gaps, including adjudication, rulemaking, and informal guidance. The development of these tools is designed to enable the FDA to achieve efficiencies and effectiveness of administration[78] and to adapt to changes in the food industry and society.

(1) Administrative Adjudication

Under the 1906 PFDA, the FDA policed the food system by using its investigative powers to examine food for evidence of adulteration or misbranding. If the FDA believed they had found a violation, they referred the case to a US attorney for either civil or criminal prosecution. Although Section 701 of the 1938 FDCA expressly provides the

---

by OPEN Government Act of 2007, Pub. L. 110–175, 121 Stat. 2524 (2007) (codified as amended at 5 U.S.C. § 552).

[74] Administrative Procedure Act, Pub. L. 79–404, 60 Stat. 237 (1946) (codified as amended at 5 USCA §§ 551 to 559, 701 to 706, 1305, 3105, 3344, 4301, 5335, 5372, 7521 (2012)).

[75] Rebecca L. Goldberg, *Administering Real Food: How the Eat-Food Movement Should-and Should Not-Approach Government Regulation*, 39 ECOLOGY L.Q. 773, 787 (2012).

[76] *See generally* Peter Barton Hutt, *The State of Science at the Food and Drug Administration*, 60 ADMIN. L. REV. 431, 446 (2008).

[77] *See* William E. Forbath, *Politics, State-Building, and the Courts, 1870–1920, in* THE CAMBRIDGE HISTORY OF LAW IN AMERICA 643, 650–4, (Michael Grossberg & Christopher Tolins eds., 2008).

[78] *See* Peter Barton Hutt, *Philosophy of Regulation under the Federal Food, Drug and Cosmetic Act*, 28 FOOD DRUG COSM. L.J. 177, 178 (1973) ("[T]he Act must be regarded as a constitution … The mission of the [FDA] is to implement [its fundamental] objectives through the most effective and efficient controls that can be devised.").

FDA with authority to promulgate formal and informal regulations, the perception at the time was that the agency's power to do so was limited. As a consequence, the FDA from 1938 to the 1970s relied upon administrative adjudication to bring enforcement actions against parties for violation of the FDCA, which approach provided court decisions that established general rules defining what types of behavior were in compliance with the FDCA and regulations.[79] In the 1970s, as the problems and issues facing the FDA became more complex, the FDA changed its principal method of policymaking from case-by-case adjudication to rulemaking.[80]

Although the FDA no longer relies on the tool of administrative adjudication to make policy, it should be noted that the APA generally allows agencies to make policy through case-by-case adjudication, whereby an agency conducts its own trial-like procedure against parties for violating the provisions of either a statute or a promulgated regulation that the agency is responsible for administering.[81] Such adjudication constitutes a final agency action, which is subject to judicial review pursuant to Section 706 of the APA.[82] While agencies such as the FTC rely solely on adjudication as tool to make policy,[83] the FDA does not have an adjudicatory branch and no longer engages in this type of policymaking.

(2) Formal Rulemaking

Section 701(e) of the FDCA empowers the FDA to engage in formal rulemaking.[84] The rules issued under Section 701(e) are binding, substantive rules with the force and effect of law.[85] For rules issued under this authority, Congress imposed detailed procedural safeguards and required that the rules be based on "substantial evidence in the administrative record."[86] FDA actions subject to Section 701(e) requirements include standards of identity for foods and regulations setting tolerances for unavoidable poisonous or deleterious substances in food.[87] Formal rulemaking under Section 701(e) is subject to formal procedural constraints embedded in the section. In addition, Section 701(e) rulemakings are subject to the requirements of the APA for formal evidentiary hearings.[88] Thus, the formal rulemaking (as well as administrative adjudication) by the FDA is subject to the substantial evidence test standard of review conducted under APA §§ 556 and 557. Under the substantial evidence standard, which was later incorporated

---

[79] Thomas W. Merrill & Kathryn Tongue Watts, *Agency Rules with the Force of Law: The Original Convention*, 116 Harv. L. Rev. 467, 557–8 (2002).

[80] Peter B. Hutt & Richard A. Merrill, Food and Drug Law: Cases and Materials 1236–7 (2d ed. 1991).

[81] See 5 U.S.C. §§ 553–554, 556.

[82] See 5 U.S.C. § 706.

[83] Paul R. Verkuil, *The Purposes and Limits of Independent Agencies*, 1988 Duke L.J. 257, 263 (1988) (noting FTC's heavy reliance upon adjudication).

[84] 21 U.S.C. § 371(e).

[85] U.S. v. Articles of Drug, 634 F. Supp. 435 (N.D. Ill. 1985).

[86] Under Section 701(e)(2) and (3), a person who would be "adversely affected" by the action is given the opportunity to file formal objections to a proposed regulation, which stays the effective date. FDA is required to hold a public hearing and to issue a report containing detailed findings of fact, which becomes the basis for the regulation. 21 U.S.C. § 371(e)(2) and (3).

[87] 21 U.S.C. § 371(e)(1).

[88] See U.S. v. Fla. E. Coast Ry. Co., 410 U.S. 224 (1973) (Section 701(e) rulemakings are subject to the requirements of 5 U.S.C. §§ 556–557).

into the APA, an agency is held to a higher burden to justify its actions. The reviewing court is directed to hold unlawful and set aside agency action, findings, and conclusions that are unsupported by substantial evidence on the record as a whole.[89] The substantial evidence test is not a quantitative test, but requires relevant evidence that a reasonable mind would accept as adequate to support the agency's conclusion.[90] In effect, it is the same standard applicable to a trial court in taking a case from the jury or in reviewing a jury verdict on a judgment notwithstanding the verdict.[91]

(3) *Informal Rulemaking*

In the two decades following the enactment of the APA in 1946, formal rulemakings as well as administrative adjudications dominated the administrative law landscape for federal agencies, including the FDA. However, those regulatory mechanisms proved to be inappropriate for implementing the mass of new legislation passed in the late 1960s and early 1970s that sought to address health, safety, and environmental problems. Informal rulemaking quickly became the preferred means of instituting these new far-reaching governmental policies. Its procedures were less demanding and more democratic than those of adjudication and it made more sense to develop. The FDA followed this pattern. Beginning in the 1960s and 1970s, the FDA – primarily in an effort to free itself from the formal procedural constraints that attached to the FDCA's specific rulemaking grants under Section 701(e) – began to assert that Section 701(a) authorized it to issue legislative rules using only informal notice-and-comment rulemaking procedures.[92]

Under Section 701(a), Congress empowered FDA to promulgate regulations "for the efficient enforcement of the Act" but did not stipulate any particular standard of judicial review. The APA sets forth six standards of judicial review of agency action.[93] The "arbitrary and capricious" standard of the APA, the most deferential standard of review, was made applicable to all then-existing grants of informal rulemaking authority, including Section 701(a) of the FDCA. Under this standard the reviewing court will uphold an agency's actions, unless the agency action is found to be "arbitrary, capricious, an

---

[89] *See id.*

[90] Consol. Edison Co. v. NLRB, 305 U.S. 197, 229 (1938).

[91] Corning Glass Works v. Int'l Trade Comm'n, 799 F.2d 1559 (4th Cir. 1986).

[92] Merrill & Watts, *supra* note 79, at 558.

[93] The APA provides that

[t]he reviewing court shall –

(2) hold unlawful and set aside agency actions, findings, and conclusions found to be –

(A) arbitrary, capricious, an abuse of discretion, or otherwise not in accordance with law;

(B) contrary to constitutional right, power, privilege, or immunity;

(C) in excess of statutory jurisdiction, authority, or limitations, or short of statutory right;

(D) without observance of procedure required by law;

(E) unsupported by substantial evidence in a case subject to Sections 556 and 557 of this title or otherwise reviewed on the record of an agency hearing provided by statute; or

(F) unwarranted by the facts to the extent that the facts are subject to trial de novo by the reviewing court.

In making the foregoing determinations, the court shall review the whole record or those parts of it cited by a party, and due account shall be taken of the rule of prejudicial error.

Pub. L. No. 79–404, 60 Stat. 237 (1946) (codified at 5 U.S.C. §§ 551 et seq.).

abuse of discretion, or otherwise not in accordance with law."[94] The arbitrary and capricious standard is a less exacting standard than the substantial evidence standard under 701(e) formal rulemaking. Absent a mistake of law or clear error of judgment, a court will reverse only if the agency action lacks a rational basis.[95] Eventually, Section 701(a) became the agency's principal rulemaking vehicle. Courts have upheld FDA's authority to issue binding substantive regulations under the authority of Section 701(a).[96]

Rulemaking by the FDA is subject to APA minimum procedural safeguards. Notice of any proposed rule must be published by the proposing agency in the Federal Register. A comment period must follow. In some cases, public hearings must be held with an official record and formal rules. Public comments must be reviewed and considered by the agency before final adoption of a regulation. Final regulations must be published at least 30 days before they are to take effect, to allow an opportunity both for legal challenge and for adjustments necessary for compliance with the regulation.[97]

Notwithstanding that the 701(a) informal notice-and-comment procedure became the preferred way of rulemaking, concerns emerged some of which applied to notice-and-comment rulemaking in general. One concern was the ossification of notice and comment rulemaking.[98] Although recent literature suggests that ossification was not as serious or as widespread as believed,[99] many agencies, including the FDA, responded to this ossification concerns by engaging in other forms of policymaking.[100] Another concern was that the technological advances in food render it urgent to solve a problem quickly without resorting to the more lengthy process of rulemaking. Even if the regulatory issue does not need immediate attention, by the time the FDA completes a rulemaking to address the issue, the rule may be moot.[101] Finally, rulemaking also has become increasingly expensive, which renders that tool burdensome when budgets are tight.

FDA has adopted various strategies to decrease the time between notice of a proposed rule and promulgation of a final rule. One such strategy is direct final rulemaking, which permits an agency to publish an uncontroversial rule, effective within a few months unless the agency receives significant adverse comments.[102] Only if the agency does receive negative comments will it proceed with normal notice and comment rulemaking. Another strategy is the use of interim final rulemaking, whereby an agency publishes a rule that becomes immediately effective, and then solicits and responds to comments from the public and industry.[103] If the comments call the reasoning behind the rule into

---

[94] 5 U.S.C. § 706(2)(A).

[95] National Ass'n of Mfrs. v. U.S. Dep't of Interior, 134 F.3d 1095 (D.C. Cir. 1998).

[96] *See, e.g.,* Weinberger v. Hynson, Westcott & Dunning, Inc., 412 U.S. 609 (1973).

[97] *See A Guide to the Rulemaking Process,* OFFICE OF THE FED. REGISTER.

[98] *See generally,* Thomas O. McGarity, *Some Thoughts on "Deossifying" the Rulemaking Process,* 41 DUKE L.J. 1385, 1410–12 (1992) (the first academic work to articulate the phenomenon of ossification).

[99] Jason Webb Yackee & Susan Webb Yackee, *Testing the Ossification Thesis: An Empirical Examination of Federal Regulatory Volume and Speed, 1950–1990,* 80 GEO. WASH. L. REV. 1414, 1420–1 (2012).

[100] *See generally* Richard J. Pierce, Jr., *Seven Ways to Deossify Agency Rulemaking,* 47 ADMIN. L. REV. 59, 60 (1995).

[101] *See* K. M. Lewis, *Informal Guidance and the FDA,* 66 FOOD & DRUG L.J. 507, 525 (2011).

[102] *See* Guidance for FDA and Industry: Direct Final Rule Procedures; Guidance for FDA and Industry: Direct Final Rule Procedures, 62 Fed. Reg. 62,466, 62,466 (November 21, 1997).

[103] *See* Ronald M. Levin, *Direct Final Rulemaking,* 64 GEO. WASH. L. REV. 1, 2 (1995).

question, the agency can then withdraw or amend the rule. Another tool used by other agencies and to a limited extent by the FDA is negotiated rulemaking.[104] Negotiated rulemaking is a consensus-based process through which the agency develops a proposed rule by using a neutral facilitator and a balanced negotiating committee composed of stakeholders.[105] The objective is to allow stakeholders to agree on the main features of a rule before the agency proposes it in final form. Despite burdens on the efficiency of its informal rulemaking, FDA has been reticent to embrace negotiated rulemaking.[106]

(4) *Informal Guidance*

One response to concerns of agency ossification has been to implement a rulemaking tool that is less formal than administrative adjudication and rulemaking and nimble enough to respond to emerging public and societal concerns. The tool that has crystalized is informal guidance, which has replaced rulemaking as the principal method of policymaking for the FDA.[107] Informal guidance is policymaking through less formal means whereby policy is announced by FDA in guidance documents, informal opinions, operating manuals, interpretive letters, or even press releases.[108] This type of policymaking typically lacks the procedural safeguards of administrative adjudication and rulemaking that protect both regulated enterprises and regulatory beneficiaries.[109]

Informal guidance does not bind regulated enterprises or the FDA. Instead, guidance documents represent FDA's current thinking on a topic. Thus, guidance can be used in a court or administrative proceeding to illustrate acceptable standards, but not as establishing a legal requirement.[110] Although the FDA cannot base an enforcement action solely on a regulated enterprise's noncompliance with a guidance document, the agency's interpretations of the law are often reflected in guidance documents or in responses to petitions that are not part of a marketing-authorization process. It is apparent then that despite guidance's nonbinding status, guidance documents have regulation-like effects because they indicate how the FDA will implement a program or enforce a rule.[111]

---

[104] *See generally* Julia Kobick, *Negotiated Rulemaking: The Next Step in Regulatory Innovation at the Food and Drug Administration?*, 65 FOOD & DRUG L.J. 425 (2010).

[105] *What Is Negotiated Rulemaking*, USDA, AGRICULTURE MARKETING SERV. (June 25, 2014).

[106] FDA does have one regulation requiring that any petition to establish or amend a reference amount customarily consumed (RACC) under 21 C.F.R. § 101.12(b) include a statement of feasibility of negotiated rulemaking.

[107] *See* Lewis, *supra* note 101.

[108] *See generally* M. Elizabeth Magill, *Agency Choice of Policymaking Form*, 71 U. CHI. L. REV. 1383, 1386 (2004).

[109] *See* James Hunnicutt, *Another Reason to Reform the Federal Regulatory System: Agencies' Treating Nonlegislative Rules as Binding Law*, 41 B.C. L. REV. 153, 157–76 (1999).

[110] 42 Fed. Reg. 4709, 4710 (January 25, 1977).

[111] *See* Lewis, *supra* note 101. While the primary use of informal guidance, especially guidance documents, is of recent vintage by the FDA, the agency and its predecessors have been using guidance documents to further their regulatory objectives for over a century. Beginning in 1902, the Bureau of Chemistry, an early prototype of FDA, began issuing Food Inspection Decisions (FIDs) to respond to questions by regulated enterprises. *See id.* at 509. Starting in the 1930s, the FDA issued advisory opinions in the form of trade correspondences (TCs) to advise enterprises on how to comply with statutory requirements. As a result of the APA's emphasis on procedural rigor, the FDA stopped using TCs after 1946 to avoid subjecting these communications to the strictures of the APA. *See id.* at 511.

Section 701(h) of the FDCA directs FDA to establish uniform procedures for issuing guidance documents.[112] The FDA has increased the uniformity and formality of guidance by promulgating a regulation establishing "Good Guidance Practices" (GGPs) to follow when formulating and issuing informal guidance.[113] The GGPs establish two tiers of guidance, Level 1 and Level 2. Level 1 documents set forth interpretations of statutory or regulatory requirements; major changes in interpretation or policy; and changes in interpretation or policy that are significant, including complex scientific issues or highly controversial issues. The procedures for issuing a Level 1 guidance document are similar to, but less rigorous than, the requirements for informal rulemaking established in the APA. FDA must publish a notice in the Federal Register after a draft guidance is available, make its draft guidance available on the Internet and in hard copy, and invite and review comments on the proposed guidance. Unlike rules promulgated through notice and comment, Level 1 guidance does not require the agency to respond to the comments it receives. Level 2 guidance documents are those guidance documents that do not fall within the Level 1 category, including those documents that set forth existing practices or minor changes in interpretation or policy. Level 2 guidance documents are less rigorous than the procedures for Level 1 documents: FDA need not publish notice in the Federal Register for Level 2 documents; it need only make the document available on the Internet and in hard copy. While FDA may not begin implementation of a Level 1 document until interested parties have had an opportunity for comment, FDA may implement Level 2 documents the instant they are issued, as long as the agency is receptive to any comments it may subsequently receive. Interested parties may at any time submit comments requesting that specific guidance documents be revised or withdrawn or may suggest topics for new guidance documents.[114] The GGPs explicitly state that guidance documents "do not legally bind the public or FDA."[115]

An area of confusion has to do with a subset of guidance documents known as advisory opinions, which "represents the best advice of FDA on a matter at the time of its issuance"[116] and are sometimes used to create broadly applicable policies.[117] FDA has drafted and published a proposed amendment that would have rendered advisory opinions nonbinding, but did not finalize it in the Code of Regulations.[118] It has been pointed out that this development is odd given FDA's previously stated intention "that guidelines have the same legal status as advisory opinions."[119] As matters stand, there are two distinct categories of informal guidance: advisory opinions, which could bind FDA, and guidance documents, which officially do not.[120]

What the future holds for informal guidance is unclear. Concerns about the use of informal guidance by the FDA as a matter of policymaking – its use as a de facto rule, the complaint that FDA enforces guidance statements as though they were legally binding rules,

---

[112] FDA Report on Good Guidance Practices: Improving Efficiency and Transparency, U.S. Food & Drug Admin. (December 2011).

[113] See 21 C.F.R. § 10.115.

[114] See FDA Report on Good Guidance Practices, *supra* note 112 at 2.

[115] 21 C.F.R. § 10.115(d)(1).

[116] 57 Fed. Reg. 47314 (October 15, 1972).

[117] Lewis, *supra* note 101, at 526.

[118] See Fed. Reg. 47314, *supra* note 116.

[119] Lewis, *supra* note 101, at 524.

[120] *Id.*

and the lack of the agency's discretion all raise questions about the place of informal guidance as a regulatory tool used by the FDA to regulate food in the modern food system. Notwithstanding these concerns, informal guidance has proven to be a nimble tool, allowing the FDA to adapt to changing circumstances.

(5) Informal and Public and Private Meetings

In addition to hearings described in FDA's regulations, the agency provides many opportunities for informal public and private meetings. Public meetings on developing scientific issues often take the form of workshops, where experts and others exchange information and views. FDA also holds educational meetings for industry and for members of the public on regulatory requirements or public health matters.[121] At the agency's discretion, it also may convene public meetings on pending matters, with broad opportunities for public participation.[122] Members of the public may also request private meetings with FDA. Although those requesting such meetings are not entitled to meet with agency officials, the agency is to "make reasonable efforts to accommodate" such requests.[123] A public record is kept of those who request and attend the meetings.[124]

(6) Citizen Petitions

FDA's regulations on citizen petitions, which are rooted in the First Amendment's recognition of the "right of the people ... to petition the Government for a redress of grievances,"[125] are codified at 21 C.F.R. Part 10. These regulations permit any interested person to petition the FDA Commissioner to issue, amend, or revoke a regulation or order or take or refrain from taking any other form of administrative action.[126] Unless the form of the petition is specified in another regulation,[127] the form of a citizen petition must follow the specifications of 21 C.F.R. § 10.30(b). These specifications contain not only format requirements, but also content requirements for petitions submitted to FDA. Once filed, petitions and supporting materials are available for the public to review and to comment on.[128] During the course of its review, FDA may choose to solicit further comment through a notice in the Federal Register, public meetings or hearings, or other processes.[129] FDA is required to respond to a citizen petition within 180 days of receipt of the petition by approving the petition, denying the petition, or providing a tentative response indicating why the agency has not yet decided.[130] Resource constraints make it difficult for the FDA to respond rapidly to citizen petitions. The agency explicitly stated that its responses to petitions would reflect

---

[121] See, e.g., Educational Workshops on Good Manufacturing Practices, 72 Fed. Reg. 53,778 (September 20, 1977).

[122] See 21 C.F.R. § 10.65(b).

[123] 21 C.F.R. § 10.65(c).

[124] See Michelle Simon, Behind Closed Doors: Who's Taking Meetings with FDA on Food Safety?, CENTER FOR FOOD SAFETY (December 2, 2013).

[125] U.S. CONST. amend. I.

[126] 21 C.F.R. § 10.25(a). An "administrative action" is defined as "every act, including the refusal or failure to act, involved in the administration of any law by the Commissioner, except that it does not include the referral of apparent violations to U.S. attorneys for the institution of civil or criminal proceedings or an act in preparation of a referral." 21 C.F.R. § 10.3(a).

[127] The form for a food additive petition is set forth in 21 C.F.R. § 171.1.

[128] 21 C.F.R. §§ 10.20(j)(1), 10.30(c)(d).

[129] 21 C.F.R. § 10.30(h).

[130] 21 C.F.R. § 10.30(e)(2).

agency resources, priorities, and statutory deadlines.[131] When a decision is made, the agency may grant or deny the petition, in whole or in part, and may grant other relief or take other action as warranted by the petition.[132] Any interested person, including the petitioner, may ask the agency to reconsider a decision on a citizen petition.[133] As a general rule, FDA's final decision on citizen petition, a petition for reconsideration, or a petition for stay of action is final agency action reviewable in court.[134]

(7) *Additional Petitions and Tools*

Any interested person may ask the agency to stay the effective date of any administrative action for a specific or indefinite period of time.[135] Also, FDA's interpretations of the law are reflected in its enforcement actions and policies. FDA exercises its authority and conveys its views through communications during inspections, warning letters and other regulatory correspondence, initiation and prosecution of administrative actions and civil and criminal judicial actions, and import-detention actions. Like other federal agencies, FDA also uses many information communication tools – such as press or other media communications, speeches, and responses to letters – to inform and educate the regulated industry and the public. It may be that as technology advances, the FDA will depend on social media messaging more in the future.

[c] Calls for Single Food Safety Agency

Appraisal of the fragmented structure of the federal food regulatory system has over the course of several years generated considerable debate of whether there should be a single food agency, especially for the administration of food safety. Proponents of a single food safety agency argue that the existing fragmented system is ill equipped for meeting the challenges of food safety.[136] They assert that a single agency would be more focused and efficient in delivering information, incentives, and penalties. For years, the GAO also has unequivocally recommended consolidation of federal food safety programs. The GAO has testified and issued numerous reports highlighting the current fragmentation and inconsistent organization of the various agencies involved in food safety oversight, and has recommended repeatedly establishing a single, independent food safety agency to administer a unified, risk-based food safety system. In May 1994 testimony before Congress, the GAO cited that its testimony supporting a single food safety system is "based on over 60 reports and studies issued over the last 25 years by the GAO, agency Inspectors General, and others."[137] In March 2004, the GAO reiterated its call for a single, independent food safety agency in testimony before Congress: "[e]stablishing a single food safety agency

---

[131] 21 C.F.R. § 10.30(e)(1).
[132] 21 C.F.R. § 10.30(e)(3) (the petitioner must be notified of the decision in writing).
[133] 21 C.F.R. § 10.33. The agency may also initiate the reconsideration of a matter. 21 C.F.R. § 10.33(a), (h).
[134] 21 C.F.R. § 10.45(d).
[135] 21 C.F.R. § 10.35(b).
[136] *See* Timothy M. Hammonds, *It Is Time to Designate a Single Food Safety Agency?*, 59 Food & Drug L.J. 427, 427 (2004).
[137] Testimony of John W. Harman, GAO, before the Human Resources and Intergovernmental Relations Subcommittee, Committee on Government Operations, House of Representatives *in* Gao, Food Safety: A Unified, Risk-Based Food Safety System Needed 1, GAO/T-RCED-94–223, (Washington DC, May 25, 1994).

responsible for administering a uniform set of laws would offer the most logical approach to resolving long-standing problems with the current system, addressing emerging threats to food safety, and ensuring a safer food supply."[138] In February 2015, as part of the US president's 2016 budget plan, President Barack Obama proposed consolidating the US food safety operations into one agency within the DHHS. The agency would be independent from the FDA and would be responsible for food safety inspections, enforcement, applied research, and responses to food-poisoning outbreaks.[139]

It is not just that the current complex and fragmented system creates gaps and overlaps. Each one of the agencies invested in the food regulatory system uses a very different approach – often mandated by law – to address the very same issues depending on jurisdiction. Products that are perceived as identical in the minds of consumers often are regulated by different agencies administering different approaches because jurisdiction frequently is split. Drawing on the aforementioned example of pizza in this chapter in which it was noted that the FDA regulates pizza until the toppings reach 2 percent or more of cooked meat or poultry, a plant that produces only cheese pizza is subject to inspection by FDA, which is likely to occur only infrequently, whereas a plant that produces pepperoni pizza is subject to daily inspection by the USDA, even though the agency already has inspected the animal from which the pepperoni is made and the processing of the meat into pepperoni. To complicate matters further, inspectors from both the USDA and FDA, operating under two very different sets of guidelines, simultaneously regulate an integrated pizza processing plant.[140] Sometimes authority for approval and administration is handed off in mid-stream. For example, jurisdiction over eggs changes several times along the farm-to-table continuum. FDA is responsible for the safety of eggs on the farm; the USDA has authority over the safety of eggs during handling and transportation; and FDA is responsible for eggs again at retail. Moreover, although FDA is given jurisdiction over shell eggs, the safety of processed or liquid eggs is the responsibility of the USDA.[141]

Opponents of a single food agency believe that the cooperative system has historically worked well and that moving from a long, settled system to a new entity would generate confusion and pose a security threat that would outweigh any supposed benefits that would accrue with a single agency.[142] Opponents stress that consolidation could increase accountability and allow regulatory flexibility in the long run, most of the benefits of consolidation would not come primarily from the unification of agency responsibilities itself. Rather, consolidation would only be beneficial if the entire system were transformed by a legislature with a renewed regulatory spirit and a willingness to give additional funding and authority. Opponents conclude that many of the benefits that are portrayed as likely to result from

[138] Testimony of Lawrence J. Dyckman, director, Natural Resources and Environment, GAO, before the Civil Service Subcommittee, Senate Governmental Affairs Committee, US Senate in Gao, Federal Food Safety And Security System: Fundamental Restructuring Is Needed to Address Fragmentation and Overlap 17, GAO-04-588T, (Washington DC, March 30, 2004).

[139] Ron Nixon, *Obama Proposes Single Overseer for Food Safety*, N.Y. Times (February 21, 2015) at A12.

[140] *See* Lawrence J. Dyckman, US GAO, GAO/T-RCED-256, U.S. Needs a Single Agency to Administer a Unified, Risk-Based Inspection System 6 (August 4, 1999).

[141] 7 C.F.R. § 56.4.

[142] *See* Stuart M. Pape et al., *Food Security Would Be Compromised by Combining the Food and Drug Administration and the U.S. Department of Agriculture into a Single Food Agency*, 59 Food & Drug L.J. 405, 414 (2004).

consolidation would probably occur only if consolidation were accompanied by an overall legislative fervor to resolve the system's inadequacies through such improvements. In contrast, a simple combination of agencies without these improvements would only serve as a short-term drain on resources for a system that can hardly afford it.[143]

[2] *Government Programs*

 [a] USDA Mission

As shown in chapters 5 and 6, government programs regulate the distribution of food assistance, the nutrition education of consumers, and various aspects of the food system. Given the gravity of the social consequences from food production and consumption, it should be no surprise that the government is involved in the regulation of food beyond the regulation of safety and quality. The lack of food can create political volatility; hence, it is natural that in addition to regulation, the government develops and funds programs intended to foster the production and distribution of food. The obesity epidemic also provides impetus for nutrition programs.

 While the FDA has regulatory authority over most food product, the USDA has responsibility for most programs that pertain to food. The USDA mission statement states that the department "provide[s] leadership on food, agriculture, natural resources, rural development, nutrition, and related issues based on sound public policy, the best available science, and effective management."[144] The department's vision statement is ambitious and broad, setting forth a number of priorities: (1) expand economic opportunity through innovation; (2) help rural America thrive; (3) promote food production to nourish Americans and feed the world; and (4) preserve and conserve natural resources.[145] These priorities are enshrined in a strategic plan that lists a number of key activities, most of which are program-driven and most of which affect to various degrees all of the stakeholders, including consumers, in the food system chain.[146]

 [b] US Farm Bill

The USDA programs intersect with law in numerous ways. Many of the programs are created by legislation, including the US Farm Bill, which Congress renews every five years. The importance of the farm bill for the administration of food law cannot be overstated. The farm bill is the closest thing the United States has to a national food policy. The farm bill is an omnibus, multiyear piece of authorizing legislation that governs an array of agricultural and food programs.[147] Although agricultural policies sometimes are created and changed by freestanding legislation or as part of other major laws, the farm bill provides a predictable opportunity for policymakers to address comprehensively and periodically agricultural and food issues. Since the 1930s, farm bills traditionally have

---

[143] The Harvard Law Review Association, *Reforming the Food Safety System: What If Consolidation Isn't Enough?*, 120 HARV. L. REV. 1345, 1366 (2007).

[144] *Mission Statement*, US DEP'T OF AGRIC. (APRIL 15, 2014, last modified)

[145] *Id.*

[146] *See Strategic Plan FY 2014–2018*, US DEP'T OF AGRIC.

[147] For a complete library of US Farm Bills and general resources related to the farm bills, see the online archive of the National Agricultural Law Center, located at the University of Arkansas.

focused on farm commodity price and income support for a handful of staple commodities – corn, soybeans, wheat, cotton, rice, and dairy. Yet farm bills have grown in breadth in recent decades. Among the most important additions have been nutrition assistance, conservation, horticulture, and bioenergy programs.[148] As noted by the Congressional Research Service:

> The omnibus nature of the farm bill can create broad coalitions of support among conflicting interests for policies that individually might not survive the legislative process. This also can stir fierce competition for funds. In recent years, more parties have become involved in the farm bill debate, including national farm groups, commodity associations, state organizations, and nutrition and public health officials, as well as advocacy groups representing conservation, recreation, rural development, faith-based interests, local food systems, and certified organic production.[149]

The Agricultural Act of 2014,[150] now known as the 2014 Farm Bill, is the most recent omnibus farm bill. It was enacted in February 2014 and succeeded the Food, Conservation, and Energy Act of 2008 (2008 Farm Bill).[151] The 2014 Farm Bill contains twelve titles including commodity price and income supports, farm credit, trade, agricultural conservation, research, rural development, energy, and foreign and domestic food programs.

[3] International Food Governance

[a] Dynamic System of Systems

The modern global food system in which the US food system is firmly entrenched is a complex, dynamic system of systems of national states that in turn consists of multiple systems. The overarching framework that regulates food to some extent on an international level comprises international standards that are used to regulate food trade, harmonize food rules among different countries, and remedy trade conflicts.

[b] Legal Instruments

As elucidated in Chapter 2, the international regulation of food is governed by a series of international legal instruments of which the United States is a signatory. The World Trade Organization (WTO) Sanitary and Phytosanitary Agreement (SPS Agreement) names the Codex Alimentarius Commission (Codex) specifically as the organization that is "to harmonize sanitary and phytosanitary measures on as wide a basis as possible"[152] by setting "international standards, guidelines or recommendations."[153] Organized by the United Nation's Food and Agricultural Organization (FAO) and the World Health Organization (WHO),

---

[148] *See* Ralph M. Chite, CONG. RESEARCH SERV. R43076, THE 2014 FARM BILL (AGRICULTURAL ACT OF 2014 P.L. 113–179): SUMMARY AND SIDE-BY-SIDE (2014).

[149] *Id.*

[150] Agricultural Act of 2014, P.L. 113–179, H. Rept. 113–133 (2014).

[151] Food, Conservation, and Energy Act of 2008, P.L. 110–246 (2008).

[152] Agreement on the Application of Sanitary and Phytosanitary Measures (SPS Agreement), Introduction (April 15, 1994), Marrakesh Agreement Establishing the World Trade Organization, Annex 1A, 1867 U.N.T.S. 493, 33 I.L.M. 1125.

[153] SPS Agreement, art. 12, para. 4.

Codex is headquartered in Rome, Italy, and has 186 member states, including the United States.[154] Codex issues and publishes two types of standards that affect food: safety standards (SPS standards) and technical standards, which are the basis for non-SPS standards, such as labeling requirements. These Codex standards are the basis for national legislation in member states;[155] the WTO relies on Codex standards to help it apply the SPS Agreement and the TBT Agreement in food safety and trade disputes.[156] National food standards that comply with Codex standards will be deemed to comply with the SPS Agreement and not be in breach of the GATT.[157]

Although use of Codex standards creates favorable presumptions under the international legal instruments, states are not required to implement Codex standards into national regulation. Codex standards are subject to FDA review. The FDA will decide whether to accept the Codex standards, accept them with modifications, or not accept them at all.[158] Because Codex standards are not mandatory, various interest groups are able to petition the FDA to apply (or not apply) certain standards. For example, the American Beekeeping Federation and others petitioned the FDA to apply Codex standards to honey but with certain deviations with regard to pesticide residue levels and heavy metal contaminants.[159]

Delay in creating or revising standards is one of the greatest criticisms of Codex. In some instances, Codex's delay in setting standards has resulted in continued dispute. For example, Codex struggled to set a standard for beef hormones, which contributed to the EU and the US disagreement on beef hormones referred to in Chapter 3. There are several reasons for delays in setting standards. One reason is that with so many member states participating and with so much at stake, agreement is not easy. These 186 members have different priorities, needs, and levels of social and economic development. Another reason is the time it takes to make scientific and risk-assessment assessments. In addition to the complexity of the science, the review process can also create delay. An independent expert scientific committee jointly administered by the FAO and WHO – the joint FAO/WHO Expert Committee on Food Additives (JECFA) – performs risk assessments and provides advice to FAO, WHO, and the member countries of these organizations. Delay by JECFA due to infrequent meetings and other logistical problems can be considerable.

National government organizations (NGOs) may attend Codex Commission sessions as observers if invited by the directors-general of the FAO or WHO. Codex has also recognized the importance of consumers' rights and consumer organizations' participation in Codex, especially in developing countries. NGO participation and consumer group participation is recognized as being particularly important for disseminating Codex information to consumers.[160]

---

[154] *About Codex*, CODEX ALIMENTARIUS COMM'N (2013).

[155] SPS Agreement, art. 3, para. 1.

[156] European Communities – Measures Concerning Meat and Meat Products, WT/DS26/AB/R, APPELLATE BODY REPORT (January 16, 1998).

[157] SPS Agreement, art. 2.4.

[158] 21 C.F.R. § 130.6(a).

[159] Citizen Petition from Kristen C. Gunter, Counsel for Petitioners, to FDA, Docket No. FDA-2006P-0101/CP1 (March 8, 2006).

[160] CODEX ALIMENTARIUS COMM'N PROCEDURE MANUAL, Rule VII: Relations with Other Organizations (12th ed. 2011)

When adopting standards, Codex aims to reach agreement by consensus but can adopt standards by voting if consensus fails.[161] Codex standards are created and revised by scientists, international risk assessment bodies, and ad-hoc consultations organized by the FAO and WHO working together. Standards are based on scientific analysis and must be made with regard to consumer health protection and, as noted in Chapter 2, with regard to preserving and promoting free trade.[162] Codex standards cover a variety of topics, including food hygiene, additives, residues of pesticides and veterinary drugs, contaminants, labeling, and import and export inspection.[163]

[4] New Governance

[a] Theoretical Underpinnings

Variant forms of food law identified in this treatise such as self-governance, voluntary standards, private standards, corporate social responsibility standards, codes of conduct, and third-party verification can be categorized loosely under the category of "new governance."[164] New governance measures generate legal mechanisms for the development of food standards and build accountability for stakeholders in the imposition of the standards. The theoretical underpinnings of new governance have been laid out in legal scholarship on the regulatory state in recent years.[165] The role of new governance in the modern food system is part of a larger issue of the overall role of government in the post–New Deal regulatory state that has relied on a command-and-control model that has been criticized in the past few decades for the inefficiency of the rulemaking process and for low compliance levels.[166]

A fundamental question is whether new governance constitutes law. This issue engenders interesting and provocative debate over the concept of law, as well as the relationship between new governance and "law in the sense of holding officials accountable for their acts and assuring that citizens are otherwise secure in the enjoyment of their rights."[167] A justification for considering self-governance as law is grounded in a doctrine called "legal pluralism" that suggests that "more than one body of laws or set of norms can exist within a legal jurisdiction."[168] This neoliberalism notion has long subscribed to the view that "private groups should be entitled to exercise within the area of their competence an authority so effective as to justify labeling it as a

---

[161] *Id.* at Rule XII, para. 2.

[162] Statement of Principle Concerning the Role of Science in the Codex Decision Making Process and the Extend to Which Other Factors Are Taken into Account, Codex Alimentarius Comm'n, Decision of the 21st Session of the Commission, 1995.

[163] Codex Procedural Manual, *supra* note 160 at 28 (General Principles of the Codex Alimentarius) (12th ed.).

[164] *See generally* Jason M. Solomon, *Book Review Essay: Law and Governance in the 21st Century Regulatory State & The Regulatory and Administrative State: Materials, Cases, Comments*, 86 Tex. L. Rev. 819, 822 (2008).

[165] *See, e.g.*, Gráinne de Búrca & Joanne Scott, Law and New Governance in the EU and the US (Gráinne de Búrca & Joanne Scott eds., 2006).

[166] *See* Jody Freeman, *Collaborative Governance in the Administrative State*, 45 UCLA. L. Rev. 1, 3 (1997) ("Regulation is currently under attack from all quarters as inefficient, ineffective, and undemocratic.").

[167] *Id.*

[168] Orley Lobel, *The Paradox of Extralegal Activisim: Critical Legal Consequences and Transformative Politic*, 120 Harv. L. Rev. 938, 966 (2007)).

sovereign authority."[169] The outcome of this notion in the global market context is an extralegal model that results in self-governance measures. Aside from the theoretical considerations of new governance, it is clear that as a practical matter new governance approaches to food law increasingly affect stakeholders in the modern food system, including consumers.

[b] Approaches

These new governance approaches, which appear intermittently through this treatise, are described briefly in the following pages in the context of how they apply to the modern food system. It is noted that these approaches are largely conceptual and overlap with one another in varying degrees. Hence, these forms are particular forms or elements of the broader model of new governance. The advantage to delineating the approaches from one another is that the terms often place different emphasis on a particular characteristic of new governance.

- Self-regulation

Self-regulation can be defined broadly as actions by food enterprises to develop and enforce rules and standards governing their behavior in the food sector. Self-regulation often involves food enterprises into nutrition regulation. For example, as noted in Chapter 4, front-of-pack labeling standards developed by a cluster of food companies have been a popular labeling device in conveying information to consumers.

- Voluntary Standards

Voluntary standards are rules set by a food enterprise that set standards for the enterprise or affirm that enterprise's commitment to a particular practice. These standards may affect other enterprises who in order to supply to the announcing enterprise must meet the voluntary standard. An example of a voluntary standard is the announcement of Walt Disney Company to phase junk food advertising out of its television and radio programming targeted at children. All foods marketed on Disney's channels must meet the company's nutrition guidelines that purportedly align with the 2010 Dietary Guidelines for Americans.[170]

- Private Standards

The term "private standards" is frequently interchangeable with voluntary standards. The nomenclature of private standards is particularly relevant to the usage of voluntary standards in food value chains.[171] These standards typically relate to food safety,

---

[169] *Id.* (quoting Owen E. Hernstadt, *Voluntary Corporate Codes of Conduct: What's Missing?*, 16 Lab. Law. 349, 349 (2001)).

[170] Gretchen Goetz, *Disney Bans Junk Food Marketing from Its Network Kingdom*, Food Safety News (June 6, 2012).

[171] *See generally* Michael T. Roberts, *The Compatibility of Private Standards with Multilateral Trade Rules: Legal Issues at Stake*, in The Evolving Structure of World Agricultural Trade: Implications for Trade Policy and Trade Agreements 253 (Alexander Sarris & Jamie Morrison eds., FAO 2009).

environmental impact, and animal welfare. NGOs often urge food enterprises to adopt and enforce private standards to effect changes in the food supply chain. Private standards are imposed on the supply chain in the form of contract and obligate suppliers in the food chain to meet specified standards. Private standards are so widespread in the global food market as to have become de facto mandatory for suppliers.[172] As noted in Chapter 3, the Global Food Safety Initiative is the leading developer and conveyor of private standards and has enormous influence in regulating the behavior of the food industry. Also, as noted in Chapter 2, private standards have come under severe criticism particularly in developing countries where the concern is that the standards create undue hardships to small farmers and invoke barriers to trade in violation of the SPS and TBT agreements.

- Codes of Conduct

Codes of conduct are developed by food enterprises to establish obligations for the enterprise to engage voluntarily in certain conduct generally involving environmental or social objectives. An example of code of conduct in the food sector is the human-rights-based code of conduct used in the Florida tomato industry.[173] This code of conduct provides a wage increase for farm workers via a price premium paid by retailers who purchase Florida tomatoes.

- Corporate Social Responsibility (CSR)

CSR statements as implemented by food enterprises integrate social and environmental concerns in their business operations and interactions with their stakeholders. CSR is generally understood as the way through which an enterprise achieves a balance of economic, environmental, and social imperatives, while at the same time addressing the expectations of shareholders and stakeholders. In the global food system, there has in recent years been a sharp escalation in the social roles large food enterprises are expected to play. The enterprises face increasing pressure to engage in public-private partnerships and to be accountable not only to shareholders, but also to stakeholders such as employees, consumers, local communities, and society at large.

- Third-Party Verification

Third-party verification refers to an external private auditor or consultant who is paid by the regulated food enterprise to verify compliance with a voluntary standard. Enterprises may employ third-party audits to prove their safety or environmental claims are true. Third-party verification also denotes a system in which governmental agencies rely on these third parties to verify regulatory compliance. This tool is incorporated in FSMA where third-party auditors are called on to certify that food produced abroad complied with FDA standards.[174]

---

[172] *Private Standards: Relevant Definitions and a Typology*, FOOD & AGRIC. ORG. OF THE UNITED NATIONS.
[173] *See Fair Food Code of Conduct & Selected Guidance*, FAIR FOOD STANDARDS COUNCIL (June 26, 2014).
[174] Tacy Katherine Hass, *New Governance: Can User-Promulgated Certification Schemes Provide Safer, Higher Quality Food?*, 68 FOOD & DRUG L.J. 77, 78 (2013).

[c] Praise and Concern of New Governance

These forms of new governance have been praised as contributing to the governance of the modern food system. First, the rules in new governance forms tend to be less prescriptive and more focused on learning through monitoring than compliance with rules enshrined in government code or regulations.[175] Second, new governance brings together agency and industry representatives to define and revise standards.[176] Public agencies and private actors "interact in increasingly complex and collaborative ways to address problems of public policy."[177] The organic certification as developed by USDA, shown in Chapter 6, serves as a model of a public governance scheme that delegates governing authority to third parties. Under this model, private producers pay private certifiers to conduct inspections. Third, new governance approaches allow industries to self-regulate when threatened by possible government regulation and public scrutiny. For example, as referenced in Chapter 5, the food industry has engaged in self-regulation since 2006 by issuing a series of highly publicized pledges and initiatives that address beverages and foods in schools, marketing to children, and menu labeling.[178] Fourth, self-governance also helps remedy regulatory fragmentation in the food sector. New governance forms overcome regulatory fragmentation by taking the conflict outside of the legal and regulatory system, as with the voluntary labeling of GE food. Fifth, private standards fill gaps, especially on the global level. For example, multinational food companies that are either frustrated with delays at Codex or simply want to gain a competitive advantage have progressively developed and implemented food safety norms on their own initiative.

Despite the popularity in some quarters of these new governance forms, concerns have emerged, including that these governance forms to varying degrees contribute to the devolution of the state, function without accountability, is less transparent than traditional regulation, and give larger food enterprises unchecked control over the food supply chain. Evaluation of new governance forms calls for standards to maximize the likelihood that self-regulation will incorporate transparency, meaningful objectives and benchmarks, accountability and objective evaluation, and oversight.[179]

[5] *State and Local Regulation*

[a] Police Power

As demonstrated through the treatise, state and local authorities regulate parts of the food system. The role of states and municipalities in regulating food is framed by the doctrine of federalism, which includes the "police power" of the state.[180] The police power of the

---

[175] Solomon, *supra* note 164, at 823.

[176] *See* Freeman, *supra* note 166, at 33–34 (the process where regulated entities negotiate the substance of a rule with the regulating agency is "increasingly common in environmental and health and safety regulation").

[177] *Id.*

[178] Lisa L. Sharma et al., *The Food Industry and Self-Regulation: Standards to Promote Success and to Avoid Public Health Failures*, 100 AMERICAN J. OF PUBLIC HEALTH 240 (2010).

[179] Roberts, *supra* note 171, at 253.

[180] Historically, states have been viewed as having the inherent sovereignty to safeguard community welfare. LAWRENCE O. GOSTIN, PUBLIC HEALTH LAW: POWER, DUTY, RESTRAINT, 79 (2d ed. 2008).

states exists alongside the Supremacy Clause, though, which declares that the federal constitution is the supreme law of the land.[181] In analyzing the Supremacy Clause, courts have opined that "it is basic to this constitutional command that all conflicting state provisions be without effect."[182] In other words, federal law supersedes both state law and local law – local laws are analyzed in the same way as state laws for the purposes of preemption.[183]

Unlike state governments, municipal governments do not possess a broad, inherent power to govern. Municipal governments derive their power to govern and make laws from the powers of the state that are expressed in the Tenth Amendment. Traditionally, local governments have possessed only those powers necessary for the purposes of their incorporation or explicitly delegated to them by the state. This relationship between states and their municipalities is often referred to as Dillon's Rule, which is a canon of statutory interpretation requiring that the powers of municipal corporations be interpreted narrowly.[184]

However, most states have transitioned from Dillon's Rule to a form of local government known as "home rule," which allows municipalities greater authority to self-govern and relieves state legislatures of handling issues that are primarily local in nature. States that adopt home rule statutes delegate to municipalities the authority to make local laws on a broad array of topics affecting the health, safety, and welfare of communities.[185] Local governments must not exceed their lawmaking powers granted to them by the state, though, or make laws that conflict with state laws.[186]

The unique aspects of the police power of states are fleshed out in this treatise where relevant, i.e., food safety regulation and the regulation of urban agriculture.

[b] Assisting Federal Regulation

State agencies can assist federal agencies to regulate food in significant ways as demonstrated in the various phases of food law. For example, Chapter 3 shows how state agencies assist the FDA and USDA perform their responsibilities under the federal safety acts by inspecting food plants and administering in the enforcement of the acts. Chapter 5 notes that state and local agencies administer the federal Supplemental Nutrition Assistance Program (SNAP), including determining and distributing benefits. Chapter 6 explains how state environmental agencies work with the EPA to implement and enforce the Clean Water Act.

[c] Laboratories for Innovation

State and local agencies often lead out on the development of new, innovative regulatory tools involving food, especially in the areas of nutrition and food systems. Chapters 4 and 5 provide numerous examples of innovative regulatory tools that have applied in marketing and nutrition, including the following: (1) prohibiting certain establishments in

---

[181] U.S. Const. art. VI, § 2.
[182] Maryland v. Louisiana, 451 U.S. 725, 746 (1981).
[183] Hillsborough Cnty. v. Auto. Med. Labs, Inc., 471 U.S. 707 (1985).
[184] J. F. Dillon, The Law of Municipal Corporations § 9b at 93 (2d ed. 1873).
[185] 56 Am. Jur. 2d Municipal Corporations, Etc. § 109.
[186] See Id. at § 113.

selling sodas and other sugary drinks in containers larger than sixteen ounces; (2) prohibiting fast-food restaurants in certain areas; (3) barring use of SNAP benefits to purchase sweetened beverages; (4) prohibiting restaurants from providing free toys in meals for children that do not meet established nutritional requirements; (5) taxing unhealthy food, especially sugar-sweetened beverages (SSBs); (6) requiring warning labels on the fronts of all cans and bottles of soda and juice drinks that have sugar added; (7) addressing hunger through the creation of food banks and various service meal programs; (8) requiring menu labeling for restaurants; and (9) banning use of trans fats by certain food enterprises. Chapter 6 provides numerous examples of innovative state and municipal measures that have addressed food system issues, including the following: (1) prescribing on-farm animal treatment standards; (2) guarding against urban sprawl by passing of what are known as "right-to-farm" laws; (3) protecting the local environment by regulating the emerging aquaculture industry; (4) exempting local producers from licensure and inspection laws through what are known as "food cottage laws"; (5) shaping local food policy via purchasing contracts; and (6) creating and mobilizing local food councils.

States and local governments have also protected the food industry from alleged intrusive legal tools or practices. For example, Chapter 5 documents how states have protected the food industry from obesity litigation by giving immunity to restaurants through what are known as "cheeseburger bills." Chapter 6 notes the development in some states to protect the animal farm industry from undercover videos of animal abuse by passing what are known as "antigag" laws to forbid the practice.

[d] Preemption Considerations

This treatise addresses the preemptive effect of federal food legislation – express, implied, or occupying the field – in the context of each act. The preemptive effects of federal food act preemption are patchwork and largely depend on the intent of Congress in dealing with specific food problems. In terms of how preemption affects the development of food law in states, however, a few general observations can be made. First, federal food law may expressly allow for states to carve out regulation over a particular regulatory regime. For example, states may create own organic program under certain conditions, including receiving approval from USDA. Second, in other cases, federal law exhibits flexibility for state and local community improvisation. For example, under SNAP, states and local communities may implement the programs in ways that maximize their impact.

[6] *Litigation*

[a] Legal Tool

Regulation by litigation is a recently recognized trend in American legal governance that develops differently in each economic sector it affects.[187] While regulation usually anticipates harm and is therefore prophylactic in design, litigation is usually a retrospective tool that assigns responsibility for harm that has already occurred.

---

[187] William M. Sage, *How Litigation Relates to Health Care Regulation*, 28 J. HEALTH POL. POL'Y & L. 387, 387 (2003).

Consumer class actions especially have been a prominent feature of US consumer protection law since the 1960s and are unique in their prevalence, scale, and economic impact.

Given the changing social conditions related to food in the modern food system, it is no surprise that the role of litigation is becoming more pronounced in recent years in the realms of food safety, marketing, nutrition, and systems. For example, there has been a legal pandemic of consumer class action lawsuits against food enterprises in recent years. Many of these lawsuits challenge labeling claims as misleading under state laws intended to prohibit deceptive trade practices. The popularity of such cases among plaintiffs' class action bar stems in part from a void left by the absence of FDA regulation and enforcement in the key areas of food labeling, such as a rule on the definition of "natural." Class actions fill in for FDA by bringing actions alleging that various food labels violate state consumer protection laws. Thus, gaps in the regulation of food have given risen to the use of litigation as a legal tool to provide remedy and effect change. In this vein, litigation is viewed by some as both a useful counterpart to government regulation and as a way to propel further regulation.

[b] Federal Acts: No Private Right of Action

An important constraint on the tool of litigation being used to affect change in the food system is the absence of a private right of action under the FMIA, the PPIA, and the FDCA.[188] The omission of this tool in the food regulatory regime contrasts with its inclusion in the environmental regulatory regime.[189] The major federal environmental statutes enacted between 1970 and 1980 all contain provisions allowing private citizens to bring suit against alleged violators of the statutes.[190] Citizen-suit provisions introduce accountability into the regulation, as citizens are able to take on the role of law enforcement by suing polluters and the government. Notwithstanding the application of private rights of action in federal environmental statutes, there does not appear to be any momentum to the implementation of this tool in the food regulatory system.

Thus, there is nothing in the FDCA that provides a proper basis for per se negligence. Permitting a negligence per se action predicated on alleged FDCA violations would allow a private litigant to avoid Congress' intent not to allow FDCA-based private rights of action by pleading an FDCA claim as a state law tort. The US Supreme Court assumed in its 1986 *Merrell Dow v. Thompson* decision, however, which considered federal subject matter jurisdiction over FDCA-related tort allegations, that Congress did not intend to allow private rights of action under the FDCA.[191] The Court went on to observe that federal jurisdiction and use of FDCA violations as the basis for state law causes of action would "flout congressional intent."[192] Since 1986, the assumption in

---

[188] *See* Mario's Butcher Shop & Food Ctr., Inc. v. Armour & Co., 575 F. Supp. 653, 654 (N.D. Ill. 1983) (addressing FMIA); Rogers v. Tyson Foods, Inc., 308 F.3d 785, 790 (7th Cir. 2002) (addressing PPIA).

[189] *See* Lisa Heinzerling, *The Verities and Limits of Transparency of U.S. Food Law* 70 FOOD & DRUG L.J. 11, 23 (2015) (recommending that the government authorize citizen suits for violation federal food law).

[190] *See, e.g.*, Clean Water Act (CWA), 33 U.S.C. § 1365; Toxic Substances Control Act (TSCA), 15 U.S.C. § 2619; and the Endangered Species Act (ESA), 16 U.S.C. § 1540(g).

[191] Merrell Dow Pharm., Inc. v. Thompson, 478 U.S. 804, 811 (1986).

[192] *Id.* at 811, 827.

Merrell Dow regarding the congressional intent of the FDCA has become the established legal rule.[193]

[c] Administrative Procedure Act

A viable alternative for plaintiffs is to sue under the APA. Section 702 of the APA provides
that "[a] person suffering legal wrong because of agency action, or adversely affected or
aggrieved by agency action within the meaning of a relevant statute, is entitled to judicial
review thereof."[194] Suits under this provision of the APA cannot be brought for money
damages, but only for declaratory or injunctive relief, and must challenge "agency action
made reviewable by statute and final agency action for which there is no adequate remedy
in a court."[195] Section 701 carves out two exceptions to judicial reviewability: (1) when
"statutes preclude judicial review"; or (2) when "agency action is committed to agency
discretion by law."[196] Litigants bringing suit under Section 702 of the APA must still meet
constitutional and prudential standing requirements, including demonstrating injury in
fact and meeting the zone of interests test.

An example of a legal challenge per the APA involving food interests was the 1998
case of *Alliance for Bio-Integrity v. Shalala*, in which a group of concerned citizens sued
the agency over its 1992 policy on GMO foods.[197] In addition to substantive claims,
the suit claimed that in drafting the 1992 FDA Policy the agency failed to abide by
the public notice-and-comment procedures of the APA. The US District Court of the
District of Columbia disagreed that the 1992 FDA Policy had been improperly promulgated and noted that a policy, as opposed to a formal agency action, is not subject to
the notice-and-comment requirements.[198] Although ultimately the court's decision made
clear that critics of the FDA's policy had little ground on which to stand, the case did
heighten public awareness of GE foods and led to a series of public hearings in 1999,
which attracted a large amount of public attention.[199]

Another example was in 1987, when a consortium of organizations and private citizens filed suit against FDA's action level for aflatoxins in corn in which it was alleged
that the action level violated the APA because it constitutes a legislative rule issued without the requisite notice-and-comment procedures. The US Court of Appeals for the
District of Columbia Circuit in *Community Nutrition Institute v. Young* determined that
the agency had not followed the procedures of the APA and that its action levels were
consequently invalid.[200]

---

[193] *See e.g.*, PDK Labs, Inc. v. Friedlander, 103 F.3d 1105, 1113 (2d Cir. 1997); Bailey v. Johnson, 48 F.3d
965, 967 (6th Cir. 1995); Gile v. Optical Radiation Corp., 22 F.3d 540, 544 (3rd Cir. 1994).
[194] 5 U.S.C. § 702.
[195] *Id.* § 704.
[196] *Id.* § 701.
[197] 116 F. Supp.2d 166 (D.D.C. 2000).
[198] *Id.* at 170, 172.
[199] Press Release, US Department of Health and Human Services, FDA Announces Public Meetings on
Bioengineered Foods (October 18, 1999).
[200] 818 F.2d 943 (1987).

2 Regulation of Food Commerce

§ 2.01 Introduction

The distribution of food generates a number of issues, which are addressed in each of the chapters in this treatise; this chapter focuses solely on the economic regulation of food distribution or what may be called the regulation of food commerce. The laws that govern the commerce of food can be organized into two distinct categories: (1) laws that ensure the authenticity and integrity of food that is distributed to consumers and (2) the standards, rules, and laws that regulate the international trade of food. The complexities of problems that give rise to the adaptation of laws to regulate food commerce evidences the challenges of the modern, global food system.

§ 2.02 Regulation of Economically Motivated Adulteration (EMA)

[1] *Background*

[a] Perpetual Problem of Food Systems

Ensuring the integrity of the commercial food supply invariably requires law to deal with a form of food fraud or cheating known as economic adulteration or economically motivated adulteration (EMA). EMA includes the padding, diluting, and substituting of food product for the purpose of economic gain, which may or may not compromise the safety of the product.[1] Food fraud in the form of EMA has plagued food commerce throughout history. A brief accounting of this history demonstrates the role of law in ensuring the integrity of food and the food system from which the food is derived.

Reports of EMA date back to the Greek and Roman eras. The Greek botanist Theophrastus (370–295 BC) reported on the use of artificial flavors in the food supply and on the use of adulterants for economic reasons in some items of commerce.[2] The physician Galen (AD 131–201) listed food products in Rome that were particular targets of adulteration, including grains, spices, wine, and preservatives.[3]

In the Middle Ages, staple foods like meat, bread, and wine were targets for adulteration. The "medieval nose" was particularly sensitive to the smell of decay, and was used to catch suppliers of putrid meat.[4] Bread was more difficult to manage, as catching a wily baker could be a challenge. Cheating bakers sold underweight bread, the price of a loaf being fixed in relation to its weight.[5] Such cheating led to regulations like the "Assize of Bread and Ale," which dictated what went into everyday food goods.[6] Guilds comprising ale conners, pepperers, and garblers enforced these purity laws with

---

[1] Grocery Mfrs. Ass'n et al., Consumer Product Fraud: Deterrence and Detection i (2010).
[2] Am. Spice Trade Assoc., Spice Adulteration White Paper 2 (June 28, 2014).
[3] *Id.*
[4] Reay Tannahill, Food in History 162 (Three Rivers Press rev. ed., 1988).
[5] *See id.* at 163.
[6] Bee Wilson, Swindled: The Dark History of Food Fraud, from Poisoned Candy to Counterfeit Coffee 67 (2008).

considerable effectiveness.[7] A particular enforcement action suited to the sensibilities of early fourteenth-century London was used against bakers selling underweight bread: the offending loaf would be slung around the neck of the condemned baker and he would be drawn through the dirtiest streets in town on a mobile pillory to be jeered at and targeted by flying debris hurled from fellow citizens.[8]

Industrialization increased the scope and sophistication of EMA. The regulatory system conceived in the Middle Ages to control food adulteration gradually crumbled in the eighteenth and nineteenth centuries.[9] As the power of the guilds waned and urban entrepreneurs gained greater control of the market, the buying and selling of food came to be ruled by the law of caveat emptor.[10]

Notwithstanding the challenges in controlling food adulteration during the industrial era, many enterprising scientists exposed cases of food fraud to the public. In 1820, German-born chemist Friedrich Accum published *A Treatise on Adulterations of Food, and Culinary Poisons*.[11] The text contained startling revelations about adulteration in the English food system, including vinegar mixed with sulfuric acid, pickles colored with copper, sugary confections dyed red with lead and pepper mixed with floor sweepings.[12] In 1850, Arthur Hill Hassall, a chemist, and Henry Lethaby, a dietician, published a series of articles in England reporting on the extraneous matter found in samples of food products they randomly purchased in London shops.[13] With the aid of a microscope, they uncovered disturbing fraudulent practices and showed that loaves of bread were adulterated with alum, a mineral salt whitening agent, and that coffee was diluted with chicory, acorns, or a type of beer called mangelwurzel.[14] Hassall worked with Thomas Wakely, founder and editor of the *Lancet*, to publish the names and addresses of the shops selling adulterated goods.[15] A few savvy manufacturers soon recognized that the new focus on purity might pay dividends. When Hassall praised provisioner Crosse & Blackwell for no longer adding copper to its pickles, the company began to market their products as "natural."[16] Not leaving the dealing of EMA solely to enterprising scientists and the marketplace, the government responded in 1860 by enacting the first comprehensive English food safety legislation, the Adulteration of Food and Drink Act.[17]

[b] US Regulatory Response: 1906 and 1938 Food Acts

The United States followed much the same historical food regulatory trajectory as England: prior to the passage of the 1906 Pure Food and Drug Act (PFDA), there was no federal control over the processing of food, let alone the authenticity and integrity of

---

[7] *Id.* at 88–93.

[8] Tannahill, *supra* note 4, at 163–4.

[9] *See id.* at 85–9.

[10] *Id.* at 34.

[11] *See* Frederick Accum, A TREATISE ON ADULTERATIONS OF FOOD, & CULINARY POISONS (Ab'm Small ed., 2d ed. 1820).

[12] *See id.* at 212.

[13] Tannahill, *supra* note 4, at 294.

[14] *Id.*

[15] Wilson, *supra* note 6, at 124–32.

[16] *Id.* at 143.

[17] Charles Lister, *Discord and Change: An Assessment of the European Community's Food Packaging Laws*, 48 FOOD & DRUG L.J. 589, 589 n.4 (1993).

food. Early colonial laws served mainly trade interests, set standards of weight, and provided for inspections of exports like salt meats, fish, and flour.[18]

In the last half of the nineteenth century, problems associated with adulteration in the United States began to develop as food production shifted from the home to the factory.[19] Developments in chemistry facilitated this shift, bringing advancements in food science and new food additives, colorings, and means of adulteration.[20] The lack of government regulation led to tampering with products by substituting cheap ingredients for those represented on labels.[21] In some cases, such tampering led to serious food contamination problems, such as the serious milk contamination problem in New York City in 1858 that reportedly killed up to 8,000 children in a single year.[22]

Food quality and safety scandals and the publication of Upton Sinclair's *The Jungle* moved President Theodore Roosevelt in June of 1906 to sign into law both the PDFA[23] and the Federal Meat Inspection Act (FMIA),[24] thus commencing the modern era of US food regulation. While the primary purpose of the PDFA was to prevent the use of potentially harmful constituents, a secondary objective was to protect the public from the possibility that valuable ingredients would be watered down or left out of basic foods in favor of cheaper substitutes.[25] Following the 1906 Act, food identity standards became the legal tool of choice by the FDA to combat EMA following the 1938 FDCA, only to fall out of favor because of the difficulties and expense in implementation and because the FDA moved to labeling to prevent consumer deception and to issues of higher priority, namely, safety and nutrition.

[c] Law's Evolving Adaptation to EMA

Although the problem of EMA has been surpassed in the twentieth century as a regulatory priority by food safety and nutrition, a new paradigm for EMA – a modern global food system marked by the trade flow of a variety of food products and ingredients from multiple locations in the world – increases the level of EMA, especially for imported premium products, and has positioned this form of adulteration once again as a priority for regulators and as a challenge for the legal system.[26]

---

[18] *See* Wallace F. Janssen, *The Story of the Laws Behind the Labels*, FDA Consumer (June 1981).

[19] *See* Neal D. Fortin, Food Regulation: Law, Science, Policy, and Practice 155 (2009).

[20] *Id.* at 5.

[21] *Harvey W. Wiley: Pioneer Consumer Activist*, FDA Consumer, January–February 2006.

[22] The increase from 90,000 to 120,000 quarts of milk per day entering New York City in the 1850s was due to dairies padding their milk with water, and then restoring its richness with flour. Bee Wilson, *The Swill Is Gone*, N.Y. Times, September 30, 2008, at A27. In time, however, the preferred adulterant became "swill milk, a filthy, bluish substance milked from cows tied up in crowded stables adjoining city distilleries and fed the hot alcoholic mash left from making whiskey." *Id.* The mash itself was doctored "with plaster of Paris to take away the blueness, starch and eggs to thicken it and molasses to provide a buttercup hue of honest Orange County milk." *Id.*

[23] Pure Food and Drug Act, ch. 3915, § 6, 34 Stat. 768 (1906) (repealed 1938).

[24] Federal Meat Inspection Act, Pub. L. No. 59–242, 34 Stat. 1260 (1907), amended by the Wholesome Meat Act, Pub. L. No. 90–201, 81 Stat. 584 (1967) (codified as amended at 21 U.S.C. §§ 601–695 (2012)).

[25] *See* Richard A. Merrill & Earl M. Collier, Jr., *"Like Mother Used to Make": An Analysis of FDA Food Standards of Identity*, 74 Colum. L. Rev. 561, 564 (1974).

[26] *See generally* U.S. Gov't Accountability Office, GAO-12–46, Food & Drug Admin.: Better Coordination Could Enhance Efforts to Address Economic Adulteration and Protect the Public Health (2011).

The link between EMA and public health in the modern food system has increased the attention given to the regulation of EMA. This link was vividly demonstrated by the melamine scandals in China that rocked consumer confidence worldwide and that triggered a FDA-public meeting in April of 2009, to address the threat of EMA.[27] The purpose of the meeting was to stimulate discussion on how industry could predict better and prevent EMA.[28] The FDA's principal concern at the meeting was the effect of the importation of foods on EMA. Two of the four examples of EMA provided by the FDA's Federal Register notice announcing the meeting involved melamine (melamine is a widely used chemical found in hard plastic dishes and the linings of food containers) in China. The first of these two examples was the contamination in 2007 of pet food containing ingredients labeled as wheat gluten and rice protein concentrate that included melamine and melamine-related compounds.[29] Melamine was allegedly added to the pet food to boost its protein content. The second adulteration was found from the 2007 investigation into Chinese pet food. It was discovered that the addition of melamine to infant formula by Chinese milk dealers and suppliers, in an effort to increase protein content and profits, resulted in 50,000 infant hospitalizations and six infant deaths in China.[30]

The melamine scandal triggered further attention to EMA and food fraud.[31] For example, a 2010 report issued by the Grocery Manufacturer's Association estimated that economic and counterfeiting of global food and consumer products costs the industry $10–$15 billion per year.[32] The US Pharmacopeial Convention (USP), a nonprofit scientific organization that develops standards to help ensure the identity, quality, and purity of food ingredients, dietary supplements, and pharmaceuticals, has created a database that compiles reports and information on EMA.[33] Commonly adulterated products include fish, olive oil, milk, honey, saffron, orange juice, coffee, and apple juice.[34] Headline stories on EMA throughout the world continue to draw attention to the problem. The discovery of horsemeat in processed beef products sold by a number of UK supermarket chains in March of 2013 resulted in a series of product recalls and threw the spotlight on the food industry's supply chain.[35] Oceana, an international nonprofit organization dedicated to ocean conservation, following a seafood fraud investigation, issued a report in 2013 announcing that one-third of the fish sampled during a US survey was incorrectly

---

[27] *See* FDA Notice of Public Meeting on Economically Motivated Adulteration, 74 Fed. Reg. 15,497 (April 6, 2009).

[28] *See id.*

[29] *See id.* at 15,498.

[30] The other two examples of EMA were also linked to mainland Chinese manufacturers. *Id.* The first incident involved the contamination in 2008 of heparin products used in pediatric dialysis patients with a heparin-like molecule known as oversulfated chondroitin sulphate that was manufactured in China. *Id.* The second incident involved the adulteration of toothpaste, cough syrup, and other drugs with diethylene glycol, which is used to replace glycerin in those products. *Id.*

[31] *See, e.g.*, Catherine Zuckerman, *Food Fraud: Labels on What We Eat Often Mislead*, National Geographic (July 12, 2013).

[32] Grocery Manufacturers Ass'n et al, *supra* note 1.

[33] US Pharmacopeial Convention Food Fraud Database (internet source); *see also* Jeffrey C. Moore et al., *Development and Application of a Database of Food Ingredient Fraud and Economically Motivated Adulteration from 1980 to 2010*, J. Food Sci., Apr. 2012 at R118.

[34] *See id.* at R121.

[35] *Q&A: Horsemeat scandal*, BBC News UK (April 10, 2013).

labeled.[36] Finally, China continues to struggle with fake-food scandals, including fake chicken eggs made of resin, starch, pigments, and fox meat sold as donkey meat.[37]

Notwithstanding the emerging recognition that economic adulteration of food is a problem not to be ignored, the challenges in regulating EMA in the global food system are daunting: increasing imports, sophisticated technology, complexities in the supply chain, scarcity of resources and information, and overall regulatory inertia present unique detection and enforcement barriers.

Despite these significant hurdles, as awareness of EMA increases, government agencies of all stripes likely will experience escalating pressure from watchdog organizations, media, and consumer advocacy groups, and food companies who are honest purveyors of food product, to enforce. Government agencies may begin to think creatively on how to enforce, not just in adopting additional technological tools, but also in collaborating with industry and other governments. At some point, the approach to EMA may fundamentally change. Instead of EMA being treated as a type of adulteration whose risk may be low, EMA may eventually be seen as criminal activity where enforcement is more robust.[38] Also, food companies themselves need to consider the liability implications of sourcing imported ingredients or components of food products that are economically adulterated.

A significant emerging area of food fraud involves dietary supplements, which is covered in Chapter 5.

[2] *Statutory Basis*

[a] Actions Constituting EMA

Prior to examining the legal tools that address EMA, it is useful to understand what constitutes EMA. A definition of EMA comprises two parts – first, the acts or the methods of the adulteration, and second, the motivation or incentives of the adulteration. The 1938 FDCA does not expressly define EMA. Nor does the FDCA set forth precise standards as to what constitutes EMA. Instead, the act envelops the critical components of EMA in the overall definition of "adulteration" found in Section 402(b).

Under Section 402(b), the range of actions that constitute EMA is broad. These actions and examples of each action are delineated as follows:

1. The omission of any valuable constituent in whole or in part. Such omission includes dilution, which reduces the amount of a valuable component, an example of which is where water is used to dilute milk.
2. The substitution of any substance in whole or in part. Such substitution typically occurs when a substance is replaced with something less valuable, an example of which is where beet sugar is used instead of honey.

---

[36] Kimberly Warner et al., *Oceana Study Reveals Seafood Fraud Nationwide*, Oceana (February 21, 2013).

[37] Patrick Boehler, *Bad Eggs: Another Fake-Food Scandal Rocks China*, TIME (November 6, 2012); Michael Moss and Neil Gough, *Food Safety in China Still Faces Big Hurdles*, N.Y. TIMES (July 23, 2014).

[38] *See generally* Chris Elliott, Elliott Review into the Integrity and Assurance of Food Supply Networks – Final Report (2014) (This report, generated in response to horse meat fraud in the United Kingdom, refers to economic adulteration as a crime and recommends it be treated as such).

3. The concealment in any manner of damage or inferiority. An example of concealment that constitutes EMA is where known salmonella contamination is concealed in peanuts.
4. The unapproved enhancement of food product by the addition of any substance to increase the product's bulk or weight, or to reduce the product's quality or strength, or to make the product appear better or of greater value than it is. An example of an unapproved enhancement is where melamine is added to milk to enhance the protein value.

Like the FDCA, the FMIA does not define EMA, but in addition to describing the conditions or acts of adulteration in a similar fashion to Section 402(b) of the FDCA, the FMIA expressly prohibits a category of adulteration that meets the description of EMA:

> The term "adulterated" shall apply to any carcass, part thereof, meat or meat food product ... if any valuable constituent has been in whole or in part omitted or abstracted therefrom; or if any substance has been substituted, wholly or in part therefor; or if damage or inferiority has been concealed in any manner; or if any substance has been added thereto or mixed or packed therewith so as to increase its bulk or weight, or reduce its quality or strength, or make it appear better or of greater value than it is.[39]

This definition is identical to the definition of this form of adulteration under the Poultry Products Inspection Act.[40]

Although EMA can be the cause of food safety concerns, EMA is distinguishable from other adulterations of food defined in Section 402(a). These adulterated foods are generally poisonous, deleterious, filthy, decomposed, or contaminated.[41] Foods that are economically adulterated do not necessarily have these dangerous characteristics and may be healthy and nutritious. The problem is one of economic cheat with the incidental danger to health.[42]

[b] Intent Basis: Economic Motivation

In addition to the acts of adulteration enumerated in FDCA Section 402(b), EMA refers to "intent" or the purpose of the perpetuator of the adulteration. In a notice of a public hearing on EMA in 2009, the FDA defined EMA as "the fraudulent, intentional substitution or addition of a substance in a product for the purpose of increasing the apparent value of the product or reducing the cost of its production, i.e., for economic gain."[43] Presumably in response to a 2011 report issued by the US Government Accountability Office (GAO) that recommended the FDA to define EMA,[44] the agency via a working

---

[39] 21 U.S.C. § 601(m)(8); see Federal Food, Drug, and Cosmetic Act (FDCA), Pub. L. No. 75–717, § 402(b), 52 Stat. 1040 (1938) (codified as amended at 21 U.S.C. §§ 301–95 (1994)) ("[T]he omission or abstraction of any 'valuable constituent,' the substitution of any substance, the concealment of damage or inferiority, or the addition of substances to increase bulk or weight or to reduce quality or strength or to make it appear better or of greater value is a form of adulteration.").

[40] See 21 U.S.C. § 453(g).

[41] See 21 U.S.C. § 402(a).

[42] See, e.g., Van Liew v. United States, 321 F.2d 664 (5th Cir. 1963) (where the government conceded that defendant's orange drink was just as healthy and palatable as freshly squeezed orange juice, but that the confusion caused by economic adulteration may result in dangers to health in some situations).

[43] FDA Notice of Public Meeting on Economically Motivated Adulteration, 74 Fed. Reg. 15,497.

[44] See U.S. Gov't Accountability Office, supra note 26.

group formed later that year to address EMA expressly adopted this definition of EMA.[45] Although this definition promulgated by the FDA does not include each of the actions listed in Section 402(b), it is widely recognized that each of these actions when performed intentionally for economic gain constitutes EMA.

The intent to adulterate food for purposes of defining EMA is generally driven by financial gain. The first and most obvious motivation for food manufacturers is to increase profits. A manufacturer may use cheap filler that is easily disguised to increase the volume sold to cut the cost and increase the ultimate profit margin. Another incentive is competition. If a manufacturer cannot meet a customer's quality criteria it may adulterate the product in an attempt to either meet a specification or to compete by offering an inferior product at a lower price. Customers wind up believing they are getting a bargain. EMA may also be market driven, resulting from pressure to cut costs. As customers squeeze their suppliers to reduce costs, there comes a point when the supplier may adulterate the product to lower the cost and maintain a workable margin. Incentives for EMA in the world food and beverage market are especially appealing for higher-value food products.

[c] Distinguishing EMA from Other Forms of Adulteration and Fraud

Whereas EMA is premised on a motivation for financial gain, it should be noted again that the FDCA technically does not distinguish among motives or require motive to be established to determine whether a product is adulterated.[46] Nevertheless, FDA commonly distinguishes between EMA from other forms of adulteration in order to address specifically EMA.[47] For example, EMA is distinguishable from bioterrorism or sabotage, whose primary purpose is to cause harm. EMA is also distinguishable from counterfeiting, another category of food fraud, which involves the unauthorized representation of a registered trademark carried on goods similar to goods for which the trademark is registered, with the intent to deceive the purchaser into believing that they are buying the original food product.[48]

[3] *Regulatory Tools to Address EMA*

[a] FDCA Section 402(b): Enforcement

Upon passage of the 1906 PDFA – prior to the enactment of Section 402(b) – the government sought enforcement against EMA in criminal cases. Convictions were secured in numerous criminal cases.[49] Although the PDFA appeared adequate to address blatant

---

[45] *See id.* at 24 (in response to the GAO's recommendations, the Department of Health and Human Services stated that the Working Group on Economically Motivated Adulteration will use the working definition of EMA that FDA proposed at its May 2009 public meeting on the topic.).

[46] *Id.* at 8.

[47] *Id.* at 8–9.

[48] Grocery Manufacturers Ass'n et al, *supra* note 1, at 1.

[49] *See, e.g.,* Union Dairy Co. v. United States, 250 F.2 31 (7th Cir. 1918) (milk diluted by water); Frank v. United States, 192 F. 864 (6th Cir. 1911) (pepper diluted by corn); United States v. Frank, 189 F. 195 (S.D. Ohio 1911) (lemon extract diluted by alcohol and water); United States v. South Hero Creamery Ass'n, White & Gates 1142 (D. Vt. 1925) (butter with less than 80 per cent milk-fat); United States v. Atlantic Macaroni Co., White & Gates 793 (E.D.N.Y. 1917) (macaroni dyed yellow to conceal

cases of EMA, the concern became focused on imitation products. The concern was that with advancements in food technology, manufacturers could produce new products that resembled, but were not identical to, traditional foods.[50] However, absent formal standards, courts held that fabricated food products were not adulterated, but were a pure and distinct separate food product. The government suffered a number of defeats on the treatment of imitation products. Especially problematic for the government's prosecutorial efforts was the Eighth Circuit's decision in *United States v. Ten Cases, More or Less, Bred Spred*, which found that "Bred Spred" was not an adulterated version of jam, even though it closely resembled jam and had less than half as much fruit, because there was no authoritative standard for comparing "Bred Spred" with jam and no misleading statements on the "Bred Spred" labeling.[51]

Inclusion of Section 402(b) in the 1938 FDCA was therefore due to a marketplace in the 1930s that was replete with substandard food products being sold to consumers, who could not depend on the label or appearance of processed food to guarantee its contents or quality.[52] Section 402(b) grants the FDA clear authority to act in cases involving EMA. The FDA has authority to act even if the EMA poses no known risk to public health.

Regardless of FDA's authority under Section 402(b) and the momentum of events that led to the enactment of Section 402(b), the provision has rarely been enforced. A primary reason for the lack of enforcement of Section 402(b) following its enactment was the growth of modern food technology that hinged on the improving of food in appearance and taste. The narrowing of the application of Section 402(b) to accommodate developing food technology is explained in the third edition of *Food and Drug Law* as follows:

> Applied literally, the economic adulteration provisions of the FD&C Act would render most modern food technology problematic. Many functional ingredients – color additives, preservatives, emulsifiers – are intended to improve the appearance of the product and thus could be challenged as making food appear "better than it is." Food producers would claim that these ingredients in fact improve the food and only make it appear to be as good as it genuinely is. Without purporting to resolve this debate, FDA has virtually abandoned enforcement of section 402(b) except in cases of outright fraud, which are rare. The agency has embraced[,] though never publicized, the philosophy that, notwithstanding the proper legal interpretation of the statute, informative labeling can cure "economic adulteration."[53]

Nevertheless, in cases of outright fraud, there are a few well-known precedents where the FDA exercised its statutory responsibility to enforce against the perpetuators. Enforcement led to a $100,000 fine and five-year prison sentence for the former president and chief executive officer of an orange juice company that put more than forty million gallons of adulterated orange juice on the US market over eleven years.[54]

---

inferiority); United States v. German American Specialty Co., White & Gates 459 (S.D.N.Y. 1913) (eggs diluted by skim milk).

[50] *See* Christopher Chen, *Food and Drug Administration Food Standards of Identity: Consumer Protection Through the Regulation of Product Information*, 47 FOOD & DRUG L.J. 185, 192–3 (1992).

[51] United States v. Ten Cases, More or Less, Bred Spred, Etc., 49 F.2d 87, 90–91 (8th Cir. 1931).

[52] Suzanne W. Junod, *The Rise and Fall of Federal Food Standards In The United States: The Case of The Peanut Butter and Jelly Sandwich, in* THE FOOD AND DRUG ADMINISTRATION 35 (Meredith A. Hickmann ed. 2003).

[53] Peter Barton Hutt et al., FOOD AND DRUG LAW: CASES AND MATERIALS 159 (3rd ed. 2007).

[54] *See* Paula Kurtzweil, *Fake Food Fight*, FDA Consumer, March–April 1999.

Fines and forfeitures totaling $120,000 were issued on a seafood company and two of its principals for adding water to scallops to increase their weight and thus net profit since scallops are priced according to weight. Fines of $20,000 each and prison terms of nineteen months and thirty months were issued to two Mississippi brothers for adulterating pure honey and pure maple can and sorghum syrups that were sold in old-fashioned tins at farmers' markets and produce stands around the country. A $2.18 million fine was issued to Beech-Nut Nutrition Corporation – an established baby food manufacturer – for selling a product labeled "100 percent" apple juice but which actually contained only sugar, water and flavoring.[55] In the early 1990s, when this fine occurred, it was estimated that 10 percent of fruit juice sold in the United States was not all juice.[56] Notwithstanding the determination by FDA Commissioner David A. Kessler at the time to prosecute adulteration cases, the FDA's efforts were plagued by the enduring problem of inadequate resources and an institutional tradition of putting a low priority on prosecuting cases of EMA.[57]

[b] FDCA Section 401: Standards of Identity

A legal tool whose use has ebbed and flowed in dealing with EMA is the implementation of a standard of identity. Standards of identity are used as a yardstick by which to measure economic adulteration. Although standards of identity have fallen out of favor by the FDA, in recent years they have found support by a few states.

Section 401 gives the FDA broad authority to establish identity standards for foods:

> Whenever in the judgment of the Secretary such action will promote honesty and fair dealing in the interest of consumers he shall promulgate regulations fixing and establishing for any food, under its common or usual name so far as practicable, a reasonable definition and standard of identity.[58]

An FDA standard of identity defines the composition of a food and may prescribe a method of production or formulation. The resulting standard closely resembles a recipe. As part of the standard, the FDA assigns a name under which all conforming products shall be sold. Section 401 of FDCA was designed to avoid the upshot of the *Bred Spred* case – that labeling requirements would combat EMA.[59] The FMIA sets forth standards of identity as well, often pertaining to meat content, prescribed ingredients, and required product names.[60]

The consequences of violating a standard of identity are spelled out in FDCA 403(g): a food shall be deemed misbranded [i]f it purports to be or is represented as a food for which a definition and standard of identity has been prescribed unless (1) it conforms to

---

[55] *Id.*

[56] *See* Diana B. Henriques, *10% of Fruit Juice Sold in U.S. Is Not All Juice, Regulators Say*, N.Y. TIMES, October 31, 1993.

[57] *See id.*

[58] 21 U.S.C. § 341.

[59] *See also* United States v. 88 Cases, More or Less, Containing Bireley's Orange Beverage, 187 F.2d 967, 971 (3d Cir. 1951) (although adding yellow coal tar dye changed the orange drink's [contained 6 percent orange juice, 2 percent lemon juice, 87 percent water and artificial coloring] naturally unattractive appearance into a rich orange color, the court denied that a product can appear better than it is within the meaning of the FDCA unless the food is made to appear to be some defined superior product).

[60] *See* 9 CFR § 319.

such definition and standard and (2) its label bears the name of the food specified in the definition and standard.[61] Accordingly, a product that "purports to be or is represented as" a standardized food either must meet the standard or it may not be sold. From 1938 through the 1960s, the FDA promulgated highly detailed "recipe" standards of food identity.[62]

In the 1970s, standards of identity began to lose favor with the FDA, as the rapid increase in the variety of food products available in the marketplace caused the standards to be viewed as unwieldy and time consuming.[63] This view was punctuated by decade-long hearings on the identity of peanut butter that commenced in 1959.[64] Later, Vice President Al Gore's expression of shock at learning that the FDA set forth precise standards for the shapes in which canned green beans could be sold spurred a 1995 advance notice of proposed rulemaking to solicit comments on the viability of food standards.[65] A consensus emerged that food standards are of limited use and do not benefit consumers.[66]

While standards of identity have shown little life from the 1970s, activity in this area on a state and federal level to stop the import of economically adulterated food product has been employed recently for certain products. An example of this effort is honey. Honey is a prime target for economic adulteration – a problem that has been exasperated by the increase of foreign imports.[67] Economic adulteration in honey typically occurs when other ingredients such as cane sugar or corn syrup are added (a process called stretching). In an attempt to stop the importation of adulterated honey, in 2006, the US honey industry (the American Beekeeping Federation and several other honey associations) in a citizen's petition asked the FDA to establish a standard of identity for honey that would essentially adopt a standard established by the Codex Alimentarius Commission.[68] The Codex honey standard defines honey sold as such in part as not having added to it any food ingredient, including food additives.[69] Two years later the FDA responded that, due to other pressing matters, it would not be able to review the petition. Florida then instituted a state standard of identity that prohibits any additives, chemicals, or adulterants in the honey produced, processed, or sold in Florida.[70] In 2009, Congress stepped in, and as recorded in the June 23, 2009, House Agriculture Appropriations Committee Report accompanying the 2010 Agriculture Appropriations bill, the committee references the problem of economically adulterated honey entering the US market and directs FDA as follows:

---

[61] 21 U.S.C. § 343(g).

[62] See Chen, *supra* note 52, at 185.

[63] Traci S. Takaki, *Temporary Marketing Permits: The Hidden Regulation in Market Testing*, 48 FOOD & DRUG L.J. 675, 680 (1993).

[64] See Junod, *supra* note 55.

[65] See Stuart Pape, *Food Standards – Are They Obsolete?*, Prepared Foods, June 1996, at 33.

[66] See id.

[67] See Andrew Schneider, *Asian Honey, Banned in Europe, Is Flooding U.S. Grocery Shelves*, Food Safety News (August 15, 2011).

[68] See Citizen Petition from American Beekeeping Federation et al. to Andrew C. von Eschenbach, commissioner of Food and Drugs, Food & Drug Administration, Docket *2006P-0101/CP* (submitted March 3, 2006) (on file with author).

[69] Codex Alimentarius International Food Standards, CODEX STAN 12–1981 (2001) (cited as Exhibit C, *id*).

[70] See *Bronson Announces First Regulation in the Nation Banning Additives in Honey*, Pine Island-Eagle (July 13, 2009).

Honey. – The Committee recognizes that honey is produced in the United States, traded internationally and consumed as both a packaged food and as a food ingredient. However, there have been instances where manufacturers have been marketing products illegally as "honey" or "pure honey" that contained other ingredients. The Committee believes that guidance about the composition and labeling of honey is needed to protect consumers and the domestic honey industry from misbranded honey about the misbranding and adulteration provisions of the Federal Food Drug and Cosmetic Act. It is the Committee's understanding that FDA intends to respond to the pending citizen petition proposing a standard of identity for honey, and the Committee expects the agency to do so.[71]

Similarly, the July 7, 2009, Senate Agriculture Appropriations Committee report accompanying the companion Senate bill included the following directive:

Standards of Identity – The committee recognizes that honey is produced in the United States, traded internationally and consumed as both a packaged food and as a food ingredient, and believes that FDA needs to work to prevent misbranded honey and honey-derived products from entering the US market. The Committee is aware that the FDA has been in receipt of a proposed standard of identity for honey for three years, and directs FDA to respond to this proposal and, if deemed appropriate, begin working toward a US standard of identity for honey.[72]

Although it appears that Congress is willing to direct an otherwise resistive FDA to take enforcement action for EMA involving the importation of adulterated food even where no safety risk is present, the FDA appears to be wedded to relying on the misbranding provisions in FDCA that require food to be properly labeled rather than adopt a standard of identity. In October of 2011, FDA denied the 2006 citizens petition because it concluded that no standard of identity was needed. The FDA expressly noted that "to the extent that consumers are confused about what honey is and what it contains, the food label provides the relevant information to alleviate consumer confusion."[73] In response to the query of what happens when consumers do not read the label, the FDA elucidates:

To the extent that consumers do not have knowledge of honey or do not read the label, FDA has concluded that establishing a standard of identity for honey would not eliminate consumer's confusion on what honey is, since individual consumers would be unlikely to be aware that a standard of identity exists, nor would they be likely to seek it out as a means of addressing their confusion.[74]

In response to high-profile reports on the adulteration of imported honey, in April 2014, the FDA issued draft guidance on the proper labeling of honey. The draft guidance provides that adding sweeteners to honey requires the label to be marked as a "blend." The label "pure honey" is reserved for honey products that do not contain added sugar, corn syrup, or other sweeteners.[75] The guidance does not address whether honey that has

---

[71] H.R. Rep. No. 111–181, at 63 (2009).

[72] S. Rep. No. 111–139, at 109 (2009).

[73] Letter from Donald W. Kraemer, acting deputy director for operations, Center for Food Safety and Applied Nutrition, to Kristen C. Gunter, Counsel to American Beekeeping Federation et al. (October 5, 2011) (on file with author).

[74] *Id.*

[75] The FDA broadly defines honey as "a thick, sweet, syrupy substance that bees make as food from the nectar of flowers and store in honeycombs." FDA Notice of Draft Guidance for Industry: Proper Labeling of

been subjected to ultrafiltration, removal of pollen, and so on qualifies as honey. Instead, it focuses on the labeling of honey with added sweeteners and other substances, and on the possible contamination with illegal pesticides. The FDA notes in the guidance document that it has a long-standing import alert for the surveillance of honey for adulteration with cane or corn sugars.

Another example of the contemporary use of standards of identity is the case of olive oil. In recent years, the demand for olive oil has exploded. Much of this demand has been generated by olive oil becoming over recent years a gourmet must-have item, and by the higher-graded olive oil being touted for its heart-health properties and taste. The higher-grade extra virgin oil is one of the most frequently economically adulterated food products.[76] A citizen's petition was made to the FDA for a standard of identity based on a standard set by the Olive Council (IOC).[77] The standard is twofold: first, an objective chemical test considers the level of fats and oils present in the olive oil; second, a subjective organoleptic test (i.e., taste, smell, and appearance) checks the purity of the olive oil product.[78] Although the FDA has not responded favorably to the citizen petition, Connecticut and California have created standards for olive oil, including extra virgin oil, that follow the IOC standards.[79]

[c] Import Alert: Border Enforcement

The import alert is a tool that the FDA has shown a willingness to use in recent years to enforce against EMA of imported foods. FDA's authority over imported food is derived from Section 801 of the FDCA: Section 801(a) prescribes that a food may be refused entry into the United States if it appears to be manufactured, processed, or packed under unsanitary conditions or if it is adulterated or misbranded.[80] An import alert is an administrative remedy that allows for a specific food article to be detained without physical examination.[81] Import alerts are guidance documents that inform FDA field personnel that the FDA has sufficient evidence about a product, producer, shipper, or importer to determine that the food article is unsuitable for import.[82] Examples of import alerts for adulterated food include an import alert from the 1990s that still remains in effect, issued for apple juice and apple juice concentrate that contained an undeclared sweetener that rendered the products both economically adulterated and misbranded;[83] an alert in August 2007 that detained farm-raised catfish, bass, shrimp, dace, and eel products from

---

Honey and Honey Products; Availability, 79 Fed. Reg. 19620 (2014). The floral source of honey may be included on the label (e.g., "orange blossom honey," "clover honey"), provided that (1) the particular plant or blossom is the chief floral source of the honey; and (2) the producer, manufacturer, processor, packer, or distributor can show that the designated plant or blossom is the chief floral source. *Honey – Source Declaration, in* Food & Drug Admin., Compliance Policy Guide § 515.300 (1980).

[76] *See* Tom Mueller, *Slippery Business: The Trade in Adulterate Olive Oil,* NEW YORKER (August 13, 2007).

[77] Citizen Petition from N. Am. Olive Oil Assoc. to Margaret A. Hamburg, commissioner of Food and Drugs, Food & Drug Administration (submitted July 9, 2012) (on file with author).

[78] *See* Trade Standard Applying to Olive Oils and Olive-Pomace Oils (Int'l Olive Council 2015)

[79] Cal. Health & Safety Code § 112875.

[80] *See* 21 U.S.C. § 381(a).

[81] *See* Food & Drug Admin., Regulatory Procedures Manual 9–19, 9–50 (2011).

[82] *See id.* at 9–19, 9–21, 9–50.

[83] *See* Detention Without Physical Examination of Apple Juice and Apple Juice Concentration Containing an Undeclared Sweetener, FDA Import Alert No. 20-02 (October 7, 2011).

China after the discovery of unapproved drug residues and food additives;[84] import alerts in 2008 for vegetable protein and milk products tainted with melamine from China;[85] an alert in 2009 for morel mushrooms, due both to microbial contamination and substitution of less valuable mushrooms for a portion of the morels;[86] an import alert in 2013 for adulterated honey that listed firms and products from India, Malaysia, New Zealand, Saudi Arabia, Turkey, and Vietnam (the same import alert noted that in the mid-1990s, detentions of imported honey from Brazil, Mexico, and the Soviet Union occurred);[87] and an import alert in 2014 against a Turkish company and Iranian company for adulterated pomegranate juice and concentrate products that contained undeclared ingredients like "black currant, apple, pear or cherry juices in place of pomegranate juice."[88]

[d] Bioterrorism Act: Traceability

Another useful tool for the FDA for import control of food product is the Public Health Security and Bioterrorism Preparedness and Response Act (Bioterrorism Act), enacted by Congress in 2002.[89] Under the Bioterrorism Act and the Final Rule issued on November 7, 2008 (effective from May 6, 2009) importers are required to submit to FDA "prior notice of food, including animal feed, that is imported or offered for import into the United States."[90] Although the Bioterrorism Act does not stop the importation of EMA food product, prior notice allows the FDA to work closely with the Customs Border Patrol to identify and trace back imports of adulterated product.

[e] FSMA: Preventive Controls

Section 106 of FSMA is titled "Protection Against Intentional Adulteration."[91] FDA has issued a proposed rule to implement Section 106. The scope of the proposed rule is limited to acts of intentional adulteration that are high risk, meaning "acts intended to cause massive public harm, including acts of terrorism."[92] The proposed rule excludes from its scope economically adulterated food. The FDA announced in its proposed rule that EMA

---

[84] *See* Detention Without Physical Examination of Aquacultured Catfish, Basa, Shrimp, Dace, and Eel from China – Presence of New Animal Drugs and/or Unsafe Food Additives, FDA Import Alert No. 16–131, (January 14, 2010).

[85] See Detention without Physical Examination of All Vegetable Protein Products from China for Animal or Human Food Use due to the Presence of Melamine and/or Melamine Analogs, FDA Import Alert 99-29 (November 7, 2014); *see also* Detention without Physical Examination of All Milk Products, Milk Derived Ingredients and Finished Food Products Containing Milk from China due to the Presence of Melamine and/or Melamine Analog, FDA Import Alert 99-30 (October 30, 2014).

[86] *See* Detention without Physical Examination of Morel Mushrooms due to Adulteration and Substitution, Food and Drug Administration, FDA Import Alert 25-02 (March 18, 2011).

[87] *See* Adulteration of Honey, FDA Import Alert 36-01 (October 16, 2014).

[88] *See* Detention without Physical Examination of Juices and Juice Concentrates that Are Adulterated or Misbranded due to Substitution, FDA Import Alert 22-04 (December 17, 2014).

[89] *See* Public Health Security and Bioterrorism Preparedness and Response Act of 2002, Pub. L. No. 107–188, 116 Stat. 594 (codified as amended in scattered sections of 42 U.S.C.).

[90] Prior Notice of Imported Food under the Public Health Security and Bioterrorism Preparedness and Response Act of 2002, 68 Fed. Reg. 58,974 (October 10, 2003).

[91] *See* Food Safety Modernization Act (FSMA), PL 111–353, § 106, 124 Stat. 3885, 3897 (2011) (codified in scattered sections of 21 U.S.C.).

[92] *Id.*

would be addressed under the hazard analysis and risk-preventive controls (HARBPC). Because the proposed preventive controls, however, do not address intentional adulteration, such as EMA, FDA "plans to provide new language and an analysis of costs" with any intentional adulteration provisions added to those rules, and to seek comment.[93]

The incorporation of EMA provisions into the preventive controls may require covered facilities to identify hazards that are reasonably likely to occur, such as melamine from China, even if there is no known history of the specific supplier. The potential for economic adulteration of products exempt from the preventive controls rules – seafood, juice, and dietary supplements – would be addressed likely through amendment of the HACCP and GMP regulations for these particular products. It is difficult to assess at this point the implications of incorporating EMA provisions into the FSMA preventive controls rule. For example, it is interesting to contemplate whether the horsemeat scandal in the United Kingdom – where horsemeat was substituted for beef without a human health threat – would constitute an FSMA violation once the preventive control rules are finalized. The test may hinge on the connection between "hazard" as defined in the final rule and the potential for public health harm.[94]

It is also possible that FSMA's overall strengthening of the FDA border enforcement may contribute to enforcement activity against EMA. FSMA enhances FDA enforcement on imported foods in several ways. FSMA authorizes FDA to enter into agreements with foreign governments to facilitate the inspection of foreign facilities.[95] Although it is unclear to what extent FSMA will bear on EMA, arguably more attention will be focused on the overall compliance of imports. Under FSMA, for the first time importers have explicit responsibility to verify that their foreign supplies have adequate preventive controls in place and that the food they ship to the United States is otherwise safe. The agency also has the power to establish a third-party program for certifying that foreign food facilities comply with US food safety standards, to require certification as a condition of entry for certain high-risk foods, and to reject entry of food if the foreign facility or country refuses an inspection by FDA or its designee. Significantly, FSMA also explicitly encourages arrangements with foreign governments to leverage resources, such as mutual recognition of inspection results, sharing electronic data, and training of foreign governments to build their regulatory capacity.[96]

[f] Development of Technology and Standards

In 2013, the USP proposed new quality standards for a trio of food products – pomegranate juice, spirulina (the dried biomass of the cyanobacterium *Arthrospira platensis* – rich in protein and considered safe for consumption by humans and animals, and cultivated and used as a food source worldwide), and Brilliant Black PN (a synthetic food color used in jams, chocolate syrup, and candies).[97] For pomegranate juice, the new standard

---

[93] Focused Mitigation Strategies to Protect Food against Intentional Adulteration, 78 Fed. Reg. 247 (December 24, 2013).

[94] *See generally* John Spink, *Review of EMA Aspects of New FDA FSMA Preventive Controls Rule*, Michigan State University Food Fraud Initiative (September 19, 2014).

[95] FSMA § 306(a), 124 Stat. 3897 (January 4, 2011).

[96] *Id.*

[97] *See* Press Release, U.S. Pharmacopeial Convention, New Standards for Pomegranate Juice, Spirulina and Other Food Ingredients Proposed for Food Chemicals Codex (July 2, 2013).

not only describes a food ingredient, but also allows for the testing for components that can help manufacturers and formulators make sure that their ingredients are not adulterated. The standard will be posted in a new FCC Identity Standard, which gives a description of the ingredient as well as a series of identification tests and acceptance criteria.[98] It may even be advisable for the FDA to issue a guidance to suggest to the food industry that these standards developed by USP could be used as benchmarks for enforcement actions against economic adulteration. An interesting question is raised as to whether the development of the preventive control rules will obligate food facilities to monitor USP's database as part of HARBPC.[99]

[g] Enhanced Coordination

In 2011, the Government Accountability Office (GAO) issued a report examining the FDA's approaches to detecting and preventing EMA of food and medical products, and the challenges the FDA faces in detecting and preventing such adulteration.[100] To enhance the FDA's efforts to combat EMA, GAO recommends that the FDA take three actions: (1) officially adopt a working definition of EMA (the GAO noted that without such a definition, when FDA detects adulteration, it is more difficult for the agency to distinguish EMA from other forms of adulteration in order for the agency to be more proactive about economic adulteration); (2) provide written guidance to agency centers and offices on the means of addressing EMA; and (3) enhance communication and coordination of agency efforts on EMA.[101]

In response to the GAO draft report, the FDA explained that it viewed EMA as a "subset of cases within the broader concept of adulteration, and believes that a holistic approach toward understanding and addressing adulteration is the best course forward."[102] The FDA also noted that FSMA provided it with increased authority to promulgate broad regulations to prevent adulteration "with enhanced focus on risk-based resource allocation."[103] Finally, FDA established the Working Group on Economically Motivated Adulteration (WEMA), which held its first meeting on September 23, 2011. The working group adopted the recommended working definition of EMA and continues to hold meetings to encourage collaboration and communication to address public health issues.[104]

[h] FTC: Unfair Method of Competition

FTC has the authority to stop "unfair methods of competition in commerce"[105] and "unfair or deceptive acts or practices in commerce."[106] Arguably, EMA is an "unfair method of competition" and an unfair or deceptive act or practice" and as noted in

[98] *See id.*
[99] *See* Ricardo Carvajal, *USP, Food Fraud, and FSMA*, FDA LAW BLOG (April 16, 2012).
[100] *See* U.S. GOV'T ACCOUNTABILITY OFFICE, *supra* note 26.
[101] *See id.* at 23.
[102] *See id.* at 24.
[103] *See id.*
[104] *See id.*
[105] 15 U.S.C. § 45(a)(1)-(2).
[106] 15 U.S.C. § 45.

Chapter 4 the FTC has concurrent jurisdiction with the FDA over this practice. Indeed, the FTC has acted to prevent the sale of debased foods, which deceive the public and divert trade from honest competitors.[107] The interest of the FTC, however, appears to be a historical footnote, as the agency has deferred to the FDA in the handling of EMA. A Working Agreement established in 1954 between the FDA and FTC provides that unless the agencies otherwise agree, the FTC will exercise sole jurisdiction over all advertising of food and the FDA will exercise sole jurisdiction over all labeling of these products.[108] It is likely that FTC regards EMA of food primarily as a deceptive labeling problem and thus an FDA problem.

[i] Litigation

Litigation can be used as a tool to address EMA, especially by food enterprises whose vested interest is threatened by adulterated product and whose requests to the government for enforcement are unheeded. An example of where litigation has been a tool against EMA is the case of pomegranate juice. POM Wonderful, a grower and manufacturer of pomegranate juice in the United States, brought to the attention of the FDA that a pomegranate juice competitor, Purely Juice, Inc., was selling pomegranate juice labeled "100 pomegranate juice" that was produced from pomegranate concentrate from suppliers in Iran and other Middle Eastern countries. When the FDA notified POM Wonderful that it lacked the resources both to investigate and develop sufficient sophisticated methodology to analyze the alleged adulteration, POM Wonderful filed an action against Purely Juice claiming that the company was deceiving consumers by selling adulterated pomegranate juice.[109] The court agreed with the test results from seven different laboratories, which concluded that Purely Juice's juice could not have been 100 percent pomegranate juice since it contained foreign sugars, colorants, and filler juices.[110] The court found that "it was widely known in the super premium juice industry that there were serious issues of adulteration with pomegranate juice concentrate originating from outside the United States."[111] The court determined that Purely Juice engaged in false advertising and misleading marketing and ordered Purely Juice to pay an approximate $1.5 million toward damages.[112]

Olive oil presents an interesting case study on the prospects of EMA litigation or fraud litigation in general and the complexities involved in determining a litigation strategy.[113] The North American Olive Oil Association (NAOOA), a trade association representing the interests of the olive oil industry, in 2013 brought false advertising claims,

---

[107] Wesley E. Forte, *The Food and Drug Administration and the Economic Adulteration of Foods*, 41 Indiana L. J. 346, 348 n.11 (1966) (citing Fresh Grown Preserve Corp. *v. FTC*, 125 F.2d 917 (2d Cir. 1942) (FTC alleges unfair competition to label as "preserves" a food not containing at least 45 percent fruit); FTC v. Good-Grape Co., 45 F.2d 70 (6th Cir. 1930) (FTC alleges "Good-Grape" soft drink with no natural grape flavor)).

[108] 3 Trade Reg. Rep. (CCH) ¶ 9850 (1954), 2010 WL 254582.

[109] POM Wonderful LLC v. Purely Juice, Inc., No. CV-07-02633, 2008 U.S. Dist LEXIS 55426 (C.D. Cal. July 17, 2008), *aff'd*, No. 08-56375, 2009 U.S. App. LEXIS 28478 (9th Cir. December 28, 2009).

[110] *See id.* at *4.

[111] *Id.* at *5.

[112] *See id.* at *14–15.

[113] *See generally*, Thomas Mueller, Extra Virginity: The Sublime and Scandalous World of Olive Oil (2011) (documenting the nature and extent of olive oil fraud).

among other claims, and sought a preliminary injunction under the Lanham Act in the Southern District of New York against Kangadis Food ("Kangadis").[114] NAOOA alleged that Kangadis had falsely and deceptively marketed a product as "100% Pure Olive Oil" when it contained Pomace, an industrially processed oil produced from olive pits, skins, and pulp. The court preliminarily enjoined Kangadis from selling as 100% Pure Olive Oil any product containing Pomace and from selling any product containing Pomace without so indicating on the label. The court reserved ruling, however, on several issues and allowed for supplemental briefing. Following the briefing, the court in April 2013 entered an order that refused to extend its previously entered injunction due to NAOOA's failure to introduce any extrinsic evidence of consumer confusion.[115] Although it was clear that Kangadis violated federal and state standards by selling refilled oil as 100 percent Pure Olive Oil, NAOAA failed to seek direct enforcement of the standards, which are either nonbinding or unenforceable through a private action, and could not show that a reasonable consumer's understanding of olive oil aligned with the standards. A consumer could view 100 percent Olive Oil as being silent on whether it was virgin or refined.[116] The court's decision underscores that violation of an industry standard alone may not be sufficient to obtain preliminary injunction on a false advertisement claim in the case of economic adulteration of food: evidence may need to be shown as to how the ordinary consumer perceives the advertisement.[117]

In an ongoing case of *Kumar v. Salov North America Corp.*, a federal district court in California allowed many of the putative false labeling claims against Salov, the maker of Filippo Berio brand olive oil, to survive dismissal. [118] Claiming violations of various California consumer protection statutes, common law fraud and deceit, breach of contract, and breach of the implied covenant of good faith and fair dealing, the plaintiff alleged Salov deceptively labeled its olive oil as "Imported from Italy" when the olives were not grown or pressed in Italy, and as "extra virgin" when the way the oil is bottled, transported, and stored allows it to degrade so that it may not be extra virgin by the time of sale or by the "best by" date.

[j] International Law

Under the WTO framework, the United States is able to keep out foods that have been subject to EMA, even when the food does not pose a health risk, because there is a

---

[114] *See* N. Am. Olive Oil Ass'n v. Kangadis Food Inc., 962 F. Supp. 2d 514 (S.D.N.Y. 2013).

[115] The court also ordered the defendant to distribute stickers to be affixed to unsold tins of oil containing Pomace (subsequently modified to allow the defendant to affix stickers or recall the product) and denied plaintiff's request that defendant provide notice of its past mislabeling via its website because it would not remedy the harm that had already occurred when the mislabeled product was purchased. *See id.*

[116] *See id.*

[117] Another case analogous to EMA was brought in 2004 by the California Olive Oil Council against Napa Valley Trading Company for deceptive marketing practices in the sale of Napa Valley Naturals olive oil. Under California law, olive oil labeled with the name of a state-approved wine region must have at least 75 percent of the oil from that locale. The suit alleged that Napa Valley Naturals olive oils have no legitimate connection to Napa Valley, but were marketed in a manner to falsely state or imply that the olive oils were produced in Napa Valley from olives grown in Napa Valley). *See* David Ryan, *Marin Company Sued for Use of Napa Name on Olive Oil Label*, Napa Valley Register.com (November 1, 2004).

[118] No. 14-CV-2411-YGR (N.D. Cal.).

legitimate state interest in preventing deceptive practices.[119] If adulterated foods pose a health risk, the United States can use the SPS Agreement to prevent importation.[120]

The practical international dimensions of EMA should be considered. For example, in the infant formula scandal in China, even though the milk was contaminated in China and sold in China, the adulteration had wide-reaching international effects. First, the adulteration gave way to trade barrier claims. At a WTO meeting in October 2008, China criticized countries that had banned their dairy products claiming it was an unnecessary barrier to trade.[121] Shortly after the case became public, the FDA recalled many contaminated foods and tested milk-based products imported from China.[122] Secondly, the adulteration led to personal injury compensation claims. Fonterra, a New Zealand company with offices in Hong Kong, owned 43 percent of Sanlu, the company that was responsible for the contamination. Sanlu went bankrupt in 2008 in an effort to pay the Chinese government for its share of the claimant's compensation scheme.[123]

[k] Private Standards

A private standard setting body, the Global Food Safety Initiative (GFSI), has released a paper on food fraud – defined as deceiving consumers using food products, ingredients, and packaging for economic gain – stating that this food problem can be more dangerous to consumers because the contaminants can be unconventional and because the fraudsters may not know the extent of the public harm potential, as was the case in the China melamine scandal.[124] The paper notes that GFSI will recommend that the food industry add two steps to its private standard protocols: (1) food enterprises will need to perform a food fraud vulnerability assessment; and (2) food enterprises will need to have a control plan in place. GFSI recommends that during a food safety certification audit, an auditor will review documentation related to the vulnerability assessment and confirm that a plan has been devised and implemented. The GFSI paper opines that it will take time for food firms to perform these steps and recommends that GFSI not ask firms to meet these requirements until the full version is released, along with practical guidelines that will be published.[125]

[l] Criminal Enforcement

The trend internationally to prosecute EMA as a crime may have implications on enforcement strategies in the United States. In February of 2014, more than 1,200 tons

---

[119] Agreement on Technical Barriers to Trade (TBT Agreement), art. 2.2, April 15, 1994, Marrakesh Agreement Establishing the World Trade Organization, Annex 1A, 33 I.L.M. 1125.

[120] Agreement on the Application of Sanitary and Phytosanitary Measures (SPS Agreement), art. 2.1, April 15, 1994, Marrakesh Agreement Establishing the World Trade Organization, Annex 1A, 1867 U.N.T.S. 493, 33 I.L.M. 1125.

[121] *China protests ban in milk imports at WTO Meeting*, International Herald Tribune, October 9, 2008.

[122] Press Release, Food & Drug Admin., FDA Updates Health Information Advisory on Melamine Contamination (September 26, 2008).

[123] Edward Wong, *Company at Core of China's Milk Scandal Is Declared Bankrupt*, N.Y. Times (December 24, 2008).

[124] Global Food Safety Initiative, GFSI Position on Mitigating the Public Health Risk of Food Fraud (2014).

[125] *See id.*

of fake or substandard food and nearly 430,000 liters of counterfeit drinks were seized in an Interpol-Europol coordinated operation that spanned across thirty-three countries in the Americas, Asia, and Europe, including in the United States.[126] The operation resulted in the arrest or detention of ninety-six people. The operation involved police, customs, national regulatory food bodies, and private firms and was carried out in shops, markets, airports, seaports, and private homes. The operation was linked to the overall effort in the EU against international smuggling and organized crime.[127]

§ 2.03 Food Trade

[1] *Background*

[a] Tension between Free Trade and Protectionism

The US laws that govern the trade of food are of increasing importance in a global food society. These laws reflect a tension in food trade policy between two competing views. The first view is that the expansion of food trade is good for consumers, farmers, and the United States as a whole. This view holds that consumers have come to expect the world food system to provide them with a wide choice of products and that changes in consumer taste have encouraged the emergence of global markets and added to the significance of trade.[128] This view also posits that trade enables farmers to build markets for surplus food and has helped maintain in the United States a competitive domestic food market. Those who subscribe to this first view favor free trade policies based on a market model in which food trade between the United States and other countries flows without restrictions imposed by government. The competing view is that the expansion of food trade threatens food safety, food security, farms and food enterprises, the environment, and culture. There is also the concern that food trade encapsulates the inequity between the industrialized nations and the poorer, predominantly rural countries. Those who oppose trade liberalization of food favor restrictions to trade.

This tension between the two competing views – free trade versus protectionism – presents challenges for the regulation of food trade. In essence, the US regulatory system faces the dual challenge of protecting public health by maintaining high national food quality and safety standards and protecting other interests, while at the same time meeting US obligations to eradicate trade restrictions and trade barriers under international trade agreements.

[b] International Agreements

International agreements create law for the parties of the agreement. There are numerous international agreements relevant to food. These agreements attempt to regulate how governments relate to one another on a host of issues, which regulation ultimately

---

[126] *Thousands of Tonnes of Fake Food and Drink Seized in Interpol-Europol Operation*, Europol (February 13, 2014).

[127] *Id.*

[128] *See US Food Imports: Overview*, Econ. Research Service, U.S. Dept. of Agric. (last updated February 14, 2015) (as Americans become wealthier and more ethnically diverse, consumers demand variety, quality, and convenience in the foods they consume).

affects the legal relationships between stakeholders in the global food supply chain and the food consumed by consumers. Trade agreements are among the most common types of international agreements that contribute to international food law and that enable a robust food commerce system.

Under the US Constitution's Commerce Clause, Congress has exclusive power to regulate international trade.[129] To this end, Congress ratifies trade treaties and passes trade legislation, which includes establishing both import barriers and export promotion programs. The executive branch implements these laws and programs, conducts foreign relations, and negotiates international trade arrangements with foreign nations. A number of government agencies at the executive level have jurisdiction over some aspect of international food trade, including the US Trade Representative (USTR), the Department of Commerce, US Customs and Border protection, the FDA, and the USDA.

The foundational food trade agreement is the General Agreement on Tariffs and Trade of 1947 (GATT).[130] GATT was an international agreement that created a multilateral trading system and established rules among participating nations to assure the efficient international trade of goods, including food products. According to its preamble, the purpose of GATT was the "substantial reduction of tariffs and other trade barriers and the elimination of preferences, on a reciprocal and mutually advantageous basis."[131] GATT fostered the liberalization of trade through the reduction of protectionist policies; however, exemptions and exceptions for agriculture limited its effects. Countries that were members of GATT developed an international trade system through a series of trade negotiations that are commonly referred to as "rounds" that bear the name of the meetings' locale. The Uruguay Round (launched in Punta del Este, Uruguay in September 1986) was the eighth round of multilateral trade negotiations conducted within the framework GATT, spanning from 1986 to 1994 and embracing 123 countries, referred to as "contracting parties." The agreement establishing the World Trade Organization (WTO) of 1994[132] was part of the Final Act of the 1986–1994 Uruguay Round, the last GATT round. The WTO became a successor of GATT and assumed control of the multilateral trading system in 1995. However, GATT is still used by the WTO as the principal source of rules and agreements for this trading system. In addition to GATT, other WTO rules and agreements that today provide the legal framework for international food trade were also produced during the Uruguay Round. These agreements include the Agreement on Sanitary and Phytosanitary Measures (SPS), the Agreement on Technical Barriers to Trade (TBT Agreement), the Agreement on Agriculture (AA), and the Agreement on Trade-Related Aspects of Intellectual Property Rights (TRIPS).

---

[129] U.S. Const. art. 1, § 8.3; *see also* Gibbons v. Ogden, 22 U.S. 1, 193–194 (1824) ("No sort of trade can be carried on between this country and any other, to which this power [to regulate commerce with foreign nations] does not extend."); Board of Trustees v. United States, 289 U.S. 48, 56 (1933) ("It is an essential attribute of [Congress's power over foreign commerce] that it is exclusive and plenary.").

[130] General Agreement on Tariffs and Trade, October 30, 1947 (GATT 1947).

[131] *Id.* at preamble, 61 Stat. A5, 55 U.N.T.S. 188.

[132] *See* Agreement Establishing the World Trade Organization, art. 14.1, Apr. 15, 1994, Marrakesh Agreement Establishing the World Trade Organization, 33 I.L.M. 1125.

[2] *GATT and WTO Regime*

[a] Trade Rules for Food Products

The current version of GATT is the result of the WTO Uruguay Round in 1994. GATT sets out four main trade rules. These rules apply to the trade of goods but not services. First, GATT creates a schedule of concessions. A state cannot enact a tariff that exceeds the maximum amount for a specific product number.[133] Second, there is a general prohibition on nontariff barriers to trade, such as quantitative restrictions.[134] Article XX of GATT provides exceptions to this general prohibition. For example, a nation can impose nontariff barriers to trade based on national security reasons,[135] human, animal, or plant safety,[136] conservation of natural resources,[137] or public morals.[138] Measures taken for technical reasons, such as to prevent consumers from being misled, must comply with the TBT Agreement. Third, GATT prohibits states from favoring one WTO state over another state.[139] This is known as the Most-Favored Nation (MFN) status. The purpose of this prohibition is to prevent trade diversion and political friction between states.[140] Fourth, GATT prohibits discrimination between imported and domestically produced goods. States cannot apply different internal charges or taxes to imported goods.[141]

[b] WTO Dispute Resolution

The WTO provides a forum for dispute resolution when disagreements inevitably arise between trading nations. Countries are encouraged to settle disputes between themselves and are permitted to do so during any portion of the formal dispute resolution process. Only the member governments of the WTO can participate in disputes as parties or as third parties.[142] Settlement of any dispute goes through several stages, including consultation and mediation between the disputing countries, expert review of the dispute, a series of hearings, reports, and a ruling.[143] An appeals process before an Appellate Body is also available.[144] If a country loses a dispute, it is expected to change its laws or policies to conform to WTO agreements and the dispute ruling. If the appropriate changes are not adopted within a reasonable time period, the complainant may request negotiations for compensation, which compensation usually involves the lifting of trade barriers (e.g., tariff reduction, increase of import quotas) by the losing party.[145] If satisfactory compensation is not agreed upon

---

[133] GATT 1947, art. II, 61 Stat. A-11, 55 U.N.T.S. 194.
[134] *Id.* at art. XI.
[135] *Id.* at art. XXI.
[136] *Id.* at art. XX(b).
[137] *Id.* at art. XX(g).
[138] *Id.* at art. XX(a).
[139] *Id.* at art. I.
[140] There are two exceptions to this prohibition: (1) free trade areas and custom unions (*id.* at art. XXIV) and (2) safeguard agreements (*id.*).
[141] *Id.* at art. III, ¶ 1.
[142] *Introduction to the WTO Dispute Settlement System: 1.4 Participants in the dispute settlement*, World Trade Org.
[143] World Trade Org., Understanding the WTO 56–7, 59.
[144] *Id.* at 57, 59.
[145] *Id.* at 58.

within the requisite time period, the complaining party may request countermeasures, which may include retaliatory measures.[146] Retaliatory measures have been used by the United States in high-profile food dispute cases, involving bananas[147] and meat products subject to hormones.[148]

[c] SPS: Trade Barrier Exception

(1) *Protection of Human, Animal, or Plant Health*

The most prevalent of the Article XX exceptions in food trade disputes is the exception in Article XX(b) to protect human, animal, and plant health. Entered into force on January 1, 1995, the SPS Agreement elaborates on the scope of Article XX(b)[149] and more specifically defines what is necessary for the assessment of risk to health.[150] Measures invoked for the purpose of protecting human, animal, or plant health that result in a trade barrier must therefore conform with the SPS Agreement in order to comply with Article XX(b) of the GATT.[151]

The SPS Agreement expressly allows countries that are members of the WTO to adopt scientifically based measures in order to protect human, animal, and plant life or health. These measures are referred to as sanitary measures or SPS measures. The agreement defines an SPS measure as any measure that is applied

   (i) to protect animal or plant life or health within the territory of the member from risks arising from the entry, establishment, or spread of pests, diseases, disease-carrying organisms, or disease-causing organisms;

  (ii) to protect human or animal life or health within the territory of the member from risks arising from additives, contaminants, toxins or disease-causing organisms in foods, beverages, or feedstuffs;

 (iii) to protect human life or health within the territory of the member from risks arising from diseases carried by animals, plants, or products thereof, or from the entry, establishment, or spread of pests; or

 (iv) to prevent or limit other damage within the territory of the Member from the entry, establishment, or spread of pests.[152]

An SPS measure may take the form of a law, decree, regulation, requirement, or procedure related to food safety.[153] Examples of common SPS measures include the regulation of foods derived from biotechnology, meat, and poultry processing standards to reduce pathogens; residue limits for pesticides in foods; restrictions on food and animal feed additives and toxic substances in food or drink; labeling requirements related

---

[146] *Id.*

[147] *See* Recourse by the United States to Article 22.7 of the DSU, European Communities – Regime for the Importation, Sale and Distribution of Bananas, WT/DS27/49 (April 9, 1999).

[148] *See* Recourse by the United States to Article 22.7 of the DSU, European Communities – Measures Concerning Meat and Meat Products (Hormones), WT/DS26/21 (July 15, 1999).

[149] SPS Agreement, *supra* note 120 at preamble.

[150] *Id.* at art. 5.

[151] *Id.* at art. 2.4.

[152] SPS Agreement, *supra* note 120 (According to Article 1(3) of the SPS Agreement, the Annexes are an integral part of the agreement.).

[153] *Introduction to the SPS Agreement: 1.3 What Is an SPS Measure?*, WORLD TRADE ORG.

directly to food safety; and sanitary requirements for imported pallets used to transport animals.[154] The decisive factor in determining whether a measure is an SPS measure is whether the purpose of the measure is to protect human, animal, or plant life or health. This subjective criterion leaves open the question as to whether a measure qualifies as an SPS measure if it has several purposes, with health protection being only one of them.

Members are allowed to apply their SPS measures on a discriminatory basis, provided they "do not arbitrarily or unjustifiably discriminate between Members where identical or the same conditions prevail."[155] SPS measures should be applied only to the extent necessary to protect health and not in a manner that would constitute a disguised restriction on international trade. "Necessary" has been interpreted to mean "nearly indispensable."[156] The appropriate level of SPS protection hinges upon demonstration by a member that their SPS measures are based on an appropriate risk assessment to human, animal, or plant life.[157] Such an assessment requires a scientific justification for the standard.[158] In other words, the measure must be reasonably supported by scientific evidence.[159] Such scientific evidence must include data and factual studies rather than social value judgments.[160] The assessment also has to be appropriate to the circumstances and take into account the risk assessment techniques that have been developed by relevant international organizations.[161] In cases where the relevant scientific evidence is not available, a country may provisionally adopt SPS measures on the basis of available information.[162]

One of the ways to ensure that measures are not disguised restriction on trade is the harmonization of SPS measures. In order to achieve harmonization of SPS measures, the SPS Agreement encourages members to base their measures on international standards (established primarily from the Codex Alimentarius Commission, as well as the World Organization for Animal Health [OIE], and the International Plant Protection Convention), guidelines, and recommendations, where they exist.[163] The SPS Agreement offers an incentive for the adoption of international standards by presuming that a national SPS measure that conforms to these international standards is consistent with the provisions of SPS and GATT.[164] The result of this presumption is that

---

[154] Michael T. Roberts, *Technical Regulations and Trade: Current Issues, Trends and Long-Term Prospects*, in THE EVOLVING STRUCTURE OF WORLD AGRICULTURAL TRADE 179, 183 (Alexander Sarris and Jamie Morrison eds. 2009).

[155] SPS Agreement, *supra* note 120 at art. 2.3.

[156] *Id.* at art. 2.2.

[157] *Id.* at arts. 3.3, 5.

[158] *Id.* at art. 3.3.

[159] *See Id.* at arts. 5.1, 5.2.

[160] *See* Appellate Body Report, EC Measures Concerning Meat and Meat Products (Hormones), WT/DS26/AB/R, WT/DS48/AB/R (January 16, 1998), para. 181 (hereinafter Appellate Body Report, EC – Meat and Meat Products).

[161] *See* SPS Agreement, *supra* note 120, at art. 5.1.

[162] *Id.* at art. 5.7.

[163] *Id.* at § 3.1.

[164] *Id.* § 3.2. Also, art. 2.4 provides: "Sanitary or phytosanitary measures which conform to the relevant provisions of this agreement shall be presumed to be in accordance with the obligations of the Members under the provisions of GATT 1994 which relate to the use of sanitary or phytosanitary measures, in particular the provisions of Art. XX(b)."

while the standards adopted by the Codex Alimentarius Commission (Codex) are not binding on its members, the explicit incorporation of its standards into the trade system as a compliance benchmark has projected Codex into greater significance. While Codex standard setting is predicated upon science, the linkages between trade interests and Codex standards raise a question as to the institution's ability to stave off nonscientific influences and the intervention of political and industrial pressure.[165] This tension is evident in the narrow vote by Codex on July 5, 2012, to adopt the maximum residue levels for ractopamine hydrochloride, a controversial veterinary drug used in animal feed that boosts growth and promotes leanness in pigs and cattle. This Ractopamine controversy is addressed in Chapter 3, but for purposes of this chapter, it is noted that the narrow vote reflected the tension between the political acceptability of the substance as well as the politicization of the underlying science. There was serious concern that this case would likely weaken the legitimacy and overall effectiveness of Codex in governing food safety and quality.[166]

Although the SPS Agreement prescribes that members base their measures on international standards, they may introduce or maintain measures that would result in a higher level of protection than would be achieved by international standards or they may introduce measures if international standards do not exist. If a country introduces such measures, there must be a scientific justification for doing so, or it must be a consequence of the level of SPS protection that country determines to be appropriate.[167]

Additional requirements in the SPS Agreement involve equivalence and transparency. Under certain conditions, member countries are required to recognize other member countries' equivalent SPS measures.[168] Member countries shall notify changes in their SPS measures by publishing and reasonable questions from other member countries.[169]

If a country enacts a food safety measure that might not comply with the SPS Agreement, another country can bring a complaint under the WTO. The first of two examples of SPS cases involved the United States and Canada complaint against the EU's import prohibition of meat treated with growth hormones.[170] This case is analyzed more fully in Chapter 3. The EU promulgated a series of directives that banned the sale and marketing of beef treated with any of the six growth hormones that the FDA had approved as safe. The United States viewed the directives as protectionist discrimination because hormone treatments of beef were commonly used outside the EU. The Appellate Body held that EU import prohibition of beef treated by the growth hormones was inconsistent with Articles 3.1 and 5.5 of the SPS Agreement. A second example is the Japan Fruit Case of 1998.[171] Japan had a policy to prevent the entry of "quarantine pests" (flies, moths,

---

[165] *See* Kuei-Jung Ni, *Does Science Speak Clearly and Fairly in Trade and Food Safety Disputes? The Search for an Optimal Response of WTO Adjudication to Problematic International Standard-Making*, 68 FOOD & DRUG L.J. 97, 97 (2013).

[166] Alberto Alemanno & Giuseppe Capodieci, *Testing the Limits of Global Food Governance: The Case of Ractopamine*, 3 EUR. J. RISK REG. 400 (2012).

[167] SPS Agreement, *supra* note 120 at art. 3.3.

[168] *Id.* at art. 4.

[169] *Id.* at art. 7.

[170] Appellate Body Report, EC – Meat and Meat Products, *supra* note 160.

[171] Panel Report, Japan – Measure Affecting Agricultural Products, WT/DS7/R (October 27, 1998).

etc.). This policy required all imported plant products be accompanied by a phytosanitary certificate, that foreign farms be subject to growing-site inspection, and that imported plant products be inspected upon entry to Japan. The United States claimed this policy barred US fruit exports and violated the SPS Agreement.[172] Siding with the United States, the WTO found Japan's measure was disproportionate to the risk because the policy was not based on scientific evidence.[173]

There have been continuing disagreements between the EU and the United States on SPS measures, especially where rBST[174] and GMOs[175] are concerned. These disputes have not only drawn the United States and the EU into conflicts at the WTO level – as shown in Chapter 3 – but have also threatened the ongoing United States and EU agricultural treaty talks.[176] The root of these disputes has been one of interpretation. Europe follows the "precautionary principle" when it comes to adopting SPS measures and interpreting the SPS Agreement.[177] The United States follows the "reasonable certainty of no harm" approach to food safety.[178] The precautionary principle is the theory that protective action should be taken when there is no scientific proof of the absence of risk.[179] This was seen in the beef hormones dispute where the EU argued that the precautionary principle supported their restrictions on US beef.[180] In the GMO cases, the European Communities argued that the precautionary principle had "become a fully-fledged and general principle of international law."[181] The US approach that protective actions should be used only when there is scientific evidence of a risk is difficult to reconcile with the precautionary principle. As a result, there has been continued dispute over SPS measures, beef hormones, and GMOs.[182]

The OIE contributes to food law by adopting international standards about animal health and adopts resolutions about animal disease control.[183] These standards are recognized as references for animal health and zoonotic disease by the SPS Agreement[184] and by the SPS Committee that works with the OIE in setting SPS Standards.[185] The WTO's

---

[172] *Id.* at para. 4.19.

[173] *Id.* at paras. 4.57, 4.74.

[174] Appellate Body Report, EC – Meat and Meat Products, *supra* note 160.

[175] Panel Report, European Communities – Measures Affecting the Approval and Marketing of Biotech Products, DS/291R, DS/292R, DS293/R (September 29, 2006).

[176] *See* Desmond Butler, *New US-EU talks Threatened by Agriculture Spats*, Huffington Post (March 23, 2013).

[177] Appellate Body Report, EC – Meat and Meat Products, *supra* note 162.

[178] *See* Mills v. Giant of Maryland, LLC, 441 F.Supp.2d 104, 109 (D.D.C. 2006), *aff'd*, 508 F.3d 11 (D.C. Cir. 2007) (citing 21 C.F.R. 170.3(i), FDA has defined "safety" of food additives to mean 'that there is a reasonable certainty in the minds of competent scientists that the substance is not harmful under the intended conditions of use.").

[179] World Trade Org., *supra* note 143, at 30.

[180] Appellate Body Report, EC – Meat and Meat Products, *supra* note 160.

[181] Panel Report, EC Communities – Biotech Products, *supra* note 175, at para. 4.523.

[182] Butler, *supra* note 176.

[183] *Procedures used by the OIE to set Standards and Recommendations for International Trade, with a focus on the Terrestrial and Aquatic Animal Health Codes*, World Org for Animal Health (2011).

[184] SPS Agreement, art. 5, para. 1.

[185] Report on the Activities of the WTO SPS Committee and Other Relevant WTO Activities in 2011 and the First Quarter of 2012, CAC/35 INF/3, Codex Alimentarius Commission, Rome, Italy: July 2–7, 2012 at 5.

recognition of OIE health standards as international sanitary rules renders the standards as significant guidelines for national legislation and regulations.[186]

(2) *Prevention of Deceptive Practices*

Under GATT Article XX(d), a country can impose a nontariff barrier to trade if it is necessary to prevent deceptive practices. This exception is the next most common exception used in food after the exception for the protection of human, animal, or plant life or health in Article XX(b). Article XX(d) allows a country to impose restrictions on labeling, marketing, and food quality. As with Article XX(b), a trade barrier imposed under Article XX(d) must not discriminate or be arbitrary. It must also meet further criteria in (d) by being for "the prevention of deceptive practices" and "necessary." For example, when the United States made a WTO complaint against Korea alleging that Korea discriminated against imported beef by limiting how it could be displayed and where it could be sold, the Appellate Body held Korea's restrictions did not meet the exception in Article XX(d) because they were not necessary or nearly indispensable.[187] In each case assessing whether a measure is necessary will require a balancing of the common interests of values protected by the law against the impact of the law on exports or imports.[188]

[d] TBT: Regulations and Standards

(1) *Purpose*

The TBT Agreement ensures that technical regulations, voluntary standards, and conformity assessment procedures – except when these are SPS measures as defined by the SPS Agreement or, in other words, except when a measure is adopted to safeguard human, animal, or plant health – do not create unnecessary obstacles to trade.[189] The TBT Agreement is separate, but closely related to GATT. The TBT Agreement is also closely linked to the SPS Agreement, which was signed the same year and has similar goals. The TBT agreement is becoming increasingly important in global food markets as governments, including the United States, promulgate more regulations and standards in response to growing consumer demands for products with specific quality attributes (in other words, nonsafety attributes) or for information about those attributes.

(2) *Technical Regulations*

The TBT Agreement uses the term "technical regulation" to cover regulations that apply to product, process, or production methods or standards with which compliance is mandatory. Annex 1 of the TBT states as follows:

> "Technical Regulation" – Document which lays down product characteristics or their related processes and production methods, including the applicable administrative

---

[186] *About Us: Objectives*, WORLD ORG FOR ANIMAL HEALTH.

[187] Appellate Body Report, Korea – Measures Affecting Imports of Fresh, Chilled and Frozen Beef, WT/DS161/AB/R, WT/DS169/AB/R (December 11, 2000), paras. 172–174, 186.

[188] *Id.* at para. 164.

[189] Roberts, *supra* note 154, at 184 ("The determination of whether the TBT or SPS is the applicable agreement depends on the objective of the regulation. If a regulation is adopted to safeguard human, animal or plant health, it would trigger an SPS provision and be considered a SPS measure; however, if the regulation is not a SPS measure, but is adopted to ensure the compositional integrity of a product, it would be governed by the TBT agreement.").

provisions, with which compliance is mandatory. It may also include or deal exclusively with terminology, symbols, packaging, marking or labeling requirements as they apply to a product, process or production method.[190]

TBT technical regulations include the labeling composition or quality of food and drink products; quality requirements for fresh food; and the volume, shape, and appearance of packaging of food products. For example, beef quality regulations are based on attributes such as marbling (the amount of fat interspersed with lean meat), color, firmness, texture, and age of the animal, for each grade. Quality regulations for each food product may describe the entire range of quality for a product, and the number of grades varies by commodity.[191]

The TBT Agreement prohibits technical regulations created in order to limit trade, as opposed to technical regulations created for legitimate purposes such as consumer protection. To this end, the TBT Agreement sets forth key principles by WTO members in Article 2 of the agreement: (1) members must not discriminate against imported products from other WTO members; (2) members must not adopt measures that are more trade-restrictive than necessary to fulfill a legitimate purpose; (3) members must monitor and review measures to address changes in circumstances and objectives; (4) members must base measures on international standards when available and where appropriate; (5) members must give positive consideration to recognizing other members' measures is equivalent to their own, even if different, provided that they are satisfied that another country's measures adequately fulfill the objectives of their own regulations; and (6) members must base measures, where appropriate, on product performance requirements rather than design or descriptive characteristics. Also, the preparation, adoption, and application of a technical regulation shall be done in as transparent a way as possible.[192]

In the implementation of the TBT agreement, the appropriate use of labels for food product to signify quality attributes has created considerable contention. For example, a highly contentious case involving the TBT Agreement was concerning the 2012 United States proposed mandatory country or origin labeling (COOL) measure, which would require labels to say where meat was raised and slaughtered.[193] Canada claimed that this labeling requirement was inconsistent with Article 2 of the TBT Agreement. The Appellate Body found that the COOL requirements for meat violated WTO rules because the US COOL scheme discriminates against imported livestock (this case is more fully analyzed in Chapter 4).

(3) Standards

In contrast to a technical regulation, a "standard" is defined by the TBT Agreement as a provision that applies to product process or production methods with which compliance is voluntary, not mandatory.[194] Thus, the basic difference between a technical regulation and a standard lies in the area of compliance: while compliance with a technical regulation is compulsory, in case of a standard, it is voluntary.[195]

---

[190] TBT Agreement, *supra* note 119, at Annex 1.
[191] Roberts, *supra* note 154, at 182.
[192] TBT Agreement, *supra* note 119, at arts. 2.1–2.11.
[193] Appellate Body Report, US – Certain Country of Origin Labeling (COOL) Requirements, WT/DS384/AB/R, WT/DS386/AB/R (June 29, 2012).
[194] TBT Agreement, *supra* note 119, at Annex 1.
[195] *Id.*

Article 4 of the TBT Agreement prescribes that central government standardizing bodies accept and comply with the Code of Good Practice for Preparation, Adoption and Application of Standards (the Code of Good Practice).[196] The members are also required to ensure that local government and nongovernmental bodies accept and comply with this Code of Good Practice. In order to do this, they are required to take such reasonable measures as may be available to them. The Code of Good Practice incorporates many of the fundamental requirements of the TBT Agreement, such as nondiscrimination, transparency, and avoidance of unnecessary obstacles to trade.

Unlike the SPS agreement, the TBT agreement does not reference specific international standards. Instead, it refers to "relevant international standards," a term it does not explicitly define.[197] The WTO prefers the international standards of organizations that adhere to the principles established by the TBT Committee in the Decision of the Committee on Principles for the Development of International Standards, Guides and Recommendations.[198] These principles include transparency and openness, impartiality and consensus, effectiveness and relevance, and coherency and attention to the needs of the developing countries. A diffuse set of public and private organizations promulgate international food standards, including the Organization for Economic Cooperation and Development (OECD), which operates the Scheme for the Application of International Standards for Fruits and Vegetables; the International Dairy Federation (IDF), a private organization that drafts standards for milk products; and the International Organization for Standardization (ISO). These public and private institutions collaborate on various levels. For example, IDF drafts standards for milk products in the Codex Committee for Dairy Products. Although these international standards are voluntary, when they are incorporated into national regulations or through voluntary contracts of private firms, such standards have the potential to affect trade significantly.

(4) *Conformity Assessment Procedures*

Another important provision in the TBT Agreement relates to conformity assessment procedures. In order to ascertain whether or not a product complies with a certain technical regulation or standard, there have to be procedures for assessing conformity. Annex I of the TBT Agreement defines "conformity assessment procedures" as "[a]ny procedure used, directly or indirectly, to determine that relevant requirements in technical regulations or standards are fulfilled." Such procedures include procedures for sampling, testing, and inspection; evaluation, verification, and assurance of conformity; and registration, accreditation, and approvals.[199] Although access to such procedures may be open to all producers from any country and be just a formality, they may also be very elaborate and difficult hurdles to cross, especially for producers from developing countries.

The TBT also contains provisions to ensure that these conformity assessment procedures do not become or are applied in a manner that would constitute an unnecessary

---

[196] *Id.* at Annex 3.

[197] *Id.* at art. 2.4.

[198] Panel Report, European Communities – Trade Description of Sardines, WT/DS231/R (May 29, 2002), para. 7.91.

[199] TBT Agreement, *supra* note 119, at Annex 1, note to Definition 3.

obstacle to international trade. Article 5 of the TBT Agreement inserts most-favored-nation and national-treatment obligations on the members through the preparation, adoption, and application of conformity assessment procedures. The WTO members are required to ensure that conformity assessment procedures are undertaken and completed as expeditiously as possible.[200] They must publish the standard processing period or communicate the anticipated processing period to the applicant upon request.[201] Information requirements should be limited to what is necessary to assess conformity and such information should be treated confidentially in such a manner that legitimate commercial interests are protected.[202]

Conformity assessment bodies must use relevant guides and recommendations of international standardizing bodies as a basis for their conformity assessment procedures, except where these guidelines are inappropriate for the country concerned because of such things as national security concerns, prevention of deceptive practices, protection of human health or safety, and so on. If there are no relevant guidelines or recommendations from international standardizing bodies or the proposed conformity assessment procedure is not in accordance with relevant guides and recommendations, notification of any proposed conformity assessment procedure is required for other members of the WTO.[203]

[3] *Additional International Agreements*

[a] Agreement on Agriculture

The Agreement on Agriculture was created by GATT member states during the Uruguay Rounds in an attempt to reduce trade distortion in the food sector.[204] Trade distortion is defined as higher or lower prices and higher or lower quantities of goods being produced, bought, or sold than would exist in a competitive market. The Agreement on Agriculture has three main features. The first is to limit or end export subsidies.[205] New export subsidies are banned and existing subsidies are to be phased out over agreed upon time periods.[206] Developed countries, such as the United States, must reduce their export subsidies by the greatest amount over the shortest period of time, followed by developing countries, and no reductions are required of lesser developing countries.[207] Certain instances of highly subsidized exports in the form of food aid to poor nations are permitted.[208]

The Agreement on Agriculture's second function is to limit or reduce domestic support policies that distort trade.[209] Members commit to reduce domestic support of agriculture with the exception of "Green Box" and "Blue Box" measures.[210] "Green Box"

---

[200] *Id.* at 5.2.8.
[201] *See id.* art. 5.2.2.
[202] *See id.* art. 5.2.4.
[203] *Id.* at art. 5.
[204] *See International Agricultural Trade: Overview*, NAT'L AGRIC. LAW CTR. (electronic reading room).
[205] Agreement on Agriculture, art. 9, April 15, 1994, Marrakesh Agreement Establishing the World Trade Organization, Annex 1A, 1867 U.N.T.S. 410 [hereinafter Agreement on Agriculture].
[206] *Id.* at art. 6, paras. 4(a)(i) and (ii).
[207] *Id.* at art. 9, para. 2(iv), art. 15, para. 2.
[208] *International Agricultural Trade, supra* note 204.
[209] Agreement on Agriculture, *supra* note 205, at arts. 6, 7.
[210] *Id.* at art. 6, para. 1.

measures are policies where domestic support does not distort trade. The measure must be funded by government program and must not provide price support to producers.[211] Examples of Green Box measures include the funding of agricultural research or training, pest control, marketing services, and infrastructural services.[212] Domestic food aid may qualify, if clearly defined by nutritional objectives and if government buys food at market price.[213] Also included in the Green Box are direct payment to producers such as income support, insurance, safety net programs, natural disaster relief, retirement programs, investment aids, and assistance for complying with governmental environmental programs.[214] WTO requirements set no ceiling on the amount of Green box subsidies a government can provide. "Blue Box" measures are where support is not subject to commitment to reduce domestic support, even if it distorts trade, when support is limited to certain criteria.[215] A third box – the Amber box – is for policies that have a direct impact on production, which causes trade distortion, and are required to be reduced. The reduction is based on the total aggregate measure of support that is calculated from each country's level of support to agriculture in 1986–1988.[216] The Amber box category also exempts payments of up to 10 percent of output value, which are regarded as too small to warrant control.[217]

The Agreement on Agriculture's third function is to increase market access.[218] Members agree to reduce tariffs and abolish custom duties. There are two exceptions. First, under Article 5, a member can impose special safeguard measures if there is a high volume of imports of a particular product or if there is import of a product at a very low price.[219] These duties can last only one year[220] and members must inform the Committee on Agriculture about measures within ten days of implementing the action.[221] Second, under Article 5 of the Agreement on Agriculture the limit on customs duties does not apply to "designated products" as long as they make up less than 3 percent domestic consumption.[222] Members can apply for extensions of special treatment of "designated products."[223]

An exception to the prohibition on quantitative imports is the Special Safeguard Provisions in Article 5. If there is a surge of an agricultural product from another

---

[211] *Id.* at Annex 2, paras. 1(a) and (b).
[212] *Id.* at Annex 2, paras. 2 (a)–(g).
[213] *Id.* at Annex 2, para. 4.
[214] *Id.* at Annex 2, paras 5–13.
[215] *Id.* at art. 6, para. 5.
[216] Subsidies in developing countries that are part of development programs aimed at helping low-income producers are not required to be included in a Member's calculation of Current Total AMS. *Id.* at art. 6, para. 2.
[217] *International Agricultural Trade, supra* note 204.
[218] Agreement on Agriculture, *supra* note 205, at art. 4.
[219] *Id.* at art. 5, para. 1.
[220] *Id.* at art. 5, para. 4.
[221] *Id.* at art. 5, para. 7.
[222] *Id.* at Annex 5.
[223] *See* Modifying the Nomenclature and Most-Favored Nation (MFN) Rates of Duty on Various Agricultural Products as Provided for Under the Tariff and Customs Code of 1978, as Amended, in Order to Implement the Philippine Commitment on Rice under the World Trade Organization (WTO) Agreement on Agriculture, Exec. Ord. No. 627 (Phil.) (gives effect to import restriction of rice based on the Annex 5 special treatment provision).

country[224] or if a product is being imported below the "trigger price,"[225] Article 5 allows a country to impose a temporary duty to the imported products.[226] Countries can impose a duty against an agricultural product that is imported at below the average price. The "import price" is assessed as CIF (cost + insurance + freight) price not including import duties.[227]

[b] TRIPS

Negotiated at the end of the Uruguay Round of the GATT in 1994, TRIPS is an international agreement administered by the WTO.[228] The TRIPS Agreement introduced intellectual property into the international trading system for the first time. The TRIPS Agreement is intended to regulate ideas and knowledge as part of trade and to provide society with benefits received from encouraging invention, innovation, and research. The TRIPS Agreement mandates that members protect intellectual property either through patents or the development of other intellectual property rights protection systems.[229] Intellectual property rights are especially important for food in the areas of biotechnology, conventional species breeding, and agricultural input products such as pesticides and mechanical equipment. Intellectual property issues were also raised in the beginning of the Doha Round.[230] Specifically, some states have called for clarity in the WTO rules as applied to food products of new technologies.

[c] Anti-Dumping Agreement

Under Article VI of the GATT, if one state can show that another state is exporting a product below the price of producing it, they can use anti-dumping measures to impose a tariff to offset the difference. These were a huge area of dispute in the pre-WTO era of the GATT.[231] The Tokyo Round code (or the Anti-Dumping Agreement) provided more detail on what dumping and injury was and tighter procedures for investigating dumping charges.[232] In the United States, the Anti-Dumping agreement is applied by the Tariff Act.[233] Under the Tariff Act, an industry can request relief for dumping if they can show: (1) an import is being sold at less than its fair value;[234] (2) there is actual or threatened "material injury" to the industry;[235] and (3) the "material injury" is caused by dumping.[236]

---

[224] Agreement on Agriculture, *supra* note 205 at art. 5.1(a).

[225] *Id.* at art. 5.1(b).

[226] *Id.* at art. 5.

[227] Appellate Body Report, European Communities – Measures Affecting the Importation of Certain Poultry Products, WT/DS69/AB/R (July 13, 1998), para 153.

[228] World Trade Org., *supra* note 143, at 39.

[229] *Id.*

[230] *See Developments Since the Fourth WTO Ministerial Conference*, Doha Round Briefing (INT'L CTR. FOR TRADE & SUSTAINABLE DEV., Geneva, Switz.), February 2003.

[231] John H. Barton et al., THE EVOLUTION OF THE TRADE REGIME 115 (2006).

[232] *Id.*

[233] 19 USCA § 1673.

[234] § 1673(1).

[235] §§ 1673(2), 1677(2).

[236] §1673(2); *see also* Iwatsu Electric Co. Ltd. v. United States, 758 F.Supp. 1506 (Ct. Int'l Trade 1991).

[d] Doha Round

The current WTO trade negotiations (the Doha Round) commenced in November 2001. As of yet, member countries have been unable to come to any agreement. Disagreement on agriculture and food trade is one reason for the failure of the Doha round.[237] US agricultural subsidies have been an area of heated debate at the Doha Round as well as a source of WTO litigation.[238] The EU wants the United States to reduce trade-distorting agricultural subsidies.[239] The United States has refused to give way on its position on agricultural subsidies and wants the EU and developing countries also to reduce tariffs.[240]

The stalled Doha Round impacts US national food policies by relieving pressure for US farm policy change. This may, in turn, increase WTO litigation over allegations that US farm subsidies are harming other WTO countries.[241] Another consequence of the failed Doha Round is that the United States (as well as other countries) is increasingly pursuing bilateral and regional free trade agreements as an alternative to WTO trade agreements.[242]

[e] Regional and Bilateral Trade Agreements

The trade agreements the United States has with individual countries and multiple countries within a region are generally free trade agreements that eliminate tariff and nontariff barriers affecting trade between the parties to the agreement or agreements that address specific issues or products such as poultry or rice.

The North American Free Trade Agreement (NAFTA) is a well-known example of a regional free trade agreement. Its implementation began on January 1, 1994. This agreement removes most barriers to trade between the United States, Canada, and Mexico. Between the United States and Mexico, all nontariff barriers to agricultural trade were eliminated and many tariffs were immediately eliminated, with a gradual reduction of other tariffs to be accomplished over different periods of time, up to fifteen years for some tariffs. Between the United States and Canada, the agricultural provisions of the US-Canada Free Trade Agreement were incorporated into NAFTA. With only a few exceptions, all tariffs affecting agricultural trade were removed. Between Mexico and Canada most agriculture-related tariffs were removed immediately or over a period of years; however, tariffs on dairy, poultry, eggs, and sugar remain.

Other US regional free trade agreements include the Free Trade Area of the Americas, the Central America-Dominican Republic Free Trade Agreement, the United States-Southern African Customs Union, the Middle East Free Trade Area Initiative,

---

[237] *The Doha Round ... and Round ... and Round,* ECONOMIST, August 2, 2008, at 37.

[238] Appellate Body Report, US – Subsidies on Upland Cotton, WT/DS267/AB/R (March 3, 2005).

[239] CHARLES E. HANRAHAN & RANDY SCHNEPF, WTO DOHA ROUND: THE AGRICULTURAL NEGOTIATIONS 2 (2013).

[240] *Id.* at 3.

[241] *Id.* at 4.

[242] *Id.* at 5.

and the Asia-Pacific Economic Cooperation. The United States has entered bilateral free trade agreements or negotiations with Australia, Panama, Chile, Colombia, Peru, Israel, South Korea, Singapore, Thailand, and other countries.

There are distinct benefits to bilateral and regional free trade agreements: parties reach agreement quicker than in multilateral trade agreements, especially after the failed Doha Round. Bilateral trade agreements can be reached in subject areas where opposition from other WTO members would make multilateral trade agreements impossible. Bilateral trade agreements can act as a solution to unresolved or continuing WTO trade disputes. For example, the United States and Korea have had WTO disputes over the access of US beef in Korea, but the US Free Trade Agreement (KORUS FTA) detailed maximum duties and safeguard trigger levels for beef, thereby resolving this dispute.[243] Finally, bilateral trade agreements can also have the effect of creating alliances between countries on multilateral agricultural trade issues. Bilateral trade agreements cannot deal, however, with the effects of dumping and agricultural subsidies because these are multilateral trade problems that affect all WTO members. Codex standards are referenced in NAFTA,[244] and in bilateral trade agreements[245] and are important in preventing and resolving trade disputes.

A prominent prospective regional trade agreements is the Trans-Pacific Partnership, which the United States announced in 2009 its plans to participate. The TPP involves Australia, Chile, New Zealand, Malaysia, Peru, Singapore, Vietnam and Brunei, and Japan (China is not included).[246] Because the United States does not have FTAs with Brunei, Malaysia, New Zealand or Vietnam, it is negotiating market access for agriculture in those countries.[247]

Another prospective trade agreement that could have a profound impact on food regulation in the United States is the Transatlantic Trade and Investment Partnership (TTIP), a proposed free trade agreement between the European Union and the United States. TTIP negotiations were launched in June 2013 and an agreement is not expected before 2016. Due to the divide between the European Union and the United States over the precautionary principle, TTIP is most contentious in the food sector, particularly on issues related to SPS measures.[248] The FDA reportedly has even attempted to remove the transatlantic SPS regulatory cooperation and harmonization provisions from TTIP.[249]

---

[243] Free Trade Agreement between the United States of America and the Republic of Korea, U.S.-S. Korea, June 30, 2007, Annex 3-A(3)(a).

[244] North American Free Trade Agreement, United States – Canada – Mexico, December 17, 1992, 32 I.L.M. 289, art. 713 (1993).

[245] For example, Codex is quoted in these bilateral trade agreements: United States – Australia, 2005. Mexico-Bolivia, 1995.

[246] *Engagement with the Trans-Pacific Partnership to Increase Exports, Support Jobs*, OFFICE OF THE U.S. TRADE REP. (February 2011).

[247] Ian F. Fergusson et al., CONG. RESEARCH SERV. R42694, THE TRANS-PACIFIC PARTNERSHIP NEGOTIATIONS AND ISSUES FOR CONGRESS (2015).

[248] *See* Debbie Barker, *Trade Matters: Transatlantic Trade and Investment Partnership (TTIP) Impacts on Food and Farming* 3-4 (May 2014).

[249] Steve Suppan, *Analysis of the draft Transatlantic Trade and Partnership (TTIP) chapter on food safety, and animal and plant health issues (proposed by the European Commission, as of June 27, 2014)*, Institute for Agriculture and Trade Policy 2 (July 23, 2014).

Numerous food regulatory issues covered elsewhere in this treatise could be affected by TTIP, including domestic subsidies, GMO food (production and marketing), organic food, animal welfare, beef hormones, antibiotics for growth purposes in animal rearing, and geographical indications.[250]

---

[250] *See* Tim Josling and Stefan Tangermann, *Agriculture, Food and the TTIP: Possibilities and Pitfalls*, Centre for European Policy Studies, 19-23 (December 2014) (identifying the potential outcomes of the TTIP negotiations in food and agriculture).

3   Regulation of Food Safety

§ 3.01 Introduction

[1] *Scope of Food Safety Challenges*

The governance of food safety in the United States is complex. Although technology and science have helped provide safer food, safety risks exist at numerous points within the global food system, giving rise to what the FDA's Center for Disease Control and Prevention (CDC) refers to as "foodborne illness" or "foodborne disease."[1] On the basis of the estimates made by the CDC, each year in the United States, about 48 million people get sick, 128,000 are hospitalized, and 3,000 die as a result of foodborne diseases.[2] These diseases range from gastrointestinal symptoms such as diarrhea, vomiting, and sometimes dysentery to more severe symptoms (induced by *Salmonella* and *E. coli* bacteria), such as autoimmune thyroid disease, inflammatory bowel disease, neuromuscular disorders, and heart damage.[3] The sources of foodborne risks are numerous, but can be grouped into three broad categories: (1) contaminated, diseased, or otherwise harmful materials that are not detected and removed or remedied; (2) inadequate storage, handling, or processing, which fails to detect and exclude harmful food materials or contaminants of food materials; and (3) purposeful introduction into the food supply of potentially harmful materials (including additives, toxins, chemicals and pesticides, animal drug residues, and packaging materials).[4]

[2] *Law and Science: Evolving Response to Safety Risks*

The fragmentation of food regulation referred to in Chapter 1 is especially evident in the regulation of food safety risks in the United States: the result is a multilayered, cooperative endeavor that involves many international, federal, state, and local government agencies – all with different levels of responsibilities (which sometimes overlap) and resource allocations (which do not always correspond with the levels of responsibilities). Although this fragmented regulatory regime has adapted to emerging safety risks, the process has proven cumbersome and slow. State regulation, litigation, and new governance tools increasingly fill regulatory gaps created by the fragmentation. The result has been a governance system that is nuanced, complex, and disjointed.

Notwithstanding the fragmentation of the food safety regime, a constant aspiration in the regulation of food safety by government agencies across all levels is management of a food safety system based on science and analysis of risk.[5] For example, the passage of the 1958 Food Additives Amendment was a technology-driven event intended to improve the safety of added and natural substances and reduced the risks associated with the use of food additives.

---

[1] The CDC defines a "foodborne-disease outbreak (FBDO) … as an incident in which two or more persons experience a similar illness resulting from the ingestion of a common food." Michael Lynch et al., *Surveillance for Foodborne-Disease Outbreaks – United States, 1998–2002*, *in* MORBIDITY & MORTALITY WKLY. REP. (Ctr. for Disease Control and Prevention, Washington, D.C.), November 10, 2006, at 1.

[2] Press Release, Centers for Disease Control and Prevention, CDC Reports 1 in 6 Get Sick from Foodborne Illnesses Each Year (December 15, 2010).

[3] A complete index of foodborne illnesses is listed on the website (A-Z *Index for Foodborne Illness*) for the Centers of Disease Control and Prevention.

[4] *See* Richard A. Merrill & Jeffrey K. Francer, *Organizing Federal Food Safety Regulation*, 31 SETON HALL L. REV. 61, 69–90 (2000).

[5] *See generally*, INSTITUTE OF MEDICINE, ENSURING SAFE FOOD: FROM PRODUCT TO CONSUMPTION 2–15 (1998).

As knowledge of the science of food safety increases, many rational, science-based regulatory philosophies are adopted (i.e., hazard analysis critical control points [HACCP])), some of which rely on quantitative risk assessment (e.g., QPRAM and FDA-iRISK®)).[6] It is fair to say that law, science, and food safety are inextricably linked.

The response of science-based regulation of food safety to changing or emerging risks in the food safety is marked by a series of federal acts that have accumulated over a century into major legislation, culminating in the most recent notable legislation – the 2011 Food Safety Modernization Act. These acts have been the basis for the promulgation of regulations, rules, and guidance by federal agencies and have helped usher in distinguishable and notable eras of federal food safety regulation.

This chapter will briefly summarize these regulatory eras and frame the constant regulatory benchmark of food safety: adulteration. It will focus on the two regulatory categories of adulteration, namely, the regulation of the composition of food and the numerous legal tools and methods provided by the federal acts designed to reduce or prevent safety risks. This chapter will also address the international standards that influence food safety regulation in the United States and the regulatory gap fillers of self-governance and litigation.

§ 3.02 Federal Regulatory Eras

[1] 1906 Federal Acts' Era

Although the early food laws in the United States were designed predominantly to protect purchasers from fraud, in the late 1800s, public awareness of health hazards in the food industry increased, leading to public demand for further regulation. Contaminated food, milk, and water caused many foodborne infectious diseases during this time, including typhoid fever, tuberculosis, and scarlet fever.[7] Three key individuals emerged to play important roles in the development of the first major food safety regulation: a scientist – Dr. Harvey Wiley; a journalist – Upton Sinclair; and a powerful politician – President Theodore Roosevelt.

In 1883, Dr. Wiley became the chief chemist of the US Bureau of Chemistry, which was then part of the US Department of Agriculture (USDA).[8] Dr. Wiley helped spur public concern over food safety and quality by his publications and by campaigning for a national food and drug law. Wiley specifically focused on chemical preservatives as adulterants through his highly publicized "poison squad," which in 1902 comprised young men who tested on themselves the effects of chemicals and adulterated food.[9] The efforts of the poison squad, which by today's standards would be considered reckless, revealed that many of the chemicals used in food production were harmful to human health.

---

[6] QPRAM is a virtual laboratory that predicts and characterizes risks from consumption of fresh produce that result from specific behaviors and practices on farms during the processing and consumption of crops. FDA-iRISK® is an interactive tool that compares and ranks public health risks from multiple food hazard combinations, to inform FDA's risk prioritization and resource allocation. *See Risk Analysis at FDA: Food Safety*, U.S. FOOD & DRUG ADMIN.).

[7] *See* JAMES HARVEY YOUNG, PURE FOOD: SECURING THE FEDERAL FOOD AND DRUGS ACT OF 1906 40 (1989).

[8] *See* Dale A. Stirling, *Profiles in Toxicology: Harvey W. Wiley*, 67 TOXICOLOGICAL SCI. 157 (2002).

[9] *See* Carol Lewis, *The "Poison Squad" and the Advent of Food and Drug Regulation*, U.S. FDA CONSUMER MAG., November–December 2002, at 1.

In 1906, Upton Sinclair, a muckraking journalist, published his novel *The Jungle*.[10] The book highlighted the horrible working conditions of the nation's working class by describing in lurid detail the filthy conditions and adulteration of meat that was common in the Chicago meat industry. Whereas Sinclair's intent was to expose the "inferno of exploitation" of the typical American factory worker, the public was more horrified at the thought of rats and other undesirables mixed in with their sausage than by the poor treatment of workers.[11] The resulting publicity generated support for further regulatory action. Sinclair later wrote, "I aimed at the public's heart and by accident hit it in the stomach."[12]

Shortly after, and in response to, the publication of *The Jungle* and the work of Dr. Wiley, Roosevelt appointed a commission to make a thorough investigation of meat-packing houses.[13] The commission submitted a report, which in part, observed:

> We saw meat shoveled from filthy wooden floors, piled on tables rarely washed, pushed from room to room in rotten box carts, in all of which processes it was in the way of gathering dirt, splinters, floor filth, and the expectoration of tuberculosis and other diseased workers.[14]

The ensuing public furor led Congress to pass the Pure Food and Drug Act (PDFA)[15] and the Federal Meat Inspection Act (FMIA),[16] both of which were signed into law by Roosevelt on June 30, 1906, thus commencing the modern era of US food safety regulation. These two food acts prohibited the adulteration (and misbranding) of food.

The FMIA protected consumers by "assuring that meat and meat food products are wholesome, not adulterated, and properly marked labeled, and packaged." The act established sanitary standards and mandated continuous inspection of cattle, sheep, goats, and equines before, during, and after slaughter. The PDFA forbade the adulteration of foods (other than the meat products covered by FMIA) in interstate commerce. The PDFA did not mandate continuous inspection of food and had further limitations, one of which, as noted in Chapter 2, was that since it did not set standards as to what exactly should be in a particular food, it was almost impossible to prove the adulteration of a food.

[2] 1938 FDCA Era

By the 1930s, the weaknesses of the PFDA prompted the FDA to recommend that Congress enact a new legislation. Fueling the drive for new, comprehensive legislation were the publications that stirred the public's ire at the condition of the food that they were eating.[17] The FDA took its message directly to the people when it developed the exhibit, the "Chamber of Horrors," which led to the 1936 publication of *The American*

---

[10] *See* Upton Sinclair, The Jungle (Penguin Books, 2006) (1906).

[11] Mark Sullivan, Our Times 222 (Dan Rather ed., 1996).

[12] Upton Sinclair, *What Life Means to Me*, Cosmopolitan Mag., October 1906, at 594.

[13] *Id.*

[14] *Id.* at 19.

[15] Pure Food and Drug Act (PFDA), ch. 3915, § 6, 34 Stat. 768 (1906) (repealed 1938).

[16] Federal Meat Inspection Act (FMIA), Pub. L. No. 59–242, 34 Stat. 1260 (1907).

[17] *See, e.g.*, Arthur Kallet & F.J. Schlink, 100,000,000 Guinea Pigs: Dangers in Everyday Foods, Drugs, and Cosmetics (1993).

Chamber of Horrors by the FDA's chief educational officer, Ruth deForest Lamb.[18] Lamb recounted some of the lurid, behind-the-scenes details of the food industry. She noted that the PDFA was outdated due to new modes of living, new kinds of products, new methods of manufacturing and selling, new tricks of sophistication, and new scientific discoveries, all of which demanded a more modern method of control. As notable as were the efforts by Lamb and others, the immediate catalyst for new food (and drug legislation), however, was the death of 107 people who unwittingly ingested an untested drug, elixir of sulfanilamide.[19] Shortly thereafter, in 1938, Congress passed the Federal Food, Drug, and Cosmetic Act (FDCA),[20] which has since served as the statutory basis for food safety regulation.

The FDCA continued with many of the intentions of the 1906 Act, but broadened the scope of federal regulation. For the first time, the law defined adulteration to include bacteria or chemicals that are potentially harmful, allowed the FDA to inspect food manufacturing and processing facilities, prohibited the sale of food prepared under unsanitary conditions, gave the FDA the authority to monitor the use of drugs in farmed animals, and authorized mandatory standards for foods.[21] The 1938 Act has been amended many times since its original passage. The most noteworthy amendments have enlarged FDA's substantive authority in response to food safety concerns: for example, the Miller Pesticides Amendment of 1954 empowered the FDA to establish tolerances for pesticides on food in order to alleviate escalating concerns over the use of pesticides.[22]

[3] *2011 FSMA Era*

Heralded as the most significant food legislation in the United States since the 1938 FDCA, the 2011 Food Safety Modernization Act (FSMA) introduced a new regime of federal food safety regulation. FSMA was passed in response to food safety concerns related to both imported and domestic food. The ever-increasing dependence of the United States on food imports triggered public pressure for legislation that strengthens US law on imported food. At the time of FSMA's passage, imports accounted for 15 percent of the US food supply, including 75 percent of seafood and 60 percent of fresh produce.[23] These numbers have and likely will continue to rise. In addition to increasing imports, the domestic food supply faces sizeable food safety challenges. Leading up to the FSMA, new foods were linked to outbreaks of foodborne illness in the United States, including bagged spinach, pot pies, carrot juice, canned chili sauce, peanut butter, hot

---

[18] *See* Ruth deForest Lamb, American Chamber of Horrors: The Truth About Food and Drugs (1936).

[19] *See Significant Dates in U.S. Food and Drug Law History*, Ctrs. for Disease Control & Prevention (December 19, 2014, last update).

[20] Federal Food, Drug, and Cosmetic Act of 1938 (FDCA) 9, Pub. L. No. 75–717, 52 Stat. 1040 (codified as amended at 21 U.S.C. §§ 301–393).

[21] Solomon H. Katz & William Woys Weaver, Encyclopedia of Food and Culture, 5 (Charles Scribners & Sons 2002).

[22] *Id.* at 14.

[23] Leavitt Partners, US Food Safety Modernization Act: Overview and Impact for Importers and Exporters 2 (August 2012).

pepper, broccoli powder, white pepper, dog food, and raw cookie dough.[24] The culmination of these food safety pressures helped build support for the FSMA from a broad coalition of actors – food safety and consumer groups, as well as industry trade groups of food producers and grocery stores, and the US Chamber of Commerce – underscoring the notion that a preventive approach to food safety is prudent for both public health and for the economic viability of the food industry.

FSMA emphasizes a preventative approach to food safety. According to a senior FDA official, the FDA's purpose under FSMA is to help food companies voluntarily comply with the act. For example, agency inspections would shift from collecting data for enforcement actions to focusing on prevention, via a risk-based approach.[25] On a specific level, FSMA requires the FDA to engage in the following areas:

o Hazard analysis and risk-based preventive controls
o Clarification of activities that subject a farm to facility registration requirements
o Science-based minimum standards for the safe production and harvesting of fresh fruits and vegetables
o Protection against intentional adulteration
o Sanitary transportation of food
o Foreign supplier verification
o Standards for third-party audits.

Given the sweeping mandate for rules, the paucity of resources allotted to the FDA, and the political and legal challenges, it should not be a surprise that the FDA has missed the deadlines imposed by the act to complete its rulemaking. In August 2012, the Center for Food Safety and the Center for Environmental Health filed suit in the Northern District of California to compel the FDA and the Office of Management and Budget (OMB) to implement the FSMA provisions.[26] The suit contends that proposed rules to implement several of the act's provisions have been pending at OMB beyond the time allotted under the executive order, which mandates review of regulations by OMB within specified timeframes.[27] A series of orders entered by the court illustrate the challenges of implementing regulations of FSMA.[28]

Notwithstanding FSMA, a US Government Accountability Office (GAO) report issued in February 2013 expressed continued disappointment in a lack of coordination

---

[24] *Id.* at 3.

[25] Joan Murphy, *Taylor promises gentler FDA inspectors under FSMA, Adding Prevention to Enforcement Role*, Food Chemical News 9 (March, 2013).

[26] Press Release, Center for Food Safety, Center for Food Safety Lawsuit Targets FDA, OMB on Stalled Food Safety Act (August 30, 2012).

[27] *See* Compl. for Decl. and Inj. Relief, Ctr. for Food Safety v. Hamburg, 954 F. Supp. 2d 965, 966 (N.D. Cal. 2013).

[28] In April 2013, the court ruled that the FDA violated the FSMA and the Administrative Procedure Act when it failed to issued FSMA regulations by the FSMA-established deadlines. *See id.* at 970. In June 2013, the court issued an order for injunctive relief, which set deadlines for the FDA to publish proposed regulations by November 30, 2013, close to the comment periods by March 31, 2014, and publish the final regulations in the Federal Register by June 30, 2015. *See* Order Granting Inj. Relief (on file with author). In August 2013, the court extended the deadline for the proposed sanitary transport rule to January 31, 2014, extended the comment period for the same rule to May 31, 2014, and denied an extension request by FDA for promulgation of the intentional adulteration rule. *See* Order (on file with author).

across the federal agencies that are responsible for food safety.[29] The GAO report acknowl-edged that although FSMA strengthens a major part of the food safety system by shifting the focus of food safety regulation to prevention and FSMA has several provisions that require interagency collaboration on food safety oversight, the act does not apply to the federal food safety system as a whole or address USDA's authorities, which remain sepa-rate and distinct from FDA's. The report also stated that because FSMA was not yet fully implemented and a number of the regulations required under the law were still under development or review, it was premature to assess the impact of the legislation on the federal oversight of food safety.[30] The GAO report specifically criticized the agencies for failing to develop a government-wide performance plan for food safety that included results-oriented goals and performance measures and information about resources. Such a plan, according to the GAO, is important when resources are limited.[31]

An additional development of interest in the FSMA regulatory era is the emer-gence of the interplay between social media and the regulation of food safety. As consumers become more aware and concerned about the food supply, bloggers and social media participants are increasingly vocal about the safety and efficacy of their food products. An example of this phenomenon involved the pejorative term of "pink slime," which applies to lean, finely textured beef and boneless lean beef trimmings, addressed at the end of this chapter. In 2001, the USDA's *Food Safety and Inspection Service* (FSIS) approved this product for limited human consumption and it was used as a food additive to ground beef and beef-based processed meats. In March 2012, on the heels of a consumer blogging campaign against "pink slime," ABC News ran a series of news reports on the matter. The concern generated by the reports led restaurants and grocery retailers to pledge to stop carrying the product and led to a change in USDA policy, which resulted in school districts stopping the serving of ground beef with the filler.[32] (Chapter 4 analyzes the disparagement law-suit brought by Beef Products, Inc. against ABC News and others for their reports on pink slime). It is expected that social media will continue to play a role as an influ-encer on the regulation of safe food.

§ 3.03 "Adulteration" Scheme

[1] *Adulteration: Regulatory Benchmark*

The regulatory benchmark in the United States for what constitutes safe food is whether based on certain enumerated criteria food is adulterated. "Adulteration" is a broad legal term that includes safety, quality, aesthetic, and authenticity concerns. It is unlawful for food that is adulterated to enter into commerce for human food use. The three enabling food acts – FDCA, FMIA, and PPIA – incorporate food safety criteria into the definition of adulteration (Section 402 of FDCA, Section 601(m) of FMIA, and Section 453(g) of PPIA).

---

[29] *See* U.S. Gov't Accountability Office, GAO-13–283, High-Risk Series, an Update 196–200 (2013).

[30] *See id.* at 196.

[31] *See id.* at 197.

[32] *See* Joe L. Greene, Cong. Research Serv., R42473, Lean Finely Textured Beef: The "Pink Slime" Controversy. 6 (August 6, 2012).

Generally speaking, food is adulterated if any one of the following, sometimes related, events occur: (1) it contains a harmful substance that may pose a safety risk; (2) it contains an added harmful substance that is acquired during production or cannot be reasonably avoided and exceeds acceptable levels; (3) it contains a substance that has been intentionally added to the food but that has not been approved or otherwise sanctioned for use by a regulatory agency or one of the food safety statutes; or (4) it has been handled under unsanitary conditions, creating a risk of contamination with a substance that may pose a safety threat.

These criteria, which are encapsulated and enumerated in the three food acts (FDCA, FIA, and PPIA) and the aggregation of food safety regulations, rules, and guidance, can be organized into two broad analytical categories: first, safety issues posed by the composition of the food; and second, the legal tools and methods designed to prevent food safety threats.

[2] *Composition of Food*

The first category addresses food composition by distinguishing between substances inherent or naturally present in the food and those that are added and by applying a different standard for adulteration for these two scenarios. This distinction lays the foundation for addressing the emerging technologies that have been applied to the development of food and food products in the modern food system. Added substances are regulated through either a food additive system or by a tolerance system. The question of composition also applies to safety concerns of pesticide residues, veterinary drug residues, and carcinogens. Controversial, complex composition issues include food and food products developed via genetic engineering, cloned animals, and nanotechnology. The issues related to these emerging food technologies encompass a broad range of societal concerns, but the focus in this chapter will be restricted to food safety concerns.

[3] *Tools and Methods*

The second category for food safety focuses mainly on the manufacturing or processing of food. Tools and measures are developed in regulations and voluntary guidance documents and apply to registration, inspection, reporting, risk analysis, prevention controls, and enforcement actions. Compliance with the regulations and guidelines established by the agencies ensure that food is legally considered safe. High-profile food contamination and disease-related outbreaks that evince limitations to these agencies' food safety and enforcement authorities turn public and congressional attention to the need to provide the agencies with additional tools to confront and deal with emerging food safety problems. For example, FSMA, the latest and most comprehensive amendment to the FDCA, is intended to offer a new public health paradigm for the FDA's food safety program – the shifting of the food safety focus from reaction to prevention – by providing new tools to the government and industry.[33] Although this platitude is exaggerated, as the food safety regulatory focus has long been oriented toward prevention, FSMA certainly

---

[33] *See* Michael Taylor, Deputy Comm'r for Foods, Food and Drug Administration, Address at the 2012 FDA Science Writers Symposium: Progress on FSMA, Changes within the FDA Foods Program, and on Partnerships (September 11, 2012).

promotes the systematic building of preventive measures across the food system. Within this category, the FDA sets science-based, prevention-oriented standards and works to ensure industry compliance, with a special focus on regulating the increasing volume of imported foods.

§ 3.04 Regulation of Composition of Food

[1] *Substances: The Division*

The foundational issue in determining whether food is adulterated (or unsafe) is whether substances in the food are either added or inherent in the food. "Substance" is a term that is used in food regulation to refer to materials that comprise food products. In a modern food system where foods are typically processed, the term substance has particular relevance. The division between substances naturally present in food and added substances in terms of what constitutes adulteration is developed in the FDCA in Section 402(a)(1):

> If it bears or contains any poisonous or deleterious substance which may render it injurious to health; but in case the substance is not an added substance such food shall not be considered adulterated under this clause if the quantity of such substance in such food does not ordinarily render it injurious to health.[34]

Although untangling the triple negative in Section 402(a)(1) can be a challenge, the interpretation is that a food that "contains any poisonous or deleterious substance" is not necessarily adulterated: a finding of adulteration depends initially on whether the substance is added or is naturally present in the food. If added, the food that contains the poisonous or deleterious substance is subject to a "may-render-injurious" standard, which establishes adulteration by proof of the possibility of harm.[35] The question of whether an added substance meets the may-render-injurious standard is a question of fact for the jury.[36] Courts have interpreted the may-render-injurious standard to take into account vulnerable groups, such as the young or the elderly or individuals allergic to various protein sources, such as peanuts.[37] If the substance is not added, but instead is naturally present in the food, then an "ordinarily-injurious-to-health" standard applies. Rather than explore possibilities, the ordinarily injurious standard focuses on probabilities, requiring some certainty of harm when considering the customary use of that food.[38] Also, rather than consider vulnerable groups, the ordinarily injurious standard evaluates the effects of a substance on the food-consuming population in general.[39]

For both the may-render-injurious standard and the ordinarily injurious standard, the quantity, rather than quality, of a substance is likely to determine whether the substance may be harmful. For example, in the US Supreme Court case of *Lexington Mill & Elevator Co.*, the Court held that when a food contains a small amount of a poisonous or deleterious substance – in this case, flour treated with nitrogen peroxide gas – if there

[34] 21 U.S.C. § 342(a)(1).
[35] United States v. Lexington Mill & Elevator Co., 232 U.S. 399, 410 (1914) (interpreting Section 7 of the Food and Drug Act of 1906, which declared adulterated any food that contained "any added poisonous or other added deleterious ingredient which may render such article injurious to health.")
[36] United States v. Forty Barrels and Twenty Kegs of Coca Cola, 241 U.S. 265, 284–5 (1916).
[37] *See id.*
[38] United States v Lexington Mill & Elevator Co., 232 U.S. at 411.
[39] *Id.*

could not be any possibility, when the facts are reasonably considered, that such food may injure the health of a consumer, it cannot be considered adulterated under the act.[40]

[2] Added Substances

The FDCA does not define "added." Because the evidentiary burden for the FDA under the ordinarily injurious standard is greater than under the may-render-injurious standard, it should be no surprise that the FDA regulations define "added" broadly: a substance is added to a food if it is not an inherent constituent of the food (e.g., the caffeine in coffee).[41] The practical effect of such a broad definition is that any environmental or accidental contaminant is an added substance.

Notwithstanding the FDA's expansive definition of "added," a few courts have more narrowly required that the presence of a substance be attributable in whole or in part to the acts of man before considering the substance added. For example, the Fifth Circuit in *United States v. Anderson Seafoods, Inc.* determined that before all of the mercury found in swordfish could be treated as an added substance, at least a portion of the mercury must come from industrial pollution.[42] Similarly, the US Court of Appeals for the District of Columbia Circuit, in *Continental Seafoods Inc. v. Schweiker*, found that because *Salmonella* in shrimp, stemming from improper sanitary and handling conditions, was attributable to the acts of man, the substance was added.[43]

The FDA has not recognized this attributable-to-man test and other court decisions have deferred to the regulations' broad definition as to what constitutes added. For example, in *United States v. Boston Farm Center Inc.*, the Fifth Circuit found that aflatoxin in corn (aflatoxins are neither added by human intervention nor inherent in the natural state of the food; instead, aflatoxins result from mold growing on food) was considered as added under FDA regulations.[44] Other courts have expressly upheld the not-an-inherent-natural constituent test, finding, for example, that *Listeria Monocytogenes*[45] in seafood is an added substance simply because it is not an inherent natural constituent.[46] Even natural field insects gathered with the harvested food, or insects in the storage facilities, may be considered added contaminants.[47]

The FMIA and PPIA contain similar provisions for meat and poultry products;[48] however, the USDA has not adopted any regulatory definition or policy as to what constitutes

---

[40] *Id.*

[41] The regulations state that a substance is added if it is not "an inherent natural constituent of the food"; is the "result of environmental, agricultural, industrial, or other contamination"; or if the natural amount of the inherent substance has been increased to abnormal levels by mishandling or other intervening acts. 21 CFR § 109.3.

[42] 622 F.2d 157, 159–61 (5th Cir. 1980). *Compare with* United States v. An Article of Food Consisting of Cartons of Swordfish, 395 F. Supp. 1184, 1186 (S.D.N.Y. 1975) (stating that mercury in swordfish is an added substance because it is not an inherent natural constituent).

[43] 674 F.2d 38, 43–4 (D.C. Cir. 1982).

[44] 590 F.2d 149, 152 (5th Cir. 1979).

[45] *Listeria Monocytogenes is* a bacterium found in some animals that when consumed via food causes Listeriosis, a serious infection and important public health problem in the United States. *See Listeria (Listeriosis)*, Ctrs. For Disease Control & Prevention (December 19, 2004, last update).

[46] *See* United States v. Blue Ribbon Smoked Fish, Inc., 179 F. Supp. 2d 30, 46–8 (E.D.N.Y. 2001).

[47] United States v. Corbi, Food Drug Cosm. L. Rep. (CCH) ¶38040 (D. Md. 1979).

[48] *See* 21 U.S.C. § 453(g), 601(m).

an added poisonous or deleterious substance. An interesting interpretative distinction though separates the USDA from FDA: whereas the FDA does not distinguish between pathogens it considers adulterants or not, the USDA is willing to do so, at least in the case of *E. coli* 0157:H7 – a kind of *E. coli* that can cause disease by producing a Shiga toxin – to declare a type of added substance an adulterant.[49]

[3] *Tolerance Levels, Action Levels, and Regulatory Limits*

While the legal nuances associated with the distinction between added and inherent in terms of food safety findings can be interesting, it has become clear over the years that in a modern food processing system, some environmental and accidental contaminants cannot be avoided. To balance the need to accommodate the presence of some contaminants while preserving food safety, Congress provided the FDA a regulatory tool known as a "tolerance" under Section 406 of the 1938 FDCA. A tolerance level under Section 406 is the level at which a substance may be present in a food that the agency has determined is consistent with safe for consumption. The determination of a tolerance level requires a balance of considerations: whether the substance cannot be avoided by good manufacturing practice (a production and testing practice that helps ensure a quality product), whether the substance is required in the production of the food, how the consumer may be affected by the substance or related substances, and whether foreseeable technological changes in the production process would affect the appropriateness of the tolerance.[50] While the tolerance tool indicates regulatory leniency, violation of a tolerance is a per se showing of adulteration, thus relieving the FDA from having to prove that a substance in food is injurious to health. The incentive to establish tolerances is significantly dimmed, however, by the fact that to set tolerances for poisonous and deleterious added substances, the FDA must go through a formal rulemaking procedure, a time-consuming and resource-intensive process, and any person who objects to a tolerance must be given a formal administrative hearing. (The burden of this formal administrative process is described more fully in Chapter 2 of this treatise.)

To ease the administrative process, FDA adopted "action levels" as an alternative to be used in place of tolerances. Action levels differ from tolerances in that the FDA does not need to go through formal rulemaking procedures in order to establish action levels; to do so, the FDA simply needs to give notice by publication in the Federal Register.[51] The FDA's preference for using action levels in place of setting of tolerances was tested in *Young v. Community Nutrition Institute*, where the US Supreme Court determined that the FDA was not required to establish contaminant tolerances through formal rulemaking procedures, as opposed to simply setting action levels.[52]

---

[49] *See* Notice, Microbiological Testing Program for *Escherichia coli* in Raw Ground Beef, U.S. Dep't of Agric., Food Safety Inspection Serv. (Final Draft, October 11, 1994) (stating that to stimulate a reduction of *E. coli* 0157:H, FSIS will commence a microbiological testing program). A Citizens Petition was filed by Concerned Science for Public Interest that requested USDA to issue an interpretative rule declaring that certain strains of *Salmonella*, when found in ground meat and ground poultry, be considered adulterants under FMIA and PPIA. *See* Complaint for Declaration, and Injunctive Relief, Center for Science in the Public Interest v. Vilsack, et al., No. 14–895 (D.C. Cir. filed May 5, 2014).

[50] *See also* 21 C.F.R. § 109.6 (b) (1)–(3).

[51] *See* 21 C.F.R. § 109.4(c)(2).

[52] *Young*, 476 U.S. 974 at 975 (1986).

The Supreme Court referred back to the lower court, however, for clarification on whether the FDA must adopt action levels through informal (notice-and-comment) rulemaking. The US Court of Appeals for the District of Columbia Circuit held that action levels were legislative rules and therefore had to be promulgated using notice-and-comment rulemaking procedures.[53] As a result, the FDA revised its regulations and declared action levels to be prosecutorial guidelines, rather than substantive rules, removing them from notice-and-comment rulemaking, but also as a result rendering them not binding on the agency or industry.[54]

In search of a middle ground between tolerance and action levels, the FDA subsequently established what is known as "regulatory limits." Unlike action levels, regulatory limits follow informal notice-and-comment rulemaking, thus making regulatory limits binding on the food industry, the FDA, and the courts.[55] The same criteria required for tolerances are also required for both action levels and regulatory limits.

§ 3.05 Regulation of Food Chemicals

[1] Increasing Focus on Food Chemicals

The advances in American food processing, preservation, and packaging – especially following advances made during World War II – sparked wide interest in new food chemicals, including ingredients and processing agents, which were used in the composition of food. During this period, the FDA and USDA did not require advance approval for any of these food chemical technologies. Consequently, in 1952, Congress established a select committee, chaired by Representative James Delaney of New York, to examine the escalated use of chemicals in food. Following hearings, a series of amendments to the FDCA were adopted that addressed these concerns: the Food Pesticide Amendment (1954), Food Additive Amendment (1958), and the Color Additives Amendment (1960) increased FDA control over the growing list of food chemicals entering the food supply, putting the onus on manufacturers to establish their safety. At the same time, apprehension over carcinogens in food moved Congress to enact the Delaney Clause in 1958 as an amendment to the FDCA.[56]

The Delaney Clause is found in Section 409(c)(3)(a) of the FDCA and provides that "[n]o additive shall be deemed to be safe if it is found to induce cancer when ingested by man or animal, or if it is found after tests which are appropriate for the evaluation of the safety of food additives, to induce cancer in man or animal." Named after Representative Dalaney, the Delaney Clause is incorporated in three parallel provisions applicable to three classes of food constituents: food additives,[57] color additives,[58] and animal drug residues.[59] However, because the Delaney Clause appears as a proviso to the general

---

[53] Cmty. Nutrition Inst. v. Young, 818 F.2d 943, 946–7 (D.C. Cir. 1987).

[54] See Action Levels for Added Poisonous or Deleterious Substances in Food, 55 Fed. Reg. 20782 (May 21, 1990).

[55] See id.

[56] See Food Additives Amendment of 1958, Pub. L. No. 85–929, 72 Stat. 1784, 1785 (1958); 21 U.S.C. § 348(c)(A).

[57] 21 U.S.C. § 348.

[58] 21 U.S.C. § 376.

[59] 21 U.S.C. § 360b.

standard for evaluating food additives, the Clause literally applies only to substances that are food additives. For example, it does not automatically proscribe FDA approval of animal carcinogens that are not food additives, even if they might be present in or added to food. It is not clear whether in 1938 members of Congress appreciated the full significance or even the presence of this limitation.

It is likely that more attention will be given to the possible ways that consumers are exposed to chemicals that are found in food. A report issued by the PEW Health Group in January 2013 suggested four steps that the FDA could take to improve exposure assessments: (1) food consumption data should incorporate longer-term surveys of people's eating patterns; (2) children and pregnant women should be more rigorously evaluated in safety assessments; (3) the cumulative effects from all dietary sources should be considered in a consistent manner; and (4) the FDA should more robustly coordinate with other agencies responsible for public health and chemical regulation, including the USDA and Environmental Protection Agency (EPA).[60]

[2] Additives

[a] Expansive Definition and Exceptions

Additives are a type of food chemical that are typically added to food to make it more appetizing, to preserve it, and purportedly to make it more healthier.[61] The development of more complex additives for foods in the 1940s and 1950s raised concerns about the safety of food additives, which led to the Food Additives Amendment of 1958. Now, section 409 of the FDCA requires the FDA to approve new food additives before they can be used in foods.

The FDCA defines in expansive terms a "food additive" as

> any substance the intended use of which results or may reasonably be expected to result, directly, or indirectly, in its becoming a component or otherwise affecting the characteristics of any food (including any substance intended for use in producing, manufacturing, packing, processing, preparing, treating, packaging, transporting, or holding food; and including any source of radiation intended for any such use).[62]

This broad definition encompasses any substance, including nonedible items, such as adhesives, packaging, and food contact surfaces, that are intended or may reasonably be expected to become a component of a food or would otherwise affect the characteristic of any food.

Notwithstanding this expansive definition, two groups exclude certain substances from the reach of the regulations governing the safety of food additives. The first group consists of specific items that are separately regulated under the FDCA, including pesticides, color additives, animal drugs, and some new food technology components. The second group consists of substances that are generally recognized as safe (GRAS).

---

[60] See The PEW Charitable Trusts, Comprehensive Reviews in Food Science and Food Safety (January 2013).
[61] Alan Davidson, The Oxford Companion to Food 4 (Tom Jaine & Jane Davidson eds., 2d ed. 2006).
[62] 21 U.S.C.A § 321(s).

[b] Prior Approval

If a substance does not fall within any of the exceptions and otherwise meets the definition of "food additive," it must receive prior FDA approval, recognizing its safety, before
it can be used.[63] To meet this requirement, FDA established a process by which an individual can petition the FDA to request approval of a food additive. Meanwhile, use of
additives without approval is per se adulteration. The approval process for food additives
is housed in Section 409 and is viewed by some in the food industry as cumbersome,
expensive, and time-consuming. Section 409 provides a formal petition process that
applies a science-based safety standard to review food additive petitions. At a minimum, a
food additive petition must include the name of the substance; its chemical identity and
composition; the proposed conditions of its use; proposed labeling; physical effects data;
technical effects (and levels) data; information on the manufacturing process, facilities,
and controls; methods of detecting and determining the quantity of the additive in the
finished food; the result of safety investigations; and an environmental assessment.[64] The
agency considers the probable levels of consumption of the additive, and the cumulative
effect of the additive and related substances in the diet in arriving at its determination.
Approval of the additive is given when there is a reasonable certainty in the minds of
competent scientists that a substance is not harmful under its intended conditions of use.
The toxicological testing requirements for food additives are the subject of a guidance
document, known as the Red Book.[65] If FDA finds an additive to be safe, it issues a regulation specifying the conditions under which the additive may safely be used.[66]

[3] *GRAS*

[a] Significant Exclusion

By specifically excluding from the definition of food additive in Section 201(s) those
substances that are classified as GRAS, the 1958 Food Additives Amendment obviates
the rigorous preapproval process for certain additives. Two groups of substances qualify
as GRAS. On the basis of the notion that the use of substances in food for a substantial
period of time supplies a reasonable basis for deeming them safe, substances used in
food prior to January 1, 1958 – the year in which the Food Additives Amendment was
enacted – are grandfathered in as GRAS. FDA later modified its regulations to state
that pre-1958 overseas use of a substance is sufficient to establish grandfather in GRAS
status.[67] The second group consists of those substances where a GRAS status is accorded
via scientific determination. There are two routes for determining GRAS status pursuant
to this scientific test. First, a party may request the FDA to review relevant scientific information and agree that a substance is GRAS. Second, a party may self-determine that a

---

[63] 21 U.S.C. § 321(a)(1).
[64] 21 C.F.R. Part 171.
[65] The Redbook was first developed and published in 1982. Following various revisions, the Redbook is
now available on the FDA/CFSAN Internet website and is now titled, "Toxicological Principles for the
Food Safety Assessment of Food Ingredients." *See* FDA, Guidance for Industry and Other Stakeholders
Toxicological Principles for the Safety Assessment of Food Ingredients, Redbook 2000 (July 2007, revised)
[66] *See* 21 C.F.R. Parts 172–178.
[67] 21 C.F.R. § 170.30(c)(2).

substance is GRAS, which is typically done by convening a GRAS panel of experts who review available information about a substance and, if appropriate, prepare a written report indicating that, in their view, the substance is GRAS.[68] A finding of GRAS requires the same quantity and quality of scientific evidence as is required to obtain approval of a substance as a food additive.[69] Although there is some risk that the FDA will disagree with a GRAS self-determination, this route permits the immediate marketing of a substance as such, which avoids the costly and protracted preapproval process for food additives. Notwithstanding GRAS status, substances remain subject to regulation by FDA under the may-render-injurious standard.[70]

[b] Oversight of GRAS Exception

Concerns about the lack of oversight over the GRAS process, in 1997, the FDA issued a proposed rule related to GRAS determinations.[71] The proposed rule would replace the process of issuing GRAS affirmation regulations in response to voluntary petitions with a notification procedure, whereby any person may notify the FDA of a determination that a particular use of a substance is GRAS. Although the proposed rule has never been finalized, FDA accepts voluntary notifications. It should be noted that the FDA does not reach a conclusion about the GRAS status of the intended use of a substance, but determines whether there is adequate scientific support for the notifier's GRAS determination.

GRAS status is not a permanent status or invested right. A substance may be revoked of this classification if its safety is called into question by new scientific evidence. For example, the FDA revoked GRAS for cyclamate, a sweetener used in the 1960s and 1970s that was suspected to be a carcinogen.[72] Once a substance is no longer classified as GRAS, it loses its exempt status and is considered a food additive, subject to regulation. Unlike food additives, which can have their approvals revoked only after certain procedural steps have been followed, a GRAS regulation issued by FDA can be revoked after a notice-and-comment rulemaking.

Although the GRAS system is lauded for its efficiencies, it is not without criticism, which at some point may lead to change. In addressing concerns about the safety of GRAS following its review of eleven citizen petitions, the GAO recommended that the FDA issue guidance to companies on how to document their GRAS determinations and that the FDA monitor GRAS determinations through random audits.[73] Whether the FDA ever adopts the recommendations of the GAO report remains to be seen; until

---

[68] It should be noted that in addition to reviewing the safety of a particular substance in response to a GRAS affirmation petition, FDA has been conducting, albeit unsuccessfully, since the 1970s, its own review of GRAS substances. *See* 21 C.F.R. Part 184. Some substances are listed in FDA's regulations at 21 C.F.R. Parts 182, 184, and 186. Section 182.1, however, explicitly states that "it is impracticable to list all substances that are generally recognized as safe for their intended use." This statement recognizes that substances not listed by FDA as GRAS nevertheless may be determined GRAS for their intended use.

[69] 21 C.F.R. § 170.30(b).

[70] 21 U.S.C. § 342(a)(1).

[71] *See* Substances Generally Recognized as Safe; Proposed Rule, 62 Fed. Reg. 18937 (April 17, 1997).

[72] *See* 21 C.F.R. § 189.135; Cyclamic Acid and Its Salts, 34 FR 17063 (October 21, 1969).

[73] U.S. Gov't Accountability Office, GAO-10-246, FDA Should Strengthen Its Oversight of Food Ingredients Determined to Be Generally Recognized as Safe (GRAS) 16–17, 35 (February 2010).

then, GRAS will continue to pave the way for the expeditious introduction of food additives and to raise concerns about the safety of these substances, or at least the lack of strictures imposed upon the GRAS process.

[4] *Food Contact Substances*

[a] Type of Food Additive

A type of food additive that is regulated in a unique manner under the FDCA is what formerly was referred to as an indirect additive, but what is now referred to as a food contact substance (FCS).[74] Section 409 defines an FCS as any substance that is intended for use as a component of materials used in manufacturing, packing, packaging, transporting, or holding food, if such use of the substance is not intended to have any technical effect on the food. Although FCSs are often used in food packaging, the additive includes components of food processing equipment and other substances used to process food. Common types of FCSs include coatings, plastics, paper, and adhesives, as well as colorants, antimicrobials, and antioxidants found in packaging.[75]

[b] Notification Process

Historically, all FCS that were additives required premarket approval by the FDA. In 1997, the Food and Drug Administration Modernization Act (FDAMA) amended Section 409 to establish a notification process that expedites the review and approval of FCS food additives. Section 409 requires sufficient scientific information to demonstrate that the FCS additive, which is the subject of the notification, is safe for its intended use.[76] In an effort to ensure the safe use of these substances, FDA established a Food Contact Notification (FCN) Program within the Center for Food Safety and Applied Nutrition's (CFSAN) Office of Food Additive Safety. The notification process under Section 409 has unique features. For example, unlike general food additive approvals where the approval is applicable to all food enterprises, approvals under the FCN process are proprietary. Section 409(h)(1)(C) of the FDCA states that an FCN is effective only for the manufacturer and substance identified in the notification. Notification is not required for a food contact substance that is GRAS or has otherwise been sanctioned for its intended use in contact with food.

[5] *Color Additives*

[a] No GRAS Exception

An interesting anomaly in the regulatory treatment of food additives is that there is no GRAS exemption to the definition of a color additive: a color additive is always subject

---

[74] "Direct" or "indirect" additives are not defined by FDCA or the regulations. The terms were used by FDA and others to identify food additives, and may or may not be food contact substances.

[75] *See* Anna P. Shanklin & Elizabeth R. Sánchez, *Regulatory Report: FDA's Food Contact Substance Notification Program*, FOOD SAFETY MAG. October/November 2005.

[76] FDA, Final Guidance, Preparation of Food Contact Notifications: Administrative, (May 2002, revised).

to premarket approval requirements.[77] Having a long, rich history,[78] a color additive is a dye, pigment, or other substance, which is capable of imparting color when added or applied to a food, unless the substance is used solely for a purpose other than coloring (e.g., flavoring).[79] The FDCA also expressly exempts from the definition of a "color additive" agricultural chemicals, such as pesticides and plant nutrients, which are added to a commodity or to soil to enhance physiological properties (e.g., growth, resistance to insects), although they may affect the commodity's color before or after harvest.[80]

[b] Early Regulation and Development of Color Additive Amendment of 1960

By the time the 1906 PFDA passed, many foods were artificially colored, oftentimes with blatantly poisonous materials such as lead, arsenic, and mercury. The USDA – the enforcement agency at the time – had issued a list of seven straight colors approved for use in food and established a voluntary certification program. When the responsibility for enforcing the 1906 Act was given to the newly established FDA, the list of approved colors had expanded to fifteen straight colors. The 1938 FDCA made mandatory the previously voluntary certification program for batches of listed colors, thus effectively requiring the listing of coal-tar colors that were harmless and suitable for use in foods (as well as for drugs and cosmetics).

Public attention became focused on color additives following an outbreak of illness among children in 1950 as a result of eating an orange Halloween candy containing 1–2 percent FD&C Orange No. 1, a color additive approved for use in food.[81] This event, coupled with the hearings held by Representative Delaney on the possible carcinogenicity of food additives, prompted the FDA to reevaluate all of the listed color additives and to terminate the listings of several that were found to cause serious adverse effects.[82]

This heightened attention to the safety of color additives eventually led to the Color Additive Amendments of 1960, which defined "color additive" and required that only color additives listed as suitable and safe for a given use could be used in foods. The 1960 Amendments did not include a grandfather provision for colors that were on the market at the time. To resolve the potential problem of having all color additives suddenly banned from use, the FDA implemented a provisional listing mechanism, pursuant to which all color additives on the market were provisionally approved, with the

---

[77] 21 U.S.C. § 321(t).

[78] The history of the use of color additives is documented from ancient times when naturally occurring color additives from vegetable and mineral sources (i.e., paprika, turmeric, saffron, iron, lead oxides, and copper sulfate) were used to color foods. *See* Brenda Seidman, *The Grays of Medical Device Color Additives*, 69 Food & Drug L.J. 491, 494 (2014). Experts have long known that color plays a crucial role in the taste and perception of food. In the nineteenth century, synthetic organic dyes that became known as "coal-tar colors" were discovered and became used to color foods. *See* Adam Burrows, *Palette of Our Palates: A Brief History of Food Coloring and Its Regulation*, 8 COMPREHENSIVE REVIEWS IN FOOD SCI. & FOOD SAFETY 394, 396 (2009).

[79] *Id.* Color additives are classified as straight colors, lakes, and mixtures. For a detailed explanation of these categories, *see* Julie N. Barrows et al., *Color Additives: FDA's Regulatory Process and Historical Perspectives*, FOOD SAFETY MAG., October/November 2003.

[80] *Id.*

[81] *Id.*

[82] *Id.*

expectation that the FDA would proceed either to permanently list the colors or remove them from the market.

[c] Current Approval Process

The regulatory approach provided by the FDCA for approval of color additives is similar to the premarket approval process for food additives. The FDA lists new color additives or new uses for listed color additives that have been shown to be safe for their intended uses, conducts a certification program for batches of color additives that are required to be certified before sale, and monitors the use of color additives in products in the United States, including product labeling.[83] An unapproved color additive renders a product containing the additive adulterated as a matter of law. When evaluating the safety of a new color additive or a new use for a listed color additive, the FDA considers such factors as probable consumption or exposure from its use, cumulative effect on the diet, evaluation by qualified experts, and the availability of the analytical methods for determining the color additive's purity and acceptable levels of impurities. Once a new color additive is listed, the FDA continually monitors its safe use by assuring the consideration of new data and safety information.[84]

[6] Delaney Clause

[a] Absolute Ban

Found in Section 409(c)(3) of the FDCA, the Delaney Clause states that "[n]o additive shall be deemed to be safe it is found to induce cancer when ingested by man or animal, or if it is found after tests which are appropriate for the evaluation of the safety of food additives, to induce cancer in man or animal."[85] Thus, unlike the food additives amendment of 1958, which merely requires that a food additive be shown safe before it can be approved, a literal reading of the Delaney Clause imposes an absolute bar on FDA approval of any carcinogenic food additive.[86]

The Delaney Clause prohibition appears in three separate parts of the FDCA: Section 409 on food additives, Section 512 on animal drugs in meat and poultry, and Section 721 on color additives. Although the three versions differ in language, they all seek to prohibit the addition of any substance in food that induces cancer in humans or lab animals.

Passage in 1958 of the Delaney Clause reflected a growing concern not only of food additives in general, but specifically of the connection between food chemicals and cancer.[87] The Delaney Clause was enacted at a time when carcinogenic substances were difficult to detect and all detectable carcinogens were extremely dangerous. This concern over the connection between food chemicals and cancer prompted debate over whether a threshold margin of safety could be determined for carcinogens in food.[88]

---

[83] *See* 21 U.S.C. § 379e; 21 C.F.R. Part 74.
[84] The process for submitting petitions is described in detail in 21 CFR Parts 70 and 71, which describe the format, the administrative requirements, and the information and data required.
[85] 21 U.S.C. § 348(c)(3)(A).
[86] Public Citizen v. Young, 831 F.2d 1108, 1108 (D.C. Cir. 1987).
[87] *Id.* at 1113.
[88] *Public Citizen*, 831 F.2d at 1114–16.

The Department of Health, Education, and Welfare (DHEW, the predecessor agency to the Department of Health and Human Services) initially opposed a specific ban against carcinogens, but withdrew objection when Representative Delaney's proposed amendment was revised to confirm the FDA's scientific discretion in interpreting the results of animal tests.

[b] Challenges in Administration

As it has turned out, the Delaney Clause has proven to be highly controversial and difficult to administer. For nearly its first twenty years, the Delaney Clause had little influence on FDA actions, since only a very small number of additives had been shown to cause cancer in animal experiments. Indeed, it appeared that implementing the Delaney Clause might have engendered little controversy if the universe of food additives had remained well defined and if technology had held still. However, the factual premise has changed: first, the universe of food additives has expanded; and second, emerging technology makes it possible to detect at least a small possibility of carcinogenicity in a vast number of food additives that would otherwise be considered safe. Improvements in the detection methodology have made it possible to measure substances in parts per trillion and it is likely that advancements in science will likely enhance the toxicologist's ability to identify carcinogenic substances still further. Even foods that are not additives today can be carcinogenic: apples, for example, contain acetaldehyde, which is a probable human carcinogen.[89] In some cases, carcinogenic substances gained market acceptance long before their carcinogenicity was discovered. Although the FDA does not recognize any known carcinogenic substance as GRAS, the reality is that because many natural foods such as apples are carcinogenic to some degree, the FDA permits a natural substance to remain GRAS even if it contains substances found to cause cancer in test animals.[90]

• Saccharin Example

The polemics involved in the debate over the application of the Delaney Clause and the interplay between science, politics, and consumer interests is exemplified in the controversy over saccharin, a nonnutritive sweetener.[91] When Harvey Wiley proposed a ban on saccharin in 1908, President Teddy Roosevelt, drawing upon his personal experience, responded: "Anyone who says saccharin is injurious to health is an idiot. Dr. Rixey gives it to me every day."[92] For the next sixty-plus years, saccharin remained on the market, enjoying GRAS status. A ban in 1969 on cyclamates, a nonnutritive sweetener often mixed with saccharin, prompted the FDA to investigate saccharin for possible

[89] *See* Chemical Summary for Acetaldehyde, Office of Pollution Prevention and Toxics, U.S. Environmental Protection Agency (August 1994).

[90] David M. Feinberg, *A Cookbook for a Consistent Food Safety Standard for Carcinogenic Foods*, at 81 (Food and Drug Law: An Electronic Book of Student Papers, Harvard Law) (1995, Third Year Paper)

[91] *See* Richard A. Merrill & Michael R. Taylor, *Saccharin: A Case Study of Government Regulation of Environmental Carcinogens*, 5 VA. J. NAT. RESOURCES L. 1, 1 (1985).

[92] Jesse Hicks, *The Pursuit of Sweet: A History of Saccharin*, CHEMICAL HERITAGE MAG. (2010).

carcinogenicity.[93] At the same time, the FDA started a program to review all GRAS substances employing the most current science and technology. In 1972, toxicological studies indicated possible bladder cancer caused by saccharin. In response, the FDA removed saccharin from the GRAS category and issued an interim food additive regulation allowing but limiting the use of saccharin in foods while waiting for additional study results.[94] Subsequent studies linking saccharin to bladder tumors in rats led the FDA to propose in 1977 a ban on saccharin as a food additive via the Delaney Clause.[95] This proposal precipitated intense public controversy. Health organizations contended that saccharin provides enormous health benefits to persons, such as diabetics, who must restrict their intake of sugar. Congress placed a moratorium on the ban for two years to allow for additional research. In lieu of the moratorium, labeling requirements were established to warn individuals of the possible risk of cancer associated with the use of saccharin, based on laboratory animal studies. At the time, no other nonnutritive sweetener was approved for use in the United States. Further research prompted the FDA formally to withdraw its 1977 proposal to ban the use of saccharin. In 2000, the Department of Health and Human Service's (DHHS) National Toxicology Program removed saccharin from its list of carcinogens and legislation was passed that repealed the warning label requirement for products containing saccharin. In 2001, the FDA formally declared saccharin safe for consumption. Nearly a decade later, in 2010, the EPA officially removed saccharin and its salts from their list of hazardous constituents and commercial chemical products and declared that saccharin is no longer considered a potential hazard to human health.[96] As part of its press release, the EPA noted that when the agency proposed to remove saccharin and its salts from the lists on April 22, 2010, it did not receive any comments opposing the proposal.[97]

[c] Limits to Application

The problems with the scope and application of the Delaney Clause – demonstrated by the saccharin saga – have caused the FDA to limit its application. The FDA has adopted something akin to a *de minimis* exception in applying the Delaney Clause, thereby excluding from enforcement the high numbers of commonly eaten foods that have trace amounts of a known carcinogenic substance present, either naturally or added. In response to a DC Circuit holding that there is administrative discretion inherent to the FDCA scheme to deal appropriately with *de minimis* situations,[98] the FDA asserted that

---

[93] Cyclamate was banned fairly quickly and with relatively little controversy on less-than-certain evidence of its carcinogenicity. A plausible reason for the stronger resistance to banning saccharin was that if the ban had occurred consumers would have been left without having an artificial sweetener on the market. *See generally, id.*

[94] *See* Saccharin and Its Salts: Removal from Generally Recognized as Safe List: Provisional Regulation Prescribing Conditions of Safe Use, 36 Fed. Reg. 12,109, 12,110 (June 12, 1971) (codified at 21 C.F.R. § 121.4001) (superseded by the Saccharin Study and Labeling Act, 21 U.S.C. § 348).

[95] Saccharin and Its Salts Proposed Rule Making, 42 Fed. Reg. 19996-01 (April 15, 1997).

[96] Press Release, U.S. Environmental Protection Agency, EPA Removes Saccharin from Hazardous Substances Listing, (December 14, 2010).

[97] *See id.*

[98] Monsanto Co. v. Kennedy, 613 F.2d 947 (D.C. Cir. 1979).

it could disregard carcinogenic chemicals in noncarcinogenic additives if tests demonstrated that a reasonable certainty of no harm would result from the additive.[99]

However, based on the clear language of the Delaney Clause and the legislative history, the DC Circuit in *Public Citizen v. Young* found that FDA did not have the authority to apply the *de minimis* doctrine to approve color additives whose carcinogenic risk is trivial.[100] The court found that the FDA needed to request relief from Congress rather than the court.[101] Additional narrowing of application of the Delaney Clause occurred when FDA began to use what it called the "constituents approach" to distinguish between the actual additive and its constituents in order to determine when the Delaney Clause would be triggered.[102] Courts have upheld FDA's applying the Delaney Clause to the additive per se, instead of a constituent of the additive (e.g., starting materials).[103] Thus, with color additives, if the additive as a whole did not cause cancer, then carcinogenic components of the color additive present in minute quantities was determined to be acceptable, even though these components caused cancer in lab animals when tested separately.[104]

[7] Pesticide Residues

[a] Fractured and Evolving Regulation

Pesticides are broadly defined by the Federal Insecticide, Fungicide, and Rodenticide Act (FIFRA), which Congress enacted in 1947, as "any substance or mixture of substances intended for preventing, destroying, repelling, or mitigating any pest."[105] The regulation of pesticides is fractured: three federal agencies have a special responsibility to administer and enforce the major federal pesticide laws, the FDA, EPA, and USDA. The EPA regulates pesticides through FIFRA, as well as the FDCA.[106] FIFRA regulates pesticide sale, distribution, and use; a pesticide cannot be sold or distributed unless first registered by EPA. EPA may register a pesticide only if it determines the pesticide will not cause "unreasonable adverse effects on the environment."[107] USDA and FDA monitor the application of pesticides to ensure that the tolerances established by EPA are met. Once a pesticide is found in or on a raw agricultural commodity or a processed food, the FDA, per its general oversight responsibility under Section 408 of the FDCA, enforces the safety of pesticide residue. States also have enacted statutes that regulate the sale, manufacture, registration,

---

[99] Policy for Regulating Carcinogenic Chemicals in Food and Color Additives: Advance Notice for Proposed Rulemaking, 47 Fed. Reg. 14464 (April 2, 1982).

[100] *Public Citizen*, 831 F.2d at 1122. The Delaney Clause has also served as the poster child for criticisms of textualism. *See e.g.*, Cass R. Sunstein, *Interpreting Statutes in the Regulatory State*, 103 HARV. L. REV. 405, 422–4 (1989) (arguing that because the premise under which the statute was originally written no longer holds true, it is by no means obvious that the statutory text should be understood in accordance with its original meaning, even if that concept were unproblematic).

[101] *Public Citizen*, 831 F.2d at 1122.

[102] Policy for Regulating Carcinogenic Chemicals in Food and Color Additives, *supra* note 99.

[103] Scott v. FDA, 728 F.2d 322 (6th Cir. 1984).

[104] *See id.* at 325 (6th Cir. 1984).

[105] 7 U.S.C. § 136(u).

[106] *See* 7 U.S.C. §§ 136–136y.

[107] 7 U.S.C. § 136a(a). In determining what adverse effects are unreasonable, the EPA is to consider "the economic, social, and environmental costs and benefits" of a pesticide's use. 7 U.S.C. § 136(bb).

and distribution of pesticides. States are generally permitted to enact legislation that restricts pesticide use more than federal law requirements.

The food safety focus on pesticides involves the residue of the pesticide on the food. Pesticide residues can result in a multiple of ways: from direct treatment of a pesticide on the target crop or to the seed stock of the crop; from using antimicrobial pesticides in food processing; from crop rotation where the pesticide was used on the previous crop; from pesticide run-off into bodies of water; from "spray drift," that is, when sprayed deposits inadvertently on other crops; from livestock, later processed into meat, milk, poultry, or eggs, eating feed with residue; and from postharvest pesticide applications when the products are stored for shipping or processing.[108] The regulation of the safety of pesticide residues is similar to that for intentionally added substances, in that it is predicated upon the employment of the regulatory tools of tolerances, registration, monitoring, and risk assessment. The development of pesticide regulation has been marked by an evolving reaction to scientific advances and public perceptions of risk.[109]

FIFRA, passed in 1947, initially focused on fraudulent claims about product performance and expedited the allowance of new pesticides into the market quickly. Over time, however, the focus of pesticide regulation shifted away from commercial interests to the protection of human health and the environment. The Delaney House Committee hearings in 1950–1 were the first government hearings to address pesticide safety. The hearings resulted in the Pesticides Control Amendment (PCA) of 1954, which introduced rules on safety limits for pesticide residues on food. Growing awareness and concerns of potential human health and environmental health effects from pesticides would continue to percolate, leading to legislative and regulatory activity and culminating in the Food Quality Protection Act (FQPA) in 1996, which amended both the FDCA and FIFRA. The FQPA mandated a single standard for pesticide residue in food, regardless of the type of food, and specifically addressed concerns about children's susceptibility to pesticides.[110]

[b] FQPA: Tolerances

The FQPA mandates the expedited registration of "reduced-risk pesticides,"[111] which have lesser impacts on human health and nontarget organisms or on groundwater than traditional pesticides.[112] To qualify as a reduced-risk pesticide, the pesticide must

---

[108] See Pesticide Registration Manual, Chapter 11, Tolerance Petitions, U.S. ENVIRONMENTAL PROTECTION AGENCY (March 6, 2015, last update).

[109] See Frederick M. Fishel, *Pest Management and Pesticides: A Historical Perspective*, INSTITUTE OF FOOD AND AGRICULTURAL SCIENCES, UNIVERSITY OF FLORIDA EXTENSION 3 (December 2009, revised February 2013) (accounting for civilization's battle against pest throughout history, including during World War II, when dichloro-diphenyl-trichloroethane (DDT), a synthetic chemical, played an important role in saving Allied soldiers from insect-transmitted disease and was hailed as the insecticide to solve all insect problems. Countless other synthetic organic pesticides followed, marking a new era in pest control in which the use of pesticides became the primary means of pest control).

[110] For concerns about pesticide exposure in children, see James R. Roberts, Catherine J. Karr, & Council on Environmental Health, *Pesticide Exposure in Children*, American Academy of Pediatrics (December 6, 2012).

[111] See Food Quality Protection Act of 1996 (FQPA), Pub. L. No. 104–170, §250(G)(10)(B)(iv), 110 Stat. 1489, 1511 (1996).

[112] NATIONAL RESEARCH COUNCIL, THE FUTURE ROLE OF PESTICIDES IN U.S. AGRICULTURE 154 (2000).

demonstrate reduced risk using one mechanism, such as a lower potential for contaminating ground water or lower pest-resistance potential.[113]

If the product's intended use causes, or is likely to cause (directly or indirectly) pesticide residues on particular crops, and if the pesticide does not fall into one of the exemptions from tolerance-setting, the EPA must set a tolerance for the pesticide.[114] That is, for each type of food crop or feed crop on which a particular pesticide is used, the EPA must establish a pesticide tolerance, or maximum legally allowable residue limit for that pesticide, in order for the food to be marketable.[115] If no tolerance is set for a particular proposed pesticide, pesticide applicants must petition the EPA to establish an appropriate tolerance for the pesticide or request an exemption from the tolerance-setting requirements.[116] A pesticide residue is deemed unsafe unless it has a tolerance for the specific crop or is exempted from the tolerance requirement.[117]

The EPA is required to amend or renew tolerances every fifteen (15) years and to evaluate registrant proposals to increase pesticide dosage rates or the frequency of applications, which will result in higher residue levels in the food products.[118] In order to amend the tolerance, the registrant must submit an amendment application to EPA.[119] The EPA issues tolerance amendments and renewals under 40 CFR part 180.[120] The process and necessary materials required to apply for a tolerance or an amendment to a tolerance are described in 40 CFR part 180.7.[121] Applicants may submit requests for exemptions from tolerance-settings, and may need to provide data on the level of residue expected.[122] The granting of an exemption is conditional upon the total amount of residue not being hazardous to human health.[123]

The EPA uses the safety standard established by the FQPA to set tolerances.[124] The standard is defined as "a reasonable certainty that no harm will result from aggregate exposure to the pesticide chemical residue, including all anticipated dietary exposures and all other exposures for which there is reliable information."[125] A pesticide tolerance for a processed food is typically the same as it is for a raw commodity, unless

---

[113] *See id.*

[114] 40 C.F.R. § 152.50(i).

[115] *See id.* Tolerances are usually measured in parts per million (ppm). *See* Pesticide Registration Manual, *supra* note 108.

[116] 40 C.F.R. § 152.50(i); Pesticide Registration Manual, *supra* note 108 at Introduction.

[117] 21 U.S.C. § 346 (b)(2)(A).

[118] 40 C.F.R. § 155.40; 7 U.S.C. § 136a-1 and § 136w; Pesticide Registration Manual, *supra* note 108.

[119] Pesticide Registration Manual, *supra* note 108.

[120] 40 C.F.R. § 180.

[121] The applicant must submit the name, chemical identity, and composition of the pesticide chemical. *See* 40 C.F.R. § 180.7 (b) (3); Pesticide Registration Manual, *supra* note 108. EPA will need information on the manufacturing process, chemical analysis of the active ingredient, and analytical methods to determine the chemical composition of the pesticide. *See* 40 C.F.R. § 158.300–158.355. Applicants are encouraged to use EPA's store of study profile templates to develop their chemical analysis. *Study Profile Templates*, U.S. ENVIRONMENTAL PROTECTION AGENCY (October 28, 2014, last update).

[122] Pesticide Registration Manual, *supra* note 108.

[123] *See* 40 C.F.R. § 180.900.

[124] FQPA at § 405 (2)(A)(ii).

[125] 21 U.S.C. § 346a. The term "aggregate exposure" incorporates dietary exposure from all the food and feed tolerances established for the pesticide, as well as all nonoccupational sources, such as drinking water. *Id.* In addition, EPA must look at the cumulative effects of pesticide residues, as well as "other substances that have a common mechanism of toxicity." *See Assessing Pesticide Cumulative Risk*, U.S. ENVIRONMENTAL PROTECTION AGENCY (February 2, 2014, last updated).

the processing concentrates the pesticide residue levels. If the pesticide residues in processed foods exceed the tolerance for raw commodities, EPA will require a separate processed-food tolerance.[126] Pesticide tolerances set by the EPA also applies to all fresh and processed foods imported into the United States.[127] However, because imported foods are infrequently inspected, the amount of pesticide residues on imported foods is unchecked.[128] Tested imported foods are frequently found to have higher levels of pesticide residues than domestic samples.[129] (The regulation of pesticide residues on imported foods is covered later in this chapter under the international regulation section.)

The reasonable-certainty-of-no harm standard eliminated for the most part the role that assessing the potential benefits of pesticides played in setting pesticide tolerances, where, for example, economic and health benefits of pesticides used to be weighed against potential health risks in determining whether pesticides could be used.[130] Now, the FQPA directs the EPA to consider the benefits to society in determining pesticide tolerances only for eligible pesticides, that is, carcinogenic pesticides whose minimal risks are slightly above an annual risk allowance of ten-in-a-million and a cumulative lifetime risk of no more than two-in-a-million.[131] For such eligible pesticides, a tolerance may be established if the pesticide's use would protect consumers from a different adverse health effect whose risks are greater than the use of the pesticide, or if using the pesticide is necessary to produce a safe, economical food supply. The EPA must review tolerances based on benefits every five years.[132]

The tolerance-setting process by the EPA has come to require a hundredfold safety factor beyond the determined level of no observe adverse effect (NOAEL).[133] In calculating NOAEL, and therefore where residue tolerances should be set, the EPA employs a quantitative assessment (QRA), which assesses the risk of harm from pesticide exposures and sets an upper level of acceptable risk.[134] The QRA calculation process involves four steps: (1) hazard identification – because pesticides are intentionally designed to harm: the pesticide is invariably determined to be dangerous;[135] (2) dose-response assessment of the chemical – the result of this assessment is the NOAEL: the EPA takes each pesticide's NOAEL and divides it by the safety factor of one hundred to determine the Acceptable Daily Intake (ADI), which is the maximum "safe" daily residue exposure that a person can safely consume under the FDCA; (3) the exposure pathway assessment, which identifies and measures the manner in which people are exposed to the pesticide residue and the intensity and duration of these exposures, resulting in a theoretical maximum residue contribution (TMRC); and (4) risk characterization, which calculates

---

[126] Id.

[127] Charles M. Benbrook, *Apples, Kids, and Core Science*, 15 CHOICES 21, 23 (2000).

[128] Laurent Belsie et. al., *Food Safety: How to Keep Our Global Menu Off the Recall List*, CHRISTIAN SCI. MONITOR, 1, 2 (October 25, 2010).

[129] Id.

[130] Linda-Jo Schierow, *FQPA: Origin and Outcome*, 15 CHOICES 18, 19 (2000).

[131] LYNN L. BERGESON, BASIC PRACTICE SERIES: FIFRA 32 (2000).

[132] Id.

[133] H.R. Rep. No. 104–669, Part 2, at 29 (1996).

[134] *See Assessing Health Risks from Pesticides, supra* note 125.

[135] If the pesticide is not deemed dangerous, the EPA can exempt the pesticide from the tolerance requirement under 21 U.S.C. § 346a(c)(2)(A)(i).

whether the TMRC exceeds the ADI, and if that is the case, then the use of that pesticide is considered safe.[136]

The FQPA also accounts for those who face greater risks from pesticide exposure. More specifically, the FQPA established an extra tenfold safety factor to account for the risks faced by women during pregnancy and children when pesticide tolerances are calculated.[137] However, if the EPA administrator determines, using reliable data, that a particular pesticide tolerance is safe for infants and children, the tolerance does not necessarily have to be ten times lower than it would be for adults.[138] The FQPA further requires that tolerances account for aggregated risks from all routes of pesticide exposure, including through drinking water.[139] The EPA must also consider the cumulative effects of pesticide residues and "other substances that have a common mechanism of toxicity" on children.[140]

In some ways, the FQPA weakened regulatory controls. By excluding chemical pesticide residues from the definition of food additives,[141] the FQPA limits the scope of the Delaney Clause. Consequently, the regulatory regime now permits the presence of pesticide residues that pose some risk of cancer. The FQPA also extends the scope of preemption of state regulations. Specifically, the FQPA preempts more stringent state regulation of pesticide residues in food.[142] FIFRA expressly authorizes states to regulate pesticide use, but it also prohibits states from imposing any labeling requirements beyond those imposed by the EPA.[143] There is no federal private right of action to redress FIFRA violations because only the EPA has the standing to enforce it.[144] Thus, if a state merely adopts as its standard of care that which is already required under federal law, no additional obligation is imposed and FIFRA does not preempt plaintiff's per se claims.[145]

[c] Monitoring

Although EPA sets the tolerances for the maximum amount of pesticide residues that can remain on food, the agency does not have authority to enforce the tolerances.[146] Instead, the FDA and USDA have the enforcement authority to enforce tolerances. Both the FDA and USDA monitor the food products under their jurisdiction: the USDA's FSIS under the department's National Residue Program monitors meat, poultry, and egg products for pesticide residue and enforces where tolerance levels are exceeded; the FDA monitors the food products under its jurisdiction, which includes fruits and vegetables, foods on which the use of pesticides is paid particular attention.[147] The USDA's Agricultural

---

[136] *See Assessing Health Risks from Pesticides, supra* note 125.
[137] FQPA at § 405(vi)(c)(ii)(II).
[138] *Id.*
[139] FQPA at § 405 (2)(A)(ii).
[140] *Id.*
[141] *See* 21 U.S.C. § 321(s).
[142] *See* 21 U.S.C. § 346(n)(4).
[143] 7 U.S.C. § 136v99(a)–(b); 7 U.S.C. § 136v(a).
[144] No Spray Coalition, Inc. v. City of New York, 252 F.3d 148, 150 (2d Cir. 2001).
[145] In re StarLink Corn Products Liab. Litig., 212 F. Supp.2d 828, 836 (N.D. Ill. 2002).
[146] U.S. Gov't Accountability Office, GAO-15-38, FDA and USDA Should Strengthen Pesticide Residue Monitoring Programs and Further Disclose Monitoring Limitations 1 (October 2014).
[147] *Id.* at 2.

Marketing Service (AMS) implements the Pesticide Data Program in conjunction with state agencies to survey pesticides on fruits, vegetables, and other foods.[148] The data in the most recently published Pesticide Data Program (2012) shows that according to AMS "overall pesticide residues found in foods are at levels below the tolerances set by the [EPA]."[149] Notwithstanding the positive report, a separate report issued by the US GAO in 2014 recommended that both the FDA and USDA strengthen their pesticide residue monitoring programs and disclose monitoring limitations.[150] The GAO report found that FDA targeted few high-risk foods for pesticide residue testing and found that undisclosed limitations in the data collected by the AMS 2012 Pesticide Data Program may lead users of the data to misinterpret the information and draw erroneous conclusions.[151]

[8] Animal Drugs

[a] Key Definitions and Public Health Concerns

Another general category of intentional additives, one that is of increasing concern to public health officials, is animal drugs and the residues that they may leave in animals used for food. The concern is that ingestion of the pesticide residue in these animals may cause resistance to antimicrobial drugs.

Comprehension of the regulation of animal drugs starts with key definitions. The FCDA defines the term "drugs" as "articles intended for use in the diagnosis, cure, mitigation, treatment, or prevention of disease in man or other animals" and "articles (other than food) intended to affect the structure or any function of the body of man or other animals."[152] "Antimicrobials" is a broad term that refers to compounds, including antibiotics, sanitizers, disinfectants, a number of food preservatives and other substances, which act to either inhibit the growth of or kill microorganisms.[153] "Antibacterial drugs," commonly called "antibiotics," are one category of antimicrobial drugs, and are used to treat infectious diseases in humans, animals, or plants. They work by inhibiting the growth of or killing microorganisms causing the disease. Antibiotics are used in animals for the same reason as for people: to treat and control diseases.[154]

Many of the animals reared for food in the US agricultural system are administered antibiotics in order to treat and prevent disease. When an animal is treated with a drug, all of the bacteria in and on that animal are also exposed to the drug. Some of the exposed bacteria may become resistant, meaning that the drugs, and possibly other similar drugs, will no longer work against those bacteria.[155]

---

[148] Id.

[149] Pesticide Data Program Annual Summary, Calendar Year 2012, Dear Reader Page, U.S. Dep't of Agric. (February 2014).

[150] GAO, FDA and USDA Should Strengthen Pesticide Residue Monitoring Programs, supra note 146.

[151] Id. at Highlights of GAO Report (the GAO report notes that AMS's sampling methodology does not meet the Office of Management and Budget's best-practice principle of product sampling to ensure that the data is nationally representative).

[152] 21 U.S.C. § 321(g)(1)(C).

[153] Questions and Answers: Animal Antibiotics, Antimicrobial Resistance and Impact on Food Safety, International Food Information Council Foundation (May 23, 2014, modified).

[154] Id.

[155] FDA's Strategy on Antimicrobial Resistance – Questions and Answers, U.S. Food & Drug Admin. (March 28, 2014, last update).

Public health officials are increasingly concerned about the link between the use of antibiotics with animals and antibiotic resistance in humans and public health. In 2003, the FDA issued Guidance No. 152, wherein the agency acknowledges the problem of agricultural antibiotic use: "[t]he FDA believes that human exposure through the ingestion of antimicrobial resistant bacteria from animal-derived foods represents the most significant pathway for human exposure to bacteria that have emerged ... as a consequence of antimicrobial drug use in animals."[156] The CDC reports a direct link between antibiotic use in food-producing animals and the occurrence of antibiotic-resistant bacteria in humans. The CDC estimates that 23,000 people die every year from antibiotic-resistant infections.[157]

Because antibiotic resistance is attributed in part to the zealous use of antibiotic treatment for food animals, a greater emphasis is being placed on judicious antibiotic use to preserve its efficacious use in both veterinary and human medicine.[158] Calls to prohibit use in food animals in deference to human health concerns have escalated.[159] Conversely, the consolidation of animal agriculture operations gives rise to disease transmission, and defenders of consolidated operations argue that efficient, industrialized production of huge quantities of food is an inescapable necessity.[160]

[b] Approval Authority for New Animal Drugs

The FDCA gives FDA the legal authority to approve and regulate drugs for animals. New animal drugs are approved and regulated by the FDA's Center for Veterinary Medicine (CVM). The CVM is made up of six offices that work together to approve new animal drugs and monitor the drugs after they are on the market. The Office of New Animal Drug Evaluation is the preapproval office, meaning that it is the lead office for reviewing the information about a new animal drug before it is approved.[161]

The statute governing the approval of antibiotics by the FDA requires they pass a proof of safety standard for humans and animals, but does not expressly limit or allow benefit analysis.[162] In the past, the FDA considered benefits to animal health, the environment, and the economy as well as potential harm resulting from prohibitions; however, the FDA commissioner now determines that benefits are not to be considered when the agency reviews a new animal drug application (NADA) for

---

[156] Dennis G. Maki, *Coming to Grips with Foodborne Infection – Peanut Butter, Peppers, and Nationwide Salmonella Outbreaks*, 360 NEW ENG. J. MED. 951, 952 (2009). The issue of animal drugs extends beyond the borders of the United States; for World Health Day 2011, the World Health Organization (WHO) called for governments and drug regulatory agencies to coordinate a response to the problem of antibiotic drug resistance. Margaret Chan, WHO Director-General, World Health Organization, Statement, World Health Day 2011 (April 6, 2011).

[157] *National Antimicrobial Resistance Monitoring System*, CTRS. FOR DISEASE CONTROL & PREVENTION (SEPTEMBER 4, 2014, LAST UPDATE).

[158] *Id.*

[159] *See, e.g.*, Sabrina Travernise, *Farm Use of Antibiotic Use Defies Scrutiny*, N.Y. TIMES, September 3, 2012, at D1.

[160] Maki, *Coming to Grips with Foodborne Infection, supra* note 156.

[161] *From an Idea to the Marketplace: The Journey of an Animal Drug through the Approval Process*, U.S. FOOD & DRUG ADMIN. (January 14, 2015, last updated).

[162] 21 U.S.C. § 355(b)(1).

food animals when the drug potentially exposes humans to safety risks through food consumption.[163]

For each new submission proposed for a new animal drug, a drug sponsor submits to the CVM extensive scientific studies that evaluate the efficacy and safety of the drug in animals and to safety for humans who consume foodstuffs derived from treated animals. Any organization, or even one person, can be a drug sponsor, including scientific research groups or academic organizations, but typically, drug sponsors are pharmaceutical companies.

As part of the submission process, the drug sponsor generally conducts what are called human food safety studies. A goal of human food safety studies is to ensure that the level of chemical residues in or on food made from treated animals will not harm people. A second goal is to minimize the number of antibiotic-resistant bacteria that enter the food supply via food products made from treated animals.[164] In its 2013 guidance document, the FDA recommended that sponsors of new drugs evaluate their proposed animal drugs on the basis of three criteria: (1) release (or the probability that resistant bacteria will result from the drug's use); (2) exposure (the probability that humans will ingest the resistant bacteria from the source in question); and (3) consequence (the probability that human exposure to the resistant bacteria will result in adverse health conditions).[165]

The FDA evaluates these and all relevant studies and then makes a determination as to whether the drug is effective in preventing or treating disease, and whether it poses a risk to consumers of animal products. The FDA also imposes any necessary rules on how the drug must be utilized to ensure safety for both people and animals. For each approved drug, the FDA reviews and approves the routes of administration (in water, in feed, or by injection), the particular species for which it can be used, and the specific diseases that the antibiotic should be used to treat. Approved antibiotics may, in some instances, be used for different species and diseases, which is referred to as off-label or extra-label use. The FDA has specific guidelines on the circumstances under which extra-label use of drugs may occur, but in some instances, the FDA prohibits off-label use to protect human or animal health or both.[166]

As part of the drug approval process, the FDA also establishes tolerance levels: what levels of each drug's residues are acceptable in edible tissues. The tolerance levels are then set at 1,000 or 100 times below the "no-effect" level. If no safe threshold has been established, the tolerance is zero. A tolerance for any known carcinogenic substance is legally zero.

For meat, poultry, and egg products, the tolerances are set by the FDA and applied by the FSIS in its regulatory programs. The official source of tolerances for animal drugs is found in Title 21, Part 556 (21 CFR 556). The FSIS does not permit concentrations of residues in meat and poultry that exceed the published tolerances or action levels.

---

[163] *See generally*, Food & Drug Admin. Comm'r, Docket No. 2000N-1571, Final Decision on the Withdrawal of Approval of the New Animal Drug Application for Enrofloxacin in Poultry 3 (July 27, 2005).

[164] *Id.*

[165] FDA, Guidance for Industry, No. 152, Evaluating the Safety of Antimicrobial New Animal Drugs with Regard to Their Microbiological Effects on Bacteria of Human Health Concern (October 23, 2003).

[166] *FDA's Strategy on Antimicrobial Resistance Q&A, supra* note 155.

[c] Withdrawal Authority for Prior Approvals

In addition to giving the FDA the authority to approve new animal drugs, the FDCA grants the agency the authority to withdraw prior approvals.[167] In a withdrawal proceeding, the FDA has the initial burden of production. The burden is imposed by FDCA § 512(e) (1), also called the "safety clause," which gives the FDA commissioner the authority to withdraw approval for animal drugs whenever "new evidence … evaluated together with the evidence available … when the application was approved, shows that such drug is not shown to be safe for use."[168] Courts have interpreted this to mean that the FDA has the burden of initiation, with the appropriate level of evidence,[169] to show that there are serious questions as to a drug's safety.[170] To raise serious questions regarding a drug's safety, the FDA must provide a "reasonable basis from which serious questions about the ultimate safety of [a drug] may be inferred."[171] Once the FDA has met the burden of production, the burden of persuasion shifts to the drug's sponsor to show that the drug is safe.[172] The drug's safety, both in human and animal health, must be evaluated by the initial approval standards set forth in the FDCA: "adequate tests by all methods reasonably applicable."[173]

On July 28, 2005, the FDA withdrew approval for Baytril®, a drug used for poultry therapeutically, rather than for growth-promoting purposes. The FDA primarily based its decision on concerns about antibiotic-resistant illnesses in humans.[174] This decision marks the first time that the FDA withdrew approval for a livestock antibiotic primarily based on concerns about the development of antibiotic illnesses in humans.

In response to a perceived failure by the FDA to withdraw approvals of subtherapeutic uses of penicillin and tertracyclines in animal feed, the National Resources Defense Council (NRDC) and other nonprofit advocacy organizations filed in May 2011 a citizen petition seeking a court order to compel FDA to follow through on proceedings the agency initiated in 1977.[175] Plaintiffs alleged that FDA, in violation of Section 706(2) of the Administrative Procedure Act (APA), failed to comply with the agency's statutory duty to withdraw approvals of these drugs as required by the "safety clause" – FDCA § 512(e) (21 U.S.C. § 360b(e)(1)) – and as the agency proposed in 1977.[176] The US District

---

[167] 21 U.S.C. § 360b(c).

[168] 21 U.S.C. § 360b(e)(1)(B).

[169] Hess & Clark, Inc. v. FDA, 495 F.2d 975, 992 (D.C. Cir. 1974).

[170] Rhone-Poulenc, Inc. v. FDA, 636 F.2d 750, 752 (D.C. Cir. 1980).

[171] FDA, Final Decision – Enrofloxacin, *supra* note 163.

[172] *Id.* at 8.

[173] 21 U.S.C. § 360b(d)(1)(A) (stating grounds for approval or denial of animal drug application, including definition of "substantial evidence" standard by which applications must be evaluated).

[174] *See* Withdrawal of Approval of New Animal Drug Application Enrofloxacin in Poultry, Docket No. 2000N-1571 (July 28, 2005), U.S. DEP'T OF HEALTH AND HUMAN SERVICES.

[175] *See* Natural Res. Def. Council, Inc. v. U.S. Food & Drug Admin., 884 F. Supp. 2d 127 (S.D.N.Y. 2012).

[176] *See id.* at 137. The 1977 proposal to withdraw approval was based upon the recommendations of a 1970 commission composed of members from the FDA, National Institutes of Health, USDA, CDC, as well as industry members. In 1972, the commission task force concluded that: (1) subtherapeutic antibiotic use in animal feed favors the development of antibiotic resistance, (2) animals can pass these bacteria on to humans, (3) the number of bacteria resistant to multiple antibiotics has increased due to subtherapeutic use, (4) antibiotic-resistant bacteria has been found in meat, and (5) "the prevalence of antibiotic resistant bacteria in humans has increased." *Id.* The commission recommended "antibiotics used in human medicine be prohibited from use in animal feed unless they met safety criteria established by the FDA and several specific drugs, including penicillin and tetracyclines, be reserved for therapeutic use." *Id.* at 132–3.

Court for the Southern District of New York granted the plaintiffs' motion for summary judgment and held that, pursuant to 21 U.S.C. 360b(e)(1), once the FDA found that the subtherapeutic use of penicillin and tetracyclines in animal feed was unsafe to humans, the agency was statutorily obligated to withdraw approval of those uses unless drug sponsors demonstrated the safety of those drugs.[177]

The NRDC filed a second suit against the FDA alleging a violation of the FDA's procedural duty to take the citizen petitions seriously.[178] Specifically, the NRDC alleged that the FDA violated Section 706(2) of the APA (arbitrary and capricious) and FDCA § 512(e) (21 U.S.C. 360b(e)(1)) when it denied two citizen petitions requesting withdrawal of approval for subtherapeutic use of certain classes of antibiotics in food-producing animals.[179] The FDA responded the same to both petitions: (1) detailing the complex nature of the problem and the FDA's limited resources and the alternative means by which they were attempting to tackle the problem; (2) stating that withdrawal must be considered on a drug-by-drug basis; and (3) denying the requests based on the fact that no hearings had been held, based on the time and expense withdrawal would take, and based on the alternative strategy the FDA was pursuing.[180] In this second suit the US magistrate granted summary judgment relief to the plaintiff's first claim for relief – that the FDA withheld agency action in violation of both the APA (arbitrary and capricious) and the FDCA § 512(e) by failing to implement withdrawal proceedings.[181]

In July 2014, the Second Circuit reversed both the lower court decisions and held that these courts could not force FDA to restart its plan because FDA has discretion on proceedings to withdraw approval of animal drugs.[182] The Second Circuit read FDCA § 512(e) (21 U.S.C. § 360b(e)(1)(B)) to require the FDA to withdraw approval of an animal drug only "after due notice and opportunity for hearing" has been afforded and then only "if the secretary finds" that the drug is not shown to be safe. The Second Circuit found that this language more naturally refers to a finding that is issued as a result of the hearing rather than based on the agency's internal investigations of the scientific evidence. Plaintiffs had asserted that after reaching an initial conclusion that the drug is not safe, the agency is required to institute proceedings and effectuate them through a hearing, after which, if the evidence presented at the hearing sustains the finding, the secretary must issue an order of withdrawal. The Second Circuit also rejected plaintiff's alternative argument that FDA's citizen petition denials and withdrawal of the 1977 NOOHs violated the APA as arbitrary and capricious. According to the court, "the decision to whether to institute or terminate a hearing process that may lead to a finding requiring withdrawal or approval for an animal drug is a discretionary determination left to the prudent choice of the FDA." A lengthy dissent to the Second Circuit decision

---

[177] See id. at 151.

[178] See Natural Res. Def. Council, Inc. v. U.S. Food & Drug Admin., 872 F. Supp. 2d 318, 321 (S.D.N.Y. 2012).

[179] The first petition was in 1999 and requested that the FDA rescind approvals for subtherapeutic uses in livestock of any antibiotic used in human medicine' … it named several specific classes of antibiotics for which it sought withdrawal, including penicillin and tetracyclines. The 2005 petition made a similar request. Id. at 324–6.

[180] Id.

[181] Id. at 340–1.

[182] See Natural Resources Defense Council v. United States Food and Drug Administration, Docket Nos. 12–2106–cv(L), 12–3607–cv(CON) (2d Cir. July 24, 2014).

argued that the decision allows the FDA to openly declare that a particular animal drug is unsafe but refuse to withdraw approval of that drug and gives the agency discretion effectively to ignore a public petition asking it to withdraw approval from an unsafe drug.

[d] Phase Out Strategy

It has become clear that the FDA's approach to the use of antibiotics in food-producing animals rests on a two-prong approach: (1) engage drug companies to phase out voluntarily certain uses of antibiotics in animal feed and water and (2) bring the remaining uses under the oversight of a veterinarian. The FDA first outlined this approach in a 2009 guidance document addressing the "judicious use of medically important antimicrobial drugs."[183] In December 2013, the FDA issued two significant documents: a Final Guidance 213 document[184] and a Veterinary Feed Directive draft rule.[185]

The final guidance of 2013 explains how drug companies proceed to remove voluntarily growth promotion from product labels. In recognition of the rule that FDA must approve any changes to approved drug product labels, the final guidance asks the drug companies to notify the FDA of their voluntary decisions to phase out production uses of their products. The guidance clarifies that drug companies can change use claims and marketing status without submitting additional safety or effectiveness data unless they are claiming new treatment uses or changing the makeup of a drug. The guidance also provides that new drug uses must have a specific dosing duration and level for an unidentified disease and be available only to certain animals, rather than an entire herd. The final guidance anticipates that the phasing out these claims will take up to three years. FDA reaffirms in the guidance that it is not asking drug companies to withdraw the use for purposes of disease prevention. The FDA expects that veterinarians will approve the use of medically important antibiotics for "prevention purposes" only to "prevent diseases based on specific, known risk." The agency establishes the criteria to justify the use of antibiotics for disease prevention; however, it appears that veterinarians are afforded broad discretion in administering antibiotics to food animals for prevention uses.

The proposed rule on the veterinary feed directive requires veterinary feed directives (VFDs) for the use of certain medically important antibiotics in animal feed that are currently available over the counter.[186] The proposed rule contemplates the states defining what constitutes a valid veterinary-client-patient relationship for purposes of the veterinarian issuing a VFD, which conceivably could enable the issuance of a VFD without a visit on the premise by the veterinarian. The proposed rule sets a default expiration date for a VFD of six months unless otherwise indicated.

The FDA's stated goal of the two-prong strategy "is to protect public health and help curb the development of antimicrobial resistance and in turn help to reduce the number

---

[183] FDA, Guidance for Industry, No. 209, The Judicious Use of Medically Important Antimicrobial Drugs in Food-Producing Animals, Guidance for Industry (April 13, 2012).

[184] FDA, Guidance for Industry, No. 213, New Animal Drugs and New Animal Drug Combination Products Administered in or on Medicated Feed or Drinking Water of Food-Producing Animals: Recommendations for Drug Sponsors for Voluntarily Aligning Product Use Conditions with GFI #209 (December 2013).

[185] Veterinary Feed Directive, 78 Fed. Reg. 75,515 (proposed December 12, 2013) (to be codified at 21 C.F.R. pts. 514, 558).

[186] In 1996, the FDA added a new class of medications for addition to animal feeds, known as "veterinary feed directive" (VFD) drugs. 21 C.F.R. §558.3(b)(6)-(7).

of infections in humans that are difficult to treat because existing antibiotics have become ineffective."[187] Whereas FDA officials hope that the new strategy will result in significant reductions in agricultural antibiotic use, critics view the strategy as flawed because it rests on voluntary industry efforts.[188]

[e] Imported Food Tolerances

In January 2012, as part of its implementation of the Animal Drug Availability Act of 1996 (ADAA),[189] the FDA published a proposed rule to establish procedures by which a person may request that the agency establish, amend, or revoke tolerances for unapproved new animal drugs in edible portions of animals that are imported into the United States.[190] The ADAA was designed to accelerate the new animal drug and medicated feed approval process in order to increase the number of animal drugs available to the industry. The portion of the ADAA that addresses import tolerances was designed to improve international harmonization of regulatory standards on the use of animal drugs in food animals. The FDA's proposed rule would permit, once an import tolerance is established, enterprises to import animal food products that were produced using drugs not approved for use in the United States, provided that the unapproved drugs were used legally in another country and that the amount of the drug contained in the product is below the established import tolerance amount. In practical terms, under the proposed rule, if a product seeking an import tolerance has a permanent Codex MRL, the product is eligible to be reviewed by FDA, which will determine if the Codex MRL information is sufficient or if more information is necessary to determine the safety of the product for human.

[f] Mandatory Reports

Section 105 of the Animal Drug User Fee Amendments of 2008 (ADUFA)[191] amended Section 512 of the FDCA to require that sponsors of applications for new animal drugs that contain an antimicrobial active ingredient submit an annual report to the FDA, detailing the amount of each such ingredient in the drug that is sold or distributed for use in food-producing animals, including information on any distributor-labeled product. This legislation was enacted to assist the FDA in its continuing analysis of the interactions (including drug resistance), efficacy, and safety of antibiotics approved for use in both humans and food-producing animals.[192] Section 105 of ADUFA also directs the FDA to make annual summaries of the reported information publicly available. The

---

[187] FDA, *Strategy on Antimicrobial Resistance Q&A, supra* note 155.

[188] *See* Gardiner Harris, *U.S. Tightens Rules on Antibiotics Use for Livestock*, N.Y. TIMES, April 11, 2012, at A-19. *See also* Lisa Heinzerling, *The FDA's Continuing Incapacity on Livestock Antibiotics*, 33 Stanford Env. L.J. 325 (2014) (recommending the FDA to complete regulatory proceedings to withdraw approvals for the mass administration of medically important antibiotics to food-producing animals).

[189] Animal & Veterinary, Animal Drug Availability Act of 1996, Pub. L. No. 104–250, 110 Stat. 3151 (1996).

[190] Import Tolerances for Residues of Unapproved New Animal Drugs in Food, 77 Fed. Reg. 3653 (January 25, 2012)(to be codified at C.F.R. Parts 10, 20, 25, and 510).

[191] Animal Drug User Fee Amendments, 110 P.L. 316; § 105, 122 Stat. 3509, 3513 (2008).

[192] Summary Report on Antimicrobials Sold or Distributed for Use in Food-Processing Animals in 2011, U.S. FOOD & DRUG ADMIN. (February 5, 2013).

FDA report is not publicized, and it provides only the bare numbers, excluding information that would assist public understanding. The FDA's 2011 report marked the release of the third year's data (since the amendment of 2008). The report shows that penicillin and tetracyclines sold for animal use increased for the second year in a row and that use of antibiotics in animals overall also continues to rise.

[g] State Legislation

Emerging state legislation has attempted to regulate antimicrobial resistance in farm animal production.[193] Such state legislation may be subject to preemption claims. The FDCA requires that the FDA must approve the use of any new animal drug[194] and any animal feed containing a new animal drug.[195] In *Animal Legal Defense Fund Boston, Inc. v. Provimi Veal Corp.*, the plaintiff, Animal Legal Defense Fund (ALDF), a non-profit charitable corporation, sued veal producers in Massachusetts, claiming that selling veal from calves that had been served subtherapeutic levels of antibiotics violated Massachusetts consumer protection law and constituted an unfair and deceptive trade practice.[196] The court in *Provimi* dismissed ALDF's complaint, holding that ALDF's state law claims were preempted because the FDCA and FMIA occupied the field of antibiotic use in animals and are intended to prohibit states from supplementing federal requirements.[197] It is unclear what precedential weight would be afforded to *Provimi*. The federal government's policy toward the use of antimicrobial drugs in farm animal production as evidenced by Guidance #209 and #213 has changed considerably: the goal now is to phase out the use of medically important antimicrobials in food animals for production purposes and to bring the therapeutic uses of such drugs under the supervision of licensed veterinarians. Although the goal is not to remove these drugs from the marketplace, the change in government policy may render *Provimi* distinguishable.

---

[193] *See* California AB-1437, Cal. 2013–2014 Reg. Sess. (Cal. 2014) (bill would prohibit the sale in California of livestock or poultry products derived from livestock or poultry that was administered a medically important antimicrobial for nontherapeutic use; California Governor Jerry Brown vetoed compromise bill SB-835 on September 29, 2014, stating that "[m]ore needs to be done to understand and reduce our reliance on antibiotics"); Pennsylvania SB 531, S.B. 531, 2013–2014 Reg. Sess. (Pa. 2013) and HB 1195, 2013–2014 Reg. Sess. (Pa. 2013) (companion bills known as the Safe Food and Safe Families Act, would prohibit any person from administering a nontherapeutic amount of specified antimicrobials to any animal or administering any antimicrobial to any animal for purpose of growth promotion); New York S233, S.B. 233, 236th Legis. Sess. (N.Y. 2013) and A769, A.B. 769, 236th Legis. Sess. (N.Y. 2013) (companion bills would ban the nontherapeutic use of antimicrobials in animals intended for food production); Minnesota SF 1285, S.F. 1285, 88th Legis. Sess. 1st Reg. Sess. (Minn. 2013); HF 1290, H.F. 1290, 88th Legis. Sess., 1st Reg. Sess. (Minn. 2013); and SF 1638, S.F. 1638, 88th Legis. Sess., 1st Reg. Sess. (Minn. 2013) (SF 1285 and HF 1290 would prohibit both the nontherapeutic use of antimicrobials in food-producing animals and the sale within the state of food products derived from animals subject to nontherapeutic use of antimicrobial agents; SF 1638 would prohibit the sale, purchase, or use of animal feed that contains antimicrobials important to human medicine for a nontherapeutic use).

[194] 21 U.S.C. § 360(a)(1).

[195] 21 U.S.C. § 360b(a)(2).

[196] 626 F. Supp. 278 (D. Mass. 1986).

[197] *Id.* at 284. The decision in *Provimi* was affirmed by the First Circuit in an unpublished opinion. 802 F.2d 440 (1st Cir. 1986).

[h] Changes in Procurement Policies

Efforts are now emerging to use the power of government procurement to limit the use of antimicrobial drugs on animal farms. For example, in Los Angeles, the Los Angeles Food Policy Council (LAFPC) created the Good Food Purchasing Pledge (GFPP) initiative that requires a GFPP participant who purchases meat products to purchase meat products produced without the subtherapeutic use of antibiotics.[198] In 2012, the City of Los Angeles and the Los Angeles Unified School District signed the GFPP.[199] In December 2014, the Urban School Food Alliance, a coalition of the largest school districts in the United States that includes New York City, Los Angeles, Chicago, Miami-Dade, Dallas, and Orlando announced an antibiotic-free standard for companies to follow when supplying chicken products to its schools.[200] Restaurants and food service providers are also listing menu items derived from antibiotic-free meat; supermarkets are offering private label brands of "anti-microbial free" animal products; and large institutions, such as schools, hospitals, and airports are purchasing more food products derived from animals without antibiotics.[201]

[9] *Genetically Modified Food*

[a] Safety Concerns

By altering the composition of food, biotechnology generates considerable regulatory attention and scrutiny. Such altered food product is commonly referred to as genetically modified food (GM food or GMOs) or genetically engineered food (GE food). As noted in the introductory chapter, a GE food is a food whose genetic makeup has been altered through the insertion of a gene from a different organism. Notwithstanding the distinctiveness of the category of genetically modified or engineered food, the FDA considers GE foods as equivalent to conventional food.

Definition considerations aside, the composition of GE food raises food safety issues, as well as labeling, environmental, intellectual property, ethical, religious, and trade issues. The application of law to biotechnology in food is complicated by the tension between science and culture. In addition to altering the composition of food, biotechnology in food also fundamentally alters the food system itself by affecting the size of farms, the ownership of seeds and product, and the characteristics of food animals. The ensuing debate over the role of biotechnology thus translates into a larger controversy over the makeup of the food system, giving way to cultural expressions, political countenances, moral considerations, and consumer confusion. It may very well be that the continued introduction of enhanced technology into the food supply will engender further controversy. Although to a large extent, the primary controversy over the role of biotechnology in food is a systems issue that hinges on holistic attitudes toward food and agriculture, this chapter focuses strictly on food safety. (However, the background provided in this chapter will apply to the other issues.)

---

[198] Los Angeles Food Policy Council Good Food Purchasing Guidelines 18.
[199] Good Food Purchasing Program, Los Angeles Food Policy Council (2012).
[200] PR Newswire, *Nation's Largest School Districts to Procure Antibiotic-Free Chicken* (December 9, 2014).
[201] The PEW Charitable Trusts, Top Food Companies Moving Away from Overuse of Antibiotics on Industrial Farms (August 11, 2014).

GE food is pervasive in the United States. The first GE commercial food item, the Flavr Savr tomato (a slow-ripening tomato), was introduced in 1994. Although the GE tomato did not prove commercially viable, GE foods since then have become widespread. In 1996, GE soybeans, corn, and cotton became commercially available and now dominate in these food product categories.[202] Roughly 70 percent of food on grocery store shelves contains ingredients from genetically modified crops, in everything from cereals and crackers, to juice and soda, to salad dressing and sauces.[203] GE crops are likely to become more varied and pervasive. The first generation of crops was altered primarily to provide agricultural benefits, such as pest resistance and herbicide tolerance. It is hoped that next generation crops may be manipulated to create more nutritious foods, and to produce plants that grow nonfood products, such as pharmaceuticals, vaccines, vitamins, and industrial compounds.[204]

The touted potential upside to food biotechnology is that GE food may help ameliorate some of the greatest crises currently facing the United States and the world, including hunger and malnutrition,[205] environmental degradation, and widespread disease. The projected downsides to food biotechnology include health concerns of new allergens or toxins, widespread environmental and ecological damage resulting from the introduction of invasive species or the loss of biodiversity, and unforeseen injury arising from the unintentional release of pharmaceuticals or industrial compounds into the food supply. Critics of biotechnology, as well as other forms of food technology, applied to food urge a precautionary approach. The rationale is that a lack of evidence of harm should not be interpreted as an affirmation of the safety of GE products.[206]

Advocates and defenders of GE food point out that "[t]here is no reliable evidence that ingredients made from current GE crops pose any health risk whatsoever."[207] The World Health Organization (WHO), however, has identified four food safety concerns of consuming GE food: allergenicity, toxicity, antibiotic resistance, and outcrossing.[208] Because allergenic proteins can be transferred by genetic modification from one organism to another, the introduction of novel genetic material creates the possibility of introducing an allergen into a previously nonallergenic product.[209] Moreover, where genetic engineering involves inserting genes from sources that historically have not been human food,

---

[202] *See Adoption of Genetically Engineered Crops in the U.S.*, ECON. RESEARCH SERVICE, U.S. DEP'T OF AGRIC. (July 14, 2013, last update) (statistics for corn, soybean, and upland cotton varieties in the US).

[203] Gregory N. Mandel, *Gaps, Inexperience, Inconsistencies, and Overlaps: Crisis in the Regulation of Genetically Modified Plants and Animals*, 45 WM. & MARY L. REV, 2167, 2177 (2004).

[204] *Id.*

[205] Increasing farm productivity and alleviating hunger is generally recognized as an often cited myth of the benefits of GE food. Gregg Jaffee, *What You Need to Know About Genetically Engineered Food*, THE ATLANTIC (February 7, 2013).

[206] Comment from Consumer's Union to FDA (October 6, 2006) ("Lack of evidence of harm should not be a proxy for reasonable certainty of safety") (on file with author).

[207] Jaffe, *supra* note 205. It is worth noting, however, a few notable examples of the detrimental effects of a rush to technology: dangerous pesticides like DDT were initially thought to be safe when they entered the market in the 1950s and 1960s, whereas regulations addressing their environmental and human health impacts (e.g., the Toxic Substances Control Act of 1976) did not emerge until at least a decade later, after the damage was already done. Asbestos is another example of the potentially disastrous results that insufficient safety studies and delayed regulation can cause.

[208] *See 20 Questions on Genetically Modified Foods*, WORLD HEALTH ORGANIZATION.

[209] Premarket Notice Concerning Bioengineered Foods, 66 Fed. Reg. 4706, 4709 (January 18, 2001).

the potential allergenicity of the GE product is likely unforeseeable.[210] Genetic modification also raises the possible introduction of new toxins or increases in the amounts of naturally occurring toxins.[211] The transfer of antibiotic resistance is where antibiotic resistance genes, used in creating GE food, are transferred to the consumer.[212] Although the probability of transfer is low, a joint WHO-FAO expert panel has encouraged the use of biotechnology on food without antibiotic resistance genes. Finally, the indirect risk of outcrossing, or crop contamination, is where the inadvertent transfer of genes from GE plants into conventional crops may introduce novel genes not approved for human consumption into the food supply and trigger further risks for allergenicity and toxicity.[213]

In addition to the scientific merits behind the safety of GE foods, there is the separate issue of consumer trust in the safety of GE foods. US consumers are more accepting of GE foods than are consumers in other countries; however, surveys show that the level of trust among the general public in GE foods remains low.[214] It may be that unease among consumers, as a result of regulatory oversight insufficient enough to build trust with consumers that GE foods are safe, healthy, and environmentally viable, will prevent biotechnology from achieving its full potential (the environmental impacts associated with GE foods – pesticide and herbicide tolerance and loss of biodiversity – are addressed in Chapter 6).

[b] Coordinated Regulatory Approach to Safety

No single statute and no single federal agency regulate the safety of GE food. Instead, the safety of GE food products rests on a coordinated, risk-based system comprising three federal agencies: the FDA, EPA, and USDA.[215] The FDA is responsible for food safety issues surrounding GE plants and animals; the EPA is responsible for the health and environmental effects of pest-protected plants; and the USDA is responsible for the effects of GE plants on other plants and animals.

Owing to the overlapping responsibilities and concerns of potential inconsistencies in the agencies' approach to GE regulation, the Reagan administration expressly created the Domestic Policy Council Working Group to draft a framework to regulate biotechnology.[216] The result was the 1986 promulgation of the "Coordinated Framework for Regulation of Biotechnology" by the White House Office of Science and Technology Policy (OSTP). The objective of the Coordinated Framework was to provide a "comprehensive federal regulatory policy for ensuring the safety of biotechnology research and products."[217] This Coordinated Framework is an administrative creation and is not legally binding.

---

[210] *Animal Biotechnology: Science-Based Concerns*, NAT'L RESEARCH COUNCIL (2002).

[211] See Nancy Podevin & Patrick du Jardin, *Possible Consequences of the Overlap between the CaMV 35S Promoter Regions in Plant Transformation Vectors used and the Viral Gene VI in Transgenic Plants*, GM CROPS AND FOODS (August 15, 2012).

[212] WHO, 20 *Questions, supra* note 208.

[213] *See id.*

[214] PUBLIC SENTIMENT ABOUT GENETICALLY MODIFIED FOOD, PEW INITIATIVE ON FOOD AND BIOTECHNOLOGY (2007).

[215] See Coordinated Framework for Regulation of Biotechnology, 51 Fed. Reg. 23302 (June 26, 1986).

[216] See, GUIDE TO U.S. REGULATION OF GENETICALLY MODIFIED FOOD AND AGRICULTURAL BIOTECHNOLOGY PRODUCTS 5, PEW INITIATIVE ON FOOD AND BIOTECHNOLOGY (2001).

[217] Coordinated Framework, *supra* note 215 at 2330.

At the time the Coordinated Framework was established, in 1986, there was considerable debate as to whether biotechnology regulation would require entirely new laws and a new agency specifically dedicated to its regulation. The Coordinated Framework rejected that approach: it reflected a belief that food biotechnology could be adequately regulated through the existing federal infrastructure and by adapting existing laws to new technologies.[218] The premise for this decision was an assessment that the process of biotechnology was not inherently risky, and therefore, only the products of biotechnology, not the process itself, required oversight. On this basis, the Coordinated Framework determined that existing laws and regulations were sufficient to handle the products of biotechnology.[219] The decision was also partly based on a desire to avoid regulations that could hamper the development of a promising and fledging industry.[220] The three-prong agency framework has seen little change since its introduction.

A fair question is whether the Coordinated Framework oversimplifies the regulation of biotechnology. It instructs the agencies – the FDA, USDA, and EPA – to rely on laws that were enacted long before rDNA genetic engineering was even scientifically conceivable. As a result, agencies must interpret old statutes and stretch old legal frameworks in order to incorporate new biotech food products.[221]

[c] FDA 1992 GRAS Strategy

The FDA's role under the Coordinated Framework and pursuant to Section 402 of the FDCA is to ensure the safety of GE foods introduced into the market. The strategy employed by the agency to meet this objective relies on a unique consultative process with sponsors of GE food. The strategy originated in 1992, when on May 29, the FDA published a *Statement of Policy: Foods Derived from New Plant Varieties* (New Plant Policy), announcing that it would presume all GE foods, produced through modern rDNA techniques, were GRAS under the FDCA, and therefore not subject to regulation as food additives. The FDA's 1992 policy does not require companies to submit their products for review to the FDA prior to marketing. Rather, the agency considered the objective characteristics and intended uses of the food or its components.[222] More specifically, the FDA has stated that "substances intentionally added to food via biotechnology to date have been well-characterized proteins and fats, and are functionally very similar to other proteins and fats that are commonly and safely consumed in the diet and thus are presumptively GRAS" and, therefore, not subject to premarket review as food additives. FDA made this decision based on its determination that "[a]ny genetic modification technique has the potential to alter the composition of food in a manner relevant to food safety, although, based on experience, the likelihood of a safety hazard is typically very low."[223]

---

[218] Neil A. Belson, *US Regulation of Agricultural Biotechnology: An Overview*, J. of 3 Agrobiotechnology Mgmt & Econ.AgBioForum, (2000).

[219] Coordinated Framework, *supra* note 215 *at* 23302–3.

[220] *Id.*

[221] *See* Issues in the Regulation of Genetically Engineered Plants and Animals 10–11, Pew Initiative on Food and Biotechnology (2004).

[222] Statement of Policy – Foods Derived from New Plant Varieties, 57 Fed. Reg. 22984, 22986 (May 29, 1992).

[223] *Id.*

The Coordinated Framework also marked the beginning of a construct that has been used to regulate genetically engineered products for food safety and labeling purposes – the product/process distinction. This distinction places a regulatory emphasis on the characteristics and unique features of genetically modified products, rather than on their means of production. This standard, known as "substantial equivalence," looks only at the final product and does not address its source or the risks involved in the process of production. In other words, according to the substantial equivalence theory, as long as a genetically engineered product is substantially the same as its conventional equivalent, it is not subject to separate regulation.[224] Substantial equivalence has never been legally defined or provided with a legal standard for implementation.[225]

The practical effect of the substantial equivalence doctrine, which permeated the 1992 guidelines, is to allow manufacturers of GE foods to avoid any safety testing beyond that necessary to demonstrate substantial equivalence. The legal rationale for this position is that the process used to create the new variety of food, be it genetic engineering or traditional plant breeding techniques, is simply not material if the end products are substantially equivalent.

Notwithstanding the substantial equivalence doctrine, the FDA has recommended that food enterprises voluntarily consult with the agency before marketing GE foods.[226] The FDA published guidance documents in 1996[227] and again in 2006[228] describing the procedures for such consultations.[229] In this voluntary consultation process, the FDA requests that firms provide the agency a summary of their food (or feed) safety and nutritional assessment and discuss these results with FDA scientists prior to beginning commercial distribution. FDA scientists will review this material to verify that safety concerns have been addressed. Specifically, the FDA seeks to evaluate whether the GE food contains no new allergens, no increased levels of natural toxicants, and no reduction of important nutrients. The 2006 guidance document encourages the developer of a novel GE food product to submit an "early food safety evaluation" when it meets with the FDA.[230] This consultation process considers only the safety risks to humans from consumption; it does not consider environmental and ecological risks. In addition, the FDA does not evaluate the safety of transgenic plant-pesticides, such as Bt toxins or the genetic material responsible for their production, which is considered to be the EPA's responsibility under FIFRA. The FDA does not formally approve an application or conclude whether the GE food is safe or not. Instead, the agency issues a memorandum summarizing the GE food's features and how they may affect safety concerns. In line

---

[224] Although organic products are an exception to this rule because they cannot be genetically modified under the USDA National Organic Program 7 C.F.R. § 205.201.

[225] Debra M. Strauss, *The International Regulation of Genetically Modified Organisms: Importing Caution into the US Food Supply*, 61 Food & Drug L.J. 167, 174 (2006).

[226] *See* Statement of Policy, *supra* note 222, at 22,991.

[227] FDA, Guidance on Consultation Procedures: Foods Derived From New Plant Varieties (October 1997, revised).

[228] FDA, Guidance for Industry: Recommendations for the Early Food Safety Evaluation of New Non-Pesticidal Proteins Produced by New Plant Varieties Intended for Food Use (June 2006).

[229] In 1995, the FDA conducted a safety review of the first GE food product to be commercialized: the Flavr Savr tomato. This review was conducted at the request of the manufacturer, who was attempting to build confidence. *See* John Henkel, *Genetic Engineering: Fast Forwarding to Future Foods*, FDA Consumer Mag. (April 1995).

[230] *Id.*

with substantial equivalence standards, the memorandum indicates whether the new food is materially different in composition from the unmodified version of the same food. Even though the consultation with FDA is strictly voluntary, there are strong commercial pressures for a developer of a new GE food to voluntarily consult with the FDA, such as increased market acceptance as well as increased protection against potential future legal liability.[231]

On January 18, 2001, the FDA published a proposed rule to replace voluntary consultations with mandatory premarket consultations.[232] The FDA's proposed new regulations would require developers of GE foods to provide a "premarket biotechnology notice" to the FDA at least 120 days prior to marketing such products. The information required in the notice generally would be similar to that provided in present consultations. However, the information submitted would be publicly available, except for information designated as confidential business information. Within 120 days of the filing of the premarket biotechnology notice, the FDA would respond with its conclusion about the regulatory status of the proposed GE food.[233] To date, this rule has yet to be enacted. Nevertheless, as of May 2013, the FDA reports to having completing 96 consultations on GE crops.[234] A complete list of all completed consultations and responses from the FDA are housed in a published inventory on a database maintained by the agency.[235]

[d] Court Challenge to FDA 1992 Policy

In September 2000, in the case of *Alliance for Bio-Integrity v. Shalala*, a federal court dismissed a challenge to the FDA's 1992 policy on genetically engineered foods.[236] The case had been filed by a coalition of public interest and environmental groups, including scientists concerned about the safety and marketing of GE foods, against the FDA and their policies regarding such foods. Plaintiffs challenged the New Plant Policy on several grounds, including the FDA's presumption that GE foods are GRAS. The court found, given that the existing evaluative framework was established when Congress passed the FAA in 1958, which obviously could not account for GE food technologies, the FDA's interpretation was a permissible construction.[237] The court validated the FDA's interpretation, claiming that in order for a substance to be GRAS, it must meet two criteria: it must be supported by technical evidence of safety, usually in the form of published scientific studies, and that this technical evidence must be generally known and accepted in the scientific community.[238] The court held that plaintiffs failed to provide sufficient evidence that the GRAS presumption was inconsistent with the statutory requirements.[239] In other words, the court upheld the FDA's position that GE foods do not require

---

[231] Belson, *supra* note 218.
[232] Premarket Notice Concerning Bioengineered Foods, 66 Fed. Reg. 4706 (January 18, 2001).
[233] *Id.*
[234] *See FDA's Role in Regulating Safety of GE Foods*, UPDATE, U.S. FOOD & DRUG ADMIN. (May 2013).
[235] *See* Biotechnology Consultations on Food from GE Plant Varieties, U.S. FOOD & DRUG ADMIN. (March 20, 2015, last update).
[236] See Alliance for Bio-Integrity v. Shalala, 116 F. Supp.2d 166 (D.C. Cir. 2000).
[237] *Id.* at 177.
[238] *Id. See also* 21 C.F.R. § 170.30(a–b); 62 Fed. Reg. 18937, 18940 (April 17, 1997).
[239] *Alliance*, 116 F. Supp.2d at 177–8.

premarket review, approval of a food additive petition, or special labeling based on the process used to develop them.

Although the case has garnered much attention for its support of the FDA's presumption of GRAS status for GE foods, the reach of the case should not be overstated. The court did not rule that GE foods have actually been shown to be safe or that the FDA could justifiably continue to presume that GE foods are safe. The court's decision was limited to the particular exercise of discretion made by the FDA in its 1992 statement.

[e] Starlink Litigation: Contamination Test Case

The FDA's regulatory regime for GE food was further tested in a GE contamination case that resulted in *StarLink Corn*.[240] This case demonstrates the workings of the coordinate framework for the regulation of GE food and the potential market and legal consequences of contamination.[241]

Aventis distributed genetically engineered corn seeds (sold under the name "StarLink"), which produced Cry9C protein, a substance known to be toxic to certain insects.[242] Per the Coordinated Framework for the regulation of biotech food, Aventis applied to register StarLink with the EPA, which is responsible for regulating insecticides under FIFRA.[243] Because of EPA concerns over the similarities between certain characteristics of Cry9C and a known human allergen, in May 1998, Aventis was granted only limited registration (known as a "split" registration) that did not permit the company to use StarLink for human consumption;[244] instead, StarLink could only be used "for such purposes as animal feed, ethanol production, and seed increase."[245] StarLink corn was not approved for human consumption because its transgenic genes expressed a protein containing some attributes of known human allergens;[246] because the FDA determined that no safe threshold could be established, the agency denied the request to establish a tolerance level.[247] These proteins had never been part of the human diet before, and therefore, it was unknown whether they would cause severe and potentially life-threatening allergic reactions in some humans.

Consequently, segregating StarLink corn from non-StarLink corn, which was deemed fit for consumption, became of utmost importance.[248] In light of the typical commingling of corn in the food system via the gathering, storing, and shipping of corn from thousands of farms and local, regional, and terminal grain elevators, the EPA required special procedures to prevent Starlink from getting into the human food chain. For example, the EPA imposed isolation distances for planting (between StarLink and non-StarLink corn), so

---

[240] In re StarLink, Corn Products Liab. Litig., 212 F. Supp.2d 828 (N.D. Ill. 2002).

[241] Alejandro E. Segarra & Jean M. Rawson, CRS Report for Congress, StarLink Corn Controversy: Background (January 10, 2001).

[242] In re StarLink, 212 F. Supp.2d at 833–4.

[243] *Id.* at 834.

[244] Giving split registration is a common practice with conventional chemical pesticides, as each registration (or tolerance) specifies the crops on which use is allowed. Segarra & Rawson, CRS Report, *supra* note 241 at 3.

[245] *Id.*; In re Starlink, 212 F. Supp.2d at 833–4.

[246] *Id.* at 834.

[247] *See* National Research Council, Genetically Modified pest-protected plants: Science and Regulation (2000). *See also* In re Starlink Corn, 212 F. Supp. 2d at 834–5.

[248] *In* re Starlink Corn, 212 F.Supp. 2d at 834–5.

that cross-fertilization would not occur.[249] It also introduced channeling requirements so that StarLink would be prevented from entering the human food chain.[250] Despite the agency's preventative procedures, after being distributed throughout the United States from approximately May 1998 through October 2000,[251] StarLink was detected in various food products, most notably in Kraft Foods' Taco Bell-brand taco shells sold in grocery stores. Many food and grain recalls as well as suits or claims by various entities that handled, processed, or sold corn grain or food products resulted.[252] More specifically, following numerous reports that human food products had tested positive for Cry9C, Kraft and numerous manufacturers issued recalls for corn products.[253] In subsequent litigation brought by the producers of non-StarLink corn, the court found that the plaintiffs' allegations presented viable claims for harm, which entitled the plaintiffs to "compensation for certain economic losses" provided that they could establish "direct harm to their own property."[254]

The StarLink ruling was significant for a couple of notable reasons, in addition to showcasing the Coordinated Framework. First, there was no indication in the court's opinion that it's reasoning was based on the GMO corn's potential harm to human health. The harm outlined was economic rather than personal injury. Second, *StarLink* caused a ripple effect throughout the international community, causing widespread concern for the unintentional comingling of GE food with conventional food.[255]

[f] Genetically Modified Animals

There is no specific legislation that expressly regulates animal breeding, including of animals and animal-derived products that enter the food supply. Hence, like the FDA's regulatory authority over GE food, the agency regulates GE animals under the Coordinated Framework and FDCA. In 2009, the FDA issued guidance where it claims primary regulatory authority over GE animals by virtue of its "new animal drug" authority under the FDCA.[256] The statutory provisions allow the FDA to evaluate new animal drugs' safety with "reference to the health of man or animal,"[257] which has been interpreted to include environmental effects that impact the health of humans or animals other than those intended to receive the new drug.[258] Thus, the development of GE animals is subject to the New Animal Drug Application (NADA). Under NADA, the applicant must demonstrate via sufficient testing a reasonable certainty that no harm will come to

---

[249] *Id.* at 835.

[250] *Id.* (explaining channeling requirements).

[251] *Id.* at 834.

[252] Peter L. Resnik et al., *Food Fights: Genetically Modified Food and the Law*, 36 THE BRIEF 1, 1 (2007).

[253] *In re* StarLink, 212 F. Supp. 2d at 835.

[254] *Id.* at 842–3.

[255] *Id.* at 835.

[256] *See* FDA, Guidance for Industry No. 187, Regulation of Genetically Engineered Animals Containing Heritable Recombinant DNA Constructs (January 15, 2009). When the FDA released Guidance No. 187, it received roughly 29,000 comments during the sixty-day comment period, the vast majority of which were critical of the proposed regulatory process for GE animals. Response to Public Comments, U.S. FOOD & DRUG ADMIN. (May 23, 2011).

[257] 21 U.S.C. § 321(u).

[258] CASE STUDY NO. I: GROWTH-ENHANCED SALMON, OFFICE OF SCI. & TECH. POL'Y (OSTP) 13–14, EXECUTIVE OFFICE OF THE PRESIDENT 13–14 (2001).

individuals who use the product under its prescribed conditions. Assuming that the FDA is satisfied with the demonstration, the FDA will issue a permit, enabling the developer to commercialize the product.[259]

Whereas the regulatory framework presumes the safety of food already in the food supply (or substantial equivalence), thus obviating the need for the FDA to pre-approve GE food, in contrast, the FDCA does not afford new animal drugs the presumption of safety. These products cannot be sold until the FDA determines the safety of the additive or the safety and efficacy of the new-animal drug. FDA evaluations are set against a backdrop, in which modern animal biotechnology develops in conjunction with the public experience of plant biotechnology, which often engenders controversy. The debate may be a continuing feature of animal biotechnology development, not least because of the closer connection between humans and some animals and the belief that techniques developed for animals are only a step away from application to humans.[260]

Unlike GE crops, a GE animal has yet to be approved by the FDA for human consumption. The FDA has appeared, however, posed to approve the first GE animal: an Atlantic salmon modified with genetic material from the Chinook salmon and the ocean pout.[261] The GE salmon, named AquAdvantage salmon, has been developed to grow twice as fast as conventional, non-GE salmon.[262] The AquAdvantage salmon is created by inserting genes from an ocean pout (an eel-like fish, distantly related to salmon) into growth hormone genes from a Chinook salmon, and then inserting this altered growth hormone gene into an Atlantic salmon.[263] If approved by the FDA, AquaBounty plans to sell its GE salmon eggs to aquaculture companies, where the salmon would grow for the purpose of being sold for human consumption.[264]

The approval process has been lengthy. In 1995, AquaBounty submitted preliminary data on its GE salmon to the FDA. Over the years, the company continued to gather and submit information on ten generations of GE salmon, ultimately completing in 2009 its submission to the FDA. The CVM convened its Veterinary Medicine Advisory Committee in September 2010 to obtain independent expert advice on the GE salmon and to hold a public hearing to gather detailed information about the salmon.

As GE salmon becomes closer to being approved, the process has not been exempt from the usual debate surrounding genetically modified food. As is typical with issues of food biotechnology, disagreement over the potential gains of GE salmon (economic, societal, and sustainability benefits) and potential risks (food safety, animal health, and environmental harms) are compounded by disagreement as to whether the FDA

---

[259] *Id.* at 41.
[260] Geoffrey S. Becker & Tadlock Cowan, Cong. Research Serv., RL33334, Biotechnology in Animal Agriculture: Status and Current Issues, (2009).
[261] Les Blumenthal, *Company Says FDA Is Nearing Decision on Genetically Engineered Atlantic Salmon*, Washington Post, August 2, 2010.
[262] *See generally* Briefing Packet, AquAdvantage Salmon, 1, 8 U.S. Food & Drug Admin. Ctr. for Veterinary Medicine (September 20, 2010).
[263] Henry C. Clifford, AquaBounty Technologies, Pioneering Application for a Genetically Modified Food Animal, International Society for Biosafety Research (August 20, 2012).
[264] Michael Bennett Homer, *Frankenfish ... It's What's for Dinner: The FDA, Genetically Engineered Salmon, and the Flawed Regulation of Biotechnology*, 45 Colum. J.L. & Soc. Probs. 83, 107 (2011).

evaluation of the potential risks is adequate or whether the FDA's approval delay under-mines the agency's credibility and American competitiveness.[265] Meanwhile, legislators continue to introduce bills that are designed to require labeling of GE salmon or to ban the sale of GE salmon.[266]

[10] Animal Cloning

[a] FDA Presumption of Safety

The FDA defines animal cloning as "a complete process that lets one exactly copy the genetic, or inherited, traits of an animal."[267] While genetic engineering of animals essen-tially alters an animal's DNA by inserting the DNA of another animal to form a new version of creature, cloned animals are created as exact genetic copies of their model animals, with no significant changes or alterations to their DNA strands.[268] To produce a clone, the nucleus of a donor egg is removed and replaced with the DNA of a cow, pig, or other animal that is being reproduced. Cloning is the newest and most complex form of assisted reproductive technology.[269]

The first mammal cloned from an adult cell was Dolly the sheep in 1996. The pro-cess that created Dolly is called somatic cell nuclear transfer (SCNT). Since then, many other species have been cloned using SCNT, including cow, pig, goat, horse, mule, dog, cat, rabbit, mouse, rat, deer, buffalo, camel, and ferret. Today, the existence of approxi-mately several thousand farm animal clones are estimated worldwide.

The difference in regulation between a cloned animal and a GE animal is that clones are covered by FDA's January 2008 risk assessment and guidance – as just clones, they are considered copies of individual conventionally bred animals because they do not contain any rDNA constructs. What can be confusing is that an animal clone can be genetically engineered (i.e., have an rDNA construct introduced into it), and a GE ani-mal can be reproduced by cloning. The 2009 FDA guidance in 2009 covers GE animals, regardless of whether they were reproduced by cloning, but does not cover animal clones that do not contain an rDNA construct.[270]

Animal cloning elicits strong reaction over concerns of food safety, as well as ecologi-cal, animal health, moral, and ethical concerns. The FDA does not consider the ethics of animal cloning: it expressly states that its charge is limited to concerns about food safety.[271] Nevertheless, the FDA gives little credence to food safety concerns of cloning.

---

[265] See Timothy Schwab, *Is FDA Ready to Regulate the World's First Biotech Food Animal?*, 3 FDLI's FOOD AND POL'Y FORUM (July 24, 2013); Allison L. Van Eenennaam et al., *Is Unaccountable Regulatory Delay and Political Interference Undermining the FDA and Hurting American Competitiveness?*, 3 FDLI's FOOD AND POL'Y FORUM (July 24, 2013).

[266] See, e.g., S. Amdt. 2108 to S. 3187 (Food and Drug Administration Safety and Innovation Act, Pub. L. No. 112–144, 126 Stat. 993 (2012)) (this Senate Bill Amendment was designed to require mandatory participation of the National Oceanic and Atmospheric Administration in the FDA's regulatory process).

[267] A Primer on Cloning and Its Use in Livestock Operations, U.S. FOOD & DRUG ADMIN. (April 25, 2013).

[268] *Id.*

[269] For centuries, livestock breeders have used reproductive technologies, including artificial insemination, and more recently, embryo transfer, embryo splitting, and in vitro fertilization. *See id.*

[270] See *General Q&A Genetically Engineered Animals*, U.S. FOOD DRUG & ADMIN. (June 10, 2014).

[271] *Id.*

In October 2003, the FDA released an executive summary of its assessment of the safety of animal cloning.[272] The agency concluded that the risks somatic cell cloning posed to animals were not "qualitatively different from those encountered by animals involved in modern agricultural practices ... although the frequency of the risks appears to be increased in some species during the early portions of the life cycle of animal clones."[273] In addressing the food consumption risks that clones pose to humans, the FDA report emphasized that information on the composition of clone-based meat or milk is extremely limited and concluded, based on the current limited information used in risk analysis, that food consumption risks were negligible. The report noted that the current weight of evidence suggests that there are no biological reasons, either based on underlying scientific assumptions or empirical studies, to indicate that consumption of edible products from clones of cattle, pigs, sheep or goats poses a greater risk than consumption of those products from their nonclone counterparts. The report also found that the one study of the composition of milk from bovine clones does not indicate any food safety concerns.[274]

In December 2006, the FDA issued a draft guidance document alongside a risk assessment and risk management plan for public comment.[275] The 2006 draft guidance essentially elaborated on its previous position that the FDA planned to regulate food products containing cloned animals with no additional precautions. The rationalization was that since cloned animals were molecularly identical to noncloned members of their species, they were the same and no additional regulatory action was needed.[276] The public's reaction to the draft guidance was strong. Consumer groups and traditional agricultural stakeholders were concerned about the safety and viability of the new technology. Consumers, in particular, remained skeptical of the idea of eating clones. Many had an instant negative reaction that researchers termed the "yuck factor."[277] Consumers voiced, in a number of recent studies, strong aversion to all types of cloned foods. For example, a 2005 study by the International Food Information Council showed that 63 percent of Americans would be unlikely to buy meat, milk, and eggs from cloned animals even if the FDA determined they were safe.[278]

Two years later, in January 2008, the FDA released its final determinations regarding the safety of food products derived from cloned animals and their progeny.[279] In the form of a 968-page risk assessment report filled with scientific data on cloned animals and their progeny, the FDA concluded that (1) cloning poses no unique risks to animal

---

[272] *See* Press Release, U.S. Food & Drug Admin. FDA Issues Draft Executive Summary of Its Assessment of Safety of Animal Cloning; Current Voluntary Moratorium on Releasing Animal Clones Remains in Effect (October 31, 2003).

[273] Animal Cloning: A Risk Assessment, Draft Executive Summary 1, 5, U.S. Food & Drug Admin. (October 21, 2003).

[274] *Id.* at 10.

[275] *See* Press Release, U.S. Food & Drug Admin., FDA Issues Draft Documents on the Safety of Animal Clones (December 28, 2006).

[276] FDA, Draft Guidance No. 179, Use of Edible Products from Animal Clones or their Progeny for Human Food or Animal Food (December 28, 2006).

[277] Press Release, FDA, *supra* note 275. The comment period closed on April 2, 2007. *Id.*

[278] *See, e.g.,* Justin Gillis, *Clone-Generated Milk, Meat May Be Approved,* Washington Post, October 6, 2005.

[279] FDA, Guidance for Industry No. 179, Use of Animal Clones and Clone Progeny for Human Food and Animal Feed, (January 15, 2008).

health, compared to the risks found with other reproduction methods, including natural mating; (2) the composition of food products from cattle, swine, and goat clones, or the offspring of any animal clones, is no different from that of conventionally bred animals; and (3) there are no additional risks to people eating food from cattle, swine, and goat clones or the offspring of any animal clones traditionally consumed as food.[280] The agency noted, however, that due to the lack of information on clone species other than cow, goat, and pig (i.e., sheep), other clone species should not enter the human food supply.[281]

Thus, the approach taken by the FDA focuses on monitoring cloning methods, rather than taking a proactive testing of food safety by monitoring the food products themselves.[282] The premise in the Coordinated Framework's regulatory scheme is extended to animal cloning: the FDA has found that like GM products, clones are presumed safe because "[c]loning doesn't put any new substance into an animal, so there's no 'new' substance to test."[283]

Further buttressing the FDA's conclusions is a report issued by the European Food Safety Authority (EFSA) in July 2012. Upon request by the European Commission (EC), the EFSA published a report that purported to take into consideration the latest research on animal clones and their offspring for food production purposes. With respect to food safety, the report found no indications that differences exist between food products derived from healthy clones or their offspring – in particular milk and meat – from those of healthy, conventionally bred animals. Nevertheless, EFSA recognizes that animal health and welfare concerns continue to be associated with this technology.[284]

While the FDA continues to treat animal clones the same as conventional food, the argument has been made that because a clone is an entirely new biological entity, it should be tested as such, and not merely compared to its conventional counterpart. Hence, the question is not whether the clone is distinguishable from its conventional counterpart, but what the risk is to humans eating cloned animal products.[285] Despite the FDA's approval, some in the United States remain concerned about the safety of animal cloning and they advocate a cautious approach to the commercialization of such products.[286]

[b] Voluntary Moratorium

Notwithstanding the 2008 FDA report that determined that food from cattle, swine, and goat clones were safe to eat, a voluntary moratorium has remained intact since June 2001, when the FDA's CVM issued a voluntary request to producers of livestock clones not to introduce food from clones or their progeny into commerce until the agency assessed

---

[280] *Animal Cloning and Food Safety*, U.S. Food & Drug Admin. (January 2008).
[281] *Id.*
[282] Jennifer E.F. Butler, *Cloned Animal Products in the Human Food Chain: FDA Should Protect American Consumers*, 64 Food & Drug L.J. 473, 481 (2009).
[283] *Animal Cloning and Food Safety, supra* note 280.
[284] *EFSA Reiterates Safety of Derived Food Products but Underscores Animal Health & Welfare Issues*, European Food Safety Agency (July 5, 2012).
[285] Butler, *supra* note 282, at 496.
[286] Becker & Cowan, *supra* note 260.

whether production of cattle, swine, sheep, or goats by somatic cell nuclear transfer (SCNT) posed any unique risks to the animal(s) involved in the process, humans, or other animals by consuming food from those animals, compared with any other assisted reproductive technology currently in use.

USDA supported the moratorium and issued the following statement:

> USDA will join with technology providers, producers, processors, retailers and domestic and international customers to facilitate the marketing of meat and milk from clones. We'll be working closely with stakeholders to ensure a smooth and seamless transition into the marketplace for these products ... the USDA has encouraged technology providers to maintain their voluntary moratorium on sending milk and meat from animal clones into the food supply during this transition time.[287]

[11] *Irradiation*

[a] Food Safety Function

Food irradiation exposes food products to ionizing radiation.[288] Irradiation is considered a food additive because it is a process that "can affect the characteristics of the food."[289] There are many different foods that are currently approved for and treated with irradiation, including poultry, beef, spices, many fruits and vegetables, pork, shell eggs, molluscan shellfish (oysters, clams, mussels, and scallops), lettuce, spinach, and seeds for sprouting (e.g., alfalfa sprouts).[290] Even with the possibility of a broader application of irradiation, consumers traditionally are reluctant to accept food irradiation.[291]

The FDA cites five purposes for irradiation: the prevention of foodborne illness, extended shelf life of foods, destruction of insects in and on tropical fruits imported into the United States, delaying of sprouting and ripening of fruit, and sterilization of foods to enable storage without refrigeration. Indeed, irradiation can reduce the pathogens that account for many of the most severe foodborne illness. Many experts believe that irradiation can effectively ensure the safety of the food against pathogens once in the food supply.[292] Yet others have expressed concerns that irradiation has negative health effects.[293] A major concern is that although irradiation may reduce unwanted pathogens in food, it does not address the underlying problem – the unsanitary food production that introduces those pathogens.[294] In fact, some argue that irradiation creates a disincentive for producers to worry about contamination prevention, since it allows them to mask the unsanitary practices of factory farms.[295]

---

[287] *Statement on FDA Risk Assessment on Animal Clones*, U.S. Dep't Of Agric. (January 15, 2008).

[288] U.S. Gov't Accountability Office, GAO-10-309R, Federal Oversight of Food Irradiation (February 16, 2010).

[289] Presentation, George H. Pauli, U.S. Regulatory Requirements for Irradiating Foods (May 1999).

[290] *See* Ionizing Radiation for the Treatment of Food, 21 C.F.R. § 179.26 (2005); *Food Irradiation: What You Need to Know*, U.S. Food & Drug Admin. (March 7, 2014).

[291] Michael Hanson, Comments of Consumers Union on the Food and Drug Administration's Docket no. 2005N-0272, Irradiation in the Production, Processing and Handling of Food (July 3, 2007).

[292] FDA, *Food Irradiation: What You Need to Know, supra* note 290.

[293] *See, e.g., About Food Irradiation*, The Center for Food Safety.

[294] Marion Nestle, New Technologies Supplant Old Precautions with High-Tech Shortcuts, in Food: Current Controversies 102, 107 (2008).

[295] *Irradiation and Food Borne Illness*, The Center for Food Safety.

Irradiation of food in the United States began in 1921, when the USDA suggested that X-rays be used to inactivate trichinae in pork. However, it was not until the 1950s that the increased availability of suitable isotopes, under President D. Eisenhower's Atoms for Peace program, triggered major international collaboration on food irradiation. Since then, irradiation has caught global attention. After international investigation and the development of irradiation potential, Codex adopted a code of practice for the use of irradiation on food products.[296] In 1994, the WHO stated that "irradiated food produced in accordance with good manufacturing practice can be considered safe and nutritionally adequate."[297]

According to the International Atomic Energy Agency, fifty-six countries currently allow the irradiation of food products. The safety of irradiated foods has been extensively studied and has been endorsed by the WHO, CDC, USDA, and FDA. The GAO has also urged the use of irradiation to reduce foodborne illness.[298] Despite regulatory approval, the amount of food irradiated has been relatively steady or even slowed since 2000. This may be explained by the low acceptance of irradiated food, which has been documented and is a matter of concern for the GAO.[299]

[b] Dosage Limits: Meat and Poultry

In November 2012, in response to petitions filed by the USDA's FSIS in December 1999, the FDA amended food additive regulations to increase the maximum allowable dosage of irradiation in meat and poultry products.[300] The new rule also removed the limitation that any packaging used during irradiation should not exclude oxygen.

[12] *Nanotechnology*

[a] Regulatory Challenges

Nanotechnology is potentially the technology that will create the most challenges for the regulation of food. Nanotechnology has the potential to revolutionize the food industry by creating new functional materials and food formulations, altering food packaging and storage materials, and enabling food processing at microscale and nanoscale levels.[301] Specifically, nanotechnology has the potential to enhance the flavors and texture of food, reduce fat content, encapsulate nutrients, increase shelf life, and generate new food products. Nanotechnology also has the potential to make packaging that keeps

---

[296] *Codex General Standard for Irradiated Foods and Recommended International Code of Practice for the Operation of Radiation Facilities Used for the Treatment of Foods*, (1984), CODEX STAN 106–1983.

[297] WORLD HEALTH ORGANIZATION, SAFETY AND NUTRITIONAL ADEQUACY OF IRRADIATED FOOD (1994).

[298] *See, e.g.,* U.S. GOV'T ACCOUNTABILITY OFFICE, GAO-10-309R, FOOD IRRADIATION: FDA COULD IMPROVE ITS DOCUMENTATION AND COMMUNICATION OF KEY DECISIONS ON FOOD IRRADIATION PETITONS (February 16, 2010) (noting that on the basis of extensive scientific studies and the opinions of experts, the GAO reported in 2000 that the benefits of food irradiation outweigh the risks); *see also* U.S. GOV'T ACCOUNTABILITY OFFICE, GAO/RCED-00-217, FOOD IRRADIATION: AVAILABLE RESEARCH INDICATES THAT BENEFITS OUTWEIGH RISKS (August 24, 2000).

[299] U.S. GOV'T ACCOUNTABILITY OFFICE, GAO-10-309R, FEDERAL OVERSIGHT OF FOOD IRRADIATION (February 16, 2010).

[300] Irradiation in the Production, Processing and Handling of Food, 77 Fed. Reg. 71316 (November 30, 2012).

[301] Jochen Weiss et al., *Functional Materials in Food Nanotechnology*, 71(9) J. FOOD SCI. 107–8 (2006).

the product inside fresher for longer. Intelligent food packaging that incorporates nano-sensors could even provide consumers with information on the state of the food inside and alert consumers when a product is no longer safe to eat. Sensors could also inform consumers about the content's exact nutritional status. Applications of nanotechnologies to food structuring may allow for targeted nutrition for different lifestyles and conditions (e.g., obesity).[302] Supporters of nanotechnology are concerned that if the FDA institutes a moratorium on nano-based products while science plays catch-up, as the agency has done with cloned food animals, it will run the risk of instilling unwarranted fear in the public and erecting a major barrier to the diffusion of beneficial nano-based technologies in the future.

Even if generalized fears about nanotechnology are unfounded, the FDA still has to overcome the hurdle posed by the public's perception of risk. Past experience suggests that transparency and openness with the public may go a long way toward smoothing the road for the consumer's acceptance of emerging nano-based products.

[b] Evaluation and Safety Review

In August 2006, the FDA formed an internal Nanotechnology Task Force to survey nano-technology and propose a course for FDA action. In 2007, the task force issued a report, opining that the existing regulatory framework was sufficient to manage FDA products (including food) that employed nanotechnology and that the FDA would continue to deal with these products on a case-by-case basis.[303] In June 2011, the FDA published a guidance document that addresses the issue of how the FDA determines when and whether a product that it regulates contains nanoscale materials or uses nanotechnology.[304] The FDA's CFSAN has published another draft guidance document focused on the use of nanotechnology in food (as well as cosmetics). Although the term nanotechnology does not appear in the title, it is the guidance document's primary focus.[305]

Neither guidance document defines what constitutes "nanotechnology." The June 2011 Nanotech-Consideration Guidance begins with a disclaimer that the document is not intended to formally define "nanoscale materials" or "nanotechnology." Instead, the Nanotech-Consideration Guidance is "intended to help industry and others identify when they should consider potential implications for regulatory status, safety, effectiveness or public health impact that may arise with the application of nanotechnology in FDA-regulated products."[306] Rather than define nanotechnology, the FDA in the guidance documents looks at two parameters: (1) whether an engineered material or end product has at least one dimension in the nanoscale range (approximately 1 nm to 100 nm); or (2) whether an engineered material or end product exhibits properties or phenomena, including physical or chemical properties or biological effects, which are

---

[302] See Bhupinder S Sekhon, *Food Nanotechnology – an Overview*, 3 NANO TECHNOL. SCI. APPL. 10 (2010).

[303] See Nanotechnology: *A Report of the U.S. Food and Drug Administration Nanotechnology Task Force*, U.S.FOOD & DRUG ADMIN. (July 25, 2007).

[304] See Considering *Whether an FDA-Regulated Product Involves the Application of Nanotechnology*, U.S. FOOD & DRUG ADMIN. (June 2011).

[305] See FDA, Guidance for Industry: Assessing the Effects of Significant Manufacturing Process Changes, Including Emerging Technologies, on the Safety and Regulatory Status of Food Ingredients and Food Contact Substances, Including Food Ingredients that Are Color Additives (June 2014).

[306] *Id.*

attributable to its dimensions, even if these dimensions fall outside the nanoscale range, up to one micrometer.[307] These two parameters apply not only to newly created products, but also to existing food products that have undergone manufacturing changes involving the use of nanotechnology. The FDA has carefully selected its words. "Engineered material or end product" means those products specifically created to use nanoscale materials or applications, not those that incidentally use nanomaterials, existing nanoparticles, or materials already naturally existing on the nanoscale, such as microorganisms or proteins. Regarding novel or unique properties, the FDA defines these as "dimension-dependent properties or phenomena" used to enhance a product's effectiveness. Examples include improved drug performance, pathogen detection, food packaging, and delivery of food nutrients.

Regarding its focus on materials up to 1000 nm in dimension, the FDA recognizes that the technical definition of "nanoscale" ends at the upper size range of 100 nm, but concludes that this should not be a hard and fast limit for the FDA's purposes. The agency reasons that regulated products may conceivably exhibit unique or novel phenomena attributable to the use of nanotechnology even if their smallest components are larger than 100 nm. Accordingly, in the absence of a suitable bright line test, FDA believes it is prudent to examine products on a case-by-case basis to determine whether they involve the use of nanotechnology, as long as those products contain components up to 1000 nm in size and exhibit size-dependent phenomena.

The Nanotech-Safety Guidance applies to food ingredients, color food additives, and food contact substances. The guidance does not categorically consider food substances containing nanomaterials or otherwise involving application of nanotechnology as intrinsically harmful. The guidance provides that safety reviews for nanotechnology-derived food products follow the same process as conventional foods. Thus, products employing nanotechnology are evaluated on a case-by-case basis where the intended use of the finished food product is examined. The guidance recommends early consultation with CFSAN where a significant change in the manufacturing process occurs or where doubt or uncertainty exists about whether such a change has occurred.[308]

The agency may conclude that the intended use of the food substance is safe and lawful, even after the change in the manufacturing process. However, if the identity, condition of use, or safety evaluation is significantly changed to remove the substance from its existing clearance, a new regulatory submission may be necessary. The guidance specifically notes that a nano-engineered food substance would likely not be covered by an existing GRAS determination for a related food substance manufactured without using nanotechnology.

[c] Pesticide Classification

In December 2014, several consumer and environmental groups, including the Center for Food Safety and Center for Environmental Health, filed a lawsuit against the EPA seeking declaratory and injunctive relief for EPA's alleged failure to respond to the group's 2008 petition calling for the regulation of consumer products containing

---

[307] Id.
[308] See id.

nano-sized versions of silver.[309] According to the complaint, the 2008 petition requested that EPA classify nano-silver products as pesticides. EPA opened a comment period on the matter in 2008, but allegedly failed to take further action. The petition included an index of products that contained nano-silver, including food storage containers, food and produce cleaners, cutlery, cutting boards, and ingestible health drink supplements. The complaint asserts that nanomaterials "create unique human health and environmental risks, which require new health and safety testing paradigms."[310]

[13] *Synthetic Meat*

The future of food technology assuredly will raise challenges and novel legal issues. One example of this dynamic is synthetic meat – meat grown in a laboratory rather than as an animal. The promise lies with processed meats, while growing fully formed, complex muscle structures – such as steaks – continues to face technical difficulties. The technology is still in progress. It is widely touted as a response to environmental pressure, ethical concerns, and human health.[311]

If and when synthetic meat becomes a scientific and marketable reality, several food safety regulatory issues may arise. Time will tell how the regulatory bodies charged with overseeing food safety will respond to this new technology. The first issue is one of jurisdiction. A threshold question is whether synthetic meat would in fact qualify as "meat" within the meaning of the FMIA. If it does, the USDA could claim jurisdiction over its processing. The agencies will be forced to evaluate how synthetic meat squares with the regulatory definition of meat.[312]

Synthetic meat is constructed by seeding a scaffold or tissue culture with cells taken from an animal,[313] and therefore would appear to satisfy the statutory definition of meat as being "made wholly or in part from any meat"[314] Assuming, however, that synthetic meat, which begins with only a few original animal cells, contains meat in such a small proportion – from the skeletal muscle directly from the animal – which would be less than 2 percent of original animal cells, the question is whether those proliferated cells qualify as meat as well. Because animals are involved only at the very earliest stage, and the killing of an animal is not involved, the enterprise involved in the production of synthetic meat falls more directly in line with the FDA, as USDA agents, generally responsible for observing the slaughter of live animals and the processing of carcasses to make meat products, would not be needed.

Additional issues may include whether synthetic meat would be considered a food additive (i.e., prepared with other active ingredients, such as spices or breaded coatings) and thus present the issue as to whether the product is injurious to health – or raise GRAS considerations, whereby the manufacturer may attempt to avoid the need for a food additive petition through a self-determination.

---

[309] *See* Center for Food Safety v. EPA, No. 14–2131 (U.S. Dist. Ct., D.C., filed December 16, 2014).

[310] *Id.*

[311] *See* Tom Levitt, *Lab-Grown Meat Gives Food for Thought*, CNN, August 13, 2012.

[312] *See* 21 U.S.C. § 601(j).

[313] *See* Thomas Boland et al., *Cell and Organ Printing 2: Fusion of Cell Aggregates in Three Dimensional Gels*, 272 ANAT. REC. 497–502 (2003).

[314] 21 U.S.C § 601(j).

§ 3.06 Federal Tools

[1] *Food Facility Registration*

[a] Bioterrorism Act and FSMA

A recently growing awareness of the need for information about food enterprises that participate in the US food system has led to registration requirements aimed at increasing food safety. The information is seen as necessary to assess risk, identify problems, facilitate coordination, and incorporate traceability capability in the multifaceted global food supply and distribution chain.

Registration requirements for food enterprises were first introduced in response to the tragic terrorist act of September 11, 2001, which highlighted the need for the enhanced security of American infrastructure, including that of the food supply.[315] The seeming ease of a terrorist attack on the United States evoked the question of what steps the government should take to minimize the threat of food terrorism.[316] In part, Congress determined that an important step to prevent terrorist activity in the food system was to require food enterprises to register, thereby creating an information trail linking the registration to the registrant.[317]

Accordingly, Congress enacted and signed into law the Bioterrorism Act in June of 2002.[318] The Bioterrorism Act included a food facility registration requirement, which requires domestic and foreign facilities that manufacture, process, produce, pack, or hold food for human consumption in the United States to register with the FDA.[319] Continued concerns over food safety and food imports in particular resulted in a strengthening of the registration rules under FSMA. FSMA amended Section 415 of the FDCA (21 U.S.C. § 350d) and made important changes to the food facility registration system, which increased the frequency of registration and the scope of information disclosed in the registration.[320] The purpose of FSMA registration requirements is to provide information to FDA to facilitate inspections and investigations in the event of a food safety problem.

[b] Covered Facilities

In addressing the registration requirements, the first query is who must register. The answer is that the owner, operator, or agent in charge of a domestic or foreign facility that

---

[315] Michael T. Roberts, *Role of Regulation in Minimizing Terrorist Threats Against the Food Supply: Information, Incentives, and Penalties,* 8 Minn. J.L. Sci. & Tech. 199–200 (2007).

[316] *See Id.* at 201. A World Health Organization report defines "food terrorism" as "an act or threat of deliberate contamination of food for human consumption with chemical, biological or radionuclear agents for the purpose of causing injury or death to civilian populations and/or disrupting social, economic, or political stability." Terrorists Threats to Food: Guidance for Establishing and Strengthening Prevention and Response Systems 4, World Health Organization (2002). In a similar vein, a Congressional Research Service report to Congress defines "agroterrorism" as "the deliberate introduction of an animal or plant disease with the goal of generating fear, causing economic losses, and/or undermining stability." Jim Monke, Cong. Research Serv., RL32521, Agroterrorism: Threats and Preparedness 1 (2004).

[317] Roberts, *supra* note 315 at 208.

[318] *See* Public Health Security and Bioterrorism Preparedness and Response Act of 2002 (Bioterrorism Act), Pub. L. No. 107–188 (codified in scattered sections of 42 U.S.C.).

[319] *See* 21 C.F.R. §§ 1.225–1.243.

[320] FSMA, § 102(c).

manufactures or processes, packs, or holds food for human or animal consumption in the United States, or an individual authorized by one of them, must register that facility with FDA.[321] A domestic facility must register even if its products do not enter interstate commerce.[322] Foreign facilities must register if products are exported to the United States, unless the food from that facility undergoes further processing (including packaging but excluding minor changes such as labeling) by another foreign facility before the food is exported to the United States.[323] A foreign facility subject to registration requirements must designate a US agent (e.g., a facility's importer or broker), who must live or maintain a place of business in the United States and be physically present in the United States, for purposes of registration.[324]

A food facility is defined as "any factory, warehouse, or establishment (including a factory, warehouse, or establishment of an importer) that manufactures, processes, packs, or holds food."[325] Excepted from the definition and therefore from the registration requirements are certain farms, restaurants, retail food establishments, and nonprofit food establishments in which food is prepared and served directly to consumers, or fishing vessels (except for vessels engaged in processing).[326]

The definitions of these establishments exempted from the registration requirements under Section 415 of the FDCA are provided in the following paragraphs.

o Exempted "farms" are defined as facilities located in one general physical location that are devoted to the growing and harvesting of crops, the raising of animals (including seafood), or both. Washing, trimming of outer leaves, and cooling of produce are considered part of harvesting.[327] Determining which activities trigger the facility registration for a particular farm is one of the most confusing aspects of FSMA. The FDA guidance document that answers questions regarding food facility registration provides a number of examples of what farm activities are exempt from the registration requirements.[328] Revisions to proposed rules in the implementation of FSMA eliminate the initial proposed rule that a farm would be required to register as a food facility if it packs or holds raw agricultural commodities grown on another farm under a different ownership.[329] Farms under this qualification, however, would still be subject to the Produce Safety Rule, as shown elsewhere in this chapter.

o Exempted "restaurants" are facilities that prepare and sell food directly to consumers for immediate consumption, including pet shelters, kennels, and veterinary facilities that provide food directly to animals.[330] Facilities that provide food to interstate

---

[321] 21 C.F.R. § 1.225(a).

[322] 21 C.F.R. § 1.225(b).

[323] 21 C.F.R. § 1.226(a).

[324] *Fact Sheet on FDA's New Food Terrorism Regulation: Interim Final Rule – Registration of Food Facilities Protecting the Food Supply*, U.S. FOOD & DRUG ADMIN. (September 21, 2013, last updated).

[325] 21 U.S.C. § 350d(b). Food is defined as the standard FDA definition of "food" in section 201 of the FDCA (21 U.S.C. § 321(f)). *See* Chapter 1 for a further explanation of this statutory definition.

[326] 21 C.F.R. § 1.227(b)(2).

[327] 21 C.F.R. § 1.227(b)(3).

[328] *See*, FDA, Guidance for Industry: Questions and Answers Regarding Food Facility Registration (6th ed.) (November 2014).

[329] Current Good Manufacturing Practice and Hazard Analysis and Risk-Based Preventive Controls for Human Food, 79 Fed. Reg. 5831 (September 29, 2014) (to be codified at 21 C.F.R. Parts 16, 117, and 507).

[330] 21 C.F.R. § 1.227(b)(10).

conveyances, such as commercial aircraft, or central kitchens that do not prepare and serve food directly to consumers, are not exempt.[331]

o Exempted "retail food establishments" sell food directly to consumers as their primary function, meaning that annual sales directly to consumers are of greater dollar value than annual sales to other buyers.[332] Examples of exempted retail food establishments include grocery stores, convenience stores, vending machine locations, delis, and roadside stands.[333] FSMA required FDA to amend the definition of "retail food establishment" to clarify that the sale of food directly to consumers includes the sale of food at a roadside stand or farmers' market, sale and distribution of food through a community supported agriculture program, and sale and distribution of food through any other direct sales platform as determined by FDA.[334]

o Exempted "nonprofit food establishments" are charitable entities that meet the terms of Section 501(c)(3) of the Internal Revenue Code and that prepare or serve food directly to the consumer or otherwise provide food or meals for consumption by humans or animals. Examples of nonprofit food establishments required to register include food banks, soup kitchens, and nonprofit food delivery services.[335]

In addition to the express exemptions of particular food establishments, it is important to remember that the Bioterrorism Act of 2001 and FSMA and thus Section 415 of the FDCA apply to FDA, not USDA. This means that exceptions to the registration requirements of Section 415 of the FDCA include facilities regulated exclusively by the USDA, that is, facilities handling only meat, poultry or egg products. Because the definition of "food" under the FDCA excludes food contact substances and pesticides, facilities that produce food contact substances and pesticides also are exempt from registration. However, if the food contact substance is used as a direct food additive, which is often the case, the facility dealing with the food contact substance must be registered.

[c] Registration Frequency

A facility must be registered only once under the Bioterrorism Act.[336] FSMA increases the required frequency of registration: food facilities that are required to register with FDA are required to renew such registrations biennially, between October 1 and December 31 of each even-numbered year.[337] Required registration information that changes must be updated.[338] FDA provides an abbreviated renewal process for

---

[331] *Id.*

[332] 21 C.F.R. § 1.226(c).

[333] 21 C.F.R. § 1.227(b)(11).

[334] FSMA, § 102(c).

[335] 21 C.F.R. § 1.227(b)(7).

[336] Registration may be done electronically, mail, fax, or CD-rom for multiple submissions. *Food Facility Registration and Registration Cancellation by Paper (Mail or FAX) or CD-ROM*, U.S. FOOD & DRUG ADMIN.

[337] *Registration: 2014 Food Facility Biennial Registration Renewal*, U.S. FOOD & DRUG ADMIN. (September 25, 2014, last updated).

[338] *See* 21 C.F.R. 1232 (addresses various permeations of changes –from information change to ownership change).

facilities that have had no changes in their registration information since the previous renewal.[339]

[d] Registration Information

Under the Bioterrorism Act of 2001, facilities that register are required to submit the following information: the name, full address, and phone number of the facility; the name, address, and phone number of the parent company; and the addresses and phone numbers of the owner, operator, and agent in charge.[340] For a foreign facility, the name, address, phone number, and emergency contact phone number of its US agent is required.[341] The Bioterrorism Act of 2001 also requires the disclosure of the general food product categories of any food manufactured, processed, packed, or held at the facility.[342]

FSMA requires the following new registration information in the form of email addresses and assurances: the email address for the facility's contact person (or, in the case of a foreign facility, the email address of the facility's US agent) and consent to permit FDA inspection of the registered facility at times and in the manner permitted by the act.[343] Under the final guidance document for FSMA, the general food categories that were identified by the Bioterrorism Act of 2001 were expanded.[344]

[e] Registration Enforcement

The failure to register, to update registration information, or to renew registration is a prohibited act under Section 301(dd) of the FDCA and may subject a food facility to criminal prosecution.[345] While the law is not totally clear whether goods imported without a valid facility registration on file are also barred from importation as adulterated products, the FDA is expected to interpret the law that way.

If FDA determines that there is a reasonable probability that food from a facility could cause serious adverse health consequences or death to humans or animals, FDA may suspend the registration of (1) any facility that created, caused, or is otherwise responsible

---

[339] 21 U.S.C. § 350d(a)(3). Under FSMA, FDA may require that food facility registrations be submitted in an electronic format, but such requirement may not become effective until five years after the date of enactment of the FSMA. 21 U.S.C. § 350d(b)(5)(B).

[340] 21 C.F.R. § 1.232(a–c).

[341] 21 C.F.R. § 1.232(d).

[342] 21 U.S.C. § 350d(a)(2); 21 C.F.R. § 170.3(n).

[343] 21 U.S.C. § 350d(a)(2). FSMA in various sections substantially changes the role and responsibility of agents for foreign establishments. No longer is someone who merely answers the phone on behalf of a foreign registrant an agent, as was the case under the Bioterrorism Act of 2001. Under FSMA, the agent is now responsible for paying reinspection fees associated with the foreign firm, and if the foreign firm imports food into the United States without a US-based owner or consignee, the agent is defined as the "importer" (who is therefore responsible for performing the responsibilities of an importer, such as foreign supplier verification). *See Fees under FSMA*, U.S. FOOD & DRUG ADMIN. The responsibility of the agent also extends to being responsible (along with the owner or operator) for ensuring that preventive controls are in place. Thus, the US agent acting for the foreign facility is put into a position of high responsibility and liability. *Facility Registration Now Open: What's New?*, Acheson Group (October 25, 2012).

[344] *See* FDA, Guidance for Industry, Necessity of the Use of Food Product Categories in Food Facility Registrations and Updates to Food Product Categories (October 2012).

[345] 21 C.F.R. § 1.241.

for such reasonable probability; or (2) any facility that packed, received, or held such food and that knew of, or had reason to know of, such reasonable probability.[346] FDA is required to issue regulations on implementing 21 U.S.C. § 350d(b), which deals with suspension of registration, but may do so on an interim final basis. Subsection § 350d(b) will become effective on the date that FDA issues implementing regulations or 180 days after the date of enactment of the FSMA, whichever is earlier.[347]

Under FSMA, FDA is required to provide the registrant an opportunity for an informal hearing on the actions required for the reinstatement of the facility's registration. The hearing is to be held as soon as possible but not later than two business days after issuance of the suspension order, or such other time as agreed upon by FDA and the registrant. If FDA determines that the suspension remains necessary, the registrant must submit a corrective action plan, and FDA is required to review the plan within fourteen days of submission or such other time period as determined by FDA. If FDA determines that adequate grounds do not exist to continue the suspension, FDA is required to promptly vacate the suspension order and reinstate the facility's registration or modify the order, as appropriate.[348]

No person may import, offer to import, or introduce into interstate or intrastate commerce any food from a facility whose registration has been suspended.[349] An article of food offered for import shall be refused admission if it is from a facility whose registration has been suspended.[350]

FDA will cancel a registration if the agency independently verifies that the facility is no longer in business or has changed owners, and the owner, operator, or agent in charge of the facility fails to cancel the registration, or if FDA determines that the registration is for a facility that does not exist. If FDA cancels a facility's registration, FDA will mail a confirmation of the cancellation to the facility at the address provided in the facility's registration.[351]

[2] Inspection of Enterprises

[a] Warrantless Search

Inspection of food enterprises has long been the centerpiece of food safety regulation. Regulatory inspections of food enterprises involve the official examination of facilities, property, product, and documents. The authority for inspections is derived largely from federal statutes that are designed to support the enforcement provision of food safety laws by determining compliance with the law and to gather evidence for enforcement against noncompliance. It is settled that warrantless inspections by closely regulated industries are fully consistent with Fourth Amendment freedoms from unreasonable searches and seizures of property.[352] In a case involving the inspection authority pursuant to the Gun

---

[346] 21 U.S.C. § 350d(b)(1).

[347] 21 U.S.C. § 350d(b)(6).

[348] 21 U.S.C. § 350d(b)(2–3).

[349] 21 U.S.C. § 350d(b)(4).

[350] 21 U.S.C. § 381(l).

[351] See Food Facility Registration User Guide: Additional Capabilities, U.S. FOOD & DRUG ADMIN. (June 16, 2015).

[352] EMILY M. LANZA, CONG. RESEARCH SERV., R43794, FOOD RECALLS AND OTHER FDA ADMINISTRATIVE ENFORCEMENT ACTIONS 3–4 (2014).

Control Act of 1968, the US Supreme Court in *US v. Biswell* held that a warrantless inspection by the government is reasonable under the Fourth Amendment when a statute provides the authority to conduct an inspection in a carefully limited manner.[353] Fifteen years later, the Supreme Court in *New York v. Burger* found that an owner of commercial premises in a closely regulated industry has a reduced expectation of privacy regarding inspections by the government, thereby affirming the principle articulated in *Biswell* that a warrantless government inspection of a commercial premise might be reasonable under the Fourth Amendment.[354] The Court set forth three criteria for what would constitute a reasonable warrantless government inspection (referred to by the court as the *Colonnade-Biswell* doctrine): (1) a substantial government interest must support the regulatory inspection scheme; (2) the warrantless inspections must be necessary to advance or further the regulatory inspection scheme; and (3) the statute must function as a warrant by limiting the discretion of the inspecting officers and by advising the owner of the commercial enterprise that the government may conduct a search within the properly defined scope of the law.[355] In applying these criteria, lower courts have consistently found a federal interest in food safety and have upheld warrantless FDA inspections as reasonable. For example, in *US v. New England Grocers Supply Co.*, the District Court in Massachusetts, found that FDA's interest in public health was served by warrantless searches and that the agency conducted the searches of defendant's warehouse of foodstuff reasonably as to time, manner, and scope.[356] Accordingly, the court held that neither warrant nor consent was required to inspect the defendant's warehouse.[357]

The FDA and USDA bear the major responsibility for inspection at the federal level. The split in jurisdiction and resource disparity between these two agencies on food safety are most evident in their respective inspection authority.

[b] FDA Inspection Authority: Reasonableness

The FDA has the authority, under Section 704 of the FDCA, to inspect any food enterprise whose food or drink products are regulated by FDA. Section 704 authorizes the FDA's duly designated officers or employees, upon presenting appropriate credentials and a written notice, to enter and inspect a food enterprise, including a factory, warehouse, establishment, or vehicle.[358] The inspections must be conducted at a reasonable time, within reasonable limits, and in a reasonable manner.[359]

The touchstone for Section 704 "reasonableness," as it regards time, place, and manner, has been delineated into various rules. The reasonable time requirement generally alludes to an enterprise's normal operating or business hours.[360] Justification of inspection outside of business hours would likely be special circumstances such as food poisoning by food product. Inspections are ordinarily unannounced. The requirement of

---

[353] 406 U.S. 311, 315–16 (1972).
[354] 482 U.S. 691, 701–2 (1987).
[355] *Id.* at 702–3.
[356] 488 F.Supp. 230, 238–9 (D.Mass 1980).
[357] *Id.* at 239. *See also* U.S. v. Bus. Builders, Inc. 354 F. Supp. 141, 143 (N.D. Okla. 1973); U.S. v. Del Camp Baking Mfg. Co., 345 F.Supp. 1371, 1376 (D.Del. 1972).
[358] 21 U.S.C. § 374(A).
[359] 21 U.S.C. § 374(B).
[360] *See e.g.*, Durovic v. Palmer, 342 F.2d 634 (7th Cir. 1965), *cert. den.*, 382 U.S. 820 (1965).

within "reasonable limits" generally means that the area or goods inspected should have relevancy to the object of the inspection. Generally speaking, factories, warehouses, and vehicles may be inspected. More specifically, Sections 373 and 374 enumerate the objects subject to FDA's inspection authority. These objects are organized into the following categories: (1) all pertinent equipment, including manufacturing plant and storage facilities; (2) finished and unfinished materials; (3) containers; and (4) labels and labeling products (including catalogs, brochures, fliers, advertisements, and other promotional materials sent to customers). As for the requirement that inspections be conducted in a reasonable manner, Section 704(a)(1) of the FDCA obligates FDA inspectors to present their credentials in order to gain entry into regulated facilities. In addition, FDA inspectors are required to issue the firm a Notice of Inspection form at the beginning of the inspection. However, the act does not require FDA to include the reasons for the inspection in the notice.[361]

At the close of an inspection, the inspector will normally supply a Form 483, or an Establishment Inspection Report (EIR), which lists the FDA's observations during the course of the inspection. Food firms have no obligation to respond to the observations listed. EIRs are public documents that can be accessed through the Freedom of Information Act (FOIA); many such documents are publicly available on FDA's website. Refusal to permit an FDA inspection to enter and inspect a registered facility violates FDCA and may lead to FDA seeking judicial enforcement, such as an inspection warrant issued by a district court.[362]

[c] Access to Company Records

The FDA's statutory inspection authority under Sections 414 and 704 includes the authority to obtain access to records of the interstate transport of foods.[363] These sections were amended by Section 306 of the Bioterrorism Act of 2002 and by FSMA.[364] The FDCA has provided FDA with express authority to inspect specific records for certain products, including infant formula,[365] low-acid canned foods,[366] acidified foods,[367] seafood products subject to HACCP requirements,[368] and fruit and vegetable juice products.[369]

The authority of FDA to inspect food enterprises for food not enumerated specifically in FDCA is restricted, so that the agency is unable to access certain records, including recipes, financial data, pricing data, personnel data, research data, or sales data (other than shipment data regarding sales).[370] A "recipe" is defined as "the formula, including ingredients, quantities, and instructions necessary to manufacture a food product."[371]

---

[361] See U.S. Food and Drug Administration Investigations Operations Manual 2014, Exhibit 5-1, Example of a Notice of Inspection.

[362] 21 U.S.C. § 331(f). See FDA Investigations Operations Manual 2014, supra note 361.

[363] See generally, FDA, Draft Guidance, Records Access Authority under Sections 414 and 704 Federal Food, Drug, & Cosmetic Act: Questions and Answers (February 2012).

[364] Id.

[365] 21 U.S.C. 350a(b)(4)); 21 C.F.R. Part 106).

[366] 21 C.F.R. § 113.

[367] 21 C.F.R. §114.

[368] 21 C.F.R. §123.

[369] 21 C.F.R. § 120.

[370] 21 U.S.C. § 350(c).

[371] 21 C.F.R. § 328.

FDA states that any confidential or trade secret information contained in records it obtains under Section 414 will be protected from public disclosure. The agency considers trade secrets to include a firm's manufacturing processes and precise product formulations.[372]

The Bioterrorism Act provides that, if FDA has a reasonable belief that a particular article of food is adulterated and presents a threat of serious adverse health consequences or death to humans or animals, the agency may, upon presenting credentials and a written notice, inspect and copy all records relating to that particular article of food that are needed to determine whether, in fact, the food is adulterated and presents the suspected risk of serious health consequences or death.[373] FSMA reaffirmed this provision for FDA[374] and expanded the agency's access authority in a number of ways, including the following:

○ During an active investigation of a foodborne illness outbreak, or if FDA determines it is necessary to prevent or mitigate an outbreak, FDA may request an owner, operator, or agent of a farm to identify potential immediate recipients (other than consumers) of an article of food that is the subject of investigation if FDA reasonably believes such article of food is adulterated, was adulterated on a particular farm, and presents a threat of serious adverse health consequences or death to humans or animals. The owner, operator, or agent of the farm would be required to provide the requested information in a prompt and reasonable manner.[375]

○ Registered food facilities that are required to have a preventive controls plan are required to make such plans and related records (including records of monitoring, verification, and corrective actions) available to FDA upon written or oral request.[376]

○ Importers are required to maintain records related to their Foreign Supplier Verification Program for at least two years and to make them available to FDA upon request.[377]

Although the law circumscribes what the FDA is entitled to review during an inspection, it places no limits on what an inspector may seek to inspect. For example, if a document falls outside the scope of FDA jurisdiction and is not relevant to FDA's investigation, the failure to object to its production is deemed a permanent waiver of the right to object.[378]

[d] Issue of Photography

One of the more contentious issues in inspections of food enterprises is the taking of photographs. FDA has long taken the position that its inspectors may take photographs inside an inspected plant. The food industry has disagreed with FDA's position, asserting that the FDCA and case law do not support the FDA's position.[379] In 2012, the FDA revised

---

[372] *Trade Secrets*, U.S. FOOD & DRUG ADMIN. (June 1, 2010, last update).
[373] Bioterrorism Act § 306.
[374] 21 U.S.C. § 350c(a)(1).
[375] 21 U.S.C. § 321(f).
[376] 21 U.S.C. § 350g(h).
[377] 21 U.S.C. § 385(d).
[378] *See, e.g.*, United States v. Gel Spice Co., 601 F.Supp. 1214 (E.D.N.Y. 1985).
[379] Neal D. Fortin, *Is a Picture Worth More than 1,000 Words? The Fourth Amendment and the FDA's Authority to Take Photographs under the Federal Food, Drug, and Cosmetic Act*, 2 J. FOOD L. & POL'Y 239 (2006).

a section of its Investigations Operations Manual (IOM) on "In-plant Photographs." The manual directs inspectors not to request permission from management to take photographs during an inspection. When the food enterprise refuses to allow the taking of photographs during an inspection, the manual instructs investigators to

> obtain name and contact information for the firm's legal counsel, and advise your district manager immediately. If the firm does not have legal counsel on retainer, collect the name and contact information for the most responsible individual. District management will inform their ORA Regional Counselor in the Office of Chief Counsel (OCC) of the situation, and OCC will then contact the firm's legal counsel or most responsible individual to discuss FDA's legal right to take pictures during inspections. OCC will relay the results of this conversation to district management.[380]

This language marks a shift from previous versions of the IOM, which instructed investigators to "advise your supervisor so legal remedies may be sought to allow you to take photographs, if appropriate."[381] The shift in language signals that investigators are likely to be more aggressive in asserting their legal right to take photographs.

The FDCA does not explicitly authorize FDA investigators to take photographs during the course of food establishment inspections. Nor is there is any case law that clearly permits photography inside an inspected plant. FDA relies on two cases, cited in its 2012 IOM, as the basis for its authority. In the first case, *Dow Chemical v. United States*, the US Supreme Court upheld the taking of aerial photographs as a valid exercise of EPA inspectional powers under the Clean Air Act.[382] In its opinion, the Court stated "[w]hen Congress invests an agency with enforcement and investigatory authority, it is not necessary to identify explicitly each and every technique that may be used in the course of executing the statutory mission."[383] FDA interprets this language to apply to any regulatory agency taking photographs in any context; however, *Dow Chemical* did not address FDA authority under the FDCA or the taking of photographs inside a plant during an establishment inspection. In the second case, *United States v. Acri Wholesale Grocery Co.*, the District Court for the Southern District of Iowa in a criminal matter admitted into evidence photographs taken by FDA inspectors because they were taken during the course of a reasonable inspection to which the defendants fully consented and the investigators made no effort to conceal the taking of photographs.[384] While this opinion does support the idea that photographs taken with a company's consent during an inspection may be used in criminal prosecution, it does not directly support FDA's assertion that it has the right to take photographs, absent consent during an establishment inspection.

Because direct judicial support for FDA's claimed authority to take photographs during inspections is lacking, it has long been industry practice to deny investigators consent to take photographs. However, the agency's patience with company objections to in-plant photography appears to be waning. The IOM does not even hint at the possible

---

[380] FDA Investigations Operations Manual 2014, *supra* note 361 at 5.3.4.1 – In-Plant Photographs 242.
[381] *See* Gary C. Messplay and Colleen Helsey, *Photo Shop: Facility Photographs and FDA Inspection Authority*, CONTRACT PHARMA 22, 22 (2009) (referencing language).
[382] 476 U.S. 227 (1986).
[383] *Id.* at 233.
[384] 409 F.Supp. 3d 529 (S.D. Iowa 1976).

need to obtain a warrant in the absence of consent. Accordingly, refusal could arguably constitute a criminal act punishable by fines or imprisonment.[385]

[e] Federal-State Cooperation

The FDCA does not contain general preemption language related to state involvement in food safety matters. As a result, FDA has encouraged cooperative relationships with state agencies and, in some cases, has left the major enforcement activities primarily in the hands of the states. Given its modest resources, the FDA is unable to inspect facilities it regulates in the same manner as USDA. Instead of having inspectors on site at all times, as is required for firms that fall under the jurisdiction of the USDA, FDA inspectors rely on periodic unannounced inspections. Limited resources further cements FDA's dependency on enhanced partnerships with state and local regulators in the domestic arena and on foreign governments and third parties in the foreign arena.

[f] FSMA and Risk-Based Inspections

FSMA adds a new Section 421 to the FDCA (21 U.S.C. § 350j) to target high-risk inspections. FDA is required to identify high-risk facilities and to allocate resources to inspect registered facilities according to their risk profile, based on the following factors: the known safety risks of the food manufactured, processed, packed, or held at the facility; the facility's compliance history, including recalls, outbreaks, and violations; the rigor and effectiveness of the facility's hazard analysis and preventive controls; whether the facility or its food have been certified by an accredited third-party auditor; whether the food manufactured, processed, packed, handled, prepared, treated, distributed, or stored at the facility meets the criteria for priority under FDCA Section 801(h)(1) (i.e., possible intentional adulteration); and any other criteria deemed appropriate by FDA.[386]

FSMA also establishes inspection frequency predicated upon risk. A minimum inspection frequency of once every five years is required for domestic food facilities. FDA is required to inspect high-risk domestic facilities at least once during the five-year period following the date of enactment, and at least once every three years thereafter. FDA is required to inspect domestic facilities that are not high-risk facilities at least once during the seven-year period following the date of enactment, and at least once every five years thereafter.

Inspection of food imports is also based on risk. FDA is required to allocate resources to inspect imported foods according to their risk profile, based on the following factors: the known safety risks of the imported food; the known safety risks of the countries or regions of origin and transport of the imported food; the importer's compliance history including recalls, outbreaks, and violations; the rigor and effectiveness of the importer's Foreign Supplier Verification Program; whether the importer participates in the Voluntary Qualified Importer Program; whether the food meets the criteria for priority under FDCA Section 801(h)(1) (i.e., possible intentional adulteration); and whether the food or the facility that manufactured, processed, packed, or held the food

---

[385] 21 U.S.C. §§ 331(f), 333(a).
[386] 21 U.S.C. § 350j(a)(1).

has been certified by an accredited third-party auditor; and any other criteria deemed appropriate by FDA.[387]

[g] Inspection of Foreign Facilities

FSMA provides that FDA may enter into agreements and arrangements with foreign governments to facilitate inspection of foreign food facilities. If, upon request, the owner, operator, or agent in charge of a foreign factory, warehouse, or other establishment, or the government of a foreign country refuses to permit entry of US inspectors or other individuals duly designated by FDA to inspect such enterprises, food from that enterprise shall be refused admission into the United States. For purposes of this provision, an owner, operator, or agent in charge will be deemed to have refused an inspection request if such person does not permit an inspection during the twenty-four-hour period after a request is made, or after such other time period as agreed upon by FDA and the enterprise.[388] FDA is required to inspect at least 600 foreign facilities during the first one-year period following the date of enactment, and to inspect at least twice the number inspected during the previous year in each of the next five years.[389] Budget constraints and logistical problems will make it difficult for the FDA to meet this mandate.[390]

[h] Inspection of On-Farm Operations

Under FSMA, FDA is required to conduct a science-based risk analysis of the types of manufacturing, processing, packing, and holding activities that occur on farms. On the basis of that risk analysis, FDA is required to exempt from the mandatory inspection frequency in Section 421, or modify the inspection frequency for, facilities that are small businesses or very small businesses engaged in specific types of on-farm manufacturing, processing, packing, or holding activities that FDA determines to be low risk or involving specific foods that FDA determines to be low risk. This exemption is addressed in this chapter in connection with the Produce Safety Rule.

[i] Food Safety and Inspection Service (FSIS)

(1) *Federal Inspection Acts*

The FSIS has broad statutory authority under three separate acts: the Federal Meat Inspection Act of 1906 (FMIA),[391] the Poultry Products Inspection Act of 1957 (PPIA),[392] and the Egg Product Inspection Act of 1970 (EPIA).[393] The duties of FSIS under these acts are primarily carried out through mandatory inspections at plants that slaughter livestock and poultry and that process eggs. The agency follows the products through processing to assure wholesomeness and proper labeling. Under both FMIA and PPIA,

---

[387] 21 U.S.C. § 350j(b).
[388] 21 U.S.C. § 388(c)(2)(A).
[389] 21 U.S.C. § 350j(a)(2).
[390] *See* Ted Agres, *FDA Inspections in 2014: Big Ambitions Hampered by Limited Resources*, FOOD QUALITY AND SAFETY MAGAZINE, February/March 2014.
[391] 21 U.S.C. §§ 601 et seq.
[392] 21 U.S.C. §§ 451 et seq.
[393] 21 U.S.C. §§ 1031 et seq.

if state inspection programs are at least as strict as the federal programs, FSIS will cooperate with the states to allow the states to administer their own inspection programs for
intrastate transactions. However, if the state does not operate a program that is at least
as stringent as the federal requirements, the state may be "designated" and, if so, certain
programs of the various Acts become applicable to intrastate transactions.[394]

(2) FMIA

FMIA requires that certain animals (cattle, sheep, swine, goats, horses, mules, and other
equines) are visually inspected before entering a slaughter facility.[395] In addition, the carcasses and parts are subject to a postmortem inspection.[396] A federal inspector conducts
antemortem and postmortem inspections on all animals slaughtered. At the facilities that
process meat food products, the inspection is done regularly and daily, but the inspector is not present at all times. In addition to this inspection of the animals, carcasses,
and meat food products, FSIS also imposes detailed facility, equipment, and sanitation
requirements and the inspectors are responsible for checking compliance with these
requirements.

Under FMIA, three exemptions from the inspection requirements exist. The first
is the custom exemption: the owner of animals may slaughter animals for household
use (not for sale) or may have the slaughter done by custom slaughterers who prepare the carcass for the owner's use without inspection.[397] The second exemption is for
operations conducted at traditional retail-type establishment (including restaurants).
This exemption does not extend to central meat-cutting facilities of chain grocery stores
or central kitchen facilities of chain restaurants where meat processing occurs.[398] The
third exemption is the territorial exemption: the slaughter of animals and other attendant activity in any territory that due to its location is determined impracticable for
inspection.[399]

FMIA contains provisions for both criminal penalties and civil sanctions. In addition,
FSIS has the authority to withdraw, deny, or suspend inspection services to establishments under specific circumstances. This refusal of authority is most often used when
the recipient of inspection services has been convicted of crimes related to the food transactions. The act provides for the refusal or withdrawal of inspector services for enumerated violations, enabling USDA effectively to shut down plants its inspectors perceive
as noncompliant by vacating the plant or withholding the federal seal. This leverage
provides a good deal of power to USDA inspectors. Refusal may occur in instances in
which an applicant does not have a HACCP plan; does not have Sanitation Standard
Operating Procedures;[400] has not demonstrated that adequate sanitary conditions exist
in the establishment; has not demonstrated that livestock will be handled and slaughtered humanely; or is unfit to engage in any business requiring inspection as specified in

---

[394] 21 U.S.C. § 661c(1), (3), § 454c(1). Designation of states is published in the Federal Register. The list
appears in 9 C.F.R. § 331.2, 331.6, and 9 C.F.R. 381.221. The trend is toward "designation" since such
states no longer pay a share of the program costs.
[395] 21 C.F.R. § 603.
[396] 21 C.F.R. § 604.
[397] 21 C.F.R. § 623(a).
[398] 21 C.F.R. § 661(c)(2).
[399] 21 C.F.R. § 623(b).
[400] 21 C.F.R. § 671.

Section 401 of the FMIA.[401] FSIS can rescind approval even after it has inspected and approved products if there are false or misleading marks, labels, sizes, or form of any container used for any meat or poultry product under Section 7 of the FMIA or Section 8 of PPIA.[402]

(3) PPIA

PPIA requires that poultry and poultry products capable for use as human food be inspected.[403] The act defines "poultry" to include chickens, turkeys, ducks, geese, and guineas but refers more broadly to "any domesticated bird."[404] Under the act, "poultry product" includes the carcass or part thereof or any product made "wholly or in part from a poultry carcass or part thereof."[405] The inspections include antemortem inspections of the poultry on the day of slaughter to determine if they "plainly show" any disease or condition that should cause them to be condemned.[406] The act does not mandate such ante-mortem inspections but leaves it to the agency to determine the extent to which such inspections are considered necessary. By contrast, the act requires postmortem inspections on a bird-by-bird basis whenever processing operations are being conducted.[407] Each carcass is examined under one of four approved systems of inspection, depending on the type of bird and type of operation. Poultry products are subject to processing inspections, as necessary, to assure compliance with the applicable regulations. This examination may be accomplished in accordance with approved sampling plans developed for individual products. The specific plan will depend on the kind of product, the type of preparation, procedures followed, and whether the product is in containers.[408] Finished product inspection may also be required.[409]

In August 2014, USDA published a final rule to amend the department's poultry slaughter inspection process to offer a new inspection system available for US plants to voluntarily adopt.[410] According to the final rule, modernization of poultry slaughter inspections will reduce *Salmonella* and other poultry pathogen contamination, by allowing better use of agency resources.[411] The new final rule allows FSIS to assign fewer inspectors for online inspections and allow inspectors to conduct more food-safety-related off-line inspections in facilities operating under this new poultry inspection system.[412]

The exemptions under PPIA from inspection requirements are similar to those under FMIA. There is a general exemption from all provisions of the act for small poultry producers who slaughter not more than 1,000 poultry each year raised on their own farm, do not buy or sell poultry products other than those from poultry raised on their own farm,

---

[401] 9.C.F.R. § 500.7.
[402] 9 C.F.R. § 500.8. Such hearings are conducted in accordance with the Uniform Rules of Practice, 7 C.F.R. Subtitle A, Part 1, Subpart H.
[403] 21 C.F.R. § 451 et seq.
[404] 21 C.F.R. § 453(e).
[405] 21 C.F.R. § 453(f).
[406] 9 C.F.R. § 381.70, 381.71.
[407] 21 U.S.C. § 455(b).
[408] 9 C.F.R. § 381.145.
[409] 9 C.F.R. § 381.309.
[410] Modernization of Poultry Slaughter Inspection, 79 Fed. Reg. 49566 (August 21, 2014).
[411] *Id.*
[412] GAO, Food Safety, GAO-14-744 17, USDA Needs to Strengthen Its Approach to Protecting Human Health from Pathogens in Poultry Products (September 2014).

and sell only intrastate.[413] A similar exemption allows one who slaughters and processes his own poultry raised on the premises to do so without inspection so long as the poultry or poultry products are sold intrastate and the person slaughters or processes the products of no more than 20,000 birds annually.[414] The custom exemption allows the slaughter, without inspection, of poultry delivered by the owner for custom slaughtering provided the custom slaughterer does not engage in the business of buying and selling of poultry products capable of use as human food and provided the final products are for the personal use of the owner.[415] Retail stores and restaurants are exempt from the inspection requirements of the act if the only processing that occurs is for direct sales to consumers and sales are only in "normal retail quantities" or only for sale or service in meals to individual consumers. Retail dealers are also exempt if the only processing is the cutting up of birds for direct sale to consumers on the premises where the birds are sold.[416] A special exemption is available to those who slaughter, process, or handle poultry or poultry products as required by recognized religious dietary laws.[417]

PPIA also grants USDA broad authority to regulate the conditions under which poultry products are stored and handled by anyone engaged in "the business of buying, selling, freezing, storing or transporting" such products[418] and authorizes, in certain circumstances, cooperation with appropriate state agencies conducting inspection programs that meet or exceed its requirements.[419] It requires that imported slaughtered poultry and poultry products be subject to inspection and sanitary standards equivalent to US standards and to random inspections and testing.[420]

Enforcement under PPIA is similar to that under FMIA: provisions for both criminal and civil sanctions and the withdrawal of inspector services may be used as leverage for violations. Also, under PPIA, FSIS has the same rescission authority as under FMIA.[421]

(4) EPIA

EPIA imposes specific inspection requirements for two categories of eggs – egg products and shell eggs. "Shell egg" or "egg" is defined under EPIA to include eggs of the domesticated chicken, turkey, duck, goose, or guinea.[422] "Egg product" means "any dried, frozen, or liquid eggs, with or without added ingredients" but does not include products that contain eggs in only a "relatively small proportion" or that have not historically been considered products of the egg food industry.[423] EPIA gives enforcement authority both to USDA and FDA.[424] Emblematic of the fragmented regulatory framework governing food safety in the United States, FDA has authority over shell eggs, while USDA, acting

---

[413] 9 C.F.R. § 381.10(c).
[414] 9 C.F.R. § 381.10(a)(5).
[415] 9 C.F.R. § 381.10(a)(4).
[416] 9 C.F.R. § 381.10(a)(1), (d).
[417] 9 C.F.R. § 381.11.
[418] 21 U.S.C. § 463(a).
[419] 21 U.S.C. § 454(a).
[420] 21 U.S.C. § 466(d)(1)(A), (d)(4).
[421] 9 C.F.R. § 500.8.
[422] 21 U.S.C. § 1033(g).
[423] 21 U.S.C. § 1033(f).
[424] 21 U.S.C. § 1034 (directing the Secretary of Health and Human Services to inspect egg handlers "other than plants processing egg products"); 21 U.S.C. § 1043.

through FSIS, has authority over egg products. Under EPIA, FDA inspectors visit shell egg packers at least every three months to ensure compliance with EIPA's terms. As with the other food products regulated by USDA, inspection of egg products is more rigorous than inspection of shell eggs: the act directs USDA to inspect continuously operations at plants that break and process shell eggs into dried, frozen, or liquid egg products.[425] An official inspector must be present at all times when eggs are being processed and examine the eggs both before and after breaking.[426] A limited exemption exists under EPIA for small producers.[427] The exemption is directed toward poultry producers who sell eggs from their own flocks directly to household consumers. Each such sale is limited to thirty dozen eggs and only if it occurs door-to-door or at a site away from the site of production, and restrictions on loss and leaker eggs still apply.[428] Like its meat and poultry counterparts, EPIA also requires affected establishments to implement the relevant sanitary practices established by the secretary of agriculture, and it provides for the withdrawal of inspection services for noncompliance, effectively giving USDA the ability to shut down any facility it believes is noncompliant.[429] In response to recall actions involving salmonella poisoning from eggs, the FDA commissioner urged for Congress to close the enforcement between the USDA and FDA by giving the agency additional preventive authority.[430]

[j] US Customs and Border Protection (CBP)

CBP was created as an agency of the Department of Homeland Security in March 2003.[431] It took over the now-defunct US Customs Service and Immigration and Naturalization Service, as well as some of the responsibilities formerly handled by the US Border Patrol and the Animal and Plant Health Inspection Service.[432] In addition to traditional border control responsibilities, CBP is charged with preventing the introduction into the United States of hazardous, toxic, and noxious products and diseases, including those carried by or in food, that threaten the nation's food and agriculture.[433] When such food reaches a US port of entry, the importer of record applies for entry with the CBP, whose Agriculture Program and Liaison Office performs a first-tier inspection.[434] CBP then conditionally releases the shipment to the relevant agency for reinspection.

---

[425] 21 U.S.C. § 1034(a).

[426] 9 C.F.R. § 420.

[427] 21 U.S.C. § 1044; 7 C.F.R. § 59.100.

[428] A "loss" egg generally refers to an egg that is unfit for human food because it is smashed or broken so that its contents are leaking; or overheated, frozen, or contaminated; or an incubator reject; or because it contains a bloody white, large meat spots, a large quantity of blood, or other foreign material. A "leaker" egg means an egg that has a crack or break in the shell and shell membranes to the extent that the egg contents are exposed or are exuding or free to exude through the shell. See, e.g., IOWA ADMIN. CODE r. 481-36.1 (2008).

[429] 21 U.S.C. §§ 1035, 1047.

[430] In Face of Egg Recall, FDA Calls for More Authority, NPR (August 23, 2010).

[431] CBP PUBLICATION NO. 0000-0504, IMPORTING INTO THE UNITED STATES: A GUIDE FOR COMMERCIAL IMPORTERS 1 (2006, last revision)

[432] Id.

[433] See generally, Protecting Agriculture, U.S. CUSTOMS AND BORDER PATROL.

[434] See generally, Fulfilling CBP's Agricultural Mission, U.S. CUSTOMS AND BORDER PATROL.

[k] National Marine Fisheries Services

The National Marine Fisheries Service (NMFS), a subsidiary of the US Department of Commerce's National Oceanic and Atmospheric Administration (NOAA), is responsible for seafood quality and grading, as a result of the Agricultural Marketing Act of 1946. It operates a voluntary inspection program for fish in conjunction with FDA. FDA regulates seafood processing but NMFS is responsible for the promulgation of grade standards, as well as the inspection and certification of fish and shellfish. NMFS also operates a voluntary fee-for-service Fish Meal Inspection Program through its National Seafood Inspection Laboratory (NSIL). Federal or state inspectors inspect participating facilities, evaluating sanitation and collecting and testing samples for salmonella.[435]

[3] *System Prevention Approaches*

A tool referred to as system prevention approaches has emerged as a significant preventive measure in ensuring food safety. This tool has taken on various forms, but emphasizes the front end of the food supply. The implementation of this tool is predicated upon the belief that reliance on end-product testing and inspections is relatively resource-intensive and inefficient because it is reactive rather than preventative. The best-known system-prevention approach is the HACCP that is required for meat, seafood, juice, and acid and utilized on a volunteer basis for other food products.

[a] Development and Application of HACCP

HACCP is a systematic preventive approach to food safety that addresses physical, chemical, and biological hazards at each stage of the food production process (including raw material production, procurement, and handling, as well as manufacturing, distribution, and consumption) rather than relying solely on finished product inspection.[436] HACCP is used in the food industry to identify potential food safety hazards so that key actions, known as Critical Control Points (CCPs), can be taken to reduce or eliminate the risk that are realized as hazards. HACCP should properly be characterized as a method of regulation, rather than a body of regulations. Accordingly, USDA regulates meat HACCP systems whereas the FDA regulates seafood and juice HACCP systems. Currently, in other food industries regulated by the USDA, the use of HACCP is voluntary. Although both federal regulators and industries have struggled in transitioning to a HACCP system, regulators continue to view HACCP with favor.

   HACCP was developed in the late 1950s and early 1960s by the Pillsbury Company, with participation of the National Aeronautics and Space Administration (NASA), with the goal to produce food that would be safe to eat in space.[437] When it became apparent that traditional end product testing was inadequate to guarantee the food's safety with complete assurance, NASA mandated the application of CCPs that it had already employed

---

[435] Nat'l Marine Fisheries Serv., Nat'l Oceanic & Atmospheric Admin., Seafood Inspection Program.
[436] *See generally, Hazard Analysis & Critical Control Points* (HACCP), U.S. FOOD & DRUG ADMIN. (November 26, 2014, last updated).
[437] *See* FOOD CODE 2001, *Recommendations of the United States Public Health Service, Food and Drug Administration* 424, U.S. FOOD & DRUG ADMIN. (2001).

in engineering management to food processing and manufacturing. Outside their collaboration with NASA, when Pillsbury confronted a serious food safety problem with an ingredient in their baby food, the company responded by introducing the HACCP system for the systems-wide production of their foods.[438] In the decades since its development, HACCP has become widely recognized by the scientific community as the best approach for improving food safety.[439] In 1985, the National Academy of Sciences recommended "government agencies responsible for control of microbiological hazards in foods should promulgate appropriate regulations that would require industry to utilize the HACCP system in their food protection programs."[440] These recommendations led to the formation of the National Advisory Committee on Microbiological Criteria for Foods in 1987, which expanded the HACCP protocol to include the seven principles that are now widely accepted as the standard. By 1988, international and foreign governments had endorsed the HACCP systems for food production, processing, and handling.[441] As concern about pathogen contamination of the food supply increased during the early 1990s, the FDA adopted the HACCP principles for the inspection of seafood in December 1995, with the USDA following suit for meat and poultry inspection beginning in January 1997.[442]

The food industry has supported voluntary adoption of HACCP but generally opposes its mandatory imposition. In both the seafood and juice processor industries, however, when their specific food products became the source of significant contamination with pathological microorganisms and the object of intensive media focus, the relevant trade associations requested the FDA to undertake HACCP programs to regain public confidence. Segments of the food industry that have not had similar problems have seen no compelling need for additional regulation.[443]

[b] HACCP: Seven Principles

HACCP is predicated upon several principles, as enumerated in the following section.[444]

1) Conduct a hazard analysis

A hazard analysis assesses food safety hazards and identifies the preventive measures to control these hazards. A food safety hazard is any biological, chemical, or physical

---

[438] William H. Sperber and Richard F. Stier, *Happy 50th Birthday to HACCP: Retrospective and Prospective*, FOOD SAFETY MAG. (2009/2010).

[439] *See, e.g.,* INSTITUTE OF MEDICINE, NATIONAL RESEARCH COUNCIL, NATIONAL ACADEMY OF SCIENCES, ENSURING SAFE FOOD: FROM PRODUCTION TO CONSUMPTION 29–30 (1998) ("It is widely accepted by the scientific community that use of HACCP systems in food production, processing, distribution, and preparation is the best known approach to enhancing the safety of foods.").

[440] AN EVALUATION OF THE ROLE OF MICROBIOLOGICAL CRITERIA FOR FOODS AND FOOD INGREDIENTS 329, NAT'L RES. COUNCIL, NAT'L ACAD. OF SCI., (1985).

[441] 61 Fed. Reg. 38,806, 38,814 (July 25, 1996) (codified in scattered sections of 9 C.F.R.).

[442] 60 Fed. Reg. 6774 (February 3, 1995), 61 Fed. Reg. 38806 (July 25, 1996) (codified at 9 C.F.R. Part 417); 64 Fed. Reg. 28351 (May 26, 1999), 66 Fed. Reg. 12589 (February 27, 2001), 68 Fed. Reg. 34208 (June 6, 2003); 62 Fed. Reg. 45593 (August 28, 1997), 63 Fed. Reg. 20450 (April 24, 1998), 66 Fed. Reg. 6137 (January 19, 2001) (codified at 21 C.F.R. Part 120).

[443] PETER HUTT ET AL., FOOD AND DRUG LAW 354 (2007).

[444] FDA Food Code 2009: Annex 4 – Management of Food Safety Practices – Achieving Active Managerial Control of Foodborne Illness Risk Factors.

property that may cause a food to be unsafe for human consumption. The hazard analysis step should include an assessment of both the likelihood that such a hazard will occur and its severity if it does occur. This analysis should also involve the establishment of preventive measures to control identified hazards.

2) Determine the CCPs

A CCP is defined as any controllable point in a specific process where loss of control may result in an unacceptable risk. Many organizations and HACCP authorities have defined additional types of control points. Points in the manufacturing process that may be CCPs include cooking, chilling, specific sanitation procedures, product formulation control, prevention of cross contamination, and certain aspects of employee and environmental hygiene.

3) Establish critical limits

Critical limits must be established and met for each CCP to ensure that the system effectively controls the identified hazards. Critical limits are the tolerance limits or safety margins for each CCP to ensure prevention or control of a hazard. Examples of criteria used for CCPs include time, temperature, humidity, water activity, and pH level.

4) Establish monitoring procedures

Monitoring is defined as a planned sequence of observation, testing, or measurement to ensure that the CCP is under control. Monitoring helps to track the process and assists in detecting adverse trends that, if not corrected, can lead to a loss of control.

5) Establish corrective actions

A critical deviation must be addressed promptly by a clearly defined and assigned plan of action. This may involve adjustment to the process upstream or the addition of corrective steps in the subsequent process. The plan must address disposition of any product that was produced during critical deviation in control.

6) Establish verification procedures

Verification procedures are necessary to ensure that the HACCP-based system implemented complies with the HACCP plan, as designed for that process. Verification may include documentation checks as well as testing, and the manufacturer or the regulatory agency may perform audits. Any significant changes in the process, materials, or packaging will require an appropriate review in order to keep the program effective and current.

7) Establish recordkeeping and documentation procedures

According to a study completed by the US Department of Commerce, correcting problems without recordkeeping could lead to a recurrence of the same problems. The seventh principle requires the preparation and maintenance of a written HACCP plan that lists the hazards, CCPs, and critical limits identified by the firm, as well as the monitoring, recordkeeping, and other procedures that the firm intends to use to implement the plan. This principle also requires the maintenance of records generated during the operation of the plan.

[c] Limitations in Enforcement

USDA maintains the ability to initiate a withholding, suspension, or withdrawal action based on sanitation or HACCP violations, including the failure to develop or implement a required HACCP plan. This proposition was tested in *Supreme Beef Processors, Inc. v. USDA*, which weakened USDA's enforcement mechanisms.[445] USDA asserted that *Salmonella* is an indicator organism that measures a HACCP plan's effectiveness against not just *Salmonella*, but all pathogens. Thus, *Salmonella* tests "serves as a proxy for the presence or absence of pathogen controls, such that a high level of *Salmonella* indicates" adulteration.[446]

In 2001, the US Court of Appeals for the Fifth Circuit handed down its decision prohibiting the USDA from suspending inspection services based solely upon failure of the *Salmonella* performance standard.[447] The Court of Appeals ruled that *Salmonella* is not a per se adulterant because it is found in all meat and meat plants and thus does not constitute evidence of unsanitary conditions. The decision was seen as a blow to the enforcement authority of FSIS, although USDA inspectors continued to inspect in order to ensure clean meat factories. The only change was the ability to shut down a meat plant based solely on results of the *Salmonella* tests.

[d] Low-Acid Canned Food and Acidified Foods

Although FDA did not nominally adopt HACCP as a regulatory tool until the mid-1990s, HACCP principles served as the framework for FDA's regulation of low-acid canned foods and acidified foods in the 1970s. These regulations resulted from a 1971 petition to the FDA by the National Canners Association (NCA), urging the agency to adopt good manufacturing practices (GMP) for low acid foods in "hermetically sealed containers which are processed by heat either before or after being sealed in the container."[448] NCA was spurred into action by several outbreaks of botulism due to consumption of improperly processed canned foods.[449] In 1971, botulism toxin in Bon Vivant soup caused one death and one severe illness, prompting coordinated efforts between NCA and FDA to recall the remaining cans and notify consumers.[450] Seeking to quell public concern over canned food, NCA proposed rulemaking that would allow FDA to regulate more effectively the manufacturing of low-acid foods and prevent botulism.[451] In 1979, the

---

[445] 275 F.3d 432 (5th Cir. 2001).
[446] *Id.* at 440.
[447] *Id.* at 442–3.
[448] Manufacture and Processing of Canned Foods, 36 Fed. Reg. 21688 (November 12, 1971).
[449] U.S. Food Safety System Country Report, Annex II Precaution in U.S. Food Safety Decision Making, at Paragraph 69, Food & Drug Admin., U.S. Dept. of Agric. (2000).
[450] Edward Dunkelberger, *The Statutory Basis for the FDA's Food Safety Assurance Programs: From GMP, to Emergency Permit Control, to HACCP,* 50 Food & Drug L.J. 357, 364–5 (1995).
[451] *Id.* at 366.

FDA finalized its good manufacturing practice provisions for low-acid foods and acid-ified foods.[452] Those provisions are currently codified at 21 C.F.R. Parts 113 (low-acid foods) and 114 (acidified foods). Emergency permit control regulations, including the general provisions (subpart A) and the provisions specific to low-acid foods (subpart B), were also finalized in 1979 and are codified at 21 C.F.R. Part 108.[453]

[e] Seafood Processors

FDA regulations require that seafood processors implement HACCP plans for any food safety hazard "reasonably likely" to occur in their product.[454] A seafood processor is any person engaged in the commercial, custom, or institutional processing of fish or fishery products in the United States or a foreign country. FDA regulations require seafood pro-cessors to make the HACCP plans and other HACCP records (e.g., monitoring records) available "for official review and copying at reasonable times."[455]

HACCP provides an overarching process for seafood regulation. A food processor must identify within its HACCP plan food safety hazards that are "reasonably likely to occur," including environmental factors such as natural toxins, chemical contaminants, and pes-ticides.[456] HACCP plans must be specific to each kind of seafood product processed.[457] HACCP seafood regulations include, as an augmentation to the general HACCP regu-lations, a subpart specific to the processing of shellfish.[458] This special subpart refers to the National Shellfish Sanitation Program, which is a federal-state cooperative program to improve the sanitation of shellfish moving in interstate commerce.[459] The program streamlines and unifies regulation, as states, FDA, EPA, and NOAA, and foreign govern-ments engage in program activities, including developing guidance and certification programs and evaluating state programs.[460]

[f] Juice Processor Inspections

Like seafood processors, juice processors are required to implement HACCP plans for any food safety hazard reasonably likely to occur in their product. FDA proposed HACCP regulations for juice in 1998. The proposal was prompted, in part, by a series of high-profile cases of microbial contamination – in particular, a 1996 outbreak of *E. coli* in unpasteurized apple juice that resulted in the death of a child.[461] The proposed

---

[452] Thermally Processed Low-Acid Foods Packaged in Hermetically Sealed Containers, Final Rule, 44 Fed. Reg. 16209 (March 16, 1979); Acidified Foods, Current Good Manufacturing Practice, Final Rule, 44 Fed. Reg. 16230 (March 16, 1979)
[453] Emergency Permit Control Acidified Foods, Final Rule 44 Fed. Reg. 16204 (March 16, 1979).
[454] 21 C.F.R. § 123.6(b).
[455] 21 C.F.R. § 123.9(c).
[456] 21 C.F.R. § 123.6(c).
[457] 21 C.F.R. § 123.6(b).
[458] 21 C.F.R. § 123.20.
[459] *National Shellfish Sanitation Program*, U.S. FOOD & DRUG ADMIN.
[460] *Id.*
[461] Hazard Analysis and Critical Control Point (HACCP); Procedures for the Safe and Sanitary Processing and Importing of Juice; Food Labeling; Warning Notice Statements; Labeling of Juice Products; Proposed Rules, 63 Fed. Reg. 20449, 20450, 20452 (April 24, 1998).

regulations revealed other potential hazards that concerned the agency, including the presence of pesticides and contaminants from soil, cans, and the manufacturing process in juice products.[462]

Over protests from the juice industry, FDA adopted the juice HACCP regulations in 2001, declining to adopt more limited regulatory options proposed at the time by the juice industry, such as increased inspections, new GMP regulations, mandatory pasteurization, better labeling, or increased industry education.[463]

[g] Requirements under FSMA for Food Safety Plan

FSMA added Section 418 to the FDCA, which requires registered facilities to perform a hazard analysis and implement a preventive controls plan.[464] Section 418 applies to all foods, except those foods that are in compliance with other FDA government prevention programs – the Seafood HACCP, the Juice HACCP, the Thermally Processed Low-Acid Foods Packaged in Hermetically Sealed Containers standards of the FDA, and the Section 419 fresh produce standards.[465]

[h] General Requirements: Written Plan

The owner, operator, or agent in charge of a facility must conduct a written hazard analysis and develop and implement a written preventive controls plan to significantly minimize or prevent the occurrence of such hazards and provide assurances that their food is not adulterated. The written plan per FDCA § 418 must include the elements listed in the following pages:

o **Hazard Analysis** – In writing, known or reasonably foreseeable hazards with the facility must be identified and evaluated. These hazards cover those that occur naturally or those that may be unintentionally introduced.[466]

o **Preventive Controls** – Preventive controls must be identified and implemented to provide assurances that known or reasonably foreseeable hazards identified in the hazard analysis will significantly be minimized or prevented.[467]

o **Monitoring of Effectiveness** – The preventive controls must be monitored to assure their implementation is achieved.[468]

---

[462] *Id.* at 20451–2.

[463] Hazard Analysis and Critical Control Point (HACCP); Procedures for the Safe and Sanitary Processing and Importing of Juice; Final Rule, 66 Fed. Reg. 6137, 6140 (January 19, 2001).

[464] 21 U.S.C § 350g.

[465] 21 U.S.C. § 350g(j).

[466] 21 U.S.C. § 350g(b). Examples of reasonably foreseeable hazards include biological, chemical, physical, and radiological hazards, natural toxins, pesticides, drug residues, decomposition, parasites, allergens, and unapproved food and color additives.

[467] 21 U.S.C. § 350g(o)(3). The term "preventive controls" means "those risk-based, reasonably appropriate procedures, practices, and processes that a person knowledgeable about the safe manufacturing, processing, packing, or holding of food would employ to significantly minimize or prevent the hazards identified under the hazard analysis ... and that are consistent with the current scientific understanding of safe food manufacturing, processing, packing, or holding at the time of the analysis." *Id.*

[468] 21 U.S.C. § 350g(d).

- ○ **Corrective Actions** – If the preventive controls are not implemented or are found to be ineffective, appropriate action must be taken to reduce the likelihood of the recurrence of implementation failure.[469]
- ○ **Verification** – The implemented preventive controls must be verified to ensure they are sufficiently adequate to control the identified hazards in the hazard analysis.[470]
- ○ **Recordkeeping** – Certain records are required to be maintained by the facility for at least two years and be made available to FDA promptly upon oral or written request.[471]

[i] Exemptions from General Requirement

A point of confusion from the original proposals by the FDA in its implementation of FSMA has been the definition of farm and the activities that may change the status of a farm operation to a manufacturer or processor. The revised proposed rules implementing Section 418 of FSMA provide that in general, on-farm packing and holding of produce would not be subject to the food preventive controls rule. Such activities may trigger the proposed Produce Safety Rule, as noted in this chapter. The revised rules also provide that farms that pack or hold produce from other farms would not be subject to Section 418. Farms that conduct additional processing or manufacturing – beyond on-farm packing and holding of food – may be subject to preventive controls rule for those activities.[472]

Certain small facilities (referred to as "qualified facilities") are also exempt from the general requirements of Section 418. A "very small business" would be defined as firms having less than $1 million in total annual sales of human food, adjusted for inflation.[473] Such a small facility (also known as "qualified facility") is required to submit documentation that demonstrates that the owner, operator, or agent in charge of the facility has identified potential hazards associated with the food being produced, is implementing preventive controls to address the hazards, and is monitoring the preventive controls to ensure that such controls are effective. In lieu of this demonstration, a qualified facility may submit documentation that the facility is in compliance with state, local, county, or other applicable nonfederal food safety law.

FDA may withdraw the exemption for a qualified facility if an active investigation of a foodborne illness outbreak is directly linked to that facility, or if FDA determines under the circumstances that withdrawing the exemption is necessary to protect public health and prevent or mitigate a foodborne illness outbreak.[474]

In addition to being confusing, the qualified facility exception has proven controversial. On the one hand, large growers argued that food safety guidelines should apply to all growers regardless of size, because there is no exception for food safety. On the other hand, small

---

[469] 21 U.S.C. § 350g(e).
[470] 21 U.S.C. § 350g(f) (subsection lists numerous verification activities).
[471] 21 U.S.C. § 350g(g) (the required records include documenting the monitoring of the preventive controls, instances of nonconformance material to food safety, the results of testing and other appropriate means of verification, corrective actions, and the efficacy of preventive controls and corrective actions).
[472] Current Good Manufacturing Practice and Hazard Analysis and Risk-Based Preventive Controls for Food for Animals, 79 Fed. Reg. 58476, 58481-85 (September 29, 2014)
[473] *Id.* at 5801-02.
[474] 21 U.S.C. § 350g(l)(3).

farm advocates believed that further regulations on small farmers would increase costs and make them less able to compete in the marketplace, and in addition, most food safety lapses occurred in big industrial facilities, not on small farms.

Additional exemptions to Section 418 are facilities in the following categories:

- **Dietary Supplements** – Any facility that manufacturers, processes, packs, or holds dietary supplements is exempt, if such facility complies with the Current Good Manufacturing Practices and adverse event reporting requirements for dietary supplements.[475] facilities solely engaged in the production of food for animals,
- **Certain Specialized Facilities** – Any facility that is solely engaged in the production of food for animals other than man, the storage of raw agricultural commodities (other than fruits and vegetables) intended for further distribution or processing, or the storage of packaged foods that are not exposed to the environment.[476]
- **Alcohol Related Facilities** – Any facility that manufactures, processes, packs, or holds alcoholic beverages, even if they also receive and distribute nonalcohol foods, provided that such nonalcohol foods are prepackaged to prevent direct human contact and constitute no more than 5 percent of the facility's overall sales.[477]

[4] *Third-Party Verification*

[a] Form of New Governance

The development of third-party verification as a tool in the regulation of food safety signifies recognition of the expanding global supply chain, where the continuous increase in the foreign importation of food products and the limited resources and challenges of government agencies interface to make effective enforcement difficult.[478] The term "third-party" refers to an external auditor and "third-party verification" denotes a system in which governmental agencies rely on these third parties to verify regulatory compliance. Private third-party verifiers essentially act in the place of government agents to conduct inspections and make regulatory compliance determinations. Government agencies, in turn, take on new roles in coordinating and overseeing these private actors. This partnership or hybridization of private and public is a form of the "new governance" addressed in the introduction of this treatise.[479]

[b] Accrediting Third Parties

Section 307 of FSMA added Section 808 to the FDCA and required FDA to establish a system for accrediting third parties that conducts audits to certify foreign facilities or

---

[475] FSMA § 103(g).

[476] 21 U.S.C. § 350g(m).

[477] FSMA § 116(b).

[478] A GAO report notes that from 2000 to 2011, imported food as a percentage of all food consumed in the United States increased from about 9 percent to over 16 percent. Fruits, vegetables, and seafood in particular are more likely to come from foreign rather than domestic sources. *See* GAO, Food Safety, GAO-12-933 5, FDA Can Better Oversee Food Imports by Assessing and Leveraging Other Countries' Oversight Resources (September 2012).

[479] *See* Orly Lobel, *The Renew Deal: The Fall of Regulation and the Rise of Governance in Contemporary Legal Thought*, 89 Minn. L. Rev. 342, 343–4 (2004). Third-party verification is not a new concept. In addition to food safety, third-party verification is also being incorporated in climate control and environmental law regulatory frameworks.

imported foods under the agency's jurisdiction. Under this system, accreditation bodies are responsible for accrediting the third parties that certify that a foreign food product or facility complies with US requirements, including new preventive control requirements. Section 302, the Voluntary Qualified Importer Program (VQIP) and Section 303 of FSMA authorize FDA to require certification for entry of imported foods that pose a food safety risk.[480] This system contemplated by Section 307 of FSMA includes model standards that accreditation bodies use to evaluate and accredit third parties. The FDA itself may only directly accredit such third parties if it has not recognized an accreditation body within two years of establishing the accreditation system. Foreign governments, as well as foreign cooperatives that market the products of growers or processors, private firms, and individuals may qualify as third parties. Under FSMA, FDA has the authority to withdraw accreditation from an accredited third party or revoke recognition of an accreditation body. FDA must also establish procedures to reaccredit third parties and reinstate the recognition of accreditation bodies.[481]

On July 29, 2013, FDA published a proposed rule on the accreditation of third-party auditors.[482] The proposed rule contains requirements and procedures for recognition and accreditation for both accreditation bodies seeking recognition by FDA and third-party auditors seeking accreditation. According to FDA, these requirements will help to ensure the competence and independence of participants. The proposed rule also contains requirements on auditing and certification of foreign food facilities and food under the program. The proposed rule provides for consultative audits, performed for internal purposes to determine whether an entity meets FDA requirements, and regulatory audits, performed to determine eligibility for food certification with a report submitted to FDA. Importantly, the third-party auditors and certification bodies must immediately notify the FDA of "any condition that could cause or contribute to a serious risk to the public health," regardless of whether the risk is discovered in a consultative or regulatory audit.

The comment on the proposed rules is now closed. Separate from this proposal, FDA will issue draft Model Accreditation Standards that will specify the required accreditation qualifications for certification bodies.

The efficacy of third-party audits as a legal tool to be used by the FDA likely will be scrutinized closely. In September 2013, the FDA held a public meeting to discuss its proposed accreditation rule. Consumer advocacy groups expressed concern over the FDA using third-party audits as a replacement for inspections conducted by the agency itself.[483] To illustrate their concerns, the advocates focused on several high-profile outbreaks at enterprises that had received passing or strong scores on third-party audits.[484] There is also the concern of a conflict of interest where auditors are paid by the enterprise they audit, in addition to concerns about insufficient standards, auditor incompetence, and inconsistency of audits.[485]

---

[480] *See also* 21 U.S.C. § 301.

[481] GAO FOOD SAFETY, *supra* note 478 at 12.

[482] *See* Accreditation of Third-Party Auditors, 78 Fed. Reg. 45782 (July 29, 2013).

[483] *FDA Holds Public Meeting on FSMA Import Proposed Rules*, HOGAN LOVELLS MEMORANDUM (September 25, 2013).

[484] *See Id.* at 2.

[485] Timothy D. Lytton & Lesley K. McAllister, *Oversight in Private Food Safety Auditing: Addressing Auditor Conflict of Interest*, 2014 WIS. L. REV. 289, 294 (2014).

[5] *Traceability*

  [a] Evolution as a Legal Tool

Traceability has long been debated as a tool in the regulation of food safety.[486] The FDA defines traceability, or product tracking, as a system that documents "the production and distribution chain of product so that in the case of an outbreak or evidence of contaminated food, a product can be traced back to a common source or forward through distribution channels."[487] The regulation of the traceability of food has been developed piecemeal and is still evolving. Efforts at product tracking are largely fueled by liability and food safety considerations, but product tracking is a complex challenge that requires individuals, departments, and food enterprises to work collaboratively throughout the food supply chain. Indeed, private actors, often in concert with government agencies, are working to further develop food traceability systems and technology. These efforts have been beset by legal and political complications.

FDA initially explored traceability in its 1998 guidance for the food safety for fruits and vegetables.[488] In these nonbinding recommendations, FDA acknowledged that the ability to identify the source of a product through trace-back serves as an important complement to good agricultural and management practices in order to prevent the occurrence of food safety problems. FDA suggested that at a minimum an effective trace-back system should document the source of a product and have a mechanism for making or identifying the product that can follow the product from the farm to the consumer. Specifically, FDA sought information on the date of harvest, farm identification, and who handled the produce from grower to receiver.

In 2002, the National Institute for Animal Agriculture (NIAA) organized a task force to produce a National Identification Work Plan.[489] Their mission was to ensure the health of the nation's animal herd, improve the ability to respond to biosecurity threats, add value to meat products,[490] and compete with international trading partners who were implementing animal traceability systems.[491] The work plan was drafted and accepted by the United States Animal Health Association, which, in response to the work plan, also passed a resolution requesting USDA's Animal and Plant Health Inspection Service

---

[486] Within the EU, traceability has been enshrined in a number of regulatory initiatives. The EU General Food Law Reg. EC No. 178/2002 defines traceability as: "The ability to trace and follow a food, feed, food-producing animal or substance intended to be or expected to be incorporated into a food or feed, through all stages of production, processing and distribution." In general, the US food industry has been uncomfortable in the past with the broad scope of the EU definition for traceability, but is moving closer to the EU model.

[487] *Product Tracing: Frequently Asked Questions*, U.S. Food & Drug Admin. (February 3, 2014).

[488] FDA, Guidance for Industry, Guide to Minimize Microbial Food Safety Hazards for Fresh Fruits and Vegetables (October 26, 1998).

[489] *See* USDA and Industry Developing National Animal Identification Plan, US Dep't of Agric., Animal and Plant Health Inspection Service (2003).

[490] Market incentives to keep records tracking food production and distribution include differentiating and marketing foods with subtle or undetectable quality attributes. *See* Elise Golan et al., *Traceability in the U.S. Food Supply: Economic Theory and Industry Studies*, Econ. Research Service, U.S. Dep't of Agric. (March 2004).

[491] Canada, New Zealand, and the European Union and Great Britain had at the time developed mandatory animal identification programs. Japan was fine-tuning and expanding its mandatory program, while Argentina, Brazil, Mexico, and Uruguay had begun to implement national animal identification systems. Clint Peck, *Around the ID World*, Beef (December 1, 2003).

(APHIS) to establish a national animal identification development team. The resolution indicated that the development team was to establish a national plan using the NIAA's work plan as a guide.[492] Accordingly, in the spring of 2003, the development team completed the United States Animal Identification Plan (USAIP). USAIP's objective was to develop a trace-back system that identifies all animals and premises that are potentially exposed to a diseased animal within forty-eight hours after discovery.[493]

The December 2003 discovery of a cow with Bovine Spongiform Encephalopathy (BSE or "mad cow disease") in the state of Washington accelerated efforts to implement a national identification program for animals. In response to criticism over delays in tracing the affected livestock in question, and general concerns about the agency's inability to trace livestock used for food product, USDA began to promote the implementation of a national animal identification program (NAIS) as a major policy priority for mad cow disease prevention.[494]

Two legal issues complicated the implementation of a NAIS: first, the confidentiality of the information collected and stored; and second, the exposure of producers to liability.[495] Some livestock producers and livestock industry participants raised concerns about who would be able to access the information provided to NAIS. Their confidentiality concerns were that: (1) establishing a centralized database might allow others in the industry, either the producer's direct competitors or packers, to know information about their operations; (2) government agencies such as the Internal Revenue Service, Bureau of Land Management, or EPA may access the data; and (3) people who have designs to harm animal agriculture might access the information.[496] With respect to liability, the concern arose from the recognition that a key component of a lawsuit is knowledge of who caused the harm. The industry's fear was that NAIS would allow people to find out who owned an animal at the time that the animal acquired the condition that caused the harm. In 2010, the USDA abandoned NAIS, earning the praise of the livestock industry and raising concern among others in the food community.[497]

[b] One Step: Bioterrorism Act

As noted previously in this chapter, traceability is a major provision in the Bioterrorism Act, which requires that enterprises keep records of all foods they receive and release, thereby establishing a chain of custody. Firms (other than farms and restaurants) are required to provide specific information to the FDA regarding the immediate previous sources of a product as well as the immediate subsequent recipients of a product (other than consumers). This is commonly referred to as the one-up/one-back requirement and is a basic traceability rule based on the EU traceability model.

---

[492] See APHIS, National Animal Identification Plan, *supra* note 489.

[493] See United States Animal Identification Plan: A Work in Progress, NATIONAL IDENTIFICATION DEVELOPMENT TEAM (December 2003).

[494] See Scott Kilman, *Mad-Cow Crisis Spurs Rules Change*, WALL ST. J. (December 31, 2003).

[495] Michael T. Roberts & Harrison M. Pittman, *Legal Issues in Developing a National Plan for Animal Identification*, THE NATIONAL AGRICULTURAL LAW CENTER (February 4, 2004).

[496] Michael T. Roberts & Doug O'Brien, *Animal Identification: Confidentiality of Information*, LIVESTOCK MARKETING INFORMATION CENTER (October 8, 2004).

[497] *Id.*

[c] FSMA: Traceability Requirements

Section 204 of FSMA is intended to provide a more stepped-up and standardized traceability system to food. Section 204 requires that prior to establishing a tracing system, that the FDA conduct at least two pilot projects (one or more for processed foods, and one or more for fresh produce) to evaluate methods for improving traceability and then report to Congress on the findings of these pilot projects. FDA is also required to engage in additional data gathering, including assessing the costs and benefits of several different product tracing technologies and evaluating domestic and international tracing practices in commercial use.[498]

Section 204 directs the FDA, after the pilots are completed and additional data are gathered, to initiate rulemaking on recordkeeping requirements for high-risk foods in order to facilitate better tracing. The FDA must define high-risk foods, considering such factors as the known risks of a food based on foodborne illness data, the likelihood that a particular food has a high potential risk of contamination, and the likely severity of an illness attributed to a particular food.[499] These high-risk foods will be a focus of the new tracing system.

[d] Private Traceability Initiatives

Private sector traceability initiatives at the level of the individual supply chain are numerous, sophisticated, and varied. These systems have emerged in response to perceived market premiums for quality assurances that can be verified through traceability. The systems emphasize whole-chain traceability, which includes internal and external visibility, from the grower, through the distributor, to the retailer.[500] Whole-chain traceability allocates risks and establishes contractual relationships between stakeholders.

Given the modest traceability mandate imposed on the food industry by FSMA (focusing mostly on "high-risk foods"), it is likely that private traceability initiatives will continue to thrive – from retail to the producer – in response to consumer demand for greater transparency and quality and safety assurance.[501] Certainly, the liability implications of traceability are relatively clear. For example, as shown in this chapter, the Food Allergen Consumer Protection Act holds manufacturers strictly liable for not labeling any top allergens contained in the product, known or unknown. Thus, manufacturers must have knowledge of their raw material contents and their sources, in order to avoid the liability associated with any detectable amount of allergens in the final product. As another example, non-GMO certification requires a verification process that relies on rigorous traceability, documentation, and segregation practices for products. This process relies on a robust traceability system.

---

[498] FSMA at § 204(a)(b).

[499] *Product Tracing under FSMA*, U.S Food & Drug Admin. (February 3, 2014).

[500] *See, e.g.*, *The Produce Traceability Initiative (PTI)*, U.S. Food & Drug Admin. (seeks supply chain-wide adoption of electronic traceability of every case of produce).

[501] *See e.g.*, FMI and ReposiTrak™Partner to Provide Food Safety Traceability Platform for Food Retailers, Leavitt Partners (December 9, 2013, announcement).

[6] *Reporting Requirements*

[a] Reportable Food Registry Act

The Reportable Food Registry (RFR), available on the FDA.GOV website since September 8, 2009, is an electronic portal for the food industry to report in when there is reasonable probability that an article of food will cause adverse health consequences.[502] Congress created RFR as part of the FDA Administration Amendments Act of 2007.[503] The act required FDA to establish an electronic portal, in which responsible parties must submit instances of reportable food within twenty-four hours and where public health officials may submit reports. The portal provides FDA with an information-gathering tool in order to track patterns of adulterated products. The RFR applies to all FDA-regulated categories, except dietary supplements and infant formula.[504] Products regulated exclusively by USDA under FMIA, PPIA, or the EPIA are not subject to RFR requirements.[505]

[b] Basic Reporting Requirements

Under Section 417 of the FDCA, a "responsible party" is required to report to the FDA if it determines that a food it has manufactured, processed, packed, or held is a "reportable food." The RFR requires a responsible party to submit a report to FDA through RFR as soon as practicable, but in no case later than twenty-four hours after determining that an article of food is a reportable food.[506] The reporting, such as that outlined in the Bioterrorism Act, includes a one step up and one step back requirement, where food companies must identify both their suppliers and customers to FDA through the web portal.

In designating the responsible party who must submit instances of reportable food under Section 417, the statute indicates that it is the same party who submits the registration under Section 415(a) of FDCA (21 U.S.C. 350d) for the food facility where the article of food is manufactured, processed, packed, or held.[507] As noted in this chapter, persons who are required to submit a facility registration under Section 415 of FDCA are the owner, operators, or agent in charge of a domestic or foreign facility engaged in manufacturing, processing, packing, or holding food for consumption in the United States. These persons may include individuals, partnerships, corporations, or associations.[508]

When enacted, the RFR required submission of the companies and products involved, a description of the problem leading to the report, how the company learned of the problem, a description of the investigation, affected product information, and whether any adverse events had been reported. In June of 2012, FDA announced that it significantly expanded the information it will seek from the reporting company.[509] The information

---

[502] Reportable Food Registry for Industry, U.S. Food & Drug Admin. (June 17, 2014).
[503] 21 U.S.C. § 350f.
[504] *Id.*
[505] FDA, Draft Guidance for Industry: Questions and Answers Regarding the Reportable Food Registry as Established by the Food and Drug Administration Amendments Act of 2007 (2d ed.) (May 2010).
[506] 21 U.S.C. § 350f(d)(1).
[507] 21 U.S.C. § 350(d).
[508] 21 U.S.C. § 301.
[509] *FDA Improves the Reportable Food Registry by Adding New Data Elements,* Update, U.S. Food & Drug Admin. (June 4, 2012).

expanded to include why the product is being reported; a root cause analysis; justification as to the company's selection of particular lots or batches being reported; corrective
actions; whether the product underwent an antimicrobial treatment and, if so, a description of that treatment; whether a bacterial isolate is available for FDA collection; and
whether the company has already notified its suppliers and customers.[510]

[c] Reportable Food

A reportable food is a food (other than a dietary supplement or infant formula) for
which there is a reasonable probability that use or exposure will cause serious adverse
health consequences or death to humans or animals.[511] The FDA provides several examples of reportable food in draft guidance, including peanut butter contaminated with
Salmonella, ice cream that did not declare peanut-derived ingredients but contained
peanut butter as an ingredient, pet food contaminated with elevated levels of melamine
and cyanuric acid, and baby food that poses a choking hazard.[512]

   If a reportable food is discovered, the responsible party (registered facility) is required
to submit a report unless the adulteration that originated with the responsible party was
detected prior to the affected product's transfer to another person, and the responsible
party either corrected the adulteration or destroyed the affected articles of food. There
is often some confusion over the transfer requirement. The FDA's draft guidance states
that "[a] transfer to another person occurs when the responsible person releases the food
to another person."[513] The FDA's draft guidance further notes that "person" is defined
in FDCA Section 201(e) "as including individuals, partnerships, corporations, and associations," and that a "warehouse operator is a distinct legal person."[514] FDA considers a
transfer any change in the custody of the product, regardless of whether actual ownership
changed. The FDA does not consider an intracompany transfer in a vertically integrated
company to constitute a transfer to another person, where the company maintains continuous possession of the article of food. The FDA may eventually move away from
interpreting "transfer" through the lens of possession and broaden its view toward an
interpretation based on issues of control. Control of the product arguably reflects more
accurately the reality of food production and thus promotes more effectively the safety of
food and the intent behind the RFR. Whether the FDA will move toward "control" will
be revealed in the FDA's expected amendments to its draft guidance.

[d] FSMA Changes

FSMA requires some changes to the RFR to allow for consumer level notification,
the largest impact of which will be on grocery stores. The responsible party (registered

---

[510] *Id.*

[511] FDCA §§ 201(ff), 417(a)(2). The FDA interprets the definition of reportable food to include those foods
that would meet the definition of a Class I recall situation, where there is a reasonable probability that
the use of, or exposure to, a violative product will cause serious adverse health consequences or death.
See FDA, Questions and Answers - Reportable Food Registry, *supra* note 505.

[512] *See id.*

[513] *Id.*

[514] *Id.*

facility) must submit consumer-oriented information for any new product, including the following: a description of the article of food, its product identification codes (*e.g.*, UPC, SKU, or lot numbers), contact information for the responsible party, and any other information the FDA deems necessary to enable consumers to accurately identify the reportable food. FDA is also required to prepare this information in a standardized one-page summary and post it on the FDA website in a format that can be easily printed by a grocery store for purposes of consumer notification. Any grocery store that sold the reportable food and that is part of a chain with fifteen or more locations is required to prominently display pertinent FDA notices within twenty-four hours after it is posted on the FDA website and maintain such display for fourteen days. FSMA also required FDA to develop and publish a list of acceptable conspicuous locations and manners for providing such notice (e.g., the in-store location of the reportable food, at or near the cash register), and grocery stores will be required to post the notice using at least one of these. The knowing and willful failure to comply with this consumer notification requirement is a prohibited act, subject to injunction and criminal prosecution.[515]

[e] Legal Considerations

As a relatively new tool for FDA, the RFR is likely to undergo modifications. Also, while RFR reports have always been considered "safety reports" and therefore not admissible in court proceedings to show a product was contaminated or caused illnesses, these new data elements raise serious concerns for future litigation. In particular, since RFR reports are subject to Freedom of Information Act requests, potential litigants may use the expanded RFR reports as a roadmap for compiling their complaints. Finally, it important to note that even an unintentional failure to report in compliance with 21 U.S.C. §350f constitutes a criminal violation of the FDCA.

[7] *Reaching the Farm: Produce Safety*

[a] FDA Responsibility

Although the FDA has had jurisidicion over food safety on the farm, the agency historically has had little to nothing to do with farming. Under FSMA, this is no longer the case. FSMA expanded FDA's food safety responsibilities to extend to certain activities on the farm. Section 105 of FSMA directed FDA by way of formal rulemaking to "establish science-based minimum standards for the safe production and harvesting of those types of fruits and vegetables, including specific mixes of categories of fruits and vegetables, that are raw agricultural commodities for which the Secretary has determined that such standards minimize the risk of serious adverse health consequences or death."[516] Ordinarily, USDA, not FDA, has claimed expertise and resources in regulating farm activity, certainly at least with livestock farming. Some commentators lamented FDA's mandate, given that the agency's expertise lay in the science of food processing, while USDA has better grasp on how farming works.[517] Nevertheless,

---

[515] 21 U.S.C. § 331.

[516] 124 Stat. at 3899–3900 (codified at 21 U.S.C. § 419(a)(1)(A)).

[517] *See, e.g.*, Bob Goodlatte, *Keep FDA Authority Out of Farm Practices*, The Hill (June 4, 2009).

Congress decided to delegate the authority to FDA to regulate farm activity for purposes of ensuring safe food.

[b] Proposed Rule

In January 2013, FDA issued a proposed rule implementing the produce safety provisions of FSMA.[518] In response to extensive comments received on the proposed order, the FDA on September 2013 issued a supplemental rule that revises language on several key provisions of the proposed produce safety rule.[519] The proposal establishes new requirements for domestic and foreign farms that grow, harvest, pack, or hold raw or unprocessed fruits and vegetables for human consumption in the United States. The produce safety rule establishes science-based minimum standards to target microbiological hazards that arise with fruits and vegetables. The proposed rule does not extend to chemical, physical, or radiological contamination. Unlike microbiological contamination, these forms of contamination are rare and do not fit within the agency's risk-based approach to improve produce safety.

The proposed rule encompasses only fruits and vegetables grown for human consumption in their raw or natural unprocessed state. Foods that are rarely consumed raw, intended for commercial processing, or intended for on-farm consumption would not qualify as covered produce, and thus would not be subject to the proposed rule. FDA also proposes that covered produce exclude grains, which are commercially processed, but includes under coverage foods not commonly thought of as fruits and vegetables, such as mushrooms and tree nuts. Also the revised proposed rules allow farms to pack or hold raw agricultural commodities grown on another farm under a different ownership, without being considered a food facility subject to the produce safety rule.[520]

[c] Exemptions for Certain Farms

The proposed rule exempts certain small farms from the produce safety provisions. Farms with average sales no more than $25,000 during the previous 3-year period would be completely excluded from the rule's coverage.[521] For farms that do not meet this exemption, FDA proposes a "very small business" exemption that applies where the average annual monetary value of produce sold during the previous 3-year period is no more than $250,000. For farms that do not meet this exemption, a qualified exemption is proposed for farms that (1) have an average annual monetary value of food sold during the previous 3-year period no more than $500,000;[522] and (2) sell the majority of the food directly to a "qualified end-user," which is defined as a consumer or a restaurant or a

---

[518] *Standards for the Growing, Harvesting, Packing, and Holding of Produce for Human Consumption,* Proposed Rule, U.S. FOOD & DRUG ADMIN. (March 2013).

[519] Standards for the Growing, Harvesting, Packing, and Holding of Produce for Human Consumption, 79 Fed. Reg. 58434 (September 29, 2014) (to be codified at 21 CFR Part 112).

[520] *Id.*

[521] The FDA first proposed to exempt from the produce safety rule farms with an average monetary value of all food (instead of produce) sold during the previous 3-year period of more than $25,000. The FDA declined to apply the $25,000 limit to the average monetary value of covered produce.

[522] Although the definition of a "small business" under the supplemental proposed rule for this qualified exemption applies to produce sold at the $500,000 threshold, the FDA did not make a corresponding

retail establishment (grocery store) that is located in the same state as the farm or is not more than 275 miles from the farm. The qualified exemption allows farms that are considered "very small businesses" (having sales of $25,000–$250,000 of produce) four years after the produce safety rule is effective to comply. The farms that are considered "small businesses" (having sales of $250,000–$500,000 of food) have three years. All other farms have two years. An additional two years is allowed beyond these dates for compliance with water quality standards imposed under the proposed rule.

The supplemental proposed rule also expands the definition of the term "farm" such that packing or holding others' raw agricultural commodity (RAC) produce on a covered farm would now be subject to the produce safety standards.[523] The FDA's supplemental proposed rule also proposes additional amendments to the definitions of "farm," "holding," and "packing," consistent with proposed changes in the amended proposed rule on preventive controls for food and seeks further comments on key issues related to the definition of "farm."

Under the proposed rule, all farms – including qualified exempt farms – are prohibited from selling adulterated food under the general provisions of FDCA. Thus, FDA could withdraw a qualified exemption if (1) there is an active investigation of a foodborne illness outbreak that is directly linked to a qualified exempt farm; or (2) FDA determines that it is necessary to protect the public health and prevent or mitigate a foodborne illness outbreak based on conduct or conditions associated with the farm that are material to the safety of the covered produce grown, harvested, packed, or held on the farm.

It is not clear what precisely is the evidentiary standard or conditions for issuing a withdrawal order. The subject farm owner, operator, or agent receiving the order must comply within sixty days or appeal the order. The preamble of the supplemental proposed rule explains that FDA views the withdrawal as a last resort and (1) may consider alternative actions before withdrawing a qualified exemption, including a warning letter, recall, administrative detention, suspension of registration, seizure, and injunction; and (2) before withdrawing a qualified exemption, FDA must first provide notice in writing of the circumstances that may lead FDA to withdraw the exemption, provide the farmer with ten calendar days to respond to the notification, and consider the actions taken by the farm to address the circumstances that may lead FDA to withdraw the exemption. The supplemental proposed rule also establishes a process whereby a farmer can have a qualified exemption reinstated. A qualified exemption can be reinstated if (1) the withdrawal resulted from the farm being directly linked to an ongoing foodborne illness investigation and the investigation concludes and determines that there was no direct link; or (2) the farm resolves the conditions or conduct that caused FDA to issue the withdrawal, and withdrawal is no longer necessary to protect public health or prevent or mitigate a foodborne illness outbreak.

---

change to the eligibility criteria for a qualified exemption because the statutory language specifies that all food must be considered in calculating sales.

[523] Under the initial proposed rule, packing or holding of produce would be subject either to the preventive controls rule or the produce safety regulation, depending on whether or not the produce was grown or harvested on a farm under the same ownership. Presumably because this distinction lacks a public health basis and would be logistically difficult to enforce, the FDA agreed that ownership is irrelevant and that hazards associated with packing or holding activities would best be addressed under the produce safety standards, rather than under the preventive control rule.

[d] Summary of Standards

The proposed rule sets forth the following standards for the safe growing, harvesting, packing, and holding of product:

○ **Agricultural Water** – The proposed rule requires that all water intended or likely to come in contact with the harvestable portion of covered produce or a food contact surface be of safe and sanitary quality for its intended use. This requirement involves recordkeeping, inspection, maintenance, and follow-up actions for the agricultural water, water sources, and water distribution systems used in growing, harvesting, packing, and holding covered produce. The supplemental proposed rule provides that a farm may meet the requirements related to agricultural water testing by using the farm's own test results or data collected by a third party or parties in certain circumstances.

○ **Biological Soil Amendments** – The proposed rule establishes standards for the use and treatment of animal waste and prohibits the use of human waste in growing covered produce, except when such use is permitted by other regulations.

○ **Domesticated and Wild Animals** – The proposed rule requires that procedures be established for circumstances in which animals are allowed or are reasonably likely to enter areas where covered produce is grown. The proposed rule requires an adequate waiting period between any such grazing or work and harvest and monitoring of the area for intrusion. The supplemental rule proposal explicitly provides that the regulation would not authorize or require covered farms to take actions that would constitute the "taking" of threatened or endangered species in violation of the Endangered Species Act, or require covered farms to take measures to exclude animals from outdoor growing areas, or destroy animal habitat.

○ **Equipment, Tools, and Buildings** – The proposed rule establishes requirements for any equipment and tools that are intended or likely to come in contact with covered produce as well as for any facilities involved in growing, harvesting, packing, and holding covered produce.

○ **Worker Training and Hygiene** – The proposed rule subjects all workers who handle produce to qualification and training requirements. FDA also requires that sanitation and hygiene procedures be established to prevent contamination of produce.

[8] *Transportation*

[a] Coverage

FSMA authorized FDA to develop regulations for the safe transportation of food, thus encompassing the complete post-farm-gate supply chain (with the rather large exception of food products falling under exclusive jurisdiction of USDA) within the FDCA. In February 2014, FDA published a proposed rule regarding the sanitary transportation of food.[524] The proposed rule on sanitary transportation covers domestic and foreign entities, although the scope of the rule is not the same for both. Shippers, receivers, and carriers who transport food in the United States by motor or rail vehicle are subject

---

[524] Sanitary Transportation of Human and Animal Food, 79 Fed. Reg. 7006 (February 5, 2014).

to requirements under the rule, even if the food does not enter interstate commerce. Exporters outside of the United States are also subject to the new rule if they (1) ship food to the United States in an international freight container by oceangoing vessel or in an air freight container; (2) arrange for the transfer of the intact container in the United States onto a motor or rail vehicle for transportation in US commerce; and (3) if the food will be consumed or distributed in the United States. The proposed rule excludes from the definition of "transportation operations" fully packaged shelf-stable foods, compressed food gases (such as carbon dioxide used for carbonating beverages), live food animals, and raw agricultural commodities when they are transported by farms. The proposed rule also would exempt entities engaged in food transportation operations with less than $500,000 in annual sales. In addition FDA would allow entities that otherwise would be subject to the rule to request waivers if they can show that the agency's grant of this waiver would not result in the transportation of food under conditions that would be unsafe for human and animal health and would not be "contrary to the public interest."[525]

[b] Summary of Proposed Rules

The proposed rule on sanitary transportation applies a risk-based approach to contamination concerns in the transportation of food. FDA identifies the greater risks in the transportation of food to include food that is not completely enclosed by its container (such as fresh produce in vented boxes) and foods that require time or temperature control to ensure their safety (such as meat, poultry, or seafood) or to prevent microbial spoilage (such as pasteurized juice). The requirements for the proposed rule include the following:

- **Vehicles and Transportation Equipment** – The proposed rule would require that vehicles and transportation equipment used in the transportation of food be suitable and adequately cleanable for sanitary transport. This provision extends to the maintenance of these vehicles and transportation equipment to prevent food from becoming unfit for consumption or rendered injurious to health.
- **Transportation Operations** – The proposed rule defines "transportation operations" as "all activities associated with food transportation that may affect the sanitary condition of food," subject to the listed exemptions. These activities include cleaning, inspection, maintenance, loading and unloading, and the operation of vehicles and transportation equipment. The proposed rule requires that transportation operations be conducted "under such conditions and controls necessary" to prevent the food from becoming unfit for food or rendered injurious to health from any source.
- **Information Exchange** – The proposed rule includes provisions that require shippers and carriers to exchange information to maintain the sanitary condition of food.

---

[525] *Id.*

○ **Training** – The proposed rule would require carriers to provide training to employees addressing issues and best practices connected to food safety in the transport of food. Carriers must also maintain records of these trainings.

○ **Records** – Shippers and carriers will need to retain records, including the information exchanged with one another and their written agreements.

[9] *Enforcement*

[a] Array of Tools

Each of the major food safety statutes contains specific enforcement provisions: Section 301 of FDCA, Section 610 of FMIA, Section 458 of PPIA, and Section 1037 of EPIA. Section 301 of the FDCA prohibits causing any of the prohibited acts as well as the act itself. Private actions citizens do not have the right to sue to enforce the food safety statutes.[526] The regulatory action for food safety violations involves an array of enforcement tools available to FDA and USDA in varying degree and scope: administrative enforcement actions, such as inspections, warning letters, and adverse publicity; and judicial enforcement actions, such as suspension, recall, injunction, seizure, retention, and criminal prosecution. The administrative enforcement actions are initiated and carried out solely by the agency, while judicial enforcement actions may require some type of involvement by the courts. These enforcement tools are not mutually exclusive and may build upon one another.[527] FSMA has increased the regulatory authority of the FDA for several of these enforcement tools.[528]

[b] Inspections

Although inspections of regulated facilities was covered in the previous section of this chapter as a major tool for food safety regulation, it is useful to note here for purposes of delineating food safety enforcement tools that the federal food safety acts grant the FDA and USDA respectively with the enforcement authority to inspect both facilities and records.

[c] Warning Letters

A warning letter is another of the administrative tools that the FDA uses to address violations of the law. Because warning letters are generally issued for violations that are not intentional or flagrant, pose little probability of injury or death, and are not part

---

[526] In re Orthopedic Bone Screw Products Liability Litigation, 193 F.3d 781, 788 (3d Cir. 1999) (citing "no private right of action" under the FDCA); Rogers v. Tyson Foods, Inc., 308 F.3d 785, 790 (7th Cir. 2002) (same, for PPIA).

[527] Michael T. Roberts, *Mandatory Recall Authority: A Sensible and Minimalist Approach to Improving Food Safety*, 59 Food & Drug L.J. 563, 565 (2004).

[528] Those involved in the regulation of food safety recognize that food safety tools are useful to achieve safer food, but that ultimately, to improve the food safety performance of an organization, people's behaviors need to change. Traditional food safety management focuses on developing a food safety program; behavior-based food safety management is focused on creating a food safety culture. Frank Yiannis, Food Safety Culture: Creating a Behavior-Based Food Safety Management System 79, 81 (2010).

of a history of repeated or continued misconduct, warning letters have primarily been used for labeling violations (the regulatory process for the issuance of warning letters is covered in Chapter 4). Warning letters are increasingly used, however, in matters of non-labeling-related, food safety violations. For example, in November 2010, the FDA issued a warning letter to Plusion Projects, makers of a popular Four Loko malt liquor beverage, on grounds that the product's high caffeine content was not GRAS and that the caffeine was therefore an unsafe food additive.[529] In May 2012, the FDA issued a warning letter to Florida's Finest Seafood Company after the agency's inspection of the company's seafood processing facility revealed that its seafood HACCP plan lacked adequate controls for pathogenic bacteria growth, C. botulinum growth, or toxin formation in its crabmeat and smoked salmon products.[530] In August 2012, the FDA issued warning letters to dairy and meat farms in California after unacceptable levels of drug residues were found in the cattle that they sold for slaughter. The FDA had visited each establishment to inspect operations there and to examine records to track animals that were slaughtered.[531]

[d] Adverse Publicity

Under 21 U.S.C. § 705, adverse publicity consists of disseminating information that a company is not cooperating with enforcement officials.[532] Section 705 of the FDCA provides the FDA with the authority to seek publicity in order to warn the public of violative products and the possible adverse consequences associated with the use of such products. While the FDA does not generally issue adverse press releases, it can occur. Adverse publicity of this nature can be devastating to a business or a product. Such publicity can cause more damage than the cost of the action proposed by the agency. Adverse publicity affects not only the short-term problem an enterprise faces; it also may extend to future product liability claims.

[e] Recall

(1) *FDA Recall Authority*
Recall is an enforcement tool that has been used frequently by FDA and USDA for food safety violations. A reoccurring and divisive issue in the regulation of food safety in the United States is whether the government should have the authority to order companies to recall unsafe food from commerce.[533]

---

[529] Letter from Joann M. Givens, Acting Director, Office of Compliance, Controller for Food Safety and Applied Nutrition, to Jaisen Freeman, Chris Hunter & Jeff Wright, Phusion Projections, LLC (November 17, 2010).

[530] Letter from Emma R. Singleton, Director, Food and Drug Administration Florida District, to Gregg Jaffy, Vice President, Florida's Finest Seafood Company (April 3, 2012).

[531] Julia Thomas, *High Drug Residues Found at California Meat and Dairy Operations*, FOOD SAFETY NEWS (August 24, 2012).

[532] *See* Michael T. Roberts, *Anatomy of the Government's Role in the Recall of Unsafe Food Products*, NATIONAL AGRICULTURE LAW CENTER 6 (May, 2004).

[533] Roberts, *Mandatory Recall*, *supra* note 527, at 563. The US government has mandatory recall authority for numerous nonfood products: the Consumer Product Safety Commission (CPSC) has the authority to order a recall of an unsafe consumer product; the Environmental Protection Agency (EPA) has the authority to order a recall of a dangerous chemical; in addition to its new authority under FSMA, FDA

The use of recalls by FDA started accidentally when the agency asked a company involved in a poisoning incident to remove the dangerous product from the market. After that, the FDA asked companies to recall products sparingly and in only the most serious of cases, but starting in the late 1960s, the number of recalls exploded, quickly becoming the most common method of enforcement for the FDA.[534]

Prior to FSMA, FDA did not have the authority to mandate a recall of unsafe food. While the development of food safety in the United States has included the debate whether the government should have the authority to order companies to recall unsafe food from commerce,[535] the debate is now settled, under the FSMA, at least for FDA-regulated food. Section 206 of FSMA gives FDA, for the first time, mandatory recall authority. The agency may request that a food enterprise voluntarily cease distribution of, and recall a food, other than infant formula,[536] when there is a reasonable probability that the food is adulterated (under Section 402) or misbranded (under Section 403) and will cause serious adverse health consequences or death (Class I Recall).[537] If the responsible party refuses to cease distribution of or recall such a food, the FDA may issue an order mandating that the party cease distribution of the food and immediately notify any distributes.[538] The company may appeal this order and, if it elects to appeal, it will be granted an informal hearing within two days, after which time, the FDA will either confirm or rescind the order.[539]

The FSMA left intact the FDA guidelines that categorize recalls into one of three classes according to the level of hazards involved. Class I Recalls are the most severe type of FDA recall; a Class I recall is issued when there is a potential for serious injury or death.[540] Class II Recalls are issued on products that have a lower chance of causing major injuries or death, but where there is still the possibility of serious enough adverse events to have irreversible consequences.[541] Class III Recalls are not very likely to cause adverse health consequences, but because a chance remains, the product is therefore recalled.[542] Notably, FDA's mandatory recall authority

has the authority to order a recall for a number of medical products; the National Highway Traffic System Administration (NHTSA) of the US Department of Transportation has the authority to order a recall of a motor vehicle product; and the US Coast Guard (USCG) has the authority to order a recall of recreation boats and related equipment. *See id.*, 527, at 53 n.7.

[534] Michael Kenneth, *Does Congress Take Note When the FDA Expands Its Enforcement Authority?* (Food and Drug Law: An Electronic Book of Student Papers, Harvard Law) (April 2007, Third Year Paper)

[535] Roberts, *Mandatory Recall, supra* note 527. For example, on December 12, 2002, the USDA held a public meeting on the topic of "Improving the Recall Process." The meeting included a lively discussion on the implications of mandatory recall authority. Transcript of Proceedings: Improving the Recall Process, Washington, D.C., U.S. Dep't of Agric., Food Safety Inspection Service (December 12, 2002).

[536] Prior to the FSMA, FDA only had mandatory recall authority on four types of products: infant formula, medical devices, human tissue products, and tobacco products.

[537] FDA Food Safety Modernization Act, Pub. L. No. 111–353, § 206(a), 124 Stat. 3885, 3940.

[538] *Id.*

[539] *Id.* at 3885, 3940–1.

[540] *See* Roberts, Anatomy of the Government's Role in the Recall, *supra*, note 532 at 8 n. 54. An example of a Class I recall would be meat that is contaminated with pathogenic bacteria, such as *Listeria monocytogenes* in a ready-to-eat product or *Escherichia coli* 0157:H7 in raw ground beef. *Id.*

[541] *Id.* An example of a Class II recall would be the presence of dry milk as an ingredient in sausage without mention of the dry milk on the label. Another example is the presence of undeclared allergens such as milk or soy products. *Id.*

[542] *Id.* An example of Class III recall would be improperly labeled processed meat in which added water is not listed on the label as required by the federal regulations. *Id.*

provided by FSMA is limited to Class I recall situations of death or adverse health consequences.

In the recall order, FDA is required to specify a timetable, including a schedule for the recalling company to make periodic progress reports to the agency. When undertaking a recall, a company must provide notice to every entity involved in the manufacturing, processing, packing, transporting, distributing, receiving, holding, or importing and selling the food, or to whom the food has been distributed, transported, or sold. FDA must ensure that a press release, as well as alerts and public notices, are published, which provide consumers and retailers with information on the name of the food, the risk associated with it, as well as information on similar articles of food that are not affected.[543] In addition, if available, pictures of recalled foods must be published on FDA's website. Furthermore, FDA must update its website to include a search engine that provides the public with access to recall information. The order to cease distribution may be limited in terms of geographic area and markets affected.[544] FDA terminates a recall when the firm has completed all recall activities.[545]

Failure to comply with a mandatory recall order is a prohibited act under the FDCA and may result in civil penalties. Specifically, the FSMA amended Section 303(f)(2)(A) of the FDCA to provide that failure to comply with a recall order may result in the assessment of civil penalties of up to $50,000 for an individual and $250,000 for any other person (defined as an individual, partnership, corporation, or association)[546] that violates the recall order.[547] Penalties are capped at $500,000 for all violations that are adjudicated in a single proceeding. Furthermore, the FDA may impose fees for action undertaken by the agency conducted on behalf of a responsible party when the responsible party fails to comply with an initial recall order.

(2) USDA Recall Authority

The mandatory provisions of FSMA do not extend to the food products exclusively under the jurisdiction of the USDA/FSIS. USDA's procedures for recalls of defective meat are found in an FSIS Directive.[548] When FSIS learns that adulterated or misbranded meat or poultry may be in commerce, it conducts a preliminary investigation to determine whether a recall of the food product is warranted. If FSIS determines that a recall is necessary, it convenes a meeting of its Recall Committee, which comprises FSIS scientists, technical experts, field inspection managers, enforcement personnel, and communication specialists.[549] The Recall Committee evaluates the available information and, based on the health risk of the food product, categorizes the recall into one of three classes that are similar to those three classes used by the FDA: a Class I recall where a strong likelihood exists that the product will cause serious adverse health consequences or death, a Class II recall where a remote possibility exists of an adverse health consequence resulting from consuming the meat or poultry

---

[543] 21 C.F.R. § 7.53.

[544] 21 U.S.C. § 350l(b).

[545] *Regulatory Procedures Manual*, 7-8-1, U.S. Food & Drug Admin. (2010).

[546] 21 U.S.C. § 321(e).

[547] FSMA at § 2006(c)–(d).

[548] *See* Recall of Meat and Poultry Products FSIS Directive 8080.1 Rev. 4, U.S Dep't of Agric. (May 24, 2004).

[549] *See id.*

product, or a Class III recall where the consumption of the product will not cause adverse health consequences.

The Recall Committee also recommends the depth and scope of the recall. FSIS and the recalling company conduct effectiveness checks to determine the adequacy of notice about the recall and the success in removing the product.[550] FSIS notifies the public of recalls in two ways: a press release and a Recall Notification Report (RNR). RNRs provide the public with detailed information about meat and poultry recalls. RNRs are sent by facsimile and electronic mail to food safety and public health officials throughout the country.[551] FSIS also posts recall notification reports on its website and sends these reports to food safety and public health officials throughout the country.[552]

Support for the current voluntary recall system for products regulated by the USDA/ FSIS rests on two predicates, which also supported arguments against extending to FDA mandatory recall authority: first, that it effectively removes unsafe food products from commerce; and second, that it engenders cooperation between government and industry. Defenders believe that companies have generally initiated recalls without delays, either on their own initiative or in response to requests to do so voluntarily.[553] USDA officials often comment that there have been no instances in which companies delayed or failed to initiate a recall; however, a US General Accounting Office (GAO) report questions this claim on the grounds that it is purely anecdotal.[554] In spite of the GAO criticism of USDA's claim, USDA officials continue to make that claim, and credit this alleged success to the implicit threat of government enforcement, adverse publicity, and liability exposure.[555] Given this presumed success, mandatory recall statutory authority is generally considered unnecessary because the USDA arguably has more than enough authority and leverage to require the recall of unsafe food products without it.

[f] Market Withdrawal and Stock Recovery

In addition to recalls, other actions may be taken by a food company to remove a product from commerce, including market withdrawal and stock recovery. Market withdrawal is the removal of a distributed product that involves a minor violation that would not be subject to legal action by FDA or FSIS, or when the company wishes to remove a product from distribution for other reasons, such as when a product does not meet the company's internal specifications.[556] Stock recovery removes products that have not yet been placed in retail distribution channels but are still under the direct control of the food company.[557]

---

[550] *See* U.S. Gov't Accountability Office, Rep. No. GAO/RCED-00-195, Food Safety: Actions Needed by USDA and FDA to Ensure That Companies Promptly Carry Out Recalls (August 2000).

[551] *FSIS Food Recalls*, U.S. Dep't of Agric., Food Safety Inspection Service (October 2011).

[552] The RNRs are posted on the FSIS Recall website.

[553] Roberts, *Mandatory Recall, supra* note 527, at 53.

[554] GAO, Food Safety, *supra* note 550, at 37.

[555] Transcript of Proceedings: Improving the Recall Process at 20–1, U.S. Dep't of Agriculture, Food Safety Inspection Service (December 12, 2002).

[556] 21 C.F.R. § 7.3(j).

[557] 21 C.F.R. § 7.3(k).

[g] Suspension

Section 102 of FSMA authorizes FDA to suspend the registration of a food facility under Section 415(b) of FDCA.[558] If the FDA determines that food manufactured, processed, packed, received, or held by a facility has a reasonable probability of causing serious adverse health consequences or death to humans or animals, the agency may suspend the registration of the facility that (1) created, caused, or was otherwise responsible for such reasonable probability; or (2) knew of, or had reason to know of, such reasonable probability, and packed, received, or held such food.

A suspension action effectively shuts down a food facility because the facility whose registration is suspended is prohibited from introducing food into commerce, or from importing or exporting food.[559] The FDA will provide a registrant subject to an order of suspension of registration with an opportunity for an informal hearing, to be held as soon as possible but not later than two business days after the issuance of a suspension order, unless an alternative time period is agreed upon by FDA and the registrant.[560] The informal hearings cover the actions required for reinstatement of registration and why the registration that is subject to suspension should be reinstated.[561] If FDA determines that the suspension remains necessary, the agency will require the registrant to submit a corrective action plan to demonstrate how the registrant plans to correct the conditions found by FDA.[562] Upon determining that adequate grounds no longer exist to continue suspension, or that such a suspension order should be modified, the FDA will vacate the order and reinstate the registration of the facility subject to the order, or modify the order, as appropriate.[563]

Suspension, in effect, allows FDA injunctive relief without the need to involve the judicial process or the potentially time-consuming activities involved in obtaining an injunction. In November 2012, the FDA suspended the food facility registration of Sunland, Inc., a producer of nuts and nut and seed spreads. This was the first time that the FDA used its registration suspension authority under FSMA. The suspension against Sunland, Inc. occurred because peanut butter made by the company had been linked to an outbreak of Salmonella Bredeney that sickened forty-one people in twenty states, coupled with Sunland's history of violations.[564]

FDA has yet to issue regulations for implementing the registration suspension provisions of FSMA. However, in the absence of regulations, the agency is following the protocol set forth in the statute and the agency's preexisting regulations in 21 C.F.R. Part 16, on regulatory hearings. FDA's letter to Sunland concerning suspension gives some insight to the content of future regulations. If Sunland were to desire a hearing to be held within two business days, FDA's letter requires them to submit a written request for such a hearing within one business day. If Sunland were to desire a hearing to be held at some other agreed upon time period, Sunland must submit its

---

[558] FSMA § 102(b).
[559] FSMA § 415(b)(4).
[560] FSMA § 415(b)(2).
[561] Id.
[562] FSMA § 415(b)(3)(A).
[563] FSMA § 415(b)(3)(B).
[564] Letter from LaTonya M. Mitchell, Director, U.S. Food & Drug Admin. Denver District, to Jimmie D. Shearer, President, Sunland, Inc. (May 17, 2013).

request within three business days after the issuance of the order. If no written request is submitted within three business days, Sunland will be deemed to have waived its right to request a hearing. The letter also states that in lieu of a hearing contesting the suspension order, the company may apply for reinstatement based on corrective actions taken. There is no deadline for the company to utilize this option. Although the FDCA does not establish a threshold requirement to qualify for a suspension hearing, the FDA's letter specifies that a hearing request must present specific facts showing that there is a "genuine and substantial issue of fact that warrants a hearing."[565] A Presiding Officer, who is designated by the agency, will make the determination of whether this standard is met.[566] The FDA also explains in the letter that the hearing will be closed to the public.

[h] Injunction

An injunction is initiated to stop or prevent violation of the law, such as to halt the flow of violative products in interstate commerce, and to correct the conditions that caused the violation to occur.[567] The FDCA expressly authorizes district courts to grant injunctive relief to enforce its provisions,[568] and the FDA may use that authority to enjoin, either temporarily or permanently, the production or distribution of adulterated or misbranded food products.[569] If FDA (or USDA) seeks an injunction, they must go to the US attorney where the company is located. If the prosecutor agrees to take the case, he or she will file a request for an injunction with the US District Court. An injunction can also compel a food enterprise to take some action (e.g., register a facility with FDA or conduct a recall). Traditionally, injunctions are used when a food enterprise has been continuously unable or unwilling to comply with the law, and other sanctions may not be practicable. Injunctions against food firms for food safety violations are very rare. The FDA Regulatory Procedures Manual notes that the agency may seek an injunction action "[i]f a firm has a history of violations, and has promised correction in the past, but has not made the corrections."[570]

[i] Seizure

Section 304 of the FDCA provides FDA with seizure authority.[571] A seizure is an action where the court condemns the article and declares forfeiture for violation of law. The offending article of food is the actual defendant in the case.

---

[565] *Id.*

[566] As defined in 21 C.F.R. § 16.42 (2014), a presiding officer is an appropriately authorized FDA employee or an administrative law judge.

[567] *Id.* at 6-2-2.

[568] 21 U.S.C. § 332(a).

[569] *See, e.g.,* United States v. Union Cheese Co., 902 F. Supp. 778, 787–790 (N.D. Ohio 1995) (granting preliminary injunction against cheese factory because of presence of *L. monocytogenes*). *See also,* United States v. Syntrax Innovations, Inc., 149 F. Supp.2d 880, 882–891 (E.D. Mo. 2001) (granting government's motion on summary judgment for misbranding in violation of the FDCA and imposing permanent injunction barring plant operation until specific steps taken to remedy condition).

[570] *Id.*

[571] 21 U.S.C. § 334.

Asserting seizure authority requires a civil court action against a specific lot of goods to remove them from the channels of commerce. Because FDA's seizure authority involves a mandatory judicial process, it is rarely invoked. Once seized, the product cannot be moved without the court's permission. The government will also file a complaint requesting that the product be "condemned" and thereby destroyed.

Civil court action ensues when FDA recommends seizure to the US attorney in the state where the product is located. If the Department of Justice (DOJ) accepts the FDA's recommendation, the US attorney files a complaint in federal district court on behalf of the FDA. A seizure is an *ex parte* order[572] obtained from the federal court under rules dating back to early admiralty law through an *in rem*[573] action against the named goods. After the complaint is filed, the federal district court issues a warrant for the arrest (seizure) of the product. Seizures run against the goods, not the company that owns them.[574] Due Process restrictions in seizure actions are viewed narrowly because of the public health and safety concerns underlying FDA powers.[575]

If a seizure is contested, the FDA has the burden of proving its case by a preponderance of the evidence.[576] As a practical matter, owners of seized food would find it in their best interest to resolve the seizure quickly: reconditioning (resolving the violation)[577] – if it will be permitted – cannot begin until the product is first condemned and while the contested case proceeds, perishable foods will lose value.[578] As long as the government's action was reasonable, the claimant who wins a contested seizure case is not likely to recover the lost value of perishable goods.

[j] Detention

Administrative detention of foods is intended to protect consumers by preventing movement in commerce of adulterated or misbranded food until the FDA has had time to consider further appropriate enforcement action.[579] FSMA significantly expanded the FDA's power to administratively detain foods. Prior to FSMA, FDA was required to have "credible evidence or information" that an article of food "presents a threat of serious adverse health consequences or death to humans or animals" to detain that article of food. This high evidentiary bar has made detaining food a challenge for FDA. The usual approach was to rely on the states to embargo products of concern.[580]

---

[572] *Ex parte* means that a judge may make a decision without all the parties present.

[573] *In rem* means the action is against the things, rather than against the person.

[574] 21 U.S.C. § 334.

[575] *See* United States v. Article of Device …Theramatic, 715 F2d 1339 (9th Cir. 1983).

[576] *See, e.g.,* United States v. 60 28-Capsule Bottles … "Unitrol," 325 F. 2d 513 (3d Cir. 1963).

[577] Once a federal court orders goods to be seized, the company may attempt to reclaim them for purposes of reconditioning; otherwise, they may be destroyed. If FDA approves a reconditioning plan, the result usually will be a consent decree for reconditioning. FDA inspectors then oversee the relabeling or reprocessing by the company, and FDA sends the court a report of the results of the recondition. The court then can dismiss the seizure order and the goods are released to the claimant.

[578] United States v. 2,116 Boxes Boned Beef, 516 F. Supp. 321 (1981), *aff'd* 726 F.2d. 1481 (10th Cir. 1984).

[579] FDA, Guidance for Industry: What You Need to Know about Administrative Detention of Foods; Small Entity Compliance Guide (March 2013).

[580] *Prior Notice and Administrative Detention: What the New Rules Mean,* The Acheson Group (May 12, 2011).

FSMA amended Section 304(h)(1)(A) of the FDCA (21 U.S.C. § 334(h)(1)(A)) to give FDA the authority to administratively detain an article of food if FDA has reason to believe that the article of food is adulterated or misbranded. FDA intends to revise its administrative detention regulations and other relevant documents to reflect this new, easier-to-meet standard.[581] Shortly following the enactment of FSMA, the FDA implemented its expanded administrative detention authority three times: one of the administrative detentions led to a request to recondition the goods under FDA supervision, another resulted in a seizure, and another terminated when the owner voluntarily destroyed the suspect food.[582]

The administratively detained article of food must be held in the specified location and under the conditions specified by FDA in the detention order.[583] The administrative detention order may require removal of the detained article of food to a secure facility; however, movement of the detained food is permitted only after FDA has modified the detention order under 21 CFR 1.381(c).

The claimant of the detained food may file an appeal to the FDA for a review of the detention order. For perishable food, an appeal must be filed to the FDA district director whose district detained the article of food within two (2) calendar days of receipt of the administrative detention order.[584] For nonperishable food, a notice of intent to file an appeal and to request a hearing must be filed within four (4) calendar days of receipt of the administrative detention order.[585] The actual appeal must be filed within ten calendar days of the receipt of the administrative detention order.[586] The claimant may request a hearing as part of the appeal, which may be denied if no genuine or substantial issue of fact and had been raised by the material submitted.[587] A hearing will not be granted on issues of policy or law. Written notice of a determination of summary judgment will be provided, explaining the reasons for the denial of the hearing. If the FDA grants the request, then for both perishable and nonperishable foods, the hearing will be held within two calendar days after the date the appeal has been filed.[588] FDA must confirm, modify, or terminate the administrative detention order within five calendar days after an appeal is filed and after providing an opportunity for an informal hearing, if requested.[589]

The USDA has similar enforcement authority to that of FDA. Rules promulgated under the FMIA allow the USDA to detain violative products for up to twenty days or to seek a court injunction seizing and condemning such products, or both.[590] The FSIS has permanent enforcement agents on-site at beef and poultry processing facilities, and these agents have additional enforcement tools, including the issuance of warnings and

---

[581] *Inspection and Compliance*, U.S. Food & Drug Admin.

[582] *Id.*

[583] Where and under What Conditions Must the Detained Article of Food Be Held, 21 CFR § 1.380 (2014).

[584] K. M. Lewis, *Informal Guidance and the FDA*, 66 Food & Drug L.J. 507, 524 (2011).

[585] *Id.*

[586] 21 CFR 1.402 (a)).

[587] 21 CFR 16.26.

[588] 21 CFR 1.402 (d).

[589] 21 CFR 1.405.

[590] *See, e.g.*, 9 C.F.R. § 329.1 (describing food products and livestock subject to temporary administrative detention); 9 C.F.R. § 329.6 (stating that any meat or meat food product transported in commerce is subject to seizure and condemnation in a judicial proceeding if such article or livestock is capable of use as human food and is adulterated or misbranded or otherwise is in violation of the act).

citations, and the refusal to designate the product as USDA certified (the absence of which is normally crippling to a producer and is the functional equivalent of a mandatory recall). The USDA retains a product when an in-plant inspector places a tag on a product located at a federally inspected facility that he or she believes to be adulterated or misbranded. Once tagged, the product cannot be removed from the facility without USDA approval. In most instances, a product is either reconditioned or destroyed within a few days.

[k] Criminal Prosecution

The FDCA, the PPIA, and the FMIA have strong criminal provisions that are largely strict liability statutes, meaning that the government need not establish intent to violate the law in order to obtain a conviction. Two types of criminal violations exist: misdemeanors and felonies. Under the FDCA, most food violations are misdemeanors; however, the FDA can request a felony conviction if the agency can prove intent to defraud or mislead, or if there has been a prior conviction. Under the PPIA and the FMIA, any violation involving the distribution or attempted distribution of an adulterated food is a felony.

The FDA will consider criminal prosecution when a company or an official has demonstrated an unwillingness to correct a violation, despite having received notice from FDA, or when a violation is flagrant, intentionally committed, or involves a health hazard that the company did not try to prevent or correct. The FDCA's criminal provisions are tantamount to strict liability, which may be imputed to all corporate officials who, by virtue of their positions, have the authority and responsibility to ensure compliance with the FDCA and its implementing regulations. The legal standard for such individual criminal liability under the FDCA is laid out in the landmark case, *United States v. Park*, 421 U.S. 658 (1975). In *United States v. Park*, the defendant, the president of a grocery store chain, was individually convicted of causing adulteration of food. On appeal, the Supreme Court held that the trial court's instructions – which explained to the jury that the defendant need not have personally participated in the situation that caused the alleged adulteration – adequately focused on the issue of defendant's authority with respect to the conditions that formed the basis of the alleged violations.[591]

Misdemeanor convictions may result in imprisonment for not more than one year and a fine of not more than $100,000 per violation for individuals and not more than $200,000 for corporations. For felonies, conviction may result in imprisonment for not more than three years and a fine of up to $250,000 for individuals and up to $500,000 for corporations. Criminal prosecutions are very rare.

It appears, however, that the government may begin to rely more heavily on criminal prosecutions as an enforcement tool. A criminal indictment in 2013 against the Peanut Corporation of America (PCA) officials suggests that the FDA is stepping up criminal enforcement under FSMA.[592] PCA's plant in Georgia was determined to be the main source of the Salmonella outbreak in late 2008 and early 2009, which sickened more than 700 people, killing nine, and led to more than 3,900 peanut-related product recalls.

---

[591] 421 U.S. at 677–8.
[592] Joan Murphy, *PCA Indictment Not Driven by FSMA, But Other Law, Top Cop Suggests*, Food Chemical News 1, (March 22, 2013).

In January 2013, the Department of Justice, unveiled a combined seventy-six-count indictment against four former PCA officials, including charges that they conspired to ship peanuts after receiving confirmed positive tests for *Salmonella Typhimurium*. The indictment was unusual in the sense that criminal indictments usually name the CEO or president and one other person as those with authority to prevent the actions, but the Department of Justice went farther by naming several other top company officials and various management positions. Future litigation may reveal that mid-level managers will also be subject to future enforcement actions.[593]

[1] Consent Decrees

A consent decree is a final, binding judicial decree or judgment that memorializes a voluntary agreement between parties to a suit in return for the withdrawal of a criminal charge or an end to a civil litigation. In a typical consent decree, the defendant has already ceased or agrees to cease the conduct alleged by the plaintiff to be illegal and consents to a court injunction barring the conduct in the future.

In September 2013, the US District Court for the District of Idaho entered a consent decree of permanent injunction against owner Gregory T. Troost, doing business as T&T Cattle and T&T Cattle Pearl, and manager Mark A. Mourton of Parma, Idaho, for violations that included illegally administering animal drugs for uses that are not approved by the FDA.[594] During previous inspections, FDA investigators had determined that the defendants had violated several provisions of the FDCA. The defendants had offered for slaughter seven dairy cows with illegal levels of drug residues. The consent decree prohibited the defendants from selling animals for slaughter for human consumption until they have implemented acceptable recordkeeping systems to identify and track animals that have been treated with drugs. If the defendants offer any animals for sale or slaughter, they also must provide written information about the animals' drug treatment status to the recipient of the animals. The consent decree provides that the FDA may order the defendants to cease operations if they fail to comply with any provisions of the consent decree, the Act, or FDA regulations. Failure to obey the terms of the consent decree could result in civil or criminal penalties.[595]

The FDA may choose to use this tool more regularly in the future for food regulatory violations. Negotiated settlements with FDA can solve conserve the costs associated with the expenditure of effort in court for both sides.[596] There are several theoretical justifications for consent decrees. One justification for seeking large settlements under a consent decree is the disgorgement of profits wrongfully obtained from the sale of violative products. Another justification is restitution, where the money obtained from a company charged with wrongdoing is used to compensate victims of the wrongdoing. These are equitable remedies that do not require statutory language in the FDCA.[597] The third justification is deterrence of both the individual company named in the suit as well as

---

[593] *Id.*

[594] *News Release, Federal Judge Grants FDA Request for Consent Decree with Idaho Farm*, U.S. Food & Drug Admin. (September 6, 2013).

[595] *See id.*

[596] *See* Eric Bloomberg, *Abbott Laboratories Consent Decree and Individual Responsibility Under the Federal Food Drug and Cosmetic Act*, 55 Food & Drug L.J. 145 (2000).

[597] *See id.*

other entities. The FDA's policy to name individuals, including the company CEO in most consent decrees is presumably intended to hold an individual or individuals personally accountable for ensuring that corrections are made and because named individual defendants also serve as public examples.

[m] Debarment

A company or person who is convicted of certain FDCA violations can be "debarred" from future FDA – regulated activities. Debarment is a complete prohibition from importing into the United States.[598] The disbarment penalty was first enacted in 1992 in response to a generic drug scandal as a means of preventing fraud and misconduct, such as bribery. The Bioterrorism Act added a provision to FDCA, Section 306, to provide the penalty of debarment for repeated or serious food import violations. Specifically, debarment may be imposed when a "person has been convicted of a felony for conduct relating to the importation into the United States of any food; or … has engaged in a pattern of importing … adulterated food that presents a threat of serious adverse health consequences or death to humans or animals."[599] The Bioterrorism Act also prohibits the importation of food with the assistance or under the direction of a debarred person.[600]

[n] Civil Monetary Penalties

The FDA's civil penalty authority is limited. FDA's regulation, 21 CFR Part 17, sets forth the procedures for administrative civil monetary penalties. FDCA authorizes only two actions punishable by civil penalties: introduction or delivery of an article of food deemed adulterated because of pesticide residue and noncompliance with a recall order. The penalty is capped at $60,000 for an individual and $300,000 for all other persons. The total amount assessed at a single proceeding may not exceed $600,000. Persons who grew the article of food are ineligible for a penalty. Once a civil penalty is assessed, the agency may not use the criminal, seizure, or injunction remedies for the adulterated product. The FDA also has authority to assess and collect fees to recover variable enforcement costs, including reinspection costs and costs associated with "food recall activities" (including technical assistance, follow-up effectiveness checks, and public notifications). FDA has sought civil monetary penalties for continuous or repeated violations of the same or similar statutory requirements when other remedies such as seizure or injunction were not appropriate.

[o] Contempt

Contempt is the judicial power to enforce existing court orders. The FDA may bring a contempt motion when a person refuses a warrant for inspection or when an injunction or seizure has been violated. Criminal contempt can result in imprisonment.

---

[598] 21 U.S.C. § 335a(b)(1)(C).
[599] 21 U.S.C. § 335a(b)(3).
[600] 21 U.S.C. § 331(cc) ("The importing or offering for import into the United States of an article of food by, with the assistance of, or at the direction of, a person debarred under section 306(b)(3)).

[p] Whistle-Blower Protection

Presumably in an effort to protect the public from adulterated food by encouraging reporting, the FSMA grants expansive whistle-blower protection. Employees of facilities that manufacture, process, or pack food that disclose FDA violations are protected from discharge, discriminatory compensation, and discriminatory employment terms. FDA has not yet issued regulations for the FSMA provisions. There is no protection under USDA for whistle-blowers.

The reach of the FSMA whistle-blower provision is quite broad. It includes entities engaged in such diverse activities as manufacturing, processing, packing, transportation, distribution, reception, holding, or importation of food. It is unclear at this point whether the reach extends to retail establishments, such as retail stores or restaurants. In terms relatively standard to whistle-blower protections, covered employers are prohibited from taking unfavorable personnel actions by way of discharge or other adverse employment actions against an employee, including those related to compensation, terms, conditions, or privileges of employment due to an employee's protected activity. Protected activity includes both internal and external disclosures and activities in its expansive definition. Expressing no priority or preference for the particular types of protected activity it defines, FSMA protects individuals if they provide, or cause to be provided, to the employer, the federal government, or a state attorney general information that relates to any violation of, or any act or omission the employee reasonably believes to be a violation of, any provision of the FDCA or any order, rule, regulation, standard, or ban under the FDCA. FSMA also protects individuals who testify, or are about to testify, in a proceeding concerning such violation; assist or participate, or are about to assist or participate, in such a proceeding; or object to, or refuse to participate in, any activity, policy, practice, or assigned task that the employee (or other such person) reasonably believes to be in violation of any provision of the FDCA, or any order, rule, regulation, standard, or ban under the FDCA.

Assuring that its base of protection will be further broadened, FSMA provides that protected activity includes not only actions expressly initiated by the employee, but also activities that are in the ordinary course of the employee's duties or the duties of any person acting pursuant to a request of the employee.[601]

FSMA adapts its investigation procedure from the Occupational Safety and Health Administration (OSHA) and its litigation procedure from the US Department of Labor (DOL), with access to federal courts by the complaining employee if a final administrative determination does not issue after a specified period. However, FSMA is distinguishable from other recent legislation adopting the OSHA/DOL scheme.[602] For example, FSMA does not bar a waiver of rights and remedies by agreement, policy, form, or condition of employment, nor does it declare that predispute agreements requiring arbitration of whistle-blower retaliation claims will be invalid or unenforceable.[603]

---

[601] Allen B. Roberts & John Houston Pope, *Food Safety and Whistleblowing – New Federal Law May Deliver a Full Basket of Claims*, FIN. SERVICES EMP. L., (January 13, 2011).

[602] *Id.*

[603] In this respect, FSMA departs from such recent legislation as the Dodd-Frank amendments to Sarbanes-Oxley and Dodd-Frank's Consumer Financial Protection Act. *Id.*

Regardless, the scope of the whistle-blower protection is impressive simply due to the number of food enterprises and individuals involved in the food supply chain. While the substance of FSMA focuses on businesses that handle food, the whistle-blower incorporation of, and reference to, the larger statute that comprehends drugs and cosmetics suggests that the scope of FSMA whistle-blower coverage may extend beyond food products to all FSMA-covered employers. That is, if protected activity were construed to be coextensive with FDA-regulated drugs and cosmetics items, it is possible that individuals could bootstrap to expanded, non-food-related coverage by raising issues concerning drugs and cosmetics and assert entitlement to protection even more broadly than is apparent from the statute's food safety label. Future rulemaking may clarify this point.

§ 3.07 State and Municipal Regulation of Food Safety

[1] *Basis of Authority*

States and municipalities play an increasingly important role in the regulation of food safety. As referenced in Chapter 1, however, the police power of the state to protect the health, safety, and welfare of the community is trumped by the Supremacy Clause, which declares the federal constitution to be the supreme law of the land. Indeed, in the regulation of food safety, the federal constitution delegates to the federal government the power to regulate interstate commerce. The Commerce Clause sets out the basic parameters for how the federal government and states share responsibility to ensure a safe food supply.[604]

As evidenced in this chapter, federal law either explicitly or implicitly preempts numerous areas of food safety. However, the regulation of the retail segment of the food system has been left to the states. In practice, state governments do not regulate and enforce laws on retail food safety alone – they often do so in concert with local governments.[605] Given the different possible forms of relationships between municipal government and states, there is great variation throughout the country in the balance of activities divided between states and local governments to regulate and enforce retail food safety.[606] For example, some state governments are directly responsible for both the licensing inspection of retail food establishments, while others delegate these tasks with varying degrees of autonomy to local health departments.

The state regulation of increasingly popular home-based food operations (also known as cottage food operations), including sanitation and food safety, is covered in Chapter 6.

[2] *Federal Government Assisting States*

States bear the responsibility to regulate food safety at retail food establishments, with guidance and support from the federal government. The authority for the federal government to provide assistance to state and local governments is derived from a number

---

[604] U.S. Const. art. I, § 8, cl. 3.
[605] *See generally Good Laws, Good Food: Putting State Food Policy to Work for Our Communities*, Harvard Food L. & Policy Clinic 5–7 (2012) (provides a concise explanation of federalism in context.)
[606] *Profile of State Public Health*, 2, Ass'n of State & Territorial Health Officials (2011).

of statutes, including the Public Health Service Act (42 USC § 2430) (PHSA).[607] Section 311(a) of PHSA states, in part:

> The Secretary [HHS] shall … assist states and their political subdivisions in the prevention and suppression of communicable diseases, and with respect to other public health matters, shall cooperate with and aid state and local authorities in the enforcement of their … health regulations and shall advise the several states on matters relating to the preservation and improvement of the public health.

Responsibility for carrying out the provisions of the act relative to food protection was delegated to the FDA commissioner in 1968.[608] In fact, the federal government has periodically discussed direct regulation of retail food facilities by the FDA. Debates on the topic of shifting the regulatory authority back to the FDA have centered on issues of administration, namely, whether the burden on the FDA in to regulating over one million retail food establishments outweighs the need for uniformity of laws and direct federal intervention in order to establish effective sanitation requirements. For example, when a 1975 GAO report found that about 90 percent of the 14,736 establishments studied were insanitary, it noted that the FDA had jurisdiction over restaurant food shipped in interstate commerce. In reaction, the FDA proposed federal regulations on food safety in food service establishments; yet the proposal was abandoned by the agency after opposition from state officials and after the FDA recognized that with millions of meals served daily, it could not inspect or regulate effectively, therefore necessitating the primary responsibility of state and local governments.[609] In addition, state and local food safety personnel far outnumber federal, making decentralization a more attractive option.

[3] Scope of State Regulation of Food Safety

As the food consumed continues to increase at the retail level, state regulation becomes more important. The tapestry of state regulation over food safety extends to farmers' markets, direct farm sales, retail sales, restaurants, and many small types of small-scale agricultural production and processing entities.[610] In these venues, a variety of government agencies may be responsible for a different aspect of the safety of food, including those agencies with responsibilities over agriculture, consumer protection, health and human services, inspections, and social services. These state agencies may "(1) administer federal food safety programs (if the state has adopted a cooperative agreement with the federal government), (2) create, implement, and enforce state-level food safety regulations, and (3) provide guidance to industry participants on compliance with these federal and state laws."[611]

Thousands of state, local, and tribal agencies have the primary responsibility to prevent foodborne illness by regulating, licensing, and inspecting establishments within the retail segment of the food industry.[612] This includes the inspection and oversight of over

---

[607] Model Food Code, Preface, iii, U.S. Dep't of Health and Human Servs. (2013).

[608] 21 C.F.R. §§ 5.10(a)(2), (3).

[609] See 39 Fed. Reg. 35438 (October 1, 1974) and 42 Fed. Reg. 15428 (March 22, 1977).

[610] Good Laws, Good Food: Putting State Food Policy to Work for Our Communities, Harvard Food L. & Policy Clinic 91 (2012).

[611] Id.

[612] Model Food Code, U.S. Dep't of Health and Human Servs. (2009).

one million retail food establishments. State governments and local health departments are aided in promulgating and enforcing scientifically and legally sound regulations for the retail segment of the food industry by the FDA.[613]

It should be noted that food safety in the retail environment is critical in preventing foodborne illness. The retail segment of the food industry refers to the part of the distribution chain where the consumer takes possession of the food. At the retail juncture, proper preparation and presentation of food can either mitigate or enhance the risks of foodborne illness. In addition, with the number of meals eaten away from home rising steadily, retail food safety, especially in restaurants, has become even more central to preventing foodborne illness.[614]

The retail segment of the food industry includes not only restaurants, but also retail food stores like grocery stores, warehouse stores, corner stores, and vending operations. It also includes foodservice operations in institutions such as schools, hospitals, nursing homes, and child care centers.

In addition to direct responsibility for food retail operation, states may also regulate, license, and inspect food processing facilities. For example, the New York State Department of Agriculture licenses food processing enterprises.[615] State governments also play important roles that contribute to food safety in a number of other areas, where the state is not the primary regulatory body. These areas include the following:

○ **Food Manufacturing Inspections** – States conduct the majority of nonretail food establishment inspections (not including USDA-inspected meat and poultry establishments). Also, the majority of FDA inspections in food manufacturing and processing facilities are conducted by state agencies under contract with FDA.[616]

○ **Surveillance** – States participate in foodborne illness surveillance, both independently and in cooperation with the CDC, and in CDC surveillance initiatives such as PulseNet, FoodNet, and OutbreakNet.[617]

○ **Outbreak Response and Recalls** – In collaboration with local health departments, states manage large-scale outbreak investigations. Also, in collaboration with federal and local authorities, states oversee many industry recalls of food products.[618] While the FSMA gives the FDA mandatory recall authority, the agency is still required to first allow a responsible party to issue a voluntary recall.[619] Within this first voluntary, then mandatory, recall framework, states will play an important role in coordinating recall efforts.

---

[613] *Retail Food Protection*, U.S. FOOD & DRUG ADMIN. (February 25, 2015, last updated).

[614] *See* Elise Golan et al., *Traceability in the U.S. Food Supply: Economic Theory and Industry Studies*, ECON. RESEARCH SERVICE, U.S. DEP'T OF AGRIC. (March 2004).

[615] N.Y. AGRIC. & MKTS. LAW, ch. 69, ART. 20-C (Mckinney 2014).

[616] Michael R. Taylor & Stephanie D. David, *Stronger Partnerships for Safer Food: An Agenda for Strengthening State and Local Roles in the Nation's Food Safety System*, GEORGE WASHINGTON UNIV. DEPT. OF HEALTH POLICY 14 (2009).

[617] *Id.* at 16.

[618] *Id.* at 14.

[619] 21 U.S.C. § 350l.

○ **Farm Inspections** – States conduct on-farm inspections for animal health and other food safety conditions. States have primary jurisdiction for enforcement of federal pesticide use restrictions, which has a direct impact on abating potentially unsafe residues in food.[620]

States are also involved, to varying degrees, in three major areas of food safety in collaboration with federal agencies – meat, milk, and shellfish inspection. These activities take place through state-federal cooperative agreements.[621]

○ **Meat and Poultry** – Numerous states have their own meat and poultry inspection programs, which coexist through state-federal cooperative agreements with USDA's FSIS to inspect meat and poultry for intrastate commerce.[622] State programs must enforce requirements at least equal to those imposed under federal law.[623] The Federal-State Cooperative Act authorizes these state-federal cooperative agreements for the inspection of meat or poultry.[624] The meat and poultry enterprises that are inspected by state programs are typically small or very small (as the meat may not be sold in interstate commerce unless inspected by FSIS).

○ **Shellfish** – The National Shellfish Sanitation Program (NSSP) is a federal/state cooperative program recognized by the FDA and the Interstate Shellfish Sanitation Conference (ISSC) for the sanitary control of shellfish (oysters, clams, mussels, and scallops) produced and sold for human consumption via interstate commerce. Participants in the NSSP include agencies from shellfish-producing and nonproducing states, the FDA, EPA, the National Oceanic Atmospheric Administration (NOAA), foreign governments, and the shellfish industry. The NSSP generates guidelines, growing area classifications, and dealer certification programs.[625] States are able to create more stringent standards than the FDA's model ordinance, and state agencies play roles in state-level licensing and inspection of shellfish-transporting vehicles or shellfish processing facilities.[626]

○ **Milk** – The Pasteurized Milk Ordinance (PMO) and the National Conference of Interstate Milk Shippers are cooperative programs through which the FDA and USDA collaborate with state authorities and the milk industry to ensure the safety of the milk shipped in interstate commerce. The PMO is an FDA-developed model ordinance, which is generally recognized as a national standard for milk sanitation and safety. The PMO has been adopted by all fifty states and is used as the basis for the certification program of interstate milk shippers, in which the states carry out much of the monitoring and enforcement to oversee the safety and wholesomeness of fresh milk and cream.[627] State agencies typically engage in the licensing and inspection of dairy processing facilities.[628]

---

[620] Taylor & David, *supra* note 615 at 14.
[621] *See* at 16
[622] 7 U.S.C. § 450.
[623] FSIS Review of State Meat and Poultry Inspection Programs, U.S. DEP'T OF AGRIC. (2011).
[624] 7 U.S.C. § 450.
[625] *See Guide for the Control of Molluscan Shellfish*, U.S. DEP'T OF HEALTH AND HUMAN SERVS. (2013, Revised).
[626] *See, e.g.*, N.H. STAT. §143:21-a
[627] Taylor & David, *supra* note 615 at 18.
[628] *See* Milk Product Plant Licenses, CAL. DEP'T OF AGRIC.

o **Raw Milk** – While the FDA maintains the authority to prevent the entrance of adulterated or misbranded milk into interstate commerce, states are responsible for ensuring the safety of milk in intrastate sale. This distinction is critical for the issue of raw milk, a topic of increased interest in the past years. The FDA prohibited the interstate shipment of raw milk in 1987, but states retain the authority to regulate the sale of raw milk within their own borders. State regulations of raw milk vary considerably. Some prohibit the sale of raw milk, while the remaining states allow sales of raw milk. States are also divided on where sales of raw milk may occur: some states permit sales only on the farm where the milk is produced, while other states permit sales of raw milk in retail stores that are separate from the farm. A handful of states maintain regulations that allow a combination approach, such as restricting sales to farmers' markets or to "owners" of the cow through "share" agreements.[629] In 2012, a number of states introduced legislation to relax restrictions on the sale of raw milk. The CDC has responded by urging state health officials to support pasteurization.[630] The CDC cites recent research that show the strong connections between unpasteurized milk and foodborne illness outbreaks, with states that restrict the sale of unpasteurized milk reporting fewer illnesses and outbreaks.[631]

[4] *Model Food Code*

[a] Updates

The FDA's guidance to states on retail food safety began with the Grade A pasteurized milk ordinance in 1924.[632] Subsequent guidance on the regulation of other components of the retail segment of the food industry followed, including guidance for restaurants in 1934.[633] Eventually, a comprehensive model food code was issued in 1993. The model food code is not preemptive and represents the "best advice for a uniform system of regulation to ensure that food at retail is safe and properly protected and presented."[634] The FDA updates the model Food Code, with ongoing input from stakeholders, every four years with a new edition. The last all-new edition was issued in 2013. The FDA itself takes comments, but encourages engagement through representative organizations like the Conference for Food Protection.[635]

[b] Coverage of "Food Establishments"

The Model Code expressly covers "food establishments." The code defines a food establishment in two parts. The first part covers enterprises that directly convey food to a consumer:

---

[629] Stephanie David, *Raw Milk in Court: Implications for Public Health Policy and Practice,*127 Pub. Health Reports 598, (November–December 2012) (citing *NASDA Releases Raw Milk Survey*, Nat'l Ass'n of State Depts. of Agric. (July 19, 2011)).

[630] Letter from Robert Tauxe, Centers for Disease Control and Prevention (July 18, 2012).

[631] Langer et al., *Non-Pasteurized Dairy Products, Disease Outbreaks, and State Laws – United States, 1993–2006,* 18 Emerging Infectious Diseases (2012).

[632] Model Food Code, *supra* note 611 at Preface ii.

[633] *Id.* at 3.

[634] *Id.*

[635] *See id.*

(a) stores, prepares, packages, serves, vends food directly to the consumer, or otherwise provides food for human consumption such as a restaurant; satellite or catered feeding location; catering operation if the operation provides food directly to a consumer or to a conveyance used to transport people; market; vending location; conveyance used to transport people; institution; or food bank.[636]

The second part of the code definition covers enterprises that indirectly convey food to a consumer:

(b) relinquishes possession of food to a consumer directly, or indirectly through a delivery service such as home delivery of grocery orders or restaurant takeout orders, or delivery service that is provided by common carriers.[637]

[c] Identification of Risk Factors

To assist the states, the FDA identifies five major risk factors from "epidemiological data in retail food service that are related to employee behavior and preparation practice: (1) improper holding temperatures, (2) inadequate cooking, such as undercooking raw shell eggs, (3) contaminated equipment, (4) food from unsafe sources, and (5) poor personal hygiene." The Food Code, to address controls for these risk factors, establishes five key "public health interventions to protect consumer health: (1) demonstration of knowledge, (2) employee health controls, (3) controlling hands as a vehicle of contamination, (4) time and temperature parameters for controlling pathogens, and (5) the consumer advisory." The 2013 Model Food Code substantively address management and personnel; food, equipment, utensils, and linens; water, plumbing, and waste; physical facilities; poisonous or toxic materials; and compliance and enforcement.[638]

[d] Adoption

All fifty states have adopted food codes patterned after the 1993, 1995, 1997, 1999, 2001, 2005, 2009, or 2013 versions of the Food Code.[639] Many of the states incorporate the entire model code by reference. The Food Code may be enacted into statute, promulgated as a regulation, or adopted as an ordinance. After adopting a version of the model food code, states or local bodies may engage in rulemaking to update their codes based on FDA updates or updates of their own creation. For example, some states have amended their food codes to provide exemptions for cottage food operations.[640] Other states have moved beyond recommendations of the Model Food Code for Certified Food Protection Managers to the requirement that all food handlers receive training and certification.[641] Some local jurisdictions require the certification of all food handlers, in addition to the presence of certified food protection managers.

---

[636] *Id.* at 9.
[637] *Id.*
[638] *See* 2013 MODEL FOOD CODE, Supra Note 611.
[639] *Real Progress in Food Code Adoption*, U.S. FOOD & DRUG ADMIN. (2011).
[640] *See, e.g.*, 2012 Cal. Legis. Serv. Ch. 415 (A.B. 1616) (West) amending CAL. HEALTH & SAFETY CODE § 110460, among other provisions.
[641] *See, e.g.*, CAL. HEALTH & SAFETY CODE § 113948.

The issue of outdated state food codes is one of concern. The Federal Food Safety Working Group, which was convened by President Obama in 2009, led by DHHS and USDA, and tasked with developing strategies to improve food safety, identified the need for the FDA to encourage more uniform adoption of current FDA standards.[642] The FDA has included the need to "encourage widespread, uniform, and complete adoption of the FDA Food Code," as one of four action areas in its Retail Food Safety Initiative Action Plan. Its main lever to accomplish this is through public recognition, education, and encouragement.[643] However, states have been unable to keep up with the two-year cycle of FDA updates to the Model Food Code, even with FDA encouragement, potentially leaving consumers at risk. This has been an ongoing problem since the initiation of the Model Food Code of 1993. For example, nearly three-fourths of the states reported in 2001 that the biennial revisions to the Food Code acted "as a drawback to adopting the most recent Food Code."[644] Respondents also indicated "other drawbacks, including the feasibility of some of the provisions, the cost and time involved in adopting or implementing an updated version of the Food Code, and the need to rely on FDA to interpret Food Code provisions and provide other support."[645] Sixteen of the thirty-four states that did not update their codes to include the 1999 Food Code changes "indicated that the length of time and the difficulty of the adoption process inhibits them from updating their code every 2 years." Some of these states reportedly were just adopting an earlier version of the Food Code and were working on implementation issues, so they did not consider adopting the 1999 Food Code. Many states reportedly did not have the time and resources to update their retail food safety regulations at the time of Food Code changes, "especially when the new version may contain only minor changes from an earlier version of the code."[646]

[e] Exemptions

There are a number of exemptions in the Model Food Code. These exemptions are typically for low-risk foods or for situations where regulation would present a burden that is out of proportion to the potential harm.[647] They include: establishments selling only prepackaged foods that are not potentially hazardous; produce stands offering whole, uncut fresh fruits and vegetables; a kitchen in a private home, if it only prepares nonpotentially hazardous foods for sale or service at a function, like a charitable organization's bake sale; a kitchen in a private home if the home is owner-occupied, the home does not have more than six bedrooms, there are not more than eighteen guests, breakfast is the only meal offered, and the consumer is informed that the food is prepared in a kitchen that is not regulated or inspected (which typically applies to bed and breakfasts and day care facilities); and private homes that receive catered or delivered food.

There are two key categories of exemptions that the Model Food Code does not include. These are exemptions for farmers' markets and exemptions for home-based (or

---

[642] Fed. Food Safety Working Group Progress Report, White House (2011).
[643] *Retail Food Safety Initiative Action Plan*, U.S. Food & Drug Admin. (2011).
[644] Retail Food Safety, Office of the Inspection Gen. (OEI-05-00-00540 OIG) (September 2001).
[645] *Id.*
[646] *Id.*
[647] *Id.*

cottage) foods. There are also a wide variation of other exemptions contained in state food codes, including exemptions for honey and maple syrup.

Although the Model Food Code does not discuss farmers' markets, many state food codes, as referenced in Chapter 6, define and regulate farmers' markets. Where codes differ, beyond whether they mention farmers' markets, is whether farmers' markets are classified as exempt from regulations applying to food establishments. For example, California includes farmers' markets in its definition of food facility, prescribing sanitation requirements for them. Iowa, on the contrary, exempts farmers' markets from its definition of food establishments, provided that the market does not sell or distribute potentially hazardous foods. New York State also exempts farmers' markets from their definition of retail food establishment, but their food code does not mention farmers' markets.[648] While the Model Food Code does not recognize any general exemption for cottage foods, many states have included exemptions in their food codes.

[5] *State Enforcement Authority and Practices*

Typically, an enforcement agency is identified and delegated authority in a state's food code. This agency is then responsible for developing a retail food regulatory program to enforce the food code's requirements. A program usually involves the licensing of restaurants and food stores after review of plans, inspections to ensure compliance with food code requirements, and engagement in enforcement actions for noncompliance. Enforcement actions require the establishment of an administrative process to review noncompliance, and determine actions necessary to prevent a retail food establishment from selling potentially unsafe foods. States have a variety of enforcement mechanisms available, including seizure, condemnation, stop sale, health advisories, monetary penalties, suspension or revocation of license and permit, injunction, criminal prosecutions or complaints, warning letters, hearings, closures, and voluntary destruction and disposal.[649] In many states, the enforcement agency's powers to embargo or condemn food are often more robust than those that can be exercised by the FDA.

Inspections are performed at food establishments to ensure compliance with the requirements set out in food codes. Historically, these inspections occur infrequently – perhaps, one to three times per year. The Model Food Code encourages risk-based inspection programs, where the frequency of inspections is tied to the level of risk to health that is posed by the food served at an establishment. For example, retail food enterprises that sell only beverages or prepackaged foods present a low-risk for transmission of foodborne illness and therefore require fewer inspections. Other enterprises, like those that sell sushi, present a higher risk, and thus are inspected more frequently. Risk-based inspections are pragmatic, given that enforcement agencies have finite resources, therefore allocating more resources to establishments that pose a greater potential risk to the public's health is prioritized.[650]

---

[648] *Sanitary Regulations for Direct Marketing*, N.Y. DEPT. OF AGRIC. & MKTS.

[649] *State Food Safety Resource Survey*, ASS'N OF FOOD & DRUG OFFICIALS (2009).

[650] Chicago created a new risk-based inspection schedule for its food service establishments, replacing twice-yearly inspections for all restaurants. The new ordinance allows low-risk establishments, and those that have a previous record of passing inspections, to self-certify, with their reporting certified by inspectors. This change shortens the time needed to inspect low-risk establishments and allows the department to allocate more time and resources to be spent on higher-risk establishments. *See* Press Release, City of

[6] *State Delegation of Retail Regulation*

States vary in their governance structure and sharing of regulatory authority with local health departments. State food codes generally authorize state agencies, and potentially local agencies, as enforcement agents of their retail food codes. Many state health agencies share with or delegate to local agencies the licensing, inspection, and enforcement of regulations for food service establishments.[651] Some states with very centralized government structures do not delegate these activities to local health departments. Some state food codes contain language on preemption, which prevents local governments from engaging in rulemaking on particular topics. For example, California has a very broad preemption provision, stating that it is the intent of the legislature to occupy the whole field of health and sanitation standards for retail food facilities. Other states, like Pennsylvania, also preempt local jurisdictions from adopting food safety regulations.[652] Still others create preemption floors, allowing local governments to make more stringent regulations,[653] or preempt the enforcement of conflicting regulations.[654] There are also some exemptions to preemption provisions, in bodies of regulation such as the California Retail Food Code (CRFC), which specifically allows for a grading system to be adopted by local public health departments. Los Angeles County has been a leader in adopting restaurant grading[655] and has seen scores on inspections go up since the implementation of a grading system.[656] NYC has followed suit, also adopting a restaurant grading program.[657] Regardless of the structure and sharing of authority, state governments direct the roles of local health departments.

Preemption can be helpful in creating state uniformity and in preventing retail food service establishments from being regulated in a duplicative manner. For example, in Tennessee, when the state food code was adopted, the city of Memphis had a similar retail food code in place. The state chose to allow the regulatory regime already in place to exist alongside the state rules. In other instances, a nonidentical local food safety law would likely be preempted due to conflict with state law. This regulatory scheme has proved to be difficult for food establishments to navigate and some are calling for harmonization.[658]

[7] *Restaurant Grading*

According to the CDC, more than half of all reported foodborne illnesses in the United States are attributed to food service establishments.[659] Food safety regulation for

---

Chicago, Mayor Emanuel Eases Restaurant Inspections for Low-Risk Food Establishments and Improves Inspection Efficiency (November 2, 2011).

[651] *National Profile of Local Health Departments*, NAT'L ASS'N OF CITY & CNTY. HEALTH OFFICIALS (2010).

[652] 3 PA. CONS. STAT. ANN. § 5701.

[653] VT. STAT ANN., TIT. 18, § 4301.

[654] MICH. COMP. LAWS § 289.4101(3); MICH. COMP. LAWS 289.3113.

[655] Los Angeles, Cnty., Ordinance 97-0071 (February 17, 1998).

[656] Simon PA et al., *Impact of Restaurant Hygiene Grade Cards on Foodborne-Disease Hospitalizations in Los Angeles County*, 67 J. ENVIRON HEALTH 32–6 (2005).

[657] *Restaurant Grading in New York City at 18 Months*, N.Y.C. HEATH DEPT.

[658] *See Creating a More Efficient and Effective Food Safety System in Memphis and Shelby County*, HEALTH L. & POLICY CLINIC OF HARVARD L. SCHOOL (2011).

[659] South Carolina Department of Health and Environmental Control (November 6, 2011).

restaurants involves monitoring and inspecting to ensure that minimum standards of safety and hygiene are being kept. Local municipalities inspect restaurants on a regular basis with guidance from state food codes, which are usually based on the Model Food Code.[660] Restaurants have to meet minimum standards to remain open, and inspection results are often posted online at confusing, difficult to use, government websites.

A centerpiece to regulating food safety in restaurants is a letter grading system. The use of letter grading in the United States for restaurants can be traced back to the creation of the Model Milk Code by the US Public Health Service (USPHS).[661] This code contained a letter grading system for milk quality, such as "A," "B," and so forth. This type of letter grading option continued in the USPHS Code up until the 1962 Model Food Code. Sometime after this point, several states and local government began adopting their own letter grading systems. In 1995, South Carolina was the first state to enact grading requirements for restaurants that applied statewide. Tennessee also has a state-wide system, and North Carolina has enacted similar legislation, implementing the "Know the Score" program.[662] There are numerous states that do not have requirements for all of their counties to use grading systems but allow for their local municipalities to adopt these systems. California, which follows this legal structure, has a plethora of cities with grading systems, including Sacramento, San Francisco, Los Angeles, San Diego, and San Bernardino County. With the success seen by cities like Los Angeles and Toronto through the use of a letter grading system for restaurants, cities from Las Vegas to Dallas to New York adopted this popular trend since the early 2000s.[663]

§ 3.08 International Food Safety

[1] Multilateral Trade Construct

The safety of food imported into and exported from the United States is a trade issue and as explained in Chapter 2 is handled within the scope of World Trade Organization (WTO) rules and with the GATT/WTO regime, as explained in Chapter 2. This regime, being a set of trade agreements rather than health agreements, does not have any provisions regarding the active promotion of food safety. Neither GATT (*General Agreement on Tariffs and Trade*) nor the legal instruments that frame the WTO (i.e., SPS [Sanitary and phytosanitary] Agreement) require WTO members to take positive measures to enhance food safety regulation or even encourage countries to prohibit the export of unsafe food. The prohibition or restriction of exports of unsafe food products in order to protect human or animal health or life in other countries has never been an objective of the WTO/GATT/SPS regime.

[660] Paul Tour-Sarkissian & Tania Tour-Sarkissian, The essential Guide to California Restaurant Law 61 (2009).

[661] Elizabeth Pytka, *Publicly Posted Health Inspection Grade Cards*, OLR Res. Rep. (April 28, 2005).

[662] Id.

[663] Los Angeles employs a restaurant grading system that has been a model for many of the systems in existence throughout the United States. A restaurant begins each inspection with a perfect score of 100 points. As the inspection progresses, the Environmental Health Specialist goes through the facility and uses a detailed checklist called the Food Official Inspection Report to score the establishment. Violations are broken down into three sections with a point system that results in a grade card for the restaurant that is posted at the restaurant until the next inspection when a new grade card is issued. Restaurants are required to present an inspection report to a customer upon request, and the reports are available to the public online. See L.A. Pub. Health, Cty of Los Angeles.

In fact, as noted in Chapter 2 food safety measures that constitute a trade barrier must conform to the SPS Agreement in order to comply with Article XX(b) of the GATT.[664] Such measures must be based on scientific evidence,[665] must take economic factors and trade into account,[666] and must ensure that the food safety measure is the least restrictive measure possible.[667]

The compliance of a food safety measure with the SPS Agreement also depends on large part whether the measure comports with sanitary and phytosanitary standards established by Codex. While the standards adopted by Codex are not binding on members, the SPS Agreement, as elucidated in Chapter 2, explicitly requires WTO members to base their SPS measures on international standards, including those food safety measures of Codex, giving national measures that comply with Codex standards a presumption of complying with the SPS Agreement and GATT.[668]

Codex's role is limited to standard-making or rulemaking; Codex does not enforce the standards or rules. Rather, the enforcement mechanisms at the international level rests with the WTO and its Dispute Settlement Body (DSB). If a country enacts a food safety measure that might not comply with the SPS Agreement, another country can bring a complaint under the WTO.[669]

It is not surprising that in an increasingly complicated global food system, where the heightened legal role of Codex functions as a quasi-legislative standard-setting body pursuant to the SPS Agreement, Codex is becoming a politicized forum. The balance between Codex's two competing goals – protecting the health of consumers and ensuring fair practices in food trade – is a challenge to maintain. Codex member states tend to vote in a manner that would advance their trade interests rather than promote food safety. In addition to the tension that exists between competing goals, cultural fragmentation between the food systems in various countries often collides with trade liberalization, making it difficult for Codex to operate on scientific principle. In addition to Codex's scientific soundness, legitimacy, concerns over transparency and accountability raise questions about the governance future of this institution.[670]

[2] WTO Food Safety Cases

[a] Overview of Cases

This section will examine two cases handled by the DSB of the WTO that involve complex food safety and SPS issues: the EC Hormones Case[671] and the EC/GMO

---

[664] Agreement on the Application of Sanitary and Phytosanitary Measures (SPS Agreement), art. 2, section 4, April 15, 1994, Marrakesh Agreement Establishing the World Trade Organization, Annex 1A, 1867 U.N.T.S. 493, 33 I.L.M. 1125.

[665] *Id.* at arts. 5.1 and 5.2.

[666] *Id.* at arts. 5.3 and 5.4.

[667] *Id.* at art. 5.6.

[668] SPS Agreement, *supra* note 663 at art. 3.

[669] Agreement Establishing the World Trade Organization, art. 3, para. 3, April 15, 1994, Marrakesh Agreement Establishing the World Trade Organization, 33 I.L.M. 1125.

[670] *See* Ching-Fu Lin, *Scientification of Politics or Politicization of Science: Reassessing the Limits of International Food Safety Lawmaking*, 15 COLUM. SCI & TECH. L. REV. 1, 14 (2013).

[671] Panel Report, *EC – Measures Concerning Meat and Meat Products*, WT/DS48/R/CAN (August 18, 1997); Panel Report, *EC – Measures Concerning Meat and Meat Products*, WT/DS26/R/USA (August

Case.[672] This section will also address the matter of WTO approval of the controversial veterinary drug ractopamine hydrochloride.[673] These cases are salient to US interest, as it was an active party or participant. This section will then identify guideposts derived from these three matters for the application of law under the WTO regulatory construct to global food -safety disputes.

[b] EC/Hormones Case

Between 1981 and 1988, the EU[674] promulgated a series of directives that banned the sale and marketing of beef treated with any of six growth hormones, which the FDA had approved as safe.[675] The ban purportedly was enacted mainly to address the health concerns of EU citizens, but it significantly impacted beef producers in the United States, where the majority of beef cattle are given synthetic growth hormones, including those banned by the EU. US producers saw the regulation as protectionist discrimination because, although any producer could theoretically comply with the EU Directive, hormone treatments of beef were commonly used and considered safe outside the EU. Codex established standards for five of the six growth hormones in question. For three of the natural hormones, Codex found that intake levels did not have to be limited; for two other hormones, Codex established safe limits for residues at levels considered to pose no risk to human health.[676]

Following several years of unsuccessful consultation with the EU to negotiate a solution, the United States and Canada took WTO action against the EU's hormone prohibition in 1995, alleging that the EC ban violated the SPS Agreement. The EC argued that the ban was based on the precautionary principle, which justifies measures to prevent risks even if scientific evidence shows little or no risk. Refusing to recognize the precautionary principle as having a basis in international law applicable to the case at hand, the Panel and Appellate Body (AB) held that the EC measure was contrary to the SPS Agreement. The Panel found in 1997 that the ban was inconsistent with Articles 3 and 5 of the SPS Agreement. Article 3 provides that a member state must base its SPS measure on international standards and guidelines, except where the country intends to provide a higher level of protection.[677] Article 5 provides that if a member state does choose to provide

18, 1997); Appellate Body Report, *EC-Measures Concerning Meat and Meat Products*, WT/DS26/AB/R (January 16, 1998).

[672] Panel Report, *EC – Measures Affecting the Approval and Marketing of Biotech Products*, WT/DS291/R, WT/DS292/R, WT/DS293/R (September 9, 2006).

[673] *See* Helena Bottemiller, *Codex Adopts Ractopamine Limits for Beef and Pork*, FOOD SAFETY NEWS (July 6, 2012).

[674] The hormone ban was initiated under the European Economic Community (EEC), which became the European Community (EC) in 1993. The European Commission (EC) is the executive body of the European Union responsible for proposing legislation, implementing decisions, upholding the Union's treaties and day-to-day running of the EU. Though the hormone ban was initiated under the EEC, the EU as a whole continues to implement the ban.

[675] *See generally* Council Directive 88/299, 1988 O.J. (L 128) (EEC); Council Directive 88/146, 1988 O.J. (L 70) (EEC); Council Directive 81/602, 1981 O.J. (L 222) (EEC). All three were repealed and replaced by Council Directive 96/22, 1996 O.J. (L 125) (EC), which prohibited, as had the earlier three directives, the sale or import of meat products that contained any of six named hormone additives. This measure was further amended by Council Directive 2003/74, 2003 O.J. (L 262) (EC).

[676] Implementation – Dispute Settlement, 5.3, The Hormones Case, THE WORLD TRADE ORGANIZATION.

[677] *See* SPS Agreement, *supra* note 663 at arts. 3.1, 3.3.

that higher level of protection it must base its SPS measure on "an assessment, appropriate to the circumstances, of the risks" to human, animal, or plant life or health.[678] All parties appealed portions of the panel report. Issued in January 1998, the Appellate Body Report concurred with the panel determination that the ban violated the SPS Agreement, while at the same time rejecting most of the panel's legal findings that supported its determination. The Appellate Body disagreed with the panel's interpretation of Article 3 and Article 5.1, and it rejected the panel's findings of a violation of Article 5.5, which directs members to aim at achieving consistency in the application of the concept of an appropriate level of protection.[679]

The AB determined that the EC ban was not based on a risk assessment and thus in violation of Article 5.1.[680] In interpreting Article 5.1 differently from the panel, the AB stressed that, when read contextually with Article 2.2, Article 5.1 requires that the risk assessment sufficiently warrant or reasonably support the SPS measure.[681] The AB stated that the substantive requirement of Article 5.1, and the test to be applied to all future measures, is that there be a "rational relationship between the [SPS] measure and the risk assessment."[682] The AB determined that when designing a risk assessment, governments can look at qualitative as well as quantitative factors, adopt risk assessments developed by other member states or international organizations, and adopt the minority view on a scientific issue.[683] The AB concluded that the assessment of whether there is a rational relationship between an SPS measure and its risk assessment should be done on a case-by-case analysis taking into account all considerations that bear on potential adverse health effects.[684] The AB did agree with the panel on the key issue as to whether the EC had performed a risk assessment on the effects of growth hormones.[685] The AB also agreed with the panel that while the studies and evidence submitted by the EC showed the existence of the general risk of cancer, the EC failed to identify the particular risks at stake in the hormone dispute, namely, the carcinogenic or genotoxic potential of the hormone residues found in the cattle produced with growth hormones.[686] The AB also concurred with the Panel that Article 5.7 incorporated its own provisional precautionary principles, and thus application of the precautionary

---

[678] See id. at art. 5.1.

[679] The panel concluded that in violation of Article 5.5, the EC had adopted arbitrary and unjustifiable levels of protection for residues of certain hormones (natural and otherwise) used for growth promotion compared to natural hormones that occur endogenously meat and other foods. The panel found that this difference resulted in an import ban that restricted international trade and constituted a discrimination or disguised restriction on international trade. In reversing the panel's conclusion based on Article 5.5, the Appellate Body stated that the goal of Article 5.5 is not absolute or perfect consistency, but only to avoid arbitrary or unjustifiable inconsistencies. The Appellate Body rejected the panel's conclusion that the different situations involving hormones occurring naturally in meat and those that have been administered as hormones for therapeutic or zootechnical purposes were arbitrary or unjustifiable. The Appellate Body also concluded that in the case of the hormones in dispute, the measure in this case under the circumstances did not "result in discrimination or a disguised restriction on international trade." Appellate Body Report, *EC-Measures Concerning Meat and Meat Products, supra* note 670 at ¶ 246.

[680] The Appellate Body Report did find that the ban also violated Article 3.3 because of its violation of Article 5.1 (the failure to base the SPS measure on a risk assessment). *Id.* at ¶ 209.

[681] *Id.* at ¶ 193.

[682] *Id.*

[683] *Id.* at ¶¶ 187, 190, and 194.

[684] *Id.*

[685] *Id.* at ¶¶ 195–209

[686] *Id.* at ¶ 200.

principle, including that pertaining to the EC's measure, should be limited to the scope set forth in Article 5.7.[687]

The AB did not specify how the EU should comply with the SPS Agreement, including Article 5.7. This lack of guidance was most likely not an accidental omission. The AB strives to enforce compliance while at the same time seeking to respect the autonomy of the implementing body. When a party is found to be WTO-noncompliant, an implementation period is determined to establish a time frame for compliance. When the EU and United States failed to agree on a method of compliance or implementation period, they proceeded to Dispute Settlement Understanding (DSU) binding arbitration, which gave the EU until May 1999 (fifteen months) to bring its policies into compliance with WTO law. The AB arbitrator rejected the EU's application for a longer implementation period because the purpose of the period was intended only to implement the Panel ruling and not to conduct further scientific research, which appeared to be the motive in the EU application.[688] As a result of the EU's failure to bring its measures into compliance by the implementation deadline of May 1999, the WTO imposed retaliatory economic sanctions against the EU to compensate the United States for the exclusion of its hormone-fed beef from the EU market. The sanctions continued until March 2012, when the EU agreed to raise its quality beef import quota in exchange for keeping its ban on imports of hormone-treated beef.[689]

[c] EC/GMO Case

In 2003, the United States, Canada, and Argentina filed a complaint against the EC to the WTO on the ground that the EC violated provisions of the SPS by imposing a moratorium on approving the import of GMO food products. After three years, the panel published a lengthy report (over 1,000 pages) in which it approved some EC measures but invalidated some others.[690] Beginning in 1998, the EC enacted what effectively was construed as a moratorium on approving GMO products for marketing.[691] The US and other claimants argued that the EC violated provisions of the SPS because of undue delay in approval, the lack of transparency in the procedure, and the lack of sufficient scientific evidence to justify the delay in approval. The panel found undue delay in the completion of the approval procedure of twenty-four of the twenty-seven products in question, and thus a violation of Article 8 and Annex C(1)(a).[692]

Another significant issue involved the temporary safeguards applied by six EC member states (Austria, France, Germany, Greece, Italy, and Luxemburg), which prohibited the marketing of GMO products in their territories. On this issue, the EC argued that

---

[687] *See* Panel Report, *EC – Measures Concerning Meat and Meat Products, supra* note 670.

[688] *See* Award of the Arbitrator Julio Lacarte-Muró, *EC Measures Concerning Meat and Meat Products (Hormones),* at ¶ 28, WT/DS26/15, WT/DS48/13 (May 29, 1998).

[689] Press Release, *Win-Win Ending to the "Hormone Beef Trade War,"* European Parliament News (March 14, 2012).

[690] Panel Report, *EC – Measures Concerning Meat and Meat Products, supra* note 670.

[691] EC disagreed that a moratoria existed and that the "moratoria" were "measures" within the meaning of the SPS Agreement.

[692] *See* SPS Agreement, *supra* note 663, at 82 ¶ 1(a) ("Members shall ensure, with respect to any procedure to check and ensure the fulfilment of sanitary or phytosanitary measures, that: (a) such procedures are

Article 5.7 of the SPS Agreement, which permits temporary measures based on the precautionary principle, justified the temporary safeguards. The panel found that the safeguard measures taken by the EC members did not satisfy the requirements for temporary safeguards as provided for in Article 5.7. The EC-level review demonstrated that there was sufficient scientific evidence available to permit a risk assessment. Consequently, the member states could not invoke Article 5.7, which allows a country to take action only "in cases where relevant scientific evidence is sufficient."[693] The panel concluded that by maintaining the safeguards in violation of Articles 5.1 and 5.7 the EC member states also acted inconsistently with their Article 2 obligations.[694]

Although the panel's decision concentrated on the issue of undue delay and the *de facto* moratorium that the EC allegedly imposed on applications, it is important to note the panel's address of the precautionary principle involved assessing the relationship between the SPS Agreement and other principles of international law, as outlined in the WTO's dispute settlement procedure. The EC argued that WTO agreements should be interpreted in accordance with international principles, as established in international law norms outlined by the UN Biodiversity Convention and the Cartagena Protocol.[695] According to the Cartagena Protocol, the signatories can take a measure to prevent genetically modified organisms even without scientific evidence that it causes a risk to human, animal, or plant life and health or that it has a detrimental effect on the environment. The panel reasoned that it did not have to take into account the principles of the UN Biodiversity Convention and the Cartagena Protocol in this dispute because one of the parties to the dispute – the United States – was not a party to those international treaties. Article 31(3)(c) provides that the norms of other treaties should be considered in a treaty dispute, if the disputing parties are parties to those other treaties.[696] Therefore, the panel concluded that the principles of UN Biodiversity Convention and the Cartagena Protocol were irrelevant since the United States was not a party to them.[697]

[d]   Ractopamine Controversy

An international food safety issue involving the veterinary drug ractopamine hydrochloride points to the complexities and polarization in the international regulation of food. This drug is used in animal feed to boost growth and promote leanness in pigs and cattle, and, to a limited extent, promote heavier turkeys. The substance promotes leanness in pigs and cattle by helping increase muscle mass. Ractopamine is absorbed into animals' bodies and distributed to muscle tissues, moving nutrients away from fat production and increasing protein synthesis and eventually muscle fibers.[698] The end result is a more lean and heavier meat, which is more marketable and thus more valuable. Unlike

undertaken and completed without undue delay and in no less favourable manner for imported products than for like domestic products[.]")
[693] *Id.* at art. 5(7).
[694] Panel Report, *EC – Measures Concerning Meat and Meat Products, supra* note 670 at ¶¶ 7.3996–.3998.
[695] *Id.* at ¶ 4.359.
[696] *Id.* at ¶ 7.68.
[697] *Id.* at ¶ 7.71.
[698] *See* The Codex and JECFA Secretariats, FAO, Information Sheet: Discussion on Ractopamine in Codex and in the Joint FAO/WHO Expert Committee on Food Additives 1–2 (2012). *See also* Alberto Alemanno &

most veterinary drugs, ractopamine is intended for use in the final stages of these animals' lives – just prior to slaughter (finishing animals) – so there is no clearance period
that would reduce or eliminate residues upon human consumption. According to the
Joint FAO/WHO Expert Committee on Food Additives, administering ractopamine to
humans for any medical purpose is impermissible.[699]

Countries around the world are split over whether to allow the use of ractopamine in
meat production. While ractopamine has been authorized as a feed additive countries,
such as the United States, Australia, Canada, Japan, and Mexico, for growth promotion of fattening pigs and cattle, the other jurisdictions, including the EU, mainland
China, and Taiwan, ban its use on safety grounds. China has expressed concerns about
the higher concentrations of residues found in pig organs, which are part of a typical
Chinese diet; the EU has argued that the science supporting Ractopamine's safety is
flawed.[700] Unlike previous disputes arising out of the use of veterinary drugs, such as
growth hormones, the safety grounds generally invoked to substantiate the restrictions
on the use of ractopamine are not limited to human health concerns. Evidence suggests that ractopamine may also cause animal health and animal welfare issues. In
particular, animal activists suggest that the substance may cause discomfort in animals
and question whether it is essential to animal rearing.[701]

After years of scientific and political deadlock, Codex voted (69–67) in July 2012 to
adopt the first-ever maximum residue levels for ractopamine. The proposal to adopt a
standard for ractopamine was based upon scientific advice from the JECFA and the
recommendation of the Codex Committee on Residues of Veterinary Drugs in Food
(CCRVDF).[702] Prior to the vote in July, WTO members debated whether the organization's rules on food safety could be undermined by an international standard-setting
body's failure to agree on Maximum Residue Limit (MRL) for a feed additive. In particular, the SPS Committee debated whether disagreement about setting an MRL for
ractopamine endangered the scientific basis and legitimacy of WTO rules or whether
resorting only to a scientific opinion undermines the need for the rules to be more
broadly based.

Those countries that authorize the use of the substance, including the United
States, believe that scientific evidence shows that some ractopamine residues are safe
and have requested that maximum residue limits (10 parts per billion for the main
types of meat) to be approved by Codex. In addition to citing the JEFCA studies, these
members note that twenty-six countries have allowed ractopamine to be used for many
years, with no harmful effects. On the other side of the ledger, countries, such as the
EU and China, challenge the JECFA findings and that Codex requires other issues
affecting consumer health to be taken into account. It appears that notwithstanding

---

Giuseppe Capodieci, *Testing the Limits of Global Food Governance: The Case of Ractopamine*, 3 EUR.
J. RISK REG. 400, 405 (2012).

[699] *See* FAO Info Sheet Discussion on Ractopamine, *supra* note 697 at 1.

[700] Helena Bottemiller, *Codex Adopts Ractopamine Limits for Beef and Pork*, Food Safety News (July
6, 2012).

[701] *See* Alemanno & Capodieci, *supra* note 697 at 4.

[702] *See id.* at 6.

the Codex vote, ractopamine is set to become the source of another endless transatlantic trade dispute and a test case for the embryonic and sometime contentious global food governance system.

[e] Guideposts for Disputes

• Trade-driven SPS disputes are exceedingly complicated

Every SPS measure imposed to ensure safe food must be supported by solid scientific evidence. Barriers based on food safety concerns must be based on risk assessment. The complexities, both in determining what constitutes solid scientific evidence and in the risk assessment process, are compounded by the fact that countries do not share a common understanding on their perceptions of risks, scientific evidence, and proper levels of protections. Also, although developing countries share a general concern of food safety with developed countries, developing countries often have different priorities, including that of food security – ensuring adequate amounts of food for people – which take precedence over food safety.

• Free trade trumps most of the social policy agenda

While social concerns are important to member states of the WTO and to its constituencies and consumers, the WTO regime is predicated upon free trade. Thus, animal welfare concerns expressed in the ractopamine issue and the food systems' concerns expressed in the GMO issue are secondary to free trade values.

• The precautionary principle in global food safety plays a limited role

The WTO defines the precautionary principle as "a notion which supports taking protective action before there is complete scientific proof of a risk; that it, action should not be delayed simply because full scientific information is lacking."[703] The WTO holds that in food safety, taking precautionary actions in the face of scientific uncertainty has long been accepted;[704] however, so far, in all the WTO disputes on the SPS where the precautionary principle has been raised, the panels have failed to uphold it as a rule of customary international law. For example, in the WTO *Beef Hormones* case, the Appellate Body, while declining to take a position on the status of the precautionary principle, stated that:

> [T]he status of the precautionary principle in international law continues to be the subject of debate among academics, law practitioners, regulators and judges. The precautionary principle is regarded by some as having crystallized into a general principle

---

[703] SPS Agreement Training Module: Chapter 8.2. The "Precautionary Principle," THE WORLD TRADE ORGANIZATION.

[704] Examples provided by the WTO of "precautionary actions" include the sudden outbreak of an animal disease that is suspected to be linked to imports, trade restrictions must immediately be imposed while further information about the source of the outbreak and its extent are gathered. *See id.*

of customary international environmental law. Whether it has been widely accepted by [WTO] members as a principle of general or customary international law appears less than clear.[705]

The WTO notes in its training module that with respect to food safety, the Codex Committee on General Principles is developing general principles of risk analysis, which will inform whether conditions warrant adopting precautionary measures.[706] Hence, it appears that the precautionary principle, while not being recognized as a rule of customary international law on food safety disputes, is recognized by the WTO in a practical way as part of risk analysis.

- Food safety disputes are generally resolved by compromise

In addition to the well-publicized disputes (hormones and GMO cases), cases that have WTO implications have long existed and will continue to arise, requiring compromise between countries that does not quite amount to the complicated and protracted dispute settlement process. For example, in 1999, the United States banned Italian wines because certain wines in Italy were treated with procymidone, a fungicide banned by the EPA.[707] The EC complained that the measure was too broad, since it banned all Italian wines when a ban against the specific type of wine containing the fungicide would have been sufficient to protect US human health interests. The United States eventually approved an interim tolerance level of the pesticide under pressure from the EC.

- The increasing politicization of Codex presents credibility problems for international food standards

While the decision by Codex in favor of the official US position on ractopamine has been welcomed as a victory for science-based standard-setting within Codex, the conditions surrounding its adoption signal the limits faced by the actual food global governance system for food safety. While this decision may make it easier for the United States and others to challenge countries in the WTO like China, the European Union (EU), and Taiwan, for having zero tolerance policies for ractopamine residues in meat products, there remains the question of whether the weight of an international standard adopted with a one-vote difference could realistically be considered tantamount to one adopted under consensus. From a legal standpoint, this outcome does not change the status of the adopted standard. In fact, once a standard is adopted, the WTO judicial bodies do not consider the circumstances in which the standards arose. As the *Sardines* case in Chapter 2 of this treatise clearly showed, a WTO member may be bound to apply an international standard that it voted against even if it is only a voluntary norm. In other words, international standards are binding through the SPS Agreement, regardless of whether they are made by consensus. However, it is arguable that the normative values that the international food community, and in particular the WTO dispute settlement bodies, should attach to a standard adopted by a slim

---

[705] Appellate Body Report, *EC-Measures Concerning Meat and Meat Products*, *supra* note 670 at ¶ 123.
[706] SPS Training Module, *supra* note 702.
[707] *Report on United States Trade Barriers and Unfair Practices*, EUROPEAN COMMISSION (1999).

majority should not be the same as those attributed to measures adopted by consensus, or at least, a qualified majority vote.

- Harmonization of food safety standards occurs in a format devoid of institutional mechanisms

The choice of the SPS drafters to set up a "quasi-legislative" system outside of the WTO offers several advantages. The outsourcing of the harmonization system to some external organizations not only facilitates negotiations that lead to the adoption of a standard by following the softer standard of consensus, but it is also potentially capable of insulating the WTO from any criticism that may be formulated about a particular standard – notwithstanding the ractopamine case, which brought highly politicized debates. By referring to the Codex and other standard-setting organizations' activities, the WTO SPS construct aims at promoting positive integration among its members and at establishing harmonization of food safety standards via a multilateral governance structure and process for food safety. Although this setup has its advantages, it is important to recognize that it, unlike national food regimes such as the United States, does not operate in a highly developed constitutional framework where well-defined institutions share and assure the balance of power. In fact, notwithstanding its *ex post* reinforcement of the Codex standards and rules through its own enforcement mechanisms, the WTO has no general authority to directly set health and food safety policies for its members. In short, the WTO dispute settlement process tends to operate in an institutional vacuum. There is no integrated and institutionalized food safety organization involved in international food safety regulation. Given the overall free trade mandate of the WTO/GATT/SPS regime, it remains to be seen whether Codex is capable of filling this gap.

[3] *Free Trade Agreements*

In recent years, many governments have faced increasing public pressure for the establishment of better food safety management. Therefore, states have gradually shifted to alternative approaches that are pragmatic enough to address the food safety needs. More and more countries have signed a growing number of bilateral or regional food safety agreements or arrangements, or incorporating an SPS (food-safety-related) chapter into their Free Trade Agreements (FTAs). The FDA is part of this trend and has been aggressively pursuing formal and informal cooperation on food safety governance through agreements with foreign counterparts. As of 2011, the United States had 110 international arrangements (104 of which are bilateral), at least 56 of which are directly related to food safety or SPS issues.[708] In addition to a bilateral food safety agreement with China and a trilateral cooperation arrangement with China and the EU, the US FDA has also participated in the signing of seventeen different confidential

---

[708] As of 2012, there were 67 memoranda of understanding and other cooperative arrangements, and 34 confidentiality commitments under the FDA International Programs. Among these 110 international arrangements, 104 are bilateral (2 are between the United States and WHO) and 6 trilateral (5 between the United States, Mexico, and Canada, and 1 between the United States, Australia, and New Zealand). For the complete list, *see International Agreements*, U.S. Food & Drug Admin. (April 26, 2012).

arrangements on food safety/SPS issues with sixteen government authorities dispersed among twelve countries, the goal being to facilitate relevant law enforcement or regulatory matters.[709]

An example of a food safety agreement that shows how law – now in the form of international agreements – responds to increasing food safety concerns is the December 2007 food safety agreement between the US and China.[710] The US-China Food Safety Agreement serves to "establish a bilateral cooperative mechanism regarding food and feed safety"[711] through existing or future schemes of registration and certification,[712] strengthened and expedited information sharing,[713] and regulatory cooperation.[714]

As noted in Chapter 2, the negotiations for the Transatlantic Trade and Investment Partnership Agreement (TTIP), a proposed free trade agreement between the EU and the United States, involves significant food safety discussions. The negotiation around food safety is one of the thorniest issues in the negotiations. The implications of the negotiations will unfold as the negotiations continue, as it is expected that a dozen annexes will emerge that contain crucial details on how the SPS chapter of the TTIP will be implemented.[715]

[4] *European Food Safety Law*

Mirroring the first phase of the US food law – the commercial regulation of food – the creation of the European Economic Community in 1957 by the Treaty of Rome[716] established a platform whereby a common agricultural policy could be created predicated upon on freedom of movement of goods throughout the European

---

[709] *Trade Policy Review: United States*, P 143, WT/TPR/S/200, WTO Secretariat (May 8, 2008).

[710] AGREEMENT BETWEEN THE DEPARTMENT OF HEALTH AND HUMAN SERVICES OF THE UNITED STATES OF AMERICA AND THE GENERAL ADMINISTRATION OF QUALITY SUPERVISION, INSPECTION AND QUARANTINE OF THE PEOPLE'S REPUBLIC OF CHINA ON THE SAFETY OF FOOD AND FEED (December 11, 2007).

[711] *Id.* at art. I.

[712] *Id.* at annex, § II.

[713] *Id.* at art. IV. The affects of Article IV are interesting and warrant consideration for the future of bilateral food-safety agreements. Article IV requires that both parties engage in information sharing so as to improve each party's understanding of the other's regulatory systems, relevant laws, and regulations in addition to the allocation of jurisdiction. Each party is required to notify the other of significant food-safety risks to public health, manufacturing conditions, recalls, and "other instances that involve imminent or significant danger to health, or the gross deception of consumers with regard to Covered Products" within two days of the discovery of the problems. Further information regarding notifications, such as contact information for the producer, exporter, distributor, or other entities concerned, shall be provided by each party within five days upon request from the other party.

[714] *Id.* at art. V. Article V emphasizes the facilitation of foreign on-site inspection. The United States and China shall develop a streamlined process for cross-border on-site inspections, for example, by issuing a letter of invitation for visa application within five days after receiving a request from the other party. Also, a certification system under the agreement provides for the issuance of certificates showing compliance of certain Chinese food products with FDA requirements.

[715] Steve Suppan, *TTIP: Food Safety Chapter Focuses only on Resources "Necessary" for Expanding Trade*, INSTITUTE FOR AGRICULTURE AND TRADE POLICY (February 4, 2015).

[716] Treaty Establishing the European Economic Community, March 25, 1957, 298 U.N.T.S. 11.

community.[717] EC legislation did not expressly mention consumer protection until the mid-1980s, with the Single European Act of 1986.[718] However, it was not until major food scares, especially the BSE crisis of the mid-1990s, that the EC began developing a regulatory system based on scientific risk assessment and creating EU food law.[719]

The pivotal EU food law, implemented in 2002, is Regulation (EC) 178/2002, which laid down the general principles and requirements of EU food law, established the European Food Safety Authority (EFSA), and adopted procedures in food safety.[720] EFSA provides the EC and its member states with independent and transparent scientific advice on food safety, nutritional issues, labeling, and other matters.[721] EFSA also provides risk assessment. EFSA is simply a scientific source, however, and does not have enforcement authority. The EC is assisted by Regulatory Committees not encompassed within EFSA to develop food safety measures. The committees are representatives of the member states and if consulted by the EC on a particular proposal, may issue an opinion that may be adopted by the EC.[722]

EU food law contains general principles housed in Regulation (EC) 178/2002.[723] One principle is that risk assessment that is to be undertaken whenever a new food measure is proposed must be based on "the available scientific evidence and undertaken in an independent, objective and transparent manner," and must be carried out by EFSA.[724] Another fundamental principle in EU food regulation is the precautionary principle, which allows risk managers to make a decision to protect health when the science regarding the risk is inconclusive. Regulation 178/2002 Article 7 introduced this principle and provides that the measure taken be "proportionate and no more restrictive of trade than is required to achieve the high level of health protection chosen in the Community, regard had to technical and economic feasibility and other factors regarded as legitimate in the matter under consideration."[725] Although Article 7 of the Regulation 178/2002 is named the "precautionary principle" it is worded in such a way that it is compatible with the SPS Agreement.[726] This principle has been the point of divergence between the EU and United States on numerous occasions.[727] Additional general principles involve transparency; the food operator's responsibility for the safety of food they produce, transport, store, or sell; member states' responsibility to inspect food at all stages in the supply chain, and the dissemination of information to consumers in the event of a problem that might pose a risk to human health via the Rapid Alert System for Food and Feed (RASFF).[728]

---

[717] Michael T. Roberts & Emilie H. Leibouitch, Comparison of EU and US Law on Sustainable Food Processing, Alternatives To Conventional Food Processing 15–16 (Andrew Proctor ed., 2011).

[718] Id. at 16.

[719] Id. at 17.

[720] Id. at 18; art. 1(2) Regulation No. 178/2002.

[721] Id. (citing Regulation [EC] No. 178/2002, Off. J. Eur. Commun., 2002, L 31 1 (art. 22(5), p. 13.).

[722] Id. at 18.

[723] Id. at 19.

[724] Id. at 19 (quoting Regulation [EC] No. 178/2002, Off. J. Eur. Commun., 2002 L. 31 1, Fecital (19), p. 2.

[725] Id. at 19–20 (quoting art. 7, p. 19).

[726] Luigi Costato & Ferdinando Albisinni, European Food Law 7 (CEDAM 2012).

[727] Id. at 20.

[728] Id. at 20–1.

§ 3.09 Private Standards

[1] *Proliferation and Administration*

Private food safety standards proliferate in the US food supply chain. Private actors, especially multinational corporations, increasingly fill gaps in public food safety regulation by means of private regulation. The development of private food safety standards in the United States has largely been based on models established in the EU. In response to foodborne pathogen outbreaks, most notably BSE and dioxins in chickens, the EU became active in issuing directives aimed at dealing with the problems. Alongside command-and-control initiatives, retailers and suppliers began to develop private food safety schemes, such as EurepGAP, the British Retail Consortium (BRC), Global Standard for Food, and Tesco's Nature Choice, to protect brand names and calm shaken consumers. The most prominent private governance institution in the world is now GlobalGAP, a European-based retailer-led organizations that sets Good Agricultural Practice (GAP) standards for food products.

Notwithstanding EU's leadership, private food safety standards in the United States are not a new; the first private standard-setter in the area of food safety was the American Institute of Baking (AIB), founded by the American Bakers Association (ABA) in 1919, which set quality and safety standards in 1921 when it adopted an Official Code of Ethics. In the United States, major food scares have worked in conjunction with other market changes to promote the use of private standards for ensuring safety. Market changes have included the growth of food imports into the United States; advances in traceability technology, which have provided greater incentive for retailers to implement systems that absolve them from blame in the event of an outbreak; the ability of retailers to hold suppliers accountable through private certification; and the growth of private retail brands. Thus, US retailers and others in the supply chain have begun to demand private certification, especially for foreign suppliers, which they cannot adequately inspect, to protect against a case of foodborne illness being traced back to their company.[729] For example, in May 2000, the Global Food Safety Initiative (GFSI) was started by CIES (The Food Business Forum), a food industry organization that represents more than 65 percent of the world's food retailers as well as many large suppliers. The GFSI was developed as an effort to harmonize private food safety standards. Many other private, industry-led, or "third-party certified" standards have also rapidly emerged and are driven by the economic incentives for transnational food corporations to avoid reputational damage caused by food safety crises. In particular, the large transnational retail grocery corporations are increasingly demanding that their suppliers meet food safety standards, and this requirement has a broader effect as it filters all the way back to processors, traders, and agricultural producers.[730]

Demands for private certification of food suppliers by retailers have, in practice, taken the "voluntary" out of "voluntary compliance." However, by definition, compliance with private food safety standards is voluntary because there is no formal coercive mechanism,

---

[729] For example, Wal-Mart requires its suppliers to meet the food safety standards (which are usually higher than the public regulation of the relevant countries) set out by GlobalGap. Alex Goldschmidt, *Wal-Mart Announces Heightened Food Safety Standards*, WAL-MART WATCH (March 11, 2008).

[730] Jennifer Clapp & Doris Fuchs, *Agrifood Corporations, Global Governance, and Sustainability: A Framework for Analysis*, CORP. POWER IN GLOBAL AGRIFOOD GOVERNANCE 1, 14 (MIT 2009).

at least not in the United States, that forces suppliers to comply. Widespread adoption and compliance with private standards reinforces the legitimacy of such systems and consolidates their authority. Indeed, given the enormous market power that trans-national food corporations (notably giant multinational retailers) have, the standards and requirements they create may well be regarded as more effective in influencing behavior than those imposed by regulatory bodies. To be clear, the making of private standards involves more than just the standards. Private standards schemes serve five major functions: standard-setting, adoption, implementation, conformity assessment, and enforcement.[731]

[2] *FSMA and Produce*

Private food safety standards for the production of fruits and vegetables have become commonplace. An outbreak associated with *E. coli* O157:H7 in spinach in 2006 marked a turning point in the regulation of produce. As a result of the outbreak, over 100 people were hospitalized and 31 suffered from a serious complication, hemolytic-uremic syndrome, which is associated with *E. coli*. FDA's assessment of the outbreak drew attention to repeated problems with *E. coli* in fresh produce and portended future regulation focused on the safety of produce.[732] Industry groups formed to address leafy green food safety problems, including a retail-formed Food Safety Leadership Council, which proposed a standards plan for on-farm produce safety that matched or exceeded FDA guidelines and would be backed by third-party certification.[733] The leafy greens industry, in collaboration with the California state government, introduced the California Leafy Green Products Handler Marketing Agreement (LGMA), which provided a system of controls designed to minimize the risks of microbial contamination on farms producing leafy greens and to reassure consumers about the safety of leafy greens produced in California. LGMA reviews and updates food safety standards, requires members to perform certain safety operations, and works with government auditors to monitor compliance. While LGMA is a voluntary arrangement, it is binding on signatories, including the owners of farms, handlers, and shippers.[734]

As noted previously in this chapter, Section 105 of FSMA makes changes to produce safety by adding Section 419 to chapter 4 of the FDCA. These changes, referred to as preventive control measures, add a new element to the utilization of private standards. As noted in this chapter, the preventive control rules introduces mandatory on-farm

---

[731] Spencer Henson & John Humphrey, *The Impacts of Private Food Safety Standards on the Food Chain and on Public Standard-Setting Processes*, report prepared for the Joint FAO/WHO Food Standards Programme, Codex Alimentarius commission 32d Session 8 (June 29–July 4, 2009).

[732] In California, the acceptance of mandatory controls began to occur in response to persistent food safety problems. In 2004, pistachio growers supported a Federal marketing order (mandatory for all growers) to control aflatoxins and almond growers supported pasteurization following salmonella outbreaks in 2001 and 2004. Hoy Carman, *California Farmers Adapt Mandated Marketing Programs to the 21st Century*, 61(4) CAL AGRIC, 177, 187 (2007).

[733] Council members included Avendra LLC, Darden Restaurants, McDonald's Corp., Wal-Mart Stores Inc., Walt Disney World Co. and Publix Super Markets. Mechel S. Paggi, *An Assessment of Food Safety Policies and Programs for Fruits and Vegetables: Food-borne Illness Prevention and Food Security*, LEARNING ACE (2008).

[734] *See* State of Cal. Dep't of Food & Agric., California Leafy Green Products Handler Marketing Agreement (effective as amended from March 5, 2008).

preventive controls on US farms for categories of fresh produce for which the risks to human health from foodborne illness outbreaks are considered substantial. FSMA also adds that food imported into the United States must have been produced at an equivalent level of safety abroad; and the responsibility to verify this is placed on food importers. Title III of FSMA requires the FDA to rely on third-party resources to regulate food imports, including third-party auditors who inspect and certify that foreign suppliers meet US food safety requirements (via the Foreign Supplier Verification Program, outlined earlier in this chapter). The use of preventive controls backed up by audit and inspection moves US public regulations much closer to the approach used by private standards and ultimately to a level of hybridization.

[3] Future of Private Standards

While it is difficult to assess the impact of FSMA on the use of private food safety standards, it appears that such standards will thrive. The continued emphasis on preventative approaches – which FSMA continues – to food safety through the establishment of process standards and codes of practice to promote effective industry food safety management prevents or minimizes the introduction of food safety hazards into the food chain. The emergence of private food standards is to a large extent a consequence of modern preventative food safety regulatory policy. Ideally, private standards can be seen as a mechanism for implementing public policies in support of a safer food supply.[735] There is general agreement that food safety measures should not be used by the food industry as a competitive tool. Indeed, the launching of the Global Food Safety Initiative (GFSI) by leading exponents of the food retail sector in 2000, signaled that these multinationals were joining forces on issues of food safety rather than competing. The GFSI sets out to benchmark private food safety schemes so as to facilitate recognition of any one of these benchmarked schemes by any of the other GFSI members. However, it is not clear whether the GFSI goal of "once certified, accepted everywhere" is being achieved. The future of private standards raises an issue as to whether such efforts will be focused more on avoiding legal liability than on actually preventing food safety violations.

Another issue will be the extent of harmonization achieved. Private standards have evolved over time and will continue to do so. If retailers continue to stand by their own standards, it is possible to harmonize risk management, even as product differentiation allows retailers to retain their individuality and uniqueness. The costs of compliance are recognized by standards owners and certification bodies, which have moved to harmonize audit protocols between the international food standards. Although there are advantages in harmonizing the standards and reducing certification costs for the industry, there is also the risk that too much harmonization will result in these standards losing their individuality, uniqueness, and ability to protect individual retail brands. There is also a move within some international certification bodies to promote ISO 22000 for food and farming, hence reducing the power of global retailers to control standards. However, it is difficult to see such retailers giving up on their own standards and the control they currently

---

[735] There is precedence for hybridization of public and private regulation in other countries and industries. Michaela Oldfield, *Enactment of the Food Safety Modernization Act : The US FDA Within the Context of Interaction Public-Private Governance Processes* 15 (to be published by the European Journal of Risk Regulation).

exert. Amidst the struggle for private standard dominance, alternative approaches to risk management (e.g., self-assessment of risk, independent audits, and risk ranking) may be the way forward, in a similar way to how insurance risks are calculated for businesses.

§ 3.10 Food Safety Litigation

[1] *Gap Filler Role*

Food safety litigation is another legal tool that fills the regulatory gap, where despite regulation – government and self-regulation – consumers become ill from the consumption of unsafe food. Under US product liability law, consumers harmed by unsafe food products can take legal action to claim damages for their injuries. Notwithstanding the increasing number of foodborne incidents resulting from imported products, the majority of foodborne incidents still stem from domestically produced food. It may be that as consumers increasingly seek out raw foods that there will be an increase in the regulation of raw foods in response to litigation. FSMA does require the FDA to create new regulations for the producers of high-risk fruits and vegetables, but these producers are generally the least financially able to comply; in the event of an outbreak stemming from these products, recourse may fall to manufacturers. It is likely that foodborne illness litigation will increase over time, especially as technology makes it easier to trace food products to the source responsible for the hazard. It is also likely that class action lawsuits will continue to be more common for mild outbreaks of foodborne illness, particularly as identification and documentation of outbreaks improve.

Consumers made sick from eating unsafe food may recover damages from manufacturers or sellers of the unsafe food in actions brought under one or more theories of liability, including strict liability in tort, breach of implied warranty, and negligence.[736] If the consumer becomes sick from eating unsafe food, the best weapon in the plaintiff's arsenal is the strict liability claim. Hence, this section focuses primarily on the elements required for a strict liability claim.

[2] *Strict Liability*

[a] Section 402A of the Restatement (Second) of Torts

Traditional strict liability is based on Section 402A of the Restatement (Second) of Torts, which states that "[o]ne who sells any product in a defective condition unreasonably dangerous to the consumer or to his property is subject to strict liability ... if [the product] is expected to and does reach the consumer without substantial change in the condition in which it is sold."[737] Accordingly, the elements that the plaintiff must prove in order to establish a prima facie case are the following: (1) the defendant was engaged in the business of selling products of the type that caused injury; (2) the product was defective; (3) the product was defective when it left the hands of the defendant and was substantially unchanged when it was ingested by the plaintiff; (4) that because of the defect the

---

[736] Porrazzo v. Bumble Bee Foods, LLC, 822 F.Supp.2d 406 (S.D. N.Y. 2011) (allegations that tuna consumed for over a year led to elevated mercury level were pled in claims of strict liability, breach of implied warranty of merchantability, and negligence).

[737] RESTATEMENT (SECOND) OF TORTS § 402A.

product was unreasonably dangerous to the plaintiff; (5) that the plaintiff was injured; and (6) that the defective condition of the product was the cause of the plaintiff's injury. It is not necessary for the plaintiff consumer to prove that the defendant manufacturer failed to exercise all possible care in the preparation and sale of the product.[738] Nor does the plaintiff consumer need to prove that he or she purchased the product from, or had any contractual relation whatsoever with, the defendant manufacturer.[739]

There are distinct advantages to basing an action on strict liability rather than negligence or breach of warranty. In an action based on strict liability, it is not necessary to prove a breach of duty by the manufacturer or seller, as would be necessary to prove negligence. In an action based on strict liability, there is no notice requirement as might apply in a warranty action, and the rules as to the effect of disclaimers are also not applicable. The requirement of privity of contract or warranty is generally not applicable in a strict-liability action as well. Moreover, a negligence claim for defective manufacture requires the plaintiff to prove the existence of both a product defect and the defendant's negligence. A product manufacturer's or supplier's liability for breach of warranty is contractual in nature, and it is designed to enforce an agreement (either express or implied) between the parties, which may be less relevant to the food safety violations that consumers seek to litigate.

Though courts still base strict liability theory on Section 402A, the Restatement (Third) of Torts has somewhat modified the theory. Under the Restatement (Third), a seller or distributor "who sells or distributes a defective product is subject to liability if ... [the product] contains a manufacturing defect, is defective in design, or is defective because of inadequate instructions or warnings."[740] This standard is somewhat less stringent than the original Section 402A requirement that the product be "unreasonably dangerous." The comments to the Third Restatement indicate, for example, that a food product may be considered to contain a "manufacturing defect" when a can of peas contains a pebble; may be "defectively designed" when the recipe for potato chips contains a dangerous chemical preservative; or may be sold without "adequate warnings" when the seller fails to inform consumers that the dye applied to the skins of oranges contains a well-known allergen. The comments also note that while it is clear that when a plaintiff suffers harm due to the presence in food of foreign matter clearly not intended by the product seller, such as a pebble in a can of peas, the claim is easily resolved as one involving a "manufacturing defect." However, unique difficulties may pertain to cases in which it is unclear whether the ingredient that caused the plaintiff's harm is an unanticipated adulteration or an inherent aspect of the product. As noted in this section, most courts have resolved this dilemma, according to the Restatement Reporters, by adopting the "reasonable-consumer-expectations" test.

In short, the doctrine of strict liability is applicable even when the defendant has exercised all possible care in the preparation and sale of the product. The focus is not whether the food enterprise did anything wrong, but simply whether the illness in question can be traced to its food product. Finally, the rules for strict liability for all products apply to food.

---

[738] *See* RESTATEMENT (SECOND) § 402A(2)(A).
[739] *See* RESTATEMENT (SECOND) § 402A(2)(B).
[740] RESTATEMENT (THIRD) OF TORTS: PRODUCTS LIABILITY §§ 1–2.

[b] Prima Facie Case of Strict Liability

(1) *Defendant Engaged in the Business of Selling Products of the Type that*
Caused Injury

In proving that the defendant is engaged in the business of selling the food or beverage product that allegedly caused physical harm to the plaintiff, it is not necessary for the plaintiff to show that the defendant is engaged solely in the business of selling such a product.[741] It is enough for the plaintiff to prove that the defendant is the manufacturer of the product, a wholesale or retail dealer or distributor of the product, or the operator of a restaurant where the product was sold. It is not enough, however, for the plaintiff to show that the defendant is merely an occasional seller of the product.[742]

In order for liability to attach, it is also not necessary that the defendant be engaged solely in the business of selling of food products. For example, the rule of liability applies to the owner of a motion picture theater who sells popcorn or ice cream, either for consumption on the premises or in packages to be taken home. A person who is an occasional seller of food but who is not engaged in that activity as a business, for example, a person who sells a neighbor a jar of jam or a pound of sugar, is not subject to strict liability.[743]

Under § 402A of the Restatement Second of Torts, any seller of an unreasonably dangerous food product who was engaged in the business of selling such products is potentially liable for physical harm caused by the consumption of the product. In the majority of states, the rule of liability applies to any manufacturer, wholesale or retail dealer or distributor, or operator of a restaurant.[744]

(2) *Defective Product*

In attempting to determine whether a food product is defective or "unreasonably dangerous," courts have historically used two tests: the foreign-natural test and the reasonable-consumer-expectations test. Liability for injuries caused by a foreign body or substance in food that has been sold will often depend on whether the body or substance in question is considered to be truly "foreign" rather than "natural" to the food or beverage.

Under the foreign-natural test, "if the food item is contaminated by a foreign substance, the injured consumer can recover damages."[745] However, "[i]f the substance in food which caused the injury is natural to the food, the consumer cannot recover damages."[746] A classic case that employed the foreign-natural test involved a plaintiff injured by a chicken bone in a potpie.[747] The court noted that "as a matter of common knowledge chicken pies occasionally contain chicken bones. We have no hesitancy in

---

[741] RESTATEMENT (SECOND) § 402A Cmt f. (owner of movie theater who sells popcorn or ice cream is in business of selling such products).

[742] *Id.*

[743] *Id.*

[744] *See* Garrison v. Heublein Inc, 673 F.2d 189 (7th Cir. 1982) (distiller); Matthews v. Campbell Soup Co, 380 F.Supp. 1061 (S.D. Tex. 1974) (manufacturer); Slonsky v. Phoenix Coca-Cola Bottling Co., 499 P.2d 741 (Div. Ariz. 1972) (bottler); Wachtel v. Rosol, 271 A.2d 84 (Conn. 1970) (restaurant); Johnesee v. Stop & Shop Co., 416 A.2d 956 (App. Div. N.J. 1980) (retailer and manufacturer).

[745] O'Dell v. DeJean's Packing Co., 585 P.2d 399, 402 (Okla. Ct. App. 1978).

[746] *Id.*

[747] *See* Mix v. Ingersoll Candy Co., 59 P.2d 144 (Cal. 1936).

so holding, and we are of the opinion that despite the fact that a chicken bone may occasionally be encountered in a chicken pie, such chicken pie, in the absence of some further defect, is reasonably fit for human consumption."[748] Pursuant to the foreign-natural doctrine, the manufacturer will be held liable only if the substance responsible for the injury is foreign to any of the ingredients contained in the product, while pursuant to the reasonable-expectation test, which applies in certain jurisdictions, "regardless [of] whether a substance in a food product is natural to an ingredient thereof, liability will lie for injuries caused by the substance where the consumer of the product would not reasonably have expected to find the substance in the product."[749]

In an era of consumerism, the foreign-natural standard is an anachronism. It protects food processors and sellers from liability even when the technology may be readily available to remove injurious natural objects from food. The consumer-expectation test, on the contrary, imposes no greater burden upon processors or sellers than to guarantee that their food products meet the standards of safety that consumers customarily and reasonably have come to expect from the food industry.

It is important to note that in states where the "foreign-natural" test is still applied, even if an injured plaintiff can establish an otherwise legally sufficient claim of negligence, breach of implied warranty, or strict tort liability, a food processor may be free from liability as a matter of law if the deleterious object or substance in the food is natural to the ingredients of the product. However, in states where the "reasonable-expectation" test is the rule, liability might be incurred on any appropriate theory, even for a "natural" defect, if it is one not reasonably anticipated by the consumer.

In contrast to the foreign-natural test, the reasonable-consumer-expectations test, which has become the primary test adopted by most courts, states that "if the substance which caused the damage can be 'reasonably expected' to be in the food or drink, the consumer is deemed to be on guard for same and if injured the consumer cannot recover."[750] The "reasonable-expectations" test has been adopted by the Restatement Third, Torts: Products Liability, which states:

> One engaged in the business of selling or otherwise distributing food products who sells or distributes a food product that is defective ... is subject to liability for harm to persons or property caused by the defect ... [A] harm-causing ingredient of the food product constitutes a defect if a reasonable consumer would not expect the food product to contain that ingredient.[751]

The Restatement Reporters also note that the reasonable-expectations test has been favored unanimously by law review commentators and that the doctrine has become the majority rule in the United States.

In reverting to the chicken bone theme, in a case involving a woman injured from swallowing a chicken bone in soup, the Rhode Island Supreme Court in 1951 rejected the foreign-natural test and adopted a reasonable-consumer-expectations test.[752] Over the next couple of decades, courts continued to adopt the reasonable-consumer-expectations

[748] *Id.*
[749] Jackson v. Nestle-Beich, Inc., 589 N.E.2d 547 (Ill. 1992).
[750] *O'Dell*, 585 P.2d at 402.
[751] RESTATEMENT (THIRD) OF TORTS: PRODUCTS LIABILITY.
[752] Wood v. Waldorf Sys., Inc. 83 A.2d 90 (R.I. 1951).

test.[753] The Restatement (Third) of Torts' subsequent adoption of the reasonable-consumer-expectations test solidified the doctrinal shift, as courts now rarely invoke the foreign-natural test. Under the reasonable-expectation test, in an action arising from injuries caused by substances in food, the query is what is reasonably expected by the consumer in the food as served, not what might be natural to the ingredients of that food prior to preparation; as applied to an action for common law negligence, the test is related to the foreseeability of harm on the part of the defendant.

(3) Defective Product When in Hands of Defendant

The Restatement Second, Torts § 402A expresses no opinion as to whether liability may attach to sellers of products expected to be processed or otherwise substantially changed before reaching the user or consumer. It suggests, however, that the mere fact that a product is to undergo processing or other substantial change will not necessarily relieve a seller of liability. For example, a seller of coffee beans contaminated by poison would be liable to the ultimate consumer even though the beans had first been sold to a processor who roasted and packaged them for sale to the consumer.[754]

A defective condition is one "not contemplated by the ultimate consumer, which will be unreasonably dangerous to him."[755] With regard to food or beverage products, the most common grounds for finding defectiveness are contamination, decay, deterioration, or the presence of foreign objects. Improper packaging may also make a food product defective.[756]

Any product, including a food product, will be unreasonably dangerous when it is "dangerous to an extent beyond that which would be contemplated by the ordinary consumer" with ordinary knowledge as to the product's characteristics.[757]

(4) Product Reached Plaintiff in Unchanged Condition

The plaintiff has to prove that the condition of the food product was unchanged between the time the product left the defendant's possession and control and the time that the plaintiff ate or drank it.[758] This may be done by showing that the product reached the plaintiff in a sealed, unopened container. Plaintiff bears the burden of proving that the product was in a defective condition when it left the control of the seller. Unless evidence can be produced supporting the conclusion that the food or beverage was defective at that time, this burden is not sustained.[759] In *Dirsa v Martuscello*, for example, a strict liability action against the brewer and retailer of a bottle of beer that was found to contain the body of a partially decomposed mouse, there was evidence that the bottle was delivered by the brewing company in a closed carton to a beer wholesaler.[760] Without being opened, the carton was delivered by the wholesaler to the retailer. The retailer's

---

[753] Brian Daluiso, *"Is the Meat Here Safe?" How Strict Liability For Retailers Can Lead to Safer Meat*, 92 B.U.L. Rev. 1081, 1104 (May 2012).

[754] Restatement (Second) of Torts § 402A Cmt. p.

[755] Restatement § 402A Cmt. g.

[756] *See* Restatement § 402A Cmt h.

[757] Restatement § 402A Cmt i. Matthews v. Campbell Soup Co., 380 F.Supp. 1061 (S.D. Tex 1974).

[758] *See* e.g., Wachtel v. Rosol, 271 A.2d 84 (Conn. 1970); Neubauer v. Coca-Cola Bottling Co., 238 N.E.2d 437 (App. Ct. Ill. 1968). *See* Restatement (Second) of Torts § 402A(1)(b).

[759] *See* Restatement (First) of Torts § 402A Cmt g.

[760] 429 N.Y.S.2d 483 (N.Y. App. Div.1980).

employees subsequently placed the still-unopened carton in the plaintiff's automobile. The evidence was considered sufficient to meet the necessary burden. Moreover, in *Santine v Coca-Cola Bottling Co*,[761] evidence of a sealed bottle indicated what the court called a "continuity of control" over the contents of the container by the bottler. The court found that the presence of a dead insect in a sealed bottle of beverage that is sold for human consumption speaks for itself and makes out a prima facie case of negligence on the part of the bottler.

There may be a presumption that food purchased in a restaurant reached the plaintiff in an unchanged condition. In *Wachtel v. Rosol*,[762] the plaintiff stated a prima facie case in a strict liability action against a restaurant that served him an egg salad sandwich allegedly contaminated with salmonella. The court said that the sale of the sandwich for immediate consumption on the restaurant's premises carried the necessary implication that the sandwich was expected to and did reach the plaintiff without substantial change in the condition in which it was sold.

(5) Causation

Food poisoning cases are governed by the same basic rules of causation that govern other tort cases, which tends to be the central issue. A manufacturer or seller of food products will be held liable for injuries or damages sustained by a consumer of the product if the injuries or damages were "proximately caused" by a foreign substance or other defect in the product. Proof that the foreign substance or other defect in the product caused the injury in controversy is therefore a prerequisite to recovery in every products liability case whether founded on negligence, breach of warranty, strict liability in tort, or a combination of such theories.

A proximate cause of an injury is defined as a cause that, in a direct sequence, unbroken by any new, independent cause, produces the injury complained of and without which the injury would not have occurred. Proximate cause is composed of two distinct elements: (1) cause in fact and (2) legal causation. Cause in fact refers to the "but for" consequences of an act, or the physical connection between an act and the resulting injury. In contrast, legal causation "rests on policy considerations as to how far the consequences of a defendant's acts should extend [and] involves a determination of whether liability should attach as a matter of law given the existence of cause in fact." Both elements must be satisfied.

In a food poisoning case, the plaintiff must prove the existence of a causal relationship between the illness or injury and the consumption of the food. In fulfilling this burden of proof, "it is not necessary for the consumer to negate every conceivable cause but he must show that it is more likely than not that the food's condition caused the injury of which he complains."[763] Furthermore, a tort plaintiff need not show that the defendant's negligence was the *only* cause of the harm that the plaintiff suffered. As a general rule, mere correlation between ingestion and illness is insufficient as a matter of law to establish causation. Direct proof of proximate cause in food safety cases can be challenging because the food has been consumed and is often unavailable for scientific analysis. In

---

[761] 591 P.2d 329 (Okla Ct. App. 1979).
[762] Wachtel v. Rosol, 271 A.2d 84 (Conn. 1970).
[763] Crosby v. Wal-Mart Stores, Inc., 67 So. 3d 695, 697, 10–1015 (La. Ct. App. 5 Cir. 2011).

the absence of direct proof, circumstantial evidence must exclude other extrinsic causes of the accident.[764]

It is generally recognized that the plaintiff can establish proximate causation exclusively by the use of circumstantial evidence.[765] To be sufficient for that purpose, the circumstantial evidence must tend to exclude other causes of the injury or illness.[766] Absolute certainty is not required. Nor is the plaintiff required to exclude every other possibility. That is, a causal connection may be inferred by a balance of probabilities.[767] The time interval between the consumption of the food or beverage product and the onset of the plaintiff's illness may be an important piece of circumstantial evidence. In *Burr v Coca-Cola Bottling Co*,[768] the plaintiff testified that she suffered nausea, diarrhea, and chest pains after consuming a bottle of the defendant's soft drink, which was found to contain a small "wad" of some foreign substance. There was no medical testimony as to the cause of these symptoms. The court said that a showing of symptoms of illness shortly after drinking a contaminated beverage is frequently sufficient to make a jury issue on causation. The court explained that there must be a reasonable basis upon which to conclude that the subsequent illness was the natural and probable consequence of drinking the contaminated beverage. The length of time between the consumption of the beverage and the onset of the illness is not necessarily controlling, the court explained, but is of significance in determining the probability of some other cause of the illness. It may be difficult to infer a causal connection if the time interval is too long.

[c] Negligence

According to the Restatement (Second) of Torts, negligence is a failure to behave with the level of care that someone of ordinary prudence would have exercised under the same circumstances. This level of care is referred to as "reasonable care." In other words, negligence in foodborne illness cases occurs when a food enterprise fails to exercise reasonable care in producing, marketing, or selling the implicated food and as a result someone became ill. The behavior usually consists of actions, but can also consist of omissions when there is some duty to act (e.g., a duty to rescue if one is obligated to do so). Proving a prima facie case of negligence requires establishing physical harm (actual damages), the existence of a legal duty to exercise reasonable care (duty), a failure to exercise reasonable care (breach), cause in fact of physical harm by the negligent conduct (but-for causation), and a showing that the harm is within the scope of liability (proximate cause). When determining whether reasonable care was taken, one may consider the foreseeable likelihood that the person's conduct will result in harm, the foreseeable severity of the harm, and the burden of precautions to eliminate or reduce the risk of the harm. For example, where a food enterprise does not know that the apples it uses to produce unpasteurized apple juice are contaminated with *E. coli*, but does know that it is buying apples gathered from the ground in an orchard

---

[764] Wilson v. Circus Circus Hotels Inc., 710 P.2d 77 (Nev. 1985).

[765] *See e.g.*, Vuletich v. Alivotvodic, 392 N.E.2d 663 (Ill. App. Ct. 1979); Hebert v. Loveless, 474 S.W.2d 732 (Tex App. 1971).

[766] Vuletich v. Alivotvodic, 392 N.E.2d 663 (Ill. App. Ct. 1979).

[767] Hebert v. Loveless, 474 S.W.2d 732 (Tex App. 1971).

[768] Burr v. Coca-Cola Bottling Co. of Columbia, Inc.,181 S.E.2d 478 (S.C. 1971)

where animals might be present; a negligence claim could be made against the food enterprise on grounds that the enterprise should have known that the apples might be contaminated.

Failure to warn consumers of a food product's hazards or potentially dangerous condition can result in negligence claims, particularly if the product does not have the warning labels required by law. Common warnings are for foreign objects in foods (e.g., that "the product may contain" bones, shell, pits, etc.). Another example would be mandated label requirements for safe handling and cooking instructions on raw meat. Food enterprises may also be required by law to provide health warnings for raw milk and the retail sale of raw shellfish.

A related cause of action is "negligence per se," which occurs when food enterprises violate a statute or regulation that is specifically designed to prevent the type of injury a consumer suffers. Negligence per se is particularly relevant where the Hazard Analysis and Critical Control Points (HACCP) regulations or guidance documents specify or suggest prevention techniques. A food enterprise could be at risk if its food products or food service activities are covered by a HACCP regulation and the enterprise does not have a HACCP plan in place or does not follow its own written rules, standards, or procedures.

[d] Breach of Warranty

Under the Uniform Commercial Code (UCC), sellers incur obligations called warranties when they sell a product. Breach of warranty is a cause of action that may be claimed in a foodborne illness lawsuit; the cause of action applies when the food does not conform to either an express warranty or an implied warranty. In essence, plaintiffs can recover compensation if the food did not conform to a warranty and that nonconforming feature of the product caused the plaintiff's injury.

An express warranty is affirmation of fact or promise about the food, as made in sales representatives' statements or in pictures or writing on food containers, menus, or advertisements, which induces the consumer to buy the food. The warranty is breached if these representations prove to be false. For example, a company that advertises its eggs as Salmonella-free when they are not has breached an express warranty. For food products, express warranties that are commonly breached involve foreign objects in the food, such as bones.

An implied warranty requires food to be both merchantable and fit for consumption. A product is merchantable if it meets certain prescribed safety standards and is fit for the "ordinary purpose" for which it was sold. For example, raw pork is merchantable because its ordinary purpose is human consumption after thorough cooking to kill foodborne parasites such as *Trichinae*. A product must also meet an implied warranty of fitness for a particular purpose in certain representations made about it. In essence, a seller makes an implied warranty of fitness when he knows the buyer's intended purpose or use of the product, and the buyer relies on the seller's judgment or skill in selecting a suitable product. For example, if a seller told a buyer that a particular type of raw fish could be used to make sushi and the buyer became ill from consuming the sushi because it was contaminated with Anisakid parasites, this warranty would be breached.

The plaintiff is not required to show that the food seller was negligent or at fault to recover damages under the implied warranty theory. Instead, the plaintiff must only prove that the seller sold the nonconforming food and that this nonconforming feature of the food caused the plaintiff's illness. This seemingly simple proof is complicated by whether the process of determining that a food is fit for human consumption or that there has been a breach of "implied warranty of merchantability" uses the reasonable-expectation test or the foreign-natural test. As previously noted, courts now show strong preference for the reasonable-expectation test.

[e] Defenses

Several defenses can be raised in food litigation. The most common defenses include contributory negligence or comparative fault, depending on the statutes that exist in the state. Courts have struggled with the role that consumers play in their own food illness, especially with regard to meat. For example, courts have placed the responsibility for consumers who become infected with trichinosis from eating contaminated ham squarely on the consumer as responsible for the illness.[769] Indeed, consumers may not have legal recourse if they are fully aware of the product's health risks but voluntarily proceed to consume the food and are injured by the product – for example, where a person with liver disease knows the risks of eating raw oysters and yet eats them and becomes ill.

Defendants may try to weaken the alleged causal link between the food and the plaintiff's illness by providing evidence that the illness-causing pathogen can be associated with multiple foods or could have been spread via other routes, such as person-to-person contact. The further removed a defendant is from the plaintiff in the chain of food production, processing, and distribution, the more difficult it may be for the plaintiff to establish a causal link. A causal link may be easier to establish between divisions of a vertically integrated company and harder to establish if consumers or intervening parties such as middlemen could also have made food-handling errors. For example, in very rare instances, defendants may claim that the foodborne illness from home-cooked food was due to the consumers' faulty food-handling and preparation practices. They may also claim that no one else became ill while eating the same food, the food is not a commonly recognized vehicle for the pathogen, or that the timing of the illness is inconsistent with the pathogen's incubation period.

In general, if the defendant is found liable, damages may be decreased if the defendant showed that reasonable care was taken when producing, handling, and selling the implicated food; that the enterprise used state-of-the-art technology in producing the food, and that the enterprise followed laws and regulations designed to prevent the harm suffered by the plaintiff. A defendant that uses its HACCP records to show that it had exercised all reasonable preventive controls following regulatory guidelines will have a better defense than a firm that cannot.

---

[769] *See* Nicketta v. Nat'l Tea Co., 87 N.E.2d 30, 34 (Ill. App. Ct. 1949); Trabaudo v. Kenton Ruritan Club, Inc., 517 A.2d 706 (Del. Super. Ct. 1986).

4 Regulation of Food Marketing

§ 4.01 Introduction

Consumers navigate a complicated and highly regulated world of food marketing. The critical issue surrounding the marketing of food concerns information and how it is conveyed to consumers. Laws – federal and state regulation, court decisions, and private standards – address this issue in various ways. Although divergent in approach, these laws seem to share the epistemological aim of increasing truth possession and reducing error.[1] One approach is to ban false, deceptive, or misleading labeling and advertising that lead people to draw false conclusions, even if the statements themselves are not false. Another approach is to provide consumers with information, sufficient to make informed decisions about what foods to buy. This objective increases the information provided to consumers rather than avert false beliefs.

This chapter divides the regulation of food marketing into two sections – labeling and advertising. This division mirrors the treatment of food marketing in the federal regulatory system: the Food and Drug Administration (FDA) and United States Department of Agriculture (USDA) regulate food labeling for food products that fall within their respective jurisdictional mandates, while the Federal Trade Commission (FTC) is responsible for policing food advertising. This simple division of jurisdiction has been blurred at different times in the long-standing relationship between the agencies. For the most part, however, the agencies cooperate and share information freely in the course of regulating food marketing. This chapter addresses the tension between the First Amendment and restrictions on speech via food marketing regulation. National labeling regulation is

---

[1] *See* Alvin I. Goldman & James C. Cox, *Speech, Truth, and the Free Market for Ideas*, 2 LEGAL THEORY 1, 1–32 (1996) (epistemology tries to identify methods and practices that promote the acquisition of knowledge or true belief, as opposed to error or ignorance).

remarkably detailed and expressly preempts states from enacting different requirements for labels. However, this chapter will also address notable food labeling issues where states have been innovators and gap fillers in developing food labeling law. Also covered in this chapter are the important roles of private regulation and international regulation. Finally, gaps in the regulations and the enforcement by the FDA and FTC have provided the impetus for an explosion in food-marketing litigation. This chapter examines the claims, defenses, and trajectory of food-marketing litigation.

§ 4.02 Regulation of Food Labeling

[1] *Purpose of Food Labels*

Consumers rely on food labels to determine what they are consuming. A number of legal requirements govern what information must, may, and may not appear on the package label. By ensuring that information is provided and warnings dispensed, food labeling requirements aim to facilitate consumers' informed choices, prevent consumer deception, educate consumers, assure food safety and wholesomeness, and promote honest and fair dealing in the marketplace.[2] These diverse and sometimes conflicting aims render food labeling a perennially thorny issue. For example, consumers may want to be informed by labeling whether a food product is genetically engineered, but the government may be concerned that catering to this consumer desire will induce the false belief that genetic engineering makes the food product unsafe. The other problem with food labeling is that the small area available on a food product combined with the various uses of the label – from warnings, to information, to marketing – generates fierce legal and policy battles for space.

[2] *Shared Jurisdiction and Responsibility*

In the United States, the regulation of food labeling laws is a responsibility shared between several federal and state agencies. Under the Federal Meat Inspection Act (FMIA), the Food Safety and Inspection Service (FSIS) of the USDA has jurisdiction for the implementation and enforcement of food labeling laws with respect to meat and poultry products derived from domestic animals, poultry products derived from domestic birds, and liquid egg and liquid egg products produced in cracking plants. Under the 1938 Food, Drug and Cosmetic Act (FDCA), the FDA has jurisdiction to regulate food labeling with respect to all foods that enter interstate commerce in the United States and not regulated by the USDA. Hence, the FDA is responsible for regulating the majority of food labels.

[3] *Definition of Label and Labeling*

FDA has jurisdiction over "labels" and "labeling" of the food products for which the agency is responsible. The FDCA provides that "label" means information on the package, and "labeling" means information that accompanies the package, which includes the label.[3] Specifically, the term "label" is defined as "a display of written, printed, or

---

[2] Elise Golan et al., *Economics of Food Labeling*, ECON. RESEARCH SERVICE, US DEP'T OF AGRIC. Econ. Rep. No. 793 (2001).

[3] 21 U.S.C. § 321(m).

graphic matter upon the immediate container of any article," and "labeling" is defined as "other written, printed, or graphic matter (1) upon any article or any of its containers or wrappers, or (2) accompanying such article."[4] The FDA and courts have given an expansive definition to "accompanying," thereby maximizing FDA authority. The Supreme Court held in *Kordel v. United States* that even though the product and the circular were shipped in separate parcels, they nevertheless accompany each other within the meaning of the FDCA.[5] The Court stated that "[o]ne thing or article is accompanied by another when it supplements or explains it, in the manner that a committee report of the Congress accompanies a bill. No physical attachment one to the other is necessary. It is the textual relationship that is significant."[6] Thus, printed materials that are shipped entirely separately from the product nevertheless can be considered labeling for that product. No physical attachment of one to the other is necessary; the key is textual relationship.[7] Thus, all literature used in the sale of foods – printed circulars, pamphlets, brochures, and newsletters – may be considered labeling.[8] The textual relationship constitutes "accompanying," when the food and literature are part of an integrated distribution program."[9] The absence of evidence of integrated use between the product and literature will negate a finding of accompanying. For example, in *United States v. 24 Bottles "Sterling Vinegar & Honey,"* the Second Circuit declined to find that a book sold in the same store as a product for which the book made medicinal claims was labeling for that product.[10]

[4] *Misbranding*

The 1906 Pure Food and Drug Act (PFDA) declared it illegal to manufacture or transport any food that was misbranded.[11] The purpose of the provision was "to make it possible that the consumer should know that an article purchased was what it purported to be; that it might be bought for what it really was, and not upon misrepresentations as to character and quality."[12] Section 8 of the PFDA defined misbranding generally as false or misleading labeling or branding. Section 8's reach was limited, however, to statements about the identity of the food product.[13] Courts struggled with the differences in Section 8 between the terms "false" and "misleading."[14] While "false" was regarded generally as an "untruth," what constituted "misleading" was more nuanced – a literally true statement might violate the act. For example, the statement "Made from selected apples" on a vinegar product was considered misleading and hence misbranded when the vinegar was in fact made from chopped dried apples.[15] The scope of the PFDA was also limited in that a food manufacturer was only subject to sanctions upon a showing of intent to

---

[4] 21 U.S.C. § 321(k).
[5] 335 U.S. 345 (1948).
[6] *Id.* at 350.
[7] *Id.*
[8] *See* V.E. Irons, Inc. v. United States, 244 F.2d 34, 39 (1st Cir. 1957), *cert. denied*, 354 U.S. 923 (1957).
[9] United States v. Guardian Chem. Corp., 410 F.2d 157, 160–161 (2d Cir. 1969).
[10] United States v. 24 Bottles "Sterling Vinegar & Honey Aged in Wood Cider Blended with Finest Honey Contents 1 Pint Prod. of Sterling Cider Co., Sterling, Mass.," 338 F.2d 157, 159 (2d Cir. 1964).
[11] *See* Pure Food and Drugs Act of 1906 (PDFA), ch. 3915, §§ 1–2, 34 Stat. 768, 768–772 (repealed 1938).
[12] United Sates v. Lexington Mill & Elevator Co., 232 U.S. 399, 409 (1914).
[13] *See* United States v. Johnson, 221 U.S. 488, 497 (1911).
[14] *See, e.g.,* United States v. Von Bremen, Notice of Judgment No. 1949 (C.C.S.D.N.Y. 1910).
[15] United States v. Ninety-Five Barrels More or Less Alleged Apple Cider Vinegar, 265 U.S. 438 (1924).

deceive.[16] Finally, the PFDA did not require any specific label information in 1913, although the act was amended to define as misbranded any package that "the quantity of the contents be not plainly and conspicuously marked on the outside of the package in terms of weight, measure, or numerical count."[17]

The 1938 FDCA essentially retained the same misbranding standard enveloped in the 1906 PDFA.[18] FDCA Section 403(a) expressly prohibits labeling statements that are "false or misleading in any particular." The balance of Section 403 itemizes in significant detail the circumstances under which a food will be considered misbranded and thus subject to enforcement action. Notwithstanding these particular provisions, the overarching question about any food labeling is whether the labeling is false or misleading. Generally speaking, a food product may be deemed misbranded if any part of its labeling is false or misleading, and even where no specific regulatory requirement has been violated. The term "false" has its usual meaning of "untruthful," whereas the term "misleading" has become a term of art. For instance, a representation may not be false, but it may be misleading from overemphasis and exaggeration; in other words, claims might be technically true, but still misleading.[19] In determining whether a food label is false or misleading, both affirmative representations and omissions of material facts may be considered. If any one representation in the labeling is misleading, then the entire food is misbranded, and no other statement in the labeling can cure the misleading statement.[20]

Grappling with the standard of false and misleading as it relates to consumer expectations is challenging. One of the first courts to address this issue determined that whether a label is misleading should be judged based on the consumer's first impression, despite whether a more deliberate reading would correct the initial impression. Average consumers, the court reasoned, do not carefully analyze labels; instead, they rely upon "a hasty glance or cursory examination."[21] Over time, two different standards have been used to evaluate whether a label is false or misleading: the IUC standard and the "reasonable consumer" standard. The IUC standard, developed by courts after the passage of the FDCA in 1938, evaluates whether a label is misleading in reference to "the ignorant, the unthinking and the credulous."[22] Under this standard, it is irrelevant whether the reasonable consumer would understand the labeling.[23] The purpose of the FDCA is to protect the public, which includes "the ignorant, the unthinking, and the credulous who, when making a purchase, do not stop to analyze."[24]

In 2002, the FDA announced in a guidance document that it would use the reasonable consumer standard in evaluating whether labels are false or misleading.[25] This decision aligned the FDA with the FTC, which uses the reasonable consumer standard

---

[16] *See* Hall-Baker Grain Co. v. United States, 198 F. 614, 617 (8th Cir. 1912).

[17] Gould Amendment, Act of Mar. 3, 1913, 37 Stat. 732.

[18] Federal Food, Drug, and Cosmetic Act (FDCA), ch. 675, § 301(a), (b), (g), 52 Stat. 1040, 1042–3 (1938) (codified in part at 21 U.S.C. § 331).

[19] *See* V.E. Irons, Inc. at 42–3.

[20] *See, e.g.,* United States v. Hoxsey Cancer Clinic, 198 F.2d 273, 281 (5th Cir. 1952), *cert. denied,* 344 U.S. 928 (1953).

[21] United States v. Ten Barrels of Vinegar, 186 F. 399, 401 (E.D. Wis. 1911).

[22] United States v. Strauss, 999 F.2d 692, 696 (2d Cir. 1993).

[23] *Id.*

[24] United States v. El-O-Pathic Pharmacy, 192 F.2d 62, 75 (9th Cir. 1951).

[25] *See* FDA, Guidance for Industry: Qualified Health Claims in the Labeling of Conventional Foods and Dietary Supplements; Availability, 67 Fed. Reg. 78002, 78002–78004 (2002).

in the regulation of food advertising. Moreover, according to the FDA, the reasonable consumer standard "more accurately reflects that consumers are active partners in their own health care who behave in health promoting ways when they are given accurate health information."[26]

Most of the definitions or forms of misbranding specified in FDCA section 403 relate to information included in, or omitted from, the labeling of food. In various ways, these definitions of misbranding are designed to compel food enterprises to tell the truth about their products and make assumptions about the types of information that consumers need to make wise food choices. Certain provisions prohibit affirmative deceptions with respect to quality, quantity, or identity. Other provisions force manufacturers to provide information that they might otherwise omit – such as the complete ingredients or the nutritional content of a product. A food may also be deemed misbranded if any required information is not presented prominently enough for the ordinary or reasonable consumer to read and understand the information.

In contrast to the USDA, the FDA does not require approval of food labels prior to marketing and distribution of the products into commerce. Rather, the FDA's activity is limited to imposing detailed food labeling regulations, and food manufacturers are responsible for complying. The FDA monitors compliance through random (and some not so random) postmarketing surveillance that may be initiated in various ways, including complaints, consumer inquiries, and informal requests (often initiated against food companies by competitor firms).

[5] Warning Letters

In Chapter 3, it was noted that following an alleged violation, the FDA may formally communicate to a company by letter the findings of alleged violations. Such communication constitutes an official enforcement mode known as a warning letter. Warning letters are a way of establishing prior notice and provide food enterprises an opportunity voluntarily to comply with the law before FDA commences enforcement action.[27] The FDA issues Warning Letters most frequently for food labeling violations.[28]

When deciding whether to issue a warning letter, the FDA looks to three factors: (1) if evidence shows that a food enterprise is in violation of the law; (2) violations are of regulatory significance and issuance of a letter is consistent with agency policy; and (3) there is reasonable expectation that the enterprise will take prompt corrective action.[29] After FDA issues a warning letter, the receiving enterprise has fifteen business days to respond and explain the corrective actions it plans to take to correct the problem.[30] Additional time may be allowed if an adequate explanation is provided as to why more time is necessary, and a time frame for correction is provided. In September 2009, FDA instituted a closing out process for warning letters. If the response appears adequate and the FDA has verified the corrections, the agency will issue a warning letter closeout letter verifying

---

[26] *Id.*

[27] FDA, Regulatory Procedures Manual ch. 4 at 4-1 (2010).

[28] The Warning Letters issued by the FDA from 2005 to date are accessible on the FDA's website. *See Inspections, Compliance, Enforcement, and Criminal Investigations*, U.S. Food & Drug Admin.

[29] FDA, Regulatory Procedures Manual, *supra* note 27 at 4-4.

[30] *Id.* at 4–16.

that correction has been achieved.[31] If an enterprise does not correct the violations in the warning letter to the FDA's satisfaction, the FDA will consider further administrative enforcement actions.[32] The FDA is not obligated, however, to pursue a full enforcement nor is the warning letter necessarily a prerequisite to any enforcement action.[33] FDA does not consider warning letters to be a final agency action subject to judicial review.[34]

Although warning letters are not formal enforcement actions by the FDA, they pose significant implications for the receiving enterprise. Warning letters are available online thereby exposing recipients to pubic stigmatization. Plaintiffs' lawyers comb Warning Letters to seek clients and to build cases. FDA Warning Letters are often used in court cases as evidence of wrongdoing.

§ 4.03 Affirmative Requirements for the Food Label

[1] *Panels*

[a] Principal Display Panel

(1) *Location*

Most label information is required to appear on either the principal display panel (PDP) or the information panel.[35] The PDP is that portion of the product label that is often referred to as the front label panel. It is the label portion that is most readily observed by consumers at the time of purchase. For both FDA- and USDA-regulated products, the labeling statements that must appear on the PDP are the statement of identity (e.g., "meat sauce") and the net quantity statement (i.e., amount of product).[36] The label artwork that is typically included on the PDP in order to attract the attention of consumers may not hide or detract from the visibility of the required information, and the lettering must contrast sufficiently with the background so that the information is easily readable.[37] For products within the USDA's purview, the PDP must also contain the official inspection legend, the establishment number, and, if necessary, a handling statement.[38]

(2) *Statement of Identity*

Both the FDA and USDA have regulations establishing statements of identity for foods.[39] These regulations prescribe the composition of a food and specify the name of the food to be used in the labeling.[40] The statement of identity must be presented on the PDP. It is to be one of the prominent features of the PDP. As such, it should be in bold type

---

[31] *Id.*

[32] *Id.* at 4–13.

[33] *Id.*

[34] *Id.* at 4–2.

[35] *See* 21 C.F.R. § 101.1.

[36] *See* 21 C.F.R. § 101.3(a) (applying to products within the FDA's purview); 21 C.F.R. § 101.105(a) (applying to FDA regulated products); 9 C.F.R. § 317.2(d) (for meat products); 9 C.F.R. § 381.116(b) (2014) (for poultry products).

[37] 21 C.F.R. § 1.21(a)(1); 21 C.F.R. § 101.3(a); 21 C.F.R. § 101.105(h).

[38] 9 C.F.R. § 317.2(d) (for meat products); 9 C.F.R. § 381.116(b) (for poultry products).

[39] *See* 21 U.S.C. § 341 (FDCA directs the FDA to establish definitions and standards for food); 9 CFR Part 319 (FMIA directs definitions and standards of identity or composition for meat products).

[40] *See* 21 C.F.R. Parts 130–169 (FDA regulated food standards of identity); 9 C.F.R. Part 319 (standards of identity for meat products); 9 C.F.R. § 381.155–381.174 (standards for poultry products).

and the font size must be reasonably related to the most prominent printed words on the PDP. Generally, the statement of identity is parallel to the base of the package.[41] For any given food product, the statement of identity will be one of the following: (1) the name of the food as specified in the regulations, such as "ketchup," or a federal common or usual name regulation, such as "peanut spread"; (2) a fanciful name, such as "candy corn," when the nature of the food is obvious; (3) the common or usual name of the food, such as "French toast," or "rice," established by common usage; or (4) an appropriately descriptive term, such as "hard candy." If the food is sold in different forms, such as sliced, minced, whole, or halves, the statement of identity must describe the form of the packaged food, such as "whole olives," or "sliced cheddar cheese."[42] New foods that contain less protein, essential vitamins, or minerals, then the traditional food must be labeled as "imitation." For example, cheese spreads often will be appropriately labeled as "imitation cheddar cheese spread" or "imitation sliced cheddar cheese."[43] The USDA has followed the FDA's approach with regard to imitation labeling, requiring the word "imitation" to appear on the label of a food that resembles the standard product, but is nutritionally inferior.[44]

(3) *Net Quantity Statement*

The PDP must also contain a net quantity statement for both FDA- and USDA- regulated food products. The net quantity of contents identifies the amount of food contained in the package. For FDA-regulated products, it must be presented in both the avoirdupois (i.e., ounces and pounds) and metric measures.[45] For USDA-regulated products, the net contents declaration is required to appear only in avoirdupois measure.[46] The identified weight should not include the container, wrappers, or packaging materials.[47] However, water, oil, and any other liquid medium that is added to the food is included in the net quantity.[48] The quantity of the package's contents is to be disclosed in terms of weight, measure, or numerical count.[49]

[b] Information Panel

(1) *Location*

The Information Fact Panel is located on the panel immediately to the right of the PDP, as seen by the consumer facing the product. If this panel is not usable because of package design, then the Information Fact Panel is the next label panel immediately to the right.[50] Required label statements that include the nutrition facts, the ingredient list, and

---

[41] 21 C.F.R. § 101.3(d) (statement of identity should be at least half the font size of the largest print on the PDP).

[42] 21 C.F.R. § 101.3(b).

[43] 21 C.F.R. § 101.3(e).

[44] 9 C.F.R. § 317.2(j)(1) (for meat products); 9 C.F.R. § 381.1(b) (for poultry products).

[45] 21 C.F.R. § 101.105.

[46] 21 C.F.R. § 101.105(a), (e), and (f).

[47] 21 C.F.R. § 101.105(g).

[48] 21 C.F.R. § 101.105(a).

[49] 9 C.F.R. § 317.2(h) (for meat products); 9 C.F.R. § 381.121(a)(for poultry products).

[50] 21 C.F.R. § 101.2(a).

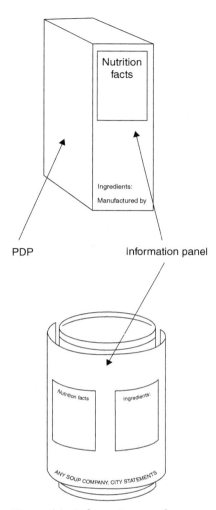

Figure 4.1. Information panel.
(*Source: FDA, Guidance for Industry: A Food Labeling Guide*)

the signature line may be placed either on the PDP or the information panel.[51] These
label statements are generally required to be placed together without any intervening,
nonessential material placed between the required labeling, such as pictures, UPC bar
code, or product claims.[52]

[2] *Nutrition Facts*

[a] Requirements

The amounts of certain nutrients present in one serving of the food product must be
presented in the Nutrition Facts label. The Nutrition Facts label is often referred to

---

[51] 21 C.F.R § 101.2(b).
[52] 21 C.F.R. § 101.2(e).

as the "Nutrition Information Panel" or the "Nutrition Facts Panel" or the "Nutrition Facts Box." As mentioned, the Nutrition Facts label may be placed either on the PDP or the information panel. On packages with insufficient area on the PDP and information panel, the Nutrition Facts label may be placed on any alternate panel that can be seen by the consumer.[53] The Nutrition Labeling Education Act (NLEA) sets forth the requirements for the Nutrition Fact Panel with respect to those foods within the FDA's purview.[54] Under the NLEA, with limited exceptions, a food regulated by the FDA is deemed misbranded unless its label bears the appropriate nutrition labeling.[55]

Nutrition facts must state the serving size and, unless the product contains only a single serving, the number of servings in the package. Nutritional content on a per serving basis, which is defined as an amount "customarily consumed," must be disclosed.[56] Serving sizes are referred to as the Reference Amount Customarily Consumed (RACC), which represents the quantity of food customarily consumed at one occasion.[57] The regulations list certain calculation and disclosure rules to be followed when determining the RACC. Only products that are under 200 percent of the RACC are required to be labeled as a single serving.[58] Otherwise, manufacturers have latitude in selecting how many servings to declare for a single food package, which directly affects the nutritional information provided.

Generally, the following nutrients must be declared, in order: calories, calories from fat, total fat, saturated fat, trans fat, cholesterol, sodium, total carbohydrate, dietary fiber, sugars, sugars alcohol,[59] protein, vitamin A, vitamin C, calcium, and iron.[60] Vitamins or minerals that are added to the food must be declared.[61] Additional nutrients may be listed voluntarily, including polyunsaturated fat, monounsaturated fat, potassium, soluble fiber, insoluble fiber, and other carbohydrates.[62]

The levels of these required and permitted nutrients (except vitamins and minerals) disclosed in the Nutrition Facts are to be declared by the quantitative amounts by weight for that nutrient (i.e., g or mg), per serving.[63] In addition, a listing of the percent Daily Recommended Value, as established by the regulations, based upon a 2,000 calorie diet, is to be provided for each nutrient, except that the percent for protein may be omitted.[64] Additional footnotes may be required, depending upon package size. As to vitamins and minerals, a statement about the percent of Recommended Daily Intake, expressed as a percent of the Daily Value, for the following is required, in order: Vitamin A, Vitamin C, Calcium, and Iron.[65] Disclosure of other vitamins and minerals that have a Recommended Daily Intake is required when they are added as nutrient supplements

[53] 21 C.F.R. § 101.9(i).
[54] 21 U.S.C. § 343-1(2010) et seq.
[55] 21 U.S.C. § 403(q).
[56] 21 U.S.C. § 343(q)(1)(A)(i).
[57] 21 C.F.R. § 101.9(b)(2).
[58] 21 C.F.R. § 101.9(b)(6).
[59] See 21 C.F.R. § 101.9(c)(6)(iii) (identifying when a listing of sugar alcohol is required).
[60] 21 C.F.R. § 101.9.
[61] For regulations regarding required and allowed reporting of vitamins and minerals, see 21 C.F.R. § 101.9(a)
    (1)–(c)(8).
[62] 21 C.F.R. § 101.9.
[63] 21 C.F.R. § 101.9(7)(i).
[64] 21 C.F.R. § 101.9(c)(7)(ii), (iii) and (c)(9).
[65] 21 C.F.R. § 101.9(c)(8)(ii); 21 C.F.R. § 101.9(c)(8)(iv).

or when a nutrient-based claim is asserted.[66] However, only those nutrients identified by the FDA's nutrient regulations, as mandatory or voluntary, can be disclosed in the Nutrition Facts.[67] If the amount of the vitamin or mineral per serving is less than 2 percent of the Recommended Daily Intake, declaration of an amount is not necessary.[68]

It is the food company's responsibility to determine the appropriate values for the required Nutrition Facts. The FDA has not specified a required number of samples that must be analyzed to ascertain accurately the nutrient data. The FDA may randomly sample and test food products in commerce to verify the accuracy of the nutrient information provided on the labels. In conducting an enforcement analysis, the FDA will use a composite of twelve samples or units.[69]

When a product is packaged with an assortment of the same types of foods (e.g., mixed nuts, mixed dried fruits) that are intended to be consumed at the same time, the manufacturer may elect to provide the required Nutrition Facts for each component separately or alternatively. It can also set forth composite values that provide one set of nutrition information based on a weighted average of the overall assortment.[70]

Single-ingredient raw meat and poultry products were long exempt from mandatory nutrition labeling requirements; however, in December 2010, the USDA issued a nutritional-labeling rule for meats and poultry.[71] Effective from January 1, 2012, the rule requires nutrition labeling of the major cuts of single-ingredient raw meat and poultry products on labels or at point of purchase.[72] Specifically, the rule requires retailers to provide nutrition information for major cuts of meat and poultry (categorically defined) either on the label or at the point of purchase (POP).[73] POP information can be provided by various methods, including posting a sign or by making the information readily available in brochures, notebooks, or leaflet form in close proximity to the food. Video, live demonstration, or other media can supplement the information. Making a nutrition claim on POP requires that all of the regulatory requirements regarding format and content must be met. For POP materials, a nutrition information declaration can be presented in a simplified format. Nonmajor cuts of single-ingredient raw products (i.e., beef flank steak, beef ribs, and chicken tenders) are not required to bear nutrition labeling. However, if processing and packaging plants or retailers voluntarily provide nutrition information for nonmajor cuts, then that information must comply with the requirements for the major cuts. In addition, the final rule required nutrition labels on all ground or chopped meat and poultry products, with or without added seasonings. Unlike the major cuts of meat and poultry, ground products are required to bear nutrition labeling on their packages. Certain products are exempted from the mandatory nutrition labeling requirements (e.g., products intended for further

---

[66] 21 C.F.R. § 101.9(c)(8)(ii).

[67] 21 C.F.R. § 101.9(c).

[68] 21 C.F.R. § 101.9(c)(8)(iii).

[69] *See* FDA, Guidance for Industry: Nutrition Labeling Manual – A Guide for Developing and Using Data Bases (Mar. 17, 1998).

[70] 21 C.F.R. § 101.9(h)(1).

[71] *See* Nutrition Labeling of Single-Ingredient Products and Ground or Chopped Meat and Poultry Products; Final Rule, 75 Fed. Reg. 82,148 (December 29, 2010).

[72] The major cuts are identified in U.S.C. §§ 317.444 and 381.444. Examples of nonmajor cuts include beef flank steak, beef ribs, and chicken tenders.

[73] *See* Nutrition Labeling of Single-Ingredient Products, *supra* note 71.

processing, products in individually wrapped small packages of less than one-half percent net weight, products that are custom slaughtered or prepared, ground or chopped meat, and poultry products that are produced by a company that qualifies for a small business exemption).[74]

Raw fruits and vegetables and raw seafood, which are frequently sold in unpackaged form, are exempt from mandatory nutrition labeling. These food products are subject to voluntary nutrition labeling guidelines that apply to retailers of these products.[75] Restaurant and food service foods also are exempt from nutrition labeling requirements.

[b] Improvements

There is constant discussion as to how the nutrition facts information required on food labels can be improved. In 2010, the Center for Science in the Public Interest (CSPI) published a well-publicized book, *Food Labeling Chaos*, which advocates for improving the Nutrition Facts label as follows: (1) calories per serving should be disclosed more prominently on the NFP; (2) extraneous information should be eliminated (e.g., "calories from fat" line); (3) serving size regulations should be updated; (4) regulations should be issued requiring that nutrition information be provided for large single servings; (5) daily value should be established for added sugars, and the term "low sugar" should be defined; and (6) fiber content disclosures should be modified.[76] CSPI has also petitioned the FDA in 1999 for proposed rulemaking seeking daily reference values[77] and in 2013 for proposed rulemaking seeking additional labeling for added sugars in soft drinks and other food products.[78]

In March 2014, the FDA issued two interrelated proposed rules that would revise the nutrition labeling of foods.[79] The proposed rules change how and what information is displayed on the Nutrition Facts label, as well as to the reference amounts for how the serving size of conventional foods will be determined. New nutrition science, new dietary recommendations, citizen petitions, and public comments received in response to FDA's advance notices of proposed rulemaking prompted the changes.[80] The FDA was particularly motivated by the current obesity epidemic.[81] The key changes in the

---

[74] *See id.*

[75] 21 C.F.R. § 101.42.

[76] *See* Bruce Silverglade & Ilene Ringel Heller, Center for Science in the Public Interest, Food Labeling Chaos: The Case for Reform (2010).

[77] *See Petition to the FDA to Require Better Sugar Labeling on Foods*, Center for Science in the Public Interest (August 3, 1999).

[78] *See Petition to Ensure the Safe Use of "Added Sugars,"* Center for Science in the Public Interest (February 13, 2013).

[79] Food Labeling: Revision of the Nutrition and Supplement Facts Labels and Food Labeling: Serving Sizes of Foods That Can Reasonably Be Consumed at One-Eating Occasion; Dual-Column Labeling; Updating, Modifying, and Establishing Certain Reference Amounts Customarily Consumed; Serving Size for Breath Mints; and Technical Amendments, 79 Fed. Reg. 11989 (proposed March 3, 2014).

[80] *See Factsheet on the New Proposed Nutrition Facts Label*, U.S. Food & Drug Admin. (February 27, 2014).

[81] *See* News Release, FDA Proposes Updates to Nutrition Facts Label on Food Packages, U.S. Food and Drug Admin. (February 27, 2014) (quoting FDA Commissioner Margaret Hamburg, "To remain relevant, the FDA's newly proposed Nutrition Facts label incorporates the latest in nutrition science as more has been learned about the connection between what we eat and the development of serious chronic diseases impacting millions of Americans").

Label Makeover

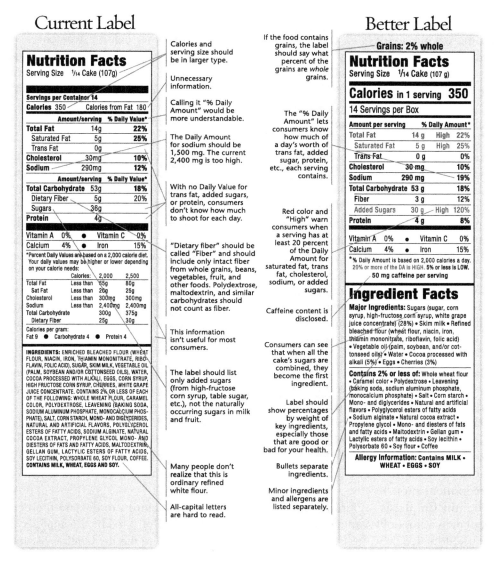

Figure 4.2. CSPI proposed nutrition facts label.
(*Source: CSPI, Food Labeling Chaos: A Case for Reform*)

two March 2014 FDA's proposed rules to revise the nutrition labeling of foods are the following:

○ **Added Sugars** – FDA proposes to require a separate declaration of "added sugars" under the current "sugars" declaration. The purpose of this change is to enable consumers to implement the 2010 Dietary Guidelines for Americans recommendation to reduce the intake of added sugars.[82] The proposed rule defines the term "added sugars" as "sugars that are either added during the processing of foods, or are packaged as such, and include sugars (free, mono- and disaccharides), syrups, naturally occurring sugars that are isolated from a whole food and concentrated so that sugar is the primary component (e.g., fruit juice concentrates), and other caloric sweeteners."[83] Added sugars content may be expressed as zero if one serving of the food contains less than 0.5 grams of added sugars. A declaration of added sugars content would not be required for foods that contain less than 1 gram of added sugars in a serving if no claims are made about sweeteners, sugars, or sugar alcohol content. The proposed rules also provide record-keeping obligations by manufacturers to verify the declared amount of added sugars.[84]

○ **Serving Sizes** – The proposed rule would require that containers of products containing less than 200 percent of the RACC would be labeled as single-serving containers. Containers of foods with at least 200 percent and up to 400 percent of the RACC, however, would include a dual-column label: one column would display the nutrition information for the entire container, and the second column would display the preexisting requirement of nutrition information for the serving size based on RACC. The proposal reiterates that the FDA is required by statute to establish RACCs based upon actual consumption habits, rather than on recommended serving sizes. The updated RACCs may have important implications for nutrient and health claims. For example, a low fat nutrient content claim may no longer qualify for that claim if its RACC significantly increases. Similarly, a food may be disqualified from making a health claim if its RACC would cause it to exceed the disqualification levels for these nutrients.

○ **Calories from Fat** – The "Calories from fat" declaration would be removed so as not to suggest that these are the only calories about which a consumer need be concerned. Labels for unsaturated, saturated, trans, and total fat would remain.

○ **Daily Values for Nutrients** – The proposed rules revise the DVs for certain nutrients, including calcium, sodium, dietary fiber, and vitamin D. The DV for sodium would be reduced from 2,400 mg to 2,300 mg. The agency determined that setting a DV for calories would not be realistic, given the need to determine a quantitative intake recommendation.

○ **Vitamin Emphasis** – Current regulations require manufacturers to declare the percent daily values of vitamins A and C, calcium, and iron. Motivated by the analysis of nutrient inadequacy, the FDA's proposed rules would require the declaration of vitamin D and potassium. The declaration of vitamins A and C would become voluntary, while the declaration of calcium and iron would remain mandatory.[85]

[3] *Ingredient List*

The FDA requires an ingredient list on the label of every food product regulated by the agency. The USDA only requires that an Ingredient List appear on labels of meat

---

[82] Dietary Guidelines for Americans, U.S. Department of Agric. and U.S. Dep't of Health and Human Services (7th ed. 2010), at 27–9.
[83] Food Labeling: Revision 79 Fed. Reg., *supra* note 79.
[84] *Id.*
[85] *Id.*

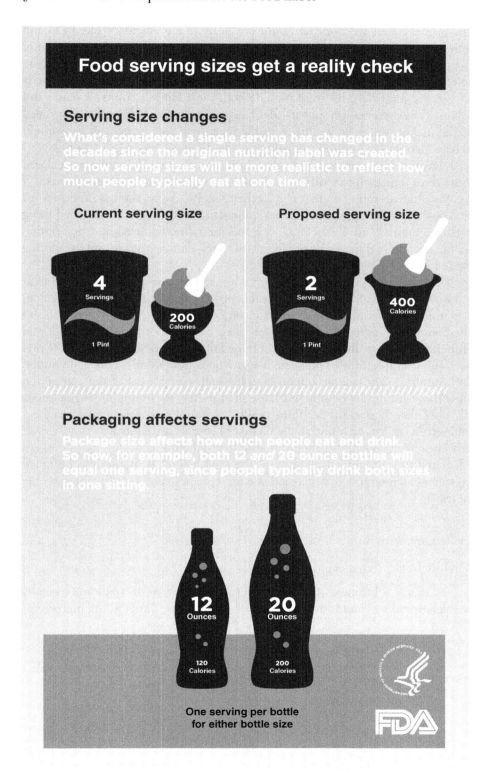

Figure 4.3. Food serving sizes get a reality check.
(*Source*: FDA, Food Serving Sizes Getting a Reality Check)

and poultry products that are fabricated from two or more ingredients.[86] The FDA and USDA both require that each ingredient present in the product be listed by its common or usual name in descending order or predominance by weight.[87] Special rules apply to the listing of certain types of ingredients. For example, when a chemical preservative is added to food, the ingredient list must include both the additive's common name and their function of the preservative, such as "BHT (a preservative)."[88] Natural and artificial flavors as well as spices may be identified in the ingredient lists by using the common name, such as "paprika" or "saffron," or generally identified as "spices," "natural flavor," or "artificial flavor."[89] However, if a spice also services as a coloring, it must be declared either by the term "spice and coloring" or by the common name, such as "paprika."[90] Certified color additives must be identified by their specific name, such as "Yellow 5" or RD&C Red No. 40,[91] but color additives not subject to certification may be listed using a generic name, such as "artificial color," or a specific name followed by a description of its function, such as "caramel color."[92] The USDA regulations with regard to coloring parallel these FDA regulations.[93]

An ingredient that itself contains two or more ingredients – sometimes referred to as compound ingredients – and which have established common or usual names or conform to a standard of identity may be listed in one of two ways. The first option is to declare the compound ingredient by the established common or usual name followed by a parenthetical listing of all ingredients contained therein in descending order of predominance – for example, "milk chocolate (sugar, cocoa butter, milk, chocolate liquor, soy lecithin, vanilla)." The second option is to list each component of the compound ingredient without listing the compound ingredient itself – for example, "sugar, cocoa buttermilk, chocolate liquor, soy lecithin, vanilla." A series of special provisions for a number of ingredients can be found in the Code of Federal Regulations.[94]

As noted later in this chapter (under notable food labeling issues), major allergens must be declared in a prescribed manner on the food label.[95] It should also be noted that added water to a food product is considered an ingredient and must be listed on the ingredient list.[96]

[4] Other Requirements

[a] Signature Line

The name and place of business of the manufacturer, packer, or distributor is typically called the "signature line" and must be presented on the same panel as the ingredients

---

[86] 9 C.F.R. § 317.2(c)(2) (for meat products); 9 C.F.R. § 381.118 (for poultry products).
[87] 21 C.F.R. § 101.4(a) (for FDA regulated products); 9 C.F.R. § 317.2(f) (for meat products); 9 C.F.R. § 381.118(a)(1) (for poultry products).
[88] 21 C.F.R. § 101.22(j).
[89] 21 C.F.R. § 101.22(h)(1).
[90] 21 C.F.R. § 101.22(a)(2).
[91] 21 C.F.R. § 101.22(k).
[92] 21 C.F.R. § 74.
[93] 9 C.F.R. § 317.2(j)(9) (for meat products); 9 C.F.R. § 381.119(b) (for poultry products).
[94] See 21 C.F.R. 101.4.
[95] Pub. L. No. 108–282, Title II, 118 Stat. 891 (February 8, 2004).
[96] 21 C.F.R. § 101.4(a) and (c).

list and nutrition facts, which is usually the information panel, unless space constraints preclude such placement. If the name given is not the actual manufacturer, the identity must be preceded by a qualifying phrase that states the firm's relation to the product, such as "manufactured for" or "distributed by." The signature line must include the firm's city (or town), state (or country, if outside the US) and zip code (or mailing code if located outside the United States). A street address must be provided unless the firm is listed in a current city or telephone directory.[97]

[b] Warning and Information Statements

Certain products are required to present warning or information statements on their labels. Examples include irradiated foods, foods that contain the fat replacer olestra, foods that contain, or are manufactured with, chlorofluorocarbon or other ozone-depleting substances, fresh eggs (in consumer packages), meat, and poultry products that require special handling to maintain wholeness and foods that contain any meat or poultry that is not ready-to-eat.

[c] Juices

Among food products that are subject to special labeling requirements, juices are singled out due to the fact that juice products are prevalent in the market. Any beverage containing fruit or vegetable juice is required to present a percent juice declaration, such as "100 percent juice" or "contains 50 percent orange juice." This declaration must appear near the top of the information panel. If a beverage contains less than 100 percent juice and its statement of identity includes the word "juice," it must also include a qualifying term such as "drink," "beverage," or "cocktail." If one or more of the juices in the product is made from concentrate, the statement of identity must be qualified with the words "from concentrate" or "reconstituted."[98]

[d] Country of Origin

Imported foods regulated by the FDA are required to bear country-of-origin marking (e.g., "product of France"). Country-of-origin marking must appear in a conspicuous place and as legibly, indelibly, and permanently as possible. Placing country-of-origin marking immediately beneath the signature line is often ideal. The FDA does not require the country of origin to be identified on the PDP. If the signature line states a US address, it should be followed by country-of-origin marking that is in close proximity to the distributor's name and address and in a font size at least comparable.[99] Imported products regulated by the USDA also must bear the name of the country of origin, preceded by the words "Product of," on the immediate and outside containers. The outside container must also bear the product name and establishment number.[100] The larger

---

[97] 21 C.F.R. § 101.5.
[98] *See, e.g.,* 21 C.F.R. § 101.30 (setting forth detailed labeling requirements applicable to the juice industry).
[99] 19 C.F.R. § 134.
[100] 9 C.F.R. § 327.14-15.

framework that regulates Country of Origin Labeling (COOL) – under the Tariff Act of 1930 and the US Farm Bill – is addressed later in this chapter.

[e] Flavor Designation

If the label or labeling for a food represents in words or pictures something about the food's primary recognizable flavor, that flavor is considered its characterizing flavor and must accompany the statement of identity on the PDP.[101]

[f] Language Specifications

All mandatory label information in the United States must appear in English. If labeling includes foreign language, then all mandatory information must appear in both English and the foreign language. Certain foreign words, however, will not trigger dual-language labeling; these words typically do not have an English equivalent (e.g., antipasto), or are used in a standard of identity (e.g., spaghetti), or are used in a brand name, motto, or trademarked design.

[5] Front of Package Labeling (FOP)

[a] Development

Concerns over the rise in obesity rates, coupled with consumer interest in simpler and more direct label information, led to an increased interest in the United States over the use of a labeling scheme largely developed in the United Kingdom known as front-of-pack (FOP) labeling. FOP labeling consists of symbols on the front of package labeling to convey certain nutritional information to consumers. The UK FOP labeling scheme relies on a traffic light logo, which is used to show favorable (green) and unfavorable (red) nutrient content.

Concerns that a similar scheme might be introduced in the United States prompted the food industry to devise its own FOP approach. Public interest groups increased their level of interest and scrutiny of industry approaches and in 2007, the FDA held a public meeting addressing concerns about industry-created FOP symbols.[102] An FDA's 2008 "Dear Manufacturer" letter cautions that certain symbols could constitute nutrient content claims that are subject to strict regulations.[103]

[b] Smart Choices Program

In 2009, the food industry began a volunteer labeling initiative called "Smart Choices," a highly touted, but quickly terminated, program developed via funding from fourteen major food companies.[104] Processed food products meeting the Smart Choices criteria could place a green seal with a check mark on the front of the package to indicate a

---

[101] See 21 C.F.R. § 101.22.
[102] See FDA, Guidance for Industry: Dear Manufacturer Letter Regarding Front-of-Package Symbols (December 2008).
[103] Id.
[104] See Rebecca Ruiz, Smart Choices Foods: Dumb As They Look?, Forbes (September 17, 2009).

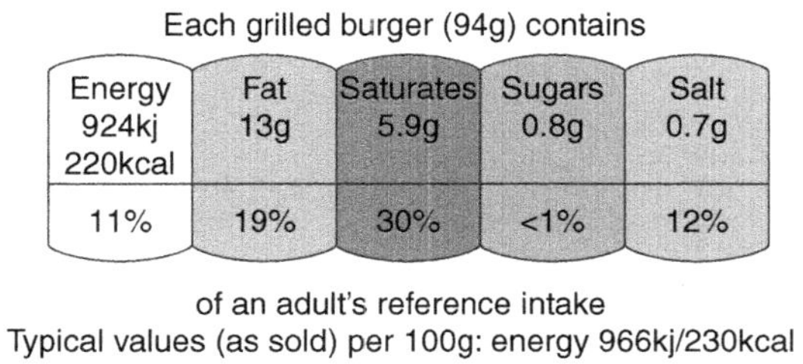

Each grilled burger (94g) contains

Energy 924kj 220kcal	Fat 13g	Saturates 5.9g	Sugars 0.8g	Salt 0.7g
11%	19%	30%	<1%	12%

of an adult's reference intake
Typical values (as sold) per 100g: energy 966kj/230kcal

Figure 4.4. Typical calorie values in grilled burger.
(*Source: Northern Ireland Chest Heart & Stroke, Ready Meals*)

healthier food product. The problem, from a nutritional standpoint, was that although the product may have contained relative high marks in one aspect (e.g., low in fat, sodium, or sugar; high in vitamins or calcium), these scores could offset relatively poor nutritional value in other areas. For example, a sixty-calorie Fudgsicle qualified for a Smart Choice label due to its low fat content. Additional examples of food that obtained a Smart Choice label include Fruit Loops and a Magical Cheese Stuffed Crust Pizza (containing 23 percent of the recommended daily salt and fat intake).[105] Media and nutrition experts openly criticized the Smart Choice labeling scheme.[106] In August 2009, FDA issued a letter expressing concern to the general manager of the Smart Choices program. Noting the proliferation of competing FOP labeling symbols and the resulting consumer confusion, the agency expressed concern that the criteria used to qualify products for the Smart Choices label was inconsistent with government dietary guidelines, could mislead consumers, and could encourage consumers to eat highly processed foods rather than healthier foods.[107] Shortly thereafter, in October 2009, the Smart Choices program voluntarily shut down the initiative.[108]

[c] FDA FOP Labeling Initiative

FDA also announced in October 2009, that it would soon propose guidance for FOP labeling and that it would involve the food industry in its development.[109] FDA announced that it would wait to issue the FOP guidance until after the issuance of a final report from the Institute of Medicine (IOM), which acts as an impartial, nongovernment advisor to the FDA on scientific issues.[110] FDA and the Centers for Disease Control and Prevention (CDC) requested IOM to undertake a two-phase review of FOP nutrition rating systems and symbols.[111] In the same month, FDA issued an open letter to industry

---

[105] *Id.*

[106] William Neuman, *For Your Health, Fruit Loops*, N.Y. TIMES, September 4, 2009, at B1.

[107] *See* Letter from Food & Drug Admin. to Sarah Krol, General Manager, Smart Choices Program (August 19, 2009).

[108] *See* Press Release, Smart Choices Program, Smart Choices ProgramTM Postpones Active Operations (October 23, 2009); *see also* William Neuman, *Food Label Program to Suspend Operations*, N.Y. TIMES, October 23, 2009, at B1.

[109] *See Front of Package Labeling Initiative*, U.S. FOOD & DRUG ADMIN.

[110] *See Background Information on Point of Purchase Labeling*, U.S. FOOD & DRUG ADMIN. (October 2009).

[111] *See* Institute of Medicine, Examination of Front-of-Package Nutrition Rating Systems and Symbols: Phase 1 Report (October 13, 2010).

Figure 4.5. Smart choices label.
(*Source: Rodale News, 'Smart Choices' Could Be Smarter*)

on the importance of accurate nutrition labeling of food products and issued warning letters to seventeen food manufacturers informing the firms that the labeling for twenty-two
of their food products violates provisions of the FDCA, including unauthorized health
claims, unauthorized nutrient content claims, and the unauthorized use of terms such
as "healthy."[112]

In October 2010, IOM released its Phase I Report on *Examination of Front-of-Package
Nutrition Rating Systems and Symbols.*[113] The report concluded that FOP labeling
would be most useful to consumers if it highlighted calories, saturated fat, trans fat,
and sodium.[114] IOM did not include sugar among this list because it found insufficient
evidence that sugar posed a public health concern, apart from their contribution of
calories.[115]

In October 2011, IOM released the second phase report on *Front-of-Package Nutrition
Rating Systems and Symbols: Promoting Healthier Choices.*[116] The report posits that there
is sufficient evidence for FDA and USDA to "consider a fundamental shift in strategy,"
beyond the prevailing "cognitive" approach which focuses on "informing consumers
about nutrition facts," to "encourage healthier choices and purchase behaviors."[117] To
this end, the report recommends that FDA develop, test, and implement a single, standard FOP symbol system to appear on all food products, in place of other systems being
used. In consideration, in part, to the DHHS and USDA's jointly published 2010 *Dietary
Guidelines for Americans*, IOM reconsidered its position on added sugar and determined
that added sugars should be included as one of the nutrient categories addressed by an
FOP rating system. Thus, the report also recommends that the symbol system should
show calories in household servings on all products and use a point system for saturated and trans fats and sodium, and added sugars that would indicate how healthy a

---

[112] *See Understanding Front-of-Package Violations: Why Warning Letters Are Sent to Industry*, U.S. Food &
Drug Admin. (November 16, 2011).
[113] *See id.*
[114] *See id.; see also* Press Release, National Academy of Sciences, IOM Nutrition Rating Systems and
Symbols on Fronts of Food Packaging Should Focus on Calories, Saturated Fat, Trans Fat, and Sodium
(October 13, 2010).
[115] *See id.*
[116] SEE Front-of-Package Nutrition Rating Systems and Symbols: Promoting Healthier Choices, Institute of
Medicine (October 20, 2011). In preparation for the Phase II report, IOM undertook a number of preliminary steps, including hosting two public sessions with expert presentations.
[117] *Id.*

food product is by the amount of points subscribed to the product.[118] The report recommended that all grocery packages carry an FOP label that displays calories per household
serving size and zero to three nutritional "points." To determine how many points a product should be able to display on the FOP label, the IOM committee has recommended
a two-step process. The first step is to determine whether the product is eligible to earn
FOP points. If a food product contains any one or more of the nutritional categories that
is inconsistent with the *Dietary Guidelines* recommendations, the product is ineligible
for FOP points (calories, saturated and trans fats, sodium, and sugar). For example, if a
product contains levels of sodium that are higher than amounts recommended in the
Dietary Guidelines, the product cannot display any FOP points even if it has low levels
of saturated and trans fat and added sugars. The second step involves a determination
of the number of FOP points a product qualifies to receive. A point would be assigned
to saturated fat and trans fats (represented by a single point), sodium, and added sugars,
with a maximum of three points being available for a food product. The report recommends that the nutritional criteria for the second step determination be more restrictive
than those that are used for the first step determination, and outlines nutritional criteria
that could be used for both the Step 1 and Step 2 determinations that are drawn from
existing FDA regulations governing nutrient content claims (e.g., "low," "healthy," "no
added sugars") and certain Nutrition Facts requirements (e.g., regarding trans fats).[119]

[d] New Industry Initiatives: Nutrition Keys

The tension that exists between the food industry and the FDA over FOP labeling is due
to their differing views over the objectives of the labeling system: FDA wants FOP labels
to emphasize nutrients to avoid (i.e., sodium, calories, and fat) while the food industry
wants to use the labels to highlight beneficial nutrients (i.e., vitamins, minerals, and
protein).

Notwithstanding this tension, the food industry has responded to the IOM reports.
For example, in January 2012, Walmart announced a new icon – The "Great for You"
symbol – to appear on food that meet nutritional criteria established by the 2010 *Dietary
Guidelines for Americans*. Walmart announced that its FOP scheme was intended to
align with the IOM reports.[120] In January 2011, the Grocery Manufacturers' Association
(GMA) and the Food Marketing Institute (FMI) unveiled an industry-wide FOP labeling system that highlights key nutritional information about many packaged foods sold in
grocery stores.[121] GMA and FMI claim to have developed the new standards directly in
response to a challenge from First Lady, Michelle Obama, who, as part of her Let's Move
healthy eating campaign, asked the industry to help consumers make healthier food
choices. This labeling program, called "Nutrition Keys," consists of four icons that will

---

[118] *See id.*
[119] *See id.* The IOM Phase II report cautions that existing FDA regulations may impose overly restrictive
FOP eligibility and qualifying criteria for certain foods who otherwise meet current *Dietary Guidelines*
recommendations. The report recommends that FDA food labeling regulations be modified "to find
an appropriate balance between restrictiveness and practicality." Appendix B: Institute of Medicine of
the National Academies Phase II Report – Examples of Front-of-Package Nutrition Rating Systems and
Symbols.
[120] Institute of Medicine, Reports, Walmart Announces "Great for You" Front-of-Package Symbol.
[121] *See* Grocery Mfrs. Ass'n., *Facts Up Front Nutrition Keys Front-of-Pack Labeling Initiative.*

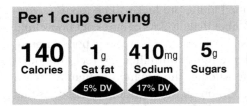

Figure 4.6. Voluntary nutrition keys label.
(*Source: FMI Facts Up Front Style Guide for Implementers*)

be prominently displayed together on the front of a food package. Each icon represents a key nutrient that dietary guidelines recommend consuming in limited quantities: calories, saturated fat, sugars, and sodium.[122] Small food packages that lack the package space to display all four icons may display only the icon containing calorie information.[123] Other manufacturers may choose to include up to two nutrients to encourage: potassium, fiber, protein, vitamin A, vitamin C, vitamin D, calcium, and iron. These nutrients may be included only if the product has more than 10 percent of the daily value per serving of the nutrient and meets the FDA requirements for a good source nutrient content claim. Nutrition Keys does not include trans fat, as recommended by IOM, may be because many food manufacturers have reformulated their products in recent years to remove trans fat. IOM also concluded that positive nutrients to encourage should not be included in FOP labeling.

[e] Moving Forward

Notwithstanding FDA's budget concerns and industry efforts to devise its own programs, it appears that FOP labeling remains a priority for the agency. The issue showcases the challenges in devising a truly educational label for consumers, as well as the coupling of consumer nutrition issues with the industry's self-interest in selling food.

Aside from the issues related to the FOP labeling schemes, there is also the issue of how effective these schemes are at changing the purchasing and eating choices made by consumers.

[6] *USDA*

[a] FSIS: Label Preapproval

USDA's FSIS is responsible for ensuring truthfulness and accuracy in the labeling of meat, poultry, and egg products that fall within the USDA's jurisdiction.[124] The FMIA, PPIA, and EPIA authorize the USDA regulations enabling FSIS to regulate labeling.[125] Similar to the FDCA, the USDA regulations define labeling in a broad manner, imposing

---

[122] *See id.*
[123] *Id.*
[124] 21 U.S.C. § 601 et seq. (FMIA, meat regulations); 21 U.S.C. § 451 et seq. (PPIA, poultry regulations).
[125] 21 U.S.C. § 601(n) (FMIA definition detailing when a meat product labeling is "misleading").

the regulations to apply not only to the traditional food label, but also to additional materials that accompany the product, such as point of purchase materials.[126]

Although the FSIS generally follows the same rules for nutrition facts labeling and nutrient content claims as the FDA, the FSIS requires prior label approval. Labels for egg products, poultry, meats, and processed foods containing significant amounts of meat and poultry must be approved for labeling information prior to marketing.[127] Prior approval of a label is based upon label applications sent to FSIS with sketch labeling. Only labeling that has received sketch approval, or is expressly permitted, may be used. Changes of a limited nature such as the name and address of the distributor need not be preapproved by FSIS. In addition, generic labeling regulations allow for the use of specified types of labels without the need to submit a sketch for prior approval, such as for single-ingredient products that have no claims. In reviewing submitted labeling information, the USDA has issued a series of policy memoranda that have been incorporated into the agency's *Food Standards and Labeling Policy Book* and the agency's online collection. These policy memoranda discuss FSIS decisions to approve or disapprove various labels and are intended to guide the food industry.

[b] USDA Regulations Unique to Meat and Poultry Labels

The USDA's labeling requirements that parallel those of the FDA include regulations requiring identity of product name, net weight statement, ingredient list, identity of manufacturer, and nutrition labeling. However, additional requirements for labels for products under USDA jurisdiction include: (1) inspection legend and establishment number (a symbol that indicates that a carcass or parts of carcasses were inspected and passed by FSIS);[128] (2) handling statement (i.e., instructions, such as "keep refrigerated" or "keep frozen," to maintain the wholesomeness of the product);[129] and (3) safe handling instructions (i.e., instructions for food product that contains raw or partially cooked meat or poultry; the USDA regulations prescribe the exact language, font, and placement of the instructions).[130]

Owing to a lack of participation in voluntary nutrition labeling efforts,[131] beginning in 2012, the USDA now requires nutrition content labels on forty of the most popular meat and poultry products.[132] Exempted from this new rule are: (1) products intended for further processing that bear no nutritional claims or nutrition information; (2) products not for sale to consumers that do not bear nutrition claims or nutritional information;

---

[126] 21 U.S.C. § 601(o) and (p) (FMIA, meat regulation); 21 U.S.C. § 453(s) (PPIA, poultry regulation).

[127] Authority for this preapproval process for food labels vested with the FSIS derives from the acts that state no food article "shall be sold or offered for sale by any person in commerce under any name or other marking or labeling ... but established trade names and other marking and labeling and containers which are not false or misleading and which are approved by the Secretary." 21 U.S.C. § 607(d) (FMIA, meat regulation); 21 U.S.C. § 457(c) (FPLA, poultry regulation). USDA has similar authority over egg products via the EPIA, 21 U.S.C. § 1036(b).

[128] 9 C.F.R. § 312 (for meat products); 9 C.F.R. § 381.96 (for poultry products).

[129] 9 C.F.R. § 317.2(k) (for meat products); 9 C.F.R. § 381.125(a) (for poultry products).

[130] 9 C.F.R. § 317.2(1) (for meat products); 9 C.F.R. § 381.125(b) (for poultry products).

[131] *See* 9 C.F.R. § 317.343 (2010) (requiring FSIS to assess retailer participation in voluntary labeling efforts every two years and requiring rulemaking for mandatory labeling if fewer than 60 percent of all companies surveyed were participating); 9 C.F.R. § 381.443 (same with respect to poultry).

[132] *See* 9 C.F.R. § 317.300 (meat); 9 C.F.R. § 381.400 (poultry).

(3) and ground or chopped meat or poultry products produced by small businesses. Also exempted are meat and poultry in small packages, custom slaughtered, intended for export, or prepared and sold at retail.[133]

Distinctive to FSIS labeling is the adoption of several standards of identity and definitions for meats and poultry. These regulations describe in great detail the permitted ingredients and additives and provide specific naming requirements for products that contain characterizing ingredients and for ingredients used in foods.[134] FSIS requires full ingredient labeling on all food. Ingredients must be listed by their common or usual name or by a name defined under regulations. The list of ingredients shall show the common or usual names of the ingredients arranged in the descending order of predominance, except as otherwise provided.[135] For multi-ingredient foods, such as pepperoni from various sources with differing formulations, a composite ingredient list may be used.

[c] Negative Labeling: FDA/FSIS Comparison

A significant area where the FSIS and FDA differ is in the regulation of negative ingredient labeling, which is where the label declares that the food does not contain certain ingredients. Although the FDA has not promulgated negative labeling regulations, such labels under the FDA's jurisdiction are allowed if they are not false or misleading. In contrast, FSIS regulations either specifically allow or disallow the use of negative labeling statements. Negative labeling statements are allowed under FSIS if: (1) it is not clear from the product name that the ingredient is not present; (2) the processor can demonstrate that the statements are beneficial for health, religious preference, or other reasons; or (3) such claims call attention to the absence of an ingredient because it is prohibited by regulation (e.g., no preservatives). An example of a negative label is "nothing artificial."[136] There are a few notable exceptions to this rule: the claims "chemical free" or "no chemicals" are not allowed;[137] the claim "no hormones added" is not allowed on pork or poultry labels unless it is followed by the statement, "Federal regulations prohibit the use of hormones."[138] However, if sufficient justification is provided, the claims "no hormones administered" may be approved on beef product labels and "no antibiotics added" may be approved on meats and poultry labels.[139]

§ 4.04 Food Labeling Claims

[1] *Health Focus*

As noted in Chapter 5, beginning in the late 1960s and early 1970s, the FDA's regulatory focus convened the connection between diet and health. In 1969, the White House Conference on Food, Nutrition, and Health addressed deficiencies in the US

---

[133] 9 C.F.R. § 317.400(a)(7); 9 C.F.R. § 381.500(a)(2)-(7).
[134] *See generally* U.S. DEP'T OF AGRIC., FOODS STANDARDS AND LABELING POLICY BOOK.
[135] 9 CFR § 317.2(f).
[136] *See* FOODS STANDARDS AND LABELING BOOK, *supra* note 134 at Policy Memo 019B (August 18, 1994).
[137] *Fact Sheets, Meat and Poultry Labeling Terms,* U.S. DEP'T OF AGRIC. FOOD SAFETY INSPECTION Service
[138] *Id.*
[139] *Id.*

diet, recommending that producers fortify foods and that the federal government create a system to identify the nutritional qualities of food.[140] The government set dietary
goals and recognized the role of diet in certain diseases.[141] The industry started developing "healthier" products and enhancing their labels so that they emphasized the health
benefits of certain foods. In 1973, concerned with the potential for false and misleading statements about health benefits, the FDA issued new regulations that effectively
restricted health claims on food. A health claim would render the food a drug under the
FDCA definition of drugs, which meant that premarket approval was required before a
health claim could be made.[142] This prohibition against health claims for food products
softened in 1987, when the FDA, largely in response to court judgments, proposed a
change to its prior rule and began allowing health claims for conventional foods without
premarket approval as long as certain criteria were met.[143] Concurrent with the proposed
rule change, the FDA stopped enforcing the requirements for health claims on food
products, and as a result health claims flooded the market.[144]

In response to the proliferation of health claims on food[145] and the growing concern for nutrition, Congress passed the Nutrition Labeling and Education Act (NLEA)
in 1990.[146] The NLEA changed food labeling in three fundamental ways: first, the
requirement of nutrition labeling on virtually all FDA-regulated food products in a
uniform format; second, prohibition of the use of a "nutrient content claim" – a claim
that characterizes the level of a nutrient present in a food such as "low calorie" or
"high fiber" – unless the FDA has defined it and the use conforms with that definition;
and third, prohibition of disease prevention claims – such as a claim that a product
"helps to reduce the risk of heart disease" – in food labeling unless it conforms with
a regulation promulgated by the FDA. This third requirement means that if an unapproved health claim is used, then, even though possibly truthful, the article is deemed
misbranded. The purpose of these changes was to assist consumers in making healthy
choices and to protect them from unfounded health claims.[147] In 1997, the Food and

---

[140] *White House Conference on Food, Nutrition and Health, Final Report* 122 (1969).
[141] *See, e.g.,* U.S. *Senate Select Comm. on Nutrition and Human Needs, Report on Dietary Goals for the
United States* (1977).
[142] *See* 38 Fed. Reg. 2128 (1973).
[143] *See* Public Health Messages on Food Labels and Labeling, 52 Fed. Reg. 28843 (proposed August
4, 1987).
[144] *See* Zachary Schiller et al., *The Great American Health Pitch: Have Food Companies Gone Overboard In
Adopting That Old Parental Refrain: "Eat It, It's Good For You"?,* Bus. Wk. October 9, 1989, at 114.
[145] FDA commissioner David Kessler signaled a new era of enforcement when the FDA in the early 1990s
threatened to seize thousands of cases of Proctor & Gamble's Citrus Hill orange juice for being misleading because the word "fresh" appeared on the label, although the juice was made from concentrate. *See* Herbert Burkholtz, The FDA Follies 179–82 (1994). Commissioner Kessler announced
that "[t]he time has come to end the din of mixed messages and partial truths on food labels." Warren
E. Leary, *Citing Labels, U.S. Seizes Orange Juice,* N.Y. Times, Apr. 25, 1991, at A18.
[146] Nutrition Labeling and Education Act of 1990 (NLEA), Pub. L. No. 101–535, 104 Stat. 2353 (codified
in part at 21 U.S.C. § 343). A prior amendment of the FDCA was the Fair Packaging and Labeling Act of
1966. It's stated purpose was similar to that of the NLEA, to prevent deceptive and unfair business practices by requiring honest and informative labeling in consumer commodities generally. Fair Packaging
and Labeling Act of 1966, Pub. L. No. 89–755, § 2, 80 Stat. 1296 (codified as amended at 15 U.S.C.
§ 1451).
[147] *See* U.S. Gov't Accountability Office, GAO-11–102, Food Labeling: FDA Needs to Reassess
Its Approach to Protecting Consumers from False or Misleading Claims (2011).

Drug Administration Modernization Act expanded the parameters for health claims by allowing manufacturers to use health claims based on authoritative statements published by a scientific body of the US government.[148]

As science and technology have established more firmly the health risks of certain food products and the connections between diet and health, nutrition labeling has garnered more and more consumer interest and media attention. This growth in interest eventually led the FDA to promulgate labeling requirements for particular areas of concern, such as allergen disclosures. The development of these labeling regimes, however, has raised preemption and First Amendment issues. Recent developments, such as proposed front-of-pack labeling, underscores the challenge of the FDA to keep up with the market demand to meet consumer expectations for clear, relevant information linking diet to health.

[2] Permissible Claims

Four types of claims are permitted on foods: health claims, nutrient content claims, structure function claims, and dietary guidance statements. Claims that go further than these imply that a food may diagnose, treat, cure, prevent, or mitigate a disease or illness are considered drug claims and thus would require that FDA approve the food as a drug.

[a] Health Claims

A health claim is any representation that characterizes the relationship between any substance and a disease or health-related condition. As noted in Chapter 3, a "substance" is a specific food or component of a food, including a nutrient or ingredient. Health claims include explicit words (e.g., "helps reduce coronary heart disease") as well as symbols (e.g., a heart symbol that implies the product is heart healthy).[149] A health claim must either be authorized by FDA regulation, or be based on an authoritative statement by a US government body, such as the National Institutes of Health.[150] Health claims require "significant scientific agreement" for approval.[151] Health claims based on an authoritative statement require premarket notification to the FDA.[152] USDA regulations currently prohibit meat and poultry products from bearing health claims.

The FDA has authorized the claims that are listed in Table 4.1.[153]

Health claims must comply with prescribed food content requirements. For example, to assert the health claim that "a diet low in total fat may reduce the risk of some cancers," the product must be low in fat, as defined by the regulations.[154] In addition to general requirements applicable to all health claims, there are also specific criteria for each

---

[148] See Food and Drug Administration Modernization Act of 1997, Pub. L. No. 105–115, 111 Stat. 2295, 2351 (amending 21 U.S.C. § 343(r)(3)(C)).

[149] 21 C.F.R. § 101.14(a)(1).

[150] Nutrition Labeling and Education Act (NLEA) § 403(r)(3)(c). The NLEA expressly provides for the use in food labeling of health claims provided the claims meet certain criteria and are authorized by an FDA regulation. See Label Claims for Conventional Foods and Dietary Supplements, U.S. FOOD & DRUG ADMIN. (December 13, 2013).

[151] 21 C.F.R. § 101.14.

[152] 21 C.F.R. § 101.9(k)(1); 21 C.F.R. § 101.14(c)-(d); 21 C.F.R. § 101.70.

[153] See Specific Requirements for Health Claims, 21 C.F.R. §§ 101.72–101.83.

[154] 21 C.F.R. § 101.73.

Table 4.1. FDA Approved Health Claims

Substance	Disease or Health-Related Conditions
Calcium	Osteoporosis
Sodium	Hypertension
Dietary fat	Cancer
Saturated fat and cholesterol dietary fiber in grains, fruits, and vegetables	Coronary heart disease
Dietary fiber in grains fruits, and vegetables	Cancer and coronary heart disease
Soluble fiber from specific food sources (e.g., oat bran, oatmeal)	Coronary heart disease
Fruits and vegetables	Cancer
Folic acid	Neural tube defects
Sugar alcohols	Dental caries
Soy protein	Coronary heart disease
Plant sterol and stanol esters	Coronary heart disease

particular health claim being made. For example, to be eligible to bear a claim about calcium (and reduced risk of osteoporosis), a food must contain at least 200 milligrams of calcium per RACC.[155] Also, to bear a health claim, a food may not contain disqualifying levels of certain nutrients – total fat (13 grams), saturated fat (4 grams), cholesterol (60 milligrams), or sodium (480 milligrams) – per RACC or per labeled serving.[156] To prevent food of little nutritional value from bearing a health claim simply because the food has been fortified, a so-called jelly bean rule requires that a food making a health claim must contain, per RACC, prior to any nutrition addition, a minimum level of at least one of the following nutrients: vitamin A (500 international units), vitamin C (6 milligrams), calcium (100 milligrams), iron (1.8 milligrams), protein (5 grams), or dietary fiber (2.5 grams).[157]

In addition to these preapproved disease relationship claims, the FDA has promulgated regulations establishing a procedure by which a firm may petition to establish new claims or modify existing ones.[158] Manufacturers may petition for a health claim, and FDA must review and provide a ruling within 540 days.[159] FDA will permit the claim if it determines, on the basis of all scientific evidence that there is "significant scientific agreement" supporting the claim.[160] Finally, it should be noted that the rules regarding health claims for supplements are regulatory in origin,[161] unlike the statutory basis for such claims for food,[162] but FDA interprets them in a similar manner.

---

[155] *See, e.g.,* 21 C.F.R. §101.72(2)(c)(ii); FDA, Guidance for Industry: Food Labeling; Health Claims; Calcium and Osteoporosis, and Calcium, Vitamin D, and Osteoporosis (May 2009).

[156] 21 C.F.R. § 101.14(a)(1)(4).

[157] 21 U.S.C. § 101.14(e)(6). The health claim that links sugar alcohols to dental caries is exempt from the "jelly-bean" rule. *See id.*

[158] *See* Petitions for Health Claims, 21 C.F.R. § 101.70.

[159] 21 C.F.R. § 101.70(j)(4)(ii).

[160] 21 C.F.R. § 343(r)(3)(B)(i).

[161] *See* 21 U.S.C. § 343(r)(5)(D) (directing the secretary to promulgate rules for health claims for dietary supplements).

[162] *See id.* § 321 (r) (setting forth the process for the approval of health claims for foods).

[b] Qualified Health Claims and Court Challenges

(1) *FDA Enforcement Discretion*

A variation of health claims permitted on food labeling is the use of what are referred to as "qualified health claims." An FDA guidance document describes the agency's process for considering petitions for the use of a qualified health claim in food labeling.[163] This process engages when there is emerging evidence for a relationship between a food substance and reduced risk of a disease or health-related condition, but the evidence is not well enough established to meet the significant scientific agreement standard required for FDA to issue an authorizing regulation. A qualified health claim petition process provides a mechanism to request that FDA review the scientific evidence and exercise enforcement discretion to permit the use of the qualified claim. If FDA finds credible evidence to support the claim, the agency issues a letter outlining the circumstances under which it intends to consider the exercise of enforcement discretion for the use of the claim in food labeling. Qualifying language is included as part of the claim to indicate that the evidence supporting the claim is limited. Although FDA's letters of enforcement discretion are issued to the petitioner requesting the qualified health claim, the qualified claims are available for use on any food or dietary supplement product meeting the enforcement discretion conditions specified in the letter. Qualified health claim petitions that are submitted to FDA will be available for public review and comment.[164]

The FDA allows such claims depending on its enforcement discretion, following submission of a health claim petition. The FDA's enforcement discretion in reviewing a health claim petition to some extent is a euphemism because the agency is constitutionally barred by case law precedent from acting against such claims supported by credible science. In fact, the impetus for the FDA's allowance for qualified health claims is the case law outlined in the following section that has compelled the agency to develop the process for the approval of these claims. The FTC defers to the FDA's decisions on qualified health claims and, so, does not take enforcement action against them.

(2) *Challenges to FDA Discretion: Central Hudson Test*

Since 1999, food firms have challenged the regulation of health claims under the Administrative Procedure Act (APA) and under the First Amendment.[165] When the FDA completely suppresses the claim, firms may request the court to review and overturn the FDA's evaluation of the scientific evidence under the APA's arbitrary and capricious standard of review.[166] A firm may request the court to evaluate the FDA of health claims under the commercial speech doctrine.[167] In addressing the First Amendment challenges, courts apply the Central Hudson four-part test. As the leading cases demonstrate, the evaluation of health claims and qualified health claims has been forced on a reluctant FDA by courts applying the rigors of the Central Hudson test and regulatory review.

---

[163] *See* FDA, Guidance for Industry: Interim Procedures for Qualified Health Claims in the Labeling of Conventional Human Food and Human Dietary Supplements (July 2003).

[164] *See id.*

[165] *See* Gerald Masoudi & Christopher Pruitt, *The Food and Drug Administration v. The First Amendment: A Survey of Recent FDA Enforcement,* 21 HEALTH MATRIX 111 (2011).

[166] *See, e.g.,* Whitaker v. Thompson, 248 F. Supp. 2d 1, 2 (D.D.C. 2002).

[167] *See* Pearson v Shalala (*Pearson I*), 164 F.3d 650, 655 (D.D.C. 1999).

While commercial speech is protected under the commercial free speech doctrine, it is given less protection and is subject to greater regulatory infringement than other types of noncommercial speech.[168] The legal framework for evaluating infringement of commercial free speech is set forth in a four-prong test set by the US Supreme Court in *Central Hudson Gas & Electric Corp. v. Public Service Commission*.[169] The first prong requires a court to determine whether the commercial speech is unlawful or misleading.[170] If the information is inherently misleading, it may be banned entirely.[171] If the commercial speech is lawful and not misleading or only "potentially misleading commercial speech," a reviewing court must employ the remaining *Central Hudson* criteria.[172] Second, the asserted government interest in regulating the commercial speech must be substantial.[173] If the government interest is not substantial, the government cannot infringe the speech. If the interest is substantial, the court next considers the third prong – whether the regulation directly advances the government's interest asserted.[174] To satisfy the third prong, the government must produce evidence showing that the regulation directly and consistently advances its goals. The speech restriction must "alleviate [the cited harm] to material degree," and the connection cannot consist of "mere speculation or conjecture."[175] The fourth prong is typically the most difficult challenge for the FDA in health claim challenges. This prong requires the court to ensure that the regulation is narrowly tailored – that is, not more than extensive than is necessary to serve the government interest asserted.[176] In determining whether the regulation is more extensive than necessary, courts have considered "whether the fit between the government's end and the means chosen to accomplish those ends is not necessarily perfect, but reasonable.[177] A reasonable fit is not a least restrictive means test.[178] The issue is not whether there is no conceivable alternative, but whether the regulation does not burden substantially more speech than is necessary to further the government's interest.[179] If the government can "achieve its interests in a manner that does not restrict speech, or that restricts less speech, the Government must do so."[180] The "government has the burden of showing that the regulations on speech that it seeks to impose are 'not more extensive than is necessary to serve' the interests it attempts to advance."[181]

---

[168] *See generally* Samantha Rauer, *When the First Amendment and Public Health Collide: The Court's Increasingly Strict Constitutional Scrutiny of Health Regulations that Restrict Commercial Speech*, 38 Am. J.L. & Med. 690 (2012).

[169] 447 U.S. 557 (1980).

[170] Thompson v. Western States Med. Ctr., 535 U.S. 357, 367 (2002).

[171] *See In re R.M.J.*, 455 U.S. 191, 203 (1982).

[172] *Pearson I*, 164 F.3d at 655.

[173] *Western States*, 535 U.S. at 367.

[174] *Id.*

[175] Edenfield v. Fane, 507 U.S. 761, 770–771 (1993).

[176] *Western States*, 535 U.S. at 367.

[177] *Pearson I*, 164 F.3d at 656.

[178] Clear Channel Outdoor, Inc. v. City of New York, 594 F.3d 94, 104 (2d. Cir. 2010).

[179] Board. of Trs. of the State Univ. of N.Y. v. Fox, 492 U.S. 469, 478 (1989).

[180] *Western States*, 535 U.S. at 371.

[181] Alliance for National Health U.S. v. Sebelius (*Alliance II*), 786 F.Supp.2d 1, 13 (D.D.C. 2011) (quoting *Western States*, 535 U.S. at 371).

(3) *Pearson Progeny*

• *Pearson v. Shalala (Pearson I)*

Pearson v. Shalala, decided by the DC Circuit Court in 1999 (*Pearson I*), is regarded as the seminal case involving the First Amendment and health claims. Relying on arguments grounded in the First Amendment and in basic principles of administrative law, the decision in Pearson I created legal and empirical challenges to the FDA's efforts to reject petitions filed in support of health claims.

At issue in *Pearson* were four claims linking the consumption of a particular supplement to the reduction in risk of a particular disease: (1) consumption of antioxidant vitamins and the reduction of the risk of certain types of cancers; (2) consumption of fiber and the possible reduction of the risk of colorectal cancer; (3) consumption of omega-3 fatty acids and the possible reduction of the risk of coronary heart disease; and (4) consumption of .8 mg of folic acid in a dietary supplement as being more effective in reducing the risk of neural tube defects than the lower amount in foods commonly consumed.[182]

The FDA rejected the claims, finding that the evidence was "inconclusive," and did not "give rise to significant scientific agreement."[183] The FDA also rejected the plaintiff firm's suggestion of a corrective disclaimer, noting that disclaimers would be "ineffective because there would be a question as to whether consumers would be able to ascertain which claims were preliminary [and accompanied by a disclaimer] and which were not."[184] The FDA argued that even claims that are only potentially misleading do not under *Central Hudson* merit a disclaimer if they lack significant scientific agreement.[185] In response, plaintiffs challenged the rejected claims under the APA and the First Amendment.

In addressing the first *Central Hudson* prong, the DC Circuit agreed that the FDA could ban the claims if they were inherently misleading; however, the court rejected what it described as the government's "paternalistic" assertion that any and all claims lacking significant scientific agreement would inherently mislead consumers because consumers could still exercise judgment in purchasing supplements.[186] The court determined that the FDA satisfied the second *Central Hudson* prong by finding that the government had substantial interests in protecting public health and guarding against deceptive marketing practices.[187] In addressing the third prong of *Central Hudson* – whether the regulation directly advanced the substantial interest – the court deferred to the FDA's evaluation of the scientific evidence. The court found in turning to the fourth point, however, that regardless of the government's interest, "disclaimers [were]

---

[182] *Pearson I,* 164 F3d at 651–2. (quotation marks omitted).

[183] *Id.* at 653 (quotation marks omitted).

[184] *Id.* at 653–4 (quoting FDA, Food Labeling; General Requirements for Health Claims for Dietary Supplements, 59 Fed. Reg. 395-01, 405 (1994)).

[185] *See id.* at 654.

[186] *See id.* at 655 (quoting In re R.M.J., 455 US 191, 203 (1982): ("[W]hen the particular content or method of the advertising suggests that it is inherently misleading or when experience has proved that in fact such advertising is subject to abuse, the States may impose appropriate restrictions. Misleading advertising may be prohibited entirely.").

[187] *See id.* at 656.

constitutionally preferable to outright suppression."[188] Thus, the court focused on the reasonable fit between the manner of restriction and the government's interest by mandating that the FDA consider corrective disclaimers rather than outright suppression of potentially misleading claims.[189]

Separate from the question of whether the FDA should consider disclaimers on health claims, the court also found that the FDA had failed to follow appropriate administrative procedures to explain why the four health claims at issue did not meet the "significant scientific agreement" standard applicable to health claims. The court emphasized the legal and practical need to provide a governing rationale for approving or rejecting proposed health claims on the basis of a lack of "significant scientific agreement."

> [T]he APA requires the agency to explain why it rejects their proposed health claims – to do so adequately necessarily implies giving some definitional content to the phrase "significant scientific agreement." We think this proposition is squarely rooted in the prohibition under the APA that an agency not engage in arbitrary and capricious action. It simply will not do for a government agency to declare – without explanation – that a proposed course of private action is not approved. To refuse to define the criteria it is applying is equivalent to simply saying no without explanation. (Citations omitted).[190]

The court remanded the case for the FDA to reconsider the proposed health claims.[191] The court directed the FDA to consider disclaimers to rectify the ambiguity or deceptiveness in any potentially misleading claims.[192] The court did not rule out the possibility that where evidence in support of a claim is outweighed by evidence against the claim, the FDA could deem the claim incurable by a disclaimer and therefore reject it as unlawful.[193]

- Pearson II

In response to *Pearson I*, FDA requested submissions of scientific data supporting the proposed health claims in *Pearson I*.[194] FDA also issued a guidance document to explain FDA's evaluation process for scientific evidence.[195] Less than two years following *Pearson I*, the FDA again refused to authorize plaintiffs' four proposed claims, deeming them "inherently misleading." FDA also stated that it would not authorize a proposed folic

---

[188] *Id.* at 657 (citing Peel v. Attorney Registration and Disciplinary Comm'n of Ill., 496 U.S. 91, 110 (1990)).

[189] *Id.* at 657.

[190] *Id.* at 600.

[191] *Id.* at 661.

[192] *Pearson I*, 164 F.3d at 658–9 (proposing disclaimer language: (1) "The evidence is inconclusive because existing studies have been performed with foods containing antioxidant vitamins, and the effect of those foods on reducing the risk of cancer may result from other components in those foods"; and (2) "The evidence in support of this claim is inconclusive").

[193] *Id.* at 659.

[194] Pearson v Shalala (*Pearson II*), 130 F. Supp. 2d 105, 110 (D.D.C. 2001). *See also* Food Labeling; Health Claims and Label Statements; Request for Scientific Data and Information, 64 Fed. Reg. 48841-02 (1999).

[195] *See* FDA, Draft Guidance for Industry on Disclosing Information Provided to Advisory Committees in Connection with Open Advisory Committee Meetings Related to the Testingor Approval of New Drugs and Convened by the Center for Drug Evaluation and Research, Beginning on January 1, 2000; Availability, 64 Fed. Reg. 71794-02 (1999).

acid claim even with clarifying disclaimers because it had found the claim to be inherently misleading as the weight of scientific evidence was against the claim.[196]

Plaintiffs rejected the alternative claims and filed suit for First Amendment and APA violations.[197] The court in Pearson II found that the FDA had failed to comply with the constitutional guidelines set forth in Pearson I and held that the proposed claim was not inherently misleading since "[t]he mere absence of significant affirmative evidence in support of a particular claim ... does not translate into negative evidence against it."[198] The court reasoned that a claim could "not be absolutely prohibited" if there was any "credible evidence" unless such evidence was "outweighed by evidence against the claim" or was "qualitatively weaker" than evidence against the claim.[199] While the court acknowledged that it is generally not the role of the courts to evaluate conflicting scientific evidence, the court's examination of the scientific literature on which FDA relied for its folic acid decision led the court to find that FDA's conclusion that the "weight" of the evidence was against plaintiff's folic acid claim was arbitrary, capricious, and otherwise violated the law.[200]

- *Whitaker v. Thompson*

In June 2001, in *Whitaker v. Thompson* the same plaintiffs in *Pearson I and Pearson II* challenged FDA's decision not to authorize an antioxidant claim for saw palmetto, a product that had been at issue in *Pearson I*.[201] FDA determined that the weight of the scientific evidence against the relationship between cancer and antioxidant vitamins was greater than the weight of evidence in favor of the relationship.[202] The FDA concluded that the claim therefore was inherently misleading and could not be cured with a disclaimer.

Following a review of the scientific data (according to the record, one-third of the 150 scientific studies the FDA considered supported the health claim), the court found that the proposed claim was not inherently misleading and that the FDA had "failed to carry its burden of showing that suppression of Plaintiff's antioxidant vitamin claim is the least restrictive means of protecting consumers against the potential of being misled by the Claim."[203] Expanding on *Pearson I*, the Whitaker court suggested that "any complete ban of a claim would be approved only under narrow circumstances, i.e., when there was almost no qualitative evidence in support of the claim and where the government provided empirical evidence proving that the public would still be deceived even if the claims was qualified by a disclaimer."[204]

Following Whitaker, the FDA separated the evaluation of health claims into qualified and unqualified claims.[205] For claims supported by significant scientific agreement, the

---

[196] *Pearson II* at 107.
[197] *Id.* at 112.
[198] *Id.* at 115.
[199] *Id.* at 114–15.
[200] *Id.* at 115.
[201] *Id.* at 7.
[202] *Id.*
[203] *Id.* at 8.
[204] *Id.* at 11.
[205] Fleminger, Inc. v. U.S. Dep't of Health and Human Servs., 854 F. Supp. 2d 192, 200 (D. Conn. 2012).

FDA considered the claim unqualified and approved it without a disclaimer.[206] If the FDA determined that the proposed claim lacked the support of significant scientific agreement, but that the weight of the evidence supported the claim, the FDA considered the claim qualified and proposed a disclaimer to reflect the appropriate value of scientific support.[207]

In 2009, FDA issued guidance describing its process for evaluating the scientific support for both qualified and unqualified health claims.[208]

- *Alliance for Natural Health US v. Sebelius*

In 2010, plaintiffs (dietary supplement manufacturers) in *Alliance for Natural Health US v. Sebelius (Alliance I)* challenged the FDA's rejection of certain health claims regarding cancer risk and selenium supplements.[209] Plaintiffs had submitted seventeen qualified health claims linking vitamins C and E with a reduction in the risk of certain types of cancer. FDA denied thirteen of the claims entirely and permitted four others to be made as qualified claims with modified language. The FDA had banned plaintiffs' claims on grounds that there was credible scientific evidence to support them and then exercised its enforcement discretion to permit qualified health claims that were supported by some credible evidence.[210]

At issue in *Whitaker* was the standard of review. The plaintiffs urged the court to adopt a heightened review because they raised a constitutional issue, while the FDA contended that "particularized findings concerning the scientific evidence" merited an arbitrary and capricious review.[211] The court concluded that it would conduct an independent review of agency decisions on constitutional issues, but noted, however, that it would be inappropriate to review the scientific evidence without some deference.[212] Notwithstanding this deference to the FDA's findings, the court held that certain aspects of the FDA's determinations were arbitrary and capricious and remanded those back to the FDA for reevaluation and drafting of disclaimers where appropriate.[213]

- Alliance II

Objecting to FDA's rewording of two proposed health claims (that Vitamin C may reduce the risk of gastric cancer and that Vitamin E may reduce the risk of bladder cancer), the same plaintiffs in *Alliance I* brought action against FDA in *Alliance for Natural Health US v Sebelius (Alliance II)*.[214] The district court continued to use the

---

[206] *Id.*

[207] *See id.*; 67 Fed. Reg. at 78003.

[208] *See* FDA, Draft Guidance for Industry: Evidence-Based Review System for the Scientific Evaluation of Health Claims (January 2009).

[209] 714 F. Supp. 2d 48 (D.D.C. 2010).

[210] *Id.* at 57–8.

[211] *Id.* at 59.

[212] *Id.* at 59–60 (quoting Ethyl Corp. v. Environmental Protection Agency, 541 F.2d 1, 36 (D.C. Cir. 1976) ("[T]he enforced education into the intricacies of the problem before the agency is not designed to enable the court to become a superagency that can supplant the agency's expert decision-maker.").

[213] *Id.* at 65, 72.

[214] 786 F. Supp. 2d 1 (D.D.C. 2011).

independent review, rather than the APA's arbitrary and capricious review. As was in the case of *Alliance I*, FDA had completely reworded and replaced two of plaintiffs' qualified health claims in an identical manner to the claims at issue in *Alliance I*.[215] The *Alliance II* court noted that the FDA's replacement and complete rewording of Plaintiffs' claims made it "difficult to tell what the original health claims are and appears to disavow FDA's own conclusions that those claims are supported by credible evidence."[216] The court interpreted *Pearson* and its progeny as standing for the proposition that "[w]here the evidence supporting a claim is inconclusive, the First Amendment permits the claim to be made; FDA cannot require a disclaimer that simply swallows the claim."[217] Plaintiffs and the FDA in May 2010 reached a settlement on the use of the qualified health claims.[218]

- *Fleminger v. US DHHS*

In this case decided by the Second Circuit in 2014, Fleminger, a manufacturer and seller of green tea, filed a petition with the FDA for the authorization of certain qualified health claims. FDA required Fleminger to include a modified disclaimer and Fleminger in turn filed a suit. Although the DC Circuit precedent in the *Pearson* and *Alliance* cases involve health claims on dietary supplements, the court in *Fleminger* concluded that the analysis is the same for health claims on food products.[219]

Fleminger proposed a health claim for its green tea products linking consumption of green tea with a reduced risk of cancer: "Daily consumption of 40 ounces of typical green tea containing 710 g/ml of natural (−) −epigallocatechin gallate (EGCG) may reduce the risk of certain forms of cancer. There is scientific evidence supporting this health claim although the evidence is not conclusive."[220] In the exercise of its enforcement discretion, the FDA proposed its own modified claim: "Green tea may reduce the risk of breast or prostate cancer. FDA does not agree that green tea may reduce the risk because there is very little scientific evidence for the claim."[221] Fleminger sued for the violation of its First Amendment commercial free speech rights.[222] Fleminger's brought action under the APA, alleging a single cause of action for the violation of the First Amendment. Fleminger did not dispute FDA's determination that "there was very little scientific evidence" for the health claim that drinking green tea may reduce the risk of breast or prostate cancer. Nor did Fleminger argue that its challenge be analyzed under Section

---

[215] The two claims were that Vitamin C may reduce the risk of gastric cancer and that Vitamin E may reduce the risk of bladder cancer. The FDA found the scientific evidence persuasive for these claims, but not conclusive. Thus, the FDA revised these claims as follows: "One weak study and one study with inconsistent results suggest that vitamin C supplements may reduce the risk of gastric cancer. Based on these studies, FDA concludes that it is highly uncertain that vitamin C supplements reduce the risk of gastric cancer." *Id.* at 24.

[216] *Id.*

[217] *Id.*

[218] *Settlement Reached for Qualified Health Claims Relating Selenium to Reduced Risk of Prostate, Colon, Rectal, Bladder, and Thyroid Cancers*, U.S. FOOD & DRUG ADMIN. (Apr. 24, 2013).

[219] 854 F. Supp. 2d 192, 195 (D. Conn. 2012).

[220] *Id.* at 203.

[221] *Id.* at 206. The FDA initially proposed claims similar to those rejected in *Alliance I*. Fleminger sought reconsideration, which was denied. Fleminger informally responded, received no response, and began using its resubmitted claim. The FDA reconsidered its rejection and proposed claims in light of the ruling in *Alliance I*, and then proposed the modified claim instead.

[222] *Id.* at 206.

706(2) of the APA, which provides that final agency action may be set aside if arbitrary, capricious, and proves to be an abuse of discretion.

The court held that the amount of scientific evidence to support a proposed health claim falls squarely within the ambit of the FDA's expertise, and the court gave deference to the FDA's assessment of the scientific evidence and to "the FDA's determination that Fleminger's articulation of the level of scientific evidence was inaccurate and misleading."[223] But the court held that such deference does not extend to the determination of whether the FDA's modified disclaimer violated Fleminger's commercial speech rights. The court found that FDA satisfied the first three prongs of *Central Hudson* and analyzed the case under the final prong (i.e., the reasonable fit of FDA's actions) to determine whether the regulation was more extensive than necessary to serve the government's interest.

The court accepted the FDA's modified claim in part and rejected it in part. According to the court, the portion stating there is "very little scientific evidence" attained a reasonable balance between permitting the claim to be made, accurately reflecting the strength of the evidence, and not burdening more speech than necessary.[224] Conversely, the court rejected the portion stating, "FDA does not agree that green tea may reduce that risk."[225] Like the rejected modifications in *Alliance II*, the court found that this statement effectively negated the relationship between green tea and a reduction in the risk of cancer and found it to be unnecessary in addition to the disclaimer "very little scientific evidence."[226] The court recommended that the FDA follow *Pearson I*'s suggestion, stating, "the FDA does not approve this claim," without the effect of negating the claim.[227]

- Observations

The FDA's regulation of health claims and *Pearson* and its progeny challenging the FDA's regulation juxtaposes two conflicting objectives: preserving commercial free speech and ensuring consumer protection. Among the important points that can be derived from these cases, the following three are especially significant. (1) While *Pearson* and its progeny mention the deferential standard of review, they frequently apply a more searching review of FDA's judgment. They also seem to go beyond the *Pearson I* holding that disclosure is preferable to suppression to almost eliminating the FDA's ability to ban a misleading claim. (2) Courts are reluctant to approve specific disclaimer language that is too strongly worded to negate the claim. At least in *Fleminger*, a compromise disclaimer that is short and easily understood by consumers was acceptable. (3) The distinction between the challenges to FDA regulation of health claims – one under the APA and the other under the First Amendment – have been blurred due to the application of a heightened standard of review to APA claims. Thus, courts are not applying the deferential arbitrary and capricious review to the FDA's conclusions regarding the evidence against an inherently misleading claim.

[223] *Id.* at 211.
[224] *Id.* at 216–17.
[225] *Id.* at 217–18.
[226] *Id.*
[227] *Id.* at 218.

[c] Nutrient Content Claims

A nutrient content claim is any representation on a food label that directly or indirectly characterizes the level of a nutrient in the product.[228] Examples of nutrient content claims include "high in fiber," "low fat," "good source," or "contains 100 calories."[229]

A nutrient content claim must comply with the specific criteria for that particular claim.[230] For example, "good source" may be used only if a food product has at least 10 percent of the Daily Value of that nutrient, while "excellent source" may be used if it has at least 20 percent of the daily value.[231] A nutrient content claim may be implied. For example, "healthy" is considered an implied nutrient content claim when used in the context of implying that a food "is useful in creating a diet that is consistent with dietary recommendations."[232] Food products that are labeled as "healthy" must satisfy certain fat, sodium, and cholesterol requirements.[233] FDA generally prohibits nutrient content claims unless they recite the exact language provided in its regulations. Some nutrient content claims are prohibited if the amount of another component (e.g., cholesterol) exceeds a certain level, and some claims are subject to additional disclosure requirements if the food contains certain nutrients (e.g., fat, sodium) above a specified level.[234]

Two forms of nutrient claims are allowed: "absolute" and "relative or comparative." The absolute form describes the level of a nutrient in a product, whereas relative claims compare the amount of the nutrient in the product with that amount in a similar product. With respect to absolute or specific nutrient content claims, such as "free," "loss," or "reduced/less," the FDA has issued regulations governing the nutrient levels required for their use. For example, to make a claim that a product has "no calories" or is "calorie free," the product must have less than five calories per RACC and per labeled serving.[235] To claim a product is "sugar free," the product must have less than five grams of sugar per RACC and per labeled serving.[236] To claim a product is "low fat," the food must contain three grams or less of total fat per RACC.[237] To claim "no added sugars," no sugar or sugar-containing ingredient can be added during processing.[238] A label statement about the actual amount or percentage of a nutrient in a food, such as "3 calories per serving" is permitted, provided it is truthful and not misleading and does not characterize the level of the nutrient in the food. If the statement implicitly characterizes the level of the nutrient, such as "just 3 grams of fat per serving," it is an implied nutrient content claim and must either meet the requirements for the implied nutrient content claim (e.g., "low fat"), or bear a disclaimer that the food does not meet those requirements (e.g., "just 6 grams of fat per serving, not a low-fat food").

For relative claims about the level of a nutrient, such as "more," "less," or "fewer," the amount of nutrient in the subject product must be compared to an amount of the same

[228] 21 C.F.R. § 101.13(b); 21 C.F.R. § 101.13(a).
[229] See, e.g., 21 C.F.R. § 101.13 (setting forth general principles for nutrient content claims).
[230] 21 U.S.C. §343(r)(2)(a)(i).
[231] 21 C.F.R. § 101.54(b); 21 C.F.R. § 101.54(e)
[232] 21 C.F.R. § 101.65(e)
[233] 21 C.F.R. § 101.65(d)(2)(ii) (healthy requirements).
[234] 21 C.F.R. § 101.13(h)(1).
[235] 21 C.F.R. § 101.60(b).
[236] 21 C.F.R. § 101.60(c).
[237] 21 C.F.R. §101.62(b)(2).
[238] 21 C.F.R. § 101.60(c).

nutrient in an appropriate reference food, as specified by the regulations. For example, to assert that a food has "reduced" sodium, the subject food must be compared to an established regular product or an average representative product.[239] When making such a relative nutrient claim, the percent of change and identity of the reference food must be declared immediately adjacent to the claim.[240] In addition, a relative claim for decreased levels of a nutrient, such as "less" or "fewer," cannot be made if the nutrient content of the subject food meets the requirements for a "low" claim for that nutrient.[241] Statements, such as, "as much calcium as milk," are permitted, provided the reference food qualifies as a "good source" of the nutrient and the labeled product has at least an equivalent level of the nutrient per serving.

The FDA exercises its authority to determine which nutrient content claims may be used in food labeling by two means: (1) FDA issues a regulation authorizing a nutrient content claim after the agency reviews the scientific evidence submitted in a nutrient content claim petition and (2) FDA prohibits or modifies, by regulation, a nutrient content claim within 120 days after it has received a nutrient content claim notification. The notification process requires a scientific basis to be established through an authoritative statement from a scientific body by the US government with official responsibility for public health protection or research directly related to human nutrition or the National Academy of Sciences.[242]

[d] Structure Function Claims

Structure or function claims (commonly referred to as "structure/function" claims) are often confused with health claims. A structure/function claim does not reference a disease or illness. Instead, it refers to a structure or function of the body. For example, a statement on a food label that "calcium builds strong bones" and "fiber maintains bowel regularity" are structure/function claims. The FDA has not issued regulations authorizing certain structure/function claims and does not preview these claims (the Dietary Supplement Health and Education Act of 1994 added section 403(r)(6) to the FDCA, which permits structure/function claims on labeling for dietary supplements).[243] However, such claims must be truthful and not misleading.[244] If a claim is associated too closely with a specific disease condition it may not be permitted. For example, "for joint function" may be acceptable, where "for joint pain" would not be. Structure/Function claims are increasingly used by food companies as a safe and cost-efficient way of making a claim. A well placed structure/function claim can still appeal to the consumer and enable the food company to steer clear of making an impermissible disease claim or engaging in the time-consuming and costly process to petition the FDA for a qualified health claim.

---

[239] 21 C.F.R. § 101.13(j)(1).
[240] 21 C.F.R. § 101.13(j)(2)(i) and (ii).
[241] 21 C.F.R. § 101.13(j)(3).
[242] *Label Claims for Conventional Foods and Dietary Supplements*, U.S. Dep't Food & Drug Admin. (December 13, 2013, revised).
[243] 21 U.S.C. § 343(r)(6); 21 C.F.R. § 101.93.
[244] *Id.*

Table 4.2. Comparison of Acceptable Claims

Types of Claims	Heart Health Claims
Health Claim	Three grams of soluble fiber from oatmeal daily in a diet low in saturated fat and cholesterol may reduce the risk of heart disease. This cereal has 2 grams per serving
Qualified Health Claim	Scientific evidence suggests but does not prove that eating 1.5 ounces per day of most nuts as part of a diet low in saturated fat and cholesterol may reduce the risk of heart disease
Nutrient Content Claim	Low fat Cholesterol free High in oat bran
Structure/Function Claim	Calcium builds strong bones Fiber helps maintain digestive regularity
Dietary Guidelines	A low-fat diet, with plenty of fruits and vegetables will promote healthy living

[e] Dietary Guidance Statements

"Dietary" guidance statements can also be made on food labels. While health claims describe the relationship between a food substance and a disease or health-related condition, dietary guidance statements do not contain both elements.[245] A dietary guidance statement generally provides dietary guidance based on the Dietary Guidelines for Americans, jointly issued by the DHHS and the USDA.[246] The guidelines were first published in 1980 and are revised every five years as new and updated scientific information becomes available. Dietary guidance statements can be made without FDA review or authorization before use, but the statements must be truthful and nonmisleading. Examples of such statements include "carrots are good for your health" or "diets rich in fruits and vegetables reduce the risk of certain cancers."

[f] Claim Comparison

A helpful comparison of the five types of claims that the FDA may find acceptable is made in Table 4.2.

[g] Functional Food Claims

As noted in Chapter 1, the food industry has created the ever-increasing popular category of "functional foods." Because there are no unique statutes and regulations for functional foods, a functional food product may be regulated as conventional food, a dietary supplement, or a drug, depending on the claims made for the product. For example, FDA will regulate functional foods as drug products where disease claims regarding the effect of the product on the diagnosis, cure, mitigation, treatment, or prevention of the

---

[245] *See* 58 Fed. Reg. 2478, 2487 (January 6, 1993).
[246] *See* HOME AND GARDEN BULLETIN NO. 232, NUTRITION AND YOUR HEALTH: DIETARY GUIDELINES FOR AMERICANS, U.S. DEP'T OF AGRIC. AND U.S. DEP'T OF HEALTH, EDUCATION, AND WELFARE (1980).

disease – unless the functional foods lawfully may bear health claims under the regulatory regime for either conventional foods or dietary supplements.

Although all foods are in some sense functional, the explosive growth of functional foods has brought increasing attention to this type of food. There is no statutory or regulatory definition of what constitutes a functional food. The Food and Nutrition Board of the National Academy of Sciences has defined functional food as "any modified food or food ingredient that may provide a health benefit beyond the traditional nutrients it contains."[247] The Institute of Food Technologists (IFT) has identified functional foods as those "substances [that] provide essential nutrients often beyond quantities necessary for normal maintenance, growth and development, and/or other biologically active components that impart health benefits or desirable physiological effects."[248] In other words, functional foods provide health benefit beyond basic nutrition.

Increasing attention to functional foods may result at some point in the future of a distinct legal category and definition for functional food. On December 5, 2006, FDA held a public hearing on the matter to gather information on regulating conventional foods marketed as functional foods.[249] The period for comment ended on March 5, 2007.[250]

§ 4.05 Notable Food Labeling Issues

[1] *Food Allergens*

[a] Development of Regulation

A sizeable percentage of Americans suffer from food allergies.[251] Over the past twenty years, incidences of food allergies and severe allergic reactions have been on the rise.[252] Thousands of people, most of whom are children, suffer anaphylactic shock from food allergies each year. Some even die from these reactions.[253] Food allergies have no cure; avoidance is the only safe strategy for food allergy sufferers.[254] Common food allergens include wheat, milk, soy, peanuts and tree nuts, fish and shellfish, and eggs. The challenge for the regulatory system is that these common food allergens are staples of most American diets and are used to prepare and process many food products.

---

[247] Inst. of Med., Opportunities in the Nutrition and Food Sciences: Research Challenges and the Next Generation of Investigators 109 (1994).

[248] Inst. of Food Technologists, Functional Foods: Opportunities and Challenges 6 (2005).

[249] *See* Conventional Foods Being Marketed as "Functional Foods"; Public Hearing; Request for Comments, 71 Fed. Reg. 62,400, 62,403 (October 25, 2006) (codified at 21 C.F.R. parts. 101 and 170).

[250] *See* Conventional Foods Being Marketed as "Functional Foods"; Extension of Comment Period, 72 Fed. Reg. 694 (January 8, 2007) (extending comment period for functional food proposed regulations).

[251] It is estimated that 4 percent of Americans (about 12 million people) suffer from food allergies. *See* Laura E. Derr, *When Food Is Poison: The History, Consequences, and Limitations of the Food Allergen Labeling and Consumer Protection Act of 2004*, 61 Food & Drug L.J. 65, 70 (2006). Generally, obtaining accurate statistics on the number of food allergy sufferers in the United States is difficult, as many sufferers may not yet have had a reaction, had only a minor reaction, or not have reported a reaction.

[252] *See id.* at 70–71; H.R. 2063, 110th Cong. §2(2) (2008) ("Peanut allergy doubled among children from 1997 to 2002.").

[253] It is estimated that 150–200 people, mostly children, die from these food allergies every year. *See* Food Labeling; Current Trends in the Use of Allergen Advisory Labeling: Its Use, Effectiveness, and Consumer Perception, 73 Fed. Reg. 46302-01 (notice of public hearing; request for comments, August 8, 2008); H.R. 2063 § 2(5), § 2(9).

[254] Derr, *supra* note 251, at 77.

As science uncovered the risks of food allergens, the FDA starting in the mid-1990s took steps to inform and protect those susceptible to allergies.[255] In 1994, FDA published *Food Allergies: Rare But Risky*, a consumer guide aimed at educating those with food allergies as to the dangers of allergen-containing foods and steps they might take to protect themselves from serious reactions. In 1996, the FDA followed this action by issuing an Allergy Warning Letter to manufacturers communicating the FDA's concerns regarding adverse consumer reactions to undeclared allergens in food.[256] The agency expressed concern that manufacturers were misinterpreting an exemption to FDA labeling requirements, which allowed for nondeclaration of incidental additives and processing aids in certain cases.[257] The 1996 Allergy Warning Letter noted that the amount of a substance that may cause an adverse reaction must be declared and encouraged voluntary declaration of allergenic ingredients otherwise exempt as colors, flavorings, and spices at the end of ingredients lists. The 1996 letter also urged manufacturers "to take all steps necessary to eliminate cross contamination and to ensure the absence" of allergens in foods.[258]

Eight years later, in 2004, the Food Allergen Labeling and Consumer Protection Act (FALCPA) was passed by Congress and enacted into law.[259] In enacting FALCPA, Congress followed up on the FDA's 1996 Allergy Warning Letter, expressly recognizing the grave dangers faced by food allergic Americans due to the insidious presence of eight major allergens in food: milk, eggs, fish, crustacean shellfish, tree nuts, peanuts, wheat, and soybeans.[260] FALCPA enacted a new regime of food allergen labeling requirements whereby manufacturers were required to list the presence of the eight major allergens in a clear and conspicuous manner.[261] These requirements were put in place by amending the FDCA to provide that a food shall be deemed misbranded unless the label either indicates below or adjacent to the list of ingredients that it contains one of the eight major allergens, or specifically lists the allergen in the list of ingredients by a name easily understandable by consumers. The act was also amended to include labeling requirements for allergens, which manufacturers were previously not required to list because they were used solely as flavorings, colorings, or incidental additives.[262]

In addition to FALCPA, other statutory and regulatory protections have been pursued for the benefit of food allergic consumers. Recognizing the special risks faced by children with food allergies, in 2010 Congress passed the Food Allergy and Anaphylaxis Management Act (FAAMA) as part of the 2011 Food Safety Modernization Act.[263] FAAMA directs the secretary of health and human services, in consultation with the secretary of education, to develop and make publicly available voluntary food allergy

---

[255] *See generally*, Jonathan B. Roses, *Food Allergen Law and the Food Allergen Labeling and Consumer Protection Act of 2004: Falling Short of True Protection for Food Allergy Sufferers*, 66 Food & Drug L.J. 225, 226 (2011).

[256] Fred R. Shank, *Notice to Manufacturers, Label Declaration of Allergenic Substances in Foods* (June 10, 1996).

[257] *See* 21 C.F.R. § 101.100(a)(3).

[258] *See id.*

[259] Food Allergen Labeling and Consumer Protection Act of 2004 (FALCPA), Pub. L. No. 108–282, Title II, §202(1)(B), 118 Stat. 905 (codified as amended in scattered sections of 21 U.S.C.).

[260] FALCPA § 202(2).

[261] FALCPA § 203(a).

[262] *Id.*

[263] Pub. L. No. 111–353, Title I, § 112, 124 Stat. 3916 (codified as amended at 21 U.S.C. § 2205 (2011)).

guidelines to manage the risk of food allergy and anaphylaxis in schools and early child-hood education programs.[264] These guidelines are purposed to reduce the risk of exposure to food allergens, assure prompt response in the event of an anaphylactic reaction, and give incentive grants to local educational agencies to assist in the adoption and implementation of these guidelines in public schools.[265]

[b] FALCPA Provisions

(1) *Misbranding*

The FALCPA requires that labels of food that contains the protein of one of eight major food allergens must disclose the presence of the allergen in "plain English."[266] Section 203(a) of the FALCPA creates a new subsection (w) in 21 U.S.C. § 343 that expands the FDCA's definition of misbranding to include a failure to identify the presence of major food allergens in a product. Explicitly closing previous exceptions, the FALCPA states that "notwithstanding ... any other law, a flavoring, coloring, or incidental additive that is, or that bears or contains, a major food allergen shall be subject to the labeling requirements of this subsection."[267] Like other labeling requirements of the FDCA, these new misbranding provisions have preemptive effect over state and local food labeling laws.[268] It is notable that due to liability concerns, many food companies began to disclose on the label the presence of the allergen prior to FALCPA.

(2) *"Major Food Allergens" – Defined*

Section 203(c) of the FALCPA defines (now in FDCA 21 U.S.C. § 321(qq)(1)) which defines the eight major food allergens as milk, eggs, fish, crustacean shellfish, tree nuts, wheat, peanuts, and soybeans, and any protein derived from these foods.[269] Tree nuts, fish, and crustacean shellfish must be labeled by their specific type of nut or species of fish or shellfish (e.g., almonds, pecans, or walnuts; bass, flounder, or cod; crab, lobster, or shrimp, respectively). Identification of tree nuts, fish, and shellfish by their specific name averts the problem of overgeneralized labeling that would preclude individuals allergic to only certain types of those foods to partake of numerous products that they otherwise could safely enjoy.

Three exceptions to the definition of "major food allergen" are carved out of the FALCPA. First, the FALCPA exempts from its allergen labeling requirements highly refined oils and ingredients derived from highly refined oils.[270] The term "highly refined oils" refers to bleached, deodorized oils, of which the oil that poses the greatest

---

[264] 21 U.S.C. § 2205(b)(1).

[265] 21 U.S.C. § 2205(b)(2), (c); 21 U.S.C. § 2205(b)(1).

[266] *See* H.R. Rep. No. 108–608, at 3 (2004). The requirement of "plain English" is due to the concern that consumers generally do not understand that many of the common or usual names for ingredients listed in the ingredient statement are derived from food allergens, such as "caseniate" or "whey" derived form milk or "albumin" derived from egg. Food Safety and Food Labeling; Presence and Labeling of Allergens in Foods, 66 Fed. Reg. 00P-1322 (notice of public hearing, July 25, 2001).

[267] 21 U.S.C. § 343(w)(4).

[268] *See id.*

[269] Congress deemed these eight allergens the "most significant" food allergens because they account for "over 90% of food allergies in the United States," H.R. Rep. No. 108–608, at 3 (2004).

[270] *See* 21 U.S.C. § 343(qq)(2)(A).

allergenicity concern is peanut oil. Second, any person can petition FDA to challenge the "major allergen" designation of ingredients they believe do not produce allergic reactions.[271] The petitioner has the burden to provide scientific evidence that demonstrates that the ingredient when derived using the method described in the petition "does not cause an allergic response that poses a risk to human health."[272] Thus, a company that is able to remove an allergenic protein from an ingredient (e.g., through distillation) could petition the secretary of DHHS (or FDA by delegation from the secretary) for an exemption. If the secretary does not affirmatively approve the petition within 180 days, it is deemed denied.[273] Finally, the FALCPA establishes a notification process whereby ingredients derived from the eight major allergens that do not contain allergenic protein or do not cause allergic reactions (as demonstrated by a manufacturer) can be exempt from the FALCPA's labeling requirements.[274] For example, if the FDA determines that a certain amount of a particular allergen is required to trigger an allergic response, companies could file a notification stating that their products contain less than the established threshold amount.[275] The notification provision also exempts from major allergen status ingredients that the secretary previously has determined, under Section 409 of the FDCA, do not cause an allergic response that poses a risk to human health (the generally recognized as safe [GRAS] notification process is not included).[276] It is presumed that the secretary has approved the exemption unless the secretary specifically notifies the company of the contrary within ninety days of receipt of the notification.[277]

(3) *Labeling Format*

Manufacturers may choose between two options for identifying the presence of a major food allergen. First, following or adjacent to the list of ingredients, a manufacturer may print in type size no smaller than the other items in the ingredient list the word "Contains" followed by the plain English name of the food source from which the allergenic ingredient was derived.[278] For example, a statement such as the following may appear at the end of a list of ingredients on a box of cereal: Contains wheat, milk, and tree nuts. Alternatively, the manufacturer may print the plain English name of the allergenic protein in an ingredient in parenthesis directly following the ingredient that contains the allergen.[279] The list of ingredients on the cereal box thus might be printed as follows: Durum (wheat), evaporated cane juice, salt, whey (milk), nut flavoring (peanuts, almonds). To avoid label clutter, the FALCPA provides that enterprises need not declare a major allergen where the parentheses presentation and the common or usual name of an ingredient already listed incorporates the plain English name of the food

---

[271] *See* 21 U.S.C. § 343(w)(6); *see also* 21 U.S.C. § 343(qq)(2)(B).
[272] 21 U.S.C. § 343(w)(6).
[273] *Id.*
[274] *See* 21 U.S.C. § 343(w)(7); *see also* 21 U.S.C.A. § 343(qq)(2)(B).
[275] *See* H.R. Rep. No. 108–608, at 17 (date) ("While the Committee recognizes that thresholds for the eight major allergens have not yet been established by the scientific community, if they are established, ingredients containing allergenic proteins below the established threshold would be eligible for the notification procedure.").
[276] *See* 21 U.S.C. § 343(w)(7)(A)(ii).
[277] *See* 21 U.S.C. § 343(w)(7)(B).
[278] *See* 21 U.S.C. § 343(w)(1)(A).
[279] *See* 21 U.S.C. § 343(w)(1)(B).

source.[280] For example, as explained in a congressional report, if "milk casein" is stated in the ingredients list then a manufacturer does not need to additionally indicate the presence of milk in parentheses beside the ingredient.[281] The FDA clarified in guidance issued in December 2005 that this exception does not apply to the "Contains" statement presentation. A "Contains" statement must include the names of all allergens in a food, whether or not the name of the allergen is stated already in the ingredient list using FALCPA-approved, plain English terminology.[282] The FALCPA also allows a manufacturer who chooses the parentheses presentation format not to declare the same allergen after any additional ingredients in which the allergen is present.[283] For instance, if milk casein or whey (milk) appears on the label, the manufacturer is not required to indicate the presence of milk in parentheses after the ingredient caseinate.[284]

[2] *Trans Fat*

Trans fats, otherwise known as "partially hydrogenated oils," are mostly created in an industrial process that adds hydrogen to liquid vegetable oils. Trans fats are relatively inexpensive, improve the texture of foods fried in them, can be used for a long time in commercial fryers, and increase the shelf life and flavor of foods. Trans fats also affect the way the body processes cholesterol and makes individuals more susceptible to heart disease, stroke, and Type 2 diabetes.[285]

The regulation of trans fat labeling has evolved over the years. When the FDA finalized the NLEA amendments in 1993, the regulations required food manufacturers to declare total fat and saturated fat contents on the NFP. However, the FDA did not require trans fat to be included in nutritional labeling. The agency concluded that it was premature to require the declaration of trans fatty acids on the panel because the scientific evidence on the dietary implications of trans fat was still inconclusive at the time.[286] In response to petitions filed by the CSPI to mandate the disclosure of trans fat information on nutrition labels, the FDA issued a proposed rule in November 1999 that would mandate trans fat labeling.[287] The 1999 proposal required food manufacturers to include the trans fat content of foods in the saturated fats amount on the nutrition label with a separate footnote indicating specific trans fat information. The FDA following heavy criticism abandoned this footnote approach. Four years later, in 2003, the FDA published a final rule – the current FDA trans fat labeling requirements.[288] Codified in 21 C.F.R. § 101.62, the final rule requires that all conventional foods and

---

[280] *See* 21 U.S.C. § 343(w)(1)(B)(i).

[281] *See* H.R. Rep. No. 108–608, at 16.

[282] FDA, Guidance for Industry: Questions and Answers Regarding Food Allergens, including the Food Allergen Labeling and Consumer Protection Act of 2004 (October 2006).

[283] *See* 21 U.S.C. § 343(w)(1)(B)(ii).

[284] *See* H.R. Rep. No. 108–608 (2004), at 16.

[285] FDA, Guidance for Industry: Trans Fatty Acids in Nutrition Labeling, Nutrient Content Claims, Health Claims; Small Entity Compliance Guide (August 2003).

[286] *See* Susan Okie, *New York to Trans Fats: You're Out!*, 356 New Eng. J. Med. 2017, 2018 (2007).

[287] Press Release, FDA Proposes New Rules for Trans Fatty Acids in Nutrition Labeling, Nutrient Content Claims, and Health Claims, U.S. Food & Drug Admin., (November 12, 1999).

[288] Trans Fatty Acids in Nutrition Labeling, 68 Fed. Reg. 41461 (July 11, 2003) (codified in 21 C.F.R. Part 101).

supplements disclose the amount of trans fatty acids on the NFP, on a separate line, immediately under the declaration of saturated fats. The trans fat amount is to be identified in increments of 0.5 grams when it is below 5 grams; but if the total trans fat content is less than 0.5 grams, then it is considered to be trans fat-free and can be declared as having 0 grams on its respective line.[289] If the trans fat content is greater than 5 grams, then it is to be expressed in increments of 1 gram.[290]

As noted in Chapter 5, in June 2015, the FDA issued its final rule that artificial trans fat is no longer GRAS and gave the industry a deadline to eliminate what remains.

[3] Genetically Engineered Food

[a] Divisive Issue

There is no more divisive issue in food law than the labeling of genetically engineered food (GE food or GMO). The principal issue is whether a food product that has been genetically engineered or contains ingredients that are genetically engineered should be required to be labeled as such. It has pitted the United States against its trading allies, and it has divided domestic constituencies on numerous points of law and policy, including a consumer's "right to know" and the role of science in determining what information is conveyed to consumers. This divide reflects not only philosophical differences concerning what information should be communicated to consumers, but also concerning the configuration of the US food system itself. (See Chapter 3 additional background on GE food and for an analysis of GE food safety issues).

[b] Materiality and FDA Statement of Policy

There is no statutory definition of what constitutes GE food. The regulatory framework that governs the labeling of genetically engineered food is predicated upon Section 201(n) of the FDCA, which requires the food enterprise to avoid the misbranding of food and to reveal all "material" facts in light of: (1) any representations made or suggested by the label or (2) any consequences that may result from use of the product. This section, along with the attendant regulations, make clear that the requirement of materiality does not mean that any and all information is subject to mandatory disclosure; the FDA can only compel disclosure of information deemed material enough that omission would make the label misleading.[291]

On the basis of this premise of materiality, as noted in Chapter 3, on May 29, 1992, the FDA issued its *Statement of Policy: Foods Derived from New Plant Varieties* to clarify the FDA's position on GE foods.[292] The FDA stated that the consumer "must be informed … if a [genetically engineered food] differs from its traditional counterpart," and accordingly, the label must disclose all material facts.[293] The FDA also made clear, and has ever since maintained, that GE foods are substantially equivalent to

---

[289] 21 C.F.R. § 101.62(c)(1).
[290] Trans Fatty Acids in Nutrition Labeling, *supra* note 288, at 41457.
[291] 21 U.S.C. §§ 343(a), 321(n).
[292] 57 Fed. Reg. 22,984 (May 29, 1992).
[293] *Id.* at 22,991.

conventional foods. The agency notes in a guidance document that "[g]enetic engineering is the name for certain methods that scientists use to introduce new traits or characteristics to an organism."[294] Hence, the FDA considers "genetic engineering" to be the more precise term than genetic modification.[295] The FDA holds that absent data or evidence showing that foods created using genetic engineering techniques differ significantly from, or lead to any greater safety risk than, other foods; the technological processes by which such foods are created are not material information. The agency believes that genetically engineered techniques are extensions at the molecular level of traditional methods and will be used to achieve the same goals pursued with traditional plant breeding.[296]

In parceling out the application of materiality to the biotech process for food, the agency does provide that a "material fact" would include the consequences that may result from the use of the genetically engineered food. For example, splicing into a tomato seed a peanut protein may be a material fact if there is insufficient information to demonstrate that the introduced protein could not cause an allergic reaction in a susceptible population. Thus, a label declaration would be required to alert consumers who are allergic to peanuts so they could avoid that tomato, even if its basic taste and texture remained unchanged. Omission of this material fact may make the label of the tomato misleading under FDCA Section 403(a).[297] However, disclosure of the technique used to genetically modify the tomato would not be necessary because of the substantial equivalence that exists otherwise between the conventional and genetically engineered tomato.

The central principle behind the Coordinate Framework is the idea of "substantial equivalence" – that GE foods are functionally equivalent to their unmodified counterparts – and should be treated accordingly. Hence, in 1992, when the FDA issued a policy statement addressing the regulation of GE food, it defined "genetic modification" as the alterations of the genotype that occurred using any technique, whether conventional plant breeding or new biotechnology techniques.[298] Under this definition by the FDA, virtually all cultivated food crops could be considered genetically modified. Thus, under the broadest definition adhered to by supporters of GE food, the use of biological sciences to develop products, conventional plant, and animal breeding techniques – the basis for agriculture advancement – fall under biotechnology.

FDA has not always consistently applied the distinction between the product and the process to evaluate the materiality of labeling information. In the case of labeling for irradiated food, for example, the FDA stated in a 1986 notice that "[w]hether information is material under [Section 201(n)] ... depends not on the abstract worth of the information but on whether consumers view such information as important and whether the omission of label information may mislead a consumer. The large number of consumer comments requesting retail labeling attest to the significance placed on such labeling by consumers."[299] The FDA also stated, "[I]n the absence of a statement that a food has

[294] *Questions & Answers on Food from Genetically Engineered Plants*, U.S. FOOD & DRUG ADMIN.
[295] *See id.*
[296] *See id.*
[297] *See id.*
[298] *See* Statement of Policy: Foods Derived From New Plant Varieties, 57 Fed. Reg. 22,984, 22,984 n.3 (May 29, 1992).
[299] FDA, Irradiation in the Production, Processing, and Handling of Food, 51 Fed. Reg.13376, 13388 (Apr. 18, 1986).

been irradiated, the implied representation to consumers is that the food has not been processed."[300] The agency later noted, in 1993, that it mandated labeling of irradiated foods because the process results in "organoleptic" changes to the food;[301] however, this point was absent from the 1986 notice. In fact, the agency stated in 1986 that "it is not relevant whether irradiation is considered a process in determining whether retail labeling is appropriate."[302] Moreover, in the case of FDA's mandatory source labeling for protein hydrolysates, the agency has stated that "the food source of a protein hydrolysate is information of material importance for a person who desires to avoid certain foods for religious or cultural reasons."[303] The FDA went on to require source labeling for protein hydrolysates out of concern for vegetarians and observant Jews and Muslims.[304]

As noted in Chapter 3, the FDA's 1992 *Statement of Policy* was challenged in court in 1998 by a coalition of consumer groups and individuals, including scientists and religious leaders, in the case of *Alliance for Bio-Integrity vs. Shalala*.[305] Plaintiffs asserted that the FDA failed to require special labeling for genetically engineered foods in accordance with section 201(n) of the FDCA. Plaintiffs claimed that the agency should have considered as "material" under the statute the "widespread consumer interest" and "the special concerns of religious groups and persons with allergies" in having GE foods labeled.[306] Finding the language of the statute unclear with respect to whether materiality pertains to both safety concerns and consumer interest, the court deferred to the FDA's reasonable interpretation that consumer interest is not "material" and that, absent unique risks to consumer health, Section 201(n) does not authorize mandatory GM food labeling. The court went further in noting that it was doubtful that FDA would even have the power under FDCA to require GE food labeling based solely on consumer demand.[307]

The court also rejected the plaintiffs' argument that the FDA's decision not to require labeling for GM foods violated their constitutional right to free exercise of religion under the First Amendment and burdened their religion in violation of the Religious Freedom Restoration Act (RFRA) of 1993.[308] The court held that the free-exercise claim could not stand because it was undisputed that FDA's policy statement was neutral and generally applicable.[309] As for the RFRA claim, the court acknowledged that the lack of labeling might inconvenience those plaintiffs whose religious beliefs required certain dietary restrictions concerning GE foods, but in denying relief the court held that the FDA statement "does not place 'substantial pressure' on any of the Plaintiffs, nor does it force them to abandon their religious beliefs or practices."[310]

---

[300] *Id.*

[301] FDA, Food Labeling; Foods Derived from New Plant Varieties, 58 Fed. Reg. 25837 (Apr. 28, 1993).

[302] 51 Fed. Reg. at 13390.

[303] FDA, Food Labeling; Declaration of Ingredients, 56 Fed. Reg. 28592, 28600 (June 21, 1991).

[304] FDA, Food Labeling; Declaration of Ingredients, 58 Fed. Reg. 2850, 2867 (January 6, 1993).

[305] 116 F. Supp. 2d 166, 166, 170 (D.D.C. 2000).

[306] *Id.* at 178.

[307] *Id.* at 178–9.

[308] *Id.* at 179–80 (citing 42 U.S.C. §§ 2000bb-2000bb-4).

[309] *Id.* (dismissing the free exercise claim).

[310] *Id.* at 180–1 (citations omitted).

[c] Voluntary Labeling

Guidance from FDA on voluntary GE food labeling gives examples of how a company that wants to say that its product is genetically engineered may label the product in ways that are not misleading.[311] The guidance also notes that most "consumers would prefer label statements that disclose and explain the goal of technology," such as "This product contains high oleic acid soybean oil from soybeans developed using biotechnology to decrease the amount of saturated fat." However, in describing the goal, the labels must not be misleading. For example, if a label contains the statement, "These tomatoes were genetically engineered to improve texture," then the label would be misleading if the consumer were not able to notice a textural difference.[312] Notwithstanding the FDA's guidance, there does not appear to be any evidence where a food company has voluntarily disclosed on a label or labeling that a food product has been genetically engineered.

The FDA guidance on GE food voluntary labeling also gives suggestions to companies that want to indicate to consumers that their product does not contain GE foods. The guidance suggests that because many people do not know the abbreviations GMO or GM, the label should spell out the meaning of this information. The guidance also suggests that "GMO free" be avoided for several reasons beyond the fact that it includes an obscure abbreviation. First, the phrase is not accurate because genetically modified is sometimes used broadly to include conventional methods of food production. Second, most foods do not contain organisms, so it is inaccurate to indicate that a food product does not have organisms as it implies that some food products do have organisms. And, finally, "free" implies "zero," which may be difficult to substantiate, and all claims on labels should be verifiable. The FDA gives suggestions of what would be appropriate, including, "We do not use ingredients that were produced using biotechnology" and "This oil is made from soybeans that were not genetically engineered."[313] The FDA has further made clear that it does not want any label to mislead people into thinking that foods that are not genetically engineered are any better than those that are genetically engineered.[314]

This approach by FDA leaves open the possibility of lawsuits against food producers wanting to show that their food is not genetically modified or engineered.[315] FDA has issued warning letters to companies using the "GMO free" label.[316] However, it is

---

[311] *See generally* FDA, Guidance for Industry Voluntary Labeling Indicating Whether Foods Have or Have Not Been Developed Using Bioengineering (2001).

[312] *Id.*

[313] *Id.*

[314] *Id.* ("[A] label statement that expresses or implies that a food is superior (e.g., safer or of higher quality) because it is not bioengineered would be misleading.").

[315] In fact, Monsanto brought just such a claim against Oakhurst Dairy in July of 2003, suing it for deceptive labeling practices. *See* Bruce Mohl, *Got Growth Hormones? Dairies Play on Fear in Marketing Milk Without the Additive,* THE BOSTON GLOBE, September 28, 2003, at J1. Oakhurst Dairy put the following label on its milk: "Our farmers' pledge: No artificial growth hormones." *Id.* Monsanto claimed that the FDA has recommended that labeling regarding this hormone should contextually or explicitly indicate that there is no difference whether we use the hormone or not, and because it does not do this, it is deceptive.

[316] *See e.g.,* Warning Letter from H. Tyler Thornburg, Dir., New Orleans District, FDA, Ann H. Randalls, Co-Owner, Aunt Lizzie's Cheese Straws, Inc. (May 17, 2005) (claims "Non-GMO" or "GMO-Free" not technically accurate and may be misleading).

unlikely that the same level of enforcement vigilance by the FDA would be found today. The growing level of consumer awareness of genetically engineered food lessens whatever confusion may occur. The marketplace has evolved over the past decade to put "GMO free" claims more in line with consumer expectations. In fact, GMO free labels are commonly found on food product in grocery stores.[317]

Further evidence of the federal government's adaptation to consumer demand for voluntary labeling on GMO free claims is the USDA's apparent development in May 2015 of a new government certification for GMO free claims. Media outlets have reported that in a letter dated May 1, 2015, USDA Secretary Tom Vilsack outlined the department's certification plan, which would allow companies to include on the label, "USDA Processed Verified."[318]

[d] Right-to-Know

At the core of the GE food labeling debate and a key legal consideration is the consumer's right to know what is in the food they eat. There is no affirmative expression of such a right to know in the US Constitution; nor is the concept expressed in any of the federal food statutes.[319] The relevancy of the concept is underscored by the growing demand by consumers for information. Surveys seem to show heightened consumer interest particularly in whether food has been genetically engineered.[320] In reviewing the more than 50,000 written comments about its 1992 *Statement of Policy*, FDA did acknowledge "there was general agreement that providing more information to consumers about bioengineered foods would be useful."[321] Adding pressure is the criticism that FDA's reasons for rejecting mandatory labeling are based mainly on "concerns about the unknown," which contrasts directly with the precautionary principle embodied in the Cartagena Protocol. Its position does not allow the "[l]ack of certainty due to insufficient relevant scientific information and knowledge" to prevent restrictions on imports in order to avoid any "potential adverse effects."[322] Adherence to the precautionary principle has led numerous countries to introduce mandatory labeling legislation for GE foods.[323] Many

---

[317] *See* Stephanie Strom, *Many G.M.O.-Free Labels, Little Clarity Over the Rules*, NY Times (January 30, 2015).

[318] Mary Clare Jalonick, *USDA Develops New GMO-Free Certification and Label for Foods*, Huffington Post (May 14, 2015).

[319] Other countries recognize a consumer's right to know whether a food is genetically engineered or contains GE ingredients. For example, in a document published on June 10, 2014, China's Ministry of Agriculture reiterated that mandatory GE food labeling in China was intended to ensure that covered GE foods are labeled appropriately in order to "fully protect consumers' rights to know and rights to choose." Ministry of Agriculture, *Further Strengthen Supervision and Management of Agro-GMO Safety* (June 10, 2014).

[320] According to some polls, more than 90 percent of the American public believes genetically engineered foods should be labeled. *See, e.g.*, Gary Langer, *Poll: Skepticism of Genetically Modified Foods*, ABC News, June 19, 2011.

[321] *Id.*

[322] Looking Behind the Curtain: The Growth of Trade Barriers That Ignore Sound Science, The National Foreign Trade Council, Inc. (May 2003).

[323] Detection Methods for Novel Foods Derived From Genetically Modified Organisms, International Life Sciences Institute (Kevin Yates ed., 1999) (summary of a workshop held in June 1998).

developed countries have laws in place that require enterprises to label GE products.[324] All European Union (EU) countries, as well as China, Brazil, and Australia, require GE labeling.[325] The EU labeling law requires that any food product containing more than 0.9 percent of GE inputs must be labeled.[326] During the development of the FDA *Statement of Policy* and follow-up guidance there was considerable discussion on how to tailor the regulation of GE food so as to minimize harm to trade while also responding to consumer concern.[327] Indeed, the FDA initially began investigating the use of voluntary labeling for GM products to ease tensions with trading partners such as the EU.[328]

Segments of the food industry itself have demonstrated their acceptance of consumer demands for labeling. Early on in the FDA assessment, some major food enterprises asked suppliers to segregate fields, grain bins, and storage elevators, with some even paying a premium for non-GM crops.[329] Frito-Lay made headlines when, in response to consumer worries, the company told its suppliers not to use genetically altered corn.[330] Farmers expressed concern that markets for unmodified grain could be threatened because crops such as maize and canola risk contamination by cross-fertilization with windborne pollen.[331]

The momentum within the food industry for private regulation in the labeling of genetically engineered food has seemingly accelerated largely in reaction to states' right-to-know campaigns, including a massive effort in California in 2012 that was encapsulated in an initiative to mandate the disclosure of genetically engineered food when included in a food product. The purpose of Proposition 37 was "to create and enforce the fundamental right of the people of California to be fully informed about whether the food they purchase and eat is genetically engineered and not misbranded as natural so that they can choose for themselves whether to purchase and eat such foods."[332] The proposed Right to Know Act would have required disclosure of GE ingredients: "Commencing July 1, 2014, any food offered for retail sale in California is misbranded if it is or may have been entirely or partially produced with genetic engineering and that fact is not disclosed."[333]

---

[324] It is reported that over 20 countries require labeling of GE foods. *See* Debra M. Strauss, *The International Regulation of Genetically Modified Organisms: Importing Caution into the U.S. Food Supply*, 61 FOOD & DRUG L.J. 167, 181 (2006).

[325] It has been suggested that neither the US nor the EU are consumers able to make informed choices. *See* Valery Federici, *Genetically Modified Food and Informed Consumer Choice: Comparing U.S. and E.U. Labeling Laws*, 35 Brook. J. Int'l L. 515, 533 (2010). In more precise terms, it has been noted that "in the United States consumers have a choice between GMO and non-GMO but no information, while in Europe consumers are guaranteed information but with no choice, since only non-GMO products can be found on the shelf." ROBERT PAARLBERG, STARVED FOR SCIENCE: HOW BIOTECHNOLOGY IS BEING KEPT OUT OF AFRICA (2009).

[326] GAIN REPORT: EUROPEAN UNION, BIOTECHNOLOGY, U.S. DEP'T OF AGRIC., FOREIGN AGRIC. SERV. (2003).

[327] *See* David G. Victor & C. Ford Runge, *Farming the Genetic Frontier*, 81 FOREIGN AFF. 107 (2002).

[328] Donna U. Vogt & Mickey Parish, CONG. RESEARCH SERV., RL30198, FOOD BIOTECHNOLOGY IN THE UNITED STATES: SCIENCE, REGULATION, AND ISSUES (January 19, 2001).

[329] *See* Alexander G. Haslberger, *Monitoring and Labeling for Genetically Modified Products*, 287 SCI. 431 (2000).

[330] *See* Associated Press, *No Genetically Altered Corn, Frito-Lay Tells Suppliers*, SACRAMENTO BEE (February 1, 2000).

[331] *See* Sally Lehrman, *GM Backlash Leaves US Farmers Wondering How to Sell Their Crops*, 401 NATURE at 107 (September 9, 1999).

[332] "Proposition 37 Text at Proposed Law," Official CA Voter Information Guide, CA Secretary of State.

[333] California Proposition 37, Mandatory Labeling of Genetically Engineered Food (2012).

Both raw food commodities and processed foods would have required labels with "clear and conspicuous" language specified in the act. Although, early on, the initiative enjoyed widespread success, major investments by the opposition food industry helped turn the tide against the initiative, which ultimately failed by a vote of 53–47 percent. Opponents of the initiative did not object to the consumer's right to know, but instead focused on the alleged complex (or convoluted) requirements of the proposed law,[334] the possibility of higher food prices, and the threat of litigation. Proponents of the failed initiative vowed to introduce the same or similar initiatives elsewhere. Initiatives in other states have been planned and the issue of state labeling has attracted national attention. A number of interested organizations have petitioned the FDA to impose mandatory labeling of GE foods.[335] A federal labeling requirement would avoid the many practical and legal issues that would accompany inconsistent state labeling laws, but FDA's conclusion that GE foods are not materially different from conventional food has boxed the agency into a position of refusal.

In the aftermath of the failed initiative in California, Whole Foods Market announced in March 2012 that by 2018, all products in its US stores would be labeled to indicate whether they contain genetically engineered substances.[336] Whole Foods calls this project the "Non-GMO Verified Program." Under this program, certifiers will be accredited as competent to perform third-party audits on the Non-GMO Project's standards. Wholefoods emphasizes that its non-GMO labeling transparency initiative includes all the products it sells, going far beyond what any of the state initiatives and legislation have proposed. Not only will meat, dairy, egg, and farmed seafood vendors need to verify whether or not animals were fed GMO corn, soy, or alfalfa, the ingredient list of each product will have to be examined for possible GMO-derived items.

[e]   Vermont Mandatory Labeling and Aftermath

Vermont passed a law in 2014 that requires the labeling of food produced entirely or partially from GMOs by July of 2016.[337] Connecticut and Maine have also passed laws mandating GMO labeling, which are conditional on neighboring states passing similar legislation. [338] The Connecticut law was enacted in June 2013, but does not become effective until four other states – including one that boarders Connecticut – adopt similar legislation.[339] The Maine law was enacted in January 2014, and requires four other contiguous states to adopt GMO labeling requirements before it takes effect.[340]

With a defined effective date and no contingencies, Vermont's mandatory GE food labeling law, Act 120, is the most significant development in state law. The stated

---

[334] Proposition 37 would have restricted the use of the word "natural" and related terms on product labels for food that is genetically engineered or processes. The term "processed" was defined broadly to include even non-GE food that is minimally processed. The proposition was also criticized for the exemption categories from Proposition 37. For example, foods sold in restaurants or otherwise prepared and packaged for immediate consumption. *Id.*

[335] *See* Docket FDA-2011-P-0723, U.S. FOOD & DRUG ADMIN.

[336] *See* Whole Food Market Online Blog.

[337] *See* VT. STAT. ANN. tit. 9, § 3043.

[338] An initiative in Washington (Initiative 522) that closely resembled California Proposition 37 failed. Ballot Measure 522 (Wash. 2013).

[339] *See* H.B. 6527, Gen. Assemb. (Conn. 2013).

[340] *See* Maine H.B. 490.

requirement of the act is intended to help consumers "make informed decisions regarding the potential health effects of the food they purchase and consume and by which, if they choose, persons may avoid potential health risks of food produced from genetic engineering."[341] Vermont's law imposes two main requirements: (1) it requires certain manufacturers and retailers to identify raw and processed food sold in Vermont that was produced, either wholly or partly, with genetic engineering; and (2) it prohibits manufacturers from labeling GE foods as "natural," "naturally made," naturally grown," "all natural," or with the term "nature."[342]

The act defines genetic engineering as "a process by which food is produced from an organism or organisms in which the genetic material has been changed" through the application of either vitro nucleic acid techniques or fusion of cells or certain hybridization techniques. The act clarifies that genetic engineering does not include a change of genetic material through the application of traditional breeding techniques, conjugation, fermentation, traditional hybridization, in vitro fertilization, or tissue culture.

The act applies both to raw agricultural commodities and processed foods. Exempt from the act are dietary supplements; medical food; food served in restaurants; food derived from animals that are fed GE food; food containing less than 0.9 percent by weight of materials produced with genetic engineering (same as the EU threshold); food that has been verified by an independent organization as not knowingly or intentionally produced from or commingle with GE food or seed (the manufacturer must obtain a sworn statement from the supplier); and certain alcoholic beverages. A failure to properly label food products containing GMOs may result in civil penalties of $1,000.00 per day per product. Consumers would be entitled to a private right of action to enforce violations of any regulations promulgated.[343]

For packaged and unpackaged GE foods, the label or signage must state "Produced with Genetic Engineering." If the food contains less than the 75% GE material by weight, the label may state: "Partially Produced with Genetic Engineering." If, after reasonable inquiry, the manufacturer does not know whether the food is produced with genetic engineering, the label may state: "May be Produced with Genetic Engineering." For unpackaged processed food, the retailer must post the appropriate statement on a label located on the bin, shelf, or container in which the food is displayed. The manufacturer need not list or identify the GE ingredients or place the term "genetically engineered" immediately before or after any common name of primary product descriptor of a food. The manufacturer who is required to make a statement may "make other disclosures about the food on its package," including that the FDA "does not consider food produced with genetic engineering to be materially different from other foods."

Several food industry trade associations, led by the Grocery Manufacturers Association, have sued the state of Vermont to overturn the new GE food labeling law.[344] The litigation is emblematic of the hurdles for states that wish to mandate labeling of GE foods. Plaintiffs argue that the act is invalid under the First Amendment, the Commerce

---

[341] Id.
[342] Vt. tit. 9, § 3043, *supra* note 337.
[343] Id.
[344] Lisa Baertlein, *U.S. Food Makers Sue to Stop Vermont's GMO Labeling Law*, Reuters (June 12, 2014).

Clause of the US Constitution, and is preempted by federal law. The plaintiffs sought a preliminary injunction to block Vermont's enforcement of the Act in its entirety pending a resolution of the claims at trial. The District Court denied the motion for a preliminary injunction because the plaintiffs failed to show that enforcement of the GE labeling law would cause irreparable harm.[345] There is little doubt that the plaintiffs will appeal the decision. The following pages summarize the main points of the court's 84 page decision.

Preemption – The court dismissed plaintiffs' claim that the Vermont Act is preempted by the FDCA and the NLEA. The court found that there is no express preemption, that compliance with both federal and state regulations is not a physical impossibility, and that Act 120 did not stand as an obstacle to the accomplishment of federal objectives because there are no federal objectives relating to the labeling of GE foods. Not surprisingly, the court found that Act 120 was pre-empted as it would apply to meat subject to the Federal Meat Inspection Act (FMIA) and to poultry subject to the Poultry Products Inspection Act (PPIA), both acts which expressly prohibit states from imposing labeling requirements in addition to, or different from, federal requirements.[346]

First Amendment - The court determined that strict scrutiny did not apply because the act neither compels political speech nor constitutes impermissible viewpoint discrimination. The court found that speech does not become political merely because it "emerged from an allegedly GE-hostile and politically-charged legislative environment." The court also noted that food company's ability to add information to the label reflecting their own views "renders it unlikely that a statute reflects impermissible viewpoint discrimination."

The focus of the court on the First Amendment dealt with whether intermediate scrutiny or the "less exacting scrutiny" of the US Supreme Court's decision in *Zauderer v. Office of Disciplinary Counsel of Supreme Court of Ohio*,[347] reasonable relationship test should apply. As set forth in *Central Hudson*, [348] intermediate scrutiny requires that a statute restricting speech be no more extensive than necessary and must directly advance a substantial government interest. In contrast, *Zauderer's* reasonable relationship test requires only that the disclosure requirement be "reasonably related to the State's interest in preventing consumers." The District Court noted that the Second Circuit had extended *Zauderer* to disclosures intended to "better inform consumers about the products they purchase."[349]

In determining which level of scrutiny to apply, the court found that product labeling requirements are commercial speech even if they effectively discourage the product's consumption. The court also found that because the mandatory labeling requirements contain only factual information, the act does not compel controversial speech. Finally, the court distinguished the case at hand from the Second Circuit's decision in *International Dairy Foods Association v. Amestoy (IDFA)*[350] that a consumer's right to

[345] Grocery Manufacturers Assoc. v. Sorrell, No. 5:14-CV-117 (D. Vt.) (April 27, 2015).

[346] 21 U.S.C. § 607(d); 21 U.S.C. § 457(c). Both laws prohibit "false or misleading" labels but permit labels approved by USDA.

[347] 471 U.S. 626 (1985).

[348] Central Hudson Gas & Elec. Corp. v. Pub. Serv. Comm'n of N.Y., 447 U.S. 557 (1980).

[349] National Elec. Manufs. Assoc. v. Sorrell, 272 F.3d 104, 115 (2d Cir. 2001).

[350] 92 F.3d 67 (2d Cir. 1996).

know did not overcome a commercial speaker's First Amendment right not to speak.[351] In *IDFA*, Vermont conceded that its only purpose in enacting a hormone disclosure requirement for the labeling of food was to satisfy consumer curiosity. In this case, the court found that the state made no such concession about its GE disclosure requirement and had instead asserted numerous rationales, including public health, religious beliefs, the promotion of consumer choice, and environmental concerns. Despite the apparent similarities between promotion of "informed consumer-decision making" and "appeasement of consumer curiosity," the court accepted the State's asserted interest. Thus, the court concluded that *Zauderer's* reasonable relationship test – the lowest level of scrutiny – should apply.

In addressing the application of *Zauderer's* reasonable-relationship standard, the court found that found the State's asserted rationales as substantial and real. The court also determined that Vermont's requirement is reasonably related to the State's substantial interest and is therefore constitutional under *Zauderer*.

"Natural" Restrictions – The court held that the restrictions on the use of the term "natural" were invalid under the First Amendment. The court noted that Act 120 did not define "natural" and rejected the state's arguments that however defined, "natural" cannot apply to GE foods because GE techniques are not "brought about by" or "existing in" nature, but rather are "manmade" and brought about by "purposeful interference" and "artificial means." The court noted that many activities in food production – fertilizing, watering, and pruning of plants – are manmade, purposeful interference, and do not exist in nature. The court also referenced the long history of altering seeds and plants from their natural state through advanced techniques, such as breeding, cross pollination, and grafting. The court concluded that Act 120's restriction on "natural" "subjects GE manufacturers to a standardless restriction that virtually no food company could satisfy.[352]

Concern about differing state GMO labeling laws led to the April 2014 introduction of the Safe and Accurate Food Labeling Act of 2014 (H.R. 4432) in Congress. The act would amend the FDCA to establish premarket notification requirements for a bioengineered organism intended for a food use application. It also would give sole authority to FDA to require mandatory labeling on GE food, if such food is found to be unsafe or materially different from foods produced without GE ingredients. H.R. 4432 would preempt any state laws that mandate the labeling of food that contains or is derived from GE ingredients.

---

[351] In IFDA, a group of dairy manufacturers brought First Amendment and Commerce Clause challenges to a Vermont statute requiring dairy manufacturers to identify products that were, or might have been, derived from dairy cows treated with a synthetic growth hormone used to increase milk production. *Id.* at 67. The Second Circuit held determined that the Vermont legislature had not satisfied the second prong of the Central Hudson test – the state having a substantial interest in regulating the commercial speech. *Id.* at 73. The court held that "consumer curiosity alone is not a strong enough state interest to sustain the compulsion of even an accurate, factual statement." *Id.* at 74. The court reasoned: (1) that if consumer interest alone were enough to compel labeling, there may be no end to the information that manufacturers would be required to disclose; and (2) that consumers interested in such information have the option to exercise their choice by purchasing products from manufacturers who voluntarily reveal the information. *Id.*

[352] *Id.*

[4] Cloning of Food Animals

Just as FDA has resisted efforts to require labeling on food products containing genetically modified plants, the agency has also resisted labeling of food products containing
cloned animals. In guidance and news releases issued by FDA in 2008, the agency made
clear that it would not be requiring any specific labels to identify food from cloned animals or their offspring. FDA states specifically that it "has found no science-based reason
to require labels to distinguish between products from clones and products from conventionally produced animals."[353]

Immediately following the 2008 announcement by the FDA, several states attempted,
but failed, to enact legislation that would regulate cloned foods.[354] The approaches taken
by the various states ranged considerably. For example, Montana proposed legislation
that would have imposed an outright moratorium.[355] New York proposed legislation that
would have required food that did not contain cloned food to be labeled as such (even
though it would seem to be much less costly to require cloned foods to be labeled,
instead of food that was not cloned).[356] California proposed legislation that passed and
was then vetoed would have required clear, prominent labeling indicating food for
humans (including milk) that was derived from an animal clone or its progeny.[357] The
proposed state action was predicated upon the consumer's right to know.[358] In addition
to state attempts to regulate the labeling of cloned animals and their offspring, some
food retailers announced that they would not intend to sell meat or milk from cloned
animals.[359]

In response to the 2008 FDA guidance document, USDA amended the National
Organic Program (NOP) and made two important findings: (1) that cloning "as a production method is incompatible with the Organic Foods Production Act (OFPA) and is
prohibited under the NOP regulations" and (2) that "[a]nimals produced using cloning
technologies are incompatible with Organic Foods Production Act and cannot be considered organic under the National Organics Program regulations."[360] Thus, the "USDA
Organic" label does not permit products bearing that label to contain any cloned animal
products.[361]

---

[353] *Animal Cloning and Food Safety*, U.S Food & Drug Admin. (January 2008).
[354] B. George Walker, *Double Trouble: Competing Federal and State Approaches to Regulating the New Technology of Cloned Animal Foods, and Suggestions for the Future*, 14 U. Fla. J. Tech L. & Pol'y 29 (2009).
[355] H.B. 326, 60th Leg., Reg. Sess. (Mont. 2007).
[356] A07421, 2007 Reg. Sess. (N.Y. 2007).
[357] S.B. 1121, 2008 Sess. (Cal. 2008). S.B. 1121 is similar to legislation that passed both houses of the California legislature in 2007, but was vetoed by Governor Schwarzenegger. *See* S.B. 63, 2007 Sess. (Cal. 2007).
[358] *California State Sen. Migden Unveils Legislation Requiring Labeling of Cloned Food Products*, Food & Drug Law Prof Blog (Apr. 12, 2007) ("People have the right to know if food is organic, if it contains pesti-cides or growth-promoting hormones, or if it's from cloned or natural-bred animals. Consumers certainly don't want to wrestle with moral issues like cloning while they're doing the family grocery shopping.").
[359] *See, e.g., Cloned Meat Q&A*, Whole Foods.
[360] *Q & As, FDA's Final Risk Assessment, Management Plan and Industry Guidance on Animal Clones and their Progeny*, U.S. Dep't of Agric. (2008).
[361] *See id.; see also NOP Statements on Cloning and Organic Livestock Production*, 11-11, USDA Policy Memorandum (January 31, 2011).

[5] *Religious Dietary Labeling (Kosher and Halal)*

  [a] Kosher

  (1) *Background: Popular and Confusing*

Kosher food in America has grown in popularity among Jews and non-Jews. In addition to religious reasons, consumers choose kosher food for reasons related to health, food safety, taste, vegetarianism, lactose intolerance, or to satisfy non-Jewish religious requirements, like halal.[362] The word kosher comes from the Hebrew meaning "fit" or "proper," and refers to foods that are fit for members of the Jewish religion to eat.[363] Technically, kosher food is regarded as kosher food because it adheres to Jewish law.[364] The "vast body of rituals, regulations, and customs surrounding the preparation and consumption of food, collectively known as the practice of kashrut,"[365] are based on only a handful of verses that appear in the Hebrew bible, or Torah.[366]

Among the different branches of Judaism, the meaning of kashrut is not uniform.[20] For example, controversy exists as to whether certain types of cheeses, wines, gelatin, birds, and fish (e.g., sturgeon, swordfish) are kosher. Generally, Orthodox Jews maintain stricter criteria for observing kashrut than do Conservative, Reform, or Reconstructionist Jews. Regardless of their differences, most Jews recognize that the laws of kashrut address three basic types of food: (1) inherently kosher food, such as fruits and vegetables; (2) biblically prohibited food, such as pork and shellfish; and (3) food that becomes kosher once processed, such as meat prepared by a ritual slaughterer (known as a shohet). Beyond merely identifying food as being kosher, the laws of kashrut are also concerned about the manner in which food is stored, cooked, served, and eaten.

Prior to the regulation of kosher, fraud in the labeling of food marked as kosher was common.[367] New Jewish immigrants were taken advantage of by "kosher crooks."[368] As early as 1887, a rabbi in New York City described the state of kosher supervision as the following: "So great is the scandal in this great city, that thousands of honest families who fear and tremble at the thought of straying into one tiny prohibition or sin never

---

[362] It has been suggested that the growing popularity of kosher food is due to the personalization of food production that kosher represents: "[t]he image of a rabbi overseeing production – motivated by a deep religious commitment to the ritual purity of food – diminishes the unease many feel about eating food manufactured in factories using industrially produced ingredients." Timothy d. Lytton, Kosher: Private Regulation in the Age of Industrial Food (2013).

[363] Sue Fishkoff, Kosher Nation 11 (2010).

[364] *Id.*

[365] The modern Hebrew pronunciation is *kashrut*. Some officials in kosher certification agencies and many Orthodox Jews favor the traditional Ashkenazic pronunciation kashrus. Lytton, *supra* note 362 at 7.

[366] The Torah establishes which animals may or may not be eaten, prohibits the consumption of blood, and forbids the cooking of a calf in its mother's milk. *Id.* Because the Torah does not explain how these dietary laws are to be put into practice, rabbis and scholars are charged with figuring out how to implement them. These determinations are compiled in scholarly writings collectively known as the Talmud, or the Oral Law. The Talmud is the "principal guide to Jewish law," and describes both slaughter practices and food preparation. For instance, based on the Torah's commandment forbidding the cooking of a calf in its mother's milk, Talmudic scholars extrapolated the idea that meat and dairy products are not to be combined. Joseph Telushkin, Jewish Literacy 635 (1991). Thus, according to the writings in the Talmud, food items such as cheeseburgers are not kosher.

[367] *See* Lytton, *supra* note 362 at 9–25; Marc Stern, *Kosher Food and the Law*, 39 Judaism 389 (1990).

[368] *Id.* at 389.

suspect that they are eating all kinds of unkosher meat."[369] In 1891, New York passed the first kosher food law. One year later, Massachusetts passed its own similar law.[370] In 1922, New York revised its kosher laws by forbidding the sale of nonkosher meat as kosher. A similar law in California was passed in 1931.[371] Once California and New York set the standard, other states looked to these statutes and drafted their own, essentially using the New York law as a template.[372]

(2) Federal Regulation of Kosher Labeling

In August 1997, FDA's informal agency policy regarding the terms "kosher" and "kosher style" in labeling was codified in the Code of Federal Regulations.[373] Section 101.29 recommended that the term "kosher" be used only on food products that meet certain religious dietary requirements, but does not provide any guidance as to what those requirements actually are. In 1997, as part of the Clinton administration's "Reinventing Government" initiative to streamline government and reduce burdens on regulated industries, FDA revoked Section 101.29 and replaced the kosher labeling provision with a compliance policy guide.[374] The agency noted that a regulation beyond the guidance provision was unnecessary because the use of the terms "kosher," "kosher style," and other terms suggesting that a food has been prepared in accordance with certain religious practices is subject to the general misbranding provisions of Section 403(a).[375] FDA made clear that "[a]side from providing this basic level of protection, FDA has no role in determining what food is kosher."[376]

(3) State Law: Constitutional Challenges

The limited regulatory oversight by the FDA has left the regulation of kosher labeling to where it started: the states. State kosher laws have been challenged in court numerous times. Several arguments against the viability of kosher designation and labeling laws have been advanced. The first argument made is that the term "kosher" is unconstitutionally vague. In 1916, in *People v. Goldberger*, a New York court held that the term kosher was sufficiently comprehensible.[377]

A few years later a variation of the same argument was advanced in *People v. Atlas*, where it was asserted that the New York kosher food law was unconstitutionally vague because the term consisted of centuries of rabbinic debates scattered across thousands of volumes of rabbinic law, which marked differing interpretations of the term and made it impossible for a purveyor to know in advance the legitimacy of the kosher design.[378] The New York Court of Appeals affirmed that the state legislature intended to use kosher as a trade-specific term rather than a term dependent on Jewish law, thus being sufficiently

---

[369] *Id.* (quoting Harold Gastwirt, Fraud, Corruption, and Holiness: The Controversy over the Supervision of Jewish Dietary Practice in New York City 1881–1940 (James Shenton ed.) (1974).

[370] Stern, *supra* note 367 at 391.

[371] Eli Schlossberg, The World of Orthodox Judaism 58 (1996).

[372] *Id.* at 65.

[373] 21 C.F.R. § 101.29.

[374] 62 Fed. Reg. 43071.

[375] *Id.*

[376] *Id.*

[377] *See* People v. Goldberger, 163 N.Y.S. 663 (Ct. Spec. Sess. 1916).

[378] 170 N.Y.S. 834, 835 (Sup. Ct. App. Div. 1918), *aff'd*, 130 N.E. 921 (N.Y. 1921) (per curiam).

well defined to be constitutionally valid.[379] In 1922, the US Supreme Court reiterated the *Atlas* holding in *Hygrade Provisions Co. v. Sherman* and rejected the assertion that kosher was unconstitutionally vague on grounds that the term kosher had a sufficiently well-defined meaning in trade, such that merchants would know what kosher meant.[380] The Court also noted that a violation of the law requires the seller to intentionally misrepresent nonkosher foods as kosher and as long as the vendor had some reasonable basis to believe that what he was selling was kosher, the malevolent intent necessary to prosecute would not be present.[381]

A second constitutional argument that has been advanced against state kosher statutes is that the statute violates the Establishment Clause of the US Constitution and state constitutions. In the early constitutional cases against kosher state statutes, the US Establishment Clause was not evoked because the First Amendment's Establishment Clause was thought to be inapplicable to state laws. Thus, US Supreme Court, in *Hygrade*, upheld the New York kosher statute without considering the Religion Clauses.[382] Now that the Establishment Clause applies to states through the Due Process Clause of the Fourteenth Amendment,[383] if such a case were to present itself to the US Supreme Court, three cases (discussed in the next few pages) invalidating kosher regulations under the Establishment Clause for excessive government entanglement with religion might be instructive.

In *Ran-Dav's County, Inc. v. New Jersey*, the New Jersey Supreme Court in 1992 struck down the state's statute that defined kosher as "prepared in strict compliance with the laws of the Orthodox Jewish religion."[384] The court found that the regulations violated both state and federal constitutional prohibitions against any establishment of religion. The court applied the three-part test articulated by the US Supreme Court in *Lemon v. Kurtzman*, requiring that any statute appearing to advance a particular religious doctrine or practice must: (1) "have a secular legislative purpose"; (2) have a "principal or primary effect that neither advances nor inhibits religion"; and (3) "not foster an excessive government entanglement with religion."[385] Focusing primarily on the third prong, the court found troubling the "close identification" between government and religion. The court noted that by requiring businesses to adhere to particular kosher standards, the statute impermissibly involved the state in the direct supervision of those religious standards.[386] Owing to the high degree of state entanglement in religious matter, the statute was found to violate the state constitution's Establishment Clause.

Subsequent to *Ran-Dav's County*, the Fourth Circuit in *Barghout v. Mayor* invalidated a Baltimore municipal ordinance, which required that all food labeled "kosher" comply "with the orthodox Hebrew religious rules and requirements."[387] The Fourth

---

[379] *Id.* at 835–6.
[380] 266 U.S. 497 (1925).
[381] *Id.* at 501.
[382] *Hygrade*, 266 U.S. at 503. State courts that have heard state constitutional Establishment Clause challenges had upheld the statutes. *See, e.g.*, People v. Goldberger, 163 N.Y.S. 663, 666 (Ct. Spec. Sess. 1916) (recasting the statute as one promoting the free exercise of religion, a right that had been hindered by the widespread fraud in the kosher food industry).
[383] *See* Everson v. Bd. of Educ., 330 U.S. 1 (1947) (holding that the Establishment Clause of the First Amendment applies to the states through the Due Process Clause of the Fourteenth Amendment).
[384] 608 A.2d 1353, 1355 (N.J. 1992).
[385] 403 U.S. 602, 612–13 (1971).
[386] *Ran-Day's County Kosher*, 608 A.2d at 1360–1.
[387] Barghout v. Bureau of Kosher Meat & Food Control, 66 F.3d 1337, 1340 (4th Cir. 1995).

Circuit held that the ordinance fostered an "excessive entanglement of religious and secular authority," and that the ordinance impermissibly advanced the tenets of Orthodox Judaism.[388] Factoring into the court's decision was that the ordinance created a six-person enforcement bureau, three of the members of whom were required to be Orthodox rabbis selected by two Orthodox associations.[389] For the *Barghout* court, such a composition unconstitutionally delegated governmental authority to religious organizations.[390]

In *Commack Self-Service Kosher Meats, Inc. v. Weiss*, the Second Circuit in 2002 applied the *Lemon v. Kurtzman* test to find that the New York kosher fraud statutes violated the Establishment Clause. The court held that the explicit reference in the statute to "orthodox Hebrew religious requirements" constituted an excessive entanglement of the state with religious authorities.[391] The court found that the statute displayed a preference for the Orthodox Hebrew view of dietary requirements over other definitions of kosher, which created an impermissible fusion of government and religion. Citing *Ran Dav's County* and *Barghout*, the Second Circuit, in *Commack*, held that the statute conflicted with the Establishment Clause's prohibition against state actions that advance or inhibit religion.[392]

As a result of the *Commack* decision, the New York Legislature passed the Kosher Act of 2004, which requires sellers and manufacturers who market their food as kosher to so label their foods and to identify people certifying the food as kosher.[393] The main part of the New York 2004 Kosher Act requires: (1) that any food establishment that sells or offers for sale food prepared on its premises, or under its control, that is represented as "kosher" post a kosher certification form on the premises; (2) that any individual packaging a product that is sold or offered for sale as "kosher" or "kosher for passover" label these products as such; (3) that any person selling both kosher and nonkosher products post a window sign indicating that both kosher and nonkosher products are sold there; and (4) that any individual certifying a food product as kosher file his or her identifying information with the Department of Agriculture (and if that individual is certifying non-prepackaged food as kosher, he or she must also file a statement of his or her qualifications for providing such certification).[394]

The new act did not define kosher or authorize state inspectors to determine the kosher nature of the products. Notwithstanding these changes, a challenge was brought in *Commack Self-Service Kosher Meats, Inc. v. Hooker* on grounds that the 2004 Act violated the Establishment and Free Exercise Clauses of the First Amendment.[395] The Second Circuit in affirming the lower court's judgment found that the act does not entangle the New York state with religion because it does not require the state to enforce laws based on religious doctrine – the term "kosher" is not defined in the statute, no religious processes are listed as being required for kosher labeling, and no particular

---

[388] *Id.* at 1344–6.
[389] *Id.* at 1339, 1342.
[390] *Id.* at 1342.
[391] 294 F.3d 415, 423–425 (2d Cir. 2002).
[392] *Id.* at 431.
[393] N.Y.McKinney's Agriculture and Markets Law §§ 201-a to 201-d.
[394] *Id.*
[395] 680 F.3d 194 (2d Cir. 2012).

branch of Judaism is given preference.[396] The court observed: (1) that the 2004 Kosher Act applies to any seller who offers products for sale as kosher, regardless of the seller's religious belief or affiliation and (2) that it impacts all consumers of kosher products, regardless of the consumer's religious belief. Thus, the court concluded that the act is a law of general applicability.

(4) *Private Regulation*

The private regulation of kosher food has been heralded as one of the most successful examples of private-sector regulation in the United States. The shortcomings of public regulation of kosher food – from constitutional limits to inaction by states – have created the need for private kosher certification. It has been argued that reform finally came with the rise of independent kosher certification agencies that established uniform industry standards.[397] These agencies provide educational programming, mentor smaller agencies, and promulgate standards.[398] It has been asserted that the kosher standards have developed in four distinct ways: (1) they sponsor educational activities that promote industry standards; (2) they exert influence through subcontracting to provide local supervision at industrial plants; (3) they use supply chain power to enforce industry standards; and (4) they promote industry standards by their influence over consumers through publications and websites.[399]

(5) *Kosher and GMO*

One issue that has divided some in the Jewish community is whether GE foods must be excluded from the kosher diet. Orthodox and Conservative Jewish legal authorities on the whole reject the notion that GE food ought to be disqualified as kosher. Some Jewish authorities argue that because GE foods directly benefit mankind, their use and development should be encouraged. A prominent kosher certification agency – Organized Kashrut Laboratories – takes the position that GE food may qualify as kosher.[400] The position taken by this agency is that genetic engineering does not affect kosher status because the genetic material is microscopic and therefore insignificant. Some take a different position, holding that the act of genetic engineering involves splicing what is

---

[396] *Id.* at 208–12 The court also found that the 2004 Act was not unconstitutionally vague. The court concluded that a person of ordinary intelligence would know how to comply with the act's labeling requirement. *Id.* at 213.

[397] To date, the kosher certification industry is governed by the five largest agencies: (1) the Kashrut Division of the Union of Orthodox Jewish Congregations of America (OU); (2) Organized Kashrut Laboratories (OK); (3) KOF-K Kosher Supervision (Kof-K); (4) Organized Kashrut Laboratories, Star-K Kosher Certification (Star-K); and (5) the Chicago Rabbinical Council (CRC); collectively known as the "Big Five." *Id.* at 72. More than 80 percent of the kosher food sold in the United States is certified by the Big Five. *Id.* at 74.

[398] *See id.* It has been suggested that the secret to the kosher certification system's success is attributable to sufficient consumer demand for companies to pay for reliable certification, fierce brand competition that counters incentives to cut corners, vigilant and active consumers who scrutinize products for certification mistakes, and interdependence among certifiers who create incentives for interagency oversight. *See* Timothy D. Lytton, *Kosher Certification: A Model of Reliable Food Label Regulation*, FOODUCATE BLOG (Mar. 25, 2013).

[399] LYTTON, *supra* note 362 at 96–7.

[400] SUE FISHKOFF, KOSHER NATION: WHY MORE AND MORE OF AMERICA'S FOOD ANSWERS TO A HIGHER AUTHORITY 155 (2010).

fundamental about living organisms and thus changes the true essence of the organism by modifying its genetic code.

[b] Halal

The consumption of halal food – the Islamic faith's analog to kosher food – is also grow-ing in popularity in the United States. This growth is largely due to the growth of the Islamic community in the United States and the demand in this community for halal food. Halal food is food that is "ritually fit for use" because it has been "sanctioned by Islamic law."[401] The Quran forbids Muslims from eating anything except food defined as being halal; however, Muslims do not agree among themselves as to the definition of halal.[402] For example, a lack of consensus exists among Muslims concerning the use of some dairy and cereal-based products, meat, fish (e.g., catfish), and seafood (e.g., mollusks, crustaceans).[403] Despite these differences of opinion, generally the following categories of food are considered impermissible: pork, blood, intoxicants, carnivorous animals, birds of prey, amphibians, snakes, the meat of dead animals, and food immo-lated unto idols.[404] Moreover, meat and poultry products must be slaughtered only in the name of Allah by a sane and faithful Muslim of proper age.[405]

There are no federal regulations that oversee the labeling of Halal food. Some states, including California, Illinois, Michigan, Minnesota, New Jersey, and Texas, have enacted statutes regulating the use of the term "halal" on food products.[406] These state statutes generally define halal to mean: "prepared under and maintained in strict com-pliance with the laws and customs of the Islamic religion" or "in accordance with Islamic religious requirements."[407] In order to protect consumers from fraud, Muslims, like Jews, have organized various private, self-regulating certification agencies to oversee the pro-duction and sale of halal products.[408]

It does not appear that any of the state statutes facially prefer one school of Islamic thought to another in interpreting what qualifies as halal food. It has been asserted, how-ever, that the laws may have the practical effect of favoring interpretations of halal by mainstream Muslims over members of minority sects.[409] Given a state's need to adjudi-cate these theological differences when determining how to enforce the laws, halal food laws should be subject to the same three-prong *Lemon* test analysis as for kosher food regulations.

[6] *Irradiation*

Notwithstanding that irradiation is a prospective food safety tool, as noted in Chapter 3, opposition to its use has led to regulation on labeling that has helped quash the acceptance

---

[401] See Mohammad Mazhar Hussaini, Islamic Dietary Concepts and Practices 25–6 (1993).

[402] Ahmad H. Sakr, Understanding Halal Foods: Fallacies and Facts 3 (1996).

[403] See Mian N. Riaz & Muhammed M. Chaudry, Halal Food Production 2–3, 4, 164 (2004).

[404] See id. at 9.

[405] Id. at 9–19, 164.

[406] Elijah L. Milne, *Protecting Islam's Garden from the Wilderness: Halal Fraud Statutes and the First Amendment*, 2 J. Food L. & Pol'y 61, 71–2 (2006).

[407] Id.

[408] Id.

[409] Id. at 80–2.

and use by consumers. FDA requires that the labels for irradiated food must contain the words "Treated with Radiation" or "Treated by Irradiation" and display the irradiation logo, the Radura.[410] FDA also requires labeling of packaged, irradiated food sold at retail stores. Irradiated whole foods sold in bulk, such as fruits and vegetables, also must display the label. No label is required for food products, however, that contain irradiated ingredients, such as spices, as long as the entire product has not been irradiated. FDA also does not require labeling of irradiated food served in restaurants.[411] Processors may add additional language to the labels to identify the source of the radiation and purpose of the treatment.

USDA's labeling requirements for irradiated foods mirror those of the FDA except that USDA requires the product's ingredient list to disclose that a particular ingredient has been irradiated, whereas the FDA does not. Irradiated, single-ingredient meat or poultry can be labeled "all," "pure," or "100%." An irradiated product cannot be labeled as natural since irradiation is considered to be more than minimal processing. Nor can irradiated products be labeled "certified Organic."[412]

As previously referenced in this chapter, FDA's treatment of the use of irradiation contrasts with its handling of GE food. Although FDA has determined that "there is no concern about the safety of such treatment," the agency has concluded that labeling of irradiated foods is necessary because such processing is a material fact that must be disclosed to the consumer in order to prevent deception. FDA has determined that irradiation can produce significant changes in certain characteristics of a food, such as the organoleptic (e.g., taste, smell, texture) or holding properties, in a manner that is not obvious to the consumer in the absence of labeling.[413] That is, in the absence of labeling indicating that the food has been irradiated, the implied representation to consumers is that the food has not been processed.[414] The notion is that consumers have a fundamental right to make fully informed decisions about what they eat, and in order to do so, they must receive reliable and accurate information about that food.[415] Mandatory labeling has resulted in many manufacturers staying away from irradiation because of the fear of scaring away customers.

FDA has proposed eliminating the labeling requirement for irradiated foods in cases where the irradiation does not cause a material change in the food – that is, when irradiation does not alter the ordinary characteristics of the food (e.g., nutritional value) – or a material change in the consequences that may result from the use

---

[410] The petals on the logo represent the food; the central circle the radiation source; the broken circle represents the rays from the energy source. *Radiation Protection: Labeling*, U.S. ENVIRONMENTAL PROTECTION AGENCY.

[411] *Id.*

[412] 7 C.F.R. §§ 205.2, 205.105(e) and (f), 205.301(f).

[413] For instance, if bananas are irradiated to delay ripening, this is a material change because it changes a sensory (taste, color, odor, or feel), nutritional, or functional property of the food. Since a consumer has an idea of how long it takes a normal banana to ripen, a consumer who was not aware a banana was irradiated would be unaware of this functional change and not be able to make banana bread in the time frame they had planned. *See* Irradiation in the Production, Processing and Handling of Food, 72 Fed. Reg. at 16293, 16294 (Apr. 4, 2007).

[414] Irradiation in the Production, Processing, and Handling of Food, 21 C.F.R. Part 179, 64 Fed. Reg. 7834 (February 17, 1999).

[415] Letter from Joseph Mendelson III et al., Legal Director, Center for Food Safety, to Div. of Docket Mgmt., FDA, at 2 (July 2, 2007).

of the food.[416] The rule would allow the terms "electronically pasteurized" or "cold pasteurized" to replace the use of "irradiated" on labels. The thought is that eliminating the word "irradiated" (and the Radura symbol) may help create a more vibrant market for irradiated foods. The GAO reports that a change by the FDA would help facilitate change by the USDA to modify its own labeling requirements for irradiated foods (although the department would have to go through its own rulemaking process before making any changes). Consumer groups, according to the GAO, do not support FDA's proposed rules and continue to support labeling requirements for irradiated foods on grounds that the consumer has a right to know if her food has been exposed to radiation, so that she can decide whether or not to purchase the food.[417]

[7] Organic Labeling Regulation

The statutory and regulatory framework governing the regulation of organic food takes a production-based approach by setting forth certain methods and requirements, which organic farmers and handlers must either follow or avoid in order to use the label "organic," as well as its derivative claims. These methods and requirements are explained in Chapter 6 of this treatise. The Organic Foods Production Act of 1990 (OFPA)[418] delegated the labeling of organic product to the USDA.[419] In 2002, the USDA promulgated the National Organic Program (NOP) and its regulations to enforce the OFPA.[420] Under the NOP regulations, there are three layers of organic products:

- **100% organic** – A product sold as "100% organic" must contain (by weight or fluid volume, excluding water and salt) "100%" organically produced ingredients.[421] A "100% organic" product may display on its packaging the certifying agent's logo and the USDA seal.[422]
- **Organic** – A product sold as "organic" must contain (by weight or fluid volume, excluding water and salt) not less than 95 percent organically produced raw or processed agricultural products.[423] An organic product may also display on its packaging the certifying agent's logo and the USDA seal.[424]
- **Made with organic** – A product sold as "made with organic," specifying which ingredients are organic, must contain (by weight or fluid volume, excluding water and salt) at least 70 percent organically produced ingredients. A product made with organic ingredients may display on its packaging the certifying agent's logo, but not the USDA seal.[425] Products that are below 70 percent organic may indicate the organic status of particular ingredients only in the ingredients statement.[426]

---

[416] U.S. Gov't Accountability Office, GAO-10-309R, Federal Oversight of Food Irradiation 5 (2010).

[417] Id. at 6.

[418] Organic Foods Production Act of 1990 (OFPA), Pub. L. No. 101–624, 104 Stat. 3935 (codified as amended 7 U.S.C. §§ 6501–6503).

[419] 7 U.S.C. § 6503.

[420] 7 C.F.R. §§ 205.1–205.669.

[421] Id. § 205.301(a).

[422] Id. § 205.303(a)(1).

[423] Id. § 205.301(b).

[424] Id. § 205.303(a)(1).

[425] Id. § 205.303(c).

[426] Id. § 205.301(d).

[8] *"Natural" Regulation*

[a] Hot Button Issue

In response to the same demand that has driven the market for organic food – the demand for foods derived from natural processes – the descriptor "natural" became ubiquitous in the food supply in the last several years, as numerous food products regulated by FDA and USDA were represented as "Natural," "All Natural," or "100% Natural." Unlike organic food, however, there is not a national uniform program that establishes processes by which a food can be considered natural.

The term "natural" on food labels has been a hot button issue for regulators. Advances in technology, including new uses for additives in food otherwise deemed natural, pose unique issues and challenges to what constitutes natural. The recent emergence of class-action litigation over the claim natural described later in this chapter not only bears light on the definitional aspects of the term, but is also directly relevant to the use of GE food and its comparative composition with conventional food products. In short, the regulation of the claim natural has much to do with the overarching debate of the food system, and the ensuing battle over what constitutes natural food reflects the challenges of food law in adapting to the idiosyncrasies of the modern food system.

It is clear that many consumers are confused about the implications of the term natural appearing on a food label. In one survey, 61 percent of consumers reported that they believed that natural meant that the product had an "absence of genetically modified foods."[427] In the same survey, a majority of respondents believed that a natural label indicates that a product does not contain pesticides, herbicides, growth hormones, artificial flavors, colors, preservatives, GMOs, or antibiotics.[428]

[b] Regulation or the Lack Thereof

(1) *FDA*

The FDA does not regulate the term "natural." In 1978, both the USDA's FSIS and FDA collaborated with the FTC in holding public hearings on matters of mutual concern including whether to formally define the term "natural."[429] The hearings did not lead to formal regulation, though FDA and FSIS later formed informal policies. FDA did note that due to the widespread use of the term and evidence of consumer confusion, the agency would consider producing a formal definition.[430] After receiving an initial set of public comments regarding the proper definition of natural, the FDA backtracked on its resolve, blaming resource limitations and other agency priorities for its ultimate decision in 1983 to terminate rulemaking on the matter. The FDA stated:

> Quite aside from the significant difficulties that would be posed in enforcing this rule, a fundamental problem exists by virtue of the fact that the context in which "natural" is used to determine its meaning. It is unlikely that consumers expect the same thing from a natural apple as they do from natural ice cream ... We should concentrate our

---

[427] *See* Hartman Group, *Where Organic Ends and Natural Begins*, Hartbeat (May 23, 2010).

[428] *See id.*

[429] *See* Food Labeling; Tentative Positions of Agencies, 44 Fed. Reg. 75,990, 76,012 (December 21, 1979).

[430] *See* Food Labeling: Nutrient Content Claims General Principles, Petitions, Definition of Terms, 56 Fed. Reg. 60,421, 60,466 (November 27, 1991).

resources on more serious consumer protection problems than addressing whether a claim that "milk is natural," is deceptive.[431]

FDA again attempted to define "natural" through a rule in the early 1990s,[432] but again ultimately concluded that resource limitations and other agency priorities precluded rulemaking. FDA stated that it would "maintain its policy regarding the use of the term 'natural' as meaning that nothing artificial or synthetic (including all color additives regardless of source) has been included in, or has been added to, an ingredient that would not normally be expected in food."[433] FDA does not define "artificial" or "synthetic ingredients" or elucidate anymore on this guidance, so the policy does little to inform what natural actually means.

In 2006, the Sugar Association filed a citizen's petition with FDA for an official definition, via rule or regulation, for the term "natural."[434] The Sugar Association specifically asked FDA to base its definition on that adopted by the USDA Food Standards and Labeling Policy Book. Seizing on the definition's requirement that the product be no more than "minimally processed," the Sugar Association asserted that "preservation of the molecular structure inherent in the raw material is an obligatory requirement before a food or beverage ingredient can be labeled as 'natural.'"[435] Although the Sugar Association's petition never mentioned corn syrup by name, under the strictures of the Sugar Association's proposed interpretation regarding minimal processing of natural foods, high-fructose corn syrup (HFCS) could not be considered a natural ingredient.[436] A year later, the Sara Lee Corporation filed a citizen's petition requesting that FDA work together with the FSIS to create a uniform policy for the use of the term natural.[437] Strongly advocating that the definition be prescribed by policy rather than regulation, Sara Lee requested a uniform definition encompassing the use of natural preservatives.[438]

The petitions from the Sugar Association and Sara Lee did not move FDA to action, neither by rulemaking nor by policy amendment. In January 2008, FDA representatives announced that the agency intended to leave "natural" formally undefined for the time being as more pressing concerns and limited resources had directed its attention to other matters.[439] As such, the FDA said it would not restrict the use of the term "natural" other than

---

[431] Termination of Proposed Trade Regulation; Rule on Food Advertising, 48 Fed. Reg. 23,270, 23,270 (May 24, 1983).

[432] FDA, Food Labeling: Nutrient Content Claims, General Principles, Petitions, Definition of Terms, 56 Fed. Reg. 60,421, 60,466 (November 27, 1991).

[433] FDA, Food Labeling: Nutrient Content Claims, General Principles, Petitions, Definition of Terms; Definitions of Nutrient Content Claims for the Fat, Fatty Acid, and Cholesterol Content of Food, 58 Fed. Reg. 2302, 2407 (January 6, 1993).

[434] Sugar Association Petition (February 28, 2006) (on file with author).

[435] *Id.* at 5.

[436] *Id.* at 5–7.

[437] *Citizen Petition Requesting FDA to Develop Requirements for the Use of the Term "Natural,"* Sara Lee Corp. (Apr. 9, 2007) (on file with author). Unlike in the case of the Sugar Association petition, Sarah Lee was not motivated by the desire to exclude corn syrup from consideration as a "natural" ingredient. *Id.*

[438] Letter of Robert G. Reinhard, Director of Food Safety/Regulatory for the Sarah Lee Corporation to FDA (Apr. 9, 2007).

[439] Lorraine Heller, *"Natural" Will Remain Undefined, Says FDA,* Food Navigator-USA (January 4, 2008) (noting that, in an interview with the publication, "Geraldine June from FDA's Food Labeling and Standards department said the agency had not put the 'natural' issue on its priority list because there is not enough evidence that the current situation means consumers are being misled").

on products containing added colors, synthetic substances, and flavors. Whether HFCS could be considered natural depended on the manner in which the corn syrup was made – products containing HFCS could carry a "natural" label when synthetic fixing agents were not in contact with the product during manufacturing. The agency provided the following, highly technical, explanation as to when the use of HFCS could be considered natural:

> [I]t is our understanding that the enzyme used to make HFCS is fixed to a column by the use of a synthetic fixing agent, gulataraldehyde. Any unreacted glutaraldehyde is removed by washing the column prior to the addition of the high dextrose equivalent corn starch hydrolysate, which undergoes enzymatic reaction to produce HFCS. Because the glutaraldehyde does not come into contact with the high dextrose equivalent corn starch hydrolysate, it would not be considered to be included in or added to the HFCS. Therefore, we would not object to the use of the term "natural" on a product containing the HFCS.[440]

This statement by FDA was immediately lauded by the Corn Refiners Association[441] and criticized by the Sugar Association.[442] However misleading or not, FDA has given no indication that it intends to convert its policy into a rule, or to alter its stated policy in any manner.

As noted previously in this chapter, FDA experienced pressure from the California GMO Initiative (Proposition 37), which included a provision (in addition to the mandatory labeling for GE food) that arguably would restrict the use of the "natural" label in the event the food had been processed.[443] The term, however, was very ambiguous, one implication being that it would undoubtedly lead to litigation efforts to clarify the vague initiative. This looming implication created some hope that FDA would define the term "natural" in order to preempt the prospective California law. The initiative failed, however, and FDA did not oblige those who hoped for a definition.

The failure to provide regulatory definitions or even formal guidance on this issue has undoubtedly fostered the current climate of active litigation in this area. The Grocery Manufacturers Association reported that as of December 2013, there were at least sixty-five class-action lawsuits involving "natural" label claims pending around the United States.[444] These suits have challenged the use of the term "natural" on labels of products containing HFCS, citric acid, and GMOs.[445]

---

[440] *Id.* FDA noted that the HFCS would not be natural if a synthetic substance or fixing agent was included in the product, or if the acids used to obtain the hydrolysate did not fit within the FDA's definition of "natural." *Id.*

[441] *Corn Refiners Welcome FDA Clarification;* WAREHOUSES FROZEN FOOD DIGEST, October 1, 2008, at 25 (citing Corn Refiners Association President Audrae Erickson as stating that "[u]pon careful review of the manufacturing process for High Fructose Corn Syrup, the FDA found that HFCS can be labeled natural.")

[442] The Sugar Association stated that it had been "deeply disappointed" with FDA's inaction, and the time had come for FDA to clearly "define 'natural' and protect consumers from misleading claims." Jane Hoback, *FDA Refuses to Define Natural,* NATURAL FOODS MERCHANDISER 29, 2 (January 22, 2008), at 9 (noting that the Sugar Association's President and CEO expressed that the Sugar Association was "deeply disappointed" in FDA's reversal).

[443] *See* California Proposition 37 Text, *supra,* note 333.

[444] Stephanie Strom, *Group Seeks Special Label for Food: "Natural,"* N.Y. TIMES (December 19, 2013).

[445] *See* Von Koenig v. Snapple Beverage Corp., 713 F. Supp. 2d 1066, 1070 (E.D. Cal. 2010) (HFCS); Ries v. Hornell Brewing Co., No. 5:10-CV-01139-PVT (N.D. Cal. Mar. 17, 2010) (citric acid); Gengo v. Frito-Lay N. Am., Inc., No. 2:11-CV-10322-SVW-FMO (C.D. Cal. filed December 14, 2011) (GMOs).

Despite several requests by courts, the FDA has declined to define "natural."[446] The FDA has made clear that if it were to amend its "natural" labeling policy, it would not do so in response to private litigation. The agency has stated that it would do so publically with a formal rulemaking process or guidance.[447] It is highly unlikely that the FDA will define "natural" under any circumstances different from its formal notice-and-comment rulemaking process. The Third Circuit held that the FDA's definition of "natural" in its guidance statement does not have the force of law.[448] The court's conclusion rests on four grounds: (1) the FDA did not undertake a formal process or receive public input on the term; (2) the FDA admitted in 1993 that it was not officially defining the term because there were still many facets that the agency needed to consider before making a definition; (3) the FDA's enforcement letters to food and beverage manufacturers telling them to remove "natural" labels were insufficient to accord the policy the weight of federal law; and (4) the FDA reissued the preexisting "natural" policy after soliciting public comments, which proves that the agency did not take any of the comments they received into account.[449]

(2) USDA

USDA guidance in this area is more nuanced than the FDA's definition, but is still not definitive. USDA's agency, FSIS, has issued a policy governing the use of "natural" claims that is set forth in the agency's *Standards and Labeling Policy Book*.[450] This standard, which was first established in 1982, stipulates that a natural claim may be used in the labeling of meat and poultry products, provided that the product does not contain any artificial flavor or flavoring, coloring ingredient, or chemical preservative (as defined in 21 CFR 101.22), or any other artificial or synthetic ingredient; and the product and its ingredients are not more than minimally processed. Minimally processed can include the following: smoking, roasting, freezing, drying, and fermenting, as well as separation, such as grinding meat, separating eggs, and pressing fruit, but does not include processing, such as solvent extraction, acid hydrolysis, and chemical bleaching.[451]

In August 2005, FSIS modified Policy Memo 055 by adding the statement that "[s]ugar, sodium lactate (from a corn source), natural flavorings from oleoresins or extractives are acceptable for 'all natural' claims." The new policy also referred to the National Organic Program's (NOP) National List of Allowed and Prohibited Substances for a list of acceptable ingredients allowed for "all natural" claims.[452] It should be noted that FSIS's issuance of Policy Memo 055 was due in part to FTC's attempt to regulate "natural" claims in the 1970s.[453] The agency terminated its rulemaking in 1983, concluding that "natural"

---

[446] *See, e.g.,* Barnes v. Campbell Soup Co., No. C-12-05185-JSW, 2013 WL 5530017 (N.D. Cal. 2013).

[447] *See* Letter from Leslie Kux, Assistant Comm'r for Policy, Food & Drug Admin. to Hon. Yvonne Gonzalez Rogers, U.S. Dist. Court for the N. Dist. Cal. et al. 3 (January 6, 2014).

[448] *See* Holk v. Snapple Beverage Corp., 575 F.3d 329, 341–42 (3d Cir. 2009). The Third Circuit is the only circuit court to address the force of the FDA's "natural" definition.

[449] *See id.* at 340–41.

[450] *See Food Safety Information:* Meat and Poultry Labeling Terms, U.S. Dep't of Agric, Food Safety Inspection Serv.

[451] *See id.*; 21 C.F.R. § 101.22.

[452] Food Standards and Labeling Policy Book, *supra*, note 136.

[453] Proposed Trade Regulation Rule, 39 Fed. Reg. 39,842 (November 11, 1974); Proposed Trade Regulation Rule, 40 Fed. Reg. 23,086 (May 28, 1975); Final Notice Regarding Proposed Trade Regulation Rule, 41 Fed. Reg. 8,980 (Mar. 2, 1976).

claims would continue to be evaluated on a case-by-case basis.[454] When FTC terminated its rulemaking, it agreed to permit a food to be represented as natural if it had not undergone more than minimal processing after harvest or slaughter and contained no artificial flavor, color additive, chemical preservative, or other artificial or synthetic ingredients.[455]

FSIS has considered issuing proposed rules or guidelines for the use of the "natural" label. In 2006, Hormel Foods filed a citizen petition, requesting that the agency undertake rulemaking to define the term natural.[456] In December 2006, FSIS responded by holding a public meeting to solicit comments on the definition of "natural" for the labeling of poultry and meat products.[457] FSIS specifically sought to determine: (1) whether a definition of "natural" should incorporate a "minimally processed" criterion; (2) the implications and/or conflicts arising from current and new food processing methods and technologies (e.g., high-pressure processing, multipurpose ingredients, and modified atmosphere packaging); (3) consumer research on views, perceptions, and beliefs about the meaning of terms such as "natural," "minimal processing," "artificial," "synthetic," and "preservatives"; and (4) whether food safety and public health interests outweigh any conflict in a definition of "natural."[458] FSIS also considered whether the "minimally processed" criterion remained viable in an age of advanced food processing technologies diverging widely by food product and industry, and whether multifunctional ingredients could be considered natural when used not only for taste, but also for preservative or antimicrobial purposes to enhance food safety.[459]

The comments given at the meeting covered a wide spectrum of subjects and opinions. Some speakers suggested that the definition of "natural" should take into account consumer expectations, which could be discerned through a USDA study on consumer perceptions. An industry representative proposed a system, under which natural claims would mimic the distinctions in organic products by attaching different descriptors to various products on the basis of differentiating levels of naturalness.[460]

Although the momentum and interest in the topic appeared to be headed toward the creation of a USDA rule defining "natural," no such rule has emerged. Nevertheless, the burdens facing producers of USDA-regulated products, due to this uncertainty, are less significant than those faced by producers of FDA-regulated products – USDA requires producers to get premarket approval for labeling.[461] It may be that USDA/FSIS evolves on this issue, especially as public interest groups remain involved.[462]

---

[454] Termination of Proposed Trade Regulation; Rule on Food Advertising, 48 Fed. Reg. 23,270 (May 24, 1983).

[455] 48 Fed. Reg. 23270 (May 24, 1983).

[456] *See* Petition for the Issuance of a Rule Regarding Natural Label Claims, Hormel Foods (October 9, 2006).

[457] *See* Product Labeling: Definition of the Term "Natural," 71 Fed. Reg. 70,503 (December 5, 2006).

[458] *Food & Drug E-Alert, FSIS Holds Public Meeting on the Definition of the Term "Natural,"* COVINGTON & BURLING (December 14, 2006).

[459] Public Meeting, Product Labeling: Definition of the Term "Natural," U.S. DEP'T OF AGRIC., FOOD SAFETY INSPECTION SERVICE 25–6 (December 12, 2006).

[460] *Id.* at 91 (statement of Tim Sontag, representing Wixom, Inc., a spice, seasoning, and flavoring manufacturer).

[461] Carolyn Fisher & Ricardo Carvajal, *What is Natural?*, FOOD TECH., November 2008, at 29–30.

[462] In 2010, FSIS "agreed to take another look at its policy after some producers, politicians and health advocates noted that about one-third of chicken sold in the U.S. was injected with additives that could represent up to 15 percent of the meat's weight, doubling or tripling its sodium content." *Disagreement Over "Natural" Label Prompts Reconsideration*, Ag and Food Law Blog, American Agricultural Law Association (July 30, 2010).

As matters stand, manufacturers must explain on the label, near the natural claim, that the product is considered natural because "it contains no artificial ingredients, and is minimally processed." Policy Memo 055 allows for a "natural" label claim on a case-by-case basis if the proposed ingredient "would not significantly change the character of the product to the point where it could no longer be considered a natural product." Manufacturers must, however, conspicuously identify the excepted ingredient on the label.[463] Where a product may not be labeled "natural," in some cases it may still bear the statement "all natural" ingredients. For example, a turkey roast cannot be called a natural product if it contains beet coloring, but it can still bear the statement "all natural ingredients."[464]

[9] Animal Raising Claims

[a] FSIS Evaluation

Animal production methods often thought by consumers to be included in the term "natural" as well as additional indications of quality or product characteristics are commonly referred to as "animal raising claims." Such claims must also be approved for use on labels and in marketing materials through USDA's FSIS. In order to facilitate this process and create some standardization on the usage of claims, the USDA's Agricultural Marketing Service (AMS) has developed proposed minimum requirements for marketing claims related to livestock and meat production.[465] These requirements are used by FSIS in its labeling approval process.

As part of its prior label approval process, FSIS evaluates labels that contain animal raising claims by reviewing testimonials, affidavits, animal production protocols, and other relevant documentation provided by animal producers to ensure that an animal raising claim in addition to comporting with AMS standards is truthful and not misleading. In addition to producer testimonials and affidavits, enterprises may also submit certifications from certifying entities to support animal raising claims. The following section provides a summary of animal claims that illustrate the requirements developed by AMS, as well as some of the issues that affect FSIS's approval process.

[b] Credence Attributes

(1) Naturally Raised

Distinguishable from the term "natural" on USDA-governed finished meat and poultry processes is the "naturally raised" marketing claim regarding livestock and meat set into a standard via guidance by AMS.[466] Under the AMS standard, livestock that "have been raised entirely without growth promotants, antibiotics (except for ionophores used as coccidiostats for parasite control), and have never been fed animal (mammalian, avian, or aquatic) by-products derived from the slaughter/harvest processes" can be certified

---

[463] *Id.*
[464] USDA, Public Meeting, Product Labeling, *supra* note 459.
[465] 67 Fed. Reg. 79552-02, 79553 (December 30, 2002).
[466] United States Standards for Livestock and Meat Marketing Claims, Naturally Raised Claim for Livestock and the Meat and Meat Products Derived from Such Livestock, 74 Fed. Reg. 3541, 3541 (January 21, 2009).

as "naturally raised."[467] Under this standard, an animal that has come from a cloned or genetically engineered stock may be labeled as "naturally raised."[468]

(2) *Raised without Antibiotics*

"No antibiotics added," "raised without antibiotics," and similar claims are approved for producers who demonstrate that their animals have been raised without antibiotics. "Antibiotic free" labeling claims are not allowed due to the fact that antibiotic-residue testing technology cannot verify that no antibiotics were ever administered.[469] FSIS does not test for the presence of antibiotic residue to verify labeling and other marketing claims. When antibiotic labeling claims are submitted for approval, they must be supported by food formulations, pharmaceutical invoices, or other appropriate documentation verifying that animals have not received antibiotics in feed or water, and whether they have been treated for illness. Procedures for handling sick animals must be documented.

An interesting case that illustrates the regulatory and competitive tensions involved in making claims for consumers, such as "raised without antibiotics," includes a major marketing campaign by Tyson Foods in June 2007 to market a new line of fresh poultry labeled: "raised without antibiotics."[470] The press release for the campaign stated that market research determined that "91% of consumers agree it's important to have fresh chicken produced and labeled 'raised without antibiotics.'"[471] Although FSIS initially approved Tyson's label based on submissions provided by the company, an issue arose as to whether ionosphores, which Tyson used in its chicken feed, were technically an antibiotic. USDA rescinded its approval for the label[472] and then approved the label "raised without antibiotics that impact antibiotic resistance in humans."[473]

Plaintiff Sanderson Farms, Inc., and Perdue Farms Inc., competitors to Tyson in the poultry sector, sued Tyson under Section 1125(a) of the Lanham Act for false advertising, claiming that Tyson's extensive "raised without antibiotics" advertising campaign was "false and misleading."[474] Plaintiffs alleged that Tyson's advertisements containing the claims "Raised without Antibiotics" and "Raised without Antibiotics that impact antibiotic resistance in humans" were false and that they misled consumers.[475] Plaintiffs specifically alleged that Tyson used ionophores in its chicken feed and that ionophores are antibiotics.[476] Tyson moved to dismiss arguing in part that the USDA's approval of

---

[467] *Id.* at 3534

[468] *See Consumers Union and Food & Water Watch Say New USDA Standard for So-Called Naturally-Raised Meat Sanctions Unnatural Practices*, CONSUMERS UNION (January 16, 2009).

[469] United States Standards for Livestock and Meat Marketing Claims, 67 Fed. Reg. 79,552, 79,554 (December 30, 2002).

[470] Press Release, Tyson Food Service, All Tyson(r) Brand Fresh Chicken to be "Raised without Antibiotics"; Products Available to Mainstream Consumers at an Affordable Price (June 19, 2007).

[471] *Id.*

[472] Press Release, Tyson Food Service, Tyson Statement on FSIS Letter on Raised Without Antibiotics Chicken Label (June 3, 2008).

[473] Press Release, Tyson Food Service, Tyson to Use New Label for Raised Without Antibiotics Chicken; Company & USDA Agree to More Informative Wording (December 27, 2007).

[474] *See* Sanderson Farms, Inc. v. Tyson Foods, Inc., 549 F. Supp. 2d 708, 709–10 (D. Md. 2008).

[475] *Id.* at 710.

[476] *Id.* at 711.

its label insulated it from the advertising challenge.[477] The district court rejected Tyson's motion, holding that USDA label approval was not a defense to the Lanham Act claim for false advertising, nor did it shield Tyson in any way from the advertising claim.[478]

As a result of the litigation, however, it was revealed that in addition to the disclosed use of ionophores, Tyson used the antibiotic Gentamicin on its eggs two or three days before they hatched.[479] A preliminary injunction was issued against Tyson's advertisements.[480] The case was subsequently settled. However, upon learning of the Gentamicin, the FSIS notified Tyson that it was rescinding its labeling authority and said that they must stop using the qualified claim.[481] Tyson objected, claiming that its administration of the antibiotic prior to hatch did not fall within the notion of "raising" a chicken. The FSIS disagreed and maintained its ruling.[482]

(3) Grass Fed

In 2002, AMS proposed standards for several livestock and meat marketing claims.[483] One proposed standard that engendered significant public comment involved "grass fed" claims. The evolution of the AMS standards for the making of a grass fed claim illustrates the complexities involved in the governance process. For most consumers, a grass-fed claim suggests that animals are raised on grass or green or range pasture. Grass feeding typically results in meat products containing lower levels of external and internal fat (including marbling) than grain-fed livestock products.[484] Consumers typically regard grass-fed meat products to be more environmentally friendly, healthier (due to higher levels of Omega-3 fatty acids), and better tasting than grain-raised meat products.[485] The 2002 proposal required grass (or grass equivalents such as green or range pasture or forage) to comprise at least 80 percent of the animal's primary energy source throughout its life cycle. To ensure the animal's health, the proposal allowed limited supplementation of grains or other non-grass-based feed during adverse environmental conditions.[486]

In 2006, as a result of comments to the 2002 proposal, AMS significantly revised its proposed grass fed labeling standards and requested additional feedback.[487] The revised standards addressed a variety of points of contention in the 2002 proposal, including grass dietary requirements, the use of stored forages, and animal confinement.[488] The

---

[477] Id. at 713.

[478] Id. at 720.

[479] Sanderson Farms v. Tyson Foods, 547 F. Supp. 2d 491, 494 (D. Md. 2008)

[480] Id. at 509

[481] Press Release, USDA, Statement by Under Secretary for Food Safety Dr. Richard Raymond Regarding the Tyson Foods, Inc. Raised without Antibiotics Label Claim Withdrawal (June 3, 2008).

[482] See id.

[483] See 67 Fed. Reg. at 79554–56 (December 30, 2002). Categories of proposed claims and standards relating to live animal production included: antibiotic claims, breed claims, free range claims, geographic location claims, grain fed claims, grass fed claims, hormone claims, livestock identification claims, pre-conditioning claims, and vitamin E claims. Id. at 79554–5. Claims related to meat product characteristics included: aged meat claims, electrical stimulation claims, and tenderness claims. Id. at 79555–6.

[484] Id.

[485] See id. at 79533; Marian Burros, New Rules Set for Meat Sold as Grass Fed, N.Y. TIMES, October 19, 2007, at A22.

[486] See 67 Fed. Reg. at 79555 (December 30, 2002).

[487] United States Standard for Livestock and Meat Marketing Claim, Grass (Forage) Fed Claim, 71 Fed. Reg. 27662, 27663 (May 12, 2006).

[488] See id. at 27663–5.

2006 proposal sought to increase the required grass and forage feed percentage from 80 percent to 99 percent of the total energy source for the lifetime of the animal.[489] AMS determined that the 99 percent standard would allow for the inadvertent exposure to nonforage feedstuffs and supplementation of diets for animal welfare purposes during periods of adverse environmental or physical conditions.[490]

AMS also considered, but rejected, a proposal to limit grass and forage consumption to only nonharvested grasses and to restrict the use of stockpiled or stored forage.[491] Supporters of this requirement argued that consumers would expect grass-fed livestock to be free range and not fed in confinement.[492] AMS acknowledged the "synergistic nature to grass feeding and free range conditions,"[493] but due to the diverse grass-feeding regimes across the nation,[494] the agency found this limitation impractical and unduly restrictive.[495]

In 2007, AMS issued a final voluntary standard for grass-fed marketing claims.[496] The grass fed standard states that grass or forage shall be the feed source consumed for the lifetime of the ruminant animal, with the exception of milk consumed prior to weaning. The standard also provides that the diet shall be derived solely from forage and animals cannot be fed grain or grain by-products and must have continuous access to pasture during the growing season. The change from 99 percent to 100 percent primarily resulted from the recognition that calculating and verifying the 99 percent standard was unnecessarily difficult, especially considering that there is little practical difference between the two amounts.[497] The final standard also allows selected vitamin supplements and minerals in order to adjust for possible diet deficiencies.[498] Under the standard, producers must obtain an AMS evaluation prior to using the grass-fed label or marketing a product as grass fed.[499]

(4) No Hormones Administered

Since all plants and animals produce hormones, a "hormone free" meat labeling claim is not allowed. However, FSIS may approve the phrase "no hormones administered" for the labeling of beef products if sufficient documentation is provided to the agency

---

[489] USDA Public Meeting Product Labeling, *supra*, note 459 at 27664.
[490] *Id.* Exceptions include milk consumed prior to weaning as well as routine mineral and vitamin supplementation. *Id.* at 27665.
[491] *Id.* at 27664.
[492] *Id.*
[493] "Granted, most grass (forage) fed livestock will also qualify as free range livestock (not fed in confinement); however, not all free range livestock will receive their entire energy source from grass or forage." *Id.*
[494] For example, in southern states with adequate rainfall and a temperate climate, year-round range feeding may be a practical alternative. In contrast, in western states with substantial dry periods and in northern states with significant snow or ice, continuous range feeding is not sustainable. *Id.* at 27664.
[495] *Id.*
[496] United States Standards for Livestock and Meat Marketing Claims, Grass (Forage) Fed Claim for Ruminant Livestock and the Meat Products Derived From Such Livestock, 72 Fed. Reg. 58,631, 58,637 (October 16, 2007).
[497] *Id.*
[498] *Id.* at 58, 634–5.
[499] Evaluation procedures are documented in the USDA's Quality Systems Verification Programs (QSVP), a preexisting set of programs designed to provide independent verification that an independent third party verifies marketing claims. *Quality Systems Verification Programs General Policies and Procedures*, U.S. DEP'T OF AGRIC. (2010).

showing no hormones have been used in raising the animals.[500] Because hormones are expressly not allowed in raising poultry or pigs, FSIS does not allow the claims "no hormones administered" or "no hormones added" on the labels of poultry or pork products unless they are followed by a statement that says, "Federal regulations prohibit the use of hormones."[501] FSIS does not test for the presence of hormones when verifying labeling claims. When hormone labeling claims are submitted for approval, they must be supported by the appropriate documentation verifying that animals have not received hormones in any form.

(5) Cage Free, Free Range, Free Roaming, Pasture Raised

AMS defines "cage free" as confinement of laying hens in a building, room, or open area with unlimited access to food and water, and with freedom to roam within these areas.[502] AMS verifies the "cage free" label by a visual inspection of the producer's facility. If a company has both "cage free" and caged hens, then AMS will also review the producer's written protocols for identifying and segregating eggs laid by "cage free" hens from those laid by caged hens.

"Free range," as it applies to eggs certified under the USDA NOP, means that the hens must be allowed access to the outdoors. However, the regulations also state that producers may confine animals temporarily for a number of reasons, including: "(1) Inclement weather; (2) conditions under which the health, safety or well being of the animal could be jeopardized; or (3) risk to soil or water quality."[503] There are also no stipulations as to a required number or size of exits, size of the outdoor area, or flock density or size. For nonorganic eggs, no term other than "cage free" is approved by the agency. Labeling claims for eggs not inspected by USDA may fall under state regulations, which vary widely, or they may not be regulated at all. To obtain approval for labels bearing the claim "free range" or "free roaming," poultry producers must provide a brief description of the birds' housing conditions when the label is submitted to the FSIS Labeling and Consumer Protection Staff for approval. The written description of the housing conditions is reviewed to ensure the birds have "continuous free access to the outdoors for a significant portion of their lives." Under the NOP, which is administered by USDA-AMS, animals raised under certified organic standards are automatically considered to be "free range" by default, as the program requires animals have access to the outdoors.

For livestock, FSIS requires that in order to obtain label approval for labels bearing claims such as "Free Roaming," "Pasture Raised," "Pasture Grown," and "Meadow Raised," it must also be shown that the livestock from which the products are derived had continuous free access to the out-of-doors area for a significant portion of their lives.[504] What is meant by terms, such as "significant portion of the animals' lives" and "outdoors," however, is not clear.

---

[500] *Meat and Poultry Labeling Terms*, U.S. Dep't of Agric., Food Safety Inspection Service.

[501] *Id.*

[502] Farm Sanctuary, The Truth Behind the Labels: Farm Animal Welfare Standards and Labeling Practices 21 (Apr. 2009).

[503] 7 C.F.R. § 205.239(b).

[504] USDA, *Meat and Poultry Labeling Terms*, *supra* note 500.

(6) *Humanely Raised*

"Humanely raised" is not a USDA-approved term. Any such claim on meat or poultry products must include an explanation of what is meant by the term. Documentation substantiating the claim must be submitted to the FSIS, and in some cases to AMS. USDA accepts third-party claims regarding humanely raised products after documentation about the independent certification program has been submitted and reviewed by FSIS and AMS staffs. Concerns and complaints about third-party certification programs received by USDA are referred to the certifying organization and any recourse taken is at the discretion of the certifier.

[10] *Country-of-Origin Labeling (COOL)*

[a] Three Regulatory Frameworks

Country-of-origin labeling (COOL) has been hotly contested at the national and international level. Navigating through the regulatory landscape is no simple task. The regulation of COOL reflects the challenges in balancing strong domestic preferences with the international free food trade obligations under the WTO regime.

There are three basic regulatory frameworks for COOL: (1) the origin labeling requirements that have been in place since the Tariff Act of 1930; (2) the origin marking requirements under FMIA and PPIA on imported containers of meat and poultry products; and, most importantly, (3) the origin labeling requirements first passed in the 2002 Farm Bill.

(1) *Tariff Act of 1930*

The Tariff Act of 1930 required every imported item to be conspicuously and indelibly marked in English to indicate its country of origin to the ultimate purchaser.[505] This means that articles arriving at the US border in retail-ready packaging must display the origin identification. The ultimate purchaser is the last person in the United States who will receive the product in the form in which it was imported.[506] Generally, consumers will see the label only if the imported goods arrive at the border in retail-ready packaging.

The 1930 provision exempts articles destined for US processors, which are slated to undergo substantial transformation.[507] If a manufacturer or processor receives the product and substantially transforms it, no COOL labeling is required, even though a new or different product is not produced. Only a minor process that leaves the identity of the imported product intact will result in a consumer being the ultimate consumer. A hot dog, for example, has likely undergone significant processing, resulting in a change of character (examples of significant processing include cooking, curing, smoking, and restructuring), or has been combined with another food component and thus does not require COOL labeling, even if its components were imported into the United States. One example of a meat item that must be labeled with the

---

[505] 19 U.S.C. § 1304. The Act requires that "[E]very article of foreign origin (or its container …) imported into the United States shall be marked in a conspicuous place as legibly, indelibly, and permanently as the nature of the article (or container) will permit."

[506] *Id.*

[507] *Id.*

country-of-origin information, because it is imported in consumer-ready packaging, is marinated lamb loins.[508]

Also exempted from the 1930 COOL provisions are products on the "J List," thus named because it is found in §1304(a)(3)(J) of the act. The act authorizes the secretary of the treasury to exempt certain classes of items. The J List includes natural products, such as vegetables, fruits, nuts, berries, and live or dead animals, fish, and birds. While this list exempts such individual items from the labeling requirements, it does still require their immediate containers to have COOL labels. The marking should make clear the country of origin with an appropriate phrase such as "Contents made in …" or "Contents product of …" where the blank is filled in with the English name of the country of origin.[509]

(2) *Meat and Poultry Products Inspection Acts*

FSIS is required to ensure the safety and proper labeling of most meat and poultry products, including imports, under FMIA and PPIA. As noted in the food safety chapter of this treatise, only manufacturing plants in countries certified by the USDA as having inspection systems equivalent to those of the United States are eligible to export products to the United States. FMIA and PPIA require that country of origin appear in English on the immediate containers of all meat and poultry products entering the United States.[510] Specifically, all individual, retail-ready packages of imported meat products (i.e., canned hams) must bear country-of-origin markings. Imported bulk products, such as carcasses or large containers of meat or poultry destined for US plants for further processing also have to bear country-of-origin marks. However, once these nonretail items have entered the country, they are deemed to be domestic products and are no longer subject to the labeling. Because Customs, under the Tariff Act of 1930, generally requires that imports undergo more extensive changes (i.e., "substantial transformation") than required by the FSIS to avoid the need for labeling – there is a potential for conflict between the two requirements. It is clear, however, that under both the Tariff Act of 1930 and the FMIA and PPIA provisions, laws that require COOL labeling are largely limited to imported food products already packaged for consumers.

With respect to foods regulated by FDA, the FDCA does not expressly require COOL. A packaged food is misbranded if it lacks a label containing the name and place of business of the manufacturer, packer, or distributor; however, this name and place of business is not an indicator of the origin of the product itself.[511]

(3) *Farm Bill*

The COOL provisions in the 2002 and 2008 US Farm Bills do not change the requirements of the Tariff Act. Instead, they were incorporated into the Agricultural Marketing Act of 1946[512] and required retail level COOL for fresh produce, red meats, peanuts, and seafood. Exempted from these provisions are further processed foods and food served at restaurant and food service establishments.[513]

---

[508] *See Country of Origin Labeling for Meat and Chicken*, U.S. DEP'T OF ARGIC.
[509] 19 C.F.R. § 134.22(c).
[510] 9 C.F.R. § 327.14; 9 C.F.R. 381.205.
[511] FDCA § 403(e).
[512] Pub. L. 107–171, §10816.
[513] GEOFFREY S. BECKER, CRS REPORT FOR CONGRESS, COUNTRY-OF-ORIGEN LABELING FOR FOODS 97-508 1 (Mar. 20, 2006).

The COOL provisions from the 2002 Farm Bill were originally slated to take effect in September 2004, but continued controversy over the new requirements, and certain events delayed the program from starting.[514] In October 2002, AMS issued voluntary guidelines for COOL.[515] While opening the door for producers and retailers to begin labeling their products with country-of-origin information, the voluntary rule did not garner significant participation.[516] The 2008 Farm Bill required COOL to take full effect in September 2008, and added additional as foods covered by mandatory COOL.[517] The final rule to implement COOL took effect in March 2009.[518]

The COOL program is neither a food safety nor a traceability program. The purpose of COOL is to convey to consumers the origin of a food product. COOL applies to: ground and muscle cuts of beef (including veal), lamb, and pork; fish and shellfish; peanuts and fresh and frozen fruits and vegetables; goat meat; chicken; pecans; macadamia nuts; and ginseng (hereinafter referred to as "covered food"). COOL requires the disclosure of whether fish and shellfish have been farm-raised or wild-caught. This method-of-production information is to be noted at the final point of sale to consumers.[519] Processed food items are exempt from COOL.[520] This category includes food items strictly used as ingredients in processed foods.[521] While a bag of frozen peas and carrots may be considered a processed food item under this exemption from COOL, if the peas and carrots are of foreign origin, the Tariff Act of 1930 requires that the country of origin be marked on the bag.[522] COOL exempts from these labeling requirements "food service establishments," such as restaurants, cafeterias, bars, and other like facilities that prepare and sell foods to the public.[523]

The meat labeling requirements are complex. It is common for meat products to be produced in multiple countries. For example, beef might be from an animal that was

---

[514] Critics of COOL asserted: (1) that passage of the provisions would trigger cost increases of food products (*See* Barry Krissoff et al., Country-of-Origin Labeling: Theory and Observation, U.S. Dep't of Agric. (2004); (2) that the USDA used faulty assumptions and incorrect data in their original calculations of the economic impact on producers, processors, and retailers (Becker, *supra* note 513 at 5.) and (3) that there was a lack of evidence that COOL labeling would provide valuable information to the consumer, leading to an increased demand for covered commodities bearing the US origin label (Letter from John D. Graham, Ph.D. to Hon. William T. Hawks, Under Secretary for marketing and Regulatory Programs, U.S. Dep't of Agric. (October 27, 2003).

[515] Guidelines for the Interim Voluntary Country-of-Origin Labeling of Beef, Lamb, Pork, Fish, Perishable Agricultural Commodities, and Peanuts in the Federal Register, 67 Fed. Reg. 63367 (August 1, 2008).

[516] Becker, *supra* note 513 at 3.

[517] *See* Appendix B of CRS COOL WTO Dispute Report for a timeline of key COOL developments.

[518] *See* Press Release, USDA, Vilsack Announces Implementation of Country of Origin Labeling Law (February 20, 2009).

[519] *Id.* COOL requires retailers who annually purchase at least $230,000 of fresh fruits and vegetables to inform consumers of origin by a label, stamp, mark, placard, or other clear and visible sign on the covered food or on the package, display, holding unit, or bin containing the covered food at the final point of sale. *Country of Origin Labeling (COOL) Frequently Asked Questions*, U.S. Dep't of Agric., Agric. Marketing Service (January 12, 2009).

[520] *See* 7 C.F.R. § 65.220 (definition of "processed food item" for purposes of the COOL exemption).

[521] The definition of a processed food item is broad. A food product that is subjected to a change that alters its basic character is considered processed. Roasting a nut or mixing peas with carrots would constitute processing. *Id.*

[522] *COOL Frequently Asked Questions, supra* note 519.

[523] Becker, *supra* note 513 at 3.

born and fed in Canada, but was slaughtered and processed in the United States. It is also common for meat products, especially ground beef, to be mixed with meat products from different countries. Thus, the designations listed in the following pages are required under COOL (the designation depends on where the animal was born, raised, and slaughtered):

○ Meats from animals that were exclusively born, raised, and slaughtered in the United States or from animals present in the United States on or prior to July 15, 2008, may bear the US origin label. The "US" label will state: "Born, Raised, and Slaughtered in the United States."
○ Meat or chicken with multiple countries of origin are to be labeled as being from all of the countries in which the animals may have been born, raised, or slaughtered. One type of label in this case could state: "Born in Mexico, Raised, and Slaughtered in the United States."
○ Meat or chicken from animals imported for immediate US slaughter are to be labeled as from both the country where the animal was imported from and the United States. A type of label that could be used would state: "Born and Raised in Canada, Slaughtered in the United States."
○ Products from animals born, raised, or slaughtered outside the United States are to be labeled with their correct countries of origin. The label in this case would state: "Product of Argentina."
○ For ground meat and chicken products, a list of all countries of origin or "all reasonably possible" countries of origin is to be designated on the label.[524]

The use of a combined US and non-US label for commingled meat has been the source of consternation for some groups and has led to various statements of clarification by the AMS.[525] In February 2009, USDA secretary Vilsack issued a letter urging the voluntary adoption of three suggested labeling changes in order to provide more useful information to consumers than that which the final rule might imply and to better meet congressional intent.[526] Vilsack stated that processors should voluntarily include information about what production step occurred in each country when multiple countries appear on the label (e.g., animals born and raised in Country X and slaughtered in Country Y might be labeled: "Born and Raised in Country X and Slaughtered in Country Y"). Vilsack also asked processors to reduce the time allowed for ground beef to bear the name of a country where the meat from that country was not present in a processor's inventory from six to ten days. Vilsack acknowledged that the "processed foods" definition in the final rule "may be too broadly drafted. Even if products are subject to curing, smoking, broiling, grilling, or steaming, voluntary labeling would be appropriate." Vilsack stated that USDA would monitor industry compliance to determine the need for additional rulemaking.[527] The letter was viewed as an effort to address concerns

---

[524] *FAQs – COOL Labeling Provisions Final Rule*, U.S. Dep't of Agric. Agricultural Marketing Serv. (September 20, 2013).
[525] *See, e.g.*, Mandatory Country of Origin Labeling of Beef, Lamb, Pork, Fish, Perishable Agricultural Commodities, and Peanuts, 68 Fed. Reg 61944 (October 30, 2003).
[526] Letter from Thomas J. Vilsack, Sec'y, USDA, to Industry Representative (February 20, 2009).
[527] *Id.*

of COOL without reopening the rule and thereby attracting renewed criticism from the meat industry and international trading partners.

In 2010 in a challenge to COOL, in *Easterday Ranches v. USDA*, a beef processing company that frequently imported Canadian cattle into the United States for slaughter argued that the COOL rules impermissibly conflicted with prior country-of-origin rules issued by the Treasury Department, which allowed cattle born or raised in Canada or Mexico but exported to the United States for slaughter to be labeled exclusively as products of the United States.[528] The COOL provisions require such cattle to be labeled first as a product of the country in which they were born or raised, and then as a product of the United States. Deciding in favor of USDA, the district court found that the COOL regulations, mandated by the 2008 Farm Bill, rather than implicitly repealing or conflicting with the Treasury marking rules, "merely [provide] for the labeling of a particular set of commodities that were previously free from any COOL requirements."[529]

[b] WTO Challenge: Undoing of COOL

Unsatisfied with the result of the consultations with the United States in December 2008 and January 2009,[530] Canada and Mexico requested WTO for a panel on grounds that COOL was inconsistent with US obligations under GATT, the Technical Barriers to Trade Agreement (TBT Agreement), and the Agreement on Rules of Origin. The WTO Dispute Settlement (DS) panel first found that COOL treats imported livestock less favorably than like US livestock (particularly in the labeling of beef and pork muscle cuts), in violation of the national treatment obligation in the TBT's Article 2.1.[531] The DS panel also found that COOL does not meet its objective of providing complete information to consumers on the origin of meat products in violation of TBT's Article 2.2. Finally, the DS panel also found that the Vilsack's letter's suggestions for voluntary action, while not a "technical regulation," went beyond COOL's obligations and constituted an unreasonable administration of COOL in violation of Article X:3(a) of the GATT 1994, which requires laws and regulations to be administered "in a uniform, impartial and reasonable manner."[532]

Following an appeal by the United States, in June 2012, the WTO's Appellate Body (AB) upheld the DS panel's finding that the COOL measure treats imported Canadian cattle and hogs, and imported Mexican cattle, less favorably than like domestic livestock. The AB, however, reversed the finding that COOL does not fulfill its legitimate objective to provide consumers with information on origin.[533]

The WTO's Dispute Settlement Body (DSB) adopted the AB and the DS panel's report, as modified by the AB, in July 2012. A WTO arbitrator set a deadline in May

---

[528] No. CV-08-5067-RHW, 2010 U.S. Dist. LEXIS 10209 (E.D. Wash. February 5, 2010).

[529] *Id.* at *2.

[530] Remy Jurenas and Joel L. Greene, Cong. Research serv., rs22955, Country-of-Origin Labeling for Foods and the WTO Trade Dispute on Meat Labeling 8 (September 16, 2013).

[531] Panel Report, United States – Certain Country of Origin Labeling (COOL) Requirements, WT/DS 384/ RWT/DS386 (November 18, 2011).

[532] *Id.*

[533] Appellate Body Report, United States – Certain Country of Origin Labeling (COOL) Requirements, II, WT/DS384/AB/R, WT/DS3861 AB/R (June 29, 2012).

2013, for the United States to comply with the WTO findings. In order to comply, the USDA issued a final rule requiring that labels show where each production step – where the animal was born, raised, and slaughtered – occurs and prohibiting the commingling of muscle cut meat from different origins. Arguing that the final rule fails to bring the United States into compliance with its WTO obligations, Canada and Mexico in August 2013 requested the establishment of a compliance panel to determine if the final COOL rule complies with WTO findings.[534]

In October 2014, a WTO compliance panel ruled against the US final rule, finding that the amended COOL measure increases the original COOL's detrimental impact on the competitive opportunities of imported livestock in the US market.[535] The ruling stated the amended COOL necessitates increased segregation of meat and livestock, entails a higher record-keeping burden, and increases the original COOL measure's incentive to choose domestic over imported livestock. The panel concluded that as with the original COOL measure, the detrimental impact of the amended rule's labeling and record-keeping rules could not be explained by the need to convey to consumers information where livestock were born, raised, and slaughtered.

Finally, in May 2015, the WTO rejected a US appeal of its decision. This final ruling triggered the WTO process to determine the level of retaliatory tariffs Canada and Mexico can impose on the US. The US will have to revise or repeal COOL in order to avoid sanctions. Legislation to repeal COOL is being considered in Congress.[536] Support for COOL seems to be waning, as a 198-page report issued by the USDA that had been mandated by the 2014 Farm Bill found little evidence that consumers are likely to increase their purchases bearing USA-origin labels.

[11] *Geographical Indicators*

[a] Form of Intellectual Property

Geographical Indicators (GIs) are a form of intellectual property that is used as a labeling mark to connect food to a reputation or characteristic of a particular geographic origin. GIs are defined in Article 22(1) of the WTO 1995 Agreement on Trade-Related Aspects of Intellectual Property Rights (TRIPS) as "indications which identify a good as originating in the territory of a Member, or a region or locality in that territory, where a given quality, reputation or other characteristic of the good is essentially attributable to its geographical origin."[537] Examples of US certification marks include: "VIDALIA" for onions, "WASHINGTON STATE" for apples, "FLORIDA" for oranges, "IDAHO" for potatoes, and "Pride of New York" for various agricultural products. Under TRIPS, any member state wishing to promote GIs abroad may implement a domestic GI regulatory

---

[534] WTO, WT/DS/384/26 Recourse to Article 21.5 of the DSU by Canada, August 20, 2013, and WT/DS/384/25 Recourse to Article 21.5 of the DSU by Mexico, August 20, 2013.

[535] Panel Report, Certain Country of Origin Labeling (COOL) Requirements, WT/DS/384/RW (October 20, 2014).

[536] *See* Catherine Boudreau, *House May Vote on Repealing COOL in June, Agricultural Chairman Says*, Bloomberg BNA (May 20, 2015).

[537] Agreement on Trade-Related Aspects of Intellectual Property Rights, article. 22(1), Apr. 15, 1994, Marraeksh Agreement Establishing the World Trade Organization, Annex 1C, Legal Instruments – Results of the Uruguay Round, 1869 U.N.T.S. 299, 33 I.L.M. 1125, 1197.

framework; states have no obligation to protect GIs that "are not ... protected in their country of origin."[538]

[b] Regulation of GI under TRIPS

TRIPS allows member states substantial leeway in devising the GI regulatory framework that best suits their needs.[539] Despite this freedom, the European and American models of domestic GI protection predominate. These two models reflect different historical approaches to the protection of geographical terms and epitomize the philosophical clash that has given rise to WTO disputes.

The EU offers a two-tiered sui generis system of public rights granted and administered by governmental agencies. The system consists of two instruments, Protected Designation of Origin (PDO) and Protected Geographical Indication (PGI), with each conferring expansive protection.[540] EU GI applications, entailing detailed product specifications and proof that the GI is protected in its home country, are sent to the European Commission either by a group of producers or processors or by the authorities of the GI's home state.[541] If the GI is registered, products bearing the GI may enter the marketplace once their compliance with the GI's specifications has been validated, typically by a designated public authority of its home state.

In the United States, on the contrary, GIs are a subset of trademarks and protected through certification marks.[542] GIs serve the same functions as trademarks because like trademarks they are source-identifiers, guarantees of quality, and valuable business interests.[543] Certification marks are owned by private certifying organizations, which license their use to other entities (i.e., the owning organization cannot itself use the mark). The certifier is responsible for submitting an application to the US Patent and Trademark Office (USPTO) and auditing the practices of users of the mark to ensure compliance with the certification mark's standards.[544] If the evidence indicates that a specific mark or sign in question has a principal significance as a generic term, registration will be cancelled, as in a case in which it was held that a generic name of a type of cheese rather than a certification mark indicated regional

---

[538] *Id.* at art. 24(9).

[539] *See id.* art. 22(3) (requiring only that each member party "provide the legal means for interested parties to prevent" the use of GIs that mislead to the geographical origin or constitute unfair competition under Paris Convention).

[540] PDOs have stricter requirements than do PDIs. PDOs are granted to products that are produced, processed, and prepared within a certain region and have qualities that are "essentially or exclusively due to a particular geographical environment with its inherent natural and human factors." *Id.* art. 2(1)(a). PGIs apply to products that need only be produced, processed, or prepared in a region and that have a "quality, reputation, or other characteristics" that is merely "attributable" to that region. *Id.* art. 2(1)(b). PGIs must be geographical terms, but PDOs need not be.

[541] CR 510/2006, art. 5(9). After scrutinizing the application, the commission publishes the GI in the Official Journal of the European Union; if six months pass without the filing of an objection, the commission registers the name as an EU GI. *Id.* arts. 6–7.

[542] *See Geographical Indications (GIs) Questions and Answers*, U.S. PATENT & TRADEMARK OFF. (explaining that certification marks have protected geographical terms since "long before the term 'geographical indications' came into use").

[543] *Geographical Indication Protection in the United States*, U.S. PATENT & TRADEMARK OFF.

[544] BERNARD O'CONNOR, THE LAW OF GEOGRAPHICAL INDICATIONS 112–114 (2004).

origin.[545] On the contrary, if use of the sign or mark is controlled by the certifier and limited to goods meeting the certifier's standards of regional origin, and if purchasers understand the sign to refer only to goods produced in the particular region, then the sign functions as a regional certification mark, as in the case where COGNAC was held to be a geographical indication for brandy from France.[546] The options for GI protection include defense against unfair competition (e.g., through trademarks).[547]

The tension between the EU and the United States in approaches to GIs has a long history that continues to divide the two systems. In 1992, the EU introduced a GI regime to provide protection throughout the EU for GIs. In 1999, the United States challenged the EU's GI legislation on two grounds, namely, discrimination against US GIs and failure to protect US trademarks. In March 2005, a WTO panel ruled that certain aspects of the EU's GI legislation were inconsistent with TRIPS and set a deadline for the EU to modify its regulation before April 2006. In March 2006, the EU adopted regulations in order to bring the EU GI system in compliance with the WTO panel.[548] The 2006 regulation effectively allowed third-party countries to submit registration applications directly to the European Commission and to object directly to applications for new registrations. In November 2012, the EU adopted new rules on EU quality schemes for food that came into force in January 2013.[549] This new regulation combines the rules for PDO, PGI, Traditional Specialties Guaranteed (TSG),[550] and optional quality terms into one single legal instrument. Registration under the different schemes is open to third-party countries and provides for the development of mechanisms to protect PDOs and PGIs in third-party countries.

In the Doha Round, the EU submitted a proposal to amend the TRIPS Agreement in order to extend the same high-level protection to food products other than wines and spirits.[551] In addition, the EU is proposing to establish a multilateral register of GIs that would be legally binding on all WTO members.[552] In the ensuing debate the EU and allies argue in favor of such an extension, asserting that the existing two-tiered system "discriminat[es]" by giving strong protection exclusively to goods that are predominantly produced by wealthy states.[553] On the other side of the debate are the United States and its allies that consider GI protection to be outright protectionism.[554] They argue that the

---

[545]   In re Cooperativa Produttori Latte E Fontina Valle D'Acosta, 230 USPQ 131 (TTAB 1986).

[546]   Institut National Des Appellations D'Origine v. Brown-Forman Corp., 47 USPQ2d 1875 (TTAB 1998).

[547]   *See* U.S. PATENT, Geographical Indications Q&A, *supra* note 543.

[548]   EC Commission Regulation 1898/2006.

[549]   European Parliament and Council Regulation 1151/2012.

[550]   A Traditional Specialties Guaranteed (TSG) applies to food with a "traditional" character. Products are eligible for registration if the product's specific character results from a traditional or processing method or if it is composed of raw materials or ingredients used in traditional recipes. The time period for a product to be considered "traditional" is set to be thirty years. An example of a TSG designation is Moazrella. *See* the EU's TSG Quality Scheme Explained, GAIN Report.

[551]   TRIPS provides a high level of GI protection to wines and spirits. TRIPS establishes a per se ban on using a GI on the labeling of nonqualifying goods (wines and spirits). TRIPS, art. 23(1). In other words, because Champagne is a French GI, a Californian winemaker may be prevented from labeling its product "Champagne-like wine from Sonoma Valley." That no consumer would think that this wine comes from the Champagne province of France is irrelevant.

[552]   *See Geographical Indications, Background and the Current Situation*, World Trade Organization.

[553]   *See Why Do Geographical Indications Matter to Us?*, Eur. Commission (July 30, 2003).

[554]   *See* Marsha A. Echols, Food Safety and the WTO: The Interplay of Culture, Science and Technology 287 (2001).

bulk of the benefit of expanded GI protection would likely accrue only to those nations with a substantial number of GIs or GI-potential. For the foreseeable future it appears that members will remain divided over this issue, unless, of course, the treaty negotiations between the EU and the United States, referenced in Chapter 2, bridge the gap between the two regulatory systems.

[12] *Special Foods Labeling Rules*

The labeling of certain special foods, referenced in Chapter 1, has particular labeling rules, as shown below.

- **Medical Foods** – Because medical foods are not drugs, they are not subject to the pre-clearance requirements of the FDCA. Medical foods may not be labeled with claims that the product will cure, mitigate, treat, or prevent disease or condition.
- **Foods for Special Dietary Use** – The regulations define food for special dietary uses where "uses for supplying particular dietary needs … exist by reason of a physical, physiological, pathological or other condition, including but not limited to the conditions of diseases, convalescence, pregnancy, lactation, allergic hypersensitivity to food, underweight and overweight," or of "age, including but not limited to the ages of infancy and childhood."[555] The regulations also include within the definition of food for "special dietary use" those foods whose "[u]ses for supplementing or fortifying the ordinary or usual diet with any vitamin, mineral, or other dietary property … regardless of whether such food also purports to be or is represented for general use."[556] It appears that these products are similar to medical foods, but they are available commercially and do not require the supervision of a health care provider. Under this definition construct, gluten-free foods, lactose-free dairy products, foods designed to aid weight loss, and infant foods may be considered foods for special dietary if the specific conditions are met.

§ 4.06 International Food Labeling Regulation

[1] *TBT Agreement: Standard or Technical Regulation*

As noted in this chapter, the United States uses the mandatory label in its regulations (as do governments in other countries) to disseminate information on food product about nutritional content, safety concerns, the place of origin, production process, and health claims. The formulation of food labeling rules is also influenced by the complex network of international conventions and agreements, which are imposed upon the United States as a member country. The most important instruments in this international framework are those presided over by the WTO and free-trade regime identified in Chapter 2, namely, the GATT, TBT, SPS, and TRIPS. These instruments were created to promote international trade, through the reduction of trade barriers. They apply to all obligations that affect international trade, including food labeling

---

[555] 21 C.F.R. § 105.3(a)(1).
[556] *Id.*

requirements. As noted in Chapter 2, the requirement to facilitate international trade is countered by recognition that countries may adopt and enforce measures necessary to protect human, animal, and plant life and to prevent deceptive practices. These concessions are subject to a condition that such measures should not be applied in a manner that amounts to arbitrary or unjustifiable discrimination or to a restriction on international trade.

The bulk of labeling issues that fall within the ambit of international trade rules involve the TBT Agreement. The TBT Agreement delineates a number of legitimate objectives that may be developed for labeling, but qualifies those with requirements of: (1) nondiscrimination; (2) the avoidance of unnecessary obstacles to international trade; (3) harmonization; (4) the equivalence of technical regulations and the results of conformity assessment procedures; (5) mutual recognition of conformity assessment procedures; and (6) transparency.

Annex 1 to the TBT Agreement divides technical requirements into two categories: technical regulations and standards. A "technical regulation" is a document, "which lays down product characteristics or their related processes and production methods, including the applicable administrative provisions, with which compliance is mandatory."[557] A "standard" is a document approved by a recognized body that provides for common and repeated use, rules, guidelines, or characteristics for products or related processes and production methods, with which compliance is not mandatory. Both technical regulations and standards include "packaging, marking or [labeling] requirements as they apply to a product, process or production method."[558]

[2] Tuna-Dolphin Labeling Cases

In the well-known cases known as Tuna-Dolphin, in which the United States was pitted against Mexico, the WTO Dispute Panel interpreted "technical regulations and standards" for the food labeling context.[559] This case involved two measures adopted by the United States concerning the importation, marketing, and sale of tuna and tuna products.[560] First, regulations promulgated under the Dolphin Protection Consumer Information Act (DPCIA) control the use of the term "dolphin-safe" when it appears on tuna products. Second, the legislation also contemplated that the secretary of commerce would develop an official mark that may be used to label tuna products as dolphin-safe in accordance with the act.

Mexico claimed that these US provisions violated Articles 2.1, 2.2, and 2.4 of the TBT Agreement. Article 2.1 introduces the national treatment and most-favored nation principles. The article requires that "in respect of technical regulations products imported from the territory of any Member shall be accorded treatment no less favorable than that

---

[557] TBT Agreement, Annex 1.

[558] Id.

[559] United States – Measures Concerning the Importation, Marketing and Sale of Tuna and Tuna Products WT/DS381/RW (September 15, 2011) (US – Tuna-Dolphin).

[560] See 16 U.S.C. § 1385 (date) ("Dolphin Protection Consumer Information Act"); 50 C.F.R. 216.91 ("Dolphin-safe labeling standards"); 50 C.F.R. § 216.92 ("Dolphin-safe requirements for tuna harvested in the ETP [Eastern Tropical Pacific Ocean] by large purse seine vessels").

accorded to like products of national origin and to like products originating in any other country."[561] Article 2.2 introduces a necessity test. Pursuant to Article 2.2, members must "ensure that technical regulations are not prepared, adopted or applied with a view to or the effect of creating unnecessary obstacles to international trade." Building on the latter requirement, Article 2.2 adds that technical regulations are not permitted to "be more trade-restrictive than necessary to fulfill a legitimate objective, taking account of the risks non-fulfillment would create." The list of legitimate objectives in Article 2.4 includes the prevention of deceptive practices and the protection of human health or safety, animal or plant, or health.

The United States argued that the TBT Agreement did not apply because the measures did not constitute "technical regulations." The Dispute Panel applied a three-tier test for determining whether a measure was a "technical regulation:"[562] (1) the measure applies to an identifiable product or group of products; (2) it lays down one or more characteristics of the product; and (3) compliance with the product characteristics is mandatory. Applying this test, the panel first found that the US dolphin-safe labeling provisions applied to an identifiable group of products, namely, tuna and tuna products that could be labeled as dolphin-safe.[563] As to the second prong of the test, the panel noted that both parties acknowledged that the US dolphin-safe labeling provisions established labeling requirements within the meaning of Annex 1 of the TBT Agreement – the labeling provisions define the qualifying conditions and criteria for a dolphin-safe label.[564] Third, the panel found that the US measures required mandatory compliance because they prescribed in a legally enforceable instrument the manner in which a dolphin-safe label could be obtained and disallowed any other use of a dolphin-safe designation.[565] The panel concluded that as the three-tier test was satisfied, the measures were "technical regulation."

Mexico claimed that the US dolphin-safe labeling provisions were inconsistent with Article 2.1 because they afforded less favorable treatment to Mexican tuna products than to US tuna products and tuna products originating in other countries. The panel used a test of whether: (1) access to the label was an advantage and (2) Mexican tuna products were denied access to it under the measures, so that they were disadvantaged on the US market compared with United States or imported tuna products originating in any other country.[566] On the first point, the panel agreed with Mexico that retailer and consumer preferences for dolphin-safe tuna products meant that the US legislation afforded an advantage to products eligible for the label.[567] On the second point, however, the panel

---

[561] TBT Agreement, Article 1.

[562] This definition had been previously developed by the Appellate Body in EC-Asbestos (Appellate Body-Report, *European Communities – Measures Affecting Asbestos and Asbestos-Containing Products*, WT/DS135/AB/R (adopted Apr. 5, 2001) and EC-Sardines (Appellate Body Report, *European Communities – Trade Description of Sardines*, WT/DS231/AB/R (adopted October 23, 2002), DSR 2002: VIII, 3359 at para. 176).

[563] 15 U.S.C. §§ 1051–1127.

[564] US – Tuna-Dolphin, *supra* note 559 at ¶ 7.74.

[565] *Id.* at ¶ 7.145.

[566] *Id.* at ¶ 7.284.

[567] *Id.* at ¶ 7.287.

held that Mexico did not prove that the US dolphin-safe provisions afforded less favor-able treatment to Mexican tuna products.[568] This decision followed the Appellate Body's holding in *Korea-Various Measures on Beef* that disadvantage was required to result from the measures themselves, rather than the consequences that arise as a result of the action of private actors on the market.[569] The panel concluded that any adverse impact felt by Mexican tuna products on the US market was the result of factors unrelated to the origin of product, including choices made by Mexico's own fishing fleet and canners.[570]

Mexico argued that the US dolphin-safe provisions violated Article 2.2 because they did not fulfill a legitimate objective or that those objectives could be fulfilled using less trade-restrictive measures. The panel agreed with the United States that the objectives of the US dolphin-safe provisions fell within two of the objectives expressly listed in Article 2.2 of the TBT Agreement, namely, the "prevention of deceptive practices" and the "pro-tection of human health or safety, animal or plant life or health, or the environment." The Appeal Board, on the contrary, ruled against the United States on grounds that it had not demonstrated that the difference in labeling conditions for tuna products was calibrated to the risks to dolphins arising from different fishing methods in different areas of the ocean.[571] As a result, nations such as Mexico, which used fishing methods outside those permitted in the legislation, were discriminatorily affected.

In April 2015, a WTO panel released a report finding that the United States had not made enough revisions to its previous labeling measure to bring it in line with the TBT and GATT agreements.[572] This decision opens the door for Mexico to petition for retal-iatory measures against the United States, pending an appeal. In June 2015, the United States notified the DSB that it would appeal certain issues developed by the compliance panel.[573]

§ 4.07 Regulation of Food Advertising

[1] *Laws Governing Food Advertising*

At the federal level, two primary sources of law govern food advertising: (1) the Federal Trade Commission Act (FTCA)[574] and (2) the Lanham Act.[575] The FTCA authorizes the Federal Trade Commission (FTC) to regulate advertisements with the goal of protecting consumers. The Lanham Act, particularly section 43(a), proscribes false or misleading statements and gives competitors standing to sue. At the state level, most states have passed Unfair and Deceptive Trade Practices Acts, with some adopting the Uniform and Deceptive Trade Practices Act to govern state-law claims, including those that involve

---

[568] *Id.* at ¶ 7.374.
[569] Appellate Body Report, *Korea-Measures Affecting Imports of Fresh, Chilled and Frozen Beef*, WT/DS161/AB/R, WT/DS 169/AB/R (adopted January 10, 2001), DSR 2001:1, 5.
[570] *US – Tuna-Dolphin, supra* note 559 at ¶ 7.379
[571] *Id.* at ¶ 297.
[572] See Panel Report, Measures Concerning the Importation, Marketing and Sale of Tuna and Tuna Products, WT/DS381/RW (April 14, 2015).
[573] The compliance panel did find that the United States was entitled to disqualify tuna caught in purse seine nets. *See id.*
[574] Federal Trade Commission Act (FTCA), ch. 311, 38 Stat. 717 (1914) (codified as amended at 15 U.S.C. § 41–64).
[575] 15 U.S.C. § 1114.

food products.[576] Some states have also passed false advertising statutes as a supplement
or alternative to the Uniform Act.[577] Finally, advertising claims may also be subject to
private standards and industry codes.

Much of food advertising law has applied to dietary supplements; however, as evidenced by the *POM Wonderful LLC. v. FTC* case decided in 2015 by the DC Circuit,[578]
advertisements of conventional foods are subject to the same legal conventions.

[2] *FTC Regulation of Food*

[a] FTCA: Relevant to Food

In recent years, the FTC per the FTCA has taken a more aggressive role in the regulation of food. The FTCA was originally enacted in 1914 to supplement and bolster
the Sherman and Clayton Acts.[579] Section 45, which originally prohibited only "unfair
methods of competition in commerce," was amended in 1938 by the Wheeler-Lea
Amendments to outlaw "unfair or deceptive acts or practices in commerce." The amendments enabled the FTC to center its attention on direct consumer protection instead of
protecting consumers only indirectly by protecting competitors.[580] Section 5 prohibits
and directs the FTC "to prevent unfair or deceptive acts or practices in or affecting commerce."[581] Section 12 of the Act includes within the prohibited category of deceptive acts
"any false advertisements" relating to "food" (among other products).[582] The act broadly
defines, as a "false advertisement," any "advertisement, other than labeling, which is
misleading in a material respect," whether through affirmative "representations made
or suggested" by the advertisement or though "a fail[ure] to reveal facts material in the
light of such representations."[583] The FTC has issued two policy statements, the 1983
FTC Policy Statement on Deception[584] and the 1984 *FTC Policy Statement Regarding
Advertising Substantiation*,[585] both of which articulate the basic elements employed by
the FTC in a deception analysis under Sections 5 and 12.

[b] Jurisdiction Blurring between FTC and FDA

Both the FTC and the FDA are empowered to take enforcement action against food
firms that engage in deceptive marketing of food. As previously noted, the FTC's authority to regulate the deceptive marketing of food derives from the FTCA, which prohibits
false and misleading advertising. The FDA's authority to regulate deceptive marketing is provided by the FDCA, which prohibits false and misleading labels and labeling. While section 15 of the FTCA defines "false advertising" as excluding labeling,

[576] *See, e.g.*, Ohio Rev. Code Ann. §§ 41.4165.01-4165.04.
[577] *See, e.g.*, Ga. Code Ann. §§ 10-1-420, -421.
[578] No. 13–1060 (D.C. Cir. January 2015).
[579] Am. Jur. 2d, Monopolies, Restraints of Trade, and Unfair Trade Practices § 736.
[580] *Id.*
[581] 15 U.S.C. § 45(a)(1).
[582] *Id.* § 52(a), (b).
[583] *Id.* § 55(a)(1).
[584] Appended to Cliffdale Assocs., Inc., 103 F.T.C. 110, 174 (1984).
[585] Appended to Thompson Med. Co., 104 F.T.C. 648, 839 (1984).

the FTC is still able to assert authority over all marketing, including labeling, under Section 5's general prohibition against unfair competition. The Second Circuit has specifically rejected the notion that a claim made only on a label was not within the FTC's authority, and only within the authority of the FDA.[586] The Supreme Court rejected the idea years ago that regulation of false advertising has been committed exclusively to the FTC, noting that "[e]very labeling is in a sense an advertisement" and that advertising can "[perform] the same function as it would if it were on the article or on the containers or wrappers."[587]

To remedy the blurring of jurisdiction between FDA and FTC over food marketing, the two agencies in 1954 agreed to a Memorandum of Understanding, under which the FTC retains primary jurisdiction over the regulation of food advertising other than labeling, while the FDA retains primary jurisdiction over food labeling.[588] The 1957 Memorandum of Understanding has since been updated with a 1971 Memorandum of Understanding, which maintains the same jurisdictional division over food marketing.[589] Thus, as a matter of policy and practice, the FDA regulates food labeling – the actual package label and any written, printed, or graphic matter that accompanies the sale of the food – and the FTC regulates food advertising, including nonlabeling marketing communications, such as television and print advertising.[590] The 1971 Memorandum of Understanding encourages joint coordination of programs and information sharing between the two agencies.[591] The memorandum stipulates that parallel proceedings against the same parties by both agencies "shall be restricted to those highly unusual situations where it is clear the public interest requires two separate proceedings."[592] Although a formal agreement similar to that between the FTC and FDA does not exist between the FSIS and FTC, generally the FSIS and FTC coordinate their activities to avoid duplication.[593] A FSIS Guide to FSIS labeling requirements recommends that firms "consult FSIS labeling regulations, rules and policies when developing advertising for meat and poultry products."[594]

Congress further clarified the agencies' roles in cases of overlapping jurisdiction in 1976, when it amended the FDCA to include Section 707, which requires FDA to notify the FTC in advance if the FDA plans to take action against a particular food product that is misbranded due to its advertising.[595] If the FTC takes action against the violators identified in the FDA's notice within sixty days, then the FDA may not initiate its own action and instead must defer to the FTC action.[596] In the pursuit of enforcement proceedings

---

[586] Fresh Grown Preserve Corp. v. F.T.C., 125 F.2d 917 (2d Cir. 1942).

[587] Kordel v. United States, 335 U.S. 345, 351 (1948).

[588] Working Agreement between Federal Trade Commission and Food and Drug Commission, 4 Trade Reg. Rep. (CCH) ¶ 9850.01 (June 9, 1954).

[589] Memorandum of Understanding between the Federal Trade Commission and the Food and Drug Administration, 36 Fed. Reg. 18,539 (September 16, 1971).

[590] See id.

[591] See id.

[592] Id.

[593] A Guide to Federal Food Labeling Requirements for Meat, Poultry, and Egg Products 12, U.S. DEP'T OF AGRIC., FOOD SAFETY INSPECTION SERV. (August 2007).

[594] Id.

[595] 21 U.S.C. § 378(a).

[596] 21 U.S.C. § 378(b).

against food advertising, the FTC still accords substantial weight to the FDA's scientific determinations.[597]

In 1994, the FTC issued the *Enforcement Policy Statement on Food Advertising*. The purpose of the statement was to harmonize the FTC's regulations of food advertising with the FDA's approach to nutrient content claims and health claims made on food labels.[598] In the statement, the FTC basically maintains its autonomy in the regulation of food advertising, while deferring to the FDA's expertise on defining certain nutritional terms.[599] The statement leaves open the possibility that, in certain limited instances, the FTC may allow in advertising under Section 5 a carefully qualified health claim that has not been authorized by the FDA for labeling. The statement makes clear, however, that such a health claim must be supported by strong scientific evidence.[600]

The rise of e-commerce complicates the jurisdiction over food advertising and food labeling for the FTC and FDA. In 2001, in response to a suggestion by the Washington Legal Foundation that information presented on a company's website could never constitute "labeling" as contemplated by the FDCA, the FDA reiterated that courts have interpreted the term "accompanying" broadly to include items, such as brochures, booklets, films, and sound recordings.[601] By way of example, the FDA noted that if a company were to promote a regulated product on its website, and allowed consumers to purchase the product directly from the website, then the website would likely be labeling. The website, in that case, would be "written, printed, or graphic matter" that supplements or explains the product and is designed for use in the distribution and sale of the product.[602]

[c]   Deceptive Advertising

(1)   *Legal Standard: Deceptive Elements*
In the FTC's 1983 *Policy Statement on Deception*, the agency enumerated three primary factors the agency considers in evaluating false advertising claims: (1) "a representation, omission or practice that is likely to mislead the consumer"; (2) "the perspective of a consumer acting reasonably in the circumstances"; and (3) "the representation, omission, or practice must be a 'material' one."[603] In sum, the *Statement* states that the FTC finds deception "if there is a misrepresentation, omission, or practice that is likely to mislead the consumer acting reasonably in the circumstances to the consumer's detriment."[604] Stated another way, the often cited Seventh Circuit case of *Kraft, Inc. v. FTC* has noted that to determine whether an advertisement is deceptive, the commission applies a three-part inquiry as to: "(1) what claims are conveyed in the advertisement; (2) are those claims false or misleading; and (3) are those claims material to prospective consumers."[605]

---

[597]   *See Thompson Med. Co.*, 104 F.T.C. at 826. (FDA final monographs for OTC drugs may form a reasonable basis for health-related advertising claims).
[598]   *Id.*
[599]   *See id.*
[600]   *Id.*
[601]   Letter from Ctr. For Food Safety & Applied Nutrition, Food & Drug Admin., to Daniel J. Popeo & Paul D. Kamenar, Wash. Legal Found. (November 1, 2001).
[602]   *Id.*
[603]   *FTC Policy Statement on Deception, supra*, note 584.
[604]   *Id.*
[605]   Kraft, Inc. v. FTC, 970 F.2d 311, 314 (7th Cir. 1992).

When identifying and reviewing the representations made by an advertisement, the commission considers the "overall net impression created by the advertisement as a whole," by evaluating "the interaction of such elements as language and visual images."[606] In other words, whether or not the advertisement is misleading is judged on the entirety of the advertisement, and not based upon any particular claim.[607] The query for the FTC is what messages would a reasonable consumer construe for a given advertisement, which involves "an evaluation of such factors as the entire document, the juxtaposition of various phrases in the document, the nature of the claim, and the nature of the transaction."[608] "[S]tatements susceptible of both a misleading and a truthful interpretation will be construed against the advertiser."[609] "An ad is misleading if at least a significant minority of reasonable consumers are likely to take away the misleading claim."[610]

Claims conveyed by an advertisement may be express or implied.[611] "Express claims directly represent the fact at issue while implied claims do so in an oblique or indirect way."[612] Proof of the meaning of an express claim is not required because the express claim itself is explicitly stated.[613] In contrast, implied claims are claims that the advertisement communicates to reasonable consumers but are not expressly stated.[614] To determine the existence of an implied claim, examination of extrinsic evidence may be required.[615] Because such claims are not stated explicitly, the FTC must find that the implied claims are likely conveyed to a significant portion of reasonable consumers.[616] This determination is made by the FTC looking at the net impression created by the ad as a whole.[617] For example, in *Kraft, Inc. v. FTC*, an advertisement stating that each slice of cheese is made with 5 ounces of milk, while truthful, still falsely implied to reasonable consumers that each slice contained as much calcium as 5 ounces of milk and was therefore held to be misleading.[618] The FTC may rely on its own reasoned analysis to determine what claims, including implied ones, are conveyed in a challenged advertisement, so long as those claims are reasonably clear from the face of the advertisement.[619]

---

[606] Daniel Chapter One, Initial Decision, at 82 (citing American Home Prods. Corp. v. FTC, 695 F.2d 681, 687 (3d Cir. 1982).

[607] *See, e.g.,* F.T.C. v. Standard Educ. Soc'y, 302 U.S. 112, 116 (1937).

[608] *FTC Policy Statement on Deception, supra* note 584.

[609] FTC v. Bronson Partners, LLC, 564 F. Supp. 2d 119, 127 n.6 (D. Conn. 2008) (quoting Country Tweeds, Inc. v. FTC, 326 F.2d 144, 148 (2d Cir. 1964)).

[610] Telebrands Corp., 140 F.T.C. 278, 291 (2005).

[611] *FTC Policy Statement on Deception, supra* note 584.

[612] *Kraft,* 970 F.2d at 318 (citing Thompson Med., 104 F.T.C. at 788).

[613] *See FTC Policy Statement on Deception, supra* note 584 at 176; *Thompson Med.,* 104 F.T.C. at 788.

[614] *See* In re Kraft, Inc. 114 F.T.C. 40, 120 (1991), *aff'd,* 970 F.2d 311 (7th Cir. 1992); *Thompson Med.,* 104 F.T.C. at 789.

[615] *See* Stouffer Foods Corp., 118 F.T.C. 746, 798–9 (1994).

[616] *FTC Policy Statement on Deception, supra* note 584. The reasonable consumer is defined often as a member of the "general populace." In re Kraft, Inc., 114 F.T.C. at 53 n 33. The reasonable consumer is to be distinguished from the particularly savvy and sophisticated consumer, and "the ignorant, the unthinking and the credulous." *See* FTC v. Balme, 23 F.2d 615, 620 (2d Cir. 1928), *citing* Florence Mfg. Co. v. J.C. Dowd & Co., 178 F. 73, 75 (2d Cir. 1910).

[617] *See* In re Kraft, 114 F.T.C. at 121.

[618] 970 F.2d at 311.

[619] *Id.* at 319.

The FTC need not prove that the advertisement caused actual deception, but rather whether the advertisement is likely to mislead.[620] An advertisement also may be deceptive by omission. Not all omissions or failures to disclose information are deceptive, even if providing the information is beneficial to consumers. Instead, the FTC will examine the overall impression created by the advertisement.[621] Even literally true statements can have misleading implications.[622] Advertisements that might be found to be misleading are construed against the advertiser.[623] The advertiser's intent to deceive is not relevant, as the FTC is concerned with protecting the public from deception rather than punishing the violator.[624]

Statements perceived as exaggeration or boasting, also known as "puffery," are generally not considered false or misleading advertising. The dividing line between puffing and misleading claims is not bright: the distinction turns on whether the statement is one of fact or opinion. A statement of fact is considered objective and not actionable; a statement of general opinion is considered subjective and thus actionable.[625] Still, the line between puffery and an actionable claim can be murky.[626] The Fifth Circuit case of *Pizza Hut v. Papa John's* shows how the overall context of an advertisement can transform seemingly puffery into an actionable statement of fact. Pizza Hut sued Papa John's for use of the advertising slogan "Better Ingredients. Better Pizza." The Fifth Circuit found both parts of the statement to be nonactionable opinion, reasoning that "it is clear that the assertion by Papa John's that it makes a 'Better Pizza' is a general statement of opinion regarding the superiority of its products over all others. This simple statement ... epitomizes the exaggerated advertising, blustering, and boasting by a manufacturer upon which no consumer would reasonably rely."[627]

(2) Applying the Unfairness Standard

In addition to deceptive acts or practices, section 5 of the FTCA prohibits acts and practices that are "unfair." According to the 1980 *FTC Policy Statement on Unfairness*, an advertisement is unfair if: (1) it causes or is likely to cause substantial consumer injury; (2) that is not reasonably avoidable by consumers, themselves; and (3) that is not outweighed by countervailing benefits to consumers or competition.[628] In 1994, Congress incorporated this three-prong "unfairness" standard into the FTCA.[629] The FTC rarely uses its unfairness jurisdiction to challenge false and misleading advertising claims; instead, the agency relies on its authority to prohibit deceptive representations or material omissions. The FTC relies on its unfairness authority to challenge practices, other than representations and omissions that cause substantial consumer injury.[630] A primary difference between unfairness analysis and deception analysis is that deception analysis

---

[620] *FTC Policy Statement on Deception, supra* note 584.
[621] *Id.*
[622] Zauderer v. Office of Disciplinary Council, 471 U.S. 626, 652 (1985); Thompson Med., 791 F.2d at 197.
[623] Giant Food, Inc. v. F.T.C., 322 F.2d 977 (D.C. Cir. 1963).
[624] *In re Kraft, Inc.*, 114 F.T.C. at 53 n.33.
[625] *See, e.g.*, Pizza Hut, Inc. v. Papa John's Int'l, Inc., 227 F.3d 489, 495–96 (5th Cir. 2000).
[626] In re Boston Beer Co., 198 F.3d 1370, 1372 (Fed. Cir. 1999).
[627] *Pizza Hut, Inc.* 198 F.3d at 498.
[628] Appended to International Harvester Co., 104 F.T.C. 949, 1070 (1984).
[629] *See* 15 U.S.C. § 45(n).
[630] *FTC Policy Statement on Unfairness, supra* note 628.

does not require a cost-benefit calculation. The deception analysis assumes that there are no countervailing benefits when a material falsehood or omission exists.

[d] Substantiation Doctrine

(1) *Reasonable Basis*

The advertiser must have a "reasonable basis" for all express and implied representations made in the advertisement. In 1972, the FTC first articulated the "substantiation" requirement in what is known as the *Pfizer* decision.[631] In *Pfizer*, the FTC held that an advertiser violates the FTCA by making an affirmative product representation without having a reasonable basis of support for that representation. The FTC explained that consumers expect advertisers to have a reasonable basis of support for their representations and therefore will be mislead by representations lacking this support. The FTC noted that advertisers are in a much better position to substantiate their representations than consumers, making the substantiation requirement economically efficient.[632] The requirement that advertisers have a reasonable basis for their representations eventually became well established and known as the "substantiation" requirement.[633] The requirement is fully embedded in the FTC's 1983 *Policy Statement Regarding Advertising Substantiation*.[634] The statement concluded that "[o]bjective claims for products or services represent explicitly or by implication that the advertiser has a reasonable basis supporting these claims. These representations of substantiation are material to consumers."[635] The absence of a reasonable basis has been held to violate Section 5 under both deception and unfairness theories.

The type of support that constitutes a reasonable basis for a particular representation depends on the type of representation and several related factors. It is important to note that FTC does not differentiate between food and other FDA-regulated products (i.e., drugs, medical devices, cosmetics, dietary supplements, and other health-related products).[636] The kind of substantiation required under the law therefore depends on the nature of the advertising claim, not on the FDA's classification of the product advertised.

The FTC determines the requisite level of substantiation by applying what have come to be known as the *"Pfizer* factors." In other words, what constitutes a reasonable basis depends on a number of factors "relevant to the benefits and costs of substantiating a particular claim."[637] These six factors, first articulated in the *Pfizer* case but later adopted in the Commission's Substantiation Policy Statement, are: (1) the type of product; (2) the type of claim; (3) the consequences of a false claim; (4) the benefits of a truthful claim; (5) the cost of developing substantiation for the claim; and (6) the amount of substantiation that experts in the field believe is reasonable.[638]

---

[631] In re Pfizer Inc., 81 F.T.C. 23, 29 (1972).

[632] *Id.*

[633] Porter v. Dietsch, 90 F.T.C. 770, 866 (1977) (quoting Nat'l Comm'n on Egg Nutrition, 88 F.T.C. 89, 191 (1976), *modified*, 605 F.2d 294 (7th Cir. 1979)).

[634] *FTC Substantiation Policy Statement, supra* note 585.

[635] *Id.*

[636] *Id.*

[637] *Id.*

[638] *Id.*

The first two *Pfizer* factors – the type of product and the type of claim – reflect the FTC's reasoning that consumers assume that health-related representations are supported by scientific evidence. Furthermore, representations for health-related products are often "credence claims," representations that may be "difficult or impossible for consumers to evaluate for themselves."[639] Consumers may be able to assess the accuracy of a claim about the taste of a product, but not be able to evaluate representations about cardiovascular health or cancer-risk reduction.

The third *Pfizer* factor – the consequences of a false claim – reflects the FTC's interest in protecting consumers from the dangers of deceptive health claims. When health claims are false or unsubstantiated, consumers may be injured. The injury may be financial. A firm's deceptive claims induce consumers to buy products that do not perform as advertised. Deceptive health representations may injure consumers by inducing them to forego proven treatments.[640]

The fourth and fifth *Pfizer* factors – the benefits of a truthful claim and the cost of developing substantiation for the claim – are often considered together "to ensure that the level of substantiation [the FTC] require[s] is not likely to deter product development or prevent consumers from being told potentially valuable information about product characteristics."[641] The commission does not exempt advertisers making health claims from the legal requirement of substantiation, even where the requisite level of research would be expensive to conduct. The cost of developing substantiation may be relevant to the nature and amount of evidence the commission may require, but it does not exempt firms from being required to substantiate their advertised claims.

The sixth *Pfizer* factor – the amount of substantiation that experts in the field believe is reasonable – has been the primary if not deciding factor in many FTC cases.[642] Where there is an existing standard for substantiation developed by a governmental agency or authoritative nongovernmental body, the FTC accords substantial deference to that standard. For representation about a food product's health benefits, the commission requires "competent and reliable scientific evidence."[643]

(2) *Major Shift in Policy*

Historically, a key characteristic of the substantiation doctrine has been its flexibility. That is, the doctrine has not been used to prescribe specific types of tests or evidence to support particular classes of advertising claims.[644] In recent years, however, this flexible standard has begun to be replaced by a more rigid standard that aligns with the FDA evidentiary standard for the approval of new drugs. FTC orders in recent years have required

---

[639] *Id.*

[640] *See, e.g.*, FTC v. QT, Inc., 512 F.3d 858, 863 (7th Cir. 2008) ("Deceit such as the tall tales that defendants told about the Q-Ray Ionized Bracelet will lead some consumers to avoid treatments that cost less and do more: the lies will lead others to pay too much for pain relief or otherwise interfere with the matching of remedies to medical conditions.").

[641] Removatron, 111 F.T.C. 206, 306 n.20 (1988), *aff'd*, 884 F.2d 1389 (1st Cir. 1989).

[642] *See, e.g., id.* at 307 n.20; *Thompson Med.*, 104 F.T.C. at 825.

[643] Conopco, Inc., 121 F.T.C. 131 (1997) (consent order) (requiring food company to possess "competent and reliable scientific evidence" to support representations that margarine or any other spread will help to reduce the risk of heart disease").

[644] J. Howard Beales III, et. al., *In Defense of the Pfizer Factors*, George Mason University Law and Economics Research Paper Series, 4 (May 2012).

two well-controlled clinical trials to substantiate certain claims, including: weight loss,[645] the duration of diarrhea and children's absence from school,[646] and reducing temporary irregularity or improving intestinal transit time.[647] Consent decrees for a case that is currently in administrative litigation have included "fencing-in" provisions (i.e., provisions directed not only against the same form of deception that was the subject of the original enforcement action, but also against other types of violations that reasonably relate to the past deception), which essentially require FDA approval of certain claims, prior to the advertisement.[648] These cases represent a significant departure from previous FTC cases, which relied upon the FTC's old flexible standard, allowing claims simply if supported by competent and reliable scientific evidence.[649] The cases are also difficult to reconcile with the FTC's previous recognition that § 5 may permit a qualified health claim that expresses the extent of the scientific support even where such claim has not yet been authorized by the FDA.[650] The FTC's approach is not entirely consistent, however. In one litigated case involving weight loss claims for acai berry products, the FTC used the traditional "competent and reliable scientific evidence" standard for substantiation.[651]

(3) POM Wonderful Action

This shift in policy was challenged in litigation, resulting in a court decision by the DC Circuit in 2015 in the case of POM Wonderful LLC v. FTC.[652] The case resulted in a partial validation and partial rejection of the FTC's new approach.

- Complaint

On September 27, 2010, the FTC initiated action against POM Wonderful, LLC. asserting that the company made false and unsubstantiated health claims about its pomegranate juice and pills.[653] The action and the appeals present a useful case study of the FTC's enforcement action against food enterprises and important implications for food advertising. The FTC alleged that POM engaged in deceptive acts and disseminated false advertising in violations of Sections 5(a) and 12 of the FTCA. The FTC challenged forty-three POM advertisements and promotional pieces, including print advertisements, newsletters, website advertisements, and public relations promotional materials. The complaint specifically alleged that POM deceptively claimed that its pomegranate juice and dietary

---

[645] See FTC v. Iovate Health Sciences USA, Inc., File No. 072 3187 (W. Dist. N.Y., July 14, 2010).

[646] Nestle HealthCare Nutrition, Inc., File No. 092 3087 (July 14, 2010).

[647] The Dannon Company, Inc., FTC File No. 0823158 (December 15, 2010).

[648] See, e.g., Nestle HealthCare, supra note 646. (claims of preventing or reducing the risk of upper respiratory tract infections); The Dannon Company, supra note 647 (claims that covered products reduce the likelihood of getting a cold or the flu).

[649] See, e.g., Sterling Drug, Inc. et al, 101 F.T.C. 375 (1983) (allowed claims that a household disinfectant could reduce the incidence and spread of colds if supported by competent and reliable scientific evidence).

[650] See FTC Enforcement Policy Statement on Food Advertising, 59 Fed. Reg. 28,388 (June 1, 1994).

[651] See, e.g., Federal Trade Commission v. IMM Interactive, Inc., Case No. 1:11-cv-02484, Northern Dist. Ill., Eastern Division (Apr. 19, 2011); Federal Trade Commission v. DLXM LLC, Case No. CV 11–1889, Eastern District of New York (May 6, 2011).

[652] No. 13–1060 (D.C. Cir. January 2015).

[653] Press Release, Fed. Trade Comm'n, FTC Complaint Charges Deceptive Advertising By POM Wonderful (September 27, 2010).

supplements would treat, prevent, or reduce the risk of heart disease, prostrate cancer, and erectile dysfunction without having a reasonable basis to substantiate such claims.[654] The complaint recommended that POM's claims must be supported by at least two well-designed, well-conducted, randomized, double-blind, placebo-controlled human clinical trials (so-called RCTs). The complaint also proposed that POM agree to pre-screening by the FDA of any claims that its products cure, prevent, treat, or reduce the risk of any disease to prevent future violations.[655]

- ALJ Determination

POM appealed the matter to the ALJ. In determining whether POM disseminated false or misleading advertisements, the ALJ as expected used the three-party inquiry: (1) whether POM disseminated advertisements conveying the claims alleged in the complaint; (2) whether those claims were false or misleading; and (3) whether those claims are material to reasonable consumers. The ALJ found that nineteen of the forty-three challenged ads and promotional materials conveyed health claims.[656] The ALJ determined that the FTC is precluded from requiring FDA preapproval of health claim advertising. The ALJ also concluded that there is no legal basis for the FTC to require RCTs to substantiate all health-related efficacy claims. The ALJ specifically stated that "[t]he required level of substantiation is a question of fact, and the evidence in this case demonstrates that [POM's] implied disease claims require 'competent and reliable scientific evidence,' which does not necessarily require RCTs, such as those required by FDA."[657] RCTs are commonly used for drug testing and can be expensive to administer.

- Appeal to FTC Commission

The order that the commission issued in January 2013 differed from that which the ALJ proposed. First, the commission found that thirty-six, rather than nineteen, ads challenged by the complaint, conveyed health claims.[658] The commission found that the challenged claims were misleading and material. Second, the commission found that the majority of POM's advertising included representations that its claims were supported by clinical or scientific evidence and were thus establishment claims. The commission found that these claims were not properly substantiated. Third, the commission ordered fencing-in relief that required that any disease-related efficacy claims or establishment claims made about POM's challenged products or in connection with POM's sale of any food or dietary supplement had to be supported by at least two RCTs. The commission did not reach the issue of the number of RCTs that will be needed in other cases to substantiate disease claims because the agency found that POM did not have a single RCT. Fourth, the commission did not impose the FTC staff recommendation that would require FDA preapproval for certain disease claims. The commission concluded

---

[654] *See* Complaint, In re POM Wonderful LLC, No. 9344 (F.T.C. September 24, 2010).
[655] *Id.*
[656] Opinion at 9, In re POM Wonderful LLC, No. 9344, (F.T.C. January 10, 2013).
[657] *Id.*
[658] *Id.*

that the Final Order's provision requiring that POM have two RCTs provides a clear bright-line standard that would render requiring preapproval by the FDA redundant.

- DC Court of Appeals

POM petitioned the DC Circuit for review, arguing that the FTC's decision violated the FTCA, APA, and First Amendment. The appellate court agreed with the FTC that the challenged POM ads were misleading under the FTCA. The court also determined that specific efficacy claims were made that the POM products treated, prevented, or reduced the risk of various health conditions, and that these claims were not substantiated.[659] The court rejected POM's contention that the FTC had adopted a new rule without following the APA notice-and-comment requirements, finding that the FTC was entitled to make decisions by adjudication rather than rulemaking.[660] The appellate court also reaffirmed the general principle that there is no First Amendment protection for deceptive or misleading advertising.[661]

The court parted company, however, with the FTC over the agency's requirement that POM substantiate any future disease-related claims with two RCTs. The court ruled that under the *Central Hudson* general test, requiring an RCT satisfied the First Amendment because the FTC had a substantial interest in ensuring the accuracy of commercial speech and that the FTC had adequately demonstrated that requiring an RCT was no more extensive than necessary to serve the stated FTC interests.[662] The court held, however, that the FTC violated the First Amendment to the extent that it imposed a blanket requirement that all disease and health-related claims be substantiated by two RCTS.[663] The court noted that the commission failed to "justify a categorical floor of two RCTs for any and all disease claims."[664] The court qualified its holding by stating that the FTC is not necessarily barred in future cases from imposing a two-RCT substantiation requirement.[665]

- Lessons Learned

A few clear and unclear points can be derived from the *Pom Wonderful* case. First, it is clear that a food advertiser or any advertiser is not permitted under the FTCA or the constitution to engage in deceptive advertising. Second, the two-RCT substantiation requirement is challengeable. As the court explains, where one RCT and other research establish proof of a product's benefit for disease prevention, "there would be substantial interest in assuring that consumers gain awareness of the dietary supplement's benefits and the supporting medical research."[666] It may be that there are fewer two-RCT orders in the future. This conclusion appears to be wholly consistent with the spirit of the *Pearson* progeny of cases. It should be noted, however, the court's order does not say that

---

[659] POM Wonderful LLC v. FTC, *supra* note 652 at 34–5.
[660] *Id.* at 29–30.
[661] *Id.* at 34.
[662] *Id.* at 37–8.
[663] *Id.* at 38.
[664] *Id.*
[665] *Id.* at 45.
[666] *Id.* at 39.

the FTC can never require two-RCTs to substantiate specific types of claims. It is not clear how the RCT standard would apply to general health claims; the court's decision was limited to disease claims. Finally, it is still not entirely clear whether there are different substantiation requirements for foods and dietary supplements versus drugs. The one point that presumably all can agree on is that it is not an easy task to formulate clear guidelines on the amount and type of evidence required to substantiate a food health claims in a manner that is understood by consumers and backed by science.

[e] Enforcement

(1) *Cease and Desist*

The FTC may enforce the FTCA through rulemaking, which affects an entire industry,[667] or adjudication, which issues a case-specific decision for an individual advertiser's practices.[668] Section 12 of the FTCA gives the FTC authority to institute administrative cease-and-desist order proceedings for the dissemination of advertisements that violate Section 12.[669] Thus, when a claim is alleged to be false or misleading, the FTC orders the advertiser to cease and desist from making such claims. Following the issuance of a cease-and-desist order, the FTC proceeds with an administrative hearing and determination, followed by the opportunity for a court appeal. Discontinuance of an offending practice is neither a defense to liability, nor grounds for omission of an order.[670] An essential feature of an administrative cease-and-desist order is a requirement that, for the next twenty years, the company file with the FTC periodic compliance reports about its marketing activities and the steps it has taken to prevent future violations of the FTCA.[671] It may also require corporate defendants to distribute a copy of the order to current and future employees or require an individual defendant to disclose the existence of the order to any future employers.[672]

(2) *Fencing-in Relief*

Almost all FTC orders include some measure of "fencing-in" relief.[673] Fencing-in relief refers to provisions in a final FTC order that are broader than the conduct that is declared unlawful. Fencing-in remedies are designed to prevent future unlawful conduct. Fencing-in relief may bar misleading ads for a particular product and across all of a firm's other unrelated product lines. The connection between this enforcement objective and the fencing-in remedy was recognized by the Supreme Court held in *FTC v. Ruberoid Company*: "If the Commission is to attain the objectives Congress envisioned, it cannot be required to confine its road block to the narrow lane the transgressor has traveled; it must be allowed effectively to close all roads to the prohibited goal, so that its order may not be by-passed with impunity."[674] Courts will overturn the "fencing-in"

---

[667] *See* 15 U.S.C. § 57(a)(1)(B).

[668] *See id.* § 45(b).

[669] *Id.*

[670] Sears, Roebuck & Co., 95 F.T.C. 406, 520 (1980), *aff'd*, 676 F.2d 385 (9th Cir. 1982), *citing* Fedders Corp. v. FTC, 529 F.2d 1398, 1403 (2d Cir. 1976).

[671] *See, e.g.*, Pfizer. Inc., 126 F.T.C. 847, 861–62 (1998) (consent order).

[672] *See, e.g.*, Laser Vision Institute, 136 F.T.C. 1. 35 (2003) (consent order).

[673] *See* FTC v. Nat'l Lead Co., 352 U.S. 419, 431 (1957) ("[R]espondents must remember that those caught violating the Act must expect some fencing in.").

[674] 343 U.S. 470, 473 (1952).

remedy imposed by the FTC "only where there is no reasonable relation between the remedy and the violation."[675] The FTC and reviewing courts consider the following three factors in determining whether an order's coverage bears a "reasonable relation" to the violation it is intended to remedy: "(1) the seriousness and deliberateness of the violation; (2) the case with which the violative claim may be transferred to other products; and (3) whether the respondent has a history of prior violations."[676] The Fourth Circuit in *Telebrands Corp.* noted that some courts have applied an additional factor: the extent to which the claim was health related or the product posed a health risk.[677]

(3) Other Remedies

In some cases, the FTC may seek full financial restitution directly to consumers. Cases involving deceptive health claims have resulted in multimillion-dollar redress orders against advertisers.[678] In the most serious cases, courts have required violators to post substantial bonds before continuing to market products to consumers, or have banned the violators outright from particular industries.[679] In addition to financial remedies, the FTC may seek informational remedies from advertisers alleged to have made deceptive claims, including corrective advertising and mandatory disclosures in future advertising. The FTC first won the right to seek corrective advertising in the landmark case of *Warner-Lambert Co. v. FTC*.[680] For decades, the marketer of Listerine mouthwash had advertised the product as effective in preventing the common cold, a claim found by the FTC and the DC Circuit to be deceptive. The DC Circuit Court found the use of corrective advertising an appropriate remedy in deceptive advertising cases where a "deceptive advertisement has played a substantial role in creating or reinforcing in the public's mind a false and material belief which lives on after the false advertising ceases."[681]

In some circumstances, the FTC may take action against others besides the corporate entity responsible for deceptive advertising. For example, corporate officers may be held individually liable for violations of the FTCA if naming them individually is necessary for the order to be effective in preventing the deceptive practices challenged by the commission.[682] To hold defendants personally liable, the FTC is not required to show that officers intended to defraud consumers.[683] Advertising agencies may also be liable where the agency was an active participant in preparing the violative advertisements, and knew or had reason to know that the advertisements were false or misleading.[684]

---

[675] Telebrands Corp. v. FTC, 457 F.3d 354, 358 (4th Cir. 2006), *citing* Atlantic Ref. Co. v. FTC, 381 U.S. 357, 377 (1965).

[676] *Id.*

[677] *Id.*

[678] *See, e.g.,* FTC v. American Urological Corp., No. 98-CVC-2199-JOD (N.D. Ga. Apr. 29, 1999) ($18.5 million judgment against marketers of dietary supplement purporting to treat impotence).

[679] *See, e.g.,* FTC v. Am. Urological Corp., No. 98-CVC-2199-JOD (N.D. Ga. Apr. 29, 1999) (imposing $6 million bond on marketer of "Vaegra," a dietary supplement purporting to treat impotence).

[680] Warner-Lambert Co. v. FTC, 562 F.2d 749 (D.C. Cir. 1977), *aff'g,* 86 F.T.C. 1398 (1975).

[681] *Id.* at 762.

[682] *See, e.g.,* FTC v. Standard Educ. Soc'y, 302 U.S. 112, 119–20 (1937).

[683] *Id.*

[684] *See, e.g.,* Campbell Mithun, L.L.C., 133 F.T.C. 702 (2002) (consent order) (challenging agency's role in advertisements claiming that Wonder Bread with added calcium could improve children's brain function and memory).

Finally, the FTC has also taken enforcement action against deceptive endorsements or testimonials. Through its *Guides Concerning Use of Endorsements and Testimonials in Advertising*, the commission has made clear that false or deceptive endorsements – whether by experts, groups, celebrities, or consumers – violate Section 5.[685] The guides are premised on the principle that, because consumers may rely on the opinions of endorsers in making product decisions, endorsements must be nondeceptive. Endorsements "may not contain any representations which would be deceptive, or could not be substantiated if made directly by the advertiser."[686]

§ 4.08 Food Marketing Litigation

[1] *Growth*

In recent years, litigation over food marketing claims has increased dramatically. This trend is due in part to gaps in the federal regulation of food labels, leaving certain issues unresolved (e.g., the lack of a regulatory definition for the term "natural"), relaxed proof requirements under state consumer fraud statutes, and the amenability to class certification. Also fueling the increase in putative class action lawsuits for food marketing claims is the active role the FTC and the FDA are taking in assessing food labeling and advertising. Regulatory enforcement, such as FDA warning letters issued to food companies to address labeling infractions and FTC enforcement actions against deceptive food advertising, help spur class action suits. That is, consumer class action complaints often follow these enforcement actions. Another impetus for consumer class action food-marketing lawsuits is investigations and media campaigns by consumer groups. For example, the Center for Science in the Public Interest triggered a consumer fraud class action lawsuit in California when it sent a letter to Unilever, the parent company to Ben & Jerry's,[687] challenging the company's use of "All Natural" claims on labels for ice creams and frozen yogurts that contained alkalized cocoa, corn syrup, and partially hydrogenated soybean oil. Ben and Jerry's removed the contested language from its products, but a class action lawsuit was still filed.[688]

[2] *Substantiation of Advertising Claims*

Private plaintiffs cannot enforce the FTCA, and, accordingly, courts have recognized that private plaintiffs – unlike the FTC – cannot state a cause of action based on an alleged failure to substantiate advertising claims. Instead, private plaintiffs in consumer fraud class actions must affirmatively plead and prove that a company's statements are false and misleading.[689] It should be noted, however, that where a company makes "establishment claims" (*i.e.*, a claim that "suggests that a product's effectiveness or superiority

---

[685] 16 C.F.R. §§ 255.0-5.

[686] 16 C.F.R. § 255.1(a).

[687] Letter from Center for Science in the Public Interest, to Paul Polman, CEO, Unilever (August 12, 2010).

[688] The court in 2014 refused to grant class certification in the suit accusing Ben & Jerry's Homemade Inc. of falsely advertising ice cream products containing a synthetic agent as "all-natural." Andrew Scurria, Ben & Jerry's Sinks Class Cert. In "All Natural" Label suit, Law 360, January 7, 2014.

[689] See, e.g., Franulovic v. Coca Cola Co., 390 F. App'x 125, 128 (3d Cir. 2010); Stanley v. Bayer HealthCare LLC, No. 11 cv 862, 2012 WL 1132920, at *3 (S.D. Cal. April 3, 2012).

has been scientifically established"), the company's lack of adequate scientific proof for its claim may render it false or misleading, in violation of consumer fraud statutes and other state laws.

[3] State Consumer Protection Statutes

[a] Usage

As noted previously in this chapter, there is also no private cause of action under the FDCA.[690] Challenges to food labeling and advertising are generally based on state consumer protection statutes, and nearly every state now has some version of one enacted in law. Consumer protection statutes vary widely, but generally prohibit unfair, deceptive, or unconscionable acts or practices.[691] These statutes are broadly drafted and, consistent with legislative intent, courts give expansive meaning to these statutory terms by applying them to prohibit a wide array of conduct that is deemed unfair, immoral, or unconscionable.[692] These statutes generally share the following characteristics that create favorable conditions for class action lawsuits: (1) minimal standing requirements; (2) the absence of a causation requirement; (3) amenability to class action certification; and (4) the authorization of attorney fees and treble damages. State consumer protection statutes have thus "eased the requirements for stating a claim and have limited the defenses that are characteristic of common law actions."[693]

A couple of cases early on demonstrated the potential expansive use of consumer protection statutes in food marketing litigation. The first of these cases was *Tylka v. Gerber Products Co.*[694] In *Tylka*, plaintiffs brought claims of common law fraud against Gerber for advertising baby food in violation of the Illinois Consumer Fraud and Deceptive Business Practices Act (ICFA) and the Uniform Deceptive Trade Practices Act (UDTPA). Although the court granted summary judgment to Gerber because plaintiffs could not show proximate cause, it noted that "the [IFCA] affords consumers broader protection than a common law fraud action because it eliminates the elements of scienter or the necessity of proof of actual reliance."[695]

The second case was *Pelman v. McDonald's* case, a highly profiled case in the media and one that struck a nerve with the public over values of personal responsibility in context of obesity while at the same time exposing the nutrition concerns of fast-food restaurants. The lasting significance of *Pelman* was that it encouraged the use of consumer protection statutes to challenge false advertising. The Second Circuit held that the district court erred in dismissing the plaintiffs' claims under New York's Consumer

---

[690] See, e.g., Murphy v. Cuomo, 913 F. Supp. 671, 679 (N.D.N.Y. 1996).

[691] *See, e.g.,* CAL. BUS. & PROF. CODE § 17200 (defining "unfair competition" as "any unlawful, unfair or fraudulent business act or practice and unfair, deceptive, untrue or misleading advertising"); N.J. STAT. ANN. § 56:8-2 (prohibiting "any unconscionable commercial practice ... or the knowing concealment, suppression, or omission of any material fact").

[692] *See* State Farm Fire & Cas. Co. v. Superior Court, 53 Cal. Reptr. 2d 229, 234–235 (1996) (quoting People v. Casa Blanca Convalescent Homes, Inc., 159 Cal. App. 3 509, 530 (1984)) (noting that an unfair business practice occurs when that practice "offends an established public policy or when the practice is immoral, unethical, oppressive, unscrupulous or substantially injurious to consumers").

[693] *See* 1 BUSINESS TORTS § 7.06 (Joseph D. Zamore et al. eds., 2001).

[694] No. 96 C 1647, 1999 U.S. Dist. LEXIS 10718, at *1 (N.D. Ill. July 1, 1999).

[695] *Id.* at *4.

Protection Act.[696] After the district court dismissed the plaintiffs' original complaint,[697] the plaintiffs filed an amended complaint based on violations of New York's Consumer Protection Statute. Plaintiffs alleged that McDonald's advertising: (1) misled plaintiffs to believe that its food was nutritious; (2) failed to adequately disclose that its processing and additives made certain foods less healthy; and (3) failed to provide nutritional information as advertised.[698] While acknowledging that § 349 of the New York Consumer Protection Statute does not require reliance on a deceptive practice, the lower court again dismissed the plaintiffs' complaint in large part because in failing to "address the role that 'a number of other factors other than diet may come to play in obesity and the health problems of which the plaintiffs complain."[699] The Second Circuit, addressing only the § 349 ("deceptive acts") claims, reversed the district court.[700] The court concluded that questions about plaintiffs' diets and exercise habits and family health history were appropriate for discovery and that the complaint's failure to answer these questions was not fatal.[701]

[b] California and New Jersey

The popular use of consumer protection statutes as the vehicle for bringing claims against food enterprises for marketing claims has found a home in two particularly friendly venues for class action lawsuits: California and New Jersey. California's Unlawful Competition Law (CUCL) prohibits unlawful, unfair, and fraudulent practices.[702] The CUCL also prohibits violations of California's false advertising statute.[703] The CUCL has been broadly construed to "borrow" violations of other laws as unlawful practices, which are then treated as independently actionable.[704] Thus, California's consumer protection statutes incorporate the requirements of the FDCA, such that violations of the FDCA are actionable under state law.[705] While the CUCL authorizes only injunctive relief and restitution, and not damages, recovery of attorney fees may occur under California's private attorney general statutes.[706] In California, a plaintiff has suffered injury in fact sufficient to bring a claim whenever he or she has "lost money or property."[707] This requirement is satisfied whenever plaintiffs "alleged that they were deceived by a product's label into spending money to purchase the product, and would not have purchased it otherwise."[708]

The New Jersey Fraud Act (NJCFA) also attracts food class action lawsuits because the New Jersey Supreme Court has held that courts should construe the state's class action

---

[696] *Pelman III*, 396 F.3d 508 (2d. Cir. 2005).

[697] *Pelman II*, No. 02-Civ.-7821, prior to 2003 U.S. Dist. LEXIS 15202, at *42.

[698] *Id.* at *6.

[699] *Id.* at *31 (quoting *Pelman I*, 237 F. Supp. 2d 512, 538–9 (S.D.N.Y. 2003)).

[700] *See Pelman III*, 396 F.3d 508, 512 (2d Cir. 2005).

[701] *Id.* at 512 (remanding only portions of the district court's dismissal).

[702] CAL. BUS & PROF. CODE § 17200.

[703] CAL. BUS. & PROF. CODE § 17500.

[704] See Farmers Ins. Exch. v. Superior Court, 2 Cal. 4th 377, 383 (1992).

[705] *See, e.g.,* CAL. HEALTH & SAFETY CODE §§ 110100, 110665, 110670 (providing that food is misbranded under California law if, inter alia, it does not conform to the requirements set forth in the FDCA or the regulations adopted pursuant thereto).

[706] *See* CAL. CIV. PROC. CODE § 1021.5

[707] Kwikset Corp. v. Superior Ct., 51 Cal. 4th 310, 317 (2011).

[708] *Id.*

rules liberally for consumer fraud class actions.[709] The NJCFA does not require plaintiffs to prove reliance, but only an unlawful act and an ascertainable loss. The Act mandates treble damages and reasonable attorney fees, and costs in most cases.[710] In addition to consumer fraud, express or implied warranty claims may be made. In a consumer food fraud action, warranty claims often turn on the issue of whether state law requires a showing of actual reliance.

[c] Defenses

(1) *Overview*

It is useful to view the array of food-marketing litigation cases through the prism of defenses advanced by the defense bar. There have been numerous defenses to consumer food fraud class actions, some more successful than others. Because food-marketing litigation is still developing, the success of plaintiffs and defendants in these cases varies. In some instances, conflicts in court cases have created confusion. In other instances, a consensus of opinion may be appearing.

At least five defense strategies have been advanced in consumer fraud cases. First, is proving the factual truth of the allegedly misleading labeling claims. Second, is arguing that the alleged misleading labeling claims are expressly or impliedly preempted by federal regulations. Third, is arguing that primary jurisdiction lies with the federal regulatory body and that the court should defer to the agency's expertise. Fourth, is arguing the failure to state a claim for relief that is plausible on its face such that the court may infer that the defendant is liable for the misconduct alleged. Fifth, is arguing failure to allege consumer fraud claims with the particularity required under Federal Rule of Civil Procedure 9(b).

In most cases, where a defense does not result in the dismissal of the case, a settlement ensues. For example, in *In re Quaker Oats Labeling Litigation*,[711] which relates to the inclusion of partially hydrogenated oils (PHOs) in Quaker Oat's products, the parties sought preliminary approval of a settlement agreement. Quaker Oats agreed to remove PHOs from its products by the end of 2014 and to thereafter label any products containing trace amounts of PHOs as containing "dietary insignificant amount of trans fat."[712]

(2) *Express Preemption*

Preemption arguments have been met with varying degrees of success. In general, if legal claims challenge labeling statements that are specifically required or permitted under the FDA's regulations, such claims are expressly preempted. On the contrary, when the FDA does not specifically define labeling terms of conditions under which they may be used, courts have rejected preemption arguments.

Although the attention in food-marketing litigation is focused on FDA-regulated food, it should be noted that the preapproval requirement of FSIS regulated labels for meat and poultry products make consumer fraud litigation for these products more susceptible to preemption defenses. In addition, the express preemption provisions of FMIA and PPIA are more expansive: allegations that a label should include more or different

---

[709] Strawn v. Canuso, 140 N.J. 43, 68 (1995).
[710] *See* N.J. Stat. Ann. § 56:8–19; Carroll v. Cellco P'ship, 713 A.2d 509, 516 (N.J. Super. Ct. App. Div. 1998).
[711] No. 10cv0502 (N.D. Cal.).
[712] *Id.*

information will likely be dismissed.[713] Also, preemptive arguments that the FSIS inspection act expresses Congress's intent to fully occupy the legislative field on product labeling would likely succeed.

The trend in food marketing litigation is that defendants can obtain dismissal of claims alleging misrepresentation of a food's benefits if those claims are expressly allowed by FDA regulations. The NLEA in particular provides strong arguments in favor of express preemption. Passed to "clarify and to strengthen [the FDA's] authority to require nutrition labeling on foods," the NLEA contains an express preemption provision that prohibits "any requirement for the labeling of food ... that is not identical to" federal regulations.[714] The FDA has interpreted "not identical to" broadly to mean "state requirements directly or indirectly impos[ing] obligations" that are "not imposed by federal law" or that "[d]iffer from those specifically imposed by federal law."[715] Thus, claims brought forth that would impose burdens not identical to federal law, as broadly construed by the FDA, are expressly preempted.

In *Young v. Johnson & Johnson*, the Third Circuit affirmed the District of New Jersey's dismissal of proposed class action plaintiffs' food labeling misrepresentation claims as preempted by federal regulations.[716] Plaintiffs alleged that the label on the butter and margarine substitutes were misleading: while the nutrition facts box and label stated that the product had no trans fat and that plant stanol esters contained in the product could help lower cholesterol, the product actually contained less than one-half gram of trans fat per serving.[717] The court held that both claims were preempted by the NLEA. Specifically, the court found that pursuant to FDA regulations, if a food serving contains less than 0.5 grams of trans fat, manufacturers are permitted to represent on the product labeling that their product contains no trans fats. The court also found that FDA regulations specifically authorize products containing plant stenol esters to make health claims as long as certain conditions are met. Thus, the claims were expressly preempted by the NLEA because they sought "to impose standards that are not identical to those set forth in the act[718] The Ninth Circuit found the same in *Carrea v. Dreyer's Grand Ice Cream, Inc.*, where the court held that the manufacturer's "0g Trans Fat" statement on ice cream product packaging was authorized by the FDA because the product contained less than 0.5 grams of trans fat per serving.[719]

The Seventh Circuit reached a similar conclusion to that reached by the Third and Ninth Circuits in *Turek v. General Mills Inc.*[720] Plaintiff alleged that General Mill's fiber bars labeled with the words "35 percent of your daily fiber" misled her because they contained "processed" fiber extracted from a chicory root.[721] The court noted the labeling provision in 21 U.S.C. § 343(q)(1) that states that the "'label or labeling of food products intended for human consumption must state 'the amount of ... dietary fiber ...

---

[713] *See, e.g.*, Meaunrit v. Pinnacle Foods Grp., LLC, No. C 09-04555, 2010 U.S. Dist. LEXIS 43858 (N.D. Cal. May 5, 2010).

[714] Nat'l Council for Improve Health v. Shalala, 122 F.3d 878, 880 (10th Cir. 1997).

[715] 21 C.F.R. § 100.1(c)(4).

[716] 525 F.App'x 179 (3d. Cir. 2013).

[717] *Id.* at 183.

[718] *Id.* at 184

[719] 475 F. App'x 113 (9th Cir. 2012).

[720] 662 F.3d 423 (7th Cir. 2011).

[721] *Id.* at 425–6.

contained in each serving size or other unit of measure.'"[722] The court found that the product was compliant with the FDA regulations related to labeling that mentions dietary fiber and the plaintiff was compliant with those regulations. Thus, plaintiff's claims were preempted.[723]

District courts have found express preemption in similar cases. For example, in *Dvora v. General Mills Inc.*, the Central District of California held that claims related to the use of fruit names and images on a product's label were preempted because FDA regulations "permit a manufacturer to use the name and image of a fruit on a product's packaging to describe the characterizing flavor" of a product "even where the product does not contain any of that fruit, or contains no fruit at all."[724] Likewise, in *Lateef v. Pharmavite LLC*, the Northern District of Illinois dismissed claims related to the gel coating on a dietary supplement as preempted because the NLEA did not require the gel to be disclosed on the product label.[725] And in *In re Pepsico Inc v. Bottled Water Marketing and Sales Practice Litigation*, the Southern District of New York held claims related to the phrase "Purified Drinking Water" were preempted based on FDA regulations governing the use of the phrase.[726]

In the case *Ang, et al. v. Whitewaves Foods Co.*, et al., plaintiff alleged that a variety of Horizon yogurt products and Silk soy and other nondairy milks were misbranded because their labels disclose evaporated cane juice as opposed to sugar or because the nondairy milks do not come from lactating cows and therefore do not satisfy the standard of identity for milk. The court dismissed the case. On the nondairy milk claims, the court found the standard of identity for milk "pertains to what milk is, rather than what it is not, and makes no mention of non-dairy alternatives such as the Silk Products." The court determined that "the names 'soymilk,' 'almond milk,' and 'coconut milk' accurately describe" the products, and found claims based on those statements preempted and implausible.[727]

(3) Implied Preemption

In situations where there are no FDA regulations directly on point, such as descriptive marketing terms for food and beverages, preemption is not as strong a defense as it is against claims related to requirements expressly governed by the NLEA and other federal laws. For example, plaintiffs have increasingly brought lawsuits alleging that certain foods are deceptively labeled as "natural," "all natural," "nutritious," or "healthful." Lawsuits challenging these types of claims have frequently involved products containing ingredients like HFCS, alkalized cocoa, factory-made ascorbic acid, and GMOs. Without regulations that can give rise to an express preemption argument, the issue is whether the NLEA or other federal law impliedly preempts these complaints. For the most part, arguments that the NLEA or other federal laws impliedly preempt state law claims have largely been unsuccessful. For example, in *Papas v Naked Juice Co.*, a California district court granted final approval to the settlement of a nationwide class

---

[722] *Id.* at 427.
[723] *Id.*
[724] No. 11-1074-GHW, 2011 U.S. Dist. LEXIS 55513, at *4 (C.D. Cal. May 16, 2011).
[725] No. 12 C 5611, 2012 U.S. Dist. LEXIS 152528, at *insert page number (N.D. Ill. October 24, 2012).
[726] 588 F. Supp. 2d 527, 537–538 (S.D.N.Y. 2008).
[727] No. 13-CV-1953, 2013 WL 6492353, at *4 (N.D. Cal. December 10, 2013).

action related to Naked Juice Co.'s practice of labeling products "All Natural," "100% Juice," "100% Fruit," "Not From Concentrate," and "Non-GMO."[728]

Plaintiffs also sued Snapple Beverage Company, alleging that its products labeled "all natural" contained HFCS.[729] Consumers have brought claims against Frito-Lay for its "all natural" claims on products (including Tostitos, Sun Chips, and bean dip) allegedly containing genetically modified corn or soy, as well as hexane-extracted soybean oil.[730] Green Giant products have also been targeted for purportedly containing GMOs.[731] Products as varied as cookies, smoothie kits, canned tomatoes, cocoa, and cooking spray have been the targets of consumer class actions challenging their labeling as "natural" based on a variety of allegedly nonnatural ingredients. As noted previously in this chapter, the lack of express preemption on the claim "natural" and "all natural" is an intentional regulatory gap: the FDA has defined "natural" only in the limited use of natural flavors.[732] The FDA has repeatedly declined to engage in formal rulemaking to define the term due to "resource limitations and other agency priorities."[733] The end result is the FDA's informal policy statement that "natural" means that "nothing artificial or synthetic (including all color additives regardless of source) has been included in, or has been added to, a food that would not normally be expected to be in the food."[734] The lack of defined standards for "natural" offers significant litigation opportunities for plaintiffs to file class actions claiming they were misled by the "natural" advertising into purchasing products that are not, in fact, natural.

In addition to the term "natural," complaints of certain health claims have avoided the preemption challenge. To avoid preemption, consumer class action suits must challenge health claim statements that fall outside of FDA-approved claims, either established by a petition process or by meeting the "substantial scientific agreement" requirement. These claims typically allege that a product is clinically proven to prevent or cure a disease or otherwise provide some health benefit. Examples of health claims that have been challenged in class action suits include: (1) claims of the antioxidant or immunity-boosting properties of foods; (2) health properties of probiotics in yogurt; and (3) claims that foods contain particular nutrients that may reduce cholesterol or prevent cancer, strokes, or heart attacks.

(4) *Primary Jurisdiction*

The primary jurisdiction doctrine is another common defense whereby a defendant argues that the relevant agency rather than the courts should perform the initial decision-making responsibility. Courts in New Jersey and California have accepted this

---

[728] LA CV11-08276 JAK, 2012 U.S. Dist. LEXIS 76067 (C.D. Cal. May 14, 2012).

[729] First Amended Class Action Complaint & Jury Demand, Weiner v. Snapple Beverage Corp., No. 07-cv-8742 (DLC), 2007 WL 4837756 (S.D.N.Y. November 20, 2007).

[730] Class Action Complaint, Deaton v. Frito-Lay N. Am., Inc., No. 1:12-civ-01029-SOH (W.D. Ark. Apr. 2, 2012); Class Action Complaint, Altman v. Frito-Lay N. Am., Inc., No. 0:12-cv-61803-WJZ (S.D. Fla. September 13, 2012).

[731] Class Action Complaint, Cox v. Gen. Mills, Inc., No. 3:12-cv-06377-WHA (N.D. Cal. December 17, 2012).

[732] 21 C.F.R. § 101.22

[733] Hitt v. Ariz. Beverage Co., LLC, Case No. 08cv809 WHQ (POR), 2009 U.S. Dist. LEXIS 16871, at *4 (S.D. Cal. February 4, 2009) (citing 56 Fed. Reg. 60466 and 58 Fed. Reg. 2407.

[734] 58 Fed. Reg. 2302, 2407.

argument and have stayed consumer fraud actions alleging that the use of the term "natural" was misleading on foods containing HFCS. The courts in these cases stayed the matters for a limited time to give the FDA an opportunity to weigh in on the issue; however, in each case the stay was lifted after the agency declined to take up the issue due to lack of agency resources.[735]

In 2013, a string of cases on the term "natural" were decided on the point of primary jurisdiction, but with varying results. In *Janney et al v. General Mills*,[736] plaintiffs alleged that General Mills' Nature Valley Products were falsely advertised as natural because they contained HFCS and similar sweeteners. The court reviewed the FDA's protracted history of not defining "natural" and the agency's refusal to rule on the issue, even when asked by courts. On the basis of this review, the court refused defendant's request to dismiss the case.[737] Conversely, in *Cox v. Gruma Corp.*,[738] the plaintiff claimed that the defendant's tortillas were falsely advertised as "natural" because they contained genetically modified organisms. Applying the primary jurisdiction doctrine, the court stayed the case for six months and referred the dispute to the FDA.[739] In *Kane et al v. Chobani*,[740] the plaintiff claimed that the defendant's yogurt was falsely advertised as "all natural" because it included fruit or vegetable juice concentrate for coloring. The court dismissed the complaint because of the clear disclosure on the labels of the presence of fruit or vegetable concentrate, rendering it not plausible that a reasonable consumer would be misled into thinking "all natural" advertising meant the yogurt did not contain added juice.

In *Pelayo v. Nestle USA Inc. et al*,[741] the plaintiff argued that the defendant's pasta was falsely advertised as "All Natural" when the products contained xanthan gum and soy lecithin, allegedly unnatural ingredients. The court dismissed the case, with prejudice, on the ground that no reasonable consumer would be misled. Specifically, the court noted that the plaintiff failed to offer an objective or plausible definition of the phrase "all natural," and the court rejected plaintiff's attempt to use the dictionary definition of "natural" (i.e., produced or existing in nature). The court also noted that the reasonable consumer is "aware that Buitoni Pastas are springing fully-formed from Ravioli tress and Tortellini bushes." The court also rejected the plaintiff's reliance on the FDA's informal guidance, noting that it did not establish a legal, binding requirement on the manufacturers. Finally, the court observed that, even if "natural" was ambiguous; the ingredient list printed on every package disclosed that the products contained the challenged ingredients, thereby preventing any reasonable consumer from being misled. Thus, in the absence of a plausible, objective definition of "natural," and the plaintiff's failure to show that reasonable consumers shared her subjective definition, the court dismissed her claims on the theory of primary jurisdiction.

---

[735] *See* Coyle v. Hornell Beverage Co., Civ. No. 08-02797, 2010 U.S. Dist. LEXIS 59467 (D.N.J. June 15, 2010); Holk v. Snapple Beverage Corp., Civil Action No. 07-3018, 2010 U.S. Dist. LEXIS 81596 (D.N.J. August 2010); Ries v. Hornell Brewing Co., Case No. 10-1139-JF, 2010 U.S. Dist. LEXIS 86384 (N.D. Cal. July 23, 2010).

[736] 944 F.Supp.2d 806 (N.D. Cal. 2013).

[737] *Id.*

[738] No. 12–6502 (N.D. Cal. July 11, 2013).

[739] *Id.*

[740] 973 F.Supp.2d 11120 (N.D. Cal. 2014).

[741] 989 F.Supp.2d 973 (C.D. Cal. 2013).

[4] *Lanham Act: Implications of POM Wonderful v. Coca-Cola Co.*

  [a] Ninth Circuit

The Ninth Circuit's decision in *Pom Wonderful LLC v. Coca-Cola Co.*, encouraged
some food and beverage firms to argue that labeling claims should be dismissed based
on implied preemption or implied primary jurisdiction.[742] Pom Wonderful, a company
that manufactures pomegranate juice, filed a lawsuit against Coca-Cola, alleging that
pomegranate juice, produced under its Minute Maid brand, misled consumer because it
actually consisted almost entirely of apple juice and grape juice.[743] In the lawsuit, it was
discovered that the subject "pomegranate blueberry" juice actually contains just 0.3 percent pomegranate juice and 0.2 percent blueberry juice.[744] In addition, Pom Wonderful
alleged that a consumer survey showed that the product's label misleads consumers,
making them believe the product contains primarily pomegranate and blueberry juice,
when it really is almost entirely cheap filler juices.[745]

  Pom Wonderful alleged that the false advertising violated the Lanham Act, a federal
statute that "broadly prohibits false advertising," as well as California's consumer protection statutes. The trial court dismissed Pom's Lanham Act claims. It reasoned that when
FDA regulations conflicted with the Lanham Act, by authorizing certain statements on
products that would otherwise be a violation of the Lanham Act, the court should defer
to the FDA's expertise.[746]

  The Ninth Circuit affirmed that decision. The court of appeals discussed the broad
statutory framework of the Lanham Act and the FDA's likewise broad regulatory mandate under the FDCA. The court then identified a conflict between the FDCA and
the Lanham Act. On the one hand, the Lanham Act "authorizes suit against those who
use a false or misleading description or representation 'in connection with any goods,'"
and suits can be brought "by any person 'who believes that he or she is or is likely to be
damaged by' the false description or representation." The FDA, on the other hand, has
"promulgated regulations that address how a manufacturer may name and label its juice
beverages," and only the FDA can act on violations of the FDCA and FDA regulations.
The court reasoned that the FDA's exclusive ability to bring suits under its regulations
squarely conflicts with the broader cause of action contemplated by the Lanham Act. It
resolved this conflict in favor of the FDA's regulations, reasoning that it should defer to
the FDA's expertise. Because Coca-Cola's labeling complied with the FDA regulations
at issue and because "[i]f the FDA believes that more should be done to prevent deception, or that Coca-Cola's label misleads consumers, it can act," the court affirmed the
district court's decision.[747] The court went on to explain that "under our precedent, for a
court to act when the FDA has not – despite regulating extensively in this area – would
risk undercutting the FDA's expert judgments and authority."[748]

---

[742] 679 F.3d 1170 (9th Cir. 2012) (hereinafter Ninth Circuit).
[743] *See* POM Wonderful LLC v. Coca Cola Co., 727 F. Supp. 2d 849, 858 (C.D. Cal. 2010) *aff'd in part,*
    vacated in part, remanded sub nom. Pom Wonderful LLC v. Coca-Cola Co., 679 F.3d 1170 (9th Cir.
    2012) *rev'd,* 134 S. Ct. 2228, 189 L. Ed. 2d 141 (U.S. 2014) (hereinafter District Court).
[744] *See* Ninth Circuit at 1173.
[745] *See* District Court at 857–8.
[746] *See* District Court at 872–4.
[747] Ninth Circuit at 1177.
[748] *Id.*

This last point emboldened some defendants to argue for implied preemption of state law labeling claims when they could not argue for express preemption. The argument did not meet with success.[749] Courts typically explained that "Pom Wonderful limited its discussions to whether the FDCA preempted Lanham Act claims that required the court to interpret FDA regulations" and "did not analyze claims brought under a state law that mirrors the FDCA."[750] Some district courts read the Ninth Circuit's *Pom Wonderful* decision and concluded that it is not even a preemption case. They reasoned that the case is implicitly about the doctrine of primary jurisdiction, which allows courts to defer to regulatory agencies regarding complicated questions within the agency's expertise.[751] For example, in *Astiana v. Hain Celestial Group Inc.*, the court addressed claims related to whether the use of the terms "all natural," "pure and natural," and "pure, natural and organic" on the label of cosmetic products was false or misleading.[752] The court relied heavily on *Pom Wonderful* to hold that it should defer to the FDA's power to regulate. First, the court construed *Pom Wonderful* as a case "actually based on the idea of deference to the FDA." It cited *Pom Wonderful* for the propositions that "issues of beverage labeling have been entrusted by Congress to the FDA" and that "for a court to act when the FDA has not – despite regulating extensively in this area – would risk undercutting the FDA's expert judgments and authority."[753] The court then reviewed the FDA's statements on the use of the term "natural" on food and cosmetic products, respectively. It explained that "[t]he only FDA statement regarding the use of the word 'natural' comes in the form of an 'informal policy statement,' and is limited to the food labeling context."[754] Because the FDA had not issued "rules or regulations (or even informal policy statements) regarding the use of the word 'natural' on cosmetics labels," the court "decline[d] to make any independent determination" of whether defendants' use of "natural" was false or misleading. Doing so would "risk undercutting the FDA's expert judgments and authority."[755]

[b] Supreme Court

In a unanimous decision, the Supreme Court in July 2014 reversed the Ninth Circuit and remanded.[756] The Court held that competitors may bring Lanham Act claims alleging unfair competition from false or misleading product descriptions on food labels regulated by FDCA. The Court made clear that the case was not a preemption case.[757] It framed

---

[749] *See* Kosta v. Del Monte Corp., No. 12-cv-01722-YGR, 2013 U.S. Dist. LEXIS 69319, at *8 (N.D. Cal. May 15, 2013).

[750] *Id.*; *See also* Khasin v. Hershey Co., No. 5:12-CV-01862 EJD, 2012 U.S. Dist. LEXIS 161300, at *5 (N.D. Cal. November 9, 2012) (limiting the holding of *Pom Wonderful* to "barring causes of action brought under the federal Lanham Act where doing so would implicate the rules and regulations set forth under the FDCA").

[751] *See, e.g.,* Syntek Semiconductor Co., v. Microchip Technology Inc., 307 F.3d 775, 780 (9th Cir. 2002).

[752] Astiana v. Hain Celestial Group Inc., 905 F. Supp. 2d 1013, 1014–16 (N.D. Cal. 2012).

[753] *Id.* at 1015–16 (quoting *Pom Wonderful*, 679 F.3d at 1177).

[754] *Id.* at 1016.

[755] *Id.* (quoting Ninth Circuit at 1177).

[756] Pom Wonderful LLC v. Coca-Cola Co., 134 S. Ct. 2228, 189 L. Ed. 2d 141, 110 U.S.P.Q.2d 1877 (2014) (hereinafter Supreme Court).

[757] The court noted that "in pre-emption cases, the question is whether state law is pre-empted by a federal statute, or in some instances, a federal agency action." Supreme Court at 2230 (citing Wyeth v. Levine, 555 U.S. 555, 563 (2009).

the case as involving preclusion of actions under one federal statute (Lanham Act) by the provisions of another federal statute (FDCA). The Court found that "[t]here is no statutory text or established interpretive principle to support the contention that the FDCA precludes Lanham Act suits" such as the one brought by POM Wonderful. Instead, the court found that "FDCA and the Lanham Act complement each other in the federal regulation of misleading food and beverage labels."[758] Noting that Congress limited FDCA's preemption to state and local requirements, the seventy-year coexistence of the two federal statutes serves as "powerful evidence that Congress did not intend FDA oversight to be the exclusive means" of ensuring truthful food labeling.[759] The Court also went a step further and noted that the two statutes complement each other in a practical way: the FDCA enables the FDA to enforce the detailed prescriptions of the implementing regulations while the Lanham Act enables food enterprise competitors to do what the FDA cannot do – assess the marketplace dynamic and sue companies for unfair competition practices – for the ultimate protection of competitors and consumers.[760] The Court found this "complementary" construct more consistent with congressional intent than Coca-Cola's assertion that FDCA precludes a Lanham Act claim because Congress intended national uniformity in food labeling.[761]

The implications of the Supreme Court decision will be evident over time. It is clear that food enterprises may now be exposed to Lanham Act claims from competitors even if they have complied with the technical labeling regulations issued by the FDA. However, it is doubtful that the Court's decision should impact the preclusive effect of the FDCA on private enforcement claims based on state law. Because the consumer class actions against the food industry are almost exclusively brought under state law, it is likely that preemption and uniformity principles – to the extent they applied previously – will continue to apply in the same manner following the Supreme Court decision.

§ 4.09 Food Disparagement Laws

[1] Response to Media Reports

One interesting outcome of the rising consumer appetite for information about the food system is the broadcasting of stories about certain food products. Such stories have given rise to food disparagement laws, also known as food libel laws or informally as veggie libel laws. A total of thirteen states have passed food disparagement laws, starting in the 1990s.

Food disparagement laws first emerged when Washington apple growers had failed in a common -law product disparagement case against CBS Broadcasting, Inc. (CBS) over a critical segment on *60 Minutes*.[762] In response, states passed food libel laws.[763] In 1998, in a well-publicized case, television talk-show host Oprah Winfrey and one of her guests were involved in a lawsuit, commonly referred to as the Amarill Texas beef trial, which rested on whether the Texas version of a food libel law applied to disparaging comments made on Winfrey's show about beef and the mad cow scare.[764] More recently,

---

[758] *Id.*

[759] *Id.* at 2237 (citing *Wyeth*, 555 U.S., at 575).

[760] *Id.* at 2238–9.

[761] *Id.* at 2239–40.

[762] *See* Auvil v. CBS 60 Minutes, 67 F.3d 816, 823 (9th Cir. 1995) (per curiam).

[763] *See, e.g.*, ALA. CODE §§ 6-5-620 to -625 (2011); OHIO REV. CODE ANN. § 2307.81 (West 2011).

[764] TEX. CIV. PRAC. & REM. CODE ANN. §§ 96.001 –.004 (West 2005).

as referenced in Chapter 1, Beef Products, Inc. (BPI) sued American Broadcasting Companies, Inc. (ABC) for food libel, defamation, and tortious interference.[765] In 2012, ABC broadcasted a segment on its evening news show regarding the manufacturing of "lean finely textured beef" (LFTB) by BPI.[766] This broadcast, as well as the follow-up reports and social media communications, repeatedly referred to LFTB as "pink slime," a term originated by a USDA employee for the processed meat. As a result of the unfavorable media exposure, the demand for LFTB declined dramatically, taking a toll on BPI, which closed three processing plants, cut hundreds of jobs, and filed for bankruptcy.

As a whole, the thirteen food disparagement state statutes allow food producers to bring a cause of action against anyone who disparages their product. While the statutes differ considerably between themselves, taken as a whole, each contains six main elements: (1) dissemination to the public in any manner; (2) dissemination of false information the disseminator knows to be false; (3) stating or implying that a perishable food product is not safe for consumption by the consuming public; (4) information is presumed false when not based on reasonable or reliable scientific inquiry, facts, or data; (5) disparagement provides a cause of action for damages; and (6) any action must be filed within one or two years.[767] Most of the statutes provide that the person who has standing to bring a food disparagement action is a "producer," which is generally defined as "the person who actually grows or produces perishable agricultural food products."[768] Georgia, though, allows "any party in the entire chain from grower to consumer" to bring a cause of action.[769] All but one of the statutes expressly requires some proof of fault from the defendant.[770] Some states require that the defendant have actual knowledge of the falsity of the statements or that the defendant "knew or should have known" that the information was false.[771] A few states impose strict liability upon the product disparagement defendant.[772] Other states require that the defendant willfully or maliciously disseminated false information to the public.[773] Each state imposes a "falsity" requirement, meaning that the disseminated information must be proven false.[774] The remedy is these statutes are compensatory damages, although Colorado imposes criminal liability.[775]

[2] Constitutional Concerns

These state statutory provisions raise a number of constitutional concerns, including First Amendment issues and upsetting the burden of proof. The Supreme Court in *New York*

---

[765] Beef Products, Inc. v. American Broadcasting Companies, Inc., No. CIV12292, 2012 WL 4017340 (S.D. Cir. September 13, 2012).

[766] Lean finely textured beef is mixed with ground beef to expand the volume of the ground beef and to yield a leaner cheaper end product that is sold to the public. *Id.* at ¶ 2.

[767] David J. Bederman, *Limitations on Commercial Speech: The Evolution of Agricultural Disparagement Statutes*, 10 DePaul Bus. L.J. 191, 195 (1998).

[768] *See, e.g.,* Idaho Code § 6–2001.

[769] GA Code Ann. § 2-16-1.

[770] *See, e.g.,* La. Rev. Stat. Ann. §§ 4501–4.

[771] *See, e.g.,* N.D. Century Code § 32-44-02.

[772] *See, e.g.,* Ala Code § 6-5-620

[773] *See, e.g.,* GA Code, *supra* note 768.

[774] *See, e.g.,* Ariz. Rev. Stat. Ann. § 3–113 (defining false information as information that is not based on reliable scientific facts and reliable scientific data).

[775] *See, e.g.,* Miss Code Ann. § 69-1-251 to 257.

Times v. Sullivan addressed the constitutional requirements imposed on a plaintiff bring-ing a defamation claim.[776] It is likely that the principles set forth in *Sullivan* would apply to disparagement actions. *Sullivan* held that for a plaintiff to succeed on a defamation claim, the plaintiff must prove the "of concerning" requirement and that the defendant acted with "actual malicious intent."[777] By replacing a strict liability standard with the burden of showing actual malice, the Supreme Court's aim was to protect a "free market-place of ideas" because "erroneous statement is inevitable in free debate."[778]

A stated food disparagement statute could be challenged on all three *Sullivan* stan-dards. First, shifting the burden of proof to the defendant may violate the first *Sullivan* tenant for defamation. Second, a state food disparagement statute could be deemed unconstitutional for eliminating the "of and concerning" requirement. The "of and concerning" requirement, which is also known as the "specific reference" requirement, limits a cause of action for defamation or disparagement to persons who are the "direct object of criticism," and denies it to those who "merely complain about nonspecific state-ments that they believe cause them some hurt."[779] Finally, by imposing a lower standard of proof or none at all, a state food disparagement statute may not meet the *Sullivan* requirement for a showing of actual malice. Notwithstanding these constitutional con-cerns, no one case brought under these state statutes has ever expressly ruled upon the constitutionality of these statutes. The Texas case involving Oprah Winfrey show did not reach the constitutional issues: the court found that the ground beef was not part of the food disparagement law because it did not decay (i.e., it could be frozen) within a lim-ited period of time, unlike fresh fruit and vegetables. The appellate court affirmed on other grounds – that the statements were not knowingly false at the time the show was taped.[780] *Beef Products, Inc. v. Am. Broadcasting Cos, Inc.* has the potential of addressing these constitutional concerns that could arise under the South Dakota statute.[781] It is also possible that if the statute is found to regulate political speech, it would be subject under the Supreme Court's 2010 decision in *Citizens United v. Federal Election Commission* to an even higher standard of review.[782]

§ 4.10 Copyright Protection of Recipes

[1] *Protecting Culinary Innovation*

The development of the food movement, the growth of the restaurant industry, the popular-ity and access of haute cuisine, the rise of celebrity chefs, and the proliferation of food blogs on the Internet have all contributed to the expansion and recognition of the new, modern culinary zeitgeist. Food in this context is about art, culture, and social change. This dynamic raises questions regarding the extent to which culinary innovation is protectable as intellec-tual property, specifically by federal copyright law.

---

[776] New York Times Co. v. Sullivan, 376 U.S. 254, 279–80 (1964).
[777] *Sullivan.*, 376 U.S. at 279–80.
[778] *Id.* at 271–2.
[779] Blatty v. New York Times Co., 728 P.2d 1177, 1183 (1986)
[780] Texas Beef Group v. Winfrey, 201 F.3d 680 (5th Cir. 2000).
[781] Rita-Marie Cain Reid, *You Say "Lean Finely Textured Beef," I Say "Pink Slime.,"* 69 Food & Drug L.J. 625(2014).
[782] 558 U.S. 310, 311 (2010).

[2] *Culinary Recipes Not Copyrightable*

The US Constitution inheres in Congress the power to "promote the Progress of Science and useful Arts, by securing for limited Times to Authors and Inventors the exclusive Right to their respective Writings and Discoveries."[783] Federal copyright statutes developed as a result to adequately protect the writings of authors.[784] The Copyright Act of 1976 provides that copyright protection requires a creative work to be (1) original; (2) an expression as opposed to an idea or procedure; (3) a nonutilitarian work or design; and (4) fixed in a tangible medium of expression.[785] Recipes and culinary dishes are not included in the list of statutorily protected subject matter. Although the federal regulations and the US Copyright Office indicate that copyright does not protect "mere listing of ingredients or contents"[786] unless accompanied by "substantial literary expression in the form of an explanation or directions" or as part of a larger work such as a cookbook, this does not entirely foreclose the possibility of copyright protection for culinary dishes and recipes.[787]

Melville Nimmer, in his highly respected treatise on copyright law, has provided a more rigid gloss on the copyrightability of recipes. Nimmer states that "because the content of recipes are clearly dictated by functional considerations, and therefore may be said to lack the required element of originality, even though the combination of ingredients contained in the recipes may be original in a noncopyrightable sense," recipes should not be copyrightable.[788] The circuit courts have relied on Nimmer in concluding that copyright looks unfavorably on culinary recipes. In *Publications International v. Meredith Corporation*, the Seventh Circuit held that individual recipes that merely listed the component ingredients were not copyrightable.[789] In *Barbour v. Head*, the federal district court noted that "to whatever extent it is instructive, [the statement issued by the Register of Copyrights] does not declare that recipes are per se copyrightable."[790] Using the standard set forth by the Register of Copyrights decreeing that recipes "accompanied by substantial literary expression" have a basis for copyright protection, *Barbour* held that "[o]f the twenty recipes identified in Defendant's Motion as being identical or similar, the Court finds that at least a few contain statements that may be sufficiently expressive to exceed the boundaries of mere fact."[791] These statements include "light-hearted or helpful commentary," which the court found satisfied the "substantial literary expression" threshold of the Copyright Register, and which was also copied verbatim in the defendant's cookbooks.[792] The upshot of these two case examples is that an individual culinary recipe, devoid of any literary accouterments, will be per se be copyrightable.

---

[783] U.S. CONST., art. I, 8, cl.8.

[784] Douglas Lichtman, *Copyright as a Rule of Evidence*, 52 DUKE L.J. 683, 689 (2003).

[785] *See* 17 U.S.C. § 102(a).

[786] 37 C.F.R. § 202.1(a).

[787] U.S. COPYRIGHT OFFICE, *Recipes*.

[788] *See, e.g.*, 1 MELVILLE B. NIMER & DAVID NIMMER, NIMMER ON COPYRIGHT § 2.18[1] (2007).

[789] 88 F.3d. 473, 482 (7th Cir. 1996) ("The recipes contained in Discover Dannon do not contain even a bare modicum of the creative expression – i.e., the originality – that is the "sine qua non of copyright" (citing Feist Publications, Inc. v. Rural Tel. Serv. Co., 499 U.S. 340, 345 (1991). *See also* Lambing v. Godiva Chocolatier, 142 F.3d 434 (6th Cir. 1998).

[790] 178 F.Supp. 2d 758, 762–3.

[791] *Id.* at 764.

[792] *Id.*

Perhaps a way of conceptually creating a colorable claim to copyright for a culinary dish is if the culinary dish is recast as an "expression" and the recipe as the mode in which it has been fixed.[793] Otherwise, copyright protection to chef-creators and their food art is to amend the copyright statute to explicitly include culinary dishes as protectable subject matter.[794]

---

[793] *See* Christopher J. Buccafusco, *On the Legal Consequences of Sauces: Should Thomas Keller's Recipes Be Per Se Copyrightable?*, 24 Cardozo Arts & Ent. L.J. 1121, 1127 (2006).

[794] Reportedly, strong social norms among chefs preclude slavish copying of recipes, sharing of recipe-related information without permission, and not giving attribution and credit. *See* Emmanuelle Fauchart & Eric Von Hippel, Norms-Based Intellectual Property Systems: The Case of French Chefs, 187, 188 (2008).

5 Regulation of Nutrition

§ 5.01 Introduction

As noted in the coverage of health claims in Chapter 4, beginning in the 1960s and 1970s, the regulation of nutrition accelerated as the relationship between diet and health became more evident to lawmakers and government officials.[1] One outcome of this acceleration was that the Food and Drug Administration (FDA) began to regulate more aggressively a significant aspect of nutrition and diet – the use of dietary supplements, which began to proliferate in the 1960s.[2] Consumers at that time and still do take dietary supplements to meet their perceived nutritional needs. These same consumers desire accurate information on the effectiveness and proper use of dietary supplements and access to the supplements of their choice. This chapter presents the unique regulatory regime under the FDA and FTC that governs dietary supplements, focusing primarily on where dietary supplements are regulated differently from conventional food.

During this same period and even more so in recent years, the emergence of the rising rates of obesity and the resulting effects on the health of US consumers' health and health care costs have prompted policymakers to consider further the connection between diet and health.[3] A number of legal tools on a local and national level have been devised to deal with nutrition problems and in particular, the national obesity epidemic.[4] The challenges in implementing these tools reflect the tension between personal responsibility[5] and charges against paternalism[6] and exemplify the complexities in adapting to the changing social conditions brought about by the modern food system.

This chapter will examine two marketing regulation movements that reflect these tensions and complexities and that involve a number of legal tools: menu labeling and marketing to children. This chapter will also outline various food prohibitions and government programs designed to promote nutrition and examine the tool of litigation as used in addressing obesity. Finally, this chapter will address two case studies on the regulation of nutrition: salt and sugar.

---

[1] Notable among the efforts by officials on addressing the importance of nutrition for consumers was the landmark 1969 White House Conference on Food, Nutrition, and Health. Many of the policy efforts emerging from this conference concerned the effects of poverty and lack of nutrition education on the well being of children in particular. National Nutrition Summit, *1969 Conference on Food, Nutrition, and Health* (1969).

[2] *See* Michael A. McCann, *Dietary Supplement Labeling: Cognitive Biases, Market Manipulation & Consumer Choice*, 31 AM. J.L. & MED. 215, 236 (2005) (describing the proliferation of dietary supplements in the 1960s and the FDA's bringing of hundreds of court cases to enforce against misleading supplement claims).

[3] The Center for Disease Control (CDC) has reported that more than one-third of American adults are obese and has identified obesity as a major risk factor for cardiovascular disease, Type 2 diabetes, and certain types of cancer. Overweight and Obesity: Adult Obesity Facts, Centers for Disease Control and Prevention (March 28, 2014).

[4] The problem of obesity stretches beyond the borders of the United States. The World Health Organization refers to obesity as "one of today's most blatantly visible – yet most neglected – public health problems." World Health Organization, *Controlling the Global Obesity Epidemic.*

[5] *See, e.g.,* Kelly D. Brownell et al., *Personal Responsibility and Obesity: A Constructive Approach to a Controversial Issue*, 29 HEALTH AFF. 378, 383 (2010).

[6] *See, e.g.,* Rebecca L. Goldberg, *No Such Thing as a Free Lunch: Paternalism, Poverty, and Food Justice*, 24 STAN. L. & POL'Y REV. 35 (2013).

§ 5.02 Regulation of Dietary and Nutritional Supplements

[1] *DSHEA: Regulatory Regime*

[a] Tension over Classification: Food or Drug?

The 1906 Pure Food and Drug Act (PFDA) did not address the regulation of dietary supplements. Under the 1938 Food, Drug, and Cosmetic Act (FDCA), FDA recognition was given to foods "for special dietary use" as well as the "vitamin, mineral, and other dietary properties" of those foods.[7] The FDA's regulation of dietary supplements proved controversial, as a tension developed, which continues today, between those who favor greater regulation over the safety and marketing of dietary supplements and those who view regulation as the anathema of consumer choice. This tension gave rise to the pivotal issue of whether dietary supplements were a drug or food. Early on, in the development of dietary supplements, the products were often classified as both a food and drug.[8] Classification of dietary supplements as a drug meant that dietary supplements were required to receive premarket approval for both safety and effectiveness.

An example of the regulatory battle over classification involved the FDA's regulation on the substantive potency of dietary supplements. In 1962, the FDA imposed new regulations restricting the sale of high-level dosage vitamins, but withdrew them in response to consumer protests. Following a protracted debate about the scope of regulation of vitamins, the FDA issued final regulations in 1973 that prohibited irrational combinations of vitamins and minerals when sold as foods, and set the maximum and minimum potency levels for nutrients.[9] If a nutrient's potency level exceeded the maximum threshold set by the FDA, the product would be deemed an unapproved drug.

These new regulations were challenged in *National Nutritional Foods Ass'n v. FDA*.[10] The Second Circuit Court in 1974 while finding that the FDA was allowed to establish limits for vitamin and mineral doses in order to protect consumers from being confused about the therapeutic effects, the court more importantly ruled that the mere fact that a nutrient is sold in high doses would not automatically subject it to status as an unapproved drug.[11] The FDA would also need to establish that the manufacturer intended consumers to use its product as a drug therapy. Congress responded to *National Nutritional Foods Ass'n* by passing the Vitamin-Mineral Amendment to the FDCA (also known as the Proxmire Amendment – named after Senator William Proxmire, D-Wisconsin).[12] Adding Section 411 to the FDCA (now codified at 21 U.S.C. § 350), the Proxmire Amendment codified the holding in *National Nutritional Foods Ass'n* that prohibited

---

[7] 21 U.S.C. § 343(j).

[8] As noted in Chapter 4, the US Supreme Court concluded in *Kordel v. United States* that the FDA could invoke its authority over drugs against dietary supplements when the information pamphlets accompanying the product suggest a use of disease prevention or treatment or a use that affects body structure or function. 335 U.S. 345 (1948).

[9] *See* Definitions and Standards of Identity for Food and Special Dietary Uses, 38 Fed. Reg. 20,730, 20,738 (1973).

[10] 504 F.2d 761, 789–92 (2d Cir. 1974).

[11] *See id.* at 789.

[12] *See* 21 U.S.C. § 350.

the FDA from using drug authority against a vitamin or mineral product merely because the level of potency exceeds the FDA recommended level.[13]

[b] DSHEA: Response to Consumer Demand

Enacted in 1994, the Dietary Supplement Health and Education Act (DSHEA) dramatically changed the regulatory approach to dietary supplements. As evidenced by the signing statement of President Clinton, the passage of DSHEA was favored limited regulation and was intended to respond to consumer demand.

> After several years of intense efforts, manufacturers, experts in nutrition, and legislators, acting in a conscientious alliance with consumers at the grassroots level, have moved successfully to bring common sense to the treatment of dietary supplements under regulation and law. More often than not, the government has been their ally. And the private market has responded to this development with the manufacture of an increasing variety of safe supplements. But in recent years, the regulatory scheme designed to promote the interests of consumers and a healthful supply of good food has been used instead to complicate choices consumers have made to advance their nutritional and dietary goals. With perhaps the best intentions, agencies of government charged with protecting the food supply and the rights of consumers have paradoxically limited the information to make healthful choices in an area that means a great deal to over 100 million people ... Simply stated, the legislation amends the [FDCA] to establish new standards for the regulation of dietary supplements including vitamins, minerals, and herbal remedies.[14]

The text of DSHEA directly addresses the concern of overregulation and presumes the safety and efficacy of dietary supplements by asserting that "the Federal Government should not take any actions to impose unreasonably regulatory barriers limiting or slowing the flow of safe products and accurate information to consumers" and that "dietary supplements are safe within a broad range of intake, and safety problems with the supplements are relatively rare" and that "legislative action that protects the right of access of consumers to safe dietary supplements is necessary to promote wellness."[15] While health and fraud problems of dietary supplements have triggered calls for expanded regulation since the passage of DSHEA,[16] the sentiment upon the signing of the Act was decidedly in favor of facilitating access to the products.[17]

---

[13] *See* Health Research and Health Services Amendments of 1976, Pub. L. No. 94–278, 90 Stat. 401 (1976) (codified at 21 U.S.C. § 350(a)(1)(A)-(C)).

[14] William J. Clinton, Weekly Compilation of Presidential Documents, Vol. 3, Issue 43, Statement on Signing the Dietary Supplement Health and Education Act of 1994, 2158 (1994).

[15] Dietary Supplement Health and Education Act of 1994 (DSHEA), Pub. L. No. 103–417, 108 Stat. 4325 (codified as amended in scattered sections of 21 U.S.C.). DSHEA, §2.

[16] U.S. Gov't Accountability Office, GAO-13-244, Dietary Supplements: FDA May Have Opportunities to Expand Its Use of Reported Health Problems to Oversee Products (2013).

[17] Since passage of DSHEA, the market for dietary supplements by all accounts has enjoyed dramatic growth. *Id.*

[c] Subcategory of Food

DSHEA created a new, broad definition of dietary supplements and identified dietary supplements as a subcategory of food. Fitting dietary supplements within the regulatory framework of food apart from drugs benefitted manufacturers by giving dietary supplements the advantage of being considered safe without requiring testing to substantiate the assumption. A dietary supplement manufacturer seeking to sell its product as a drug was required to obtain premarket approval from the FDA showing that the proposed product was safe, and effective.[18] This rigorous premarket approval process involved and still involves a significant duration of time in order to ensure that the claims are supported by "adequate and well-controlled investigations."[19]

DSHEA also created the Office of Dietary Supplements, a subagency of the FDA, which was given the power to research dietary supplements and substantiate claims made by manufacturers.[20] Under DSHEA, the labeling requirements of dietary supplements became more lenient, allowing, for example, structure or function claims to appear on the supplements.[21] DSHEA also provided statements of nutritional support for dietary supplements.[22] Finally, the burden of proving product safety shifted from the manufacturer to the FDA once the supplement was on the market.

[d] Definition of Dietary Supplement

(1) *Broadly Defined*

The DSHEA broadly defines a dietary supplement as a product that (1) is intended to supplement the diet; (2) bears or contains the following dietary ingredients: a vitamin, mineral, herb or other botanical, amino acids, and other substances or their constituents; (3) is intended to be taken by mouth as a pill, capsule, powder, tablet, or liquid; and (4) is labeled on the front panel as being a dietary supplement.[23] While under the DSHEA, dietary supplements are not considered drugs, the Act authorized the FDA to declare a dietary supplement a drug if inappropriate claims are made for it.[24] As noted in Chapter 1, a drug is defined in Section 201(g) as "articles intended for use in the diagnosis, cure, mitigation, treatment, or prevention of disease in man or other animals."[25] Like with all other foods, the labeling claims and advertising of the dietary supplements demonstrates the intended use. Even though the DSHEA specifies certain types of dietary supplements and the forms such supplements must take, the DSHEA allows dietary supplements to be sold in conventional food form so long as they are not represented as conventional food or as meal replacement and so long as they are labeled as dietary supplements.[26]

---

[18] *See* 21 U.S.C. § 321(d).
[19] 21 U.S.C. § 355(d).
[20] *See* 42 U.S.C. § 287c-11.
[21] *See* 21 U.S.C. § 343-2.
[22] *See* 21 U.S.C. § 343(r)(6).
[23] *See* 21 U.S.C. § 321(ff)(1)(A-F).
[24] See 21 U.S.C. § 321(g).
[25] 21 U.S.C. § 321(g)(1)(B).
[26] *See* 21 U. S.C. §§ 321(ff)(2)(B)-(C), 350(c)(1)(B)(ii).

Notwithstanding the distinct regulatory regime for dietary supplements, the FDA will regard a dietary supplement as a conventional food if it is represented for use as a conventional food. [27] For example, the FDA took action against the marketing of Benecol, a butter-like spread containing cholesterol-reducing stanol esters, as a dietary supplement. Though the inclusion of stanol esters gave the company a colorable argument for marketing the product as a dietary supplement, the FDA rejected the classification because, in addition to claiming the health benefits of the stanol esters, Benecol claimed a butter-like taste, butter-like flavor, and uses analogous to butter.[28] Because of these representations of conventional food attributes, Benecol could not be classified as a dietary supplement.

(2) Exception: Food Additive

After the Proxmire Amendment, the FDA mostly abandoned its efforts to regulate dietary supplements under FDCA drug provisions and instead turned to FDCA food additive provisions, which require premarket approval for food additives that are not prior sanctioned, generally recognized as safe (GRAS), or the subject of a food additive regulation.[29] The FDA took the position that a dietary supplement ingredient could be characterized as a food additive because it was added to a capsule or tablet to create the dietary supplement. The FDA often used its authority to regulate food additives as an easier means of declaring a dietary supplement ingredient unsafe or inadequately tested. If the FDA declared that the dietary supplement was not safe according to the food additive provisions of the FDCA, then the manufacturer would have the burden of proving that the supplement in question was exempt from such requirements. Courts often struck down this position by the FDA, however, finding that a substance that is simply a component of food does not meet the classification criteria of a food additive.[30] It was generally found that a substance must alter a food's characteristics to be considered a food additive.[31]

These issues were resolved when the DSHEA expressly exempted supplements from the definition of food additives under Section 409 of the FDCA.[32] Such removal has profound consequences. By avoiding being deemed adulterated under food additive provisions of the FDCA, dietary supplements bypass the need to receive specific approval from the FDA for use as food additives. Dietary supplements also bypass the need to be GRAS by the FDA or the food industry. And notably, by virtue of being excluded from the definition of food additives, dietary supplements do not have to comply with the Delaney Clause prohibiting the FDA from approving food additives that have been "found to induce cancer when ingested by man or animal."[33] Dietary supplements containing color additives, however, must still comply with the Delaney Clause.[34] (See Chapter 4 for a more in-depth discussion of food additive regulation.)

---

[27] See Ilene R. Heller, Functional Foods: Regulatory and Marketing Developments, 56 FOOD & DRUG L.J. 197, 210–11 (2001).

[28] See U.S. GOV'T. ACCOUNTING OFFICE, GAO-RCED-00-156, FOOD SAFETY: IMPROVEMENTS NEEDED IN OVERSEEING THE SAFETY OF DIETARY SUPPLEMENTS AND "FUNCTIONAL FOODS" 14 (2000).

[29] See 21 U.S.C. § 348.

[30] See e.g., U.S. v. 29 Cartons ... An Article of Food, 987 F.2d 33 (1st Cir. 1993); U.S. v. Two Plastic Drums, 984 F.2d 814 (7th Cir. 1993).

[31] See, e.g., Two Plastic Drums, 984 F.2d at 817.

[32] 21 U.S.C. § 321(s)(6).

[33] 21 U. S. C. § 348(c)(3)(A).

[34] See 21 U. S. C. § 379e(b)(5)(B)(i).

[e] Regulation of Safety

(1) *Adulteration*

DSHEA establishes separate safety standards for dietary supplements, including standards about which types of adulterations are unsafe. The government bears the burden of proof on each element of adulteration.[35] Under the DSHEA, a dietary supplement will be deemed to be an adulterated food if it presents a significant or unreasonable risk of illness or injury under conditions of use recommended or suggested in labeling or under ordinary conditions of use. Thus, the standard is the existing food standard – if it presents a significant or unreasonable risk of illness or injury – but it also requires that safety of dietary supplements be based on conditions of use, recommended use suggested on the product label, or ordinary conditions of use.[36] In addition, a dietary supplement will be deemed adulterated if it contains an ingredient that the secretary of the Department of Health and Human Services (DHHS) finds poses "an imminent hazard to public health or safety."[37]

Under DSHEA, a manufacturer and distributor is responsible for determining that the product is safe and that all claims and representations are supported by evidence to ensure they are not false or misleading. Dietary supplements do not need premarketing approval from FDA, except for a new dietary ingredient, which is required by law, to submit to premarket review for safety checks. Dietary supplement manufacturers do not have to provide FDA with the evidence they rely on when determining if their product is safe and effective both before and after they market their products. Once a product is marketed, FDA must show the product is unsafe before it can take action to restrict or remove the product from the market.[38]

(2) *Good Manufacturing Practices*

Dietary supplements are also considered adulterated if they have been prepared, packed, or held under conditions that do not meet good manufacturing practices (GMPs).[39] GMPs are strict, detailed procedures used to ensure quality – manufacturing processes of products for human consumption, such as dietary supplements.[40] DSHEA gave the FDA the authority to establish GMPs specific to dietary supplements modeled after the existing GMP for food.[41] The final regulations issued in 2007 contain sections that detail quality control proceedings and recordkeeping requirements or each step in the supplement manufacturing process.[42] The FDA noted in the final rule that "the focus of GMP is on process controls to ensure that the desired outcome is consistently achieved, and not on the inherent safety of the ingredients used."[43] GMPs for dietary supplement

---

[35] *See* 21 U.S.C. § 342(f)(1).
[36] 21 U.S.C. § 342(f)(1)(A).
[37] 21 U.S.C. § 342(f)(1)(C).
[38] *Id.*; *Dietary Supplements*, U.S. Food & Drug Admin.
[39] Current Good Manufacturing Practice in Manufacturing, Packaging, Labeling, or Holding Operations for Dietary Supplements, 72 Fed. Reg. 34,751–34,958 (June 25, 2007).
[40] *See* 21 C.F.R. § 111.
[41] *See* 21 U.S.C. § 342(g).
[42] *See* Dietary Supplement Current Good Manufacturing Practices (CGMPs) and Interim Final Rule (IFR) Facts, U.S. Food and Drug Admin. (June 22, 2007).
[43] *Id.*

applies to all domestic and foreign companies that manufacture, label, or hold a dietary supplement for import and sale in the United States.[44]

(3) *New Dietary Supplement Ingredients: Grandfather Clause*

For "new" dietary supplement ingredients – those marketed after October 15, 1994 – products can be considered adulterated if the supplement lacks information that would provide reasonable assurance that the ingredient does not present a significant or unreasonable risk of illness or injury.[45] Dietary supplements in use before October 15, 1994, are presumed safe based on their history of use by consumers and to not need to be reviewed for safety by the FDA.[46] For these grandfathered dietary supplements ingredients, manufacturers are required to maintain records that document their use prior to October 15, 1994. For supplements not grandfathered in, manufacturers and distributors must notify the FDA if they intend to market a product in the United States that contains a "new dietary ingredient." The manufacturer or distributor must demonstrate why the ingredient is reasonably expected to be safe (does not present a significant or unreasonable risk of illness or injury) for use in a dietary supplement, unless it has been recognized as a food substance and is present in the food supply.[47] Manufacturers and distributors of new dietary ingredients must also give seventy-five days premarket notification to the FDA, and provide a history of use or other evidence of safety when used under recommended conditions.[48]

The Food Safety Modernization Act of 2010 (FSMA) contained a provision that required FDA to clarify the definition of a new dietary ingredient notification (NDI) within 180 days of enactment.[49] After receiving complaints from manufacturers that the FDA's proposed draft NDI guidance in July 2011, did not comport with DSHEA, the FDA agreed in June 2012 to revise the guidance. The FDA has not yet proposed a timeline for the revisions.[50]

As an alternative to the notification requirement, a manufacturer can petition the FDA for "issuance of an order prescribing the conditions under which a new dietary ingredient under its intended conditions of use will reasonably be expected to be safe."[51] The FDA must evaluate and rule on the petition within 180 days of filing.[52] Seeking this optional approval rather than issuing a notification would likely eliminate the possibility of FDA action against the new dietary ingredient once marketing began.

(4) *Serious Adverse Event Reporting*

Because dietary supplements are not required to undergo premarket review for safety, to locate safety problems, the FDA relies on an adverse event reporting system. Replacing

---

[44] 21 C.F.R. § 111.1.

[45] 21 U. S. C. § 350b(c)).

[46] 21 U. S. C. § 342(f)).

[47] *Q & A on Dietary Supplements*, U.S. FOOD & DRUG ADMIN.; 21 U.S.C. § 350b(a).

[48] FDA, Draft Guidance for Industry, Dietary Supplements: New Dietary Ingredient Notifications and Related Issues, 79 Fed. Reg. 39,111 (July 5, 2011).

[49] FDA Food Safety Modernization Act (FSMA), Pub. L. No. 111–353, (2011) Section 113.

[50] *See* Press Release, Council for Responsible Nutrition, Supplement Associations Ask FDA to Issue Revised Draft Guidance on NDI Ingredient Identity (May 6, 2013),

[51] 21 U. S. C. § 350b(b)).

[52] *Id.*

a voluntary adverse event reporting system for supplements created by the FDA in 1993,[53] the Dietary Supplement and Non-Prescription Drug Consumer Protection Act – enacted in 2006 – required several important changes to the adverse event reporting system for dietary supplements.[54] A manufacturer, packer, or distributor must report to the FDA a "serious adverse event" with a dietary supplement within fifteen days and required the FDA to create and maintain a system to track adverse events related to dietary supplements. An "adverse event" is defined as "any health-related event associated with the use of a dietary supplement that is adverse."[55] Such an event includes death, a life-threatening experience, inpatient hospitalization, a persistent or significant disability, or a medical or surgical intervention to prevent any of the aforementioned outcomes.[56] The public may also voluntarily submit adverse event reports. All dietary supplement labels are required to list a domestic address and phone number so that a responsible person can receive event reports. While the Act does not require companies to report moderate or mild adverse events, such as gastrointestinal distress or headaches, companies may do so voluntarily. In addition, health care practitioners and consumers can submit voluntary reports of serious, moderate, and mild adverse events.

In addition to receiving adverse event reports, the FDA relies on post-market surveillance efforts to ensure safety, including reviewing consumer complaints and conducting facility inspections.[57] Once a safety concern is identified, the FDA must demonstrate that the dietary supplement presents a significant or unreasonable risk, or is otherwise adulterated, before it can be removed from the market.[58]

(5) Registration

The DSHEA does not require manufacturers to register with the FDA or identify the products they manufacture or the ingredients of those products. However, all food facilities, including manufacturers and distributors of dietary supplements, were required to register with the FDA no later than December 12, 2003, under the Public Health Security and Bioterrorism Preparedness and Response Act of 2002 (Bioterrorism Act) and implementing regulations.[59] The registration requirements under the Bioterrorism Act are delineated in Chapter 3. Essentially, the Act requires an initial registration with the FDA and updates within sixty days of any changes in information. Registration must include the name and address of the facility and an emergency contact, and facilities that manufacture or sell certain types of products, such as vitamins, must self-identify as such.

---

[53] The voluntary system reportedly provided inadequate data on adverse events, due to its voluntary nature and limited scope. *See* ADVERSE EVENT REPORTING FOR DIETARY SUPPLEMENTS: AN INADEQUATE SAFETY VALVE OFFICE OF THE INSPECTOR GENERAL, OEI-01-00-00180, DEPARTMENT OF HEALTH AND HUMAN SERVICES (April 2001).

[54] Pub. L. No. 109–462, 120 Stat. 3469 (2006) (21 U.S.C. § 379aa-1).

[55] 21 U.S.C. § 379aa-1(a)(1).

[56] *Id.*

[57] *See* U.S. GOV'T ACCOUNTABILITY OFFICE, GAO-09-250, DIETARY SUPPLEMENTS, FDA SHOULD TAKE FURTHER ACTIONS TO IMPROVE OVERSIGHT AND CONSUMER UNDERSTANDING 1 (2009)

[58] *Id.*

[59] Public Health Security and Bioterrorism Preparedness and Response Act of 2002, Pub. L. No. 107–188, 116 Stat. 594 (2002).

Supplement facts

Serving size 1 tablet

	Amount per serving	% Daily value
Vitamin A (as retinyl acetate and 50% as beta-carotene)	5000 IU	100%
Vitamin C (as ascorbic acid)	60 mg	100%
Vitamin D (as cholecalciferol)	400 IU	100%
Vitamin E (as dl-alpha tocopheryl acetate)	30 IU	100%
Thiamin (as thiamin mononitrate)	1.5 mg	100%
Riboflavin	1.7 mg	100%
Niacin (as niacinamide)	20 mg	100%
Vitamin B_6 (as pyridoxine hydrochloride)	2.0 mg	100%
Folate (as folic acid)	400 mcg	100%
Vitamin B_{12} (as cyanocobalamin)	6 mcg	100%
Biotin	30 mcg	10%
Pantothenic Acid (as calcium pantothenate)	10 mg	100%

Other ingredients: Gelatin, lactose, magnesium stearate, microcrystalline cellulose, FD&C Yellow No. 6, propylene glycol, propylparaben, and sodium benzoate.

Figure 5.1. Dietary supplement label.

(*Source: FDA, Dietary Supplement Labeling Guide: Chapter IV. Nutrition Labeling*)

[f] Marketing Regulation

(1) *Labeling*

DSHEA specifically authorized the FDA to promulgate labeling requirements specifically for dietary supplements. A failure to follow the labeling regulations for dietary supplements may result in the product being deemed misbranded under the FDCA. DSHEA requires dietary supplements to have a supplement facts panel, which is different from the nutrition facts panel required for conventional foods.[60] Regulations for the layout and content of the supplement facts panel are incorporated in 21 C.F.R. §101.36. Guidance from the FDA establishes the general display (principal display panel, or PDP) and placement requirements of dietary supplemental labeling.[61] With some notable exceptions, the basic labeling requirements for conventional foods apply to dietary supplements: the statement of identity, ingredient statement, nutritional information, the name and place of business of the manufacturer, packer, or distributor, and accurate net contents all need to be placed appropriately on the product label.[62] An example of a dietary supplement label is shown in Figure 5.1.

The notable exceptions from conventional foods for the labeling of dietary supplements include the naming requirements that oblige dietary supplements to bear the term

---

[60] 21 U.S.C. §343.
[61] FDA, Guidance for Industry: A Dietary Supplement Labeling Guide (April 2005).
[62] *See Overview of Dietary Supplements*, U.S. FOOD AND DRUG ADMIN.

"dietary supplement" in their statement of identity. The word "dietary" may be replaced by the name of the dietary ingredients in the product.[63] Most dietary ingredients should be listed by their common names. Botanicals must be listed according to the terms used in the book *Herbs of Commerce*. If a supplement contains any plant materials, the label must identify the part of the plant that was used. If the Latin name of a botanical is not in the book, the label must use the Latin name.[64]

The ingredient statement lists the name and quantity of each ingredient.[65] This requirement differs from conventional foods, where only nutrients that have daily recommendations may be listed in the nutritional information. DSHEA allows dietary ingredients for which recommendations have not been established to be listed as long as the label indicates this fact by an asterisk in the "% of Daily Value" column that refers to the footnote "Daily Value not established." The label needs to identify only ingredients present in significant quantities.[66] If the dietary supplement contains a proprietary blend of ingredients, then the label need list only the total quantity of all ingredients in the blend.[67] If the dietary supplement contains a herbal or botanical, then the label must identity "any part of the plant from which the ingredient is derived."[68]

The nutrition information is titled "Supplement Facts." Dietary supplement labels must list serving sizes, which is the amount recommended to be eaten in one occasion. This information must be stated near the top of the nutrition information after the words "serving size."[69]

Generally, DSHEA requires that if a dietary supplement purports to conform to the standards of a particular compendium, it must actually do so. Official compendiums identified by FDCA or Federal regulations include the US Pharmacopeia (USP) and the Food Chemicals Codex. Otherwise, the identity and quality of the product must be as stated on the label. If an official compendium does not cover the dietary supplement, it must contain the identity and strength that it is represented to have, and it must contain the quality, purity, and compositional specifications that it is represented to have.[70]

Section 5 of the DSHEA provides an exemption from labeling requirements for scientific journal articles, books, and other publications used in the sale of dietary supplements provided these materials are reprinted in their entirety, are not false or misleading, do not promote a specific brand or manufacturer, are presented with other materials to create a balanced view of scientific information, and are physically separate from the supplements being sold.[71] DSHEA also requires that when such third-party information is used in an establishment, it may not be displayed next to the supplement product but must be physically separated from the supplement.

---

[63] 21 U.S.C. § 343(s)(2)(B)).
[64] Neal D. Fortin, Food Regulation: Law, Science, Policy, And Practice 360–61 (2009).
[65] 21 U.S.C. § 343(b), (f), and (i).
[66] *Id.* Section 343(b) does not define "significant amount."
[67] 21 U.S.C. § 343(s)(2)(A)(ii)(II)).
[68] 21 U.S.C. § 343(s)(2)(C)).
[69] Dietary Supplement Labeling Guide: Chapter IV. Nutrition Labeling, U.S. Food and Drug Admin (April 2005).
[70] 21 U.S.C. § 343(s)(2)(E)(ii)(I-II)).
[71] Fortin, *supra* note 64.

(2) *Claims*

A dietary supplement may not bear a disease claim. In other words, a manufacturer may not state that a supplement can be used to cure or treat a disease.[72] If a claim is made that the dietary supplement does intend to diagnose, treat, cure, or prevent any disease, the manufacturer must notify the FDA of such a statement within thirty days after first marketing the product.[73] DSHEA permits statements of nutrient support to be made on a dietary supplement label. In addition, similar to food manufacturers, dietary supplements manufacturers may make nutrient content claims, structure/function claims, and health claims. Any claims statement must also include a prominently displayed disclaimer that the product was not evaluated by the FDA nor "is not intended to diagnose, treat, cure, or prevent any disease."[74] Also, any statement made by the manufacturer on the product must be truthful and not misleading.[75]

- Statements of Nutrient Support

The DSHEA took the significant step of allowing dietary supplement labeling and packaging to contain certain statements of nutritional support unavailable to conventional foods. Specifically, Section 6 of the DSHEA allowed a statement of nutritional support on the label of dietary supplements without the dietary supplement being deemed misbranded if the statement claims a benefit related to a classical nutrient deficiency disease and discloses the prevalence of such disease in the United States, describes the role of a nutrient or dietary ingredient intended to affect the structure or function in humans, characterizes the documented mechanism by which a nutrient or dietary ingredient acts to maintain such structure or function, or describes general well-being from consumption of a nutrient or dietary ingredient.[76]

The DSHEA also required that a manufacturer of a dietary supplement containing a statement of nutritional support on its label must have "substantiation that such statement is truthful and not misleading."[77] And the DSHEA further required that the label contain the following disclaimer: "This statement has not been evaluated by the Food and Drug Administration. This product is not intended to diagnose, treat, cure, or prevent any disease."[78]

- Nutrient Content Claims

A nutrient content claim is one that expressly or implicitly characterizes the level of a nutrient in a dietary supplement.[79] An expressed nutrient content claim is a direct statement about the level or range of a nutrient in the dietary supplement. An example of an expressed nutrient content claim is the statement: "contains 200 calories."[80] An

---

[72] 21 U.S.C. § 343(r)(6).
[73] 21 U.S.C. § 343(r)(6)(C).
[74] *Id.*
[75] 21 U.S.C. § 343(r)(B).
[76] 21 U. S. C. § 343(r)(6)(A)).
[77] 21 U. S. C. § 343(r)(6)(B)).
[78] 21 U. S. C. § 343(r)(6)(C)).
[79] 21 C.F.R. § 101.13(b).
[80] 21 C.F.R. § 101.13(b)(1).

implied nutrient content claim either describes the nutrient in a manner that suggests that it is absent or present in a certain amount (e.g., "high in oat bran") or suggests that the dietary supplement due to its nutrient content helps maintain healthy dietary practices and includes an express claim or statement about a nutrient.[81] The NLEA allowed nutrient content claims to be made for both conventional food and dietary supplements if the FDA first promulgated a regulation regarding such a claim.[82] The DSHEA did not change this regulatory framework. The first FDA action post-DSHEA concerning nutrient content claims for dietary supplements came in 1995. In that year, the FDA published proposed rules for certain nutrient content claims for both conventional food and dietary supplements.[83] Then, in 1997, the FDA promulgated a final version of these rules. These final rules specify several terms that can be used to describe the nutrient content in dietary supplements. First, while dietary supplements can list nutrition information for nutrients that have no RDI and DRV, the regulations make clear that "the use of defined nutrient content claims, such as 'more' and 'high,' remains limited, for both conventional foods and dietary supplements, to those dietary ingredients that have RDI's or DRV's."[84] Second, the regulations allow the following nutrient content terms to be used on dietary supplement labels: (1) "high," "rich in," or "excellent source";[85] (2) "good source," "contains," or "provides";[86] and (3) "more," "fortified," "enriched," or "added."[87] Third, a separate set of regulations issued the same day allows dietary supplements to use the terms "high potency" and "antioxidant."[88]

When the FDCA was amended by the Food and Drug Administration Modernization Act of 1997 ("FDAMA"), it allowed nutrient content claims for conventional food and dietary supplements to be made by an additional route.[89] Specifically, FDAMA allowed nutrient content claims to be made without the need for an FDA regulation if based upon current, published authoritative statements from certain scientific bodies.[90] FDAMA specified premarket notification procedures that must be met in such a case.[91] If these notification procedures are met and the FDA does not act within the specified statutory time frame, the nutrient content claim may be made.

---

[81] 21 C.F.R. § 101.13(b)(1) and (2) and 21 C.F.R. § 101.65.

[82] *See* 21 U. S.C. § 343(r). Generally, the NLEA regulation process begins with a petition from a manufacturer. 21 C.F.R. § 101.69.

[83] Food Labeling; Requirements for Nutrient Content Claims, Health Claims, and Statements of Nutritional Support for Dietary Supplements, Proposed Rule, 60 Fed. Reg. 67,176 (December 28, 1995).

[84] Food Labeling; Nutrient Content Claims: Definition for "High Potency" and Definition of "Antioxidant" for Use in Nutrient Content Claims for Dietary Supplements and Conventional Foods, Final Rule, 62 Fed. Reg. 49,868 (September 23, 1997) (codified at 21 C.F.R. §§ 101.54, 101.50).

[85] *Id.* at 49,867 (codified at 21 C. F. R. § 101.54(b)). To use these terms, the dietary supplement must have "20 percent or more of the RDI or the DRV per reference amount customarily consumed." *Id.*

[86] *Id.* (codified at 21 C. F. R. § 101.54(c)). To use these terms, the dietary supplement must have "10 to 19 percent of the RDI or the DRV per reference amount customarily consumed." *Id.*

[87] *Id.* (codified at 21 C. F. R. § 101.54).

[88] *Id.* at 49,880 (codified at 21 C. F. R. § 101.54(e)). For a list of more approved nutrient content terms, *see* 21 C. F. R. §§ 101.13, 101.54, 101.56, 101.60–101.62.

[89] Food and Drug Administration Modernization Act of 1997, Pub. L. No. 105–115, 111 Stat. 2296 (codified in scattered sections of 21 U. S. C.).

[90] 21 U. S. C. § 343(r)).

[91] 21 U. S. C. § 343(r)(2)(G)).

• Structure/Function Claims

Structure/Function claims describe the role of a nutrient or dietary ingredient's intended effect on the structure or function of the body.[92] While structure/function claims may describe how a product affects organs and systems of the body, it cannot mention any specific disease. A standard example of a standard/function claim is that "calcium builds strong bones."[93] Structure/function claims sometimes also describe a benefit related to a nutrient deficiency disease, but the producer must also state (in the same statement) how widespread such a disease is in the United States.

The DSHEA expands the scope of structure/function claims for dietary supplements over that for food.[94] Structure/function claims may appear on a label without formal review or premarket approval by the FDA (subject to notification requirements). However, statements must be truthful and nonmisleading, per FDCA requirements.[95] The manufacturer is responsible for ensuring the accuracy and truthfulness of claims.

Thus, under the DSHEA, a claim is a structure/function claim if the statement claims a benefit related to a classical nutrient deficiency disease and discloses the prevalence of such disease in the United States, describes the role of a nutrient or dietary ingredient intended to affect the structure or function in humans, characterizes the documented mechanism by which a nutrient or dietary ingredient acts to maintain such structure or function, or describes general well-being from the consumption of a nutrient or dietary ingredient.[96]

In 1996, the FDA issued proposed rules for the notification and substantiation procedure under the DSHEA for dietary supplements making structure/function claims.[97] The FDA issued its final rule pertaining to notification and substantiation in 1997.[98] This rule provides that notification must be made within thirty days of introducing the dietary supplement with the structure/function claim.[99] Further, the notification must include: (1) the name and address of the manufacturer or distributor; (2) the text of the claim made; (3) the name of the dietary ingredient that is the subject of the claim; (4) the name of the dietary supplement, including the brand name, on which the claim appears; and (5) a signature certifying that the manufacturer or distributor has substantiation that the claim is truthful and not misleading.[100]

---

[92] 21 U.S.C. §343(r)(6).

[93] *Label Claims for Conventional Foods and Dietary Supplements*, U.S. FOOD AND DRUG ADMIN. (December 2013).

[94] Prior to DSHEA, FDA also took the position that any structure/function claim made by a dietary supplement (other than a vitamin or mineral with recognized nutritional value) was an unapproved drug claim, a position that was ratified in the courts, including by Seventh Circuit in its 1983 decision in Nutrilab v. Schweiker, 713 F.2d 335 (7th Cir. 1983).

[95] 21 U.S.C. § 343(4)(6).

[96] 21 U. S. C. § 343(r)(6)(A)).

[97] Food Labeling; Dietary Supplement; Nutritional Support Statement; Notification Procedure, Proposed Rule, 61 Fed. Reg. 50,771 (September 27, 1996).

[98] Food Labeling; Requirements for Nutrient Content Claims, Health Claims, and Statements of Nutritional Support for Dietary Supplements, 62 Fed. Reg. 49860, 49833 (September 23, 1997) (codified at 21 C.F.R. §101.93).

[99] *Id.* at 49,886.

[100] *Id.*

In 1998, the FDA undertook to define the general types of structure/function claims that could be made on dietary supplement labels and attempted to distinguish such claims from disease or health-related condition claims – claims "that describe the relationship between a nutrient and a disease or health related condition."[101]

The FDA issued a final rule on structure/function claims in 2000, which distinguishes general structure/function claims (which need no FDA prior approval) from disease or health-related condition claims (which need FDA authorization, or premarket notification under FDAMA, or else are handled as new drug claims).[102] The final rule defined "disease or health-related condition in conjunction with claims made by dietary supplements: [d]isease or health-related condition means damage to an organ, part, structure, or system of the body such that it does not function properly (e.g., cardiovascular disease), or a state of health leading to such dysfunctioning (e.g., hypertension); except that diseases resulting from essential nutrient deficiencies (e.g., scurvy, pellagra) are not included in this definition.[103] The regulations also narrowed the scope of a disease or health-related condition for dietary supplement purposes: "[c]ommon conditions associated with natural states or processes that do not cause significant or permanent harm will not be treated as diseases."[104] Thus, hair loss due to aging would be eligible for dietary supplement structure/function claims. Finally, the final rule allows dietary supplement manufacturers to substantiate label claims by citing on the label the title of publication referring to a disease so long as, in the context of the whole label, the citation does not imply that "the product may be used to diagnose, treat, mitigate, cure, or prevent disease."[105]

Although FDA preapproval is not required for structure/function claims, manufacturers must have substantial backing for its claim, notify the FDA within thirty days of a product being marketed with structure/function claim on its label, and provide for the disclaimer on the supplemental label that the supplements have not been evaluated by the FDA and that the dietary supplement is not intended to "diagnose, treat, cure, or prevent any disease".[106]

- Health Claims

As noted in Chapter 4, general concern over unsubstantiated health claims helped prompt enactment of the Nutrition Labeling and Education Act of 1990 (NLEA),[107] which created a health claim approval system for the FDA including the availability of

---

[101] Regulations on Statements Made of Dietary Supplements Concerning the Effect of the Product on the Structure or Function of the Body, Proposed Rule, 63 Fed. Reg. 23,624 (April 29, 1998).

[102] *Id.* at 1001, 1050.

[103] 21 C. F. R. § 101.14(a)(5).

[104] Regulations on Statements Made for Dietary Supplements Concerning the Effect of the Product on the Structure or Function of the Body, 65 Fed. Reg. 1,000 (January 6, 2000).

[105] *Id.* at 1050 (codified at 21 C. F. R. § 101.93(g)).

[106] 21 U.S.C. § 34z3(r)(6).

[107] The Dietary Supplement Act of 1992 instituted a one-year moratorium on the implementation of dietary supplement labeling under NLEA. Prescription Drug User Fee Act of 1992 (PDUFA), Pub. L. No. 102–571, 106 Stat. 4491 (§ 202). However, Congress subsequently required FDA to create dietary supplement-specific regulations for labeling under DSHEA.

separate procedures for dietary supplement health claims.[108] Chapter 4 explains that health claims characterize the relationship between a food, food component, or dietary supplement and reduces the risk of a disease or health-related condition. An example of a health claim is "While many factors affect heart disease, diets low in saturated fat and cholesterol may reduce the risk of this disease." Manufacturers must notify the FDA of the health claims they are making within thirty days of marketing their product. If the FDA rejects the claim, it will send a letter to the manufacturer who is then advised to change or remove the claim or it will face a potential FDA enforcement action.

The DSHEA did not alter the NLEA framework regarding health claims for dietary supplements. In 1994, before the passage of the DSHEA, the FDA had issued final rules on health claims for dietary supplements.[109] These regulations stated that dietary supplements would be held to the same health claim standards as conventional foods. Rather than enact new health claim provisions for dietary supplements, the DSHEA appointed the Commission on Dietary Supplement Labels (CDSL) to issue recommendations on such health claims. The FDA was then to timely complete final rulemaking on the CDSL recommendations or else the 1994 FDA final regulations on dietary supplement health claims would be rescinded.[110] The CDSL issued its final report in 1999, specifically recommending that "[t]he process for approval of health claims as defined by the NLEA should remain the same for dietary supplements and conventional food."[111] This effectively preserved the FDA's 1994 final regulations on health claims and dietary supplements. Thus a dietary supplement may make a health claim by complying with the NLEA provisions regarding health claims for conventional foods.

While the DSHEA prohibits manufacturers from stating that a dietary supplement can be used to treat a disease, the label can describe the relationship between a supplement and disease prevention. This description constitutes a health claim (e.g., "the use of beta-carotene helps decrease the risk of cancer").[112] While the manufacturer is not required to conduct studies verifying its statements, the FDA must review and authorize any health claim made on the label.[113]

The FDA requires "significant scientific agreement" that a health claim is accurate.[114] To be clear, this standard does not derive from the DSHEA, but instead was established by the FDA.[115] The FDA has asserted that its evaluation of health claims is based on objective factors, most importantly scientific consensus as evidenced by institutional (governmental and nongovernmental) studies.[116] While FDAMA provides another means of health claim authorization for conventional foods – if a manufacturer successfully notifies the FDA of a health claim that is based on an "authoritative statement" from a scientific body of the US government or the National Academy of Sciences, then the claim's use may

---

[108] *See* 21 U.S.C. § 343.
[109] *See* 59 Fed. Reg. 395 (1994) (codified at 21 C.F.R. § 101.14).
[110] *Id.*
[111] The Commission on Dietary Supplement Labels (CDSL) Report 35 (November 24, 1997).
[112] 21 C.F.R. § 101.14(a)(1).
[113] 21 C.F.R. § 101.14(d).
[114] *Id.*
[115] 21 C.F.R. § 101.70.
[116] 21 C.F.R. § 101.14(c).

be granted – FDAMA does not include dietary supplements in the provisions for health claims based on authoritative statements.

Noting that FDAMA had created an additional health claim procedure for conventional foods but not for dietary supplement, the FDA issued proposed rules in 1999 to equalize the health claim treatment of dietary supplements and conventional foods.[117] The FDA stated that it "believes that, for health claims, conventional foods and dietary supplements should be subject to the same standards and procedures, including the notification procedure provided by FDAMA."[118] Under the NLEA and accompanying regulations, several health claims have been approved for use on dietary supplement (as well as conventional food) labels. These range from calcium-osteoporosis claims to folate-neural tube defects claims to plant stanols-coronary heart disease claims.[119]

Both conventional foods and dietary supplements may use qualified health claims.[120] As documented in Chapter 4, in response to the *Pearson* decision, the FDA issued a notice in 2000 delineating circumstances in which the agency might exercise enforcement discretion for a qualified health claim in dietary supplement labeling.[121] This notice was followed by an FDA notice in 2002 of forthcoming interim industry guidance for making qualified health claims for dietary supplements.[122] This notice further specified that these interim procedures would also be applied to qualified health claims for conventional foods.[123] In December 2002, the FDA also instituted "the Consumer Health Information for Better Nutrition Initiative, to make available more and better information about conventional human food and human dietary supplements."[124] This initiative resulted in the issuance in 2003 of the promised interim procedures for health claims in dietary supplements and conventional foods.[125]

(3) Advertising

While FDA regulates claims made on product labeling (including packaging, inserts, and information at the point of sale), the FTC has primary jurisdiction for the regulation of dietary supplement advertising.[126] FTC's area of responsibility for regulating dietary supplements ranges from broadcast advertisements, infomercials, catalogs, Internet marketing,

---

[117] *See* Food Labeling: Use on Dietary Supplements of Health Claims Based on Authoritative Statements, Proposed Rule, 64 Fed. Reg. 3,250 (January 21, 1999).

[118] *Id.* at 3251.

[119] *See* 21 C. F. R. §§ 101.72–101.83.

[120] *Id.* at 376.

[121] Food Labeling; Health Claims and Label Statements for Dietary Supplements; Update to Strategy for Court Implementation of Pearson Court Decision, Notice, 65 Fed. Reg. 59,855 (October 6, 2000).

[122] Guidance for Industry: Qualified Health Claims in the Labeling of Conventional Foods and Dietary Supplements; Availability, Notice, 67 Fed. Reg. 78,002 (December 20, 2002).

[123] *See id.* at 78,003.

[124] Release of Task Force Report; Guidance for Industry and FDA: Interim Evidence-Based Ranking System for Scientific Data; Interim Procedures for Health Claims on the Labeling of Conventional Human Food and Human Dietary Supplements; Availability, Notice, 68 Fed. Reg. 41,387 (July 11, 2003).

[125] *See id.*

[126] 15 U.S.C. § 45(a)(1).

and similar direct marketing materials.[127] The FTC's authority derives from Section 5 of the Federal Trade Commission Act (FTCA) that prohibits "unfair methods of competition in or affecting commerce, and unfair or deceptive acts or practices in or affecting commerce."[128] FTCA defines "false advertisements" as "any advertisement other than labeling, which is misleading in any material respect."[129]

FTC requires that dietary supplement claims be adequately substantiated. FTC's *Dietary Supplement: An Advertising Guide for Industry*, published in 2001, outlines the expected enforcement efforts regarding substantiation.[130] The FTC standard essentially requires that (1) advertising must be truthful and not misleading and (2) before disseminating an advertisement, advertisers must have adequate substantiation for all objective product claims. The FTC advertisement guide defines a deceptive advertisement as one that "contains a misrepresentation or an omission that is likely to mislead consumers acting reasonably under the circumstances to their detriment."[131] The guide also provides that the FTC's standard of substantiation for express and implied claims is one of "competent and reliable scientific evidence,"[132] which differs from FDA's requirements for nutrient, structure/function, and health claims. FTC and FDA have worked closely on protecting consumers from producers who market products with false or deceptive claims over the Internet.[133]

As noted in Chapter 4, there has been a major shift in policy by the FTC from the FTC's old flexible standard of allowing claims simply if supported by competent and reliable scientific evidence, to requiring two well-controlled clinical trials to substantiate certain claims. This policy was challenged in *POM Wonderful v. FTC*,[134] wherein the D.C. Circuit in 2015 held that the FTC violated the First Amendment to the extent that it imposed a "blanket" requirement that all disease and health-related claims be substantiated by two RCTS.[135] The court did state, however, that the FTC is not necessarily barred in future cases from imposing a two-RCT substantiation requirement.[136] It is likely that courts will be asked to weigh in further on the application of the two-RCT substantiation requirement for purveyors of dietary supplement products.

[g] Enforcement

By enacting DSHEA, Congress revoked most of the FDA's regulatory power over dietary supplements by making the dietary supplement regime replicate that of food products. In practice, this has meant that the FDA's involvement is more limited in that it must prove a supplement is unsafe prior to removing it from the marketplace. This contrasts with drug regulation where the manufacturer must prove the safety and efficacy prior

---

[127] Amalia K. Corby-Edwards, Cong. Research Serv., R43062, Regulation of Dietary Supplements 12 (May 6, 2013).

[128] 15 U.S.C. § 45(a)(1).

[129] 15 U.S.C. § 52.

[130] *See* Dietary Supplements: An Advertising Guide for Industry, 3, U.S. FEDERAL TRADE COMM. (2001).

[131] *Id.*

[132] *Id.*

[133] For example, in October 2009, FDA and FTC issued their first joint Warning Letter to a website that fraudulently marketed supplements aimed at preventing the H1N1 virus. FTC and FDA Warning Letter to Weil Lifestyle LLC, October 15, 2009.

[134] No. 13–1060 (D.C. Cir. January 2015).

[135] *Id.* at 38.

[136] *Id.* at 45.

to marketing a product. However, FDA has the authority to enforce against misbranded and adulterated dietary supplements in the form of warning letters, product seizures, and mandatory recalls. It may also ban an ingredient through the rulemaking process.

FDA bears the burden of proof for each element in proving that a dietary supplement is adulterated[137] or misbranded.[138] FDA must provide a manufacturer with the opportunity to present its side to the FDA before the FDA proceeds with an adulteration case to the US attorney.[139] This procedural right applies exclusively to dietary supplements. DSHEA eliminates deference to FDA interpretation for adulteration cases.[140] The standard focuses on the intended/recommended use of the product instead of the actual product itself. When the FDA wants to bring an enforcement action, it carries the burden of proving both the toxicity of the ingredients and the toxicity under recommended use. Because recommended use supersedes ordinary use in the statutory definition, a supplement hypothetically might be commonly used in an abusive manner – leading to serious health risks and even death – but nevertheless be allowed to remain on the marketplace if the FDA cannot prove that the recommended use is unsafe.[141]

[2] *Functional Foods*

Because scientists continue to strengthen the link between nutrition and health, the barrier between food and drug is becoming more and more difficult for the FDA to maintain. As noted in Chapter 1, an emerging food product called "functional foods" or "nutraceuticals" possess attributes for both foods and dietary supplements. Functional food, roughly defined, is any modified food or food ingredient that provides a health benefit beyond the traditional nutrients it contains.[142] Consumers may choose functional foods not only for their aroma, taste, or nutritional value, but also for specific dietary benefits.[143] For example, yogurt is promoted for use in weight loss programs; tomato products are promoted for their lycopene content; orange juice fortified is promoted to help maintain bone density.

The "functional food" terminology has been around for many years, however, and as noted in Chapter 4, Congress has never amended the FDCA to govern functional foods and the FDA has never established regulations unique to this product category. Because there are no specified statutes and regulations for functional foods, these products fall under the same general requirements that apply to foods, dietary supplements, and other products FDA regulates. This means that a functional food product may be regulated as dietary supplement or conventional food depending on the claims made for the product and the product's positioning in the marketplace.

---

[137] 21 U.S.C. § 342(f)(1).
[138] 21 U.S.C. § 343-2(c).
[139] 21 U.S.C. § 342(f)(2).
[140] 21 U.S.C. § 342(f)(1).
[141] Fortin, *supra* note 64 at 357–8.
[142] Food and Nutrition Board, Institute of Medicine, Opportunities in the Nutrition and Food Sciences: Research Challenges and the Next Generation of Investigators 109 (Paul R. Thomas & Robert Earl eds., 1994).
[143] U.S. Gov't Accountability Office, GAO/RCED-00-156, Report to Congressional Committees, Improvements Needed in Overseeing the Safety of Dietary Supplements and "Functional Foods" (2000).

The market for functional foods, like it is for dietary supplements, is large and likely will continue to grow, especially given the aging of the baby boom generation, an increased interest in prevention in health care, and advances in science that identify new relationships between diet and disease.[144]

[3] The Case of Energy Drinks

Energy drinks pose interesting issues for food and dietary supplement regulations. The term "energy drink" is not defined in statute or regulation.[145] The FDA interprets energy drink as "a class of products in liquid form that typically contains caffeine, with or without other added ingredients."[146]

Generally, an energy drink can be marketed as a conventional food or dietary supplement. A manufacturer may choose to market an energy drink as a dietary supplement in order to circumvent the required standards for food additives and GRAS substances (such as caffeine) in conventional foods. A manufacturer also may choose to market an energy drink as a conventional food in order to not be required to report serious adverse events in association with the product. In addition, the energy drink as a beverage may be purchased with food stamps.[147]

In a 2009–2010 report, the GAO recommended that FDA issue guidance to clarify when products should be marketed as dietary supplements or as conventional foods.[148] FDA agreed with this recommendation and has issued draft guidance on distinguishing liquid dietary supplements from beverages.[149] Adverse event reports potentially associate energy drinks with a number of illnesses, including heart attacks and convulsions, and even deaths.[150] Some members of Congress have expressed concern over energy drink regulation, specifically those with caffeine.[151] In November 2012, the FDA agreed to commission an outside panel of experts to review the safety of energy drinks.[152]

[4] Problem of Fraud

As noted in Chapter 2, economically motivated adulteration (EMA) is a form of food fraud that has plagued food systems for centuries. FDA defines EMA as "[t]he fraudulent, intentional substitution or addition of a substance in a product for the purpose

---

[144] *Id.* at 7.

[145] Corby-Edwards, *supra* note 127 at 13.

[146] Letter from Jeanne Ireland, assistant commissioner for legislation, FDA, to the Honorable Richard J. Durbin, senator (August 10, 2012).

[147] Corby-Edwards, *supra* note 127 at 14.

[148] *See* U.S. Gov't Accountability Office, GAO-09-250, FDA Should Take Further Actions to Improve Oversight and Consumer Understanding (2009).

[149] *See* FDA, Guidance for Industry: Factors that Distinguish Liquid Dietary Supplements from Beverages, Considerations Regarding Novel Ingredients, and Labeling for Beverages and Other Conventional Foods (December 2009).

[150] Corby-Edwards, *supra* note 127 at 14.

[151] *See* Letter from Richard Durbin, senator, and Richard Blumenthal, senator, to Margaret Hamburg, commissioner, FDA (September 11, 2012).

[152] Press Release, Energy "Drinks" and Supplements: Investigations of Adverse Event Reports, Food and Drug Admin. (November 16, 2012).

of increasing the apparent value of the product or reducing the cost of its production, i.e., for economic gain."[153] EMA is particularly vexing in the dietary supplement industry and has been linked to public health concerns.[154] The traditional legal tools used to regulate dietary supplements – GMPs, labeling requirements, adverse event reporting – do not effectively abrogate EMA in a complex global food system that makes it particularly difficult to ascertain the level of EMA among dietary supplements, let alone enforce against this form of adulteration. In February 2015, the New York State attorney general's office issued to major retailers a letter demanding they cease and desist from adulterated and misbranded herbal supplements.[155] Testing showed that four out of five of the products did not contain the herbs listed on their labels and that pills labeled medicinal herbs often contained cheap fillers such as powdered rice, asparagus, and houseplants.[156] It is likely that the problem of fraud with dietary supplements will continue to attract attention from policymakers and enforcement authorities.

[5] *Self-Governance*

The dietary supplement industry does engage in self-regulation via the development of standards of quality and safety and third-party certification programs.[157] For example, NSF International tests and certifies dietary supplements for quality, contamination, and label verification. Also, USP, a nongovernment organization, sets standards and verifies the quality, purity, and potency of ingredients and finished products. USP also has a consumer aid certification program (United States Pharmacopeia Dietary Supplement Verification Program) that verifies the contents of dietary supplements. USP conducts laboratory testing, gives reviews, and assesses manufacturing practices. If a company meets their standards (that the dietary supplement product contains the ingredients as indicated on the label in the stated amount and strength, that the product meets purity standards, and that the product complies with good manufacturing practices), the USP stamps its approval.[158]

§ 5.03 Menu Labeling

[1] *NLEA Omission*

The NLEA expressly exempted restaurants, food retailers, and establishments where food is served for immediate consumption – covering a broad swath of food providers – from the mandate that a food is misbranded unless its label bears accurate nutritional

---

[153] Economically Motivated Adulteration; Public Meeting; Request for Comment, 74 Fed. Reg. 15,497 (April 6, 2009).

[154] *See* Virginia M. Wheatley and John Spink, *Defining the Public Health Threat of Dietary Supplement Fraud*, INSTITUTE OF FOOD TECHNOLOGISTS COMPREHENSIVE REVIEWS IN FOOD SCIENCE AND FOOD SAFETY (2013); Steve Myers, *Will Economic Adulteration Help Bring Down DSHEA?*, NATURAL PRODUCTS INSIDER (November 12, 2009).

[155] Letter from Attorney General Eric T. Echneiderman, to GNC (February 2, 2015).

[156] Anahad O'Connor, *New York Attorney General Targets Supplements at Major Retailers*, N.Y. TIMES, February 3, 2015.

[157] *See* Corby-Edwards, *supra* note 127 at 18.

[158] *See* U.S. PHARMACOPEIA, *USP Pharmaceutical Ingredient Verification Program: Mark Usage Manual.*

information, providing mandatory nutritional information.[159] Therefore, restaurants were not required to provide the calorie content or any other nutritional facts about the food they served. A restaurant would be covered under the NLEA provisions only if it made a specific claim about its food content (such as "low salt" or "light").[160] Notwithstanding the intent by Congress in passing NLEA to provide consumers with scientifically based information so they can make informed decisions about their food purchases, Congress, at the time, believed requiring nutritional labeling at restaurants would be impractical.[161]

[2] *State and Local Menu-Labeling Laws*

[a] New York City Regulation: First Amendment Challenge

Following passage of the NLEA, state and local governments enacted laws that required disclosure of nutritional information for food served in restaurants that are similar to the NLEA requirements for FDA-regulated foods. In 2006, New York City's Board of Health passed a regulation requiring that calorie information be posted on menus and menu boards of any food service establishment that was already voluntarily publishing nutritional information somewhere other than the menus, such as on a restaurant's website or a handout. The goal of the regulation was to make published nutrition information more visible to patrons. Before the regulation went into effect, the New York Restaurant Association (NYSRA) filed suit against the New York City Board of Health challenging the city's menu-labeling regulation on grounds of federal preemption and free speech.[162] The federal district court noted that because the city's regulation's application was limited to restaurants that already voluntarily made public the caloric value of their food, the city's regulation operated precisely in the same manner as the NLEA and was therefore expressly preempted under NLEA.[163] Because the district court determined that the regulation was preempted, it did not address the NYSRA's First Amendment arguments. When the New York City Board of Health revised the regulation to require all New York City restaurants with fifteen or more locations to display calorie content on its menus and menu boards, the NYSRA filed a new suit to challenge the revised law.[164] The federal district court dismissed the suit and upheld the New York City regulation, a decision affirmed by the Second Circuit. The Second Circuit held that the revised regulation was not preempted by the NLEA's regulatory scheme.[165] The Second Circuit Court found that, even though Congress exempted food service establishments from the NLEA, it left the authority to state and local governments to require nutritional information on menus and menu boards.[166] Addressing the First Amendment claim, the Second Circuit found under the four-prong *Hudson* test for First Amendment scrutiny that the mandatory disclosures of factual information did not impermissibly infringe on the First Amendment

---

[159] 21 U.S.C. § 343(q)(5)(A)(i).

[160] 21 U.S.C. § 343(r).

[161] H.R. Rep. No 101–538, at 7 (1990).

[162] *See* N.Y. State Rest. Ass'n v. N.Y. City Bd. of Health, 509 F. Supp. 2d 351, 352 (S.D.N.Y. 2007).

[163] *Id.* at 353.

[164] N.Y. State Rest. Ass'n v. N.Y. City Bd. of Health, 556 F.3d 114, 122. (2d Cir. 2009).

[165] *Id.* at 130–2.

[166] *Id.* at 118.

rights of the NYSRA's members because the city's goal of combating obesity was reason-ably related to this regulation.[167]

[b] Other City and State Regulation

Following New York City's lead, several other local governments introduced sim-ilar menu-labeling provisions. In 2008, California became the first state to enact menu-labeling law, requiring restaurants with twenty or more locations to post calo-rie information for standard menu items on menus or menu boards.[168] In addition to California, states such as Massachusetts, Maine, Oregon, and New Jersey all promul-gated regulations or enacted statutes requiring menu labeling.[169] At the local level, numerous counties implemented menu-labeling laws, including counties in Oregon and California, which were preempted by state laws.[170]

[3] *Federal Menu-Labeling Law*

[a] Patient Protection and Affordable Care Act

In March 2010, Congress passed the Patient Protection and Affordable Care Act (ACA).[171] This health care reform legislation included Section 4205, which amended the NLEA provisions of the FDCA.[172] Section 4205 requires restaurants, retail food establishments, and vending machine operators to provide point-of-purchase nutrition information to consumers. The ACA limits its coverage to food service establishments and vending machines that are part of a chain of twenty or more locations.[173]

The ACA specifically required FDA to promulgate regulations for the following issues: (1) standards for determining and disclosing the nutrient content for standard menu items that come in different flavors, varieties, or combinations, which are listed as a single menu item; (2) any other nutrient that may be disclosed for the purpose of pro-viding information to assist consumers in maintaining healthy dietary practices; (3) rules for the registration of establishments that are not otherwise subject to the law's require-ments to voluntarily provide nutrition information; and (4) the format and manner of the nutrient content disclosure requirements. The FDA was further instructed to consider certain factors in rulemaking, including the standardization for recipes and preparation methods; variations in ingredients, serving size, and formulation of menu items; space on menus and menu boards; and human components including worker training and the possibility of human error.[174] The ACA gave FDA one year to propose regulations for

---

[167] *Id.* at 135–6.

[168] *Nutrition Labeling in Chain Restaurants, State and Local/Bills/Regulations: 2009–2010* 1–2, Center for Science in the Public Interest Newsroom (2010).

[169] *Id.* at 5–7.

[170] *See* Lainie Rutkow et al., *Preemption and the Obesity Epidemic: State and Local Menu Labeling Laws and the Nutrition Labeling and Education Act*, 36 J.L. Med. & Ethics 772, 780 (2008).

[171] Patient Protection and Affordable Care Act, Pub. L. 111–148, § 4205, 124 Stat. 119, 573–6 (2010) (cod-ified as amended at scattered sections of 42 U.S.C.).

[172] *Id.* at § 4205.

[173] *Id.* § 4205(b)(H)(ii).

[174] Amalia K. Cory-Edwards, Cong. Research Serv., R42825, Nutrition Labeling of Restaurant Menus, 7 (November 19, 2012).

enacting the provisions.[175] The mandatory requirements are not expected to take effect until the FDA finalizes its regulations.

[b] Proposed Labeling Requirements

In April 2011, the FDA issued two proposed regulations on calorie labeling on menus and menu boards in chain restaurants, retail food establishments, and vending machines with twenty or more locations.[176] The FDA purportedly was expected to issue final rules by the end of 2012.[177] The FDA then set a deadline for itself in the issuance of final rules on menu-labeling requirements in February 2014. The agency has yet to finish the final rules. In a 2013 interview, FDA commissioner Margaret Hamburg indicated that crafting the rules had become very complicated: "[t]here are very, very strong opinions and powerful voices both on the consumer and public health side and on the industry side, and we have worked very hard to sort of figure out what really makes sense and also what is implementable."[178] In February 2014, a bipartisan group of twenty-four members of Congress expressed concern in a letter to the FDA that "[t]he proposal harms both those non-restaurants that were not intended to be captured by the menu-labeling law as well as those restaurants that have the flexibility and variability in the food they offer."[179] The group requested the FDA to consider alternatives, including letting delivery operations provide the information online, limiting the rule to venues where food service is the primary source of revenue, shaving away penalties, and letting restaurants use other approaches for made-to-order or variably sized items.

The proposed rule presents two options in defining "restaurants or similar retail food establishments" to be covered by the rule. Both options define a "restaurant or similar food establishment" as a retail establishment that offers for sale restaurant or restaurant-type food, where the sale of food is the primary business activity of that establishment. Both options cover the establishment that presents itself publicly as a restaurant or a total or more than 50 percent of a retail establishment's gross floor area is used for preparation, purchase, service, consumption, or storage. The first option applies to establishments where 50 percent of the revenues are derived from food. The second option applies to establishments where "restaurant or restaurant-type food or its ingredients" is stored.[180] Both options for the interpretation of restaurants and similar retail food establishments would generally exempt movie theaters, bowling alleys, bookstore cafes, amusement parks, general merchandise stores with in-house concessions stands, hotels, and transportation carriers such as trains and airplanes – all establishments that sell restaurant-like food to consumers.[181] The second option would also exempt grocery and convenience stores. The exclusion of these entities, especially grocery and

---

[175] § 4205(b) (to be codified as amended at 21 U.S.C. § 343 (q)(5)(H)(x)(I)).

[176] Food Labeling; Nutrition Labeling of Standard Menu Items in Restaurants and Similar Retail Food Establishments, 76 Fed. Reg. 19,192 (April 6, 2011) and Food Labeling; Calorie Labeling of Articles of Food in Vending Machines; Proposed Rule, 76 Fed. Reg. 19,237 (April 6, 2011).

[177] Corby-Edwards, *supra* note 127 at 8.

[178] Mary Clare Jalonick, *FDA Head Says Menu Labeling "Thorny" Issue* (March 12, 2013).

[179] Benjamin Goad, *Uproar over ObamaCare's Menu Rules*, THE HILL (February 18, 2014).

[180] *See* Food Labeling; Nutrition Labeling of Standard Menu Items in Restaurants and Similar Retail Food Establishments, 76 Fed. Reg. 19,192 (April 6, 2011).

[181] Corby-Edwards, *supra* note 127 at 8.

convenience stores, as provided in option two, has provoked debate over the intent of Congress.[182]

The proposed rule also delineates the food that will require calorie and nutrient information. Under the ACA, covered establishments are required to provide calorie and nutrition information for "food that is a standard menu item." The ACA expressly excludes from this category custom orders (prepared in a specific manner at the customer's request), daily specials (foods that are not routinely listed on the menu), temporary menu items (food that appears on a menu or menu board for less than sixty days per calendar year), part of a customary market test (foods that are offered for fewer than ninety consecutive days to test consumer acceptance), and condiments (available for general use, such as salt, pepper, and ketchup that every customer has access to).

The proposed FDA rule further specifies the foods that would require labeling and food that would be exempt. It proposed definitions for restaurant food and restaurant-type food, standard menu items, and combination meals. Restaurant food that would be subject to the labeling requirements is food that is served in restaurants or other establishments in which food is served for immediate human consumption – that is, food to be consumed on the premises where the food is purchased or while walking away, or that is sold for sale or use in such establishment.[183] Standard menu item is restaurant or restaurant-type food that is routinely offered as a self-service food or food on display, to include multiple serving foods that are routinely included on a menu or other primary writing or routinely offered as a self-service food or food on display.[184] Combination meal is a standard menu item that consists of more than one food item.

The proposed rule lists three exempt foods: variable menu item, self-service food, and food on display. A variable menu item comes in different flavors, varieties, or combinations, and is listed as a single menu item. Self-service food is restaurant or restaurant-type food that is offered for sale at a salad bar, buffet line, cafeteria line, or similar self-service facility, and self-service beverages. Food on display is restaurant or restaurant-type food that is visible to the consumer before the consumer makes a selection, so long as there is not an ordinary expectation of further preparation by the consumer before consumption. These definitions would cover grab-and-go items, such as sandwiches or meals prepared in a restaurant or similar self-service facility. The grocery store industry disagrees with this definition.[185]

Other concerns include issues over how the calorie and nutrient information is presented and the amount of time businesses will have to implement the rule.

[c] Preemption Considerations

The ACA provides that it does not preempt any provision of state or local law unless otherwise expressly preempted by the FDCA. Section 4205 amends Section 403(a) of the FDCA that explicitly prohibits state and local governments from imposing nutrition labeling requirements not identical to federal law to exclude state and local provisions

[182] *Id.* at 9.
[183] *Id.* at 11 (citing Food Labeling: Nutrition Labeling of Standard Menu Items in Restaurants and Similar Retail Food Establishments, 76 Federal Register 19192, April 6, 2011).
[184] *Id.*
[185] *Id.* at 12.

regarding restaurant chains of less than twenty outlets.[186] The cumulative effect of these subsections of 4205 is to allow state and local governments to mandate more stringent menu-labeling requirements than those imposed by federal law on restaurants of fewer than twenty locations.

[d] Constitutional Scrutiny

It is likely that ACA would withstand constitutional issues of free speech and equal protection that were raised in the suit brought against the New York City's Board of Health regulation for menu labeling. It is likely that the Second Circuit's holding that the city's goal of combating obesity was reasonably related to this regulation and therefore not constitutionally barred by the First Amendment under the *Hudson* inquiry will be persuasive to other courts. However, the concerns of paternalism and the effectiveness of labeling requirements, which were directed in opposition to state and federal menu legislation, may continue to shape future law making of labeling for foods not originally covered by the NLEA. Empirical analysis as to the effectiveness in menu labeling also may affect future policy.[187]

[4] *Self-Regulation*

When menu labeling was first proposed, the restaurant industry adamantly opposed regulation as a tool to combat obesity. As states and municipalities began adopting menu-labeling provisions, the restaurant industry began to support legislation, especially armed with preemption provisions. In advance of the FDA's final rule on the national menu-labeling law, some establishments moved forward with their own voluntary menu nutrition labeling. Most notably, McDonald's, the largest fast food company in the US, announced in September 2012 that it would list calorie information on all restaurant and drive-thru menu boards.[188]

§ 5.04 Regulation of Marketing to Children

[1] *Scope of Legal Tools*

The Center for Disease Control (CDC) has reported that the obesity epidemic is particularly problematic with children. The rise in childhood obesity rates is strongly correlated with a rise in childhood physical health complications, including fatty liver, Type 2 diabetes, and emotional health problems.[189] Children who are overweight also have a propensity of being overweight or obese as adults.[190]

---

[186] *See id.* at 6.

[187] A recent article posits that several studies have shown that consumers do not make healthier food choices even when armed with menu labeling. Ellen A. Black, *Menu Labeling: The Unintended Consequences to the Consumer*, 69 FOOD & DRUG L.J., 531 (2014).

[188] Press Release, McDonald's USA LLC, McDonald's USA Adding Calorie Counts to Menu Boards, Innovating with Recommended Food Groups, Publishes Nutrition Progress Report (September 12, 2012).

[189] Childhood Obesity Facts, Centers for Disease Control and Prevention (childhood obesity rates have more than tripled in the past thirty years) (December 11, 2014).

[190] Stephen R. Daniels, *The Consequences of Childhood Overweight and Obesity*, 16 FUTURE OF CHILD. 47, 61 (2006).

In response to the obesity epidemic for children, much focus in the public health community has centered on restricting food-marketing practices directed at children. The legal tools employed to implement marketing restrictions include advertising restrictions, government regulation, and self-regulation. Use of these tools raises considerable tension between the notions of government's public health role, parental roles, and personal responsibility. While many advocates agree that government should play an affirmative role with respect to childhood obesity, they are very much divided over what that role should be.

[2] Restriction of Child-Directed Food Advertisements

[a] IOM Report

Much of the attention on food marketing focuses on television advertisements.[191] The Institute of Medicine (IOM) in its 2006 report, *Food Marketing to Children and Youth: Threat or Opportunity*, determined after reviewing 123 published empirical studies that "strong evidence" shows that television advertising affects the food and beverage requests and preferences of children aged two to eleven.[192] The IOM has also found that food advertising increased children's consumption of the advertised foods, at least in the short term.

> The quantity and nature of advertisements to which children are exposed to daily, reinforced through multiple media channels, appear to contribute to food, beverage, and sedentary-pursuit choices that can adversely affect energy balance. It is estimated that the average child currently views more than 40,000 commercials on television each year, a sharp increase from 20,000 commercials in the 1970's ... Dietary and other choices influenced by exposure to these advertisement may likely contribute to energy imbalance and weight gain, resulting in obesity ... [B]ased on children's commercial recall and product preferences, it is evident that advertising achieves its intended effects ...[A]n extensive systematic literature review concludes that food advertisements promote food purchase requests by children to parents, have an impact on children's product and brand preferences, and affect consumption behavior.[193]

The power to regulate television advertisements is shared by two government agencies: the Federal Communications Commission (FCC) and the Federal Trade

---

[191] Although the Internet and computer games have been growing in popularity with children, television remains a preferred electronic medium for food marketers. Susan Linn & Josh Golin, *Beyond Commercials: How Food Marketers Target Children*, 39 Loy. L.A. L. Rev. 15 (2006). Another advertising technique that is often used on children by food companies is referred to by the Federal Communications Commission as "embedded advertising." This form of advertising is used in television shows, movies, video games, and music. Embedded advertising, also known as product integration, involves incorporating the branded product into the dialogue or plot of the sponsored program. *See* Rita-Marie Cain Reid, *Embedded Advertising to Children: A Tactic that Requires a New Regulatory Approach*, 51 Am. Bus. L.J. 721 (2014).

[192] *See Overview of the IOM Report on Food Marketing to Children and Youth: Threat or Opportunity?*, Fact Sheet, Institute of Medicine of the National Academies (December 2005).

[193] *Preventing Childhood Obesity: Health in the Balance* 173, Institute of Medicine of the National Academies (2004).

Commission (FTC). Under the Communications Act, the FCC has the power to regulate broadcasting as "public convenience, interest, or necessity requires."[194] The FTC is governed by the FTCA, which states that "unfair methods of competition in or affecting commerce, and unfair or deceptive acts or practices in or affecting commerce" are unlawful.[195] The FTC regulates all unfair or deceptive advertising techniques. The FCC and FTC both have each attempted to restrict child-directed advertising.

[b] FCC Regulation: Limited

The FCC's regulatory power is limited with regard to the length of advertisements during children's programming. The FCC does not have any regulatory power over the content of advertisements geared toward children. The 1990 Children's Television Act (CTA) applies both to over-the-air commercial television broadcasters, as well as cable and digital providers. CTA established limitations on the length of advertisements permitted during children's programming.[196] CTA specifically "limits the duration of advertising in children's television programming to 10.5 minutes per hour on weekends and 12 minutes per hour on weekdays."[197] The FCC's power to review and modify limitations on advertisement length presumably could lead to further limitations on the length of advertisements during children's programming.

[c] FTC Regulation

(1) *Section 5*

As noted in Chapter 4, Section 5 of the FTCA makes unfair or deceptive acts or practices in or affecting interstate commerce unlawful. The FTC has the authority to bring cases against companies for unfair or deceptive advertising under this section of the Act, and it further has the authority to promulgate rules to address pervasive abuses. The FTC has the ability to regulate unfair and deceptive acts and practices by bringing individual actions or by undertaking rulemaking procedures authorized by the FTCA. Rulemaking is preferable in the food-marketing context because it can reach pervasive acts and practices as opposed to individual actions targeting specific practices that can result only in discrete remedial orders.

(2) *Kid Vid*

The FTC's first comprehensive efforts to regulate advertising to children were made in the 1970s. In 1977, the Action for Children's Television (ACT) and Center for Science in the Public Interest (CSPI) requested rulemaking to regulate television advertising for candy and sugared food products directed at children in 1977.[198] Consumers' Union of the United States, Inc. and Committee on Children's Television, Inc. filed a petition in

---

[194] Communications Act, 47 U.S.C. § 303.
[195] Federal Trade Commission Act, 15 U.S.C. § 41.
[196] Children's Television Act, 47 U.S.C. § 303a(b).
[197] *Id.* at § 303a(c).
[198] Children's Advertising, 46 Fed. Reg. 48,710 (October 2, 1981) (codified at 16 C.F.R. 461).

1978, which sought rulemaking to regulate all television advertising oriented to young children.[199] At that time, the advocacy stemmed from concerns over dental caries and tooth decay promoted by the consumption of high sugar foods. Childhood obesity was not yet on the horizon in terms of public health concern; however, many of the arguments about advertising to children are similar issues to those now debated.

Under its authority, FTC chose to pursue these petitions. An FTC staff report stated that "televised advertising of sugared products to children too young to understand the selling purpose violate[s] the FTC Act."[200] The staff proposed either: (1) a complete ban on advertising directed at children eight and under; (2) a ban on all ads for foods linked to poor dental health directed at children twelve and under; or (3) a requirement that ads for sugared foods contain disclosures of the health effects of the foods.[201] With this staff approval, the FTC embarked on a rulemaking that came to be known as "Kid Vid." The FTC issued a Notice of Proposed Rulemaking in 1978 that proposed major regulation of advertisements aired during children's television time.

The FTC action met opposition. The *Washington Post* carried an editorial entitled *The FTC as National Nanny*, stating in part:

> [T]he proposal, in reality, is designed to protect children from the weaknesses of their parents – and the parents from the wailing insistence of their children. That, traditionally, is one of the roles of a governess – if you can afford one. It is not a proper role of government. The government has enough problems with television's emphasis on violence and sex and its shortages of local programming, without getting into this business, too.[202]

Opposition to the FTC's action culminated in Congress passing the FTC Improvements Act of 1980, which withdrew the FTC's authority to regulate advertising to children as unfair. The Act specifically revoked the Commission's authority "to promulgate any rule in the children's advertising proceeding or in any substantially similar proceeding on the basis of a determination by the Commission that such advertising constitutes an unfair act or practice in or affecting commerce."[203] Without its unfairness jurisdiction as a basis for rulemaking, the FTC could restrict advertising only based on deception.[204] Deception requires a showing that "there is a representation, omission or practice that is likely to mislead the consumer acting reasonably in the circumstances, to the consumer's detriment."[205] The rationalization for the termination of the FTC's unfairness jurisdiction over children's advertising was that proof was lacking to show either that advertising of sugared products to children less than twelve years old adversely affected their attitudes about nutrition, or that it was responsible for the ill effects of sugared products on

---

[199] *Id.*

[200] FTC Staff Report on Television Advertising to Children 10–11, U.S. FEDERAL TRADE COMMISSION (February 27, 1978).

[201] Children's Advertising, 43 Fed. Reg. 17,967 (April 27, 1978).

[202] *The FTC as National Nanny*, THE WASHINGTON POST (March 1, 1978), at A22.

[203] F.T.C. Improvements Act of 1980, Pub. L. No. 96–252, §§ 11(a)(1), 11(a)(3), 94 Stat. 374 (codified in part at 15 U.S.C. § 57a).

[204] Children's Advertising, 46 Fed. Reg. 48,711 (October 2, 1981).

[205] J. Howard Beales, *Advertising to Kids and the FTC: A Regulatory Retrospective That Advises the Present* 5 (March 2, 2004), U.S. FEDERAL TRADE COMMISSION.

teeth.[206] As matters stand today, due to the FTC Improvements Act of 1980, the FTC can rulemake only under its deception jurisdiction in child-marketing regulation.

(3) Policy Statement on Deception: Constitutional Considerations

A ban on junk food advertising to children is a murky issue from a constitutional standpoint. According to the 1983 FTC's Policy Statement on Deception, there are three elements to finding deception: (1) there must be a representation, omission, or practice that is likely to mislead a consumer; (2) that is analyzed from the perspective of a consumer acting reasonably in the circumstances; and (3) the representation, omission, or practice must be material.[207] It is instructive to note that while judicial review of FTC factual conclusions in rulemaking has been highly deferential,[208] legal issues are subject to de novo judicial review.[209] Thus, if an FTC rule on deception in child advertising on food were to be challenged, it would be subject to First Amendment scrutiny. As shown in Chapter 4, under the First Amendment, restrictions on commercial speech are reviewed under the four-prong inquiry set forth in *Central Hudson*.[210]

Although it is reasonable to assume that the government has a substantial interest in protecting children from obesity and deceptive junk food advertisements, the *Central Hudson* test is not so easily satisfied. As the government may only regulate advertisements that are false, misleading, or otherwise deceptive, it may be difficult to find data that all junk food advertising communications are deceptive. It could be argued that because such a disproportionate number of fast food advertisements on television are misleading, and since these advertisements directly target young, impressionable children, a complete ban, or perhaps a ban on all misleading and deceptive advertisements, would be the only method to assure that such communications do not unduly influence children. The fact remains, however, that not all junk food advertisements disseminated on television are deceptive and, therefore, a blanket ban is more extensive than necessary and thus potentially unconstitutional under the fourth prong of the *Central Hudson* test.[211] Even laws that seeking to deny access of minors to obscenity or sexually explicit depictions have been struck down as unconstitutional because it would effectively suppress speech that adults have a constitutional right to receive.[212]

---

[206] Children's Advertising 46 Fed. Reg., *supra* note 204 at 48,713.

[207] *See* F.T.C. Policy Statement on Deception (1983), appended to Cliffdale Assoc., 103 F.T.C. 110, 174 (1984).

[208] Jennifer L. Pomeranz, *Television Food Marketing to Children Revisited: The Federal Trade Commission Has the Constitutional and Statutory Authority to Regulate*, 38 J.L. MED. & ETHICS 98, 106 (2010) (citing Pa. Funeral Dirs. Ass'n, Inc. v. F.T.C., 41 F.3d 81 (3d Cir. 1994).

[209] *Id.* (citing F.T.C. v. Ind. Fed'n of Dentists, 476 U.S. 447, 454 (1986)).

[210] A court must determine the following: (1) whether the expression is protected by the First Amendment, meaning that it must relate to a lawful activity and not be false, deceptive, or misleading; (2) whether the government asserted a substantial interest to be achieved by restricting commercial speech; (3) whether the regulation directly advances this interest; and (4) whether the restriction is not more extensive than necessary to serve this interest. Cent. Hudson Gas & Elec. Corp. v. Pub. Serv. Comm'n of N.Y., 447 U.S. 557 (1980).

[211] *See* Martin H. Redish, *Childhood Obesity, Advertising, and the First Amendment*, White Paper (June 8, 2011) (asserts in unequivocal terms that voluntary regulations contemplated by the Interagency Working Group on Food Marketed to Children – referenced in this section of Chapter 5 – fail the last three prongs of the *Central Hudson* test).

[212] Reno v. ACLU, 521 U.S. 844, 874 (1997).

[3] *Self-Governance*

[a] National Voluntary Initiatives

(1) *Children's Advertising Review Unit (CARU)*

The pressures of public health concerns over the obesity epidemic among children coupled with the limited range of government regulation of the marketing of food oriented to children has resulted in extensive self-regulation. The principal self-regulatory advertising body in the United States is the Advertising Self-Regulatory Council (formerly, National Advertising Review Council [NARC]) whose mission it is to foster truth and accuracy in national advertising through voluntary self-regulation and to support advertiser compliance to minimize governmental involvement in advertising regulation. In 1974, NARC established the Children's Advertising Review Unit (CARU) as a self-regulatory body to promote responsible children's advertising. Administered and funded by members of the children's advertising industry, CARU sets standards for the industry to assure that advertising directed at children is not deceptive, unfair, or inappropriate for its intended audience and takes into account the special vulnerabilities of children.[213] The guidelines developed by CARU apply to advertising targeted at children under twelve years of age in all media, including print, broadcast and cable television, radio, video, point of sale, packaging, and online advertising. Certain "Core Principles" apply to all practices covered by the CARU self-regulatory program.[214]

CARU monitors and reviews advertising directed at children, initiates and receives complaints about advertising practices, and determines whether such practices violate the program's standards. When CARU finds a violation, it attempts to secure the voluntary cooperation of the advertiser or website operator.[215] CARU performs voluntary investigations of the advertising industry. CARU announces all formal decisions through press releases. Advertisers may appeal a formal decision to the National Advertising Review Board.[216]

(2) *2005 FTC/DHHS Workshop*

In July 2005, the FTC and the DHHS jointly sponsored a public workshop on food and beverage marketing to children, self-regulation, and childhood obesity.[217] The workshop addressed food-marketing practices and the self-regulatory efforts governing food marketing to children. The report suggested expanding and enhancing the role of CARU to make it more effective.[218] The workshop also noted that Congress had directed FTC to conduct a comprehensive food- marketing study.[219] The panel discussions and the comments received for the workshop demonstrated a divergence of opinions on the value of the CARU Guidelines and the effectiveness of the self-regulatory system. Industry

---

[213] Children's Advertising Review Unit, Self-Regulatory Program for Children's Advertising 3 (2009).
[214] *Id.* at 5.
[215] *Id.* at 3.
[216] *Id.*
[217] U.S. FEDERAL TRADE COMMISSION & U.S. DEP'T OF HEALTH AND HUMAN SERVS. JOINT WORKSHOP REPORT, PERSPECTIVES ON MARKETING, SELF-REGULATION, & CHILDHOOD OBESITY (April 2006).
[218] *See id.* at i–ix (executive summary).
[219] *See id.* at 58 note 34.

members opined that the guides had worked well and had done an adequate job in protecting children from false, misleading, or inappropriate food ads. Consumer group participants were less enthusiastic about the guides, indicating that self-regulation was not working or should be abandoned.[220]

(3) 2006 Children's Food and Beverage Advertising Initiative

The Council of the Better Business Bureaus launched the Children's Food and Beverage Advertising Initiative (CFBAI) in November 2006 to provide companies that advertise foods and beverages to children with a transparent and accountable advertising self-regulation mechanism.[221] The CFBAI is a self-regulatory program with the self-pronounced goal "to shift the mix of advertising messaging directed to children under twelve to encourage healthier dietary choices and healthy lifestyles."[222] The CFBAI has five guiding "core principles" that participating companies follow: (1) companies will advertise only "better-for-you products," a unique standard developed by each company that is consistent with scientific or government standards; (2) companies will incorporate "better-for-you products" in interactive giveaways; (3) companies will only use licensed characters, celebrities, and movie tie-ins in ways that comply with their advertising promises; (4) companies will not pay for or actively seek product placements in programming geared to children under twelve; and (5) companies will not advertise branded food or beverages in elementary schools.[223] Participating companies also each create a pledge – a public commitment to advertising "that will further the goal of promoting healthy dietary choices and healthy lifestyles to children under 12."[224] These manufacturers pledged to: (1) devote at least half of their television, radio, print, and Internet advertising directed at children to encouraging healthier choices and lifestyles; limit products shown in interactive games; (2) not advertise food or beverage products in elementary schools; (3) not engage in food and beverage product placement in entertainment content; and (4) reduce the use of third-party licensed characters in advertising.[225] Each company's pledge is enforced solely by the CFBAI. If a company refuses to comply with its pledge, the CFBAI may expel the company from participation and report the expulsion to the FTC.[226] Participating companies can still use characters that they created themselves (e.g., Tony the Tiger and Ronald McDonald) to advertise any of their products, not just products that are "better-for-you."[227] Also, CFBAI sets no standards for children twelve and older. Participating companies are free to set their own definition for what constitutes a "better-than-you" product.[228] In July 2011, the CFBAI announced the

---

[220] Senator Harkin, who offered opening remarks at the workshop, expressed the view that self-regulation to date has not been effective. *Id.*

[221] Council of Better Bus. Bureau, Children's Food and Beverage Advertising Initiative, Council of Better Business Bureaus .

[222] *Id.*

[223] *Id.* at 1–3.

[224] *Id.* at 1.

[225] *Marketing Food to Children and Adolescents: A Review of Industry Expenditures, Activities, and Self-Regulation* E-2-E-15, U.S. Federal Trade Commission (July 2008).

[226] Council of Better Bus. Bureau, *supra* note 221 at 4.

[227] *Id.* at 2.

[228] Products that have qualified under these definitions include Cinnamon Toast Crunch, Lucky Charms, Fruit Loops, and Kellogg's Rice Krispies cereal. *Id.* at 6–8.

addition of "uniform nutrition criteria" to be followed by companies participating in the program.[229] The "uniform nutrition criteria," which went into effect on December 31, 2013, divide food and beverage products into ten categories that have specific calorie, saturated fat, sodium, and sugar limitations with which participating companies must comply.[230] The uniform nutrition criteria do not have categories that include snack foods or soft drinks.[231]

(4) 2009 *Interagency Working Group on Food Marketed to Children*

In 2009, Congress established the Interagency Working Group on Food Marketed to Children (IWG) through the Omnibus Appropriations Act.[232] The Act directs the FTC, the CDC, FDA, and USDA to establish an IWG. The Working Group is required to conduct a study and develop recommendations for standards addressing food marketed to children under eighteen. In April 2011, the IWG released a set of Preliminary Proposed Nutrition Principles (PPNP) geared at child-directed food marketing.[233] The PPNP covers children aged two to seventeen and is predicated around two core nutritional principles: (1) advertising and marketing should influence children "to choose foods that make a meaningful contribution to a healthful diet"[234] and (2) inspiring children by using advertising and marketing to minimize consumption of foods with significant amounts of nutrients that have a negative impact on health – sodium, saturated fat, trans fat, and added sugars.[235] IWG also recommended that companies focus on regulating food groups that are marketed most often to children.[236]

(5) *International Chamber of Commerce Standards*

The International Chamber of Commerce (ICC) has also developed and published guidelines that establish ethical standards for marketing practices aimed at children.[237] Television advertising in particular is covered by the ICC International Code of Advertising Practice, which states that advertisements should be legal, decent, honest, and truthful, not contain any statement or visual presentation which may, directly or indirectly, mislead a consumer, and clearly be distinguishable as advertisements.[238] The

---

[229] Press Release, Council of Better Business Bureaus, Council of Better Business Bureaus Announces Groundbreaking Agreement on Child-Directed Food Advertising (July 14, 2011).

[230] Category-Specific Uniform Nutrition Criteria, COUNCIL OF BETTER BUSINESS BUREAUS, INC. (July 2011). The categories are juices; dairy products; grain, fruit, and vegetable products, and items not in other categories; soups and meal sauces; seeds, nuts, and nut butters and spreads; meat, fish, and poultry products; mixed dishes and entrees; small meals; and meals. ELAINE D. KOLISH, CHILDREN'S FOOD AND BEVERAGE ADVERTISING INITIATIVE, COUNCIL OF BETTER BUSINESS BUREAUS, INC., WHITE PAPER ON CFBAI'S UNIFORM NUTRITION CRITERIA 6–7 (2010).

[231] *Id.* at 6–7.

[232] PRELIMINARY PROPOSED NUTRITION PRINCIPLES TO GUIDE INDUSTRY SELF-REGULATION: REQUEST FOR COMMENTS 1, INTERAGENCY WORKING GROUP ON FOOD MARKETED TO CHILDREN (April 28, 2011).

[233] *See* Press Release, U.S. Department of Health and Human Services, Interagency Working Group Seeks Input on Proposed Voluntary Principles for Marketing Food to Children (April 28, 2011).

[234] *Id.* at 3.

[235] *Id.*

[236] *Id.* at 7.

[237] *See* ADVERTISING AND MARKETING COMMUNICATION PRACTICE: CONSOLIDATED ICC CODE, INT'L CHAMBER OF COMMERCE (2006).

[238] *Id.* at 13–15.

"social values" section of the guidelines also states that an advertisement should not include any direct appeal to children to persuade adults to buy products for them or to confuse children as to the value or cost of a given product.[239] The goal of these rules is to protect children from advertising that exploits their nativity.[240] The ICC rarely pursues enforcement actions against violators.[241]

[b] Enterprise Self-Regulation

In addition to the FTC's attempt to regulate food advertisements targeted at children, most of the restrictions in place today are self-imposed by the food companies.[242] For example, candy-maker Mars has its own "Marketing Code" and prohibits itself from such actions as advertising to children under age twelve or placing its vending machines in primary schools. In February 2012, Mars released a statement saying that because of the ability of people to overindulge in sweets, the company will no longer be shipping any candy bar that contains more than 250 calories.[243] As evidence of sugar addiction emerges, the food industry could respond by self-regulation: some beverage companies, for example, have begun to post nutrition information next to vending machines in Chicago and San Antonio.[244]

[4] *Litigation*

A class action case that attributed marketing practices as an adverse influence on appropriate nutritional choices and connect it to a legal claim of unfair competition under consumer protection acts was *Committee on Children's Television v. General Foods Corporation*.[245] The Committee on Children's Television, along with other organizational plaintiffs and individual parents and children, sued General Foods and their marketing firms because sugar cereals were marketed toward children to make them seem nutritious, beneficial, and healthful. Calling the defendant General Foods' children's cereals "candy breakfast" because the cereals were 38–50 percent sugar by weight, plaintiffs brought a claim of deceptive marketing under the California's Consumer Protection Act.[246] Five cereals –AlphaBits, Honeycomb, Fruity Pebbles, Sugar Crisp, and Cocoa Pebbles – were targeted because they were almost half sugar and chemicals, yet marketed enticed children to believe that they were nutritious and healthful.[247] Relying on the California consumer protection statute, plaintiffs alleged that because this message was contrary to sound nutritional guidelines, General Foods should be responsible for any harm that the cereal and its marketing caused.[248] Specifically, the complaint claimed

---

[239] *Id.* at 17.

[240] *Id.*

[241] Emily Lee, *The World Health Organization's Global Strategy on Diet, Physical Activity, and Health: Turning Strategy into Action*, 60 Food & Drug L.J. 569, 577 (2005).

[242] *See, e.g.*, Marketing Code for Food, Chocolate, Confections and Gum, Mars, Inc. (2010).

[243] *See* Jacque Wilson, *Mars Puts Snickers Bars on a Diet*, The Chart, CNN Health (February 16, 2012).

[244] D. A. Kysar, *Preferences for Processes: The Process/Product Distinction and the Regulations of Consumer Choice*, 118 Har. L. Rev. 525, 525–9 (2004).

[245] Comm. on Children's Television, Inc. v. Gen. Foods Corp., 673 P.2d 660, 663 (Cal. 1983) (en banc).

[246] *See id.* at 667–71.

[247] *See id.* at 664.

[248] *See id.* at 667–70.

unfair competition, fraud, and breach of fiduciary duty.[249] The plaintiffs also asserted that corporations that engage in marketing to children breached a fiduciary duty to children and their parents.[250]

The case represents the larger issue of who bears responsibility for the consumption of unhealthy products marketed to children. The plaintiffs argued that because General Foods characterized itself as an expert source of information on diet and nutrition, that children were exploited when General Foods targeted ads that made its "candy break-fast" seem nutritious, beneficial, and uplifting.[251] This view, as set forth in the complaint, recognizes the food enterprise as having superior bargaining power over children and parents.

§ 5.05 Food Prohibitions

[1] *Trans Fat*

[a] State Bans

Perhaps the most coercive and politically divisive form of obesity regulation is an out-right ban or prohibition on foods or ingredients deemed to be particularly harmful. In this section, a sample of food prohibitions is surveyed, starting with the ban on Trans Fat. Effective in 2006, FDA labeling law requires that trans fat be listed on the Nutrition Facts panel of foods and some dietary supplements.[252] The CDC has esti-mated that a reduction of trans fat in the food supply could prevent heart disease and coronary deaths.[253] An Institute of Medicine (IOM) report has concluded there was no safe level of trans fat consumption and that it provides no known benefit to human health.[254] Trans fat raises low-density lipoprotein (LDL) or bad cholesterol, increasing the risk of CHD.[255]

New York was the first large US city to strictly limit trans fats in restaurants and sim-ilar enterprises, when in 2007 licensed food vendors – including restaurants, caterers, and street vendors – were prohibited from using artificial trans fats in foods sold to the public.[256] In addition, vendors could not use, serve, or store products with more than 0.5 grams of trans fat per serving.[257] In July 2008, California became the first state to ban trans fats in restaurants effective from January 1, 2010.[258] California restaurants were prohibited

---

[249] *See id.* at 660.

[250] *See id.* at 675.

[251] *Id.*

[252] Trans fat levels of less than 0.5 grams per serving can be listed as 0 grams trans fat on the food label. 21 C.F.R. § 101.9 (c)(2)(ii).

[253] *See FDA Targets Trans Fat in Processed Foods* – Update, U.S. Food & Drug Admin. (November 7, 2013).

[254] National Research Council, Food and Nutrition Board, Institute of Medicine of the National Academies, Dietary Reference Intakes for Energy Carbohydrate, Fat, Fatty Acids, Cholesterol, and Amino Acids, chapters 8 and 11, National Academies Press, Washington DC, 2002/2005.

[255] *See generally,* William H. Dietz and Kelley S. Scanlon, *Eliminating the Use of Partially Hydrogenated Oil in Food Production and Preparation,* 308 J. Am. Med. Ass'n. 108, 143–4 (2012).

[256] *See* N.Y. City Health Code § 81.08.

[257] *Id.* at § 81.08(a).

[258] *See* Cal. Health & Safety Code §114377 (enacted by chapter 207)

from using oil, shortening, and margarine containing artificial trans fats in spreads or for frying, with the exception of deep-frying doughnuts. As of January 1, 2011, doughnuts and other baked goods have been prohibited in California from containing artificial trans fats. Packaged foods are not covered by the ban and can legally contain trans fats.

[b] 2015 FDA Final Rule

In June 2015, the FDA issued a final rule that artificial trans fat is no longer GRAS and gave the industry a deadline to eliminate what remains.[259] Most major food enterprises, including manufacturers and restaurant chains had eliminated trans fats by this time. This effort to prohibit trans fats shifted to the federal level when in November 2013, the FDA announced a tentative determination that partially hydrogenated oils (PHOs) – the primary dietary source of trans fat – are not GRAS and are therefore food additives requiring prior approval by the FDA before being added to food.[260] As noted in Chapter 4, foods that contain unapproved food additives are considered adulterated. For a substance to be GRAS there must be a consensus among qualified experts that the substance is safe under the intended conditions of use. FDA believes there is no longer a scientific consensus to support the safety of PHOs in food.[261]

Included in the FDA's June 2015 announcement was the declaration that food manufacturers will have three years to remove PHOs from their products. This will allow companies either to reformulate without PHOs or to petition the FDA to allow specific uses of PHOs. Following the compliance period, no PHOs can be added to food without FDA approval.[262]

[2] Soda Cap

[a] 2012 New York City Cap Rule

New York City's Sugary Drinks Portion Cap Rule, proposed by Mayor Michael Bloomberg in May 2012, and approved by the New York City Board of Health in September 2012, prohibited food services establishments subject to the city's health department from selling sodas and other sugary drinks in containers larger than sixteen ounces.[263] The proposed rule defines "sugary drink" as:

> [A] carbonated or non-carbonated beverage that is non-alcoholic; is sweetened by the manufacture or establishment with sugar or another caloric sweetener; has greater than 25 calories per 8 fluid ounces of beverage; and does not contain more than 50 percent of milk or milk substitute by volume as an ingredient.[264]

---

[259] See FDA Press Release, *The FDA Takes Steps to Remove Artificial Trans Fats in Processed Foods* (June 16, 2015).

[260] See Tentative Determination Regarding Partially Hydrogenated Oils; Request for Comments and for Scientific Data and Information. 78 Fed. Reg. 67,169 (November 8, 2013).

[261] See FDA to *Extend Comment Period on Measure to Further Reduce Trans Fat in Processed Foods* – UPDATE, U.S. FOOD & DRUG ADMIN. (December 30, 2013).

[262] FDA Press Release, *supra* note 259.

[263] Vivian Yee, *Your Guide to New York's Soda Ban*, N.Y. TIMES, March 11, 2013.

[264] R.C.N.Y. tit.24, § 81.53(a) (proposed).

Thus, in addition to soda, the other sugary beverages subject to the proposed rule would include fruit-flavored drinks, sports drinks, energy drinks, presweetened black coffee and teas, and hot chocolate.[265] The rule specifically excepted out alcoholic beverages, milkshakes, fruit smoothies, mixed coffee drinks, mochas, lattes, and 100 percent fruit juices.[266] The rule would apply to New York City restaurants, movie theaters, food carts, sports stadiums, and other city-regulated food service establishments.[267] The rule would not apply to establishments, such as supermarkets and convenience stores, that are regulated and inspected by the New York City Department of Agriculture and Marketing.[268]

[b] Court Challenges: New York Courts

The portion rule was planned to take effect starting March 2013. However, the plan was struck down by the New York County Supreme Court in Manhattan.[269] The First Department of the Appellate Division of New York State Supreme Court in Manhattan upheld the New York County Supreme Court's ruling in July 2013.[270] Finally, New York State's highest court – the Court of Appeals – affirmed the Appellate Division's decision in June 2014.[271]

The litigation was pitched as a contest about the nanny state and individual liberty.[272] As noted, however, the litigation is "much more about the ability of administrative agencies to use modern regulatory techniques, which include trying to shape consumer behavior in healthier ways."[273] In a 4–2 decision, the Court of Appeals held that New York City's Board of Health had exceeded its "health" powers when it enacted the Portion Cap Rule, thereby improperly usurping the legislature's lawmaking role, and violating New York's constitutional system of separation of powers.[274] The Court of Appeals found that the City Charter restricts the Board of Health to a regulatory, not legislative role.[275] In a vigorous dissent, Justice Read conducted an exhaustive review of statutes, cases, and the history of the Board of Health, and urged that the Board's "authority to regulate the public health in the City is delegated by the New York State Legislature, and its regulation[s]

---

[265] *See* N.Y. Statewide Coal. of Hispanic Chambers of Commerce v. N.Y. City Dept. of Health & Mental Hygiene, No. 653584-12, slip op. 5505 at 9 (N.Y. App. Div. 1st Dep't, July 30, 2013).

[266] *Id.*

[267] Michael M. Grynbaum, *New York Plans to Ban Sale of Big Sizes of Sugary Drinks*, N.Y. Times, May 30, 2012, at A-1.

[268] *See* N.Y. Statewide Coal. of Hispanic Chambers of Commerce v. N.Y. City Dept. of Health & Mental Hygiene, No. 134, slip op. 4804 at 3 (N.Y. Court of Appeals, June 26, 2014).

[269] Michael M. Grynbaum, *Judge Blocks New York City's Limits on Big Sugary Drinks*, N.Y. Times, March 11, 2013, at A-1.

[270] E. C. Gogolak, *Appeals Court Rules against Bloomberg Beverage Restrictions*, N.Y. Times, July 30, 2013, at A-17.

[271] N.Y. Statewide Coal. of Hispanic Chambers of Commerce v. N.Y. City Dept. of Health & Mental Hygiene, No. 134, slip op. 4804, at 3 (N.Y. Court of Appeals, June 26, 2014).

[272] *See, e.g.,* Sarah Conly, *Three Cheers for the Nanny State*, N.Y. Times, March 24, 2013***; Karen Harned, *The Michael Bloomberg Nanny State in New York: A Cautionary Tale*, Forbes, May 10, 2013.

[273] Michael M. Grynbaum, *New York City Soda Fight, in Court, Tests Agency's Power*, N.Y. Times, June 4, 2014, at A1 (quoting Richard Briffault).

[274] N.Y. Statewide Coal. of Hispanic Chambers of Commerce v. N.Y. City Dept. of Health & Mental Hygiene, No. 134, slip op., 4804 at 1–2 (N.Y. Court of Appeals, June 26, 2014).

[275] *Id.* at 7–11.

have the force and effect of state law. The delegation granted by the state is and always has been very broad."[276]

The Court of Appeals' strict interpretation of the Board's authority has important implications for local agencies and governmental regulatory bodies that wish to deal with the obesity epidemic. Local agencies may be less inclined to adopt creative regulatory approaches that could be characterized as legislative and therefore beyond the delegated authority of the agency.

Having determined that the Board of Health's role is strictly regulation, the next question for the Court of Appeals was whether the lower courts correctly found that the Board did not properly exercise its regulatory authority in adopting the portion cap rule.

This question was addressed by using the conceptual framework set forth in a four-prong test of *Boreali v. Axelrod*, the seminal New York State separation of powers case.[277] In *Boreali*, the New York Court of Appeals held that the Public Health Council (PHC) overstepped the bounds of its authority in instituting regulations banning indoor smoking in certain establishments.[278] The four "coalescing circumstances" the *Boreali* court looked at in making its determination were: (1) whether the challenged regulation was based upon concerns not related to the stated purpose of the regulation (e.g., economic and social concerns); (2) whether the regulation was created on a clean slate, thereby creating its own comprehensive set of results without legislative guidance; (3) whether the regulation addressed a matter the legislature had previously discussed, debated, or tried to address (presence of this factor is construed as being indicative of the legislature's inability to agree on "the goals and methods that should govern in resolving" the issue); and (4) whether the regulation required the exercise of expertise or technical competence on behalf of the body passing the legislation.[279] The four Borealis factors function to frame judicial analysis of whether regulatory action exceeds the authority of an administrative body by supplanting the constitutionally allocated exclusive legislative authority of the State Legislature. In addressing the *Boreali* analysis, the Court of Appeals underscored that the focus on whether the challenged regulation attempts to resolve difficult social problems is mindful that this task is policymaking, a task reserved to the legislative branch.[280]

In utilizing the four-factor *Boreali* test to determine the constitutionality of the Soda Ban, the Court of Appeals found that the Board of Health engaged in law-making beyond its regulatory authority, under the first *Boreali* factor. The court noted that an agency that adopts a regulation like the portion cap rule that interferes with the daily activities of consumers involves "complex value judgments concerning personal autonomy and economics," which, according to the court, "is policy-making, not rule-making."[281] With respect to the second *Boreali* factor, the Court of Appeals found that "[b]ecause there was no legislative articulation of health policy goals associated with consumption of sugary beverages upon which to ground the Portion Cap Rule,"

---

[276] *Id.* at 14.
[277] 71 N.Y.2d 1 (1987).
[278] *Id.* at 6.
[279] *Id.* at 12–14.
[280] N.Y. Statewide Coal. of Hispanic Chambers of Commerce v. N.Y. City Dept. of Health & Mental Hygiene, No. 134, slip op., 4804 at 13 (N.Y. Court of Appeals, June 26, 2014).
[281] *Id.* at 17.

the adoption of the rule impermissibly involved policymaking.[282] In addressing the third *Boreali* factor, the Court of Appeals determined that inaction by the state legislature and city council constituted additional proof that the Board's adoption of the portion cap rule amounted to making new policy rather than executing legislative policy.[283] The Court of Appeals did not address the fourth *Boreali* factor because regardless of whether the Board exercised technical or professional expertise, the portion cap rule is invalid under *Boreali*.[284]

The Court of Appeals' decision has been criticized for importing federal administrative law doctrine into New York State constitutional law that in the end distorts the deferential origins of administrative law.[285] Notwithstanding its limited precedential affect due to the uniqueness of New York constitutional law, the case does call attention to the need for local public health agencies to carefully weigh the scientific and technical basis for advancing creative solutions to advance nutrition policies.[286]

[3] *SNAP for Soda*

In October 2010, New York City and New York State officials submitted a request to the USDA to operate a two-year pilot program under which benefits from the Supplemental Nutrition Assistance Program (SNAP) could not be used to purchase sweetened beverages in New York City.[287] New York argued that sweetened drinks are the single biggest contributor to the obesity epidemic, and as such they should not be subsidized with federal dollars.[288]

Under federal law, each state is responsible for administering its SNAP program, which can be operated at the local level.[289] While states and local governments have some discretion in administering SNAP, most program requirements are federal. Thus, New York first needed to request a waiver of SNAP rules from USDA. USDA denied the request in August 2011, citing various concerns about the administration of the proposal. USDA's denial letter specifically stated that the agency was denying the request because of its "longstanding tradition of supporting and promoting incentive-based solutions to the obesity epidemic, especially among SNAP recipients."[290] The letter noted that USDA was in the midst of a pilot project with Massachusetts that studied the effects of increasing SNAP benefits when used to buy produce, and that it would be "imprudent to reverse policy" while that pilot was ongoing.[291] "In 2011 and early 2012, bills were

---

[282] *Id.* at 19.

[283] *Id.*

[284] *Id.* at 19–20.

[285] Paul A. Diller, *Local Health Agencies, the Bloomberg Soda Rule, and the Ghost of Woodrow Wilson*, 40 Fordham Urb. L.J. 1859, 1860–61 (2013).

[286] *See id.* (embodying a technical or scientific regulatory approach by local public health authorities provides more explanatory heft than the predominant public choice narrative).

[287] *See* Patrick McGeehan, *U.S. Rejects Mayor's Plan to Ban Use of Food Stamps to Buy Soda*, N.Y. Times, August 19, 2011, at A15.

[288] N.Y.C. Dep't of Health & Mental Hygiene, *Removing SNAP Subsidy for Sugar-Sweetened Beverages* 2 (October 2010).

[289] *See* 7 U.S.C. § 2012 (a), (t).

[290] Letter from Jessica Shahin, associate administrator, Supplemental Nutrition Assistance Program, to Elizabeth R. Berlin, executive deputy commissioner, New York State Office of Temporary and Disability Assistance (August 19, 2011).

[291] *Id.*

proposed in nine states (including Texas, Florida, and California) to attempt to limit the purchase of unhealthy foods with SNAP benefits, often by requiring the state to seek a waiver from USDA."[292]

These efforts to deny SNAP benefits for the purchase of soda are not without controversy in the public health community. An IOM report on obesity prevention notes that the issue is complex riddled with "ethical and social justice concerns" and that "limiting food choices for SNAP recipients may be viewed as patronizing and discriminatory to low-income consumers."[293] The concern for public health advocates is that stigmatizing SNAP users may lead people to leave the program.

[4] *Toys in Meals*

In 2010, Santa Clara County and the city of San Francisco passed the first-ever local ordinances that prohibit restaurants from providing free toys in meals for children that do not meet established nutritional requirements.[294] The ordinances generated substantial concerns and criticism from the food industry and members of the public who accuse San Francisco and Santa Clara County of usurping the role of parents who have the ultimate right of determining their children's food choices.[295] There may be a question as to whether such a regulation would survive challenges under the dormant Commerce Clause on grounds that the toy bans would be unduly burdensome for nationwide restaurants.

[5] *Food Tax*

A legal and policy tool that has attracted considerable attention in response to the obesity epidemic is taxes on unhealthy food, especially sugar-sweetened beverages (SSBs).[296] In 2003, the World Health Organization (WHO) suggested a tax on unhealthy food to address concerns of "heart disease, diabetes, obesity, and other non-communicable diseases."[297] Several taxing strategies have emerged in the health and economic literature to address obesity.[298] In May 2010, a White House task force

---

[292] Rebecca L. Goldberg, *No Such Thing As a Free Lunch: Paternalism, Poverty, and Food Justice*, 24 STAN. L. & POL'Y REV. 35, 64 (2013).

[293] INSTITUTE OF MEDICINE OF THE NATIONAL ACADEMIES, ACCELERATING PROGRESS IN OBESITY PREVENTION: SOLVING THE WEIGHT OF THE NATION 266 (2012).

[294] *See* S.F., Cal., Health Code art. 8, § 471 to 9; Santa Clara, Cal., Code of Ordinances § A18-352 (2010).

[295] Former Mayor Gavin Newsom of San Francisco opposed the ban, alleging that it inappropriately interferes with the role of parents who have the ultimate right and responsibility to determine their children's food choices. *See* Michael Martinez, *Mayor Vetoes San Francisco Ban on Happy Meals with toys*, CNN, November 13, 2010.

[296] The definition of taxable SSB beverages is broad and is based on the addition of any caloric sweetener including added sugar or other caloric sweetener such as high fructose corn syrup, soda, sports drinks, fruit drinks, teas, flavored or enhanced waters, and energy drinks. KELLY D. BROWNELL & ROBERTA R. FRIEDMAN, RUDD REPORT: SUGAR-SWEETENED BEVERAGE TAXES, AN UPDATED POLICY BRIEF (2012).

[297] Anita Srikameswaran, *WHO Wants 'Twinkie Tax' to Discourage Junk Foods*, PITTSBURGH POST-GAZETTE (December 6, 2003).

[298] *See, e.g.*, Kelly D. Brownell et al., *The Public Health and Economic Benefits of Taxing Sugar-Sweetened Beverages*, 361 NEW ENG. J. MED. 1599, 1599 (2009).

on childhood obesity invited the states to experiment with taxing sugar-sweetened beverages as a way to reduce consumption.[299] These strategies are beginning to emerge in states and in local communities. Recently, the Navajo Nation implemented a 2% tax on junk food in an effort to curb high rates of obesity, diabetes, and heart disease among the tribe.[300]

Public health officials point to the success of tobacco taxes to support taxes against unhealthy foods.[301] Tobacco taxes have both decreased smoking and raised billions of dollars in tax revenues for states and the federal government.[302] However, some key distinctions between tobacco and unhealthy food should be noted in assessing the viability of a tax on unhealthy food. One of the most commonly cited justifications for tobacco taxes is the externality of secondhand smoke, which harms the health of those who abstain from smoking. Obviously, when it comes to food, there is no such thing as secondhand fat. Nevertheless, the externality of poor nutritional choices – such as increased health care costs – may align with the negative externalities found in smoking. Another distinction that may be lessening is that tobacco is addictive, while the addictive qualities of unhealthy foods are still being explored.[303] One interesting comparison to tobacco implies that food is a better candidate for a tax than tobacco. In the long term, smokers cost the health care system less than nonsmokers because smokers die earlier and thus consume fewer years of health care services than nonsmokers.[304] Because of this, a tobacco tax, while reducing smoking and its associated medical costs, actually increases health care costs in the long run. On the contrary, the same is not true of obese individuals. While obesity leads to many chronic diseases, the life span of obese individuals is not shortened so much that their overall health expenditures are less than nonobese individuals.[305]

In evaluating taxes on junk food as a legal tool, it should be noted that excise taxes on food and other products are common in the United States. An excise tax is "a duty or impost levied upon the manufacture, sale, or consumption of commodities."[306] Tobacco and alcohol are contributors to the leading causes of premature death in the United States and both are subject to federal excise taxes. A proposal for a national excise tax on soft drinks was raised in May 2009 as part of the Senate Finance Committee's negotiations on health care reform.[307] The goal of an excise tax is to increase the base price of

---

[299] Sal Gentile, *As White House Tackles Obesity, Lawmakers Eye Soda as Culprit*, NEED TO KNOW ON PBS (May 11, 2010).

[300] Nigel Duara, *Navajo Nation Sees Tax on Junk Food as a Way to Combat Health Problems*, LOS ANGELES TIMES (March 30, 2015).

[301] *See, e.g.*, James F. Chriqui et al., *State Sales Tax Rates for Soft Drinks and Snacks Sold through Grocery Stores and Vending Machines, 2007*, 29 J. PUB. HEALTH POL'Y 226, 228 (2008).

[302] Robert O. Lynch, *Should We Tax the Fat Out of America? The Trouble of Selling the Fat Tax to the Public*, 18 ANNALS HEALTH L. ADV. DIRECTIVE 172, 174 (2009).

[303] *See, e.g.*, FOOD AND ADDICTION: A COMPREHENSIVE HANDBOOK (Kelly D. Brownell & Mark S. Gold eds 2012) (assembles leading scientists and policy makers to explore and analyze the scientific evidence for the addictive properties of food).

[304] Jeff Strnad, *Conceptualizing the "Fat Tax": The Role of Food Taxes in Developed Economies*, 78 S. CAL. L. REV. 1221, 1241 (2005).

[305] *Id.*

[306] U.S. MASTER EXCISE TAX GUIDE (David Becker ed., 6th ed., CCH 2008).

[307] Christine Spolar & Joseph Easton, *Food Lobby Mobilizes, As Soda Tax Bubbles Up*, HUFFINGTON POST, November 4, 2009.

the product. For sugary beverages, for example, an excise tax would be imposed on the syrup or beverage manufacturer for beverages with added caloric sweetener.

The government has a history of taxing products associated with disease. The use of an excise tax to deter consumption was first employed in the United States on whiskey, two years after the Constitution was ratified. Alexander Hamilton, who was the secretary of treasury at that time, stated that "[t]he consumption of ardent spirits particularly, no doubt very much an account of their cheapness, is carried to an extreme, which is truly to be regretted, as well in regard to the health and morals, as to the economy of the community. Should the increase of duties tend to a decrease of the consumption of those articles the effect would be, in every respect desirable."[308] The Supreme Court has since confirmed that the government's use of power to tax is legitimate even if implemented specifically to deter behavior.[309] Excise taxes represent a significant revenue stream for the government, and are often channeled to a specific fund related to the purpose of the tax. For example, federal excise taxes placed on special motor vehicle and diesel fuels are channeled to the Highway Trust Fund to finance federal highway projects. Public health advocates argue that an excise tax on sugary beverages should be channeled for public health. For example, the funds could be used to fund public health and nutrition programs or specifically to subsidize fruits and vegetables.[310]

Central to the debate over the efficacy of junk food taxes is whether the tax actually modifies the behavior of consumers.[311] Behavior modification can be viewed from an economic perspective and a public health perspective. Economists tend to frame fat taxes in terms of a market failure or a fault-based paradigm, where up-front economic disincentives at the point of purchase are created to compensate for internal and external market failures.[312] In contrast, the public health perspective views health at a population level and seeks solutions by addressing causes at a systemic level, including socioeconomic and environmental factors in their framework.[313] The public health perspective embraces two primary purposes for a fat tax: set normative standards (disapproval of overindulgence in certain foods)[314] and improve health through improved nutrition and obesity reduction.[315]

Criticism of taxes on unhealthy foods is plentiful. One view is that such taxes are paternalistic, and that people should educate themselves sufficiently to know how to care for their own health.[316] There are also concerns that fat taxes interfere with individual

---

[308] ALEXANDER HAMILTON: WRITINGS 213 (Joanne Freeman ed., 2001).

[309] See, e.g., U.S. v. Sanchez, 340 U.S. 42, 44–5 (1950) (holding that a federal tax passed by Congress in order to deter the use and sale of marijuana is not unconstitutional).

[310] See Richard Triffin and Matthieu Arnoult, The Public Health Impacts of a Fat Tax, 65 EUR. J. CLINICAL NUTRITION, 427, 427 (2011).

[311] Preliminary reports suggest that the tax in Mexico on sodas and sugary drinks is reducing consumption. See Eliza Barclay, Mexico's Sugary Drink Tax Makes a Dent in Consumption, Study Claims, NPR (June 19, 2015).

[312] Chris L. Winstanley, A Healthy Food Tax Credit: Moving Away from the Fat Tax and Its Fault-Based Paradigm, 86 OR. L. REV. 1151, 1152–3 (2007).

[313] Id. at 1153.

[314] Nicholas Confessore, Paterson Lowers Expectations on Soda Tax, Calling Approval Unlikely, N.Y. TIMES, February 13, 2009, at A17.

[315] Strnad, supra note 304, at 1226.

[316] Winstanley, supra note 312, at 1174.

choice and autonomy.[317] The most frequently cited concern about fat taxes is that they are regressive and disproportionately burden the poor.[318] Because low-income people of color do not have access to healthy options where they live and do not have easy access to transportation to places where healthy options are sold, there is no realistic healthy choice, and the tax simply becomes a punishment.

§ 5.06 Government Nutrition Programs

[1] *Legal Basis: Police Power in Health*

The US government has long had an involvement in public health via federal programs. The connection between federal programs and public health is well established in case law as a legitimate exercise of police power. The standard for the exercise of the police power in health is expressed in *Jacobson v. Commonwealth of Massachusetts*, where the Supreme Court in 1905 upheld the states' ability to enforce compulsory vaccination laws.[319] The Court found that the state could encroach on the liberties of its citizens when "the safety of the general public may demand."[320] The Supreme Court in 2007 supported again the notion of the government intervening in matters of public health in *Massachusetts v. Environmental Protection Agency*.[321] The Court found that the EPA has the ability to regulate carbon dioxide and other greenhouse gases, noting that under the Clean Air Act, the agency has the power to set emission standards for "any air pollutant" from motor vehicles to new motor vehicle engines, which cause or contribute to air pollution that may reasonably be anticipated to endanger public health or welfare.[322] The direction from the Supreme Court has been clear: when there is a threat to the population's health and well-being, the government has the power to intervene. It follows then that when millions suffer from malnutrition and obesity, the government as the defender of public health has the ability and the obligation to implement programs to combat these health risks.

[2] *Public Health and Food: Dietary Guidelines*

The USDA administers nutrition programs in three basic areas that address hunger and obesity-related chronic diseases: dietary guidelines, nutrition programs, and school meal programs. With respect to the first area, the USDA Center for Nutrition Policy and Promotion (CNPP) has a public health mandate to develop and promote dietary guidelines that link scientific research to the nutrition needs of consumers.[323] The CNPP is a subagency of the USDA's Food, Nutrition, and Consumer Services. The history of

---

[317] Adriana Badilas, *Food Taxes: A Palatable Solution to the Obesity Epidemic?*, 23 Pac. McGeorge Global Bus. & Dev. L.J. 255, 262 (2011).

[318] Brad Schiller, *Obama's Poor Tax*, Wall St. J. April 1, 2009.

[319] Jacobson v. Massachusetts, 197 U.S. 11, 25 S. Ct. 358, 49 L. Ed. 643 (U.S. 1905).

[320] *Id.* at 29.

[321] Massachusetts v. EPA, 549 U.S. 497 (2007).

[322] *Id.* at 530.

[323] *See Improving the Nutrition and Well-Being of Americans*, U.S. Dep't of Agric., Center for Nutrition Policy and Promotion.

USDA's involvement in the development of dietary guidelines dates back to as early as 1902, when the department promulgated *Principles of Nutrition and Nutritive Value of Food* through its Farmers' Bulletin.[324] In 1943, USDA relied on the *Recommended Daily Allowances* developed by the National Academy of Sciences to create the National Wartime Nutrition Guide, introducing the "Basic Seven" food groups.[325] The culmination of efforts to develop dietary guidelines led to a congressional mandate for USDA and DHHS to jointly publish the "Dietary Guidelines for America."[326] The DHHS's Office of Disease Prevention and Health Promotion and the USDA's CNPP coordinate the effort by the two departments.[327] A draft of the 2015 Dietary Guidelines was issued in February 2015.[328] The new guidelines recommend a focus on foods rather than nutrients, suggest that cholesterol is no longer a nutrient of concern for overconsumption, emphasize the connection between nutrition and sustainability and recommend a plant-based diet that is low in red and processed meat, and recommend that added sugar products comprise no more than 10 percent of daily caloric intake. USDA and DHHS have promoted previous guidelines using "My Plate" and its predecessor the "food pyramid" that simplify the guidelines and put them in a graphic form that can be reproduced on various mediums, including posters, school textbooks, and cereal boxes.[329]

[3] *Programs Mandate: Farm Bill*

The Farm Bill, renewed by Congress every five years, is the legislative and funding platform for numerous government nutrition programs administered by the USDA. In recent years, the Farm Bill has become a significant issue in public health circles due to the complicated relationship between the Farm Bill and nutrition programs. The relationship reflects the uneasy tension between USDA's dual mission objectives of promoting food production and public health.

The 1977 Farm Bill was the first Farm Bill to completely incorporate food stamp provisions into the bill through a nutrition title.[330] Such inclusion facilitated the link between nutrition interest and the farm interest group bloc who were anxious to protect farmers and traditional subsidies, such as corn, soy, and wheat.[331] In the debates leading up to the 2008 and 2014 Farm Bills, public health and social justice advocates noted the correlation between affordability and availability of processed foods and rising rates of obesity and diet-related illnesses, especially among low-income consumers.[332] The argument was made that because sweetener high fructose corn syrup was relatively cheap as

---

[324] Lindsay F. Wiley, *The U.S. Department of Agriculture as a Public Health Agency? A "Health in All Policies" Case Study*, 9 J. Food L. & Pol'y 61, 70 (2013).

[325] *Id.*

[326] 7 U.S.C. § 531 (2012). *See also* National Nutrition Monitoring and Related Research Act of 1990, Pub. L. No. 101–445, 104 Stat. 1034 (requiring the "secretaries" to issue nutritional guidelines at least every five years).

[327] Wiley, *supra* note 324, at 72.

[328] U.S. Dep't of Agric. and U.S. Dep't of Health and Human Serv., Advisory Report, Scientific Report of the 2015 Dietary Guidelines Advisory Committee.

[329] *Id.*

[330] Nadine Lehrer, U.S. Farm Bills And Policy Reforms 67 (2010).

[331] *Id.* at 66–7.

[332] *See* Agriculture and Health Policies in Conflict: How Food Subsidies Tax Our Health, Agricultural Policies versus Health Policies, Physicians Committee for Responsible Med. (April 2011).

a result of corn subsidies, portion sizes of items such as soft drinks and sweets increased without a proportional increase in price.[333] Also, because subsidized corn and soybeans were fed to livestock, the cost of meat remained low, making a high-meat diet accessible and affordable.[334] Public health advocates increasingly argue for reprioritization of Farm Bill agricultural production incentives so that processed foods are no longer the cheapest and most convenient foods in the grocery store. The battle lines between public health stakeholders blurs, however, when these advocates conflict with antihunger groups who advocate emergency feeding programs included in the farm bill that depend on surplus commodities.

[4] *Specific Notable Programs*

  [a] The Supplemental Nutrition Assistance Program

The largest of the nutrition assistance programs mandated and funded by the Farm Bill is the Supplemental Nutrition Assistance Program (SNAP), formerly known as the Food Stamp Program. Originally authorized by the Food Stamp Act of 1964, SNAP is administered by the USDA Food and Nutrition Service (FNS). USDA's dual mission is clearly articulated in the 1964 Act: though the 1964 Food Stamp Act aimed to "promote the general welfare, ... safeguard the health and well-being of the Nation's population and raise levels of nutrition among low-income households," its first stated goal was "[t]o strengthen the agricultural economy."[335] State agencies administer the program at the state and local level under federal regulations, including determining and distributing benefits. The program provides eligible low-income families with monthly benefits calculated based on the size and income of the household.

   In the 2008 Farm Bill, Congress changed the name of the food stamp program to the Supplemental Nutrition Assistance Program.[336] Because SNAP is governed by federal regulations and administered only by the states, state and city governments are barred from instituting any new restrictions without a waiver from USDA. For example, in 2004, USDA denied a request from the state of Minnesota to waive federal regulations and allow that state to prohibit the purchase of candy and soda with food stamp benefits.[337] Previously, benefits in the SNAP were conferred in the form of paper coupons, but the 2008 Farm Bill established electronic benefit transfer cards (EBT) as the official form of benefit transfer. EBTs can be electronically swiped like a debit card or credit card in exchange for authorized products such as food items or seeds for planting food crops. To encourage farmers' markets to accept EBTs the FNS allows one farmers' market sponsor to obtain a license to accept EBTs on behalf of all farmers in the market through one centralized point of sale. Breads, cereals, fruits, vegetables, meats, fish, and dairy products are the types of food authorized. Participants cannot use SNAP benefits to buy hot food, food to be eaten in the store, or nonfood items like alcohol, tobacco products, vitamins,

---

[333] *See, e.g.*, Michael Pollan, *You Are What You Grow*, N.Y. TIME MAG., April 22, 2007.
[334] *See* Physician Committee for Responsible Medicine, *supra* note 332.
[335] Wiley *supra* note 324, at 83 (quoting the Food Stamp Act of 1964, Pub. L. No. 88–525, § 2, 78 Stat. 703.
[336] Food, Conservation, and Energy Act of 2008, Pub. L. No. 110–234, 122 Stat. 923, 1092.
[337] Letter from Ollice C. Holden, regional administrator, Food Stamp Program, Food & Nutritional Service, U.S. Dep't of Agric., to Maria Gomez, assistant commissioner, Economic and Community Support Strategies, Minnesota Dep't of Human Services (May 4, 2004).

medicines, pet food, soap, or household supplies. In addition to officially switching to EBTs, the 2008 Farm Bill made a number of other changes designed to increase the effectiveness of SNAP. These changes include an authorization for states to establish new methods of receiving application and incorporating nutrition education and fruit and vegetable promotion aspects into the program.[338]

Title IV of the 2014 Farm Bill reauthorized SNAP as the United States's largest food and nutrition assistance program. It is estimated that nearly 80 percent of the 2014 Farm Bill is for nutrition assistance.[339] The bill required a larger variety of food options at authorized retailers and established a grant program to provide incentives for the purchase of fruits and vegetables by SNAP recipients.[340] The 2014 Farm Bill also clarified SNAP eligibility and benefit rules. Funding was also provided for pilot programs and grants to boost SNAP participation and to improve program integrity by eliminating the illegal exchange of SNAP benefits for cash.

California is representative of how states can facilitate participation in SNAP. The state has taken up the federal option to offer "express enrollment" for individuals who are currently enrolled in SNAP or CalFresh in California.[341] Thus, if an individual is enrolled already in CalFresh, the state can use that eligibility information to enroll them in Medi-Cal (California's Medicaid program). No additional application is needed. Since the eligibility rules and income levels are very similar between CalFresh and Medi-Cal, a CalFresh enrollee is also eligible for Medi-Cal. The intricacies for states in administering SNAP benefits is evidenced by the fact that those who are eligible under the California program for express enrollment have to consent to the expedited enrollment, and the Department of Health Care Services will only send one letter notifying people of the opportunity.

[b] The Women, Infants, and Children Supplemental Nutrition Program

The Child Nutrition Act of 1966 started the Special Supplemental Nutrition Program for Women, Infants and Children (WIC), which is designed to help low-income pregnant, postpartum, and breastfeeding women, as well as children age five and under achieve and maintain healthy diets.[342] Unlike the USDA food stamp program, which historically had the dual purpose of improving nutrition and supporting agriculture, WIC is solely focused on health. When Congress made the program permanent in 1975,[343] its express purpose was "to provide supplemental nutritious food as an adjunct to good health during ... critical times of growth and development in order to prevent the occurrence of health problems."[344] In most

---

[338] Ed Bolen, *Summary of the 2014 Farm Bill Nutrition Title: Includes Bipartisan Improvements to SNAP While Excluding Harsh House Provisions*, Center on Budget and Policy Priorities (February 3, 2014).

[339] According to the Congressional Budget Office, the 2014 Farm Bill would spend $956 billion over the next ten years, with $756 billion for nutrition assistance and $200 billion for agriculture. Ralph M. Chite, the 2014 Farm Bill (P.L. 113–79): Summary and Side-by-Side Summary Page (February 12, 2014).

[340] Specialty Crop Farm Bill Alliance *H.R. 2642: Agricultural Act of 2014*, 2014 Farm Bill Summary.

[341] David Gorn, *CalFresh New Path to Medi-Cal Enrollment*, CALIFORNIA HEALTHLINE (February 19, 2014).

[342] *See* 42 U.S.C. § 1786(a).

[343] National School Lunch Act and Child Nutrition Act of 1966 Amendments of 1975, Pub. L. No. 94–105, 89 Stat. 511.

[344] Wiley, *supra* note 324 at 85 (quoting Pub. L. No. 94–105, § 17(a)).

states, WIC recipients receive vouchers that can be exchanged for specifically approved supplemental food items at authorized retailers.

Supplemental foods are "foods containing nutrients ... to be lacking in the diets of pregnant, breastfeeding, and postpartum women, infants, and children and foods that promote the health of the population served by the program."[345] The WIC "basket" typically includes juice, milk, cereal, cheeses, eggs, fruits and vegetables, whole wheat bread, canned fish, legumes, and peanut butter, and for infants, includes WIC formula, infant cereal and baby food fruits, vegetables, and meats. Supplemental foods are to be reviewed at least every ten years and amended to reflect emerging science, public health concerns, and cultural eating patterns.[346] The program is supposed to add on supplemental foods to the diets of women, infants, and children who are at nutritional risk. This is in addition to (not a substitution for) SNAP benefits.[347]

WIC, unlike SNAP, is a block grant program as opposed to an entitlement program. Administered by the FNS, the federal government provides block grants to state agencies to implement the WIC program. The FNS provides state agencies with considerable autonomy to operate the retail delivery systems and establish the stocking requirements for authorized WIC vendors.[348]

WIC programs allow infant formulas to bid competitively and then the formula with the lowest price becomes the WIC formula. Whenever a WIC participant purchases that formula using a WIC voucher or EBT card, the manufacturer sends WIC a rebate to pay for the discount.[349] By 2020, all states must be switched over to an Electronic Benefit Transfer (EBT) system.[350]

Legislation governing WIC is found in the Child Nutrition Act of 1966.[351] The FNS administers the program at the federal level. State agencies administer WIC programs in connection with retailers and local agencies.

To be eligible for WIC benefits, an applicant's income must be at or below 185 percent of the US Poverty Income Guideline.[352] The applicant must meet state residency requirements, and be individually determined a nutrition risk by a health professional. Owing to the millions of eligible participants, FNS has established a hierarchy of WIC participant priority. First priority is awarded to pregnant women, breastfeeding women, and infants determined to be at a nutrition risk due to a nutrition-related medical condition. The six subsequent categories focus on providing help to young children, pregnant women, and new mothers with either a nutrition-related medical condition or inadequate dietary patterns. In addition to the primary benefits available, women infants and children who have been certified to receive primary benefits are eligible to participate in the WIC Farmers' Market Nutrition Program (FMNP).[353] The

---

[345] 42 U.S.C. § 1786(b)(14).
[346] 42 U.S.C. § 1786(f)(11).
[347] 42 U.S.C. § 1786(c)(1).
[348] *See* U.S. Gov't Accountability Office, GAO-02-142, WIC Faces Challenges in Providing Nutrition services 5 (2001).
[349] 42 U.S.C. § 1786(i)(8).
[350] 42 U.S.C. § 1786(i)(12).
[351] Child Nutrition Act of 1966, Pub. L. No. 89–642, 80 Stat. 885 (codified as amended at 42 U.S.C. §§ 1771–1790).
[352] 42 U.S.C. § 1786(d)(2).
[353] 42 U.S.C. § 1786(m)(1).

FMNP provides checks or vouchers to participants, which can be used to purchase fresh unprepared locally grown fruits, vegetables, and herb. Each state complies a specific list of approved foods.

[c] Other Food Distribution Programs

Other notable food distribution programs are listed in the following section.

- **Commodity Supplement Food Program (CFSP)** – The CFSP is similar to the WIC program. Unlike WIC, however, CFSP provides food rather than vouchers. Also, unlike WIC, CFSP serves elderly people as well as women, infants, and children. Participants are restricted from participating on both programs simultaneously.[354]
- **Emergency Food Assistance Program (TEFAP)** – The TEFAP supplements the diets of low-income individuals by providing food commodities in states. The amount of assistance a state receives is based on the level of income and unemployment within the state. States that receive assistance deliver the food to local agencies that often distribute it to food banks, which then supply soup kitchens, food shelters, food pantries, and other such entities.[355]
- **Food Distribution Program on Indian Reservations (FDPIR)** – FDPIR provides food commodities to low-income Native Americans. FDPIR is federally administered by the FNS and locally administered by Indian Tribal Organizations or state agencies. Participants can select from a list of food products and receive a food package each month that is designed to help them maintain a nutritionally balanced diet. Participants may not simultaneously participate in both SNAP and FDPIR.[356]
- **Senior Farmers' Market Nutrition Program** – This program provides fresh, nutritious, unprepared, locally grown fruits, vegetables, and herbs from farmers' markets, roadside stands, and community-supported agriculture programs to low-income seniors.[357] Low-income seniors are individuals who are at least sixty years old and who meet the general WIC benefits requirement of having household incomes of not more than 185 percent of the federal poverty income guidelines.[358]
- **Farm to School Program** – USDA established this program in an effort to put fresh fruits and vegetables in the hands of children.[359] Farm to school movements have gained popularity for changing children's eating patterns and for educating children on food nutrition and farming.

---

[354] *See* 7 C.F.R. § 247.
[355] *See* Temporary Emergency Food Assistance Act of 1983, Pub. L. No. 98-8, 97 Stat. 35.
[356] *See* Food and Nutrition Service: Food Distribution Program on Indian Reservations, U.S. Dep't of Agric. (2009).
[357] 7 U.S.C. § 3007(b).
[358] Senior Farmers' Market Nutrition Program, U.S. Dep't of Agric.
[359] *See* Jean Buzby et al., Food Assistance and Nutrition Research Program, Food and Rural Economics Division, Economic Research Service, U.S. Department of Agriculture, Evaluation of the USDA Fruit and Vegetable Pilot Program: Report to Congress, iii–v, (May 2003).

[d] School Meal Programs

A significant area where the federal government attempts to regulate childhood obesity and malnutrition is through school meal programs. The focus of these efforts is the
National School Lunch Program (NSLP),[360] which enables the government to directly
affect the nutrition of millions of children every school day. The NSLP is a federally
assisted meal program operating in public and nonprofit private schools and residential
child care institutions. It was established under the National School Lunch Act to promote "the health and well-being of the Nation's children and to encourage the domestic consumption of nutritious agricultural commodities."[361] The secretary of agriculture
under the Act possessed the authority to supply schools with surplus food purchased as
part of agricultural subsidy programs, distribute funds to schools based on the number
of program meals served, and establish nutritional guidelines for meals served under the
program.[362]

The NSLP and development of school meal programs have increased over years in
response to various concerns. In 1966, the government expanded the NSLP through the
enactment of the Child Nutrition Act.[363] The Act included the Special Milk Program,
which offered federal reimbursements for milk served to children in schools. It also
established the School Breakfast Program, which provides federally subsidized breakfasts
to children at school and childcare facilities. In 1968, the Special Food Service Program
for Children was created as a three-year pilot. The pilot, which had two components,
childcare and summer care, provided grants to states to assist in providing meals to children when school was not in session. In 1969, the Food and Nutrition Service (FNS)
was created as a new agency within the USDA. The Service was established exclusively
to administer federal food programs, including the school lunch program. In 1975, the
two components of the Special Food Service Program for Children were separated and
authorized as the Child Care Food Program and Summer Food Service Program. An
extension of the Child Care Food Program was then authorized, and in 1978, it became
a permanent program. The program gives nutritious meals and snacks every day to childcare centers, day care homes, homeless shelters, and adult day care centers. The name
was changed in 1989 to the Child and Adult Care Food Program in order to reflect the
adult component of the program.[364] In response to increasing childhood obesity rates,
the Healthy Hunger-Free Kids Act was implemented in 2010.[365] The Act was part of the
reauthorization of funding of child nutrition and allowed the USDA for the first time in
over thirty years to make real reforms to the nutrition content in the school lunch and
breakfast program. The Act required the meals served in the NSLP to have fewer calories, more fruits and vegetables, fewer processed items, and less sodium.[366] Additional
school meal programs have also been developed by the FNS to provide nutritional food
to children at times when school is not in session. For example, the NSLP provides

---

[360] *See National School Lunch Program*, U.S. Dep't of Agric.
[361] National School Lunch Act, Pub. L. No. 79–396, 60 Stat. 230 (1946).
[362] Wiley, *supra* note 324, at 91.
[363] 42 U.S.C. §§ 1771–1789.
[364] *Child and Adult Care Food Program*, U.S. Food and Drug Admin.
[365] *See* Healthy, Hunger-Free Kids Act of 2010, Pub. L. No. 111–296, § 201, 124 Stat. 3183, 3215 (codified
as amended at 42 U.S.C. § 1753(b)).
[366] *Id.*

cash subsidies to help pay for after-school snacks. Another program, the School Breakfast Program (SBP), operates like the School Lunch Program, but there is no commodity distribution entitlement. The Summer Service Program provides free meals to children in an area "in which poor economic conditions exists," at a central community center such as a school or recreational facility.[367] Finally, for schools that do not participate in other school meal service programs, the Special Milk Program provides subsidies for milk served to students.

Court decisions have resolved a few operational issues involved with NSLP. In *Haddon Township Board of Education v. New Jersey Dep't of Ed*, the US District Court for New Jersey decided that the meals of NSLP must be eaten at school. Students from three school districts took their NSLP lunches home with them during the lunch break. The statutory language, on its face, can only be construed to indicate that food must be provided inside the school, highlighting that the place where the subsidized lunches are consumed is an integral part of the overall scheme of the program.[368] The US District Court for the District of Columbia in *Sargent v. Block* stated that schools are required to verify the applications for at least 3 percent of the 3,000 students, whichever is less, of students who applied for free or reduced lunch to ensure that the families meet the qualifications for the program.[369]

[e] Competitive Food in School

The healthy school meals and snacks provided through the NSLP have not made up all food that has traditionally been provided in school: "competitive foods," known in the Kids Act as "nonprogram foods," historically have been frequently sold in cafeterias, school stores, snack bars, and vending machines outside of the federal program and have constituted a significant part of students' diet.

The USDA defines competitive foods as foods offered at school, other than meals served through the school lunch, school breakfast, and after-school snack programs. With the exception of one regulation that does not allow the sale of soda or certain candy – dubbed "foods of minimal nutritional value (FMNV)" – in the food service area during mealtimes, no federal nutrition standards apply to competitive foods. The federal regulations define FMNV as soda water (commonly known as carbonated soft drinks), water ices not containing fruit or fruit juice, chewing gum, and certain candies.[370]

When USDA restricted the sales primarily of FMNV from the beginning of the school day until the end of the last lunch period, the National Soft Drink Association (later named the American Beverage Association) filed suit. While the appellate court in *National Soft Drink Association v. Block* upheld the USDA's nutrition standards, it overturned the time and place restrictions placed on the sales of junk foods to children on the ground that the USDA had overstepped its statutory bounds.[371] As a result, the

---

[367] At least 50 percent of enrolled school children or at least 50 percent of children living in a geographic region based on census data are eligible for free or reduced-price lunches. 42 U.S.C. § 1761(a). There is an emphasis for this program in rural areas. 42 U.S.C. § 1761(a)(10).

[368] Haddon Twp. Bd. Of Educ. v. N.J. Dep't of Educ. 476 F. Supp. 681, 694 (D. N.J. 1979).

[369] Sargent v. Block, 576 F. Supp. 882, 886 (D. D.C. 1983).

[370] 7 C.F.R. § 210 app. B.

[371] Nat'l. Soft Drink Ass'n v. Block, 721 F.2d 1348, 1353 (D.C. Cir. 1983).

Child Nutrition Act of 1966 was amended to reflect the court's decision, and sugary soft drinks – in addition to other FMNV, such as snack foods and fast foods – were allowed in public schools throughout the day. With federal regulatory efforts drastically weakened, state and local governments were left to create their own laws regarding school nutrition.

[5] State Discretion

The federal nutrition programs provide some flexibility for state and local communities to implement the programs in ways that maximize their impact and help end hunger. It should be no surprise, given the continuing presence of hunger, that a number of states have undertaken additional efforts to address hunger concerns. The state initiatives typically relate to improving the coordination of public antihunger programs and improving the performance of the programs that exist – in terms of their coverage and operation. State programs include food banks and various service meal programs.[372]

§ 5.07 Public Health Litigation

[1] Tool to Address Obesity Epidemic

Advocates have long used litigation as a tool to combat major public health problems.[373] Following years of failed attempts to regulate the tobacco industry, affirmative litigation by state attorneys general and private lawyers helped turn the tide in the fight against tobacco-related chronic disease.[374] Advocates of food litigation take comfort in the fact that tobacco litigation had an inauspicious start.[375] Notwithstanding research that linked smoking to cancer, hundreds of lawsuits against tobacco manufacturers from the 1950s to the 1990s met without success.[376] Tobacco litigation began to achieve success when in recent years litigation focused more on the tobacco industry's deceptive conduct regarding its knowledge about the addictive nature of nicotine and its deliberate efforts to cause individuals to become addicted to cigarettes.[377] In addition to private litigation, state attorneys general contributed via litigation. In the late 1990s, four states individually negotiated settlements to recover smoking-related Medicaid costs, and forty-six states and territories negotiated the Master Settlement Agreement securing annual payments of several billion dollars in perpetuity as repayment for smoking-related healthcare costs.[378]

---

[372] See Childhood Anti-Hunger Programs in 24 Cities, the United States Conference of Mayors and Sodexo (November 2009).

[373] Peter D. Jacobson & Soheil Soliman, Litigation as a Public Health Policy: Theory of Reality?, 30 J.L. MED. & ETHICS 224 (2002).

[374] Cara L. Wilking & Richard A. Daynard, Beyond Cheeseburgers: The Impact of Commonsense Consumption Acts on Future Obesity-Related Lawsuits, 68 FOOD & DRUG L.J. 229, 229 (2013).

[375] See generally, Stephen P. Teret & Lainie Rutkow, Legal and Policy Implications: Litigation, in FOOD AND ADDICTION: A COMPREHENSIVE HANDBOOK 401 (Kelly D. Brownell and Mark S. Gold eds., 2012).

[376] Id. at 401–2.

[377] Id. at 402. See two cases that paved the way for factual findings about smoking and addiction – U.S. v. Philip Morris USA, Inc., 449 F Supp. 2d. 1 (DDC 2006); Engle v. Liggett Grp., Inc. 945 So. 2d 1246 (Fla. 2006).

[378] Smokeless Tobacco Master Settlement Agreement, National Association of Attorneys General.

Drawing on the tobacco litigation model, litigation against food companies has been advocated as a tool to combat obesity. Litigation arguably helps transfer the cost of obesity and malnutrition back to the producer rather than the consumer. Litigation may also be useful for promoting information disclosure via the discovery process. By having access to the discovery documents, the epidemiology of the harm can be better understood by researchers. Food companies may be incentivized to provide healthier products to avoid paying a financial penalty.

Critics of the use of litigation as a tool in addressing obesity assert several points. Litigation is viewed as complex, protracted, costly, unpredictable, and inconsistent. Regulatory bodies have more experience and expertise in assessing scientific association and causation than does a jury or court. Courts are seen as less well equipped than legislatures and administrative agencies to evaluate technical information, implement regulations, monitor results, and make adjustments. Finally, it is also asserted that policies resulting from litigation may involve less public input and accountability than government regulation, serving the private or political interests of litigants rather than the public interest.[379]

Public health advocates have adapted strategies from tobacco litigation for use in litigation against the food industry.[380] Legal theories range from inadequate disclosure of health risks, misleading advertisements, targeting of children, and deceptive practices, to serving foods that are dangerous beyond the extent ordinarily understood by consumers. In many respects, the similarities between obesity litigation and tobacco litigation are readily observable. For example, both obesity and tobacco involve "a large population of affected individuals, an identifiable corporate target, widespread demands of action, and contentious legislative debates over systemic causes versus private behavior."[381]

However, differences between tobacco and obesity weaken the link between tobacco and food litigation rationale. First, while tobacco is addictive and harmful even with moderate use, the science of food addiction still needs to be developed. Second, whereas harmful health effects of smokers may be directly and singularly traced to tobacco use, the same cannot be said about obesity and food because "[m]any people are able to eat multiple types of food, including fast food and other junk food, without becoming overweight, obese, or even unhealthy."[382] Obesity is a product of many causes including, but not limited to, lack of exercise, genetics, and social and cultural environmental factors.[383] In addition, although nonsmokers are harmed by secondhand smoke, no equivalent harmful side effects may be alleged to have affected "people who are not themselves overeaters but are in close proximity to overeaters."[384] Finally, the tobacco industry is controlled by only a few major companies, and therefore was easier for plaintiffs to

---

[379] See Timothy D. Lytton, *Using Tort Litigation to Enhance Regulatory Policy Making: Evaluating Climate-Change Litigation in Light of Lessons from Gun-Industry and Clergy-Sexual-Abuse Lawsuits*, 86 TEX. L. REV. 1837, 1838 (2008).

[380] *Public Health Approaches to Obesity: Litigation, Legislation, and Lessons Learned*, 1 PITT. J. ENVTL. PUB. HEALTH L. 127, 135 (2006).

[381] *Id.*

[382] Brooke Courtney, *Is Obesity Really the Next Tobacco? Lessons Learned from Tobacco for Obesity Litigation*, 15 ANNALS HEALTH L. 61, 94 (2006).

[383] *Id.*

[384] *Id.*

pinpoint them as the source of their injuries. On the contrary, the food industry comprises numerous manufacturers, restaurants, and retailers of various sizes, making it difficult for plaintiffs to isolate and assign specific blame to any one product or company for their alleged injuries.

[2] State Attorneys General

State attorneys general have a scope of authority that lies at the intersection of law and public policy. Although their authority varies according to the state's statutory and constitutional mandates, their powers are quite broad and generally include the authority to enforce state and some federal laws, to handle or supervise criminal prosecutions, to act as public advocates in areas such as consumer protection, to represent the public interest, and issue formal opinions.[385] Therefore, state attorneys general can use their authority to make a significant contribution to public health. Attorneys general were the major initiators of and actors in the US tobacco litigation and ensuing master settlement agreement.[386] Before and since the tobacco litigation, attorneys general have also played an important role in public health matters. For example, attorneys general brought a series of cases across the states to successfully enjoin the activities of polluters and initiated investigations into misleading and deceptive labeling of food and beverage products, pharmaceuticals, and food companies to protect the public from dangerous products.[387]

[3] Obesity Litigation

[a] Pelman v. McDonald's

Tobacco-style litigation, founded on tort law, as applied to obesity litigation, requires essential elements to be proven to be successful: (1) the defendant owed a duty of care to the plaintiff; (2) the duty was breached; and (3) the breach was casually related to (4) damage suffered by the plaintiff. *Pelman v. McDonald's Corp.* is the landmark case in obesity and the forerunner to obesity lawsuits.[388] This case invoked a plethora of issues. The most important issued in the case involved causation and reliance, which ultimately illustrates how difficult food content liability is to prove.

In August 2002, the parents of two minor children filed a class action lawsuit in state court against McDonald's Corporation, McDonald's of New York, and two New York City fast food restaurants (referred to collectively as McDonald's).[389] The lawsuit was brought on behalf of all New York minors who had purchased and consumed McDonald's

---

[385] *What Does an Attorney General Do?*, National Association of Attorneys General.

[386] Michael Pertschuk, Smoke in Their Eyes: Lessons in Movement Leadership from the Tobacco Wars (2001).

[387] *See* Jennifer L. Pomeranz & Kelly D. Brownell, *Advancing Public Health Obesity Policy through State Attorneys General*, 101 Am. J. Pub. Health 425–31 (2011).

[388] *See* Theodore H. Frank, *A Taxonomy of Obesity Litigation*, 28 U. Ark. Little Rock L. Rev. 427, 429–34 (2006) (discussing the various types of lawsuits included under the umbrella of obesity litigation).

[389] *See* Pelman v. McDonald's Corp., 237 F. Supp. 2d 512, 519 (S.D.N.Y. 2003). Although the original complaint named several local franchisees, the notice of appeal named only McDonald's Corporation. *See* Pelman v. McDonald's Corp., 396 F.3d at 510 n.2. Thus, the Second Circuit Court did not address whether the McDonald's franchises should be liable for the alleged misconduct and, if so, indemnified by their franchisor.

products.[390] The suit alleged that McDonald's engaged in deceptive practices and violated state consumer protection laws. Plaintiffs also alleged negligence and deficiencies in the allegations, the court dismissed every count in the complaint, but granted leave to amend.[391] The court expressly stated that it was guided by the general principle that it was not the place of the law to protect people who knew, or ought to have known, of the dangers of eating such food.[392]

The plaintiffs then filed an amended complaint, alleging four causes of action.[393] The first three causes of action were for deceptive acts and advertisements in violation of two sections of the New York General Business Law: Section 350, which prohibits false advertising, and Section 349, which prohibits "deceptive acts or practices in the conduct of any business, trade, or commerce or in the furnishing of any service."[394] The fourth claim, which alleged negligence by McDonald's because of its failure to warn plaintiffs of the dangers and adverse health effects of eating processed foods from McDonald's, was voluntarily dropped by the plaintiffs.[395]

The district court dismissed the amended complaint principally for two reasons: first, plaintiffs failed to plead an adequate causal connection between the consumption of McDonald's food and their alleged injuries, and second, certain alleged misrepresentations in advertisements regarding McDonald's french fries and hash browns were objectively nondeceptive and therefore not actionable.[396] Refusing to grant leave a second time to amend the complaint, the district court dismissed the complaint with prejudice.[397]

On appeal, the Second Circuit reversed the district court and reinstated some of plaintiffs' claims.[398] The plaintiffs did not appeal the dismissal of their Section 350 claims for false advertising, so the Second Circuit considered only the dismissal of the Section 349 claims of deceptive acts or practices that dismissal rested entirely on the district court's conclusion that plaintiffs failed to properly allege causation.[399] The claims of deceptive acts or practices were as follows: first, that the combined effect of McDonald's various promotional representations created the false impression that its "food products were nutritionally beneficial and part of a healthy lifestyle"; second, that McDonald's failed to disclose its use of additives and how its processes of products rendered those products "substantially less healthy than represented"; and, third, that McDonald's deceptively promoted the availability of nutritional information in its stores.[400]

---

[390] See Pelman, 237 F. Supp. 2d at 520.

[391] See id. at 543. However, Count I (deceptive advertising and failure to warn) and Count II (inducement of minors through deceptive marketing) of the complaint were dismissed with prejudice to the extent they were based on the New York City administrative code. Id.

[392] See id. at 517. The author of the opinion, the Honorable Robert W. Sweet, revealed in a footnote that he had publicly opposed the criminalization of drugs and that his logic for doing so applied in the situation of fast food: as long as consumers have adequate knowledge about even harmful substances, they should be entitled to purchase them. See Pelman, 237 F. Supp. at 517 n.2.

[393] See Pelman v. McDonald's Corp., No. 02-Civ.-7821, 2003 U.S. Dist. LEXIS 15202, at *2 (S.D.N.Y. Sept. 3, 2003) vacated in part, 396 F.3d 508 (2d Cir. N.Y. 2005).

[394] See id. at *4.

[395] See id. at *2.

[396] See id. at *11–14.

[397] See id. at *14.

[398] See Pelman, 396 F.3d at 512.

[399] See id. at 511.

[400] See id. at 510.

The Second Circuit found that the district court erred by determining that the statutory claim of deceptive acts or practices was subject to the pleading-with-particularity requirements of Rule 9(b) of the Federal Rules of Civil Procedure.[401] Referring to the bare bones notice-pleading requirements of Rule 8(a) of the Federal Rules of Civil Procedure, the Second Circuit determined that the statutory claim of deceptive acts or practices has a lower pleading standard.[402] Information, such as the amount plaintiffs exercised, family medical history, and the other components of plaintiffs' diet could be obtained in discovery, rather than constitute what the district court believed requisite for plaintiffs to state a claim.[403] Thus, the Second Circuit determined that the amended complaint was properly pleaded.[404]

In October 2010, the federal district court ruled that *Pelman* could not proceed as a class action.[405] Plaintiff sought to certify a class action under Rule 23(b)(3) of the Federal Rules of Civil Procedure, which allows class certification if questions of law or fact common to the class members predominate over questions that affect only individual members of the class. The court denied certification finding that individual issues predominated on three questions central to the litigation: (1) Is there a casual connection between a person's consumption of foods of a certain nutritional makeup and certain health conditions such as obesity? (2) Was McDonald's the primary source of these types of products for each particular plaintiff? (3) Did each plaintiff rely upon McDonald's misrepresentations about its foods when deciding to eat there?[406] Each one of these questions, ruled the court, involved highly particularized inquiries into the eating habits and health of each plaintiff, and the case could therefore not proceed as a class action.[407]

[b] Causation Barrier

Proving that one single factor resulted in obesity is a high hurdle to clear. Currently, scientists do not fully understand the cause of obesity, but recognize that it is the result of a confluence of factors. The exact interplay of these factors is yet unknown, although scientists believe in some specific genes that have been identified as directly linking to obesity.[408] Nevertheless, some food products have the ability to cause harm. Calorie-dense products can cause obesity, and obesity is linked to damaging illnesses such as diabetes.

If a food product is addictive due to intentional product manipulation by the manufacturer, and if there was a failure to warn the user of the addictive nature of the product even though the manufacturer knew or should have known that overuse of the product could result in damage, then a claim may be made against a manufacturer for damage to the consumer.

---

[401] See *id.* at 511.
[402] See *id.*
[403] See *Pelman*, 396 F.3d at 511–12.
[404] See *id.*
[405] Pelman v. McDonald's Corp. 272 F.R.D. 82, 85 (S.D.N.Y. 2010).
[406] *Id.* at 93–5.
[407] *Pelman*, 272 F.R.D. at 93.
[408] University of Chicago Medical Center, '*Master Regulator*' of Obesity? Distant IRX3 Gene Appears to Interact with Obesity-Related FTO Gene Mutations, Science Daily (March 12, 2014).

[c] Immunity Legislation

In an effort to immunize the food industry from tobacco-like lawsuits, state legislation, Commonsense Consumption Acts (CCAs), euphemistically known as "cheeseburger laws," were enacted in twenty-five states between 2004 and 2012.[409]

No federal legislation has been enacted, although the House of Representatives approved legislation known as the Personal Responsibility in Food Consumption Act of 2005 ("H.R. 554"), in order "[t]o prevent legislative and regulatory functions from being usurped by civil liability actions."[410]

The underlying rationale for the CCAs is the belief that the choices of what and how much to eat are issues of personal responsibility and no single industry should be blamed for and responsible for solving the obesity crisis.[411] Widespread media coverage of obesity litigation was dominated by the themes of personal responsibility and the need for tort reform to protect businesses from frivolous litigation.[412] This sentiment of responsibility for obesity being placed on the individual is enshrined in many CCAs. For example, Colorado codified the rationale for enacting its CCA as follows:

1. Obesity and many other conditions that are detrimental to the health and well-being of individuals are frequently long-term manifestations of poor choices that are habitually made by those individuals;
2. Despite commercial influences, individuals remain ultimately responsible for the choices they make regarding their body; and
3. Excessive litigation restricts the wide range of choices otherwise available to individuals who consumer products responsibly.[413]

A court challenge has not been made against CCAs. CCAs were enacted using model statutory language that can be classified in two categories. The first category reflects the legislation in sixteen states where CCAs confer broad immunity for claims stemming from long-term consumption of food.[414] Immunity coverage in these states generally exempt claims seeking to recover for obesity-related health harms that allege knowing and willful violations of a state or federal laws governing manufacturing, marketing, distribution, advertising, labeling, or sale of food.[415] "Knowing and willful" typically means that the conduct was committed with the intent to deceive or with actual knowledge that the violation was injurious to consumers.[416] CCAs in this first category could be interpreted to depart from state Uniform and Deceptive Acts and Practices (UDAP) statutes that were designed to create statutory claims without intent requirements. The second category includes CCAs in nine states where the approach is more tailored to bar or

---

[409] See, e.g., Colo. Rev. Stat. §§ 13-21-1101 to 13-21-1106 (West 2012); La. Rev. Stat. Ann. § 9:2799.6 (2012)

[410] Personal Responsibility in Food Consumption Act, H.R. 544, 109th Cong. (2005).

[411] Sarah A. Kornblet, *Fat America: The Need for Regulation Under the Food, Drug, and Cosmetic Act*, 49 St. Louis U. L.J. 209, 217 (2004).

[412] *Id.*

[413] Colo. Rev. Stat. § 13-21-1102.

[414] Wilking & Daynard, *supra* note 374 at 232.

[415] *Id.* (citing several state statutes, including Ala. Code § 6-5-732(2); Idaho Code Ann. § 39–8703(2)).

[416] *Id.* at 233 (citing *e.g.*, Idaho Code Ann. § 39–8704(4) (2012).

shield civil liability for obesity-related tort claims.[417] A good example of this approach is the Louisiana CCA, the first to be enacted:

> for personal injury or wrongful death based on an individual's consumption of food or nonalcoholic beverages in cases where liability is premised upon the individual's weight gain, obesity, or a health condition related to weight gain or obesity and resulting from his long-term consumption of a food or nonalcoholic beverage.[418]

Unlike the broader category, these tort-based CCAs should not bar claims filed by consumers or state AGs under state UDAP statutes.[419]

§ 5.08 Food Product Focus: Case Studies

[1] *Salt*

[a] Public Health Problem: IOM Report

Two food products that illustrate the multifaceted response of the law to evolving public health concerns from overconsumption are salt and sugar.[420] The purpose of this section is limited to surveying some of the legal tools used to address the public health and nutrition concerns related to these two foods.

The IOM claims that the "major adverse effect of increased sodium chloride intake is elevated blood pressure, which has been shown to be an etiologically related risk factor for cardiovascular and renal diseases."[421] In other words, diets with excessive sodium consumption can significantly raise a person's risk for heart disease and failure. The average American consumes far more salt than recommended by the 2010 Dietary Guidelines for Americans.[422] In 2010, the IOM reported that most of the sodium in the diet of American consumers comes from salt added to processed and restaurant foods. The IOM recommended in its report gradual sodium reduction to allow consumers to adjust to new levels of sodium in their diet. The IOM report also recommended government intervention in order to achieve real reductions of sodium intake.[423]

[b] FDA Response to Citizen Petitions

Government intervention was evoked by CSPI in a petition filed in 1978 to the FDA asking the agency to revoke the GRAS status of sodium.[424] As noted in the Chapter 4, "it is the use of a substance, rather than the substance itself, that is eligible for the

---

[417] *Id.*

[418] LA. REV. STAT. ANN. § 9:2799.6(A).

[419] Wilking & Daynard, *supra* note 374 at 234.

[420] *See generally*, Michael Moss, SALT SUGAR FAT: HOW THE FOOD GIANTS HOOKED US (2013) (investigative report of the food processing industry use of salt and sugar).

[421] *Dietary Reference Intakes* 394, Inst. of Medicine (Jennifer J. Otten, et al. eds. 2006).

[422] *See Americans Consume Too Much Salt*, Centers for Disease Control and Prevention (2011); *Get The Facts: Sodium and Dietary Guidelines*, Centers for Disease Control and Prevention (2012).

[423] *See generally, Strategies to Reduce Sodium Intake in the United States*, Institute of Medicine of the National Academies (2010).

[424] *See Petition to Revoke the GRAS Status of Salt*, Center for Science in the Public Interest.

GRAS exemption."[425] Thus, a substance may be GRAS for one use but not another, or may be GRAS in one food but not others.[426] The FDA had granted GRAS status to salt, as indicated in Title 21, Part 182 of the Code of Federal Regulations, where salt is named as a "common food ingredient" that is considered safe for its "intended" uses, without conditions, along with pepper, vinegar, baking powder, and monosodium glutamate.[427]

In response to the CSPI petition, the FDA in 1982 issued a Policy Notice that announced the agency would defer action on salt's GRAS status until the impact of the sodium-labeling regulations being proposed at the time (relating to claims of "sodium free," "low sodium," and the like), and manufacturers' voluntary efforts to reduce salt and sodium content in their products, could be assessed.[428] The FDA did state that if the sodium content of process foods was not substantially reduced, it would consider additional regulatory options, including changing salt's GRAS status.[429]

Continued concerns about salt consumption in the United States has led to continued calls to change salt's GRAS status. In 2005, CSPI submitted another petition to the FDA urging the agency to revoke salt's GRAS status. In response to that petition, FDA held a 2007 public hearing on sodium intake reduction.[430] In the notice announcing this hearing, the FDA referred to the concerns it expressed in the 1982 policy notice about the many technical effects and food categories for which salt is used, and the difficulty of setting "fair use" limits for salt for all of these effects and categories that would be safe and effective for all consumers, regardless of their susceptibility to hypertension.[431] The FDA also referred to the high burden in regulating prior-sanctioned uses of salt and the small benefit of regulating the remaining uses of salt that do not meet the burden under the adulteration standard for prior-sanction uses.[432]

[c] FDA Proposed Rulemaking: Daily Value Label

In the 2007 advanced notice of proposed rulemaking issued by the FDA that requested comments about what nutrient reference values it should use to calculate the percentage daily value (DV) in the Nutrition Facts panel and Supplement Facts labels,[433] the agency asks for comments about whether sodium's DV should be based on the tolerable upper

---

[425] Substances Generally Recognized as Safe, 62 Fed. Reg. 19,938, 18,939 (April 17, 1997) (codified at 21 CFR pts. 170, 184, and 570).

[426] An example of this is the GRAS regulation for caffeine, which states that it is a GRAS at tolerance levels of up to .02 percent, "when used in cola-type beverages in accordance with good manufacturing practice." 21 C.F.R. §182.1180 (b), (c).

[427] 21 C.F.R. § 182.1(a).

[428] *See* GRAS Safety Review of Sodium Chloride; Policy Notice; Solicitation of Views, 47 Fed. Reg. 26,590, 26,592 (June 18, 1982).

[429] *Id.* at 26,592–3.

[430] Salt and Sodium; Petition to Revise the Regulatory Status of Salt and Establish Food Labeling Requirements Regarding Salt and Sodium; Public Hearing; Request for Comments, 72 Fed. Reg. 59,973 (October 23, 2007).

[431] *Id.* at 59,976–7.

[432] *Id.* at 59,977.

[433] Food Labeling: Revision of Reference Values and Mandatory Nutrients, 62 Fed. Reg. 62,149 (proposed November 2, 2007) (to be codified 21 C.F.R. pt. 101).

level of intake (UL) of 2,300 mg/day, as suggested by the 2005 Dietary Guidelines for Americans, or be based on an Adequate Intake of 1,500 mg/day, as recommended by the IOM report.[434] If the FDA were to decide to base sodium's DV on the 1,500 mg AI value, the daily value percentage appearing on nutrition labels would be significantly higher. This proposed rulemaking is still pending.

[d] USDA Rulemaking Efforts

The USDA has engaged in extensive rulemaking on salt intake.

In July 2011, the USDA issued a proposed rule to establish a common or usual name for raw meat and poultry products that do not meet the standard of identity regulations and to which solutions have been added, either through injections, marinades, or other means.[435] The USDA noted that consumers might not realize that the meat products contain these solutions, and may also be unaware that these solutions often contain salt.[436] The proposed regulations would require that the label disclose the percentage of weight that is from the added solution, and the common or usual names of the ingredients in the solution, by weight, from most to least.

In September 2011, the FDA and FSIS jointly published a notice requesting comments, data, and evidence relevant to the dietary intake of sodium and the current and emerging approaches to reduce sodium intake.

In January 2012, the USDA's FNS Program issued a final rule updating the meal patterns and nutrition standards for the National School Lunch and Breakfast Programs.[437] The new standards require schools to reduce the sodium content in meals over a ten-year period starting by the 2014–2015 school year, with two interim targets. For breakfast meals, they require a 25 percent reduction in the sodium content from baseline amounts by the end of the ten years; and for lunches they require a reduction of nearly 53 percent.[438]

In 2013, for competitive foods – vending machines, school stores, and snack bars – the USDA's interim final rule establishing minimum nutrition standards for these foods requires that starting July 1, 2014, snack items and side dishes may contain no more than 230 mg of sodium and entrees may contain no more than 480 mg. On July 1, 2016, the limit for snack items/side dishes decreases to no more than 200 mg of sodium, while the limit for entrees remains the same.[439]

---

[434] 62 Fed. Reg. at 62,170; IOM report at 10.

[435] Common of Usual Name for Raw Meat and Poultry Products Containing Added Solutions, 76 Fed. Reg. 44,855 (proposed July 11, 2011) (codified at 9 C.F.R. pts. 319, 381).

[436] *Id.* at 44,858.

[437] Nutrition Standards for National School Lunch and School Breakfast Programs, 77 Fed. Reg. 4,088 4,088 (January 26, 2012) (to be codified at 7 C.F.R. pts. 210, 220).

[438] The targets were based on ULs that were modified to be appropriate for children in various age ranges, based on IOM recommendations. *Id.*

[439] Nat'l School Lunch Program and School Breakfast Program: Nutrition Standards for All Foods Sold in School as Required by the Healthy, Hunger-Free Kids Act of 2010, 78 Fed. Reg. 39,068 (June 28, 2013) (interim final rule) (to be codified at 7 C.F.R. pt 210 and 220).

[2] *Sugar*

[a] Public Health Problem: Addiction Studies

Sugar consumption has long been linked with a host of chronic health problems, including obesity, diabetes, and cardiovascular disease. As noted in this treatise, to reduce Americans' intake, calls have been made to tax sugary products or limit access in certain environments like schools and workplaces. Assessing the legal implications of emerging sugar-addiction research is challenging given the unique roles that sugar plays in Americans' lives: sugar is ubiquitous in the American food supply and is in many respects a cultural icon.[440]

[b] Stakeholder Advocacy

The often-divergent interests of three distinctive stakeholders – public health officials, the food industry, and consumers – are particularly evident in the analysis of viable legal tools to regulate sugar. In response to evidence suggesting that sugary beverages contribute to the obesity epidemic,[441] public health officials often call for more aggressive controls on unhealthy foods in the American diet, even without conclusive proof of sugar's addictiveness. The food industry contends that isolating a singular food product or ingredient like sugar and subjecting it to regulation is overly simplistic; the industry asserts that because obesity is a complex and multifaceted problem that requires lifestyle solutions, a single type of food ought not to be penalized. The food industry demonstrated its resistance to regulation with its recent objections to the FDA's plan to test consumer responses to changes in the Nutrition Facts labels, which included a declaration of added sugar amounts.[442] Consumer interests are more difficult to access. Consumers value the freedom to choose what they want to eat; however, once consumers receive information, there is concern over their capacity to interpret and effectively use it. If sugar is proven to be addictive, then regulatory attention may turn to how much information should be provided to consumers and in what form (i.e., facts panels, warning labels, or some other dissemination device).[443]

[c] Legal Tools

The legal tools to regulate sugar are diverse and include labeling (disclosure and warning), advertising restrictions, taxes (special excise duties, value-added taxes, and sales taxes), product bans or restrictions, litigation (especially class action litigation), self-regulation, a reduction of farm subsidies and sugar programs, and the development of education programs. Thoughtful analysis of the implications of these tools must consider several

---

[440] Ashley Gearhardt, Michael Roberts & Marice Ashe, *If Sugar Is Addictive ... What Does It Mean for the Law?*, J.L. MED. & ETHICS 46, 48 (2013).

[441] David S. Ludwig et al., *Relation between Consumption of Sugar Sweetened Drinks and Childhood Obesity: A Prospective, Observational Study*, 357 THE LANCET 505–8 (2001).

[442] *See* Joan Murphy, *"FDA's Added Sugars Study Prompts Complaints from Food Industry,"* FOOD CHEMICAL NEWS, August 10, 2012, at 1. Stephanie Strom, *Pepsi and Coke to Post Calories of Drinks Sold in Vending Machines*, N.Y. TIMES, October 8, 2012, at B3.

[443] Gearhardt, *supra* note 442 at 48.

issues, including the following: (1) whether advertising restrictions on sugary food products violate the First Amendment;[444] (2) whether taxes or bans on products change consumer behavior or are an unnecessary burden and intrusion on consumers; (3) whether a reduction of farm subsidies and sugar programs effectively reduces sugar consumption; and (4) whether class action litigation furthers public health objectives by changing the production and marketing of sugar products and the consumption habits of consumers.

[d] HFCS: Sugar Wars

An interesting battle in the regulation of sugar involves the name High-Fructose Corn Syrup (HFCS). High tariffs on imported raw sugar that have over the years kept sugar prices artificially high have resulted in producers seeking alternative sweeteners that can be manufactured at a lower cost. The sweetener of choice of manufacturers has been HFCS. HFCS has been used in a variety of food staples for the US food market, such as chips and soft drinks. Sugar-sweetened beverages are the largest single source of added sugars. It has also been suggested that the granting of corn subsidies by the federal government has incentivized farmers to produce as much corn as possible, thus keeping the price of HFCS relatively low. This explanation has been questioned on grounds that several other factors decreasing the cost while increasing the utility of HFCS explain its popularity.[445] With the rise in obesity coupled with the permeation of HFCS in the food market, there has developed a link between HFCS consumption and obesity. As a result, and presumably to meet consumer preference for more "natural" products that contain sugar, many food enterprises removed HFCS from their products.[446]

In 2008, the corn industry launched a multimillion dollar advertising campaign to revamp the reputation of HFCS as the dietary equivalent to sugar, specifically corn sugar.[447] In 2010, the Corn Refiners Association (CRA) filed a Citizen's Petition with the FDA requesting the term "corn sugar" be approved as an alternative or usual name for HFCS.[448] The petition specifically requested that the Code of Federal Regulation section defining HFCS (21 C.F.R. Section 184.1866) be amended to say, "High Fructose

---

[444] *See* K. M. Sullivan, The Interagency Working Group's Preliminary Proposed Nutrition Principles to Guide Industry Self-Regulatory Efforts: Constitutional Issues, *in* COMMENTS OF VIACOM BEFORE THE FEDERAL TRADE COMMISSION Appendix A (2011) (First Amendment concerns "would unquestionably invalidate" mandatory government restrictions on food marketing to children); but cf., Open Letter on the First Amendment and the Interagency Working Group Principles to FTC, CDC, FDA, USDA, and the White House from G. D. Allison et al. (September 6, 2011) (nutrition principles, which are designed to guide industry self-regulatory efforts, do not restrain or compel anyone's speech).

[445] *See* John S. White & John P. Foreyt, Ten Myths about High-Fructose Corn Syrup, SWEET SURPRISE Foodtechnology 96 (October 2006).

[446] Starbucks, for example, removed HFCS from its line of baked goods. Wheat Thins removed all HFCS from their products and replaced it with regular sugar. *See* David Mercer, *U.S. Corn Syrup Sales Fall*, FOOD MFG., June 2, 2010; Melanie Warner, *For Corn Syrup, the Sweet Talk gets Harder*, N.Y. TIMES, May 1, 2010, at BU1.

[447] John S. White, *supra* note 447 (the CRA campaign includes efforts to address common perceptions regarding the health effects, taste characteristics, and production methods of HFCS).

[448] *See* Citizen Petition from Audrae Erickson, president, Corn Refiners Ass'n, to U.S. Food & Drug Admin., Docket No. FDA-2010-P-0491 (September 14, 2010).

Corn Syrup, also known as corn sugar, a sweet nutritive saccharide mixture."[449] The petition asserted that corn sugar is more representative of what HRCS actually is.[450]

In May 2012, the FDA denied the CRA's petition, claiming that to change the name of HFCS to corn sugar would be confusing to consumers.[451] Under the FDA's standard nomenclature, a sugar is a solid, dried, and crystallized food. A syrup, on the contrary, is used to describe an aqueous solution or liquid food. Thus, the FDA found that the use of the term "corn sugar" would suggest that HFCS is a solid, dried, and crystallized sweetener when in fact it is an aqueous solution.

CRA's petition also requested that the FDA eliminate corn sugar as an alternate name for dextrose and replace all references to corn sugar with "dextrose." The CRA reasoned that the name HFCS is confusing to consumers and that the name "corn syrup" more accurately represents consumer expectations. In addition, the CRA claimed that consumers do not currently associate corn sugar with dextrose and that the term "corn sugar" is seldom used in food labeling.

In its denial of CRA's petition, the FDA found that corn sugar has been used to describe dextrose for over thirty years and is regularly used as the term for dextrose in scientific literature and on public websites. FDA typically looks to the usage of the term in the public literature to determine whether the product name is an appropriate, common, or usual name. Finally, the term "corn sugar" has traditionally described sweeteners that can safely be consumed by individuals with hereditary fructose intolerance or fructose malabsorption. As a result, the FDA opined that changing the name of HFCS to corn sugar could pose a health concern to these individuals.

Despite FDA's denial of the petition on what the CRA calls "narrow, technical grounds," the association maintains its position that the vast majority of Americans are confused by the name HFCS.[452]

[e] Lanham Act Suit

In April 2011, plaintiff sugar producers and two of their associations sued the CRA in the California Central District Court, alleging that CRA's efforts to market HFCS as corn sugar, natural, and nutritionally equivalent to cane and beet sugar is false and misleading in violation of the Lanham Act.[453] An interesting aspect of the case is that plaintiffs allege that individual members were liable for the actions of the trade association based on vicarious/agency liability for CRA's actions or joint tortfeasor liability. Plaintiffs also alleged that the CRA members were individually liable for their own, similar, advertising statements. The CRA members filed a counter claim in September 2012, alleging that the sugar companies were themselves deceiving consumers by engaging in what

---

[449] *Id.*

[450] *See id.* at 2; *see also* Press Release, Corn Refiners Ass'n, Corn Refiners Petition for use of "Corn Sugar" as Alternate Name for High Fructose Corn Syrup: Eliminating Consumer Confusion Is the Goal (September 14, 2010).

[451] Letter from Michael M. Landa, dir., ctr. for Food Safety & Applied Nutrition, US Food & Drug Admin., to Audrae Erickson, president, Corn Refiners Ass'n (May 30, 2012).

[452] Press Release, Corn Refiners Ass'n, Statement of Audrae Erickson, president, Corn Refiners Association on the Food & Drug Admin. Denial of Petition (May 30, 2010).

[453] Western Sugar Cooperative, et al. v. Archer-Daniels-Midland Co., et al. No. 2:2011cv03473 (April 22, 2011) (Cal. Central District Court).

they called a decade-long "spin and smear conspiracy" aimed at damaging corn syrup's reputation.[454]

[f] California Warning Labels

A bill proposed in California would require warning labels on the fronts of all cans and bottles of soda and juice drinks that have sugar added and 75 or more calories per 12 ounces.[455] The label would read: "STATE OF CALIFORNIA SAFETY WARNING: Drinking beverages with added sugar(s) contributes to obesity, diabetes, and tooth decay."[456]

§ 5.09 International Regulation of Food Nutrition

As noted in Chapter 2, nutrition claims are subject to TBT Agreement for the international trade of food.[457] Under the TBT Agreement, technical barriers can be used as long as the trade restriction is done for a legitimate purpose, is applied equally to foreign and domestic goods, and is not broader than necessary to achieve a legitimate purpose. Thus, under the TBT Agreement, a nation state could restrict the importation of a food product whose nutrition value is misrepresented where prevention of deceptive trade practices is a legitimate purpose.

---

[454] *See, e.g.*, Archer-Daniels-Midland Company's Counterclaim.

[455] Lydia Zuraw, *California Senate Passes Bill Requiring Warning Labels on Some Sugar-Sweetened Drinks,* FOOD SAFETY NEWS, June 5, 2014.

[456] *Id.*

[457] Uruguay Round Agreement: Agreement on Technical Barriers to Trade Preamble, art. 1, World Trade Organization.

6 Regulation of Food Systems

§ 6.01 Introduction

[1] *Adaptation by Food Law to Food Systems' Issues*

[a] Affects in Previous Food Law Phases

The concept of "food systems" as used in this treatise refers to multiple systems: local, regional, national, and global. Two additional points flesh out the concept of food systems as used in this treatise. First, each food system comprises the production, processing, preparation, packaging, promotion, sales, preparation, distribution, and consumption of food. The shorthand descriptor of these events is known as "farm-to-fork" or "farm-to-plate," which connote a systematic way of thinking about the life cycle of a food product. Second, a "food systems approach" involves more than the acknowledgment of the multiple stages in the modern food system; it also refers to an orientation that raises normative questions about what sort of food system(s) is preferable. Discussion of these normative questions involves food policy that is beyond the scope of this food law treatise; however, the implications of the debate are germane to food law because much of emerging law governing food is shaped in response to the changing norms and social ideas about the food system(s).[1]

The adaptation by food law to food systems issues is evident in each of the phases outlined in this treatise – food commerce, safety, marketing, and nutrition. For example, a critical issue in food safety regulation is whether small enterprises should be excluded from food safety laws in order to preserve the small farm, seen by many as the foundation for a successful local food system. Emerging labeling laws determine how food credence information (i.e., organic, grass-fed, cage-less, GMO-free) is conveyed to consumers concerned about the values of the food system from which the food product is derived. Indeed, the motivation for state initiatives on mandatory labeling for genetically engineered foods is less about food safety and more about what kind of food system voting consumers prefer. Finally, laws are being used to correct the deficiencies in food system(s) that result in malnutrition and obesity.

The pressures on the law to govern the layered, complex food systems are immense. Gaps in administrative regulation give rise to additional legal tools, such as private standards, self-governance, and litigation. Preferences for one food system over another generate policy tensions and affect the type of laws that emerge.

[b] Distinctive Food Law Application

This chapter will address the distinctive food law adaptation to social change in a more structured way than that covered in the preceding chapters of this treatise. These adaptations are best understood in the context of certain concepts that mobilize values representing the choice of food systems. These concepts include local food, sustainability,

---

[1] An interesting analogue to the food systems orientation to food law is the Earth System Governance Project that helps color legal approaches to environmental law issues. The concept of Earth Systems Governance is defined as "the interrelated and increasingly integrated system of formal and informal rules, rule-making systems, and actor-networks at all levels of human society (from local to global) that are set up to steer societies towards preventing, mitigating, and adapting to global and local environmental change and, in particular, earth system transformation, within the normative context of sustainable development." Frank Biermann et al., Earth System Governance: People, Places and the Planet 22 (2009).

food security, food sovereignty, urban agriculture, and social justice and equity. Defining these terms presents a challenge. These concepts in many respects are mini-movements in a larger food movement and although they differ in specifics, they share overarching values and goals. They span issues such as GE foods, urban agriculture, ecological sustainability, sustainable diets, and food safety. As might be expected, considerable overlap and convergence between the concepts muddy definitions. Nevertheless, this chapter attempts to define each concept and identify their objectives. The policy rationales, tensions, and aspirations of the concepts are well beyond the purview of this chapter and treatise. Instead, this chapter, in addition to defining terms, makes a modest attempt to address the legal issues that intersect with the food system concepts.

[c] Consumer Role in Driving Food Law's Adaptation

As noted in Chapter 1, an important driver in food law's adaption to social change in the modern food system is that of the consumer role.[2] Rising purchasing power, education level, urbanization, and evolving lifestyles combined with the decline of food prices relative to other goods have led to changes in consumption patterns. Whereas in the past price and visual aspects were the main purchase criteria, the intrinsic quality of food has now become a much more important parameter. In addition to the physical quality of foods, consumers are increasingly demanding on the ethical dimension of food production, including its broad impacts on society and the environment and the subsequent issues of the treatment of workers, a fair return to producers, environmental impacts, and animal welfare.[3] These concerns are couched in terms of "ethical consumerism" and resonate especially in developed countries, such as the United States.[4]

The interest of consumers in food is sure to be multidimensional. For example, consumers may wish to have information about organic food because they perceive organic food to be more healthy or nutritious. Consumers may also have ethical and philosophical reasons for buying organic foods.[5] These multifaceted considerations are often beyond the purview of the regulating agencies and therefore create gaps in law. To fill the gap, private standards and other forms of self-governance, as well as litigation, have become important legal tools. For example, food retailers are assuming more of a gatekeeper role and use private standards to guarantee safety and desirable qualities.[6] Retailers (and manufacturers) also incorporate social responsibility standards that translate into private standards. A principal aim of private standards is to help retailers derive information about

---

[2] *See* Warren Belasco, *Food and Social Movements, in* THE OXFORD HANDBOOK OF FOOD HISTORY 461, 461–80 (Jeffrey M. Pilcher ed., 2012) (discussing the nature of consumer food demand).

[3] Liu Pascal, Private Standards in International Trade: Issues, Opportunities and Long-Term Prospects in The Evolving Structure of World Agricultural Trade, *in* FOOD & AGRIC. ORG. OF THE UNITED NATIONS, THE EVOLVING STRUCTURE OF WORLD AGRICULTURAL TRADE 207 (2009).

[4] Michael T. Roberts, The Compatibility of Private Standards with Multilateral Trade Rules: Legal Issues at Stake in *the* Evolving Structure of World Agricultural Trade *in* FOOD & AGRIC. ORG. OF THE UNITED NATIONS, THE EVOLVING STRUCTURE OF WORLD AGRICULTURAL TRADE 261 (2009).

[5] Rosie Mestel, *Lots of Chatter, Anger over Stanford Organic Food Study,* L.A. TIMES, September 12, 2012 (noting that nutrition is not the only reason why people buy organic foods); Peter Hoffman, *Going Organic, Clumsily,* N.Y. TIMES, Mar. 24, 1998, at A23 ("Organic food is not just about a product; it is a philosophy in which the process of production is as important as the final result.").

[6] The unprecedented retail globalization and consolidation since the 1980s has facilitated the transference of values into decisions on food systems. Pascal, *supra* note 3 at 206.

unique attributes of food product. Certification is the means by which companies derive this information and use it to align private standards with demands from consumers.[7]

This emphasis on the consumer does not negate the role of the farmer in the food system; instead, it reflects the affects of the consumer preference on farmers. Three examples illustrate this point: (1) concerns over animal cruelty have led to consumer rejection of animal products; (2) negative impacts to the environment have caused consumers to choose foods they believe are environmentally friendly; and (3) ethical concerns concerning agriculture and big business cause consumers to choose foods that they believe speak out against unethical practices.

Whether the adaptation of law to social changes surrounding food will reform the food system(s) as envisioned by many proponents of the social changes only time will tell. However, the fact that food law is adapting, even if only incrementally, is palpable. This development of "food systems" law will continue to shape food law as a dynamic, responsive discipline.

§ 6.02 Local Food

[1] *Key Concept in Food Movement*

[a] Objectives

A key concept in a food systems orientation and to the broader food movement is that of "local food." This concept has translated into the development of local food models including farmer's markets, mobile food facilities, street vending, institutional food distribution programs, and urban agriculture. The impetus and management of these models are largely done through food policy councils, which operate either at a state or local level.

The objectives of the local food movement are many: (1) provide fresh, high-quality, and wholesome food to consumers interested in promoting local sources; (2) move beyond organics to achieve sustainable food systems;[8] (3) help develop viable livelihoods for farmers; (4) generate positive economic effects on local economies; (5) remedy social justice issues such as food deserts in urban areas; (6) support development in rural areas by routing revenue away from distributors to farmers; (7) lessen the environmental footprint by shortening the length of the supply chain needed to process and transport the food; (8) provide food in a more transparent method; (9) enhance food safety by reducing opportunities for contamination; and (10) allow consumers to personally connect with the farmers who produce their food.

[b] Defining Local Food

As noted in Chapter 4, in prohibiting the sale of misbranded food, the Food, Drug, and Cosmetic Act (FDCA) defines misbranded as bearing a label "false or misleading in any particular." One "particular" on a label (or an accompanying written, printed,

---

[7] *Id.* at 207.
[8] Nina Planck, Op-Ed., *Organic and Then Some*, N.Y. Times, November 23, 2005.

or graphic matter) may be an indication the food is local. Neither the FDCA nor any other federal act (Federal Meat Inspection Act for meat and Poultry Products Inspection Act for poultry) or implementing labeling regulations defines local.

Nor is there consensus as to what constitutes local food.[9] Merriam-Webster defines "local" as characterized by or relating to a position or space.[10] Thus, something may be local if it is associated with a particular area. But this definition fails to account for the fact that the concept of local foods centers on direct marketing, rendering the social proximity between producers and consumers essential to defining local food.[11]

It is conceivable that consumer reliance on a local label would rise to the level of a "particular" under the FDCA. Thus, presumably a starting point in establishing where a food properly bears the label "local" is consumer perception.

It should be noted that Congress on at least two occasions has defined "local" in the food context. First, in the 2008 Food, Conservation, and Energy Act (2008 Farm Bill), Congress directed the secretary of agriculture to facilitate loans in support of locally or regionally produced food products.[12] In this context, the 2008 Farm Bill defined a locally or regionally produced food product as grown within 400 miles or the same state in which it is marketed.[13] More recently, as noted in Chapter 3, in the Food Safety Modernization Act (FSMA), Congress provided a carve-out for certain food safety requirements for producers selling in local markets. Congress defined "local" as products produced within a state's borders or within 275 miles,[14] which is a much narrower range than the 400 miles in the 2008 Farm Bill.

States typically define local food as food grown within state borders.[15] This is not surprising since the motivation for a local foods definition in a statute is to enhance the local and thereby the state economy. Given the commercial popularity of local food, it is also not surprising, that grocery stores, restaurants, and farmers' markets have developed their own local food definitions. These private or quasi-private (in the case of farmers' markets) entities typically base the definition of local on geographical distance or state borders.[16] For example, Raley's Supermarkets in Sacramento, California, defines local produce as that which is grown within fifty miles of its stores; Wal-Mart Stores Inc. bases local on the state where food is grown.[17]

---

[9] *See, e.g.,* Michael S. Hand & Stephen Martinez, *Just What Does Local Mean?,* CHOICES, 1st Quarter 2010, at 1. *See also* Stephen Martinez, et al., *Local Food Systems: Concepts, Impacts, and Issues,* ECON. RESEARCH SERV., U.S. DEP'T OF AGRIC. 97 (May 2010).

[10] MERRIAM-WEBSTER, COLLEGIATE DICTIONARY 730 (11th ed. 2004).

[11] *See* Clare Hinrichs, *Embeddedness and Local Food Systems: Notes on Two Types of Direct Agricultural Markets,* 16 J. RURAL STUD. 295, 296 (2000).

[12] 7 U.S.C. § 1932(g)(9)(B)(i).

[13] *See* 7 U.S.C. § 1932(g)(9)(A)(i).

[14] Specifically, Congress exempted small farms (less than $500,000 in total sales) engaged in direct farm marketing (so long as 50 percent of total farm sales were in direct sales to consumers or restaurants in the same state or within a 275-mile radius). 21 U.S.C.A. § 350(h); 21 U.S.C.A. § 350(g).

[15] *See e.g.,* 30 Ill. Comp. Stat 595/5 (2009) (defining "local farm or food products" as "products grown, processed, packaged, and distributed by Illinois citizens or businesses located wholly within the borders of Illinois.").

[16] *See* Hand & Martinez, *supra* note 9, at 13 (showing a table of the top ten grocery retailers' definitions of local foods).

[17] Tom Burfield, *Retailers Define Local Produce,* PRODUCE RETAILER (April 2, 2013).

[2] Farmers' Markets

[a] State and Local Regulation

The farmers' market is perhaps the most visible component to the local food movement. These markets now proliferate the American landscape, providing benefits to consumers, farmers, and communities. Consumers have access to seasonal, healthful, and often very affordable fresh local foods through farmers' markets; farmers have access to a greater percentage of every dollar worth of food they sell when providing access directly to consumers;[18] and communities benefit from increased community cohesion, civic revitalization, and revenue enhancement.[19]

State and local governments share the dominant roles in the regulation of farmers' markets, determining the licensing and permitting necessary to establish farmers' markets and the conditions for farmers to participate. The food sold at farmers' markets is generally not in interstate commerce. As noted in Chapter 3, food sold by small farms is generally exempted from FSMA and food sold to consumers at the retail level is typically governed by state food codes. Finally, farmers' markets most often take place on property regulated by local governments through their police power. State and local regulation of farmers' markets can vary and be multilayered.

[b] Defining Farmers' Markets

The definition of farmers' markets is an important starting point in the regulation of such markets because definitions help determine eligibility for accommodations and benefits often conferred on markets.[20] These benefits may include exemption from classification as a retail food facility by the food code or exemption from packing and grading requirements for produce. For example, California defines Certified Farmers' Markets as "locations established in accordance with local ordinances, where California farmers may transport and sell to the public California agricultural products that they produced, that are exempt from the established grade, size, labeling, packaging and other such requirements for fruits, nuts, and vegetables, and operated in accordance with this chapter and regulations adopted pursuant to this chapter."[21] A few states define farmers' markets in their agriculture codes or regulations. For example, the Massachusetts Department

---

[18] Patrick Canning, *A Revised and Expanded Food Dollar Series: A Better Understanding of Our Food Costs*, Econ Research Serv., U.S. Dep't Of Agric. 114, (February 2011).

[19] Many case studies document the dollars that the presence of farmers' markets add to local economies, from direct support of local jobs to spending at businesses nearby farmers' markets. *See* Hand & Martinez, *supra* note 9.

[20] Definitions of farmers' markets in states and local laws reflect the variations of form and purpose of farmers' markets. *See* Neil D. Hamilton, *Farmers' Markets: Rules, Regulations and Opportunities*, Nat'l Agric. L. Center (June 2002) (farmers' markets mean different things in different regions of the country). Professor Hamilton also endeavors to define farmers' markets by their common terms: "(1) Farmers selling produce and food they raise or create (2) To individual customers (3) At a temporary location, often on public property, such as a street or parking lot, (4) On a periodic basis, typically once or twice a week, (5) For a set period of time, usually 3 or 4 hours, (6) During the local growing season, usually 5 or 6 months, (7) Operated by a government or non-profit organization." *Id.* at 3.

[21] Cal. Agric. Code § 47004(b).

of Agricultural Resources defines farmers' markets as "public markets for the primary purpose of connecting and mutually benefiting Massachusetts farmers, communities, and shoppers while promoting and selling products grown and raised by participating farmers."[22] Although the Model Food Code (referenced in Chapter 3) does not define farmers' markets, some states define farmers' markets in their food codes. For example, the Iowa Inspection Food Code states "Farmers' market means a marketplace which seasonally operates principally as a common market for fresh fruits and vegetables on a retail basis for off-the-premises consumption."[23] Finally, local governments also may define farmers' markets as a use within their zoning code or within their policies as a use that is encouraged on public land. For example, Portland, Oregon's zoning code defines in detail farmers' markets as

> events where farmers, ranchers, and other agricultural producers sell food, plants, flowers, and added-value products, such as jams and jellies, they have grown, raised, or produced from products they have grown or raised. In addition, some vendors sell food that is available for immediate consumption on site, and some may be community groups, services, or other vendors or organizations. Farmers Markets occur on a regular basis in the same location. They are free and open to the public. Some markets are seasonal, while others occur year-round.[24]

[c] Regulating Farmers' Markets

(1) *Safety and Quality*

The state's regulation of retail food safety extends to farmers' markets and vendors at farmers' markets. The details vary as to how states regulate and license farmers' markets and their vendors. Many states issue permits to vendors, but some, like California, issue health permits to farmers' market itself. The California Retail Food Code requires that the market itself obtain a permit from the local health department. Individual producers of agricultural products are not required to obtain their own permits to sell at markets, but must obtain a certified producer certificate from the County Agricultural Commissioner to participate in a farmers' market. Vendors of nonagricultural products, such as foods prepared onsite, may also operate under the health permit of a farmers' market and must follow all applicable rules in the code for temporary food facilities or food processing.[25] Typically, states set the regulations for food safety for farmers' markets, which are then enforced by local governmental entities. A ten-state analysis by the Harvard Food Law and Policy Clinic of the regulation of farmers' markets found that all ten states regulated farmers' markets, with four preempting more stringent local laws, and none allowing for more lax local laws.[26]

---

[22] Bureau of Envtl. Health, Food Protection Program: Policies, Procedures, and Guidelines, Mass. Dep't of Pub. Health (April 30, 2013).

[23] Iowa Admin. Code r.481-30.2.

[24] Portland, Or., Zoning Code, ch. 33.910.

[25] Cal. Health & Safety Code § 114370.

[26] *See* Nathan Rosenberg & Emily Broad Leib, *Pennsylvania's Chapter 57 and its Effects on Farmers' Markets*, Harvard Food L. & Policy Clinic 10 (August 2012).

(2) *Land Use*

Local land use laws and municipal policy determine where, or even if, farmers' markets can exist. Farmers' markets may take place on private property, public property, or streets. Cumbersome permitting processes or vague zoning codes, however, can make it difficult for the establishment of farmers' markets. Ideally, a community will establish farmers' markets as an allowed use in the areas the community selects, which eliminates the need for a permit and increases the land available for markets.[27] In the alternative, a streamlined and affordable permitting process can also facilitate the allowance of a farmers' market. Cities often employ a variety of processes to review different types of land uses. In Los Angeles County, for example, farmers' markets are a defined use and are subject to either a director's review approval or a minor conditional use permit, depending on the zone where a farmers' market seeks to locate.[28]

If a farmers' market is not an allowed or recognized use, a market may face difficulty in locating. The market may not be allowed at all, even as a temporary use, or it may effectively be barred due to the high costs of the permitting processes (including the periodic reapplication for a temporary use permit). An example of the complexities of defined use and prohibitive costs for farmers' markets is in San Jose, California, where farmers' markets were deemed an Outdoor Private Property Special Event, needing a Special Use permit costing up to three thousand dollars annually.[29]

Land use regulation can also increase access to farmers' markets for low-income consumers. Since land use laws prescribe the conditions under which a use can exist, zoning codes can require the acceptance of various forms of payment, including Supplemental Nutrition Assistance Program (SNAP) benefits. SNAP is named CalFresh in California. Within its zoning code, Los Angeles County defines farmers' markets and sets out general provisions that they must follow. These provisions expressly provide that "[f]armers' markets shall accept CalFresh benefits via electronic benefit transfer ('EBT') card in addition to accepting other forms of payment."[30] Within its administrative code, San Francisco also requires CalFresh acceptance by all farmers' markets within the city.[31]

Public property is often an attractive location for a farmers' market, and some cities create policies to encourage the location of farmers' markets on various types of public property. Public property can often offer markets an affordable location with favorable amenities, foot traffic, and parking. Examples include the use of transit stops with large plazas for farmers' markets, space at government buildings, and locations within parks.[32] Finally, some farmers' markets operate with street closure permits. Street closure markets can be expensive to operate, requiring a weekly permit and fee to close the street.

[d] Legal Issues for Farmers' Market Management

(1) *Liability*

The management of farmers' markets face at least three categories of legal risks: liability, compliance, and fraud prevention. As a general rule, insurance is needed

---

[27] *Establishing Land Use Protections for Farmers' Markets*, Pub. Health L. & Policy (December 2009).

[28] *See* L.A. County, Cal., Zoning Code § 22.52.2610.

[29] *See* San Jose, Cal., Ordinance 29218.

[30] L.A. County, Cal., Zoning Code § 22.52.2610.

[31] S.F., Cal., Admin Code, § 9A.4.

[32] *See, e.g.,* S.F., Cal., Admin Code, § 9A.4 (providing that a farmers' market may be established on property under the jurisdiction of the Recreation and Park Commission).

that covers liability for accidents on the farmers' market site and liability for injury caused by using products sold at the market. A tragic automobile accident in 2003 at a farmers' market in Santa Monica, California, where ten people were killed, resulted in a $21 million settlement against the city, which operated the market.[33] In Fort Collins, Colorado, produce samples at a farmers' market were linked to an outbreak of *Escherichia coli* O157:H7 that sickened fourteen people and caused hemolytic uremic syndrome in two small children.[34] In addition to carrying adequate insurance, markets may want to implement rules to promote food safety and limit liability. These rules can include guidelines on the types of products that can be sold, requiring proof of insurance by vendors, and requiring vendors to execute a "hold harmless or indemnification" clause in order to commit the vendor to pay for any costs the market may experience as the result of a problem created by the vendor's conduct.[35]

(2) Compliance

Managers of farmers' markets should ensure that market participants comply with food safety requirements and that the market itself maintains all necessary conditions for operating (like access to hand-washing and bathroom facilities), and that other laws are enforced, like restrictions on smoking. Failure to comply with conditions of licenses and permits can result in citation or revocation.

(3) Fraud

Farmers' markets should also monitor and mitigate the potential for fraud. This issue has come to light in recent years in two scenarios. First, there have been some instances of farmers fraudulently representing produce that was purchased as produce they have grown. Second, farmers have been identified as mislabeling organic produce. It is necessary for farmers' market managers to conduct site visits to ensure that the land a farmer claims to grow their food on actually contains plants producing what is being sold at the market.[36]

Local governments and states have also deployed regulatory approaches to address farmers' market fraud.[37] California's certification program requires agricultural commissioners to perform at least one annual inspection on the seller's site to verify that the food product is in fact production or stored on the site.[38] Even with this type of provision, farmers' market managers should be aware that the California provision allows inspectors to verify that the product is on site, but not actually growing on site.[39]

---

[33] *See* Richard Winton & Martha Groves, *Case Is Closed on Deadly Day at Market*, L.A. Times, May 22, 2008.

[34] S. Bridges, *Two Kids Gravely Ill with E. Coli*, Ft. Collins Coloradoan, September 27, 2000 at A1-2.

[35] *See* Hamilton, *supra* note 20.

[36] Farmers' markets in Los Angeles County were found to have a number of farmers' selling produce not grown on their farms, in an investigation conducted by NBCLA. *See* Joel Grover and Matt Goldberg, *False Claims, Lies, Caught on Tape at Farmers' Markets*, NBCLA (September 23, 2010).

[37] Samuel R. Wiseman, *Fraud in the Market*, 26 Regent U. L. Rev. 367, 385 (2014).

[38] *See id.* at 386 (citing Cal. Agric. Code § 47020).

[39] *See id.*

[3] *Mobile Food Facilities*

[a] Conflicts

An old practice that has emerged in recent years and gained attention for both its potential as a way to improve food systems and its culinary novelty is mobile vending. For
centuries urban centers were filled with street vendors; however, with the push to clean
up cities and make them more organized, many cities banned or restricted the practice
of street and sidewalk vending.[40] While street vending has resurfaced in urban communities, cities still have regulatory schemes that hamper the resurgence of mobile vending.
Businesses on private property often object to mobile vending near their business, citing fairness concerns that mobile vendors have lower business costs and will take their
customers.[41]

[b] Defining Mobile Food Facilities

Mobile food facilities are considered mobile food establishments in the 2009 Model
Food Code: "[a] food establishment includes (b) An operation that is conducted in a
mobile, stationary, temporary, or permanent facility or location; where consumption
is on or off the premises; and regardless of whether there is a charge for the food."[42]

States may define mobile food facilities in their own food code. California's retail
food code directly defines mobile food facilities as "any vehicle used in conjunction
with a commissary or other permanent food facility upon which food is sold or distributed at retail."[43] Localities also define mobile food facilities in order to allow for permitting and licensing and to regulate the location and manner in which mobile food
facilities conduct business. For example, Pennsylvania's food code defines a mobile
food facility as "any stationary, movable or temporary food facility – such as a stand,
vehicle, cart, basket, box or similar structure from which food is stored, prepared,
processed, distributed or sold – which physically locates at one site or location for no
more than 14 consecutive days, whether operating continuously or not during this
time."[44]

[c] State and Local Regulation of Mobile Food Facilities

(1) *Health and Food Safety*
State food codes set out the requirements for obtaining a health permit to operate as a
mobile food facility. The requirements for mobile food facilities are risk-based like those
for other food facilities and differ to the extent necessary to adapt to the mobile environment, which typically include requirements for cleaning frequency and storage of the
vehicle.

---

[40] *See generally* Alfonso Morales & Gregg Kettles, *Zoning for Public Markets and Street Vendors*, Zoning
     Practice (American Planning Association), 2 (February 2009).
[41] *See, e.g.*, Santa Monica, Cal., City Council Report on Mobile Vending Trucks, June 21, 2011.
[42] Model Food Code §1–201.10.
[43] Cal. Health & Safety Code §114294.
[44] 7 Pa. Code § 46.3.

(2) *Location*

In terms of space, mobile vending can take place on streets, sidewalks, private property, and public property. Municipalities regulate how and when mobile vending may take place on various types of property. The question of how mobile vending is allowed within public spaces is one that produces broad policy discussions on the history and purposes of public spaces.[45] Some cities allow vending on sidewalks, but others do not. Los Angeles does not allow vending on sidewalks, per its municipal code. Most other large cities allow sidewalk vending, but also regulate some aspects of where mobile food facilities can locate. It is common for cities to designate areas for vending or particular districts. Philadelphia's code identifies the specific streets in the central business district when mobile vendors may sell from the sidewalk.[46] Cities may also restrict vendors from locating on sidewalks near schools or other food businesses. Cities may regulate where mobile food facilities can park next to a curb to vend. Some cities do not create any special requirements for food trucks, only that they must follow parking laws.[47] Other cities restrict mobile food facilities from parking within a particular distance of any other food facility.[48] Laws pertaining to any vending activity in the public right of way may also regulate the hours during which mobile vending may take place and whether vendors may remain stationary or move at certain intervals. For example, in San Jose, California, vendors may not stay in one place longer than fifteen minutes, and may only vend from 10:00 A.M. until 7:00 P.M.[49]

Mobile food facilities may locate on private property that is properly zoned for the activity and that the operator has permission to use. Food truck lots, which are parking lots when mobile food facilities gather and locate, are one way that private property is used by mobile food facilities. Raleigh, North Carolina, made changes to its zoning code to allow multiple food trucks to park together on properly zoned parking lots, provided certain distance requirements are met by the lot (i.e., the lots must be at least 100 feet from another food facility and 5 feet from any driveway or sidewalk).[50]

Municipalities may also allow access to their properties by mobile vendors. Some cities allow mobile vendors in parks with proper permits.[51] Other cities allow them at transit stops.[52] Finally, some local jurisdictions may also differentiate between types of food sold when providing access to permits or space. New York City's Green Cart program provides easier-to-obtain permits for vendors of whole, uncut fresh produce.[53] In San Francisco the city may take into account the type of food, including some aspects of the food related to health, when issuing contracts for vending in parks.[54]

---

[45] *See generally* Morales & Kettles, *supra* note 40.

[46] PHILADELPHIA, PA., BUSINESS TRADE & PROFESSIONS CODE § 9–205.

[47] *See* Report of the Chief Legislative Analyst to the City Council of Los Angeles, Cal., Regulation of Mobile Food Trucks, February 17, 2011.

[48] *See e.g.,* HEALTH & SAFETY CODE, ch 8.09, OAKLAND, CAL.

[49] SAN JOSE, CAL., BUSINESS LICENSES & REGULATIONS CODE, § 6.54.240.

[50] *Food Trucks,* CITY OF RALEIGH (September 5, 2014).

[51] *See e.g.,* Kansas City, Mo., Kansas City Parks and Recreation Vending Policy 4.7.08 (revised December 12, 2006).

[52] *See e.g.,* Recommendation of the L.A. County Metro. Transit Auth. Exec. Mgmt. & Audit Comm., Use of MTA Property for Commercial Activities (July 21, 2011).

[53] *See* NYC Green Carts, N.Y. C. DEPT. OF HEALTH & MENTAL HYGIENE.

[54] *See* SF Parks City and County of San Francisco and San Francisco Recreation and Park Commission. Request for proposals for the operation of specialty food push- carts, at various park locations citywide.

(3) *Licensing*

Local governments may require permits or licenses to operate a mobile food facility within a city, and create restrictions on where mobile food facilities can operate.

Some jurisdictions require a municipal permit to engage in mobile food vending. This permit is beyond the health permit issued by the local health department. For example, New York City required a permit for all mobile food vendors, capping the number of permits issued at 3,100 until its Green Cart program (described in the following section) was introduced.[55] The city of Pittsburgh has also required permits for all mobile vendors by law.[56] Other cities do not require a city-issued permit to vend, but may still require a public health permit.

[d] Emerging Issues for Mobile Food Facilities

(1) *Planning for Vending*

Many jurisdictions have updated their rules for mobile food facilities to streamline them and make them easier to navigate. Other local governments have created rules allowing mobile food facilities to operate for the first time. Experts in the area of mobile vending have outlined eight domains for decision making in planning for mobile vending at the local level: vending locations, exemptions, permit caps, vending area, space allocation, restrictions on certain goods, cart or design display, and fees and taxes.[57] Illustrative of various approaches, Cincinnati in 2011 created a mobile vending program to allow trucks and carts to legally operate in the central business district. As has been the case with many new programs, the city allocated vending spots to maintain greater control over the business.[58] In 2011, Boston began allowing food trucks at designated public properties. Vendors proposed their own spot for approval on private or public property. This program is unique because it also required all vendors to provide a healthier meal option on their menus.[59]

(2) *Economic Liberty Challenges*

Local laws regulating mobile food facilities that restrict mobile vending may be challenged. In *Castenada v. City of El Paso*,[60] four food truck vendors sued the City of El Paso's (Texas) over a ban of food trucks from operating within 1,000 feet of restaurants, grocers, and other food service establishments. The vendors claimed that the regulation's sole purpose was to protect established businesses, which is not a legitimate government interest that would allow the government to infringe upon the constitutional rights of food vendors. As a result of the lawsuit, El Paso agreed to repeal the regulations.[61]

---

[55] Sumathi Reddy, *Prices for Food-Cart Permits Skyrocket*, WALL ST. J., March 9, 2011.

[56] PITTSBURGH, PA., BUSINESS LICENSING CODE §719.01.

[57] *See* Morales & Kettles, *supra* note 40.

[58] *See* Report from the Cincinnati, Ohio Quality of Life Comm. to the City Manager, Mobile Food Vending Pilot Program Report – Fountain Square Zones, November 1, 2011.

[59] *Food Trucks*, CITY OF BOSTON GOV.

[60] No. 3:11-CV-00035-KC (W.D. Tex. filed January 26, 2011).

[61] Keith H. Berk & Alan D. Leib, *Food Truck Regulations Drive Controversy*, BUSINESS L. TODAY (American Bar Association), May 25, 2012.

(3) *New York City "Green Carts" Program*

In March 2008, New York City implemented the city's Green Carts program.[62] Green carts are mobile vending carts that sell fresh, unprocessed fruits and vegetables in neighborhoods that lack access to fresh produce. Products other than fresh produce, like chips or candy, cannot be sold from green carts, nor can fruits and vegetables that have been processed in any way. Operators of green carts have special permits that identify them as participants in the program and restrict the areas where they may set up their carts to the neighborhoods designated in the legislation establishing the program.[63] A few other cities have followed suit, including Philadelphia's Healthy Cart program, which provides incentives for produce carts.[64] Kansas City (Missouri) established incentives for pushcart vendors in city parks. Vendors meeting nutritional guidelines are eligible for a reduction in the cost of a vending permit or a special roaming permit that allows a vendor to operate in three parks with one permit.[65]

(4) *Mobile Groceries*

The use of mobile food facilities to sell groceries has been a typical practice in many neighborhoods for decades. Organizations and municipalities have recently begun projects to promote access to healthier foods through mobile grocery stores or produce markets. New Jersey's Fresh Mobiles Initiative establishes a pilot program for the creation of mobile farmers' markets, which are vehicles carrying fresh produce to underserved neighborhoods.[66]

[e] *Government Procurement Power*

(1) Contracting

State and local governments purchase large amounts of food. As noted in Chapter 5, much of this food goes into schools. Some of it is available to employees through cafeterias and vending machines or in commercial operations on government-owned properties. The government can use its contracting powers to decide the types of foods to purchase for distribution, and interest is increasing in the purchase of healthier foods and local foods by agencies and schools. New York City has created nutrition standards that are comprehensive and apply to all food purchased by the City.[67] Also, the Los Angeles City Council has adopted the "Good Food Purchasing Pledge," a food purchasing policy that promotes environmentally sustainable food production, local sourcing, fair labor practices, animal welfare, and nutrition through food purchasing by the city.[68] Los Angeles Unified School District has adopted the pledge as well.[69]

---

[62] N.Y., ADMIN. CODE §§ 17–306, 17–307, 17–309, 17–325.

[63] *Green Carts Will Increase Access to Healthy Foods, Improving the Health of an Estimated 75,000 New Yorkers*, N.Y.C. DEPT. OF HEALTH & MENTAL HYGIENE (February 27, 2008).

[64] Food Fit Philly, Healthy Carts.

[65] Kansas City Vending Policy, *supra* note 51.

[66] See N.J. REV. STAT. § 4:10–25.3.

[67] *Meals/Snacks Purchased and Served*, NEW YORK CITY FOOD STANDARDS (internet source).

[68] *See Directive No. 24, Good Food Purchasing Policy*, L.A., Cal., Exec. (October 24, 2012).

[69] *See L.A. School Board Adopts Comprehensive Food Policy*, L.A. TIMES, November 13, 2012.

(2) Purchasing Preferences

Local governments, through their role as market participants, often use contracts to purchase healthier food. To increase access to fresh, local foods, especially fruits and vegetables, some governments institute purchasing preferences. Whether a state or local government may promote local food systems by giving preference to purchasing local foods depends on the source of the funds used to purchase food and any restrictions on the use of the funds, and procurement laws.[70] It is typical that a state or local agency that purchases food uses a competitive process to find the supplier who can provide the lowest-priced goods. Government agencies may give a competitive preference to locally grown food. Numerous states have laws requiring state and local agencies to give preference to food grown or processed within the state.[71]

(3) School Lunch and Breakfast Programs

The 2008 Farm Bill amended the National School Lunch Act to direct the secretary of agriculture to encourage institutions operating child nutrition programs, including schools participating in the school lunch and breakfast programs, to purchase unprocessed locally grown and locally raised agricultural products.[72] In February 2011, the US Department of Agriculture (USDA) clarified that the purchasing institutions, school food agencies, child care institutions, and summer food service program sponsors have the authority to choose whether to give preference to locally grown food and, if so, to specify the geographic area within which unprocessed locally raised and grown food products will originate. This USDA statement changed its prior position that states must follow competitive procurement procedures for school lunches and that geographic preferences are illegal.[73]

(4) Local Food Councils

As part of the local food movement, states and cities create local food policy councils "in order to more systematically explore food policy issues and opportunities. The state of Connecticut was the first to create a state food policy council when legislation was enacted for this purpose in 1997."[74] A council often is created through some official government action, such as the passage of a law, the issuance of an executive order, or a proclamation. A food policy council typically comprises diverse stakeholders who come together to examine the operation of a local food system, and provide ideas or recommendations for how it can be improved. Stakeholders may include farmers, city and state officials, nonprofit organizations, chefs, food distributors, grocers, hunger advocates,

---

[70] *See* Pub. Health L. & Policy, Local Food for Local Government: Considerations in Giving Preference to Locally Grown Food (2012).
[71] *See id.*
[72] *See id.*
[73] *See* Memorandum SP 02-2007 from Director of the Child Nutrition Division of Food Nutrition Service (USDA) to all Directors of Child & Special Nutrition Programs (January 23, 2007) (discussing school districts and federal procurement regulations).
[74] Neil D. Hamilton, *Putting a Face on Our Food: How State and Local Food Policies Can Promote the New Agriculture*, 7 Drake J. Agric. L. 407, 440 (2002).

educators, lawyers, health professionals, and concerned citizens.[75] The governance of food policy councils takes various forms and is currently in flux with innovations and new democratic approaches being implemented to enable the councils to meet their goals.[76]

§ 6.03 Sustainability

[1] *Conceptual and Definitional Challenges*

Food sustainability has become an important and all-encompassing descriptor for many of the aspirations in the modern food movement.[77] Food sustainability takes a number of forms and is multifaceted. For starters, it involves the whole food supply chain, which consists of a variety of stakeholders, including producers and all of the players within the food sector, government, and of course consumers. Also, this supply chain is global, cutting across variant cultures, societies, and legal systems. Adding to the complexity is the moral dimension of food serving as the very sustenance of life and of sustainable agriculture production improving the human race and the planet. The multidimensional attributes of sustainability in the food sector are reflected in the difficulties in defining the term.[78] Sustainability broadly defined "meets the needs of the present without compromising the ability of future generations to meet their own needs."[79] This definition evokes seemingly endless boundaries.

A unique feature of food sustainability is the number of food enterprises in the global food supply chain that have adopted sustainability standards. Factors contributing to the private sector's adoption of sustainability standards include an emerging business interest in corporate social responsibility, consumer demand, and a growing awareness of all that is involved in the making of a food product.[80] A typical, broad definition of sustainability from the private sector is "a concept whereby companies integrate social and environmental concerns in their business operations and in their interaction with their stakeholders on a voluntary basis."[81]

---

[75] Harvard Law Sch. Food Law & Policy Clinic, Good Laws, Good Food: Putting Local Food Policy to Work for Our Communities (July 2012); *see also* Mark Winne, *Food Policy Councils: A Look Back at 2012*, Mark Winne (January 8, 2013).

[76] *See* Clare Fox, Food Policy Councils: Innovations in Democratic Governance for a Sustainable and Equitable Food System (December 2010) (surveying emerging food policy council trends).

[77] *See* Gracy Olmstead, *Has the Sustainable Food Movement Failed?*, The American Conservative (June 23, 2015) (asserting that the economic benefits of factory farming are trumping sustainability goals of food movement).

[78] *See generally* NAL SRB 99-02, Sustainable Agriculture: Definitions and Terms. U.S. Dep't of Agric. (2007).

[79] World Comm'n on Env't and Dev., Our Common Future, U.N. Doc. A/42/427 pt. I, ¶ 27 (G.H. Brundtland ed., 1987) (Brundtland Report).

[80] As noted by a prominent global grocer bullish on sustainability: "Customers are the most powerful agents of change there are – and [] by working with them we have some very exciting opportunities for changing society for the better … [P]erceptions of trust are increasingly being shaped not just by price or choice or convenience, but by issues like health, the environment, and social responsibility." Terry Leahy, Chief Exec., Tesco, Serving Customers 3–4, 28th Annual Campden Lecture (June 7, 2006).

[81] Comm'n of the Eur. Communities COM(2002) 347 final, Corporate Social Responsibility: A Business Contribution to Sustainable Development 5 (July 2, 2002).

Notwithstanding these definitional challenges, a consistent theme for food sustainability is its general association with environmental stewardship in a social and economic context. These connections are visible in the 1990 Farm Bill's reference to sustainability as "an integrated system of plant and animal production practices" that (1) satisfies human food and fiber needs; (2) enhances environmental quality and the natural resource base upon which the agricultural economy depends; (3) makes the most efficient use of nonrenewable resources and on-farm resources to integrate; (4) sustains the economic viability of farm operations; and (5) enhances the quality of life for farmers and society as a whole.[82]

[2] Environmental Programs

[a] Historical Perspective: Farm Programs

(1) USDA Conservation Activities and Programs

While sustainable food or agriculture did not emerge in popular usage until the late 1980s,[83] the idea of agricultural sustainability – stewarding the food production resource base for the use of future generations – is not a new phenomenon. The USDA has historically contributed to agricultural sustainability through conservation programs that encourage agricultural producers and landowners to follow conservation practices on their land.[84] The Soil Conservation Act of 1935 established the Soil Conservation Service to assist producers in planning soil management programs with the ultimate goal of protecting land resources from soil erosion.[85] A year later, the Soil Conservation and Domestic Allotment Act amended the Soil Conservation Act to allow the voluntary Agricultural Conservation Program, which gave financial assistance to producers who followed approved soil conservation practices. In 1956, the Great Plains Conservation Program was established to persuade producers to resort to conservation practices in the Great Plains.[86]

(2) EPA Strategy for Agriculture

Fifty years later, in 2006, the Environmental Protection Agency (EPA) announced the EPA Strategy for Agriculture that outlined the agency's commitment to protect the country's food, water, land, and air for future generations. The strategy aspired to "working with the agricultural sector – including production, processing and distribution – in developing and demonstrating environmental protection solutions that express the value of farmland environmental stewardship activities to the public."[87] This aspiration to work toward agricultural sustainability was again reflected in an EPA strategic plan, especially

---

[82] Food, Agriculture, Conservation, and Trade Act of 1990 (FACT Act, 1990 Farm Bill), Pub. L. No. 101–624, 104 Stat 3359, 3705–6 (1990) (codified as amended at scattered sections of 7 & 16 U.S.C.).

[83] Wes Jackson is credited with the first publication of the expression in his *New Roots for Agriculture* (1980). Fred Kirschenmann, *A Brief History of Sustainable Agriculture*, THE NETWORKER (Science & Environmental Health Network, March 2004).

[84] Michael T. Roberts & Emilie H. Leibovitch, *Comparison of EU and U.S. Law on Sustainable Food Processing, in* ALTERNATIVES TO CONVENTIONAL FOOD PROCESSING 11, 37–9 (Andrew Proctor ed., 2011).

[85] *See id.* at 37.

[86] *See id.*

[87] *National Strategy for Agriculture*, U.S. ENVIRONMENTAL PROTECTION AGENCY (April 25, 2006).

in terms of the agency's commitment to find new agricultural measures to encourage clean and affordable biofuels and monitor the use of pesticides.[88]

[b] Farm Bill Funded Operations and Programs

(1) *Applicability of Farm Bill Funding*

There is not an organized approach by the government to food sustainability; instead, the effort is hodgepodge. The most visible aspect of sustainability – preservation of the environment – is no exception. USDA administers the bulk of its sustainability efforts through various programs, which cover activities at the farm-level, via funding from farm bills. In addition to these administrative USDA programs, there are several grant programs designed to promote agricultural research for which projects devoted to the study of sustainable initiatives are expressly eligible.[89]

(2) *2014 Farm Bill*

The most recent Farm Bill, the Agricultural Act of 2014 (2014 Farm Bill),[90] was signed in February 2014, and will remain in force through 2018 – and in the case of some provisions, beyond 2018. The USDA's Economic Research Service (ERS) notes that program practices under the 2014 Farm Bill "range from conservation activities that address natural resource issues and benefit productivity of agricultural working lands, forestlands, and grasslands to wetlands restoration and temporary or permanent land retirement."[91] Government reports also describe the 2014 Farm Bill as streamlining conservation programs and cutting spending.[92] Prior to the enactment of the 2014 farm bill, the agricultural conservation portfolio included twenty-three conservation programs. The conservation title of the 2014 Farm Bill consolidates many conservation programs into new programs or merges them into existing programs, reducing the number of USDA conservation programs from twenty-three to thirteen.[93] Many of the larger existing conservation programs, such as the Conservation Reserve Program (CRP), the Environmental Quality Incentives Program (EQIP), and the Conservation Stewardship Program (CSP) – as outlined in the following section – were reauthorized under the 2014 Farm Bill, while smaller and similar conservation programs were rolled into them.[94]

Below is a summary outline of significant USDA programs that affect conservation and sustainability on the farm in the US and their status under Title II of the 2014 Farm

---

[88] 2009–2014 Strategic Plan Change Document, U.S. ENVIRONMENTAL PROTECTION AGENCY (September 30, 2008).

[89] For example, Conservation Innovation Grants (CIG) is a voluntary program that seeks to develop and stimulate the adoption of creative conservation efforts and technologies that combine federal investments into environmental resources with agricultural production. *See* Office of Environmental Markets, U.S. DEP'T OF AGRIC., FOREST SERV. (July 11, 2011). Also, working-land programs provide assistance (both technical and financial) to farmers who employ conservation practices on land used for production. *See Conservation Programs*, U.S. DEP'T OF AGRIC., FOREST SERV.

[90] Pub. L. No. 113–179, 128 Stat. 649 (2014).

[91] *Id.*

[92] *See Agricultural Act of 2014: Highlights and Implications*, U.S. DEP'T OF AGRIC, ECONOMIC RESEARCH SERV. (August 4, 2014).

[93] *Id.*

[94] *See* Ralph M. Chite, Cong. Research Serv., R43076, *The 2014 Farm Bill: A Comparison of the Senate-Passed (S. 954) and House-Passed (H.R. 2642, H.R. 3102) Bills with Current Law* (October 18, 2013).

Bill.[95] This summary illustrates the dynamic between the farm bill and sustainability efforts by the USDA.

- The Conservation Reserve Program (CRP)

CRP, USDA's largest conservation program, is administered by the USDA's Farm Service Agency (FSA). In exchange for a yearly rental payment, farmers enrolled in the program agree to remove environmentally sensitive land from agricultural production and plant species that will improve environmental health and quality. Under the 2014 Farm Bill, CRP continues through 2018 with an annually decreasing enrolled acreage cap. The contract portion of the Grassland Reserve Program enrollment was merged with CRP.

- Conservation Stewardship Program (CSP)

CSP (formerly the Conservation Security Program) is administered by USDA's Natural Resources Conservation Service (NRCS). CSP rewards farmers with payments who implement conservation practices through an enrollment and stewardship process specified in the program. The 2014 Farm Bill raises the bar for CSP enrollment and reduces the annual enrolled acres in the program from that set under the 2008 Farm Act.

- Environmental Quality Incentives Program (EQIP)

EQIP was started in the 2008 Farm Bill and is administered by the NRCS. Its purpose is to "promote agricultural production, forest management, and environmental quality as compatible goals." The program provides cost sharing, payment incentives, and technical assistance to farmers and livestock producers who make conservation and environmental improvements on land devoted to agricultural production. In the 2014 Farm Bill, EQIP continues to operate and incorporates the functions and funding of the repealed Wildlife Habitat Incentive Program, with at least 5 percent of program funding targeted to practices benefitting wildlife habitat.

- Sustainable Agriculture Research and Education (SARE) Program

SARE is a federally funded organization that helps advance farming systems that are both economically profitable and environmentally sound. SARE funds a number of sustainable agriculture programs through a project grant system in cooperation with the Cooperative State Research, Education, and Extension Service (CSREES). SARE also compiles information and results from these programs and makes them available to the public. SARE received an increase in funding under the 2014 Farm Bill.

- Agricultural Conservation Easement Program (ACEP)

ACEP provides financial and technical assistance to help conserve agricultural lands and wetlands. Under the 2014 Farm Bill ACEP consolidates the functions of previous

---

[95] *See Agricultural Act of 2014*, ERS, *supra* note 92.

programs (Wetlands Reserve Program, the Grassland Reserve Program [easement portion], and the Farmland Protection Program). Annual funding under the 2014 Farm Bill is significantly less than that provided for ACEP predecessor programs in the 2008 Farm Act.

- Regional Conservation Partnership Program (RCPP)

RCPP is a new program started under the 2014 Farm Bill. RCPP is designed to coordinate conservation program assistance with partners to solve problems on a regional or watershed scale. The RCPP consolidates functions of several existing regional programs.

- Crop Production on Native Sod ("sodsaver")

For producers who choose to till native sod, the sodsaver provision in the 2014 Farm Bill reduces crop insurance premium subsidies and limits the yield or revenue guarantee available during the first four years of crop production on native sod that had not been previously tilled. Some limitations would also apply to noninsured crop disaster assistance. The new provision applies only to native sod in Minnesota, Iowa, North Dakota, South Dakota, Montana, and Nebraska.[96]

A contentious provision in the 2014 Farm Bill was the inclusion of the federally funded portion of crop insurance premiums to the list of program benefits that could be lost if a producer is found to produce an agricultural commodity on highly erodible land without implementing an approved conservation plan or qualifying exemption, or converts a wetland to crop production. This prerequisite, referred to as conservation compliance, has existed since the 1985 farm bill and previously affected most USDA farm program benefits, but has excluded crop insurance since 1996.[97]

[c] Key Agencies: Sustainability and Environmental Programs

- Farm Services Agency (FSA)

FSA reports to the secretary of agriculture and to the Farm and Foreign Agricultural Services. Several other agencies merged to create the FSA in 1994, including the Agricultural Stabilization and Conservation Service, the Federal Crop Insurance Corporation (which is now a separate Risk Management Agency), and the Farmers Home Administration. Under the National Environmental Policy Act (NEPA) and the National Historic Preservation Act, FSA is required to consider the environmental and cultural resources effects of its actions. In addition, when deciding how to implement programs, FSA is required to consider various other environmental laws, regulations, and executive orders. FSA administers programs through state and county officers, each of which is responsible for implementing and reviewing programs in compliance with environmental regulations.

---

[96] *See* ERS, *Agricultural Act of 2014, supra* note 92.
[97] Chite, *supra* note 94, at 8.

- Natural Resources Conservation Service (NRCS)

NRCS is the USDA agency responsible for implementing and overseeing most of the conservation-based sustainable agriculture programs. NRCS also provides technical assistance for farmers and ranchers who wish to design conservation practices.

- National Sustainable Agriculture Information Service

ATTRA (formerly the Appropriate Technology Transfer for Rural Areas project) provides information and technical assistance to farmers and ranchers involved in sustainable agriculture with funds provided by a cooperative agreement between the National Center for Appropriate Technologies and the USDA's Rural Business-Cooperative Service.

- Alternative Farming Systems Information Center

AFSIC is a subset of the National Agricultural Library and specializes in identifying and compiling resources about sustainable food systems and agricultural practices.

- Office of Environmental Markets (OEM)

OEM was established in the 2008 Farm Bill and operates within the USDA. OEM, known as the Office of Ecosystem Services and Markets, helps develop markets for ecosystem services. OEM helps to create uniform national standards and a market infrastructure to facilitate a market-based approach to agriculture, forest, and rangeland conservation. Examples of emerging markets include carbon sequestration, water quality, wetlands, and biodiversity. The 2014 Farm Bill left OEM largely intact.[98]

[3] Organic

[a] Value-Based

The growth of organic food reflects the burgeoning interest by consumers in the perceived values of a certain way of growing and handling food. The practice of producing organically grown agricultural food has existed for several decades in the United States, initially as a small-scale and localized system. Early definitions of "organic food" were predicated upon a clear break from industrial agriculture and enveloped a natural approach to food. These concepts are evident in the statement by populist Wendell Berry in 1982 that "[a]n organic farm, properly speaking, is not one that uses certain methods and substances and avoids others; it is a farm whose structure is formed in imitation of the structure of a natural system that has the integrity, the independence and the benign dependence of an organism."[99]

---

[98] See ERS, *Agricultural Act of 2014, supra* note 92.
[99] Wendell Berry, THE GIFT OF GOOD LAND: FURTHER ESSAYS CULTURAL AND AGRICULTURAL (2009).

[b] Organic Food Production Act

While organic food production is marked by platitudes such as those expressed by Wendell Berry, the regulation of the product is in comparison mundane. Food that is designated as organic derives from organic production that is regulated and managed by law. Organic production integrates "cultural, biological, and mechanical practices that foster[s] cycling of resources, promote[s] ecological balance, and conserve[s] bio-diversity."[100] To facilitate the commerce of organic product, states and private agencies starting in the 1960s and 1970s granted organic certification; however, a lack of uniform standards meant that there were variations in what could count as "organic."[101] Accelerated growth of organic production coupled with general confusion as to what qualified as organic led to demand for uniform regulation. Eventually, the Organic Foods Production Act (OFPA) was enacted under the Food, Agriculture, Conservation, and Trade Act of 1990 (1990 Farm Bill), to establish "uniform national standards for the production and handling of foods labeled organic.[102] Chapter 4 outlines OFPA's labeling regime based on its certification system. OFPA has three stated purposes: (1) to "establish national standards governing the marketing of certain agricultural products as organically produced products"; (2) to "assure customers that organically produced products meet a consistent standard"; and (3) to "facilitate interstate commerce in fresh and processed food that is organically produced."[103] These purposes correct the deficiency that a lack of uniformity in standards created.[104]

USDA is responsible for the administration of OFPA. USDA delegates this duty to the department's Agricultural Marketing Service (AMS) agency. OFPA also required the USDA to establish various other programs including the National Organic Standards Board (NOSB), a fifteen-member body that makes recommendations to the National Organic Program (NOP),[105] an organic certification program that bases its requirements on NOSB findings and federal regulations. Finally, OFPA also creates a certification procedure whereby organic producers are accredited once every five years according to federal regulations and the "Meets USDA Organic Requirements."

[c] National Organic Standards Board

OFPA created the NOSB to advise the secretary of agriculture in setting standards upon which NOP is based. The secretary of agriculture has final authority to decide which regulations go to the NOP. The secretary appoints members of the NOSB who serve five-year terms. The membership NOSB is required to include four farmers, two

---

[100] *Welcome to the National Organic Program*, U.S. DEP'T OF AGRIC., AGRICULTURAL MARKETING SERV.
[101] *Organic Foods Production Act Backgrounder*, ORGANIC TRADE ASSOCIATION.
[102] 7 U.S.C. §§ 6501–6522.
[103] 7 U.S.C.A. § 6501.
[104] Various groups, including the National Association of State Departments of Agriculture, the American Farm Bureau Federation, and the Center for Science in the Public Interest, expressed concern that not having uniform standards would confuse customers and undermine the integrity of organic products. Mary V. Gold, *Organic Production/Organic Food: Information Access Tools*, NATIONAL AGRICULTURAL LIBRARY, U.S. DEP'T OF AGRIC. (June 2007). The organic food industry in particular was concerned that the lack of uniform standards impedes growth in the organic market. *See id.*
[105] *See* 7 U.S.C. § 6518.

handlers or processors, one retailer; one scientist (with expertise in toxicology, ecology, or biochemistry), three consumer or public interest advocates, three environmentalists, and one USDA-accredited certifying agent.[106]

NOSB has six committees who cover a range of topics from standards to compliance to accreditation to certification and who develop recommendations for the entire NOSB's consideration. These committees publish official proposals for NOSB with a call for public comments. NOSB meets twice a year to discuss and vote on recommendations. All meetings are free and open to the public. The NOSB then submits its final recommendations to the USDA.[107]

[d] National List

OFPA mandates the creation and maintenance of a National List of approved and prohibited substances.[108] In addition to making clear which products can and cannot be used for products to qualify as organic, the National List clarifies processing and handling requirements for organic products. In 1995, recommendations by organic producers and a review of material that organic producers rely upon became the base of the National List.

The National List is divided into three parts: (1) acceptable synthetic production materials; (2) prohibited natural production materials; and (3) acceptable nonagricultural, nonsynthetic processing aids. The NOSB convenes various Technical Advisory Panels to advise it on materials that should be included on or prohibited from the National List.[109] The Technical Advisory Panels gather and evaluate the scientific data and make recommendations to the board based on review criteria that include sustainability considerations, such as the effect on the farm ecosystem; the probability of environmental contamination during manufacture, use, and disposal; and the overall compatibility with a system of sustainable agriculture.[110]

A unique feature of the National List is that instead of listing inclusions, it contains exceptions to basic understandings within the organic industry. For example, the industry understands and expects that organic products will be produced with solely natural minerals. To avoid the problem of listing every natural material that growers might use, the National List lists exceptions.

[e] National Organic Program (NOP)

(1) Rule

NOP is the regulatory framework governing organic food. OFPA required NOP to set national standards for the production, handling, and processing organic products. In December 2000, AMS published a final rule that created the national standards, found at 7 C.F.R. Part 705.

---

[106] See id. at § 6518(b)(1)-(4).

[107] National Organic Standards Board (NOSB), U.S. Dep't of Agric., Agricultural Marketing Service.

[108] 7 U.S.C. § 6517(a), (c)(1)–(2).

[109] 7 U.S.C. § 6518(k)(3).

[110] OTA, OFPA Backgrounder, supra note 101.

(2) Key Definitions

The final rule requires that any producer or handling operation that sells, labels, or represents agricultural products as organic must comply with the national standards incorporated in the NOP.[111] A "producer" is any person engaged in the business of growing or producing food or feed. A "handler" is any person engaged in the business of selling, processing, or packing agricultural products but does not include retailers who do not process agricultural products. An "agricultural product" is any agricultural commodity or product derived from livestock that is marketed for either human or livestock consumption.[112]

(3) Organic System Plan

Producers and handlers of organic product are required to operate under an organic system plan approved by an accredited certifying agent and use materials in accordance with the National List. An Organic System Plan must include detailed growing, handling, and materials procedures and at least five years of records. Plans must also include future intentions and improvements to production methods and materials. Producers are also subject to annual on-site inspections to confirm methods and materials used. Growers and harvesters of organic wild crops are also required to submit Organic System Plans that show how their harvesting methods are not and will not be destructive to the environment or to the future productivity of the crop.[113]

(4) Certification

NOP also oversees mandatory organic certification programs. Certification is used as a means to ensure that standards and regulations set forth by the OFPA are being followed. All entities or persons who produce, handle, or sell products must be certified. The focus of certification for organic producers are the methods and materials used. There are three main requirements under the certification process dealing with methods and materials used in organic production: (1) methods and materials must meet organic standards; (2) there must be clear and continuous documentation of methods and materials used; and (3) there must be a way to trace products back to productions sites in order to verify methods and materials used.[114]

Certain operations are exempted or excluded from being required to comply with NOP certification requirements. These exempted or excluded operations must still comply with other NOP requirements (i.e., submit an organic system plan). Exempt operations include (1) enterprises with a gross annual income from sales of organic products totaling $5,000 or less; (2) retail food that handle but do not process organic products; (3) handling enterprises that handle products containing less than 70 percent organic ingredients; and (4) handling operations that identify ingredients as organic only on the label of packaged products. Excluded operations include (1) handling operations that only sell organic products that are packaged or enclosed in a container prior to receiving the product and that remain packaged or enclosed without any further processing while under the control of the handling operation, and (2) retail food enterprises that sell but

---

[111] *Organic Farming*, U.S. ENVIRONMENTAL PROTECTION AGENCY.
[112] *See* 7 C.F.R. § 205.2.
[113] *Id.*
[114] Gold, *supra* note 104.

do not process organic products (such as raw and ready-to-eat food from products previ-ously labeled as organic). Producers may also apply for a split operation if only a part of the operation is organic. However, in situations such as this, there must be separate records kept and there must be separation of organic versus nonorganic products, materi-als, and methods.[115]

NOP accredits various entities (including private businesses, organizations, and state agencies) to certify producers and handlers of agricultural products according to NOP regulations. Certifiers must be USDA-accredited agencies. They can be either state or private entities. Each certifier must have an expertise in organic farming and handling techniques. Certifiers must also be able to implement all stages of the certification pro-gram. For example, they must be able to hire an adequate number of inspectors to carry out on-site inspections.[116]

(5) National Standards

The national organic standards promulgated by NOP to govern the qualifications of organic product are detailed and technical. These standards address methods, practices, and substances used in producing and handling crops, livestock, and processed agricul-tural products. The requirements apply to the way the product is created, not to measur-able properties of the product itself. Thus, OFPA and NOP do not address food safety or nutrition.[117]

A few of the notable standards published on the NOP website and elsewhere, includ-ing those especially relevant to sustainability, are listed in the following pages:

○ In order for an imported agricultural good to be labeled and sold as organic, it must be shown that the product has been produced and handled in a manner that is least equivalent to US requirements.[118]
○ In a processed product labeled as "organic," all agricultural ingredients must be organ-ically produced, unless the ingredient(s) is not commercially available in organic form."[119]
○ The following additives are not allowed in organic processing: "sulfites, nitrates or nitrites; any ingredient known to contain higher levels of heavy metals or toxic resi-dues than permitted by federal regulation. Any nonagricultural ingredient that is not organically produced unless it is designated as acceptable on the National List." Water used in organic processing must meet all requirements of the Safe Drinking Water Act.[120]
○ Organic production methods must be evaluated based on their long-term effect on the environment instead of just whether they are synthetic or natural.[121]
○ The use of genetic engineering, ionizing radiation, and sewage sludge is prohibited.

---

[115] *Id.*
[116] *Accreditation Policies and Procedures*, U.S. Dep't of Agric., Agricultural Marketing Serv. (2000).
[117] *See* EPA, *Organic Farming, supra* note 111.
[118] 7 U.S.C.A. § 6505.
[119] EPA, *Organic Farming, supra* note 111.
[120] *Id.*
[121] *See* OTA, *OFPA Backgrounder, supra* note 101.

○ Organic farmers must create adequate buffer zones or barriers between nonorganic farms to prevent pesticides and fertilizers from entering their organic farm. If contamination occurs, the crops cannot be sold/labeled as organic and they cannot be fed to organic livestock.

○ Organic products "shall not contain pesticide residues in excess of the FDA action level or 5% of the EPA tolerance."

○ Handlers must prevent the commingling of organic with nonorganic products and protect organic products from contact with prohibited substances.

It should be noted that the Codex Alimentarius Commission establishes standards for organic labeling purportedly to help prevent consumer confusion and assist countries develop national standards on organic foods.[122]

(6) *Rules for Organically Raised Animals*

Numerous rules apply to organically raised animals. Organically raised animals may not be given hormones to promote growth, or antibiotics for any reason. Instead, preventive management practices, including the use of vaccines, are used to keep animals healthy. Producers are prohibited from withholding treatment from a sick or injured animal; however, animals treated with a prohibited medication may not be sold as organic. All organically raised animals must have access to the outdoors, including access to pasture for ruminants. They may be confined temporarily only for reasons of health, safety, the animal's stage of production, or to protect soil or water quality.[123]

(7) *Enforcement*

AMS is responsible for enforcement of OFPA. The Compliance and Enforcement Division of the AMS is responsible for ensuring OFPA compliance.[124] The Division processes and investigates complaints alleging violations of NOP regulations; conducts proactive compliance and outreach activities; and enforces organic production, handling, and labeling standards. The Compliance and Analysis Program of the AMS is responsible for (1) appeals; (2) assisting the NOP in investigating allegations of "severe and willful violations" for possible civil or criminal penalties; (3) enforcement actions; and (4) reporting to the NOP any appearance of fraud (i.e., making of fraudulent organic certificates).[125] If an operation is selling or representing their products as organic without a certificate, civil penalties and other available enforcement actions are taken. Knowingly mislabeling products as organic may result in a maximum fine of $10,000 and disbarment from the Organic Program for up to five years. Making false statements to the secretary of agriculture, a state official, or a certifying agent are subject to penalties under federal law, and could be grounds for disbarment from the program for five years. Certifying agencies that falsely or negligently certify operations as organic may lose accreditation and not eligible for reaccreditation for three years.[126]

---

[122] Guidelines for the Production, Processing, Labelling and Marketing of Organically Produced Foods, GL 32–1999, Codex Alimentarius Commission (Rome,1999).

[123] *Id.*

[124] *Compliance and Enforcement*, U.S. Dep't of Agric., Agricultural Marketing Serv.

[125] *Id.*

[126] OTA, *OFPA Backgrounder*, *supra* note 101.

[f] State Organic Programs

Approved state organic certification program may impose additional guidelines and
requirements under certain circumstances.[127] State programs are required to assume
regulatory enforcement responsibility for USDA organic operations for their state. States
may add more restrictive requirements according to conditions or necessities in that
state; however, those practices cannot conflict with the USDA national regulations. In
order for a state to create an organic program, a governing state official must submit to
the USDA a State Organic Program proposal. In addition, states cannot discriminate
against out-of-state products that only meet federal guidelines.[128] California is the only
state that has established a certification program.

[4] *Food Processing*

[a] Waste Management

The primary sustainability concern of food processing involves water and the handling
of waste. Water is abundantly used in daily food processing activities. Water serves as
ingredient, but is also used to clean the raw commodities, to transport raw materials, and
to sanitize processing plants and machinery. In addition to the water overuse issue, the
sustainability of food processing is jeopardized by water reuse, which generates wastewater and which leads to pollution and contamination. In general, sustainable practices in
food processing are where processes or product technologies include advanced wastewater treatment practices, water and wastewater reduction, improved packaging, improved
sensors, and process control and food irradiation.[129]

[b] EPA Guidelines

The EPA has issued a set of guidelines on environmental compliance that identify waste
as the main contamination source. The guidelines list provides guidance and techniques
for food processors on the use of materials, processes, or practices that reduce or eliminate the generation of pollutants or waste at the source for food processors.[130]

   The EPA has sought to promote environmental management systems (EMS), which
are sets of processes and practices that enable an organization to reduce its environmental impacts and increase its operating efficiency.[131] An example of EMS is laid out in the
EMS Implementation Guide for the Meat Processing Industry, which provides a regulatory checklist for meat processors, an advisory on the identification of environmental
impacts in meat processing, and suggestions on establishing an environmental management program for meat processing.[132]

---

[127] 7 U.S.C.A. § 6503.
[128] Information for State Organic Programs, U.S. Dep't of Agric., Agricultural Marketing Serv.
[129] Roberts & Leibovitch, *supra* note 84.
[130] *See Multimedia Environmental Compliance Guide for Food Processors*, U.S. Environmental
       Protection Agency (March 1999).
[131] *Environmental Management Systems*, U.S. Environmental Protection Agency.
[132] Environmental Management System (EMS) Implementation Guide for the Meat
       Processing Industry 1–17–1–21, U.S. Environmental Protection Agency.

Various private standards focus on sustainable practices, including specifically the management of waste.[133] Particularly helpful is the *Food Processing Environmental Assistance Center* developed via an industry-government partnership, supported by the EPA's Office of Compliance and Enforcement. Housed at Perdue University, the center provides sustainability resources in the form linkages to environmental laws and regulations specifically tailored to various types of food processing enterprises.[134]

[5] Regulation of Animals for Food

[a] Animals Feeding Operations

(1) Definitions

Animal agriculture increasingly operates on an industrial model that emphasizes efficiency and raises issues about the environment and animal welfare. This model is commonly referred to as Animal Feeding Operations (AFOs). The EPA considers an AFO as an "agricultural operation where animals are held in reserve and raised in confined situations."[135] According to the EPA, AFOs generally congregate animals, feed, manure, dead animals, and production operations on a small land area, where feed is brought in rather than allowing animals to graze.[136] A significant subset of AFOs is AFOs designated as Concentrated Animal Feeding Operations (CAFOs). The EPA defines a CAFO as an AFO that (1) confines animals for at least forty-five days in a twelve-month period; (2) in an area that does not produce vegetation; and (3) meets certain size thresholds.[137] CAFOs are usually corporate owned, which ownership interest covers the entire process, from animal rearing, to slaughter, to packaging and distribution. CAFOs represent the trajectory in the food system from small family farms to large-scale factory-style farms that have increased the efficiency of raising animal food products and raise concerns for consumers.

(2) Clean Water Act Regulation

The EPA focuses on regulating CAFOs because they generate millions of tons of manure every year. When improperly managed, the manure can pose substantial risks to the environment, including water pollution. The two main contributors to water pollution caused by CAFOs are nitrogen and phosphorus.[138]

Aimed at clean water concerns in general, the EPA, under the Clean Water Act (CWA), regulates the amount of manure and wastewater discharged into public waterways.[139] Congress created the CWA in 1972, which significantly amended the Federal Water Pollution Control Act.[140] The objective of the CWA is "to restore and maintain the

---

[133] Roberts & Leibovitch, *supra* note 84, at 57.

[134] *See Sustainability*, FOOD PROCESSING ENVIRONMENTAL ASSISTANCE CENTER.

[135] *Animal Feeding Operations*, U.S. ENVIRONMENTAL PROTECTION AGENCY.

[136] *Id.*

[137] 40 C.F.R. § 122.23(b)(2).

[138] See EPA-821-B-01-001, *Environmental Assessment of Proposed Revisions to the National Pollutant Discharge Elimination System Regulation and the Effluent Guidelines for Concentrated Animal Feeding Operations*, U.S. ENVIRONMENTAL PROTECTION AGENCY (January 2001).

[139] *Id. See also* Concerned Area Residents for the Env't v. Southview Farms, 34 F.3d 114, 117–19 (2d Cir. 1994) (application of manure onto fields by dairy operation that fell within the definition of a CAFO was a form of point source pollution).

[140] *See* 33 U.S.C. §§ 1251–1387.

chemical, physical, and biological integrity of the Nation's waters."[141] The EPA is the agency tasked with implementing and enforcing the CWA. The agency works in conjunction with state environmental agencies and the US Army Corps of Engineers. CWA prohibits the discharge of pollution to waters from any point source unless a National Pollutant Discharge Elimination System (NPDES) permit issued by the EPA authorizes the discharge (or a state delegated by the EPA).[142] Under the CWA, the EPA specifies the maximum allowable amounts of pollution that can be discharged by CAFOs. These general "effluent limitations guidelines" dictate the terms of the specific effluent limitations found in NPDES permits. The EPA places minimum effluent limitations requirements into each permit issue for CAFOs. Unauthorized discharges made from CAFOs violate the CWA, even if unplanned or accidental.[143]

(3) Clean Air Act

Although much of the interest in animal agriculture has focused on the impacts on water resources, increasing attention is focused on how AFOs can affect air quality through emissions of gases such as ammonia and hydrogen sulfide, particulate matter, volatile organic compounds, hazardous air pollutants, and odor.[144] These pollutants and compounds have a number of environmental and human health effects.[145] Gas emissions from the decomposition of animal manure stored in large quantities on CAFOs contribute to the reduction of ambient air quality.[146]

CAFOs typically escape Clean Air Act enforcement since many do not reach thresholds necessary for them to be declared major sources under the act. Plus, the EPA's regulations do not provide a clear methodology for measuring emissions from CAFOs. Negotiations between the EPA and the agricultural industry did, however, result in an Air Compliance Agreement in January 2005. According to the agreement, certain animal feeding operations (AFOs) received a covenant not to be sued from the EPA in exchange for payment of a civil penalty for past violations of the Clean Air Act and an agreement to allow their facilities to be monitored for a study on air pollution emissions in the agricultural sector. The EPA study was released in 2011.[147]

(4) State Regulation

Because many animal feeding operations are not required to seek an NPDES permit under the CWA, states may create their own programs for regulating CAFOs.[148] For

---

[141] 33 U.S.C. § 1251(a).

[142] Ass'n to Protect Hammersley, Eld, & Totten Inlets v. Taylor Res., 299 F.3d 1007 (9th Cir. 2002); 33 U.S.C. §§ 1311(a), 1342.

[143] Claudia Copeland, *Animal Waste and Water Quality: EPA's Response to the* Waterkeeper Alliance *Court Decision on Regulation of CAFOs, in* WATER POLLUTION ISSUES AND DEVELOPMENTS 77 (Sarah V. Thomas ed., 2008).

[144] Claudia Copeland, Cong. Research Serv. RL23947, *Air Quality Issues and Animal Agriculture: EPA's Air Compliance Agreement* (July 20, 2012).

[145] *Id.*

[146] *See* ENVTL. INTEGRITY PROJECT, HAZARDOUS POLLUTION FROM FACTORY FARMS: AN ANALYSIS OF EPA'S NATIONAL AIR EMISSIONS MONITORING STUDY DATA (2011) (showing that levels of some pollutants at some CAFOs, including particulate matter, ammonia, and hydrogen sulfide, are far higher than federal health-based guidelines recommend for human exposure).

[147] *See id.*

[148] *See Animal Feeding Operations – Laws, Regulations, Policies, and Guidance,* U.S. ENVIRONMENTAL PROTECTION AGENCY.

example, in Arizona, CAFOs must obtain an Arizona Pollutant Discharge Elimination System (AZPDES) permit if a CAFO discharges, intends to discharge, or has ever discharged into waters of the United States. The AZPDES permit requires CAFOs to submit a Notice of Intent to Discharge and a Nutrient Management Plan (NMP) as part of the application. CAFO compliance is regulated via on-site inspections. Facilities are subject to enforcement for violations of discharge standards.[149]

Many states have also taken it upon themselves to regulate the air pollution of AFOs. The Minnesota Pollution Control Agency regulates air emissions from AFOs through its Feedlot Program. Feedlots with a capacity of fifty or more animals must register with the agency and apply for a permit and submit an "Environmental Assessment Worksheet" with a manure management plan.[150]

(5) *CAFO Litigation*

Litigation over the regulation of CAFOs is often viewed in the larger context of what sort of food system is desired in the United States.[151] To this end, advocates against CAFOs consider litigation an important tool to achieve food sustainability goals. At the same time, the food industry has engaged in CAFO litigation to stave off alleged government regulation overreach. Notwithstanding the overarching policy debate that CAFO litigation represents, the disputes themselves are generally over the enforcement of specific rules and involve administrative law rather than on engagement on the broader policy issues.

Lawsuits opposing CAFOs arise in a number of contexts. Such suits arise by way of federal regulatory challenges under a variety of federal statutes, including the CWA and the Clean Air Act. Two main types of challenges predominate CWA lawsuits against CAFOs: programmatic challenges (either to federal rules regarding CAFOs under the CWA, or to state programs authorized by the CWA) and specific permit challenges to individual CAFOs.

The seminal case in CAFO litigation is the Second Circuit decision in *Waterkeeper Alliance, Inc. v. EPA*.[152] Environmental and farm industry groups challenged the EPA's Final Rule on CAFOs issued in 2003 and the Second Circuit in *Waterkeeper* issued a decision in a consolidated case. The Second Circuit struck down the regulations and held that the CWA gives the EPA jurisdiction to regulate and control only actual discharges from CAFOs, not potential discharges or the point sources themselves.[153] Following the court's guidance, the EPA promulgated new regulations in 2008, which shifted much of the compliance burden onto CAFOs by forcing them to apply for permits to discharge pollutants if they were already discharging or were designed or constructed to discharge into the waters of the United States.

But industry and environmental groups promptly challenged these regulations. Shortly after publishing the 2008 rule, EPA issued guidance letters helping to explain the scope of the new rule. The letters stated EPA's position that poultry growers must apply for CWA

---

[149] Reagan M. Marble, *The Last Frontier: Regulating Factory Farms*, 43 Tex. Envtl. L.J. 175, 187 (2013) (citing Water Quality Division: Permits: Concentrated Animal Feeding Operation Program (CAFO), Arizona Dep't of Envtl. Quality.

[150] *Id.* (citing provisions of Minn. R. §§ 7020.0200–7020.225 (2014)).

[151] *See* Stephanie Tai, *The Rise of U.S. Food Sustainability Litigation*, 85 S. Cal. L. Rev. 1069, 1080 (2012).

[152] 399 F.3d 486 (2d Cir. 2005).

[153] *Id.*

permits to release dust through poultry confinement house ventilation fans.[154] The industry challenged the guidance letters before the Fifth Circuit in *National Pork Producers Council v. EPA* on grounds that the guidance documents amounted to a substantive rule issued in contravention of the Administrative Procedure Act's notice-and-comment requirements. The Fifth Circuit dismissed the challenge because the letters did not constitute reviewable, final agency action. The court found that the guidance letters merely restated the CWA's prohibition against discharging pollutants without an NPDES permit and had no effect on a party's rights or obligations.[155] Thus, the guidance letters reiterated what CAFO operators always had to do under the CWA: obtain permits for manure and other litter that ventilation fans blew into farmyards.

The Fifth Circuit in *National Pork Producers* agreed, however, with the industry petitioners on the point that the EPA's 2008 rule exceeded the EPA's statutory authority.[156] Relying on *Waterkeeper*, the Fifth Circuit found that the EPA could not require CAFOs to obtain NPDES permits based on a potential discharge because the CWA gives only the EPA authority to regulate CAFOs that are discharging pollutants into navigable waters. The court also held that the EPA could not hold CAFOs liable for failing to apply for an NPDES permit. The court found that Congress explicitly spoke to the issue of liability in text of the CWA and that the statutory list of when the EPA could impose liability did not include failure to apply for an NPDES permit.[157] *Waterkeeper* and *National Pork Producers* made clear that if the EPA wished to regulate CAFOs more extensively to prevent pollution, Congress would have to amend the CWA.

In March 2011, the Michigan Court of Appeals in *Michigan Farm Bureau v. Department of Environmental Quality* upheld a Michigan Department of Environmental Quality rule that requires a CAFO to obtain an NPDES permit if the CAFO has the potential to discharge pollutants.[158] This rule was similar to the federal rule that the Second Circuit in *Waterkeeper Alliance, Inc.* found that EPA did not have the authority to impose. The Michigan Court of Appeals noted that the EPA granted the State of Michigan the authority to administer its own NPDES program and that it "may adopt discharge standards and effluent limitations that are more stringent than the federal standards and limitations."[159] Finding that the powers conferred upon the MDEQ were broader than the powers conferred upon the EPA by the CWA, the court determined that the *Waterkeeper* decision did not apply in the case.[160]

A case brought in 2014 against Washington State dairies further illustrates the role that CAFO litigation can have in shaping the animal food system. The Community Association for the Restoration of the Environment and the Center for Food Safety filed the action against Washington dairies under the Resource Conservation and Recovery Act (RCRA)'s citizen suit provision.[161] RCRA is generally enforced in the context of sanitary landfills and industrial waste disposal, not agricultural operations.

---

[154] Nat'l Pork Producers Council v. U.S. E.P.A., 635 F.3d 738, 748 (5th Cir. 2011).
[155] *Id.* at 756.
[156] *Id.* at 751–2.
[157] *Id.*
[158] 807 N.W.2d 866 (Mich. App., 2011).
[159] *Id.* at 878.
[160] *Id.* at 886.
[161] *See* John G. Dillard, *Can EPA Regulate Animal Operations as Landfills?*, Olsson, Frank, & Weeda PC Ag/FDA Blog.

However, the plaintiffs alleged that the dairies violated Section 7002(a) of RCRA by storing, handling, and disposing of manure in a manner that endangers health and the environment. Furthermore, the plaintiffs contended that the dairies' manure handling activities amount to open dumping of solid waste, which violates Section 4005(a) of RCRA. In addition to seeking recovery of their attorneys' fees, CARE and CFS sought an injunction that would require the dairies to undertake several remedial and preventive actions.[162]

The dairies sought to have the cases dismissed on grounds that manure intended for use as fertilizer is not transformed into solid waste in the event it is overapplied to fields or leaked from lagoons. In rejecting this argument, the court acknowledged that Congress did not intend for manure that is applied as fertilizer to be regulated as a solid waste under RCR, but held that it was untenable that manure could never transform into solid waste through unintentional excess application or leaking from lagoons. The case now rests on whether the plaintiffs can demonstrate that the dairies' manure storage and application activities actually led to manure runoff and leaching as well as leakage into the groundwater.

The dairy cases could have major implications for livestock, dairy, and poultry operations in the United States. Manure is a valuable by-product and a critical component for ecological and economic sustainability in animal farming operations. Animal agriculture is accustomed to regulation under the CWA. However, shoehorning livestock, dairy, and poultry operations into RCRA, a statute intended to regulate waste storage and sanitary landfills, has the potential to create confusion and possibly duplicative regulations.

[b] Animal Treatment Laws

(1) *Philosophical Underpinnings*

A central concern in the food system is how animals for food are treated in AFOs and otherwise. This concern is espoused by a broader, growing animal protection movement. The issue of how animals for food are treated is complex and generates a wide spectrum of philosophical and moral beliefs. Animal protection activists have reframed the debate within a broader policy context. They see links between animal welfare problems and other perceived ills in production agriculture such as an overdependence on chemical pesticides and fertilizers, environmental pollution, the decline of the family farm and rural areas, and unhealthy food products. This treatise does not address the merits of this linkage nor the moral and philosophical debate around the treatment of animals in agriculture except to note that there are two major strains within the animal movement: animal rights and animal welfare.[163] Animal rights are based on the philosophical view that animals have similar or the same rights as humans. Animal welfare supports the use of

---

[162] *Id.* In 2006, EPA sought to hold a swine operation liable under the Resource Conservation and Recovery Act (RCRA) on the basis that manure applied in excess of agronomic uptake rates was a solid waste under the Act. *Id.* The EPA and the swine producer resolved the matter when the producer entered into a consent decree. *Id.* The state of Oklahoma in *Oklahoma v. Tyson Foods, Inc* applied the same theory to poultry litter. "In that case, the court held that manure applied as a useful fertilizer did not *transform* into solid waste simply because its entire contents were not absorbed by crops as nutrients." *Id.* (citing Okla. v. Tyson Foods, 2010 WL 653032 at *10 (N.D.Okla. February 17, 2010)).

[163] *See* Pamela D. Frasch, *Finding Our Voice: Challenges and Opportunities for the Animal Law Community*, 14 ANIMAL L. 1, 3 (2007) (describing the lack of a uniform voice in the animal rights movement).

animals by humans and seeks to improve their treatment and well being.[164] To be clear, regardless of the debate, animals have had the same legal status since the 1800s – that of property.[165]

(2) *Animal Welfare Act*

The primary federal statute that governs the treatment of animals is the 1966 Animal Welfare Act.[166] The USDA's Animal and Plant Health Inspection Service (APHIS) administers the AWA. The act was intended to prevent pets from being stolen for sale to research laboratories, and to improve the treatment and well-being of animals intended for research. Since that time, AWA has been amended multiple times.[167] Under the AWA, businesses and others with animals covered by the law must be licensed or registered, and they must adhere to minimum standards of care. The AWA explicitly excludes farm animals from its regulatory coverage.

Legislation has been introduced on multiple times in Congress to address animal welfare. For example, in the 110th Congress, the Farm Animals Anti-Cruelty Act (H.R. 6202) would have imposed fines on producers who abuse animals in food production. Neither this bill nor other proposed legislation comprising comprehensive welfare provisions for farm animals have been enacted.[168]

(3) *Poultry*

In 2005, the USDA's Food Safety and Inspection Service (FSIS) issued a notice regarding the treatment of live poultry before slaughter.[169] This notice reminded poultry establishments that under the PPIA they must handle live poultry in accordance with "good commercial practices," which includes treating the animals humanely. The notice recognized that there are no specific federal humane handling and slaughter statute for poultry, but notes that poultry, which have been treated inhumanely, are more likely to be adulterated under the PPIA. The notice was published in response to considerable public and congressional interest in the humane treatment of poultry, and it specifically mentions that in 1995 FSIS received a petition from the Animal Legal Defense Fund requesting that FSIS amend PPIA to require humane standards of slaughter for poultry. The court denied the petition on the grounds that there is no specific federal humane handling and slaughter statute for poultry.[170]

In July 2011, the United Egg Producers and the Humane Society of the United States announced that they would work together to push for a uniform national cage production standard for the US egg industry.[171]

---

[164] *See* DAVID FAVRE, ANIMAL LAW: WELFARE, INTERESTS, AND RIGHTS (2008) (providing an overview of the historical development of animal law).

[165] PAUL WALDAU, ANIMAL RIGHTS: WHAT EVERYONE NEEDS TO KNOW 82 (2011).

[166] *See* 7 U.S.C. §§ 2131 et seq.

[167] *See* Tadlock Cowan, Cong. Research Serv., RS22493, The Animal Welfare Act: Background and Selected Animal Welfare Legislation 4–12 (June 12, 2013) (summary of amendments).

[168] *Id.*

[169] Treatment of Live Poultry Before Slaughter, 70 Fed. Reg. 56624-01 (proposed September 28, 2005).

[170] *See id.*

[171] *See* Joel L. Greene & Tadlock Cowan, Cong. Research Serv., R42534, Table Egg Production and Hen Welfare: Agreement and Legislative Proposals (February 14, 2014).

(4) Horse Slaughtering Prohibitions

In 2007, the last of three horse slaughtering facilities were closed following unsuccessful litigation challenges to state laws banning the practice.[172] Beginning in fiscal year 2006, Congress took annual actions in appropriations legislation that effectively prevented the operation of horse slaughtering facilities in the United States by prohibiting USDA's use of federal funds to (1) inspect horses being transported for slaughter and (2) inspect horses intended for human consumption at slaughtering facilities.[173] These annually renewed prohibitions via appropriations were lifted when the Consolidated and Further Continuing Appropriations Act of 2012 did not include any provision prohibiting USDA from inspecting horses.[174] USDA received up to five applications for grants of inspection from prospective horse slaughtering facilities. When one of the facilities filed a lawsuit against the USDA to speed up the decision making by the USDA's FSIS, FSIS agreed to inspect. At that point, the Human Society of the United States sued the USDA, but the Humane Society's request for an injunction was rejected by a US District Court and later affirmed by the US Court of Appeals' Tenth Circuit,[175] which triggered attention by the media.[176] Presumably in response to the public scrutiny, the 2014 omnibus spending bill reestablishes the prohibition against USDA from spending any money to inspect horse-slaughter facilities, effectively preventing horse slaughtering in the United States.[177]

(5) State Laws: Hens, Shark Fins, and Foie Gras

- Hens and Battery Cages

At the state level, laws to prevent deliberate animal cruelty sometimes apply to farm animals, but few states have prescribed on-farm treatment standards. A significant exception to this general rule is in California, where Proposition 2, the Prevention of Farm Animal Cruelty Act, amended California law to prohibit the cruel confinement of farm animals in a manner that does not allow them to turn around freely, lie down, stand up, and fully extend their limbs.[178] Although it applies to all farm animals, Proposition 2 particularly targets commercial hens that typically cannot extend their wings in battery cages.[179]

Concerned that Proposition 2 would harm California farmers economically when eggs in particular would be sold in California from states without regulations like Proposition 2, the state legislature in July 2010 passed California Bill A.B. 1437, which

---

[172] See U.S. Gov't Accountability Office, Gao-11-228, Horse Welfare: Action Needed to Address Unintended Consequences from Cessation of Domestic Slaugter 8 (2011).

[173] See Joel L. Greene, Cong. Research Serv., R42954, Animal Agriculture: Selected Issues in the 113th Congress, Congressional Research Service, 9 (February 11, 2013) (citing FY 2006 appropriations bill PL 109–97 and Consolidated Appropriations Act, 2008 P.L. 110–161).

[174] See id. (citing the Consolidated and Further Continuing Appropriations Act, 2012, Pub. L. No. 112–55, 125 Stat. 552 (2011)).

[175] See Front Range Equine Rescue v. Vilsack, No. 13–2187 (10th Cir. December 13, 2013) (order denying preliminary injunction).

[176] See, e.g., Stephanie Strom, U.S.D.A. May Approve Horse Slaughtering, N.Y. Times, March 1, 2013, at B-1.

[177] Dan Flynn, Omnibus Spending Bill Defunds U.S.D.A. Horse Slaughter Inspection, Food Safety News (January 17, 2014).

[178] Cal. Health & Safety Code § 25990.

[179] Id. at § 25991(f).

required that all shelled (whole) eggs sold in California come from cage-free hens.[180] While Proposition 2 applies only to laying hens in California, A.B. 1437 applies to all shelled eggs sold in California.[181] It is interesting that the stated purposes of this seemingly animal welfare law include the protection of human health: "It is the intent of the Legislature to protect California consumers from the deleterious, health, safety, and welfare effects of the sale and consumption of eggs derived from egg-laying hens that are exposed to significant stress and may result in increased exposure to disease pathogens including salmonella."[182] Other states have also taken action, either by legislation or ballot initiative, to ban gestation crates, veal crates, and battery cages.[183]

Lawsuits challenging California Proposition 2 on grounds that the language of the law was unconstitutionally vague under the US Constitution and the California Constitution have been dismissed.[184] In February 2014, the Missouri attorney general filed a lawsuit in a US District Court in California, challenging the 2010 California egg law on grounds that the California law violates the Supremacy Clause and also the Commerce Clause of the US Constitution, which "prohibits states from enacting legislation that protects its own citizens from competition from citizens of other states" or "regulates conduct wholly outside of the state's borders" or "places an undue burden on interstate commerce." Missouri specifically alleges that California's law would require chickens to be held in slightly larger cages than those Missouri farmers currently use, which Missouri's attorney general argues is essentially taxing out-of-state farmers without representation.[185]

- Shark Fins

Animal welfare matters have emerged in recent years on a state level involving a clash between animal welfare and food culture. The first matter involves shark fins that are obtained via "finning," where a shark is caught, its fin is removed, and the still-alive shark is dumped into the water to die. Shark fin soup is a Chinese delicacy and is consumed at significant cultural events.[186] California banned the sale, possession, and distribution of shark fins within the state. A neighborhood association and the Chinese Neighborhood Association and Asian Americans for Political Advancement sought an injunction against the ban, claiming that the law was unconstitutional and preempted by federal law.[187] The California District Court granted the state's request to dismiss the case, finding in part that the law was constitutional in that it was facially neutral. The court also found that the law did not violate the commerce clause and was not preempted by the federal

---

[180] *Id.*

[181] Cal. Health & Safety Code § 25995–97.

[182] *Id.* at § 25995(e).

[183] Jerry L. Anderson, *Protection for the Powerless: Political Economy History Lessons for the Animal Welfare Movement*, 4 Stan. J. Animal L. & Pol'y 1, 53 (2011) (citing to Maine, Oregon, and Michigan provisions).

[184] *See* Cramer v. Brown, No. 2:12-cv-03130 (C.D. Cal. 2012), *appeal docketed*, No. 12-56861 (9th Cir. October 15, 2012.)

[185] Complaint, Missouri v. Harris, No. 1:14-at-00067 (E.D. Cal. filed on February 3, 2014).

[186] William Peacock, *Shark Fin Ban Argued Before 9th Circuit; Feds Step In*, Find Law (August 19, 2013).

[187] Chinatown Neighborhood Ass'n v. Harris, No. 12-CV-03759, 2014 WL 1245047 (N.D. Cal. March 25, 2014).

Magnuson-Stevens Act, which governs marine fisheries management in US federal waters.[188] Other states have followed California's lead and have banned shark fin sales.[189]

- Foie Gras

Another animal welfare matter that has generated a dormant commerce clause challenge involves foie gras, the production of which involves the force-feeding of a duck for the purpose of enlarging the bird's liver beyond normal size. Animal advocates say the force-feeding fattening method is inhumane, while some restaurants consider foie gras a cultural expression.

In 2004, California enacted S.B. 1520, prohibited the production and sale of foie gras in California.[190] The law does not prohibit the possession or consumption of foie gras, giving it as a gift, or its importation from outside California. Although the law was enacted in 2004, it went into effect in July 2012.[191] In July 2012, a US District Court in Los Angeles in July 2012 denied petitioners' request for a temporary injunction that would have immediately suspended the foie gras ban.[192] The Ninth Circuit upheld the law, finding that it did not violate the Due Process Clause or the Commerce Clause of the US Constitution.[193]

After the Ninth Circuit ruling, the foie gras producers filed an amended complaint alleging that the PPIA preempts the ban. The district court ruled in January 2015 that the state prohibition was preempted by federal poultry standards.[194] The court noted that the PPIA expressly prevents states from imposing additional products that "unduly interfere with the free flow of poultry products" and found that the California ban "imposes an ingredient requirement in addition to or different than the federal laws and regulations."[195] The court therefore enjoined the California attorney general from enforcing the law against the producers' USDA-approved foie gras products. The court rejected the attorney general's argument that SB 1520 prohibits the inhumane treatment of birds by regulating the bird liver production process, and not the ingredients of the ultimate foie gras product. The court relied heavily on the US Supreme Court decision in *National Meat Association v. Harris*, which holds that the FMIA preempted a California law regulating the treatment and sale of nonambulatory swine.[196] California Attorney General

---

[188] *See id.*

[189] *See* Jesse McKinley, *Cuomo Signs Law Banning Shark Fin Sales*, N.Y. Times, July 27, 2013, at A15.

[190] S.B. 1520, 2003–2004 Leg., Reg. Sess. (Cal. 2004), *codified as amended at* Cal. Health & Safety Code §§ 25980–25984.

[191] California S.B. 1520 included a provision that it would take effect almost eight years after enactment, in order to allow time for techniques to be developed by which foie gras could be produced without force-feeding birds. *Id.*

[192] Association des Eleveurs de Canards et d'Oies du Quebec v. Harris, No. 12–5735, (C.D. Cal. September 28, 2012) (Order Denying Preliminary Injunction).

[193] Association des Eleveurs de Canards et d'Oies du Quebec v. Harris, No. 12-56822 (9th Cir. August 30, 2013).

[194] Association des Eleveurs de Canards et d'Oies du Quebec v. Harris, No. 12–5735, (C.D. Cal. filed July 2, 2012) (Order Denying Defendant's Motion to Dismiss and Granting Plaintiff's Motion for Partial Summary Judgment as to Preemption Claim and Partial Judgment as to Preemption Claim) (January 7. 2015).

[195] *Id.*

[196] *Id.*

Kamala Harris in February 2015 announced she would challenge the district court's overturning of the state's ban.[197]

(7) *Private Standards: Humane Meat Standards*

Presumably in response to animal welfare activists and consumer demand, food enterprises have developed humane meat standards to address their concerns. For example, Chipotle through its Food with Integrity program claims that they only purchase from ranchers who raise pigs outside or in deeply bedded pens, who never give their pigs antibiotics, and who feed their pigs a vegetarian diet.[198] A number of third-party certification schemes now exist that provides labeling information for consumers on humanely produced products.[199]

(8) *International Trade*

One of the most significant implications of humane animal treatment enforcement in the United States is the potential impact on international trade under the US international treaty commitment in GATT (see Chapter 2 for a general summary of GATT and food trade). For example, it is unclear whether a nationwide ban on the production and importation of batter cage eggs would violate WTO obligations. The *Tuna-Dolphin* cases cited in Chapter 4 demonstrate how the WTO has held that two commodities – tuna caught in seine nets (which cause high mortality rates among dolphins) and tuna caught in nets designed to reduce dolphin mortality rates are the same product and cannot be distinguished from one another based on the way they are caught.[200] Thus, arguably under GATT, the US cannot take into account the way a product is produced when determining if it is "like" another product because the production method does not change the end product. The argument would need to be made that eggs produced by battery cage hens and eggs produced by cage-free hens undergo such vastly different production methods, that they should not be considered "like" products. For example, if the hens that are fed grass at pasture (as opposed to a seed diet in battery cages) produce a healthier egg and consumers treat battery cage and cage-free eggs differently, then the WTO may construe the products different enough.

(9) *Ag-Gag Laws*

A movement involving the treatment of animals for food that is quite controversial is the passage in states of what are known as "Ag-Gag" laws. A series of undercover videos have exposed animal abuses in farms across the country. For example, a 2011 hidden camera video showed employees at a Texas cattle farm bashing cows' heads with pickaxes, leading to criminal charges for animal abuse.[201] In California, a 2008 video showed workers

---

[197] David Pierson, *California Attorney General to Appeal Reversal of Foie Gras Ban*, L.A. Times, February 4, 2015.

[198] Susanna Kim, *Chipotle: Why Hundreds of Restaurants Don't Have Pork on the Menu*, abcNews, January 14, 2005.

[199] *See, e.g.*, Animal Welfare Approved (AWA) standards, *Standards*, Animal Welfare Approved and the American Humane Certified (AHC) standards, *Science-Based Standards*, Humane Heartland.

[200] *See* Peter Stevenson, *The World Trade Organisation Rules: A Legal Analysis of Their Adverse Impact on Animal Welfare*, 8 Animal L. 107 (2002).

[201] *Mercy for Animals Announces Felony Animal Cruelty Warrants Issued*, Bradenton Herald, May 26, 2011.

pushing downed cows with a forklift to force them to stand for inspection and shooting high-intensity water sprays up their noses.[202] The California video led not only to criminal charges of animal abuse, but also to a recall of 143 million pounds of beef.[203]

In response to these events, states have passed a number of anti-whistle- blower bills known as "Ag-Gag" laws, which limit documentation of agricultural activities. Illustrative of these laws are legislation recently passed in Iowa and Utah.[204] The Ag-Gag Bill passed in Iowa in 2012, the Iowa statute, is titled "Agricultural production facility fraud" and makes it a crime to apply for a job under false pretenses, including applying for a job in order to expose animal cruelty or other harmful conditions.[205] The Utah statute, titled, "Agricultural operation interference," provides that:

> [a] person is guilty of agricultural operation interference if the person: without consent from the owner of the agricultural operation, or the owner's agent, knowingly or intentionally records an image of, or sound from, the agricultural operation by leaving a recording device on the agricultural operation; obtains access to an agricultural operation under false pretenses; applies for employment at an agricultural operation with the intent to record an image of, or sound from, the agricultural operation[.][206]

Opponents of Ag-Gag laws assert that they are unconstitutional. An Ag-Gag law that is broad, includes content-neutral restrictions, and limits distribution of recordings is likely more susceptible to a successful challenge. Ag-Gag laws that intentionally evade issues of speech and expression will be much more difficult to challenge under the First Amendment. For example, the early versions of the Iowa and Utah bills included prohibitions against recording devices left on the premises rather than being held and operated by a person; however, both were later amended to eliminate the broad prohibition against unauthorized recording. A Utah federal district court in 2014 denied a motion to dismiss a challenge to the state's Ag-Gag law.[207]

(10) Nuisance and Right to Farm

Right-to-Farm laws, which protect farmers from nuisance action with the intent of protecting smaller farms from suburban sprawl, have become tools of AFOs and CAFOs to protect their operations from nuisance claims often brought about by claims about the noise, smells, and sounds from these operations. Right-to-Farm laws may not help AFOs whose development or expansion ripens into a nuisance, as most protection against nuisance suits offered by Right-to-Farm laws only extends to agricultural operations that existed before the party claiming the nuisance arrived in the area. However, some Right-to-Farm laws contain language that protects farm areas rather than individual farm operations.[208] Such laws may be found to be unconstitutional. In 1995, the Kossuth County Board of Supervisors created an "agricultural area" of 960 acres, immunizing

---

[202] Andrew Martin, *Agriculture Dept. Vows to Improve Animal Welfare*, N.Y. Times, February 29, 2008, at C3.
[203] *Id.*
[204] Dan Flynn, *Five States Now Have 'Ag-Gag' Laws on the Books*, Food Safety News, March 26, 2012.
[205] Iowa Code Ann. § 717A.3A(1)(b).
[206] Utah Code Ann. § 76-6-112(4).
[207] Linday Whitehurst, *Judge Refuses To Throw Out Challenge To Utah's 'Ag-Gag' Law*, Huffington Post (August 8, 2014).
[208] *See, e.g.*, Ind. Code Ann. § 32-30-6-9(b).

farms within this area from most nuisance suits. The Iowa Supreme Court found that the law created an easement, resulting in an unconstitutional taking of property. The court equated the right to maintain a nuisance to a physical invasion of property, and held that a taking had occurred when a law was created that immunized farms from nuisance suits.[209]

The Iowa law involved in *Bormann* differs from most states' Right-to-Farm laws that grant agricultural operations a nearly absolute right to create a nuisance, regardless of whether the neighbors "came to the nuisance" or acquiesced in its creation. Because of the exceptional nuisance protection provided by the Iowa laws, courts have distinguished other states' Right-to-Farm laws and found them not to constitute unlawful takings.[210] For example, a Minnesota federal district court distinguished *Bormann* on grounds that the Minnesota Right-to-Farm Act created a two-year window before the immunity from nuisance suit applies. In contrast to Iowa where the Right-to-Farm law created immediate immunity from nuisance suit, neighboring landowners in Minnesota maintained their ability to bring suit for at least two years, meaning that no easement is created and the neighboring landowners are not deprived of any property rights.[211]

[c] Food Waste

Wastage of food in the United States has caught the attention of sustainability advocates in recent years.[212] A 1997 report by the USDA Economic Research Services cited that the United States could feed 20 million Americans if the nation recovered just a quarter of the edible food that was wasted in 1997. Their figures put annual waste at 5.4 billion pounds at the retail level and 91 billion pounds by consumers and foodservice, which is likely already out of date. The study also reported 32 percent of fresh vegetables in supermarkets, restaurants, and households are wasted. Moreover, the study cautions that these "estimates of . . . losses are likely understated due to limitations in the published studies on which [the] estimates were based." Finally, the report notes that the USDA was not able to quantify food losses that occur on the farm or between farm and retail levels, but speculates that such losses can be significant for many commodities.[213] A more recent study estimates that 29 percent of food is wasted in the United States.[214]

The 1996 Federal Bill Emerson Good Samaritan Act provides that as long as certain requirements are met and if a food donation later causes an injury, the donor will not be held liable for that injury.[215] The donor may be liable only for acts constituting gross negligence or for intentional misconduct. The requirements that must be met are (1) the

---

[209] Bormann v. Bd. of Sup'rs In & For Kossuth Cnty., 584 N.W.2d 309, 311, 313–14 (Iowa 1998). *See also* Gacke v. Pork Xtra, L.L.C., 684 N.W.2d 168 (Iowa 2004) (Iowa Supreme Court reaffirms the Bormann holding in a case challenging a similar right to farm statute applicable to CAFOs).

[210] *See, e.g.*, Overgaard v. Rock Cnty. Bd. of Comm'rs, No. CivA.02-601, 2003 WL 21744235 (D. Minn. July 25, 2003).

[211] *Id.*

[212] *See, e.g., Reducing Food Waste*, HARVARD FOOD LAW AND POLICY CLINIC.

[213] Linda Scott Kantor et al., *Estimating and Addressing America's Food Losses*, ECONOMIC RESEARCH SERVICE, U.S. DEP'T AGRIC. (1997).

[214] *See* Jean C. Buzby & Jeffrey Hyman, *Total and Per Capita Value of Food Loss in the United States*, 37 FOOD POLICY 561, 562 (2012).

[215] 42 U.S.C. § 1791.

donated food must be either an "apparently wholesome food" or an "apparently fit grocery product; (2) the donor must donate the items in good faith; (3) the donation must
be made to a nonprofit organization; and (4) the nonprofit organization must distribute
the donated items to needy individuals.[216] The Act does not waive state and local health
regulations: the Act expressly states that "[n]othing in this act shall be construed to supersede State or local Health regulations."[217]

In reference to the Act, the Department of Justice has stated "[w]e believe that the
legislative history of the Act, together with its express purpose and the context in which
it was enacted, indicate that Congress intended to establish a 'uniform national law' that
displaces conflicting state [G]ood [S]amaritan statutes – i.e., those that provide less liability protection than federal law."[218] To date, no state has challenged this preemption
interpretation and it is doubtful that states would disturb the Emerson Act because of the
benefits they derive from it.[219] It appears then that states are free to increase the amount
of liability protection afforded to those involved or to expand the covered activities and
personnel.[220]

[d] Aquaculture

(1) *Emerging Sustainable Development*

An emerging area of food production of interest to consumers that demonstrates the
opportunities and challenges of a sustainable food system is the development of aquaculture. The appeal of the development of aquaculture is due to several factors. First, aquaculture is driven in part by the global food system. The United States imports 91 percent
of the seafood consumed by US consumers.[221] Other countries are developing regulatory
systems and investing in aquaculture production because of the economic opportunities
that come with it. Second, aquaculture is connected to nutrition given the comparative
health benefits of consuming fish, rather than other meats, for protein. Finally, aquaculture is seen as instrumental in economic development, particularly in urban areas. On
the other side of the ledger, concerns about aquaculture largely involve its impact on the
surrounding environment.

As an emerging area of food production, the definition of "aquaculture" commands
attention. The National Aquaculture Act of 1980 (NAA) defines "aquaculture" as the
"propagation and rearing of aquatic species in controlled or selected environments,
including but not limited to, ocean ranching (except private ocean ranching of Pacific
salmon for profit in those States where such ranching is prohibited by law)."[222] Some

---

[216] *Id.* at § 1791(c)(1).

[217] *Id.* at § 1791(f).

[218] Memorandum from the Office of Legal Counsel, U.S. Department of Justice, to James S. Gilliland, general counsel, USDA 1 (March 10, 1997).

[219] *See* David L. Morenoff, *Lost Food and Liability: The Good Samaritan Food Donation Law Story*, 57
FOOD & DRUG L.J. 107, 131 (2002).

[220] James Haley, *The Legal Guide to the Bill Emerson Good Samaritan Food Donation Act*, ARKANSAS LAW
NOTES (August 8, 2013).

[221] *See NOAA Fisheries Posts Statistical Report Card for U.S. Fisheries in 2011*, NOAA FISHERIES (September
19, 2012).

[222] 16 U.S.C. § 2802. An "aquaculture facility" means any land, structure, or other apparatus that is used for
aquaculture and is located in any state, including: laboratories, hatcheries, rearing ponds, pens, raceways,
incubators, and other equipment used. *Id.*

states where the development of aquaculture is of particular interest also define aquaculture. In California, the State Fish and Game Code defines aquaculture as "that form of agriculture devoted to the propagation, cultivation, maintenance, and harvesting of aquatic plants and animals in marine, brackish, and fresh water."[223] The code expressly excludes from the definition of aquaculture "species of ornamental marine or freshwater plants and animals not utilized for human consumption or bait purposes that are maintained in closed systems for personal, pet industry, or hobby purposes."[224] The California Public Resource Code defines aquaculture as "the culture and husbandry of aquatic organisms, including, but not limited to, fish, shellfish, mollusks, crustaceans, kelp, and algae."[225] The Florida Aquaculture Policy Act defines aquaculture simply as "the cultivation of aquatic organisms."[226]

(2) Organization of Aquaculture Regulation

Congress passed the NAA to promote private aquaculture development and to help facilitate coordination among federal agencies with aquaculture programs.[227] The NAA authorizes the USDA, the Department of Commerce, and the Department of the Interior to develop a National Aquaculture Development Plan, to identify aquatic species and make recommendations to public and private sector on issues including research and development, technical assistance, extension and education services, and training.[228] Published in 1983 by the Joint Subcommittee on Aquaculture, which was created by the Act, the plan covers a number of developmental areas, including facility design, water quality management, use of waste products, nutrition and development of economic foods, life history, disease control, processing and marketing, production management, and quality control.[229] The NAA does not, however, create regulatory oversight over the development or management of aquaculture.[230]

Other than the NAA, there are no federal statutes that deal directly with aquaculture. Certain federal acts – such as the Federal Water Pollution Control Act, the Food, Drug and Cosmetic Act, the Animal Drug Availability Act, and the Magnuson-Stevens Fisheries Conservation Act – do not significantly address aquaculture, but provide the statutory framework for regulating food safety, veterinary medicines, HACCP programs, coastal zone management, and other activities related to aquaculture.

Thus, the leading food regulatory agencies – the FDA, USDA, and EPA – regulate that part of the aquaculture industry that falls within the scope of their mandated duties. The FDA regulates food safety and drug approvals; the USDA through its agency APHIS regulates the protection of aquatic animal health; and EPA regulates waste water permitting. Additional federal agencies involved in aquaculture include most significantly

---

[223] Cal. Fish & Game Code § 17.

[224] Id.

[225] Id. at § 828.

[226] Id. at § 597.0015(1).

[227] 16 U.S.C. § 2801.

[228] Id. at § 2803.

[229] See generally NATIONAL AQUACULTURE DEVELOPMENT PLAN, U.S. DEP'T OF AGRIC, NATIONAL RESEARCH SERV. (1983).

[230] See Garrett Wheeler, A Feasible Alternative: The Legal Implications of Aquaculture in the United States and the Promise of Sustainable Urban Aquaculture Systems, 6 GOLDEN GATE U. ENVTL. L.J. 295, 306 (2013).

the Department of Commerce's National Oceanic and Atmospheric Administration (NOAA) Office of Aquaculture.[231] The NOAA conducts scientific knowledge research to facilitate innovative and sustainable approaches to aquaculture, to develop connections with other bodies that regulate aquaculture, and to conduct outreach and education surrounding issues pertaining to aquaculture.[232] In June 2011, NOAA and the Department of Commerce released national aquaculture policies that establish a framework to allow sustainable approaches to aquaculture.[233] The initiatives include (1) a "National Shellfish Initiative" to increase shellfish farming and restoration; (2) a "Gulf of Mexico Fishery Management Plan for Aquaculture"; and (3) a "Technology Transfer Initiative" to foster partnerships, start private sector investments, and create employment opportunities in coastal communities – all in an attempt to promote sustainable practices in aquaculture.[234] The USDA's Animal and Plant Health Inspection Service (APHIS) has instituted programs that address both plant and animal aquaculture issues, including disease prevention, pest prevention, and wildlife damage management. APHIS is also involved in the importation and exportation of aquaculture products.[235]

A number of international arrangements and agreements to which the US is a party pertain to the development of aquaculture and may be relevant to regulation.[236] For example, in 1982, the United Nations Conference on the Law of the Sea (UNCLOS) created offshore territorial boundaries that helped to establish economic zones and rights for fisheries for coastal nations. Although some countries have not ratified the convention, UNCLOS acts as the de facto set of guidelines for the world's oceans. The UN has also developed a Code of Conduct for Responsible Fisheries that is based on UNCLOS and other international laws.[237]

The regulation of aquaculture is most robust at the state level, particularly in the states that border the Gulf of Mexico (Florida, Louisiana, and Alabama) and California. In fact it is common for the states to monitor and enforce both federal and state regulations for aquaculture.[238] It is expected that aquaculture will receive more attention by domestic and international regulatory bodies as it continues to grow and develop. As for now, federal, state, or a mixture of federal and state laws regulates the various components of aquaculture.

- Planning and Permitting

Foundational to the establishment of an aquaculture enterprise is licensing and access to land and water, two activities primarily governed by the states. The requirements for

---

[231] *Office of Aquaculture*, NOAA FISHERIES SERVICE.

[232] *See Department of Commerce and NOAA Aquaculture Policies*, NOAA FISHERIES SERVICE.

[233] *Commerce and NOAA Release National Aquaculture Policies to Increase Domestic Seafood Production, Create Sustainable Jobs, and Restore Marine Habitats*, NOAA FISHEREIES SERVICE.

[234] *Id.*

[235] Aquaculture Disease Information, ANIMAL & PLANT HEALTH INSPECTION SERVICE, U.S. DEP'T OF AGRIC.

[236] *See id.* (list of activities and agreements).

[237] *See Code of Conduct for Responsible Fisheries*, FOOD & AGRIC. ORG. CORPORATE DOCUMENT REPOSITORY (September 6, 2014).

[238] *See National Aquaculture Legislation Overview: United States of America*, FOOD AND AGRIC. ORG. OF THE UNITED NATIONS.

differing locations vary based on the needs of the regions. The owner of an aquaculture facility likely would be required to register with a state department. It is also likely that the location of the operation and the species grown will be required to be disclosed. A description of the facility and operation may be required. A license may not be issued if the operation is detrimental to native wildlife and some activities may be curtailed. For example, in Florida, operators may not use a dredge or any means other than hand tongs to remove oysters from natural or artificial state reefs or beds.[239] A license may be conditional on certain environmental considerations, as in California, where state water bottoms can be leased only if the California Fish and Game Commission determined that the lease is in the public interest

- Water

Wastewater discharge and water quality are regulated at the state and federal level. The EPA is the lead federal agency that regulates this issue. The Department of Water Resources is the lead agency in California to regulate this issue. The CWA regulates activities that discharge pollutants into navigable waters (including construction or operation of a facility) and requires that enterprises must receive a state-issued permit that certifies that the discharge of pollutants is in compliance with specified federal standards. The state must provide public notice when it receives applications for such permits and providing hearings if necessary. The California State Water Resources Control Board, which is responsible for monitoring and enforcing EPA regulations in California, can issue an NPDES permit.[240] The NPDES authorizes the EPA to permit the discharge of pollutants into "navigable waters" of the United States (i.e., rivers, lakes, and streams that cross state boundaries). The EPA also maintains a Coastal Water Quality Monitoring Program that collects scientific data that measures the quality of the nation's coastal ecosystems. The program coordinates with other federal agencies that have been similarly tasked under the CWA in order to collect data. States, such as California, that offer discharge pollutant permits to coastal aquaculture facilities must turn over data in compliance with the program.[241]

- Movement

Both federal and state authorities regulate the movement of fish. A Prior Notice of Imported Food Shipments must be filed with the FDA before fish is imported. An importer must provide written verification that the fish or fish products were processed in accordance with FDA regulations. In California, it is unlawful to import live fish, fresh or saltwater animals, or aquatic plants into the state without submitting the stock for inspection. In California, the Fish and Game Commission has the authority to regulate the movement, sale, and possession of fish and aquaculture products in order to protect native wildlife. Before importing live aquatic plants or animals, it is necessary to get written approval from the commission. The commission can inspect the aquaculture

---

[239] FLA. STAT. § 597.010(18)(a).
[240] *National Pollutant Discharge Elimination System (NPDES) – Wastewater*, CALIFORNIA ENVIRONMENTAL PROTECTION AGENCY STATE WATER RESOURCES CONTROL BOARD.
[241] *Id.*

facilities, of each person holding a permit. The commission can also require importers to receive a certificate of veterinary inspection, which certifies that the animal is healthy and shows no sign of contagious or communicable diseases.[242]

- Disease Control

The FDA, APHIS, and Fish and Wildlife Service (FWS) are together responsible for the regulation, research, and control of fish-related diseases and pests that may affect the health of the fish, other animals, or humans. States also assume responsibility for disease control. For example, in California, the Fish and Game Commission's inspection extends to entering any car, warehouse, depot, ship, or growing area where any fish are held or stored, in order to examine and to ascertain whether such fish are infected, diseased, or parasitized. If any of the diseases or parasites is found, the commission may establish a quarantine area and list the aquatic plants and animals affected by the quarantine.[243]

- Drugs

The FDA regulates the use of drugs and the use of feed additives used in aquaculture activities. When fish are diseased (due to bacteria, fungi, parasites, viruses, or poor water quality) the FDA's Center for Veterinary Medicine (CVM) is responsible for working with other government agencies, aquaculture groups, and fish health professionals to promote the proper use of legal drugs. When CVM decides to use a particular drug to treat fish sick, NEPA applies. NEPA requires CVM to consider the effects of drugs on the environment before drugs are approved for use. Drug producers are required to conduct studies and prepare an Environmental Assessment to prove that their drug is not environmentally harmful. The CVM also encourages scientific research to develop safe and effective drugs for fish.[244]

- Animal Feed

The CDFA is responsible for the regulation and manufacturing of commercial animal feed in California. Commercial feed includes all material used as feed or feed mix, but does not include feed used for domestic pets.[245]

- Pesticides

The CDFA has the authority to establish tolerances for pesticide chemicals that are considered safe for consumption in California and may inspect and take samples of any product. If the fish do not meet standards, the CDFA director must notify the state director of Health Services.[246]

---

[242] *See* Food & Agric. Org. of the United Nations, *supra* note 238.
[243] *See id.*
[244] *Aquaculture and Aquaculture Drug Basics*, U.S. Food & Drug Admin.
[245] *See* Food and Agric. Org. of the United Nations, *supra* note 238.
[246] *Id.*

- Safety

As noted in Chapter 3, all seafood processors must comply with FDA Fish and Fishery Products HACCP regulation.[247] The FDA HACCP program focuses on food safety hazards associated with fish species and processes. FDA has enforcement authority and may take regulatory action in the event of noncompliance with HACCP regulations. The federal HACCP plan must list the food safety hazards associated with fish species and processes that are likely to occur, and identify the conditions that must be controlled for each type of fish. In formulating the program, producers should give consideration to whether hazards are likely to occur as a result of natural toxins, microbiological contamination, chemical contamination, pesticides, and drug residues.[248]

- Organic

Currently, there is no US government-approved organic seafood. Some seafood products are in fact labeled as organic based on criteria set by a private certification company, or in accord with European standards. The state of California does not allow any seafood to be marketed as organic in lieu of USDA organic standards; it remains the only state to have passed such a law.[249]

Proposed rules for organic aquaculture were to be ready for public comment in early 2013,[250] but have not been released to date. It is likely that the production and use of fishmeal for fish feed will be one of the major issues during the public comment phase.

[6] *GMO Litigation*

[a] Sustainability Challenge

As shown in Chapters 3 and 4, genetically engineered food (GE or GMO food) often triggers intense objections from members of the food movement. The Center for Food Safety, a group established "for the purpose of challenging harmful food production technologies and promoting sustainable alternatives," describes the use of GMOs "as one of the greatest and most intractable environmental challenges of the 21st Century."[251] Critics of this view generally regard such GE resistance as a sort of "Frankenstein" narrative, grounded in a social construct without a scientific basis. Chapter 3 gives an accounting of the unsuccessful attempt by a coalition of public interest and environmental groups in *Alliance for Bio-Integrity v. Shalala* to challenge the FDA's presumption that GE foods are "generally recognized as safe" (GRAS). Opponents of GE food have since then attempted to use the tool of litigation to fashion a food system that recognizes a place for social values in the evaluation of GE food approval.

---

[247] 21 C.F.R. § 123.
[248] *See id.*
[249] *See* Cal. Health & Safety Code § 110827.
[250] *USDA Works to Create Organic Aquaculture Standards*, Food Safety News (May 25, 2012).
[251] *About Genetically Engineered Foods*, Center for Food Safety.

[b] Challenges to Approval

One type of challenge to GE foods is getting agency approval for the use of GE foods. The issue in these challenges is whether the USDA's APHIS failed to comply with the National Environmental Policy Act (NEPA), under which agencies must prepare an environmental impact statement (EIS) for "major federal actions significantly affecting the quality of the human environment."[252] An early example of such a challenge was a lawsuit filed by the Center for Food Safety against APHIS's issuance of permits to ProdiGene, Monsanto, H.A.R.C., and Garst Seed for the open-air testing of crops in Hawaii engineered to produce pharmaceuticals. The Ninth Circuit agreed with plaintiffs that APHIS had failed to perform a systematic determination of the effects of the permits on endangered species, emphasizing "Hawaii's extensive number of threatened and endangered species."[253] The court also agreed that some type of environmental evaluation – either an EIS or an EA – was required under NEPA, rejecting APHIS's argument that the project automatically fell under one of the regulatory categorical exclusions to NEPA.[254] The court did reject plaintiffs' assertion, however, that NEPA requires APHIS to assess the effects of the permit as part of a broader program of allowing genetically engineered plants into the environment. The court also held that APHIS's alleged inadequate response to the plaintiffs' petition was not justiciable under the Administrative Procedure Act ("APA") because APHIS's decision to avoid promulgating additional regulations or creating a public database was not the type of discrete agency action that fell under the APA provisions allowing plaintiffs to challenge agency decisions in court.[255] Finally, the planned field tests were already conducted by the time the case was decided; thus, the court could issue only declaratory relief rather than injunctive relief, as requested by plaintiffs.[256] One legal scholar concluded that notwithstanding the mixed result in the case, because NEPA allows for expression of a broader range of values than those expressed in the applicable federal statutes – CWA, CAA, and CERCLA – "the case may have also enhanced the sustainable food movement's aim of creating a food system that can honor spiritual and cultural well-being by allowing such values to be expressed and considered during the comment process."[257]

In *Monsanto v. Geertson Seed Farms*, the US Supreme Court found a nation-wide injunction against partial deregulation by APHIS of Roundup-ready alfalfa flawed because that partial deregulation could be challenged in a subsequent NEPA lawsuit and a narrower planting of GMO alfalfa might not cause irreparable harm.[258] It has been noted, however, that *Monstanto v. Geertson See Farms* "ultimately advances a number of values put forth by the sustainable food movement." The same scholar referenced in the *Center for Food Safety v. Johanns* case – Stephanie Tai – commented as follows on *Monsanto*:

> By considering relevant such factors as participation in the organic market as a part of its standing analysis, the Supreme Court gave weight to values such as consumer choice

---

[252] 42 U.S.C. § 4332(2)(C).
[253] Ctr. for Food Safety v. Johanns, 451 F. Supp. 2d 1165, 1170–1 (D. Haw. 2006); Ctr. for Food Safety v. Veneman, 364 F. Supp. 2d 1202, 1205–6 (D. Haw. 2005).
[254] *Id.* at 1184–6.
[255] *Id.* at 1195.
[256] *Id.* at 1195–9.
[257] Stephanie Tai, *The Rise of U.S. Food Sustainability Litigation*, 85 S. Cal. L. Rev. 1069, 1124 (2012).
[258] Monsanto Co. v. Geertson Seed Farms, 561 U.S. 139, 158–9 (2010).

and expressiveness, as well as economic sustainability of the food system for producers and consumers – including those in the organic community. The litigation as a whole also contributed toward availability of knowledge regarding the system through which food is produced. By achieving a requirement that APHIS, on remand, must conduct a more thorough analysis of the environmental effects of GMO alfalfa, the litigants were able to compel the production of a study that would further inform the public about the effects of a particular type of food production system (GMO alfalfa) on the environment.[259]

It may be that the more expansive drafting of NEPA, which sets forth no numerical standards, allows for greater interjection of competing social values identified with sustainable food.

[7] Sustainability and Dietary Guidelines

The Dietary Guidelines jointly issued by the DHHS and USDA in February 2015 included sustainability criteria in the Dietary Guidelines recommendations. The guidelines inextricably link sustainability to nutrition. The guidelines define sustainable diets as "a pattern of eating that promotes health and well-being and provides food security for the present population while sustaining human and natural resources for future generations."[260] The guidelines specifically "recognize[] the significant impact of food and beverages on environmental outcomes, from farm to plate to waste disposal, and therefore, the need for dietary guidance to include the wider issue of sustainability.[261] The American Farm Bureau Federation promptly criticized the recommendations "foray into sustainability issues" as "well beyond both the group's expertise and its clearly defined mission."[262] The legal significance of this linkage between nutrition and sustainability remains to be seen.

[8] Private Sustainability Standards

[a] Contract Law

Much of the development of sustainable practices in the global food supply chain is due to private standards issued by food enterprises. As noted previously in this treatise, private standards are generally imposed upon suppliers by way of contract. The contract terms often place a higher burden of performance than that imposed by regulation. As a practical matter, these contracts do not include parties with equal bargaining powers. It is difficult for players in the food chain upstream who lack leverage to bargain private standard terms in a contract that incorporates sustainability or environmental obligations. As a result, downstream players, especially retailers and national restaurant chains, are able to impose the sustainability conditions they want on suppliers.[263]

---

[259] Tai, *supra* note 257, at 1128.

[260] Scientific Report of the 2015 Dietary Guidelines Advisory Committee, U.S. Dep't of Agric. and U.S. Dep't of Health and Human Serv.

[261] *Id.*

[262] Statement by Bob Stallman, president of American Farm Bureau Federation, February 20, 2015.

[263] *See* Michael T. Roberts, The Compatibility of Private Standards with Multilateral Trade Rules: Legal Issues at Stake, *in* The Evolving Structure of World Agric. Trade 253, 262 (2009).

These private standard contracts often govern stakeholders in the global food supply chain who are either in the US or in another country. An important question in cross-border transactions is which law applies. The Uniform Commercial Code (UCC) is the primary body of commercial law for domestic transactions in the US and has been adapted in all fifty states. For international transactions involving US companies, the United Nations Convention on Contracts for the International Sale of Goods (CISG) is gradually supplanting the UCC.[264]

[b] Speech and Public Scrutiny

The widespread use of private sustainability commitments by food enterprises in a food supply chain that consists of multiple stakeholders creates a possible risk for food firms where purported sustainable practices do not meet the commitment as advertised. This speech venue risk is illustrated by the case of *Kasky v. Nike*, in which the California Supreme Court addressed statements and advertisements made by Nike over Nike's labor practices in foreign countries.[265] The California Supreme Court held that Nike's statements were not protected political speech under the First Amendment but rather commercial speech with an economic motivation to promote and protect product sales.[266] The upshot of the *Nike* decision is that factual statements made by food enterprises in corporate social responsibility statements could be construed, at least in California, as commercial speech.

[c] Trade Implications

The concerns over the international trade implications derived from private standards in the international food sector are unique and point to the complexities of food regulation in the global food supply chain that can generate unintended consequences, such as how do small producers cope with the costs of compliance with private standards in investing in upgrades and certification.

In reaction to the trend toward increasingly strict private standards, developing countries have turned to the World Trade Organization (WTO) to explore whether relief may be available under multinational international law instruments, namely, the Agreement on the Application of Sanitary and Phytosanitary Measures (SPS) and Agreement on Technical Barriers to Trade (TBT). (See Chapter 2 for an explanation of the SPS and TBT agreements.) The debate could have implications in the US over the use of private standards, including sustainability standards. The debate first took hold at an SPS Committee meeting held in June 2005, when Saint Vincent and the Grenadines, supported by Jamaica, Peru, Ecuador, and Argentina, raised concerns regarding the operation of a EurepGAP scheme (now renamed GlobalGAP) in relation to trade in bananas with supermarkets in the United Kingdom.[267] These complainants challenged the "Good Agricultural Practices" standard set

---

[264] Roberts & Leibovitch, *supra* note 84 (citing UN Convention on Contracts for the International Sale of Goods in 1980).

[265] *Id.* (citing 27 Cal. 4th 939, 964, 119 Cal. Rptr. 2d 296, 45 P.3d 243 (2002)).

[266] *Id.* (citing 27 Cal. 4th 967 (2002)).

[267] *See* Roberts, *Compatibility of Private Standards, supra* note 4.

by EurepGAP, which exceeds public standards that applied to the EC. The EC argued in response that EurepGap was a private entity and not subject to the SPS Agreement.

The WTO has not determined the legal relationship between the SPS and TBT agreements and private standards. Were a particular private standard, such as an environmental standard, to fall within the definition of a standard under the TBT Agreement, then Article 4 would apply. Under Article 4, member countries to the WTO would be required to take "reasonable measures" to ensure that nongovernment bodies accept and comply with the TBT provisions of the Code of Good Practice, which includes nondiscrimination, transparency, and other obligations. The EC argued in response that EureGAP was a private entity and as such was not subject to the SPS and TBT agreements. Thus, the application of the TBT Agreement to the governance of private standards hinges upon whether a private enterprise that imposes standards into the food supply could be considered under Article 4 as a nongovernmental body. Neither the TBT nor the SPS Agreement or any other international legal instrument defines the term "non-governmental bodies."[268] It appears that Annex 1 of the TBT Agreement and Article 13 of the SPS Agreement support the definition of a nongovernment body as one that has legal power that is derived or delegated from a member country to enforce a technical regulation. In other words, the nongovernment body and the government have a relationship that enables the nongovernment body to perform certain tasks, including enforcing TBT and SPS rules, which are rules that typically do not belong to private food enterprises.[269] Although developing countries have been favored the filing of a complaint with the WTO to challenge the legitimacy of private standards, especially those that evoked sustainability rules, it is doubtful that a challenge would prevail.

§ 6.04 Urban Agriculture

[1] *Definition*

Urban agriculture has emerged in the past decade as an integral part of the food system conversation. Urban agriculture has multiple potential definitions. The Community Food Security Coalition's (CFSC) Urban Agriculture Committees defines "urban agriculture" as "the growing, processing, and distributing of food and other products through intensive plant cultivation and animal husbandry in and around cities."[270] Municipal governments define urban agriculture in a way that helps determine the form urban agriculture will take in that jurisdiction, if any at all. For example, some cities define community gardens as subdivided plots where individuals may grow food for personal consumption,[271] while others allow for on-site sales within their definitions of community

---

[268] *See id.* at 275–6.

[269] *See id.* Even assuming that a private standard-setting body qualifies as a "non-government entity" under the SPS and TBT agreements, members would then be required under Article 13 to "take such reasonable measures as may be available to them to ensure that ... non-governmental standardizing bodies within their territories ... comply with this Code of Good Practice." Neither the TBT and SPS agreements nor WTO jurisprudence define what constitutes a "reasonable measure." *See id.* at 276–7.

[270] *CFSC Urban Agriculture Committee*, Cmty. Food Sec. Coalition (September 6, 2014) (citing Martin Bailkey & Joe Nasr, *From Brownfields to Greenfields: Producing Food in North American Cities*, Cmty. Food Sec. News, Fall 1999/Winter 2000, at 6).

[271] *See* Cleveland, Ohio, Zoning Code § 336 (2007).

gardens.[272] Another example of terminology used by cities in their zoning codes is the term "truck garden," which the city of Los Angeles uses to describe the growing of food on residential property for sale off-site.[273]

The legal and policy disposition toward urban agriculture is best understood by recognizing the distinctive American interpretive tradition of agrarianism built largely around the writings of Thomas Jefferson and in recent years by contemporary voices.[274] While agrarianism has long been embraced by rural populations and while agriculture policy in the United States still favors large industrialized farming, policy advocates increasingly point to the virtues of urban agriculture and promote its development.[275]

In addition to the notions of agrarianism and the synergies of urban agriculture to the food systems concepts elucidated in this chapter – local food, sustainability, food sovereignty, and food justice – another key driver in the interest in urban agriculture is the obesity epidemic. Increasing access to affordable fresh produce is a central strategy for local governments seeking to improve nutrition and reduce obesity rates.

Notwithstanding the growing enthusiasm for urban agriculture, the modes or urban law and planning that dominated the twentieth century have imposed barriers to urban agriculture. The food movement has helped spur the implementation of legal tools to remove barriers and to develop urban agriculture, with an objective to improving food systems in general.

[2] *Urban Agriculture and Land Use*

[a] Framework: State and Local Government Regulation

A legal framework for the discussion of urban agriculture can be centered on land use and liability. Land use law is indispensable to the development of urban agriculture. The authority to regulate land use is derived from the police power of the state to protect the health, safety, and welfare of the public.[276] The Supreme Court in *Berman v. Parker* provides a helpful explanation of the wide range of activities that can be taken under the police power: "[t]he concept of the public welfare is broad and inclusive. The values it represents are spiritual as well as physical, aesthetic as well as monetary. It is within the power of the legislature to determine that the community should be beautiful as well as healthy, spacious as well as clean, well balanced as well as carefully patrolled."[277]

Local governments in all states, with the exception of Hawaii, are delegated the authority to regulate land use by their state governments. Land use laws can span a wide variety of topics, and can apply to many activities taking place on the land. This gives local governments a large degree of control over local issues.[278] For example, urban poultry

---

[272] *See* Chicago, Ill., Zoning Ordinance § 17-9-0103.5 (2011); Kansas City, Mo., Zoning and Development Code §§ 88-312-01, 88-312-02 (2009).

[273] Los Angeles, Cal., Mun. Code § 12.03.

[274] Michael Roberts & Margot Pollans, *Setting the Table for Urban Agriculture* in Urban Agriculture: Policy, Law, Strategy, and Implementation (American Bar Association (2015)).

[275] *Id.*

[276] Zoning ordinances have been upheld as constitutional exercises of the police power. Village of Euclid, Ohio v. Ambler Realty Co., 272 U.S. 365 (1926).

[277] Berman v. Parker, 348 U.S. 26 (1954).

[278] *See generally* Lisa Feldstein, General Plans and Zoning: A Toolkit for Building Healthy, Vibrant Communities (2007).

keeping is becoming a more visible issue throughout the country. An analysis of the laws of mid-Western states found that state law was silent on the issue of urban chicken keeping, leaving the topic open to local governments for decision making. Typically, local governments handle the issue of urban chickens within their zoning codes.[279]

Local governments are often given a framework for their land use planning by state governments. For example, in California, local governments are required to create general plans that include seven mandatory elements. General plans are binding on local governments, and land use planning laws, like zoning codes, must be consistent with general plans.[280] However, local governments still exercise considerable control over the content of their policies. Through their general plans, which establish long-term goals and directions for future land use, and land use planning regulations, local governments classify types of land and land uses. Urban agriculture can be a type of land use allowed in multiple zones, but few jurisdictions holistically address its various and multiple forms within their codes. This is changing as the issue attracts greater attention. Many large and medium-sized cities have instituted major changes to their land use laws to encourage urban agriculture. For example, San Francisco, Seattle, and Chicago have updated their zoning codes to allow for many urban agriculture activities. Other jurisdictions are following suit, some with comprehensive laws, and many others with smaller changes to foster the growth of more food within cities.

[b] Land Use Tool

Land use regulations enable government entities to control permissible uses of land in order to achieve a range of goals.[281] Land use regulations are typically presented in a zoning code, "a regulatory mechanism by which a government divides a community, such as a city or county, into separate districts with different land use regulations within each district."[282] "Simply stated, zoning determines what can and cannot be built, and what activities can and cannot take place, on the parcels of land throughout a community."[283]

Local governments create definitions for types of land use, which can include community gardens and urban farms, and designate which types of areas (residential, industrial, commercial, etc.) in which these uses can exist by right or by permit. Allowing a use by right means that a landowner need not obtain a permit or special permission in order to use the land in that particular manner.

Land use laws can also prohibit expressly, or through omission, certain activities from taking place on land parcels in particular zones. For example, many municipalities prohibit the keeping of bees or goats in residential areas, regardless of whether the animals and animal products are kept for personal consumption or retail sale.[284] It is becoming

---

[279] Iowa Policy Research Organization, State and Municipal Urban Chicken Legislation (2009).

[280] Cal. Gov't Code § 65302.

[281] Peter W. Salsich & Timothy J. Tryniecki, Land Use Regulation: A Legal Analysis & Practical Application of Land Use Law 8 (Aen. W. Webster et al. eds., 2d ed. 2004).

[282] Public Health Law & Policy, Establishing Land Use Protections for Community Gardens (2010).

[283] Id.

[284] Steve Lopez, *Abuzz about Beekeeping in Los Angeles*, L.A. Times (July 14, 2012) (internet source); Pittsburgh Department of City Planning, Urban Agriculture Zoning.

much more common for local governments to allow egg-laying hens in residential neighborhoods, with many cities changing their laws in the past few years.[285]

Another example applies to home gardens, which have become the focus of increased attention. Many cities require property in residentially zoned areas to maintain proper ground cover. In some cities with zoning codes containing this requirement, zoning enforcement officials have clashed with home gardeners, maintaining that gardens of food-producing plants, or raised beds, are not proper ground cover. Some cities have even forcibly removed front-yard gardens.[286] Without other zoning code language specifically allowing gardens, residents have little recourse.

Some cities do not recognize, or prohibit, certain types of urban agriculture. Community gardens often find themselves in this in-between space, where they are neither a recognized use, nor prohibited from existing. This can either (1) prevent them from being created in the first place, as the procedures to establish a nonconforming use can be lengthy and expensive or (2) leave community gardens vulnerable to losing their ability to operate if neighbors object.[287]

These examples highlight the fundamental issue in land use planning and urban agriculture of where urban agriculture fits in to modern cities. Many of the original land use laws set out to separate agricultural, industrial, and residential uses both to protect the public's health and create a more urban or suburban aesthetic for cities. Urban agriculture, observed through one lens, seeks to reduce these separations to promote the public's health, bringing up critical questions of identity for communities, especially those communities seeking to maintain the typical residential aesthetic.

The regulation of urban agriculture through land use can be discussed by addressing two questions: (1) What types of urban agriculture activities can take place? and (2) Where can urban agriculture activities take place? These questions do not address all of the potential topics addressed in a land use regulation pertaining to urban agriculture, but do provide for exposition of the central issues.

(1) *Types of Urban Agricultural Activities Permitted*
Land use regulations typically define what type of urban agriculture activities can take place on a parcel. These descriptions can define the form of the activity (i.e., divided parcels typical of community gardens or collective growing space more typical of farms) and the content of the activity (i.e., vegetables, orchards, livestock, bees), as well as the purpose (i.e., personal consumption or retail sale) and intensity (size of parcel or growing area). Some types of urban agriculture activities, like commercial urban farming and livestock in residential areas, typically inspire greater debate as compared to less controversial uses, like community gardens.

Examples of cities adopting zoning code changes to allow a wider range of urban agriculture activities include San Francisco. The city in this case took a unique approach, creating only two categories, neighborhood agriculture and large-scale urban agriculture,

---

[285] For example, San Diego changed its zoning code in 2012 to allow chickens, bees, and goats in residential neighborhoods. *See* SAN DIEGO, CAL., MUN. CODE, § 44.0307 (2004). *See generally* Patricia Salkin & Amy Lavine, *Regional Foodsheds: Are Our Local Zoning and Land Use Regulations Healthy?*, 22 FORDHAM ENVTL. L. REV. 599 (2011).

[286] Steven Kurutz, *The Battlefront in the Front Yard*, N.Y. TIMES, December 19, 2012, at D-1.

[287] PUBLIC HEALTH LAW & POLICY, *supra* note 287.

based mainly on the size of the lot to be used.[288]"Neighborhood Agriculture" is defined as "a use that occupies less than one acre for the production of food or horticultural crops to be harvested, sold, or donated … the use includes, but is not limited to, home, kitchen, and roof gardens. Farms that qualify as Neighborhood Agricultural use may include, but are not limited to, community gardens, community-supported agriculture, market gardens, and private farms." The "Large-Scale Urban Agriculture" is defined as "the use of land for the production of food or horticultural crops to be harvested, sold, or donated that occur: (1) on a plot of land one acre or larger or (2) on smaller parcels that cannot meet the physical and operational standards for Neighborhood Agriculture."[289]

Another example is Seattle, which made major changes to its zoning code in 2010 to allow for urban agriculture in many forms. Its laws are particularly comprehensive and categorize activities into five defined urban agriculture uses: animal husbandry, aquaculture, community gardens, horticulture, and urban farms.[290]

As a final example, Los Angeles does not define urban agriculture or community gardens within its code. It does define truck gardening, though, as "the cultivation of berries, flowers, fruits, herbs, mushrooms, nuts, ornamental plants, seedlings, or vegetables for use on-site or sale or distribution off-site."[291] Changes allowing a wide variety of products to be grown were made following a conflict between the city government and a resident growing flowers in her backyard for sale at farmers' markets. Prior to the changes instituted, only vegetables could be grown in truck gardens.[292] Had the law not been changed, the resident would have needed to obtain a conditional use permit to continue selling her flowers off-site at farmers' markets, which can be an expensive and time-consuming endeavor.[293] Los Angeles's code now allows for farming (which allows for both on- and off-site sales) and truck gardening, with the primary difference between the two uses being the allowance for on-site sales.[294]

Zoning codes also may set out rules for urban agriculture on a number of topics, including farm buildings (hoop houses, cold frames, greenhouses), fencing, tool storage, and composting. The way these requirements are integrated into codes can affect the extent to which urban agriculture proliferates in a community.[295] In Chicago's changes to its zoning code, community gardens are a use by right in residential zones, and sheds, greenhouses, and hoop houses meeting applicable building requirements are allowed on properties.[296] In New Jersey the state's Uniform Construction Code exempts hoop houses meeting particular requirements from obtaining permits.[297] In cities lacking green space, roofs are potentially attractive places for food production. New York City recently changed its zoning code to allow for green roofs.[298]

---

[288]   See SAN FRANCISCO, CAL., PLANNING CODE § 102.35.

[289]   Id.

[290]   See SEATTLE DEPARTMENT OF PLANNING & DEVELOPMENT, URBAN AGRICULTURE (2010).

[291]   LOS ANGELES, CAL., MUN. CODE § 12.03.

[292]   MICHAEL LOGRANDE ET AL., DEPARTMENT OF CITY PLANNING RECOMMENDATION REPORT (2010).

[293]   Katherine Spiers, Urban Farms: Where "Vegetable" Is a Murky Term, LA WEEKLY (November 4, 2009).

[294]   See LOS ANGELES, CAL. MUN. CODE §§ 12.03, 12.05.

[295]   HEATHER WOOTEN & AMY ACKERMAN, SEEDING THE CITY: LAND USE POLICIES TO PROMOTE URBAN AGRICULTURE (2011).

[296]   See CHICAGO, ILL., ZONING ORDINANCE § 17-9-0103.5-B (2011).

[297]   See N.J. ADMIN. CODE § 5:23-3 (2012); N.J. UNIF. CONSTR. CODE §§ 3.14(b)23ii(4), 3.24(b)23ii(5).

[298]   Zone Green, NYC PLANNING.

(2) *Regulation of Where Urban Agricultural Activities Take Place*

Beyond discussing the types of activities allowed under the umbrella of urban agriculture, zoning codes also define where these activities may take place. Zoning code changes aimed at increasing opportunities for the growing of food within cities typically apply to zones other than agricultural zones, as agricultural zones allow, by definition, for the cultivation of plants or the keeping of livestock for commercial purposes, with on-site sales.

For example, Seattle's zoning code specifies where each of its five urban agriculture activities may take place. Community gardens are allowed in all zones, while aquaculture and horticulture are allowed only in commercial and industrial zones.[299] Urban farms up to 4,000 sf. ft. are permitted as an accessory use in residential zones without a permit. Urban farms are permitted in commercial and industrial zones as a primary use. By allowing urban farms only as accessory uses in residential zones, the city ensures that residential zones maintain their character as places where people live, and not where larger-scale farming takes place. Residents will not find themselves living next door to urban farms without a home on the property. Animal husbandry has the most specific guidelines. In residential zones it is not permitted, except through specific regulations related to the keeping of small animals and domestic fowl.[300]

San Francisco's two-category approach based on the size of the garden results in neighborhood agriculture (gardens less than one acre) being allowed in all zones and large-scale urban agriculture (gardens more than one acre) being allowed in commercial, industrial, and production/distribution/repair districts (not residential districts) by right. Large-scale urban agriculture may exist in other zones with conditional use authorization.[301]

Los Angeles's truck gardening regulatory regime allows farming allowed in agricultural zones, but truck gardening allowed in all zones, including residential zones, as an accessory use.[302] Finally, some cities, instead of allowing urban agriculture in other types of zones, have chosen to create specific zones for urban agriculture. Cleveland, Chattanooga, and Boston all have specific urban agriculture districts.[303] Creating a designated urban agriculture district facilitates intensive urban agriculture under specific conditions and addresses land tenure. Many community gardens and urban farms face ambiguous land tenure, for instance, if they are run by a nonprofit that leases land for a nominal sum. An urban agricultural designation can protect a garden or farm if agriculture is a particularly good use for that parcel. This rationale may apply when a parcel contains a long-established garden that serves an important social or cultural function, when an agricultural use can help to supply food to an area underserved by grocery stores, when the garden or farm serves an educational purpose, when the parcel helps to fulfill an open space goal, or when the use is in an environmentally sensitive area that should not be developed. If a city wants to protect a garden from future changes, an urban garden designation creates a hurdle for future development.[304]

---

[299] *See* SEATTLE, *supra* note 290.
[300] *Id.*
[301] *See* SAN FRANCISCO, CAL. PLANNING CODE §§ 102.35, 204.1, 209.5, 227, 234.1, 234.2.
[302] *See* LOS ANGELES, CAL., MUN. CODE §§ 12.03, 12.05
[303] NINA MUKHERJI & ALFONSO MORALES, ZONING FOR URBAN AGRICULTURE (2010).
[304] *See e.g.*, CLEVELAND, OHIO, MUN. CODE §§ 336.01–336.05.

The question of where agriculture activities may take place in a city continues to refer back to some of the fundamental questions raised by land use planning. In trying to balance the competing views on the role for agriculture within cities, municipalities create regulations that may be viewed as too restrictive or not restrictive enough depending on the perspective taken. For example, municipalities might prevent community gardens from locating in industrial areas, create regulations limiting the hours when sales may be made from urban farms in residential neighborhoods, and prohibit urban farms from using mechanized equipment not designed for household use.[305]

[c] Access to Government Property

In order to promote urban agriculture beyond simply allowing the use of private property for farming and gardens, states make their public land available in a variety of ways. New York State has fostered statewide use of public lands for community gardens through express enabling legislation. The law authorizes the state's Office of Community Gardens to provide for interagency, intergovernmental, and public and private coordination of community gardens.[306] California, Massachusetts, and Tennessee have authorized the use of public land for community gardens and provide for support and coordination of gardens.[307] California allows school districts to sell produce grown in school gardens, as long as federal, state, and local health and safety requirements are followed.[308]

Municipalities also authorize and coordinate in a variety of ways the use of municipal property for community gardens. The Department of Neighborhoods in Seattle runs a P-Patch Garden Program, which manages 76 public garden sites. The property upon which P-Patches operate is under the jurisdiction of a variety of agencies and departments, from neighborhoods, parks, and transportation. The city has authorized and support the program through a variety of resolutions and ordinances.[309] Some of the gardens are market gardens, which allow residents to sell the produce they grow. Des Moines passed legislation in 2004 allowing for the lease of city property and right-of-ways for community gardens, and enabling the director of parks and recreation to execute community garden leases to individuals and entities.[310] The Land Redevelopment Office in Columbus (Ohio) runs the Land Bank Community Garden Program that maintains inventories of properties suitable for community gardens.[311]

Beyond community gardens, many cities work to provide access to vacant, abandoned, or tax-foreclosed properties for urban agriculture. Cities that have experienced population reduction are left with the problem of abandoned properties. These properties are costly to maintain, reduce tax revenue, and have negative financial effects on neighborhoods. In Philadelphia, where losses have mounted from vacant land,[312]

---

305 *See eg.*, SEATTLE, WASH., MUN. CODE § 23.42.051.
306 *See* N.Y. AGM. LAW §§ 31-G-31H.
307 *State Statutes and Programs Concerning Community Gardens*, NATIONAL CONFERENCE OF STATE LEGISLATURES.
308 *See* CAL. EDUC. CODE § 51798.
309 *Factsheet*, P-PATCH COMMUNITY GARDENING PROGRAM (December 22, 2011).
310 Des Moines, Iowa, Ordinance No. 14,314 (February 23, 2004).
311 *The City of Columbus Land Bank Community Garden Program*, THE CITY OF COLUMBUS.
312 In recent years, Philadelphia loses an estimated $2 million in tax revenues from vacant land, spends $20 million to maintain vacant lands, and loses $3.6 billion in property values due to urban blight.

community groups have worked to use the Pennsylvania Abandoned and Blighted Property Conservatorship Act to take control of property for community gardens and urban farms.[313] Milwaukee, home of the highly successful Growing Power urban farms, and the owner of nearly 4,000 vacant properties, has developed HomeGrown Neighborhoods that make use of vacant properties to create neighborhoods that grow and sell healthy foods.[314] Finally, Detroit, with its huge inventory of abandoned properties, has been at the forefront of urban agriculture for years now. In December 2012, the Detroit City Council approved the sale of 140 acres of public land to Hantz Woodlands Farms for $300 per lot.[315] This is one of the largest urban land acquisitions of its kind and establishes a very large urban farm within city limits. The urban farming project and the sale of such a large number of acres for a below-market price was a source of controversy in the community and pitted some food justice advocates against the urban farming project.[316]

Government support of urban agriculture promotes land tenure for community gardens and urban farms, which is a critical issue for their (1) productivity, as it can take a significant amount of time to rehabilitate urban soils to increase productivity and (2) success, as investment of resources into short-term projects may not attract investment from participants and community members in the endeavor.[317] A number of conflicts have arisen stemming from land tenure for community gardens and farms, and it is important that local governments account for land tenure when planning for urban agriculture. For example, in Los Angeles, a group of urban farmers was granted permission to use a plot of land in industrial South Los Angeles after the 1992 riots. The lot had been seized from the owner in an eminent domain action. After many years, the city sold the lot back to the original owner, who in turn evicted the farmers in 2006 amid high-profile protests.[318] The farmers continued to seek resolution to their conflict with the city over the land, as of 2011 were involved with the city in decision making around a park planned for the site of the original park.[319] New York City has also had conflicts over the sale of community garden land to developers. Community garden plots were sold by the city to make way for housing, sparking conflict between the city and advocates. These conflicts concluded with an agreement between the Mayor and the New York State attorney general in 2002 to preserve 500 existing community gardens.[320]

---

[313] ECONSULT CORPORATION, PENN INSTITUTE FOR URBAN RESEARCH, VACANT LAND MANAGEMENT IN PHILADELPHIA: THE COSTS OF THE CURRENT SYSTEMS AND THE BENEFITS OF REFORM (2010).

Kia Gregory, *Under New Pa. Law, Neighbors Control Abandoned Lot*, PHILADELPHIA INQUIRER, November 4, 2010.

[314] *HOMEGR/OWN Milwaukee*, CITY OF MILWAUKEE.

[315] David Sands, *Hantz Woodlands Deal Approved by Detroit City Council 5-4*, HUFFINGTON POST (December 11, 2012).

[316] See Leslie MacMillan, *Vast Land Deal Divides Detroit*, N.Y. TIMES, December 10, 2012.

[317] Krisitin Choo, *Plowing Over: Can Urban Farming Save Detroit and Other Declining Cities? Will the Law Allow It?*, ABA J. (August 1, 2011).

[318] *See* Cindy Chang, *Anti-Development Protesters Are Arrested at Farm Site in Los Angeles*, N.Y. TIMES, June 14, 2006.

[319] Kate Linthicum, *South Central Farmers Object to L.A.'s Change in Park Plans*, L.A. TIMES, August 4, 2011.

[320] *See* Jennifer Steinhauer, *Ending a Long Battle, New York Lets Housing and Gardens Grow*, N.Y. TIMES, September 19, 2002.

[3] *Liability*

[a] Urban Agriculture and Food Safety

(1) *Environmental Contaminants*

Widespread lead contamination, as well as contamination from other metals like copper and mercury, in cities is a growing concern as urban agriculture becomes more prevalent. Environmental contaminants are a potential risk to consumer health, as some plants can absorb contaminants and contaminants can also deposit on edible plant parts.

There are no standards on soil as a growing medium, meaning that there are no regulations at the federal level on environmental contaminants, like lead, in soil used to grow food. The EPA sets a threshold at which lead concentrations are harmful to health, but does not require remediation for the use of the area.[321]

In the absence of federal regulation, local governments work to determine the best practices to protect the public's health. Seattle, which has known lead and arsenic contamination from the Tacoma Smelter Plume, advises that potential participants in urban agriculture send their soil in for free testing, but does not require testing.[322] When cities allow the use of their own property for community gardens, they may require testing or remediation. For example, Milwaukee requires raised beds be used by gardeners growing food on a community garden plot.[323] The leading edge of zoning code change is to require testing and remediation of soil. Baltimore's zoning code changes adopted in 2013 require "for any urban agriculture use that involves the cultivation of plants for human consumption, measures must be taken to test and, if necessary, remediate the soil in accordance with guidelines adopted by the department of planning."[324]

Soil testing is a complex issue to address, as evidenced by the multitude of approaches taken by local governments. As more evidence emerges, regulatory best practices will likely emerge that provide the best approach for promoting urban agriculture while also protecting the public's health. The EPA issued interim guidelines for safe gardening practice in 2011 to address the gaps in using potentially contaminated urban property for agriculture.[325]

(2) *Pathogens*

Food produced in urban areas presents many of the same risks for contamination with pathogens that cause illness in humans, like *Salmonella or E. coli,* as food produced in agricultural or rural areas. Urban agriculture does face some additional issues with potential for contamination by pathogens, as urban farms and community gardens may be in less controlled environments than commercial farms. Urban agriculture areas potentially can be accessed by more people, including passers-by, as well as by domestic and wild animals. Farmers may face civil liability if a consumer falls ill due to consuming

---

[321] Brownfields and Urban Agriculture: Interim Guidelines for Safe Gardening Practices, U.S. Environmental Protection Agency (2011).

[322] Seattle Department of Planning and Development, Client Assistance Memo 244, Urban Agriculture (2010).

[323] *See 2012 Season Garden Plot License,* City of Milwaukee.

[324] *City of Baltimore Council Bill 12–0152,* City of Baltimore.

[325] *See* Brownfields, *supra,* note 321.

products the farmer produced and thus should take certain steps to lessen the liability risk, such as using good agricultural practices and acquiring products liability insurance.

Small-scale growers, whether growing food for their consumption or to sell, may lack the knowledge, training, and resources to exercise reasonable care, and it is critical that educational resources are available for participants in urban agriculture. For example, the rise in backyard poultry has raised the issue that people without agricultural training may not possess enough knowledge about *Salmonella* and the way it is spread to safely raise fowl. Recognizing this potential problem, the Center for Disease Control has created an educational site for backyard poultry to provide education on preventing *Salmonella*.[326]

As noted in Chapter 3, FSMA exempts most urban farmers and community gardens, due to their small size and limited revenue. The Model Food Code exempts any produce stand "that only offers whole, uncut fresh fruits and vegetables" from its requirements, and so many states also exempt farm stands from their food codes as well.[327] Some states, though, like California, do not exempt fresh produce, and require sellers of produce at farmers' markets and produce stands to comply with the standards set out in the law.[328]

[b] Premises Liability

Premises liability is generally defined as "a landowner's or landholder's tort liability for conditions or activities on the premises."[329] Any recovery, generally, for a premises liability claim would be based in negligence. Thus, a claimant must prove that the landowner owed a duty of care to the claimant, failed to exercise reasonable care, and, as a result of that failure, the claimant was injured. Many urban agriculture activities have the potential to give rise to tort claims based on premises liability, including operating a farm stand at an urban farm or owning land used as a community garden.

Municipalities can limit their liability for property used and maintained by individuals or groups engaged in urban agriculture by requiring the property user (often a leaseholder) to carry insurance and indemnify the property owner. Tennessee state law requires that "any person who is granted the use of garden land shall indemnify and save harmless the state of Tennessee … against suits and any claims of liability arising out of, or in consequence of the use of vacant public land."[330] Similarly, land possessors engaged in urban agriculture owe a duty of care to those entering their property, especially for the purpose of conducting business (like customers at a farm stand), and should actively manage potential risks, ameliorate them when possible, and otherwise warn of potential hazards. All injuries cannot be foreseen, so it is likely in the best interest of urban agriculture practitioners to obtain insurance that covers premises liability, especially if they will be conducting business transactions on the property.

[326] *Keeping Backyard Poultry*, CENTERS FOR DISEASE CONTROL AND PREVENTION (March 31, 2014).
[327] UNITED STATES DEP'T OF HEALTH AND HUMAN SERVICES, MODEL FOOD CODE.
[328] See CAL. HEALTH & SAFETY CODE §114375.
[329] BLACK'S LAW DICTIONARY (9th ed. 2009).
[330] TENN. CODE ANN. § 43-24-103.

[4] *Nuisance*

  [a] Municipal Regulation

The regulation and abatement of nuisances is one of the quintessential exercises of local police power. "Nuisance" is a legal term meaning a condition, activity, or situation (such as a loud noise or foul odor) that interferes with the use or enjoyment of property.[331] Property owners have the right to the quiet enjoyment of their property, and nuisance conditions on nearby properties that interfere with this right can be enjoined by the property owner or cited by the municipality. Somerville, Massachusetts, allows the keeping of bees within city limits, but specifically states that it will refuse the keeping of honeybees on a property if they are deemed a nuisance.[332] Urban farms and community gardens must not only follow zoning regulations aimed at preventing the presence of nuisance conditions, such as a requirement that composting take place away from property lines,[333] but also take care to maintain farms and gardens in a manner that does not create nuisances unanticipated by the specific regulations within the zoning code.

  (1) *Right to Farm*

"Right-to-Farm" laws may provide some protection to urban producers. These laws protect existing farms from lawsuits by neighboring property owners seeking to curb agricultural activities. Right-to-Farm laws exist in some form in all fifty states.[334] As urban areas began to expand, existing farms were subject to lawsuits from new neighbors alleging that the agricultural activities were a nuisance. To protect existing farms from those nuisance lawsuits, states passed Right-to-Farm laws. "In its most basic form, a right-to-farm law establishes that no agricultural operation will be deemed a nuisance due to changed circumstances in the area where it is located, so long as the operation is not conducted in a negligent or unlawful manner and was not a nuisance when it was begun."[335]

[5] *Government Incentives and Assistance Programs*

  [a] Land Incentives

  (1) *Tax Incentives*

Beyond creating the conditions necessary for urban agriculture to exist legally in communities, some jurisdictions may also offer incentives for urban agriculture. These

---

[331] BLACK'S LAW DICTIONARY (9th ed. 2009).

[332] *See The ABC's of Urban Agriculture*, CITY OF SOMERVILLE'S URBAN AGRICULTURE ORDINANCE (Somerville, M.A.), September 2012.

[333] *See e.g.*, Title 12 Minneapolis, Minn. Muni. Code § 244.770; Chicago, Ill. Muni. Code § 7-28-715.

[334] Terence Centner, *Governments and Unconstitutional Takings: When Do Right to Farm Laws Go Too Far?*, 33 B.C. ENVTL. AFF. L. REV. 87 (2005).

[335] Heather Wooten and Amy Ackerman, SEEDING THE CITY: LAND USE POLICIES TO PROMOTE URBAN AGRICULTURE, CHANGELAB SOLUTIONS (2012). There is some concern that when right-to-farm laws regulate farm management practices, they may inhibit a community's ability to regulate farm management practices through their land use policies. This concern has produced some dialogue around the potential impact of Michigan's right-to-farm law on Detroit's regulation of urban agriculture. *See* John Mogk et al., *Promoting Urban Agriculture as an Alternative Land Use for Vacant Properties in the City of Detroit: Benefits, Problems and Proposals for a Regulatory Framework for Successful Land Use Integration*, 56 WAYNE L. REV. 4 (2011).

incentives can take a variety of forms. Tax incentives are an important tool to enhance land access. Tax credits or reduced tax assessments effectively lower the amount of property tax owed by a property owner, providing an incentive to property owners to use property for urban agriculture. This incentive may motivate an enterprise to develop urban agriculture within a deteriorating area by reducing the tax rate or the taxable value of the project area. Maryland's "Urban Agriculture Tax Credit," passed in 2010, allowed counties and the City of Baltimore to enact a tax credit for real property used for urban agriculture.[336] There are a wide variety of ideas currently circulating on tax incentives for urban agriculture: for example, federal tax incentives could include cultivation easements and charitable contribution deductions.[337]

(2) *Other Financial Incentives*

Access to favorable terms for the lease or acquisition of public property can also be viewed as an incentive promoting urban agriculture. Many cities extend very inexpensive leases to community gardens run by private organizations. Other cities have set up land banks to allow for the efficient acquisition and sale of abandoned and tax-foreclosed properties, which can be sold at affordable prices to urban agriculture projects.

For example, Jersey City's (New Jersey) Adopt-a-Lot ordinance[338] and program[339] allows city land to be leased for community gardening by nonprofits and community groups for one dollar per year. State legislation in 2006 gave local municipalities in Indiana the authority to create land banks to exercise greater control over vacant and abandoned properties within their jurisdictions, which created an opportunity to transfer land to local groups for community gardening and urban farming initiatives.[340]

When cities are formulating creative incentive to facilitate farming initiatives on publicly owned land, officials need to be cognizant of the potential to run afoul of state constitutional provisions preventing gifts of public funds. These types of provisions ensure that government resources cannot be used to benefit private interests, unless the public interest is primarily served by the government's actions.

[b] Agriculture Assistance Programs

Most USDA programs support farming in rural areas, and this section provides a sample of USDA and other federal programs that can support both experienced and beginning farmers within and near urban centers.

- Beginning Farmer and Rancher Development Program (BFRDP)

BFRDP provides competitive grants to organizations to provide education, training, outreach, and mentoring to beginning farmers and ranchers in rural and urban areas. For

---

[336] *See* Md. Code Ann., Tax-Prop. § 9–253 (2010) (Baltimore has yet to enact a tax incentive).
[337] *See* Kathryn Peters, *Creating a Sustainable Urban Agriculture Revolution,* 25 J. Envtl. L. & Litig. 1 (2010).
[338] *See* Jersey City, N.J. Ordinance 01-109
[339] *See,* City of Jersey City "Adopt-a-Lot" Program Fact Sheet.
[340] Bob Hersh, Edible Cities: Urban Farming in Indianapolis, Center for Public Environmental Oversight (2009)

example, a 2010 BFRDP grant funded the startup of the New York City School of Urban Agriculture, which serves as an agricultural training resource for New York City and the Northeast.[341]

- Cooperative Extension System (CES)

CES is a nationwide educational network with offices at land-grant universities and a network of local or regional offices comprising experts who convey information to agricultural producers, including those in urban areas.[342]

- Conservation Technical Assistance Program (CTAP)

CTAP is housed within USDA's Natural Resources Conservation Service and provides science-based assistance to help people voluntarily conserve, maintain, and improve their natural resources, in urban or rural settings.[343]

- Farm Programs

USDA's Farm Service Agency (FSA) delivers commodity, credit, conservation, disaster, and emergency assistance programs that are available to urban as well as rural farmers. Urban producers have access to FSA loan programs.[344]

- Sustainable Agriculture Research and Education (SARE) Program

SARE advances sustainable innovations to urban as well as rural agriculture. For example, SARE supported urban agriculturist Will Allen, now a MacArthur Genius Award recipient, to develop low-cost, high-value production from Milwaukee's urban lots in poor areas.[345]

- Specialty Crop Block Grant Program

This program provides funds to states for projects that enhance the competitiveness of specialty crops such as fruits, vegetables, nuts, and nursery crops. States have supported urban projects with funds provided by USDA, including developing community gardens and urban agriculture education and promotion. For example, in 2010 the CDFA partnered with an enterprise to develop a community garden in Woodland, California, on a half-acre lot near the city center in order to provide an opportunity for thirty to sixty gardeners to grow fruits and vegetables for their families.[346]

---

[341] Kathleen Merrigan, Memorandum on Urban Agriculture and Gardening – Supporting farm viability, building access to nutritious, affordable food and encouraging rural-urban linkages, US DEP'T OF AGRIC. (October 14, 2011).

[342] Id.

[343] Id.

[344] Kathleen Merrigan, Memorandm on Farm Service Agency Support for Local and Regional Food Systems, U.S. DEP'T OF AGRIC. (June 17, 2010).

[345] Merrigan, Memorandum on Urban Agriculture and Gardening, *supra* note 341.

[346] Id.

- Specialty Crop Research Initiative

This initiative develops and disseminates science-based tools to address the needs of specific crops and their regions. For example, a 2009 grant to the Ohio State University funded planning to facilitate and enhance the production, marketing, and utilization of specialty crops, particularly fresh vegetables and fruits, in poverty-stricken urban areas.[347]

§ 6.05 Food Security

[1] *Definition*

Food security is a condition related to the ongoing availability of food. Concerns over food security have existed throughout history. Food security practices were evident in Ancient China and Ancient Egypt when granaries released food from storage in times of famine. Yet in the modern global food system, it was at the 1974 UN's World Food Conference that the term "food security" was established as a formal concept within a broad framework. At that time, food security was understood to apply at the national level, with a state being food secure when there was sufficient food to "sustain a steady expansion of food consumption and to offset fluctuations in production and prices."[348] The World Food Summit of 1996 changed the emphasis of food security from nations to individuals by defining food security as existing "when all people at all times have access to sufficient, safe, nutritious food to maintain a healthy and active life."[349]

In a slight variance to the World Food Summit definition, the USDA defines food insecurity as "limited or uncertain availability of nutritionally adequate and safe foods or limited or uncertain ability to acquire acceptable foods in socially acceptable ways."[350] In 2006, USDA through its Economic Research Service agency (ERS) introduced a quantitative aspect to food security and developed a new language to describe ranges of severity of food insecurity. USDA made these changes in response to recommendations by an expert panel convened at USDA's request by the Committee on National Statistics of the National Academies. ERS also provides data access and technical support to social science scholars to facilitate their research on food security. ERS surveys measure food security in the United States based on the four categories of high food security, marginal food security, low food security, and very low food security.[351] The new dietary guidelines jointly issued in February 2015 for public comment by the DHHS and USDA defined "food security" as existing "when all people now, and in the future, have access to sufficient, safe, and nutritious food to maintain a healthy and active life."[352]

---

[347] *Id.*

[348] *Policy Brief: Food Security*, Food and Agriculture Organization, 1 (2006).

[349] *World Food Summit Rome Declaration on World Food Security and World Food Summit Plan of Action*, World Food Summit, Rome, Italy (1996)

[350] *Food Security in the United States*, U.S. dep't of agric., Economic Research Serv.

[351] *Food Security Status of U.S. Households in 2012*, U.S. Dep't of Agric., Economic Research Service, (2013).

[352] Scientific Report, *supra* note 260.

[2] Right to Food: Constitutional Concept

[a] Global Recognition

Integral to food security is a constitutional concept recognized globally as "right to food." In contrast to developmental goals, the right to food "is rooted in the rule of law and hence has a potential dimension of enforceability."[353] The right to food was first recognized in Article 25 of the Universal Declaration of Human Rights (UDHR), which was adopted by the UN General Assembly in 1948.[354] The right was codified in 1966 in Article 11 of the International Covenant on Economic, Social, and Cultural Rights (ICESCR), which went into effect in 1976.[355] As of 2012, the ICESCR has been ratified by 160 nation states, none of which has reservations on Article 11.[356] This article provides the following relative right to adequate food:

> The States Parties to the present Covenant recognize the right of everyone to an adequate standard of living for himself and his family, including adequate food, clothing and housing, and to the continuous improvement of living conditions. The States Parties will take appropriate steps to ensure the realization of this right, recognizing to this effect the essential importance of international co-operation based on free consent.[357]

The UN Committee on ICESCR, which monitors and implements the ICESCR in those states that are a party to it, provides an even more expansive interpretation of the right to food:

> the right to adequate food is realized when every man, woman and child, alone or in community with others, has physical and economic access at all times to adequate food or means for its procurement. The right to adequate food shall therefore not be interpreted in a narrow or restrictive sense that equates it with a minimum package of calories, proteins and other specific nutrients. The right to adequate food will have to be realized progressively. However, States have a core obligation to take the necessary action to mitigate and alleviate hunger even in times of natural or other disasters.[358]

Nation states have taken different approaches to implementing the right to food in their domestic legislation, though not all countries that have ratified have implemented the right. Some countries have created a constitutional right to food, some have adopted legislation and created a right to food,[359] and in some cases the ICESCR is directly binding as national legislation.[360] The FAO has developed guidelines to help countries

---

[353] Nora McKeon, Food Security Governance 81 (2015).

[354] Universal Declaration of Human Rights, G.A. Res. 217A, U.N. Doc A/810; GAOR, 3d Sess., 1st plen. mtg., (December 12, 1948) ("Everyone has the right to a standard of living adequate for the health and well-being of himself and his family, including food").

[355] International Covenant on Economic, Social and Cultural Rights [ICESCR], G.A. Res. 2200A (XXI), art. 11 (December 16, 1976).

[356] Treaty Collection: Status of ICESCR as at 02-05-2013, United Nations (2013).

[357] International Covenant on Economic, Social and Cultural Rights [ICESCR], G.A. Res. 2200A (XXI), art. 11(1) (December 16, 1976)

[358] Special Rapporteur on the right to food, United Nations Human Rights.

[359] See, e.g., Constitution of South Africa, Article 27. See also, Lidija Knuth, Constitutional and Legal Protection of the Right to Food around the World, 31 United Nations Food and Agric. Organization (2011).

[360] See id. at 24.

implement the right to food[361] and is working to implement the right to food at the national level. It does this through advocacy, assessment of vulnerable populations, promoting implementing legislation, assisting with food programs and policies, and monitoring development.[362]

Also giving impetus to the visibility of right to food is the establishment of the post of UN Special Rapporteur on the Right to Food. The Special Rapporteur is an independent expert appointed by the Human Rights Council to examine and report back on a country situation or a specific human rights theme.[363] The Special Rapporteur presents annual reports to the UN Human Rights Council and to the General Assembly.

[b] US Resistance to Right to Food as Constitutional Concept

While the United States is a signatory to the UDHR and has signed the ICCPR, it remains steadfast in opposition to ratifying the ICESCR and to the constitutional concept of a guaranteed right to food. In 1996, for example, the United States interpreted the concluding document of the World Food Summit by characterizing its understanding of the right to safe and nutritious food to mean only that "governments should not interfere with the effective opportunity or ability of their citizens to obtain safe and nutritious food."[364] US law does not recognize a right to food: the Supreme Court has never acknowledged an "explicit right to eat certain foods" or of a right to fight at all. The FDA responded to a lawsuit by expressly stating that there is "no fundamental right to choose your food or freedom the contract for it" and by finding that there is no right to freedom of food.[365]

This rejection of the right to food concept as a constitutional proposition comports with the US constitutional framework that accepts negative human rights but not positive human rights. With a handful of exceptions, the federal courts have consistently interpreted the US Constitution to protect only negative rights (acts that government must refrain from doing, i.e., regulating freedom of speech).[366]

[3] Regional Food Hubs: A Practical Route to Food Security

The development of local food systems has moved beyond city boundaries to the food sheds in which they exist. The food system organization at this level is known as the food hub, which has become integral to discussions of food security. The USDA defines

---

[361] See *Voluntary Guidelines on the Progressive Realization of the Right to Aadequate Food in the Context of National Food Security* (2005), United Nations Food and Agric. Organization.

[362] See *The Right to Food in Practice: Implementation at the National Level*, (2006) United Nations Food and Agric. Organization.

[363] The mandate of the Special Rapporteur on the right to food was originally established by the Commission on Human Rights in April 2000 by a resolution 2000/10. Subsequent to the replacement of the Commission by the Human Rights Council in June 2006, the mandate was endorsed and extended by the Human Rights Council by its resolution 6/2 of September 27, 2007. *Special Rapporteur on the right to food*, United Nations Office of the High Commissioner of Human Rights.

[364] George Kent, Freedom from Want: The Human Right to Adequate Food 158 (2005).

[365] Heidi Stevenson, *The FDA Says You Have No Right to Health or Freedom of Food*, Reader Supported News, June 1, 2010.

[366] *See generally*, Frank B. Cross, The Error of Positive Rights, 48 UCLA L. Rev. 857 (2001).

regional food hubs as "a business or organization that actively manages the aggregation, distribution and marketing of source-identified products, primarily from local and regional producers to strengthen their ability to satisfy wholesale, retail and institutional demand."[367]

The USDA's Regional Food Hub Resource Guide divides the structure of food hubs into a few legal organizational categories: nonprofits, many of which are producer-owned and may function as a cooperative; for-profit cooperatives; and publicly held food hubs.[368] The legal structure of a food hub can influence the operation and function of the hub, particularly in capital investment, risk management, and liability exposure. Nonprofit hubs are better positioned for grant programs and donations than are for-profit hubs. However, privately held food hubs are better positioned to access loans, revolving lines of credit, and investment. Publicly held food hubs have the advantage of leveraging member equity, but will find it difficult to qualify for grants and loan programs.[369]

These food hubs may play multiple roles within a food system, each of which poses some level of legal risk. For example, food hubs involve contracts on a number of different transactions, including distribution, services, and financing. A food hub may attempt to limit contract risks (or product liability claims) from the hub itself by having producers retain product ownership until the product is loaded into a truck for delivery to the end consumer. Another option for hubs is to assume some or all of the liability risk by purchasing insurance to cover contractual transactions made under their auspices. A food hub that engages in food processing, packing, holding, or manufacturing needs to comply with the applicable state and local food safety requirements and other requirement for commercial kitchens. If the food hub is large enough, it may also need to comply with the requirements of FSMA.

§ 6.06 Food Sovereignty

[1] *Definition: Alternate Vision for Food Systems*

Food sovereignty has emerged as an alternative vision for food systems that is distinctive from food security. Over the years, the definition of food sovereignty has evolved largely in part to its responsive character and to the increasing number of stakeholders that contribute new and differing values and goals. La Vía Campesina first coined the term "food sovereignty" in 1996 at the World Food Summit. La Via Campesina is a coalition of over 148 organizations, advocating family-farm-based sustainable agriculture.[370] It was founded in 1993 by farmers' organizations from various countries and is headquartered in Jakarta, Indonesia.[371] When La Vía Campesina first introduced the concept of food sovereignty in 1996 at the World Food Summit, discussions at the summit and at the

---

[367] James Barham et al., *Regional Food Hub Resource Guide*, U.S. DEP'T OF AGRIC., AGRICULTURAL MARKETING SERV. 4 (April 2012).

[368] *See id.* at 7.

[369] *Id.*

[370] *See Global Small-Scale Farmers' Movement Developing New Trade Regimes*, Food First News & Views (Food First, Spring/Summer 2005) at 2.

[371] For general history of La Via Campesina movement, *see* María Elena Martínez-Torres & Peter M. Rosset, *La Vía Campesina: The Birth and Evolution of a Transnational Social Movement*, 37 THE J. OF PEASANT STUDIES 149 (2010).

World Trade Organization negotiations focused on food security. The concept was presented as "an alternate paradigm to frame issues about food and agriculture" and has since then come into vogue as an alternative framework for the modern global food system. [372]

Food sovereignty in essence argues that every country and people must have the right and the ability to define their own food, farming, and agricultural policies. In other words, the "sovereign" in food sovereignty is the "people" within communities whose right to choice can then be supported by policies adopted at higher governance levels.[373] Food security defines a goal without automatically recommending a specific program to achieve it, whereas food sovereignty is a more precise policy proposal, with proponents challenging political inactivity or other failures to pursue appropriate policies.[374]

While food sovereignty has appeared in many forms around the world, six principles have been held in common since participants at the 2007 Forum for Food Sovereignty in Sélingué, Mali, developed the Declaration of Nyéléni:

○ Focuses on food for people – food sovereignty puts the right to sufficient, healthy, and culturally appropriate food at the center of food policies and rejects the proposition that food is just another commodity or component for international agribusiness.
○ Values food providers – food sovereignty values and respects the rights of food providers and rejects those policies, actions, and programs that undervalue them, threaten their livelihoods, and eliminate them.
○ Localizes food systems – food sovereignty brings food providers and consumers closer together to the center of decision making on food issues and protects consumers from poor quality and unhealthy food and food tainted with genetically modified organisms and rejects governance structures, agreements, and practices that depend on and promote unsustainable and inequitable international trade and give power to remote and unaccountable corporations.
○ Puts control locally – food sovereignty places control over territory, land, grazing, water, seeds, livestock and fish populations; and rejects the privatization of natural resources through laws, commercial contracts, and intellectual property rights regimes.
○ Builds knowledge and skills – food sovereignty builds on the skills and local knowledge that conserve, develop, and manage localized food production and harvesting systems and rejects technologies that undermine, threaten, or contaminate these, for example, genetic engineering.
○ Works with nature – food sovereignty uses the diverse, agro-ecological production, and harvesting methods that maximize ecosystem functions and improves resilience and adaptation, especially in the face of climate change and rejects energy-intensive industrialized methods that damage the environment and contribute to global warming.[375]

These broad principles underscore the mission of the food sovereignty movement to delegitimize the market ideology that supports the global food system. The concept of

---

[372] *Id.* at 160.
[373] MCKEON, *supra* note 353 at 84.
[374] *Id.* at 80.
[375] *Id.* at 78–79; Molly D. Anderson, *The Role of US Consumers and Producers in Food Sovereignty*, FOOD SOVEREIGNTY: A CRITICAL DIALOGUE, INTERNATIONAL CONFERENCE, YALE UNIVERSITY 2–4 (September 14–15, 2013).

food sovereignty is also used, however, to achieve practical ends, such as apply its principles to urban communities in order to wrestle control over land and resources in support
of regional food sheds and CSAs (community-supported agriculture), as well as build
support for SNAP benefits and food subsidies to the poor and unemployed.[376]

[2] *Local Ordinances and Preemption Challenges*

Food sovereignty, as a named movement, has emerged in the United States in the form of
local ordinances, popularly coined as "food sovereignty" ordinances.[377] In particular, the
state of Maine became a lightning rod for Local Food and Community Self-Governance
or food sovereignty ordinances.[378] In March 2011, Sedgwick, Maine, was the first town to
pass such an ordinance. Drawing on Maine's state constitution's Home Rule provisions
for authority, the ordinance asserted:

> We the People of Sedgwick have the right to produce, process, sell, purchase and con-
> sume local foods thus promoting self-reliance, the preservation of family farms, and
> local food traditions. We recognize that family farms, sustainable agricultural practices,
> and food processing by individuals, families and non-corporate entities offers stability to
> our rural way of life by enhancing the economic, environmental, and social wealth of
> our community ... We hold that federal and state regulations impede local food produc-
> tion and constitute a usurpation of our citizen's right to food of their choice.[379]

These food sovereignty types of ordinances have spread to other states and
communities–spanning Massachusetts, Vermont, California, and a couple more towns
in Maine– with varying success.[380] The ordinances are often passed in response to perceived burdensome government regulations. The Maine ordinances were focused on
regulations of on-farm poultry farming and the production of raw milk.

The basic legal thrust of food sovereignty ordinances is to exempt local producers from
licensure and inspection requirements. The ordinances also address the rights of local
communities to self-govern. The underlying premise is that local governments have the
right to shape and develop their own food system. A community self-governance ordinance, however, must be reconciled with the issue of preemption, both at a state and
national level. The issue is whether a municipality has the authority to pass an ordinance
that exempts food production, processing, or distribution transactions from specific state
and federal laws.[381] This assessment depends on large part whether the food sovereignty
ordinance countenances a food transaction that is interstate or intrastate. For example,
ordinances that exempt producers from state laws that regulate meat slaughter or raw
milk production present state law preemption issues instead of federal law preemption
issues.

---

[376] See Maggie Dickinson, *Beyond the Minimally Adequate Diet: Food Stamps and Food Sovereignty in the
U.S.*, FOOD SOVEREIGNTY: A CRITICAL DIALOGUE, INTERNATIONAL CONFERENCE, YALE UNIVERSITY
(September 14–15, 2013).

[377] Allison Condra, *Food Sovereignty in the United States: Supporting Local and Regional Food Systems*, 8 J.
FOOD L. & POL'Y 281, 303 (2012).

[378] Anderson, *supra* note 375 at 10.

[379] *Id.*

[380] Condra, *supra* note 377 at 303.

[381] *Id.* at 308–9.

This issue has been and is being tested in Maine where the State of Maine in November 2013 filed suit against a plaintiff dairy farmer for injunctive relief and civil penalties from the Maine Department of Agriculture for selling unpasteurized (raw milk) without a license.[382] Seeking safe harbor under the town's (Blue Hill) food sovereignty ordinance, plaintiff's defense goes to the heart of the food sovereignty issue. The Superior Court found summary judgment in favor of the state, finding that reading the Local Food Ordinance as permitting the unlicensed sale of milk would render the ordinance implicitly preempted as it would clearly frustrate the purpose of existing state law.[383] The court found that "a municipality may only add to the requirements of the statute," and may not loosen the requirements of the statute absent express being delegated the authority to do so.[384] The court's decision was appealed and a hearing was heard before the Maine Supreme Court in May 2014. The decision by the Maine Supreme Court could affect the food sovereignty movement in Maine and across the country. It is very likely that the food sovereignty ordinance will be found to circumvent the state's regulatory food safety regime. To reverse the Superior Court, the Maine Supreme Court may need to find that the purpose of the regulatory regime is not only to achieve sanitation and safety, but also to foster the sustainability of local agricultural practices and economy, as expressed by the local ordinance.

[3] Food Cottage Laws

[a] Exemption for Home-Based Food Operations

While the model food code does not allow for the retail sale of food made in a personal home (i.e., food not made in a licensed commercial kitchen), many states have chosen to create exemptions for home-based food operations. A majority of states now have some exemption allowing for home-based food operations to engage in retail sales. These exemptions are commonly referred to as "food cottage laws." As noted in Chapter 3, many states have adopted food cottage laws and the topic is one of significant interest among states as interest is developing in local food systems. Arizona, Arkansas, Florida, Illinois, Texas, Washington, and California all passed cottage food laws in 2011 and 2012.[385] The laws are viewed as a way to provide local jobs, promote local food systems, and encourage entrepreneurship.

[b] Definition of Cottage Food Operation

The Association of Food and Drug Officials (AFDO), a long-standing organization that has provided extensive input to the FDA on food safety issues, has recently assembled guidance on cottage food laws, providing information on the best practices for cottage food laws.[386] The AFDO defines a cottage food operation as "a person who produces cottage food products only in the home kitchen of that person's primary domestic residence

---

[382] See State v. Brown, ELLSC-CV-11–70 (Me. Super. Ct. Han. Cty., April 27, 2013) (Murray, J.).
[383] Id. at 8–9.
[384] Id. at 9.
[385] See, e.g., Home Baked and Confectionary Goods, ARIZONA DEPARTMENT OF HEALTH SERVICES.
[386] See Cottage Foods: Regulatory Guidance for Best Practices, ASSOCIATION OF FOOD AND DRUG OFFICIALS (AFDO) (April 2012).

and only for sale directly to the consumer. A Cottage food operation shall not operate as a food service establishment, retail food store, or wholesale food manufacturer."[387] A representative state definition is Illinois's definition of a cottage food operation as "a person who produces or packages non-potentially hazardous food in a kitchen of that person's primary domestic residence for direct sale by the owner or a family member, stored in the residence where the food is made."[388]

[c] Regulation of Cottage Food Operations

(1) *Scope of Sales*

Cottage foods are defined by the AFDO as "non-potentially hazardous baked goods, jams, jellies, and other non-potentially hazardous foods produced at a cottage food operation."[389] States specify a wide variety of typical nonpotentially hazardous foods that can be sold, including baked goods, jams, jellies, maple syrup, and dry herb mixes. Some states even allow pickling or canning if stringent standards are met.[390]

States typically define whether home-based food operations are limited to direct sales to consumers at farmers' markets or events, or whether home-based food operations may also sell their foods through grocery stores, restaurant, and other retail channels.[391]

Cottage food operators in California are permitted to sell directly to consumers or indirectly through restaurants or other retail establishments, subject to registration and permitting requirements.[392] By contrast, cottage food operators in Arkansas may sell their products directly only to consumers from the place the food was made, a farmers' market, a county fair, or a special event.[393]

(2) *Sanitary Requirements and Inspections*

States may prescribe the sanitary conditions under which foods are to be produced. AFDO suggests that "all food contact surfaces, equipment, and utensils used for the preparation, packaging, or handling of any cottage food products are washed, rinsed, and sanitized before each use."[394] It further recommends that "all food preparation and food and equipment storage areas are maintained free of rodents and insects" and prescribes certain personal hygiene practices.[395]

States may or may not require a license and inspection for home-based food operations. For example, Texas does not require any licensure or inspection for cottage food

---

[387] *Id.*

[388] Food Handling Regulation Enforcement Act, 410 ILCS 625.

[389] AFDO, *supra* note 386.

[390] *See* UNIVERSITY OF KENTUCKY, HOMEBASED MICROPROCESSOR LAW (explaining the pickling and canning provisions of Kentucky legislation).

[391] *See* Christina Oatfield, *Summary of Cottage Food Laws in the U.S.*, SUSTAINABLE ECONOMIES LAW CENTER (2012) (provides a helpful compilation of state laws on cottage foods).

[392] *See* California Food Retail Code 9 (2014).

[393] *Farmers' Market Vendor Guide: A Guide for Farmers and the Consumer*, ARKANSAS DEPARTMENT OF HEALTH AND ARKANSAS DEPARTMENT OF AGRICULTURE (June 2013), at 4.

[394] AFDO, *supra*, note 386.

[395] *Id.* at 5–6.

operations[396] in contrast to Washington, which requires a cottage food operator to obtain a permit annually.[397]

(3) Labeling Requirements

State cottage food law regimes commonly specify particular labeling requirements. For example, Maryland requires the name of the product, name and address of the cottage food business, ingredients of the product in descending order and the amount of each ingredient by weight, net weight or net volume of the product, allergen information (as per federal labeling rules), nutritional information that complies with federal rules if a nutritional claim is made, and the statement (printed in ten point or larger type): "Made by a cottage food business that is not subject to Maryland's food safety regulations."[398]

(4) Revenue Requirements

States may impose a cap on earnings for cottage food producers. For example, Florida sets its limit at $15,000 annual gross sales. California's cottage food law allows for annual increases in earnings, starting with $35,000 in 2013, $45,000 in 2014, and capping out at $50,000 in 2015.[399] Caps are presumably to ensure that home-based food operations remain small scale, and thus less likely to cause a widespread foodborne illness outbreak, among other reasons.

(5) Trajectory

A few general trends can be noted about home-based food operations. First is a lack of consensus around legal requirements for home-based food operations, including whether licensing and inspections should be required, as well as where home-based food operations should be allowed to sell their foods.[400] Second, states are clearly becoming more interested and more assertive in the use of their authority to regulate intrastate food safety, acting as laboratories for determining the best practices for handling emerging food safety issues, like cottage foods.

§ 6.07 Food Justice, Equity, and Ethics

[1] Definition: Expansive Prism

Concerned that the food movement has been elitist, activists speak in terms of "food justice" in order to focus on barriers that low-income or otherwise marginalized groups face in enjoying the benefits of the broader food movement.[401] The food justice movement

---

[396] *See* Texas Department of State Health Services, *Frequently Asked Questions – Cottage Food Production Operations* (the authorities in Texas may investigate a complaint regarding preparation of potentially hazardous food at a private residence).

[397] *See* Washington State Department of Agriculture, *Cottage Food Operation*.

[398] Md. Code Ann. Health – Gen. §21–330.1(c)(2).

[399] California Retail Food Code, *supra* note 392 at 9.

[400] *See generally* Nina W. Tarr, *Food Entrepreneurs and Food Safety Regulation*, 7 J. Food L. & Pol'y 35 (2011) (provides a good general exploration of food safety regulation, cottage foods, and direct sales).

[401] Rebecca L. Goldberg, *No Such Thing as a Free Lunch: Paternalism, Poverty, and Food Justice*, 24 Stan. L. & Pol'y Rev. 35, 49 (2013).

has emerged as a response to inequality in the food system. Food justice scholars Robert Gottlieb and Joshi Anupama describe food justice as follows:

> The interpretation of food justice can be complex and nuanced, but the concept is simple and direct: justice for all in the food system, whether producers, farmworkers processors, workers, eaters, or communities. Integral to food justice is also a respect for the systems that support how and where the food is grown ... The groups that embrace food justice vary in agendas, constituencies, and focus, but all share a commitment to the definition we originally provided: to achieve equity and fairness in relation to food system impacts and a different, more just, and sustainable way for food to be grown, produced, made accessible, and eaten.[402]

The food justice movement has borrowed heavily from the environmental justice movement, which responded to the perceived failure of the environmental movement to consider the plight of low-income and minority communities who were disproportionately harmed by environmental hazards.[403] The food justice movement has been criticized for lacking a coherent vision and, unlike the environmental justice movement, the legal scholarship is scant.

Food justice changes the perspective and language of the food system. Instead of speaking of the food system in terms of "obesity," the language includes "rights," "equity," "empowerment," and "cultural appropriateness." The aim of the food justice narrative is to work toward the broader food movement's goal of changing the food system, while simultaneously "reorient[ing] the food movement ... to prioritize the need to address inequities."[404]

Food justice concepts provide the intellectual and moral grist to remedying food access problems.[405] Food access is a shared value with the food security movement. Food justice, like food security and food sovereignty, lay claim to the right to food as a tool advancing its precepts.[406] Food justice covers all aspects of food law, from food safety to nutrition programs to farm worker rights to community supported agriculture (CSAs) to environmental concerns to local food to urban agriculture to food access, but does so with the perspective and prism of equity. Food councils often serve as forums for food justice concerns and inequalities to be addressed.[407]

Food equity is a concept only now beginning to emerge in the context of food systems. Food equity not yet widely used that encompasses the adverse effects of both the production and distribution of food that marginalized communities face. Food equity aims to consider all demographic axes and how the food system produces and exasperates disparities among them. Like other food system terms, food equity is intentionally broad and encompasses equity issues that span the food system (i.e., wages and working conditions to access to healthy food options).

---

[402] ROBERT GOTTLIEB & ANUPAMA JOSHI, FOOD JUSTICE 222 (2010).

[403] Goldberg, *supra* note 401 at 49–50.

[404] *Id.* at 52 (quoting Robert Gottlieb and Anupama Joshi, Food Justice 228–229 (2010).

[405] See Kate Meals, *Nurturing the Seeds of Food Justice: Unearthing the Impact of Institutionalized Racism on Access to Health Food in Urban African-American Communities*, 15 SCHOLAR 112 (2012).

[406] *See id.* at 114–16.

[407] Danielle M. Purifoy, *Food Policy Councils: Integrating Food Justice and Environmental Justice*, 24 DUKE ENVTL. L. & POL'Y F. 375, 392–7 (2014).

[2] *Eighth Amendment and Food*

An example of how these food justice concepts intersect with the law is with the role of food in prisons. Prison food can implicate the Eighth Amendment's prohibition of cruel and unusual punishment in the way food is prepared or withheld.[408] At the other extreme is the issue of whether it is cruel or unusual for prison staff to force feed a starving inmate in order to prevent death.[409] The legal tool available to prison inmates who seek to vindicate their Eighth Amendment claim of cruel and unusual punishment is litigation.[410] The Supreme Court has noted in dicta that it would be an Eighth Amendment violation to deny a prisoner an "identifiable human need such as food."[411] For a prison inmate to prevail on such a claim, they must show that (1) they suffered a sufficiently serious deprivation and (2) a prison official demonstrated a subjective "deliberate indifference" toward the inmate's needs.[412] In other words, the official must know and disregard an excessive risk to inmate health.[413]

---

[408] *See generally* Rights of Prisoners § 3:43 (4th ed.) (summarizing successful and unsuccessful Eighth Amendment and other constitutional claims regarding frequency and content of prison meals).

[409] Recently in California, inmates went on a sixty-plus day hunger strike to protest the use of Solitary Housing Units (SHU) as punishment for disobedience. The strike also prompted the CDCR to ask for a federal court to rule that forced feeding when it is required to prevent death. *See* Paige St. John & Anthony York, *Prisoners on Hunger Strike Could Be Force-Fed under Order*, L.A. TIMES, August 19, 2013. For general discussion on the constitutionality of force-feeding prisoners on a hunger strike, *see* Joel K. Greenberg, *Hunger Striking Prisoners: The Constitutionality of Force-Feeding*, 51 FORDHAM L. REV. 747 (1983).

[410] *See* Margo Schlanger, *Inmate Litigation*, 116 HARV. L. REV. 1555, 1557–58 (2003) (documenting prison lawsuits).

[411] Wilson v. Seiter, 501 U.S. 294, 304 (1991).

[412] Farmer v. Brennan, 511 U.S. 825, 825 (1994).

[413] *Id.* at 837.

Table of Cases

Index

barn
12

CPSIA information can be obtained
at www.ICGtesting.com
Printed in the USA
LVOW04s1644100118
562401LV00032B/183/P

9 781107 545762